International Conference on Game and Entertainment Technologies (GET2023), International Conference on Interfaces and Human Computer Interaction (IHCI2023), and International Conference on Computer Graphics, Visualization, Computer Vision and Image Processing (CGVCVIP2023)

Held at the 17th Multi-Conference on Computer Science and Information Systems (MCCSIS 2023)

Porto, Portugal
15-18 July 2023

Editors:

Katherine Blashki
Yingcai Xiao

ISBN: 978-1-7138-8467-5

Printed from e-media with permission by:

Curran Associates, Inc.
57 Morehouse Lane
Red Hook, NY 12571

Printed with permission by Curran Associates, Inc. (2024)

For permission requests, please contact International Association for Development of the Information Society (IADIS) at the address below.

International Association for Development of the Information Society (IADIS)
Rua Sao Sebastiao Da Pedreira
No. 100, 30, 1050-209
Lisbon, Portugal

Phone: 351 21 3151373
Fax: 351 21 3151244

secretariat@iadis.org

Additional copies of this publication are available from:

Curran Associates, Inc.
57 Morehouse Lane
Red Hook, NY 12571 USA
Phone: 845-758-0400
Fax: 845-758-2633
Email: curran@proceedings.com
Web: www.proceedings.com

TABLE OF CONTENTS

FULL PAPERS

SHORT PAPERS

REFLECTION

POSTER

FULL

PAPERS

DESIGN AND DEVELOPMENT OF ONLINE CUSTOMISED CLOTHING MARKETPLACE: A PRELIMINARY STUDY ON CONSUMER PREFERENCES

Sin Ying Ng and Pik Yin Mok
School of Fashion and Textiles, The Hong Kong Polytechnic University, Hong Kong

ABSTRACT

Fashion online shopping has rapidly evolved since the pandemic. Unlike shopping offline, customers cannot physically touch or feel the actual products, therefore, UI design for product information display is fundamentally important for online shopping of fashion. This paper aims to investigate what product information, including product detail image, product display formats, size information, and credibility cues consumers consider when shopping for clothing online by collecting survey responses from 162 respondents. The results show that displaying product in different angles and close-up product details with zoom-in functions are the key product information; displaying clothing on human models with size information, such as size chart, try-on of products on models in different sizes and body shapes and size recommendation tools are also essential. Consumers also valued the credibility cues, such as product review and comment, seller reputation and rating, and photos of products received by customers. The study will be used as a reference to prioritise product information and functions in the design and development of an online customised clothing marketplace platform. It also provides valuable customer insight to fashion brands tech companies and who are assisting brands to launch their e-shops.

KEYWORDS

Product Information, Online Marketplace, Product Page, Customer Perceptions, Credibility Cues, Online Shopping

1. INTRODUCTION

Generation Z (GenZ), a new wave of generation born from 1995 to 2012, has entered workforce with the greatest purchasing power amongst all the generations (Amed et al., 2019, Francis and Hoefel, 2018). This generation shift transforms the consumer landscape which drives fashion brands to formulate new strategies for gaining support from Gen Z consumers who are digital savvy, sustainability-conscious and looking for unique and personalised products (Francis and Hoefel, 2018). Several fashion brands and start-up leverage digital customization approaches to let the consumers purchase highly personalised fashion items and experience the process of clothing bespoke and customisation online. The emergence of digital customisation has been found in various garment categories. Anomalie, a bridal gown start-up since 2016, launched collaborative dress sketch visualizer to enable customers and designer team to co-design their own wedding gown (Anomalie, 2020). Unspun, a custom denim brand, which leveraged 360 degree mobile scanning technology to craft a tailor made jeans, choose denim fabric, thread colour, style and preview 3D finished jeans online(Unspun, 2020). These start-up brands have been supported by huge seed funding resources from investors to undergo advanced digital transformation.

However, a majority of fashion businesses are micro-sized and sole proprietors, including independent designers and tailors (Gorgels et al., 2022, Hollihan, 2021). Some of them might be interested in digital customisation, but they mostly focus on their daily operation to achieve turnover and lack time, manpower, financial resources and technical knowledge to establish and operate their own digital customisation system (Canhoto et al., 2021, Klein and Todesco, 2021).

To address their painpoints, we will design and develop an online customised clothing marketplace for small fashion businesses and consumers to conduct digital customisation and online transactions. This paper aims to understand what product information (e.g. rating, size information, detail and presentation of products) consumers consider when shopping for clothing online by collecting survey responses from 162 respondents mainly from Hong Kong. The investigated results will be used as reference to prioritise important product information and functions for the design and development of online customised clothing marketplace platform. It also provides valuable customer insight to fashion brands or tech company who assist brands to design their online presence.

2. LITERATURE REVIEW

Online fashion marketplace is a fashion e-commerce which is normally owned and operated by a third-party service provider. The marketplace gathers a network of sellers and buyers to sell and purchase products or services from each other. For each successful transaction, the third-party platform will charge seller commission fee (Yenipazarli, 2021). Renowned fashion online marketplace platforms from luxury to mass market segments, such as Farfetch, ASOS and Zalora which charges commission with charge from 10% to 30% per sale from brands (ASOS, 2023, Kansara, 2015, Tan, 2020). Oklander and Kudina (2021) highlighted various advantages of marketplace model from seller perspective, including a higher cost-effectiveness to establish online store, higher accessibility to target customers and wider market. From buyer perspective, marketplace could offer a wide selection of products, efficient information screening, product search and comparison.

Product information: Marketplace offers a wide range of product selections and consumers have to select the most suitable product amongst all the variety of choices. Product Information in the marketplace is important to tell consumers how the product will look like in the reality even they do not have chance to physically touch or feel the actual products. Consumers might need to rely on the information provided electronically by the online sellers and marketplace to make purchase decision, especially purchasing item that they have not used before. First, product information can build up trust and purchase confidence. The more accurate and detailed product information provided by the sellers, the better understanding of consumers to a product and build up trust, purchase confidence and eventually boost up sales afterwards (Davis, 1989, Hong et al., 2016). Second, a high-quality product information which is SEO-friendly can rank higher in search engines, reach more searchers, and potential consumers. Therefore, it is important for sellers to optimize their product information to drive traffic, conversions and sales. The basic product information of fashion products includes product description, product detail photography, product display formats, size information, statistic, rating and customer feedback. This paper will focus on product detail image, product display formats, size information and credibility cues.

Product detail images: In the fashion marketplaces, product details are often shown in image forms to let consumers know how the detail of product looks like. The products are often displayed in different angles (e.g. front, back, side views), close-ups and enlargement and styling with colour and fabric swatches support (Hong et al., 2016, Naegelein et al., 2019, Kim et al., 2007). Some fashion products are displayed on models in different sizes to demonstrate their diversity and inclusion which can catering the need of a large group of consumers (Rhee and Lee, 2021).

Product display format: Fashion products are often displayed into two different approaches: product itself and showcasing by models. Products can be flat laid. They can be also displayed in static images featuring mannequin, human model (with or without styling) and short catwalk video with models who strike a pose and turns around less than 20 seconds (Rhee and Lee, 2021, Kim et al., 2007, Naegelein et al., 2019, Bug and Helwig, 2020).

Size information: A survey conducted by Mckinsey in 2019 demonstrated 25% return rate on fashion online business channel, and 70% of the returns were attributed by poor fitting or style (Ader et al., 2021). Therefore, size information is crucial for fashion ecommerce. Usually a size chart with detailed measurements for different product sizes (e.g. US2, 4, 6, 8) will be listed on the product page, with some supplementary information, such as try-ons on model in different weights and heights, size comparisons from different brands and size recommendation tools (e.g. size calculator, mobile body measuring technology).

Credibility cues: In addition to the information of product details, consumers also take reference on the statistic, rating and customer feedback, namely credibility cues when they make purchase decision. The common statistic product transaction volume, repeat customers of product, seller experience, number of subscribers, number of people who add the item to favourite and number of view history of products. Rating and customer feedback includes seller reputation and rating, review and comment and photo of products received by real customers. Researches have been found that seller reputation and customer reviews (e.g. e-word of mouth, eWOM) are positively related with trust and purchase intention of customers (Malak et al., 2021, Sulthana and Vasantha, 2019, Cheong et al., 2020, Sa'ait et al., 2016, Kim and Choi, 2012).

3. METHOD

Online survey platform system Qualtrics was used for collecting questionnaires from 162 respondents. The survey was distributed in social media platform and communication tool. The survey was divided into six section: (i) online fashion shopping habits, (ii) product detail images, (iii) product display formats, (iv) size information, (v) credibility cues and (vi) demographic information. Multiple choices questions are used to collect the demographic information and online fashion shopping habits. For other questions which involved customers' opinions and judgement of statements, customers were asked to rate based on the 7-point Likert scale (1= strongly disagree to 7 = strongly agree) in order to understand what kinds of product information consumer will consider when they shop online in the fashion marketplace. Table 1 shows the demographic information of respondents. The collected information from the questionnaire was analyzed in Microsoft excel and visualized various types of charts. The Likert rating scale was plotted in a diverging stacked bar (bi-directional bar chart) because this sort of bar style was highly recommended by researchers to graphically display data of each rated scales (Robbins and Heiberger, 2011, Howorko et al., 2018, Heiberger and Robbins, 2014).

Table 1. The demographic information of respondents

Item	Type	Count	%
Gender	Male	63	39%
	Female	99	61%
Age	Under 18	1	1%
	18-25	73	45%
	26-35	63	39%
	36-45	13	8%
	46-55	8	5%
	Above 56	4	2%
Position	Student	57	35%
	Employee	105	65%
Education level	Secondary School	10	6%
	Diploma/ Higher Diploma	19	12%
	Undergraduate	93	57%
	Postgraduate	40	25%
Monthly income	HKD 0-15,000	63	39%
	HKD 15,000-29,999	57	35%
	HKD 30,000-59,999	34	21%
	>HKD 59,999	8	5%
Frequency of purchasing	Twice per month or above	26	16%
	Once every 1-2 months	65	40%
	Once every 3 months	33	20%
	Once every 6 months	24	15%
	Once per year or less	14	9%

Average monthly online	<HKD 500	96	59%
	HKD 500-999	38	23%
	HKD 1,000-1,999	17	10%
	> HKD 2,000	11	7%
Cities / Countries	Hong Kong	138	85%
	Mainland China	3	2%
	Oversea	21	13%

4. FINDINGS

4.1 Product Detail Images

We found that nearly a half of respondents believe displaying product in different angles is extremely important, followed by displaying close-up product details with zoom-in functions (41%). Previous literatures indicated that the close-up product details, zoom-in functions and displaying in various angles can provide local information-based cues of product quality (e.g. craftsmanship) and materials (e.g. fabrics) (Hong et al., 2016, Naegelein et al., 2019). This information is particularly helpful for respondents to make purchase decision for online shopping.

Respondents believed that colour and fabric swatches are less important product information. Our explanation for this finding is that the close-up details and zoom-in functions already deliver a rich information of product detail, such as the colour and fabric. Therefore, the images of colour and fabric swatches might not be necessary. Figure 1 shows the preferences of product detail images from respondents.

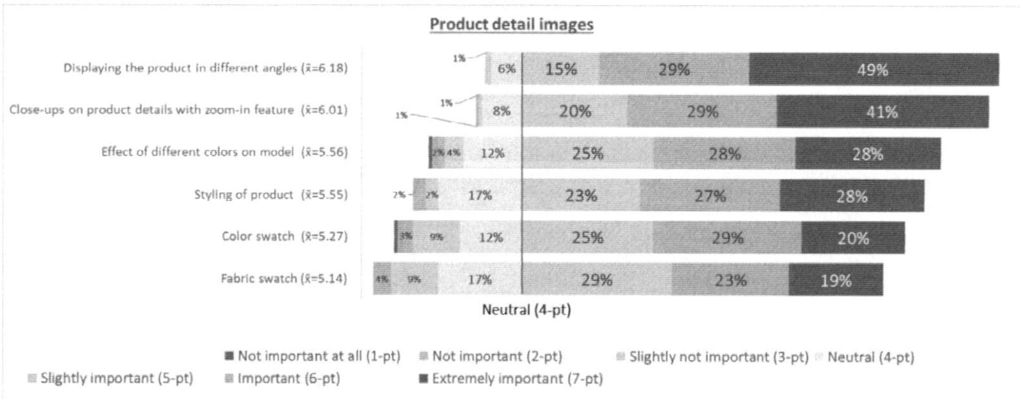

Figure 1. The preferences of product detail image types from respondents

4.2 Product Display Formats

Respondents believed that model display (without specific styling) is the most important product display format ($\bar{x}$=5.86 pt. out of 7 pt.). It can be explained that this is a basic and necessary format to demonstrate how a fashion product is worn by a human body (e.g. the drape and cutting). Figure 2 shows the preferences of product display formats from respondents.

However, it is surprised that respondents believed model catwalk in video is the least important amongst all ($\bar{x}$=4.88 out of 7 pt.). Previous literatures highlighted the advantages of videos (e.g. catwalk videos) which can demonstrate how a fashion product is worn by a model in motion and movements. It can further enhance online fashion shopping experience and purchase intention of shoppers (Bug and Helwig, 2020, Kim et al., 2007). It can be explained that videos might be attractive feature from the perspectives of consumers but they might not be the most essential part, comparing with other product display formats (e.g. model and mannequin display). Moreover, catwalk videos might be too fast and hectic without showing detail of product clearly. It is also found that video production is relatively costly and time consuming than other presentation formats (e.g. flat-lay and mannequin display) (Lee and Park, 2014, Bug and Helwig, 2020)

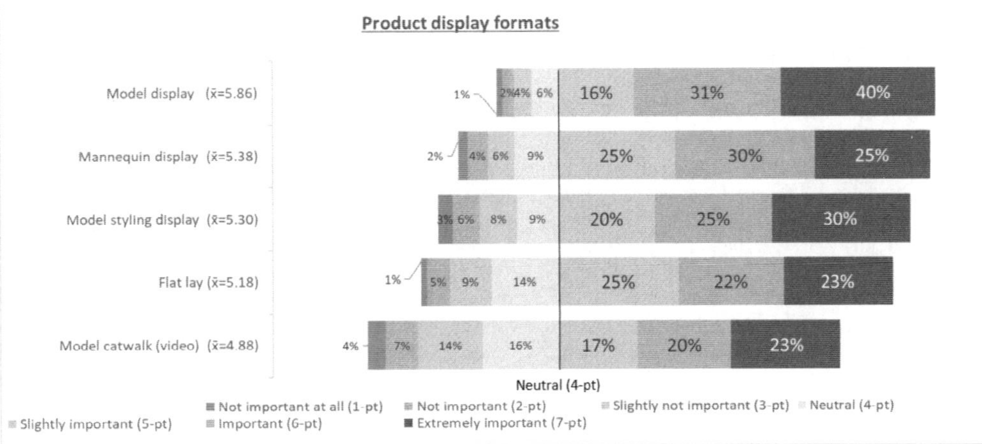

Figure 2. The preferences of product display formats from respondents

4.3 Size Information

We found that amongst all the size information, over a half of respondents believe size chart is extremely important (57%), followed by try-on of product on different sizes of models and size recommendation with over 40% of respondents agree those two size information cues are extremely important. It is not surprised that respondents believed size chart is the most important size information for fashion product because it provides numeric information to customers in order to select right size that fits on their body. A few researches highlighted that the lack of size chart will probably results perceived product risk and uncertainty over sizing which might result purchase hesitation (Masoud, 2013, Kim et al., 2006, Ariffin et al., 2018). Therefore, size chart is an essential product size information for online fashion shopping.

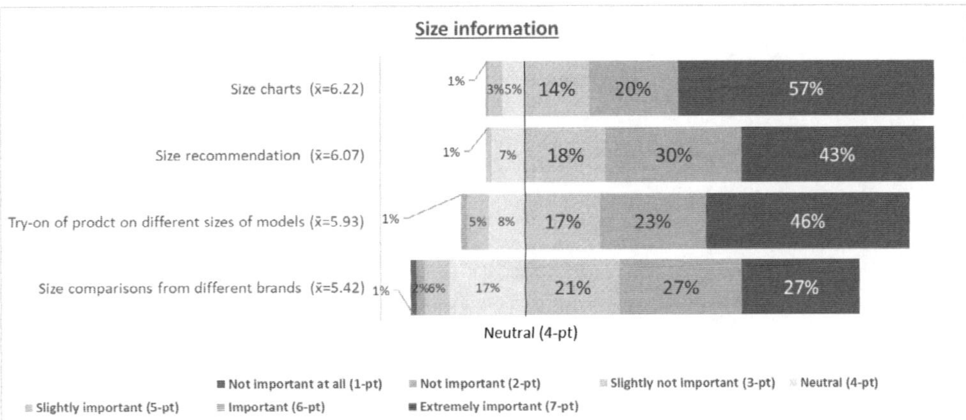

Figure 3. The preferences of size information from respondents

Although size chart is available in most of the online fashion shopping platforms, researchers found that customers are still confused to decide which size of fashion product they should purchase because there is a lack of standardized size chart with size inconsistency amongst brands and countries. Therefore, size recommendation is necessary to provide size guidance to each individual consumers based on their inputted body measurements (Lasserre et al., 2020, Guigourès et al., 2018). In addition, displaying of product on different sizes and shapes of models enable shoppers to imagine how the products look like on their bodies by taking reference from the photos of models who have similar body shapes and sizes (Rhee and Lee, 2021). Figure 3 shows the preferences of size information from respondents.

4.4 Credibility cues

Besides the intrinsic cues (e.g. colour, design and materials of product itself), credibility cues such as review and ratings, infer insight about product quality in pre-purchase stage. It is found that review and comment, seller reputation and rating and photo of product received by real customer are the top-three important information-based cues to consider from the perspectives of respondents. This finding is consistent with previous literatures which highlighted eWOM (e.g. seller reputation, ratings and customer feedback of products) determines purchase intention and reduces risk perception (Kim and Choi, 2012, Malak et al., 2021, Sulthana and Vasantha, 2019). Figure 4 shows the preferences of credibility cues from respondents.
The finding shows that "the number of view history", "the number of people who add the items to favourite" and "the number of fans and subscribers of seller" are the least important product information and cues amongst all. Our explanation of this finding is that those cues might be more related with "popularity", rather than "credibility". A product with more view history might probably due to its high-ranking in search engines with better SEO (Lewandowski, 2013). "The number of people who add the items to favourite" and "the number of fans and subscribers of seller" might not always reflect the product quality (Dias et al., 2021).

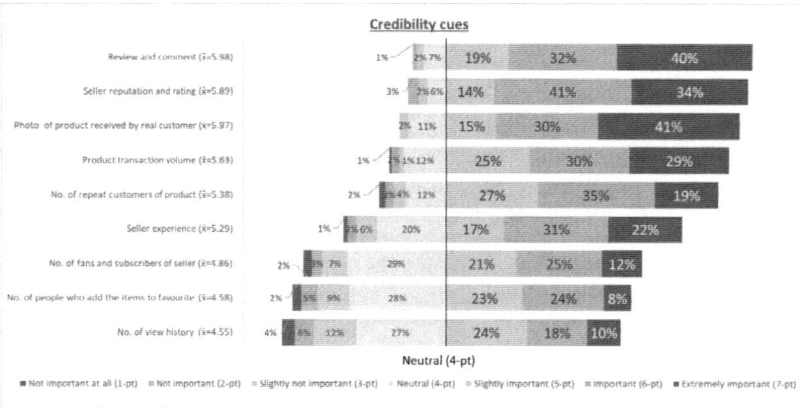

Figure 4. The preferences of credibility cues from respondents

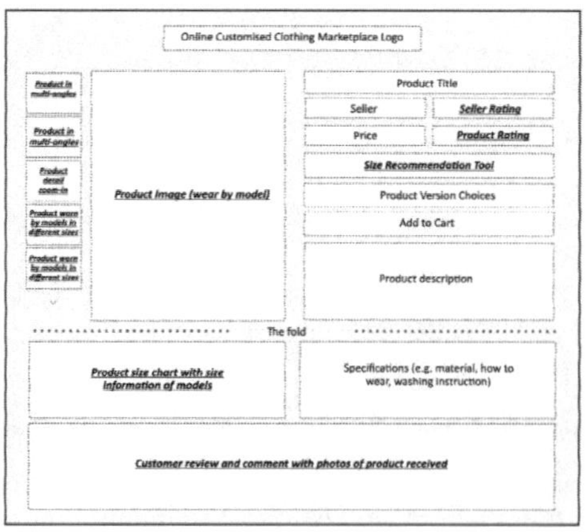

Figure 5. The demographic information of respondents

4.5 Online Customized Clothing Marketplace

By taking reference from the survey results, we designed the product page of our online customized clothing marketplace platform featuring essential product information, including images of human models in different size and body shapes who wear the fashion products in multi-angles of view, close-up detail with zoom-in feature of products, size chart, size recommendation, product review and comment, seller rating and photo of products received by customers. We will include measurement data input and clothing customization functions in the nearly future. Figure 5 shows how the overview of product page of our online customized clothing marketplace platform design.

5. CONCLUSION

This paper investigated what product information (e.g. rating, size information, detail and presentation of products) and cues customers consider when shopping for clothing online. We found out that displaying product in different angles and displaying close-up product details with zoom-in functions are the key product information for online fashion shopping. Displaying clothing on human models with size information, such as size chart, try-on of products on models in different sizes and body shapes and size recommendation tools are also essential information. Respondents also valued the credibility cues, such as product review and comment, seller reputation and rating, and photos of products received by customers. The investigated results will be used as reference to prioritise key product information and functions for the design and development of online customised clothing marketplace platform. The result also provides valuable insight for tech companies who are developing or running marketplace for online fashion shopping. In addition, some individual fashion brands who are running their fashion ecommerce business might need to decide what kind of product information should provide to customer. The information should be able to meet the need of customers without being overloaded and requiring huge investment (e.g. cost of time and money) This study is a preliminary study with relatively small sample size — only 162 respondents were involved. In the future, we will expand our increase our sample size and cover samples from various countries and cities out of Hong Kong.

ACKNOWLEDGEMENT

The work described in this paper was supported by the Innovation and Technology Commission of Hong Kong under grant ITP/028/21TP.

REFERENCES

Ader, J., Adhi, P., Chai, J., Singer, M., Touse, S. and Yankelevich, H. (2021) 'Returning to order: Improving returns management for apparel companies', *McKinsey, available at: https://www.mckinsey.com/industries/retail/our-insights/returning-toorder-improving-returns-management-for-apparel-companies (accessed 25 May 2021).*

Amed, I., Balchandani, A., Beltrami, M., Berg, A., Hedrich, S. and Rölkens, F. 2019. The influence of 'woke'consumers on fashion. *McKinsey & Company.*

Anomalie (2020) *Don't Settle. Go custom to find your dress soulmate.* Available at: https://www.dressanomalie.com/design-services (Accessed: May 24).

Ariffin, S. K., Mohan, T. and Goh, Y.-N. (2018) 'Influence of consumers' perceived risk on consumers' online purchase intention', *Journal of Research in Interactive Marketing*, 12(3), pp. 309-327.

ASOS (2023) *ASOS MARKETPLACE*. Available at: https://m.marketplace.asos.com/help/features-fees.

Bug, P. and Helwig, J. (2020) 'Overview of product presentation with moving images in fashion e-commerce', *Fashion and film: moving images and consumer behavior*, pp. 217-241.

Canhoto, A. I., Quinton, S., Pera, R., Molinillo, S. and Simkin, L. (2021) 'Digital strategy aligning in SMEs: A dynamic capabilities perspective', *The Journal of Strategic Information Systems*, 30(3), pp. 101682.

Cheong, J. W., Muthaly, S., Kuppusamy, M. and Han, C. (2020) 'The study of online reviews and its relationship to online purchase intention for electronic products among the millennials in Malaysia', *Asia Pacific Journal of Marketing and Logistics*.

Davis, F. D. (1989) 'Perceived usefulness, perceived ease of use, and user acceptance of information technology', *MIS quarterly*, pp. 319-340.

Dias, R., Martinez, L. F. and Martinez, L. M. 'How Does the Number of Instagram Followers Influence Brand Attitude: The Role of Purchase Intention, Perceived Product Quality, Referrals, Brand Trust, and Gender'. *Advances in Digital Marketing and eCommerce: Second International Conference, 2021*: Springer, 121-128.

Francis, T. and Hoefel, F. (2018) 'True Gen': Generation Z and its implications for companies', *McKinsey & Company*, 12.

Gorgels, S., Priem, M. and Blagoeva, T. M., A Milanesi, G (2022) *Annual Report on European SMEs 2021/2022 SMEs and environmental sustainability Background document:* European Comission.

Guigourès, R., Ho, Y. K., Koriagin, E., Sheikh, A.-S., Bergmann, U. and Shirvany, R. 'A hierarchical bayesian model for size recommendation in fashion'. *Proceedings of the 12th ACM conference on recommender systems*, 392-396.

Heiberger, R. and Robbins, N. (2014) 'Design of diverging stacked bar charts for Likert scales and other applications', *Journal of Statistical Software*, 57, pp. 1-32.

Hollihan, C. (2021) 'Post-Brexit, can small be beautiful for UK fashion brands?', *Vogue Business*.

Hong, L. M., Zulkiffli, W. F. W. and Hamsani, N. H. (2016) 'The impact of perceived risks towards customer attitude in online shopping', *International Journal*, 1(2), pp. 13-21.

Howorko, L., Boedianto, J. M. and Daniel, B. (2018) 'The efficacy of stacked bar charts in supporting single-attribute and overall-attribute comparisons', *Visual Informatics*, 2(3), pp. 155-165.

Kansara, V. A. (2015) 'Farfetch's Global Platform Play', *Business of Fashion*.

Kim, J., Fiore, A. M. and Lee, H.-H. (2007) 'Influences of online store perception, shopping enjoyment, and shopping involvement on consumer patronage behavior towards an online retailer', *Journal of retailing and Consumer Services*, 14(2), pp. 95-107.

Kim, M., Kim, J. H. and Lennon, S. J. (2006) 'Online service attributes available on apparel retail web sites: an E-S-QUAL approach', *Managing Service Quality: An International Journal*, 16(1), pp. 51-77.

Kim, S. and Choi, S. M. (2012) 'Credibility cues in online shopping: an examination of corporate credibility, retailer reputation, and product review credibility', *International Journal of Internet Marketing and Advertising*, 7(3), pp. 217-236.

Klein, V. B. and Todesco, J. L. (2021) 'COVID-19 crisis and SMEs responses: The role of digital transformation', *Knowledge and Process Management*, 28(2), pp. 117-133.

Lasserre, J., Sheikh, A.-S., Koriagin, E., Bergman, U., Vollgraf, R. and Shirvany, R. 'Meta-learning for size and fit recommendation in fashion'. *Proceedings of the 2020 SIAM international conference on data mining*: SIAM, 55-63.

Lee, E.-J. and Park, J. (2014) 'Enhancing virtual presence in e-tail: Dynamics of cue multiplicity', *International Journal of Electronic Commerce*, 18(4), pp. 117-146.

Lewandowski, D. (2013) 'Credibility in web search engines', *Online credibility and digital ethos: Evaluating computer-mediated communication*: IGI Global, pp. 131-146.

Malak, F., Ferreira, J. B., Pessoa de Queiroz Falcão, R. and Giovannini, C. J. (2021) 'Seller reputation within the B2C e-marketplace and impacts on purchase intention', *Latin American Business Review*, 22(3), pp. 287-307.

Masoud, E. Y. (2013) 'The effect of perceived risk on online shopping in Jordan', *European Journal of Business and Management*, 5(6), pp. 76-87.

Naegelein, P., Spann, M. and Molitor, D. (2019) 'The value of product presentation technologies on mobile vs. non-mobile devices: A randomized field experiment', *Decision Support Systems*, 121, pp. 109-120.

Oklander, M. and Kudina, A. (2021) 'Channels for promotion of fashion brands in the online space', *Baltic Journal of Economic Studies*, 7(2), pp. 179-187.

Rhee, H.-L. and Lee, K.-H. (2021) 'Enhancing the sneakers shopping experience through virtual fitting using augmented reality', *Sustainability*, 13(11), pp. 6336.

Robbins, N. B. and Heiberger, R. M. 'Plotting Likert and other rating scales'. *Proceedings of the 2011 joint statistical meeting: American Statistical Association*.

Sa'ait, N., Kanyan, A. and Nazrin, M. F. (2016) 'The effect of e-WOM on customer purchase intention', *International Academic Research Journal of Social Science*, 2(1), pp. 73-80.

Sulthana, A. N. and Vasantha, S. (2019) 'Influence of electronic word of mouth eWOM on purchase intention', *International Journal of Scientific & Technology Research*, 8(10), pp. 1-5.

Tan, Y. S. (2020) *Beauty and skincare e-commerce mobile application with advanced searching module using image processing*. UTAR.

Unspun (2020) *Unspun // beta testers wanted* https://beta.unspun.io/ [https://beta.unspun.io/]. Available at: https://beta.unspun.io/ (Accessed: May 24).

Yenipazarli, A. (2021) 'The marketplace dilemma: Selling to the marketplace vs. selling on the marketplace', *Naval .Research Logistics (NRL)*, 68(6), pp. 761-778.

INVESTIGATING AUTHENTICATION OF CHOICE USED BY SECURITY CRITICAL PROFESSIONALS IN HEALTH SETTING

Oluwadamilola Arinde, Jinjuan Feng and Ziying Tang
Towson University, Towson MD, USA

ABSTRACT

User authentication is a crucial security mechanism that plays an essential role in protecting systems and information. Numerous studies have examined users' experiences with various authentication methods. However, very few focused on granting users the freedom to select one or more authentication methods of their own choice. Limited research in this area suggested that the "Authentication of Choice" (AoC) approach can potentially serve as a usable and secure authentication solution on mobile devices. However, those studies only evaluated the AoC approach on the general population. No study examined the AoC approach as used by individuals in security-critical professions such as the military. To address this gap, we conducted an online longitudinal study with 12 military and 12 civilian participants to assess the AoC approach using a mobile app supporting healthy living. The result of the study provides insight into how users in special professions interact with and perceive the AoC approach in the context of mobile health apps.

KEYWORDS

Authentication of Choice, Usability, Security, Health Mobile App

1. INTRODUCTION

User authentication is a process employed to verify the identity claimed by a user before granting access to a system or an application. An effective user authentication method is crucial to prevent illicit access to any information service, especially health-related applications. Even though many studies have examined users' experiences with various authentication methods, very few studies have focused on the approach that grants users the freedom to select one or more authentication methods of their choice. Oluwafemi and Feng (2020) conducted studies to understand how users perceive the 'Authentication of Choice' (AoC) approach in the context of mobile applications. The results suggested that the AoC approach can serve as a usable and secure authentication solution on mobile devices. However, this work only evaluated the AoC approach on the Android platform when users executed tasks with low security and privacy concerns.

User perception about an authentication approach might differ when the nature of the tasks involves more sensitive information, such as those supported in health applications. We examine the impact of task and information sensitivity on the perception of AoC in the context of mobile health apps, and the results further confirm that users perceive multi-factor AoC as a usable and secure authentication method in the health setting (Arinde et al., 2022, pp. 228-240).

Users' perceptions may also differ depending on the nature of their profession. Users in the security-critical profession, such as the military, may have a different perspective towards authentication methods than the general public. In this paper, we report a study that aims to investigate the 'Authentication of Choice' approach used by individuals from special professions. With a split-plot design, the study assessed the performance and user perception of the AoC approach in the context of mobile health apps. 12 Military and 12 Civilian participants used three types of authentication processes: alphanumeric password, Single-Factor AoC, and Multi-Factor AoC, in 3 weeks. The results suggest the potential to adopt the authentication of choice approach in security-critical professions.

2. RELATED WORKS

2.1 Multiple Factor Authentication

In access control, validation is the initial phase. Usually, it employs authentication mechanisms categorized into three factors: something you know (knowledge factor), something you have (possession factor), and something you are (inherent factor) (Nilesh et al., 2016, pp. 246-249). An additional authentication factor is somewhere you are (location-based).

The traditional security procedure for user authentication is based on only one factor, called Single-Factor authentication (SFA) (Madhuravani et al., 2013, pp.1358-1361). The most popular SFA method is knowledge factor authentication, notably "passwords". The SFA is widely used but has several problems associated with it. Gunson et al (2011) made an argument in their study that despite the popularity of SFA methods, they are not strong enough to provide the needed level of security to the system. Numerous studies further supported this claim. (e.g., Dasgupta et al., 2016, pp. 85-116).

Multi-Factor Authentication (MFA) was subsequently proposed to provide a higher level of security by combining two or more distinct and different categories from the authentication factors (Abhishek et al., 2013). While multi-factor authentication improves the security of the authentication system, it may interfere with the usability of the system. One of the challenges is the user's lack of motivation (Das et al., 2018) because some users believe that multi-factor authentication is making the system more complex to use. Another study by Aleksandr et al (2018) classifies the usability challenges from three perspectives: task efficiency, task effectiveness, and user preference.

2.2 Authentication of Choice

To design a usable and secure system, Cranor and Buchler (2014) suggest that researchers need to go beyond using human-centered design techniques and adopt design techniques that give users the ability to make decisions. One of Ben Schneiderman's golden interface design rules, support of internal locus of control, addresses the user decision-making design approach concept. A sense of satisfaction comes with users knowing they are thought of during the design process and given the freedom to make choices in an application. Vance and Paik (2005) suggest user interface be designed so that users feel more responsible and accountable for their actions. If this is apparent in the interface, they will be less likely to misuse their access rights to the system.

As we have established that there is no perfect authentication method in terms of usability and security, this shows that no authentication method can accommodate all users. It will be challenging to design an authentication method that is universally accessible for users without the knowledge of their abilities and disabilities (Fairweather et al., 2002).

Users may also have a preferred authentication method depending on their physical abilities and cognitive skills (Belk et al., 2013, pp. 442-459). Hausawi et al (2014) proposed a choice-based authentication approach that can address the issues with current authentication methods, including security issues, usability issues, and universal access. According to the findings in (Oluwafemi and Feng, 2020; Arinde et al., 2022), the general users prefer the AoC method over the alphanumeric method. They also perceive the AoC method as easy to use, efficient, easy to remember, and secure.

2.3 Security and Usability of Mobile Health Applications

In the past decade, mobile health applications have grown exponentially due to their usefulness in telehealth, which requires remote patient monitoring. The pandemic further motivated the healthcare industry to integrate technology now more than ever for the benefit of all stakeholders ("Number of mHealth apps available in the Google Play Store," 2021).

The growth of mobile health apps has led to increasing challenges in protecting sensitive and personal data collected through those apps. Increasing vulnerabilities in the mobile health apps available have been widely reported. An assessment by Intertrust highlights significant security gaps in mHealth apps, one of them indicating that 71% of tested mHealth apps have a high-level security vulnerability ("Intertrust Releases 2020 Security Report on Global mHealth App Threats," 2020).

One of the high-level security vulnerabilities is the possibility of a data breach due to weak data encryption on the apps. Another one is 81% data leakage from COVID-tracking applications ("Intertrust Releases 2020 Security Report on Global mHealth App Threats," 2020).

With such security issues, it is understandable how the critical focus in developing mHealth apps is security. These applications' balance of security and usability is crucial for successful adoption and high-quality service.

2.4 User Authentication in Special Professions

The operations of many special professions, such as the military, first responders, and healthcare, require substantially higher security and privacy practice than the other fields. With the sensitive nature of the military, user authentication is a crucial part of its operations. Military personnel must gain access to applications using an authentication method. According to login.gov ("Authentication Options," 2023), military personnel must set up multi-factor authentication as an added layer of protection to secure information. They offer their personnel multiple authentication options, with Security Keys, PIV/CAC cards, and authentication apps being considered the most secure options ("Authentication Options," 2023).

Although the military favors Security keys and PIV/CAC, these physical objects can be misplaced, lost, or stolen. Authentication apps such as Google Authenticator are great options for the general public as they are mobile applications that can be downloaded on the phone to generate a one-time password and are considered secure. However, they may cause security implications in the military setting. Finding the balance between the security and usability provided by various options can improve military personnel's' perception of user authentication.

The longitudinal study reported in the following sections is the first study that investigated the use of Authentication of Choice in healthcare by military professionals.

3. METHODS

3.1 Study Goal

This online longitudinal study aims to examine the performance and user perception of the Authentication of Choice approach by military professionals in the context of mobile health-related applications. The study adopted a split-plot design with two participant groups (military and civilian) and three conditions for authentication:

- Alphanumeric Password: Participants signed up and logged in with email and password.
- Single-Factor AoC: Participants chose one authentication method out of five options (alphanumeric passwords, pin, phone's One Time Password (OTP), face recognition, and fingerprint authentication).
- Multi-Factor AoC: Participants chose two authentication methods from the five options listed above.

3.2 Participants

Twenty-four participants took part in the study. Twelve of the participants are members of the Military, while the other twelve are civilian participants. All the participants are between the ages of 22 – 43 years. There were nine males and three females from each group. Sixteen participants used iPhones, and eight used Android phones. Nineteen of the participants have a bachelor's degree or higher. The military participants work in various specialties such as Machinery, Intelligence, and healthcare. The civilian participants also work in various fields, such as IT, healthcare, and engineering. No financial incentive was provided for participating in the study.

3.3 HealthyCog Application

An application named "HealthyCog" was developed for this study. The application is a cross-platform application that can be used on both iOS and Android platforms. The app presents five authentication methods that are commonly adopted in commercial mobile devices:

- Alphanumeric email and password
- Personal Identification Number (PIN)
- One-Time-Password (OTP) via SMS
- Face Recognition
- Fingerprint Recognition

The application design followed general usability guidelines and underwent several rounds of testing based on user feedback. Users will create and test a different type of authentication condition each week:

- Type 1: Alphanumeric email and password
- Type 2: Single-Factor authentication of choice with five options
- Type 3: Multi-Factor authentication of choice (Two) with five options

Figure 1 below shows the user interface of the HealthyCog app featuring the home page where users can sign up or login. The sign-up button leads to the registration page where participants will select the account type to test for the week.

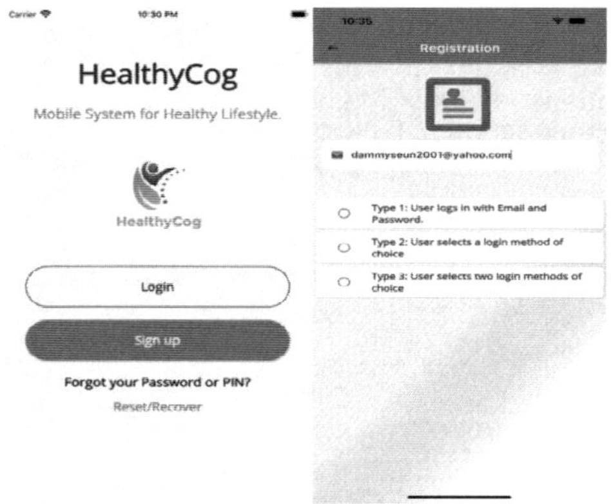

Figure 1. Home page and registration page of the HealthyCog app

4. PROCEDURE

The study was conducted online. After providing consent to participate in the study, Instructions about the study environment and procedure were emailed to participants. A demographic questionnaire was completed at the beginning of the study. Each participant used the app for three weeks, interacting with one authentication condition each week. The order of the three authentication conditions was counterbalanced among the participants to control the learning effect.

During the study, participants first installed the 'HealthyCog' app from the App Store or Google Play Store, depending on if they had an iOS or an Android phone. Following successful installation, each participant created an account on the app. The type of account created depended on the order in the instructions they received. The participants then logged into the account daily for the next seven days. After logging in, they completed one of the following health-related tasks:

— Select the 'HealthyCog Chatbot' function and schedule a tentative appointment (This is a fictional task; no actual appointment is made)

— In the 'HealthyCog Arm' function, watch an arm exercise video and, if interested, perform the arm exercise

— In the 'Med Reminder' function, add a fictional medication, set a reminder, and select a time interval for the reminder

— Visit the 'Daily Steps' function to activate the pedometer and walk for a few minutes if possible. The number of steps taken is displayed at the end of the exercise.

At the end of the first week, participants completed a questionnaire about the session via Google Forms before switching to the following account type specified in the instruction. After completing all three sessions, participants completed a post-study questionnaire where they rated their preference for each of the three authentication processes.

The app automatically logged the sign-up and log-in time for the three conditions and the authentication methods chosen during the single-factor and multi-factor Authentication of Choice processes into a secure database.

5. RESULTS

5.2 Average Login Time

A split-plot Analysis of the Variance test with login time as the dependent variable and profession and type of authentication as the independent variables suggests no significant difference in login time between the military and civilian groups ($F(1, 22) = 0.438$, n.s.). There is a significant difference in login time between the three authentication conditions ($F(2, 44) = 12{,}21$, $p < 0.001$). Figure 2 shows the average login time of the three conditions in seconds per group. Participants spent a shorter time signing into an account in the single-factor AoC condition than in the other two conditions.

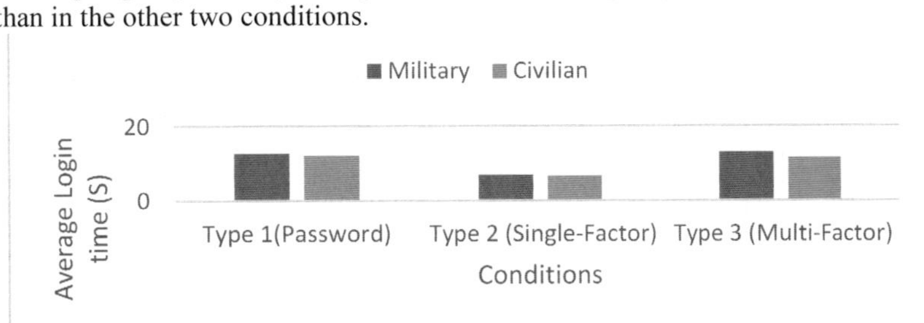

Figure 2. Average login time of the three conditions in seconds per group

5.3 Authentication Method chosen for AoC

Table 1 and Table 2 illustrate the number and percentage of military and civilian participants who chose each authentication method under the single-factor AoC and multi-factor AoC conditions. In the multi-factor AoC condition, each participant chose two methods. Therefore, the total number of participants choosing all methods is 24, and the total percentage of participants is 200% for each table.

Table 1. Number and percentages of military participants who chose each method under Type 2 and Type 3 conditions

Authentication Method	Type 2	Type 3	Type 2%	Type 3%
Password	1	2	8.3%	16.7%
Pin	5	10	41.7%	83.3%
OTP	1	6	8.3%	50%
Fingerprint	2	2	16.7%	16.7%
Face Recognition	3	4	25%	33.3%
Total	12	24	100%	200%

As illustrated in Table 1, the PIN authentication method is the most frequently chosen in both conditions at 41.7% and 83.3%, respectively. For single-factor AoC, the second most frequently chosen method was Face Recognition at 25%, and Fingerprint came third at 16.7%. The SMS OTP and the Password methods were the least chosen by 1 participant each. Similar results in the ranking were observed for multi-factor AoC for the PIN method. The OTP was the second most frequently chosen method, Face Recognition as the third, while Fingerprint and Password tied as the fourth.

Table 2. Number and percentages of civilian participants who chose each method under Type 2 and Type 3 conditions

Authentication Method	Type 2	Type 3	Type 2%	Type 3%
Password	0	3	0%	25%
Pin	3	9	25%	75%
OTP	2	6	16.7%	50%
Fingerprint	2	1	16.7%	8.3%
Face Recognition	5	5	41.6%	41.7%
Total	12	24	100%	200%

As shown in Table 2, for the civilian group, the most frequently chosen method for single-factor AoC was Face Recognition at 41.6%, the Pin method came second at 25%, while Fingerprint and OTP tied as third at 16.7% each. The Password method was not chosen in this method of AoC. For multi-factor AoC, the PIN method was the most frequently chosen, while OTP was the second. Face Recognition was the third. The Password method was selected by 3 participants making it the fourth and fingerprint the least chosen. Figures 3 and 4 show the percentages of participants who chose each method under the single-factor AoC and the multi-factor AoC conditions, respectively.

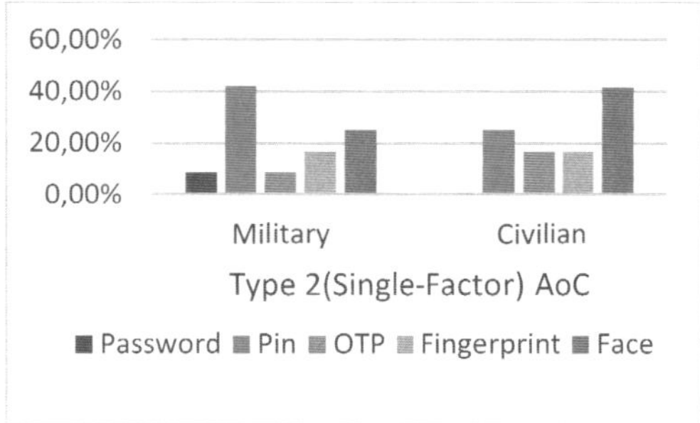

Figure 3. Percentages of participants who chose each method under Type 2 condition per group

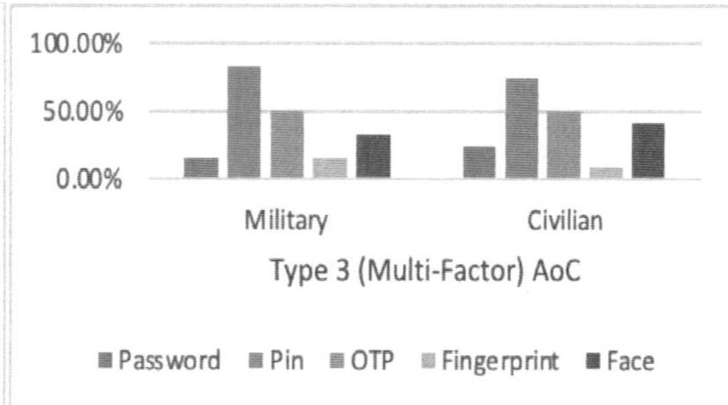

Figure 4. Percentages of participants who chose each method under Type 3 condition per group

5.4 Preferred Authentication Process

In the post-study questionnaire, we asked the participants to rank their preferences towards the three authentication processes based on all factors combined. Tables 3 and 4 illustrate how the participants ranked each process for each group.

Table 3. Number and percentages of military participants who ranked each of the three conditions as their first, second, and third choice

Rank	Alphanumeric Password number (%)	Single-Factor number (%)	Multi-Factor number (%)	Total
First	0 (0%)	4 (33.3%)	8 (66.7%)	12
Second	2 (16.7%)	7 (58.3%)	3 (25)	12
Third	10 (83.3%)	1 (8.3%)	1 (8.3%)	12
Total	12	12	12	

We can see from Table 3 above 66.7% of the Military participants ranked the multi-factor AoC as their first choice. 33.3% chose the single-factor AoC as their first choice. No one chose the alphanumeric password condition. For the second choice, 58.3% chose the single-factor AoC as their second choice, 25% selected multi-factor AoC as their second choice, and 16.7% selected alphanumeric as their second choice. The least preferred process of the three is the alphanumeric password at 83.3%, while multi-factor and single-factor tie at 8.3%.

Table 4. Number and percentages of civilian participants who ranked each of the three conditions as their first, second, and third choice

Rank	Alphanumeric Password number (%)	Single-Factor number (%)	Multi-Factor number (%)	Total
First	0 (0%)	6 (50%)	6 (50%)	12
Second	1 (8.3%)	6 (50%)	5 (41.7)	12
Third	11 (92.7%)	0 (0%)	1 (8.3%)	12
Total	12	12	12	

Table 4 shows that the Civilian participants ranked the single-factor and multi-factor AoCs as their first choice at 50% each. None of them selected the alphanumeric method. For the second choice, 50% chose the single-factor AoC as their second choice, 41.7% selected multi-factor AoC as their second choice, and 8.3% selected Alphanumeric as their second choice. The least preferred process of the three is also the alphanumeric password at 92.7%, multi-factor was selected as the least preferred by 1 participant, and none selected the single-factor as their least preferred.

5.5 Perception of Usability and Security

In the post-study questionnaire, participants were asked to rank their satisfaction with the security, speed, memorability, and ease of use of each authentication approach using a Likert scale of five points (5- strongly agree, 1 – strongly disagree). All the military group and 92% of the civilian group strongly agreed that the multi-factor AoC improved security. No participant from the military group agreed that the multi-factor AoC took too long. One participant from the civilian group strongly agreed that AoC took too much time. No participant from the military group and only one participant from the civilian group agreed that the multi-factor AoC was challenging to remember. Finally, no participant from the military group agreed that the multi-factor AoC was difficult to use. Only one participant from the civilian group strongly agreed.

When asked for their preferred choice regarding ease of use, both groups of participants ranked single-factor authentication as their first choice (100%). When asked for their preference on the most secured, 100% of the participants in both groups chose the multi-factor AoC as their first choice.

Overall, all military participants have highly positive perceptions regarding both usability and security towards the multi-factor AoC process and are likely to adopt the approach. The perception of the civilian group towards the multi-factor AoC is also positive.

6. DISCUSSION AND LIMITATIONS

We conducted the first study that investigated the use of Authentication of Choice in the healthcare context by professionals from the military. The results suggested that for all factors combined, the multi-factor Authentication of Choice is the most preferred approach by the military participants, with single-factor authentication as the second and the Alphanumeric password the lowest. For civilians, the single-factor and multi-factor AoC approaches were ranked similarly overall, while the alphanumeric approach was the least preferred. Both the military and the civilian participants' preference towards the multi-factor authentication of choice approach over the alphanumeric password suggests that participants like the freedom of choosing authentication methods during authentication. The military group's preference towards the multi-factor AoC approach over the single-factor AoC approach could be attributed to the extra layer of security that multi-factor authentication provides.

Regarding specific measures, both groups of participants perceived the single-factor Authentication of Choice as the most preferred in terms of ease of use and the multi-factor authentication as the most preferred in terms of security. Overall, the results confirmed the potential to adopt the authentication of choice approach by critical security professionals. They also further validated the findings of previous studies (Oluwafemi and Feng, 2020; Arinde et al., 2022) on the adoption of AoC in general and health-related mobile applications to improve user experience and security.

Regarding limitations, the study only investigated a limited set of authentication methods. Some commonly adopted techniques, such as gesture passwords and location-based authentication were not examined. In addition, the number of participants is fairly small and may not represent the diverse user characteristics of the general public or the military profession. We plan to include a broader set of authentication methods and larger, more diverse participants in future studies.

REFERENCES

Abhishek, S. et al., 2013. A Comprehensive Study on Multifactor Authentication Schemes, Meghanathan, N. et al., Advances in Computing and Information Technology. Vol. 177. Springer, Berlin, Heidelberg, https://doi.org/10.1007/978-3-642-31552-7_57.

Aleksandr, O. et al., 2018. Multi-Factor Authentication, A Survey. *Cryptography*, Vol. 2, issue 1, doi:10.3390/cryptography2010001.

Arinde, O. et al., 2022. A Preliminary Investigation of Authentication of Choice in Health-Related Mobile Applications. *Proceedings of 24th HCII.* Pp. 228-240.

Authentication options | Login.gov. www.login.gov. Retrieved April 18, 2023, from https://www.login.gov/help/get-started/authentication-options.

Belk, M. et al., 2013. Security for Diversity: Studying the Effects of Verbal and Imagery Processes on User Authentication Mechanisms. *Proceedings of the IFIP TC13 Conference on Human-Computer Interaction*. South Africa, pp. 442-459. 2013.

Cranor, L. and Buchler, N., 2014. Better Together: Usability and Security Go Hand in Hand. *In IEEE Security & Privacy*, vol. 12, no. 6, pp. 89-93, doi: 10.1109/MSP.2014.109.

Das, S. et al., 2018. Why Johnny Doesn't Use Two Factor a Two-Phase Usability Study of the FIDO U2F Security Key. *In International Conference on Financial Cryptography and Data Security (FC)*.

Dasgupta, D. et al., 2016. Toward the design of adaptive selection strategies for multi-factor authentication. *Computers & Security*. Vol. 63, pp. 85-116, 2016, doi: 10.1016/j.cose.2016.09.004.

Fairweather, P. et al., 2002. From assistive technology to a web accessibility service. *In International Conference on Assistive Technologies (ASSETS). ACM.*

Gunson, N. et al., 2011. User perceptions of security and usability of single-factor and two-factor authentication in automated telephone banking. *Computers & Security*. Vol. 30, no. 4, pp. 208–220, doi: 10.1016/j.cose.2010.12.001.

Hausawi, Y. et al., 2014. Choice-Based Authentication: A Usable-Security Approach, Stephanidis, C. et al., Universal Access in Human-Computer Interaction. Design and Development Methods for Universal Access. *In UAHCI Lecture Notes in Computer Science*. Vol. 8513, Springer, Cham. https://doi.org/10.1007/978-3-319-07437-5_12.

Madhuravani, B. et al., 2013. A Comprehensive Study on Different Authentication Factors. *IJERT*. Vol. 2, no. 10, pp. 1358-1361.

Nilesh, A. et al., 2016. A Review of Authentication Methods. *IJSTR*. Vol. 5, no. 11, pp. 246-249, 2016.

Number of mHealth apps available in the Google Play Store from 1st quarter 2015 to 1st quarter 2021. Statista https://www.statista.com/statistics/779919/health-apps-available-google-play-worldwide/, last accessed 2021/12/17.

Oluwafemi, J. and Feng, J., 2020. How Users Perceive Authentication of Choice on Mobile Devices. *Proceedings of 13th International Conference on Advances in Computer-Human Interactions*. Pp. 345-351.

Vance, C. and Paik, Y., 2005. Forms of Host-Country National Learning for Enhanced MNC Absorptive Capacity. *Journal of Managerial Psychology*. Vol. 20, no. 7, pp. 590–606.

Intertrust Releases 2020 Security Report on Global mHealth App Threats. www.businesswire.com. https://www.businesswire.com/news/home/20200929005146/en/Intertrust-Releases-2020-Security-Report-on-Global-mHealth-App-Threats#:~:text=Intertrust%20released%20their%202020%20Security,a%20breach%20of%20medical%20data.last accessed 2022/02/17.

ASSESSING THE USABILITY OF A MOBILE APP IN A REMOTE ENVIRONMENT: COMBINING THINK ALOUD WITH A USER EXPERIENCE SCALE QUESTIONNAIRE

Virginia Tiradentes Souto and Luiza Reolon Cabral
Design Department, University of Brasilia, Brazil

ABSTRACT

The aim of this study is to investigate an approach for evaluating the user experience of mobile applications in remote environments. The proposed approach includes both thinking aloud and a user experience questionnaire with three types of questions: personalized, scaled, and open-ended. The novelty of this study lies in the proposal of a new form with questions that not only focus on usability but also include other aspects of user experience, such as user characteristics, product features, and previous user experiences. The proposed App User eXperience Scale (AUXS) is based on SUS, but has many differences, including questions about content, visual appeal, content, user expectations, and an NPS question. The proposed approach is tested using a mobile application to promote artists and artisans. The results show that this approach can be useful not only for researchers, but also for designers to validate their creations and for companies offering mobile applications to test the usability of their applications.

KEYWORDS

User Experience, Mobile Application, Remote Environment, Think Aloud, Questionnaires

1. INTRODUCTION

Testing the user experience of mobile applications is important at various stages of product development, such as the interface design phase, the prototype phase and also after implementation and before launch. It is also important to consider how the researcher/designer can reach the target audience for participation in the study. Participants with certain characteristics or distances may be difficult to reach, and the use of remote tools may be a good option for researchers/designers, as well as in times of pandemic when laboratory testing may pose some risk.

There are several methods to test the user experience of a mobile application, such as: task completion, interviews, questionnaires, thinking aloud, heuristic tests, focus groups and more. Each of these tests is used for a specific purpose and has some advantages and disadvantages, so it must be selected considering the context and needs of the project. Among these methods, the think-aloud protocol stands out as one of the most popular methods in usability research (Nielsen, 2012). The think-aloud protocol is considered a highly valued (Fan et al. 2019) and effective method for usability testing to learn people's thoughts about mediating the completion of a task (Souto, 2013). It has been used for many years in various research areas such as cognitive psychology (Davison et al., 1997) and human-computer interaction (Ramey et al., 2006). Thinking aloud has also been used to test mobile apps (Nasruddin et al., 2018) and is considered a useful method for obtaining immediate feedback from end-users about their experience interacting with the app (Oliveira et al. 2022).

Besides the think-aloud protocol, another very common method for usability testing is the questionnaire. A specific type of questionnaire that uses a scale to measure responses is the System Usability Scale (SUS), which can be applied in a short period of time and measures user perceptions (Brooke, 1996). SUS is a widely used tool to determine usability aspects of various systems (Oliveira et al., 2022) and has also been used to evaluate the user experience of mobile apps. Each user experience testing method has advantages and disadvantages, and therefore different evaluation methods are more appropriate depending on the study. Qualitative methods such as the think-aloud protocol can be more useful for understanding user thoughts, gathering user feedback, and identifying issues that need to be addressed. On the other hand, quantitative methods such as usability scaling can provide a general measure of usability (Maramba et al., 2019).

In this study, we explored a user experience evaluation approach for mobile apps using the Think Aloud protocol and a user experience scale inspired by the SUS tool. As a case study, we use an application to promote artists and artisans that is in a testing phase and has not yet been published.

2. RELATED RESEARCH

The proposed approach for evaluating mobile applications in remote environments was based on the Concurrent Think Aloud protocol, followed by a questionnaire based on the System Usability Scale tool. Both methods are described below, as well as mixed approaches to mobile application usability assessment.

2.1 Concurrent Think-Aloud Protocol

The concurrent thinking aloud method (also referred to as classic, McDonald et al. 2016) was first introduced to the literature by Ericsson and Simon (1980) and refers to a test in which participants are asked to verbalise their thoughts while performing tasks (Souto, 2013). Another type of thinking aloud, also introduced by Ericsson and Simon (1980), is retrospective thinking aloud, in which participants verbalise their thoughts after performing tasks.

The think-aloud protocol is considered a widely researched topic (Reeves, 2019). Many researchers have studied the implementation of think-aloud protocols (Fan et al. 2021), the effect of the rater on the think-aloud test (Jacobsen et al. 1998), and also the variability with which instructions are given. For example, Hertzum, Hansen, and Andersen (2009) have shown that changing the instructions given to participants on how to think aloud affects both the assessment process and the outcome.

Many studies that focus on the usability of mobile applications have been conducted using the think-aloud method. Maramba, Chatterjee, and Newman (2019), in a review of methods used exclusively in usability testing of eHealth applications (from 2014 to 2017), found that ⅓ of the studies used the think-aloud method (45 of 133 studies), which was the most commonly used qualitative method. In addition, the think-aloud method was associated with at least one additional iteration of the developed application.

2.2 Usability Scale Questionnaires

Questionnaires are considered one of the most commonly used usability methods. Among their advantages is the fact that they are easy to conduct and analyze [25]. Quizzes are also the most common usability tests found in various literature reviews on mobile apps [11; 26]). According to the literature review by Maramba, Chatterjee, and Newman (2009), the SUS was the most commonly used questionnaire (44 out of 133 studies).

The System Usability Scale (SUS) is a commonly used questionnaire to measure the usability of human-computer interaction systems and mobile applications in particular. According to Brooke (2013), the main goals of SUS are: to provide a measure of subjective perceptions of the usability of a system, and to perform this assessment in the short time available in a session.

The SUS consists of 10 questions, each with five possible answers on a 5-point Likert scale (from "strongly disagree" to "strongly agree"). The questions relate to the ease of use and simplicity of the system being learned and concern: frequency of use, system complexity, technical support, functional integration, system consistency, system reliability, learning to systemize. The ten questions of SUS are (Brooke, 1996): (1) I think that I would like to use this system frequently, (2) I found the system unnecessarily complex, (3) I thought the system was easy to use, (4) I think that I would need the support of a technical person to be able to use this system, (5) I found the various functions in this system were well integrated, (6) I thought there was too much inconsistency in this system, (7) I would imagine that most people would learn to use this system very quickly, (8) I found the system very cumbersome to use, (9) I felt very confident using the system, and (10) I needed to learn a lot of things before I could get going with this system.

More recently, some researchers have proposed adaptations of the SUS tool to test the usability of mobile apps (Kaya et al., 2019), as well as other tools developed for specific topics, such as the specific questionnaire for health-related apps: MARS - mHealth app quality rating tool (Stoyanov et al. 2015), and MAUQ - The mHealth app usability questionnaire (Zhou et al., 2019). Some of the reasons for adapting the tool SUS are that SUS is not a specific scale for mobile apps, and while it is useful for identifying general usability issues and providing an overview, it is not intended to identify usability issues specific to mobile devices (Kaya et al., 2019). There are also some versions for specific languages, such as Spanish, to ensure conceptual, semantic, and contextual equivalence between SUS and the translated version (Sevilla-Gonzalez et al., 2020) or Indonesian adaptation through cross-cultural adaptation and reliability testing (Sharfina and Santoso, 2016), or for specific user groups, such as the SUS, adapted for testing with children (Putnam et al., 2020).

2.3 Mixing Approaches to Measuring Usability of Mobile Applications

As mentioned by Drew, Falcone, and Baccus (2018), SUS can be more useful when used in conjunction with other usability methods. There are several studies that use a mixed methods approach to mobile application evaluation. For example, O'Grady et al. (2019) used a combination of 4 methods: think-aloud tasks, task success ratings, semistructured interviews, and usability questionnaires (e.g. SUS) to assess the usability of a mobile application for guiding health professionals. To measure usability ratings of a mobile application for neuroanatomy, Ponte et al. (2019) used two types of questionnaires: SUS to determine usability and learnability; and another five questions to determine participants' perceptions of the usefulness of the application, perceived usefulness. On the other hand, Weichbroth (2019) proposes a mixed methodology for measuring and evaluating the usability of mobile applications. This methodology consists of three integrated methods: research, participant observation, and verbal protocol analysis, and aims to provide quantitative and qualitative data and a complete overview of the quality of application use and users' attitudes and perceptions.

While some authors mention the effectiveness of their mixed-methods approaches, others only address the effectiveness of the product tested. The aim of this study is to test a methodological approach to evaluate the user experience of mobile applications. The study is based on a case study of an application for promoting artists and artisans, which is described below.

3. METHOD

To test the effectiveness of combining Thinking Aloud methods with usability questionnaires in a remote environment, an empirical experiment was conducted. The mobile application used in this study, Nicho, an application to promote artists and artisans, was developed by some of the researchers who participated in this study and has not yet been launched. The methodology and results are described below.

3.1 Case study

Testing was conducted using a concurrent think-aloud protocol followed by a usability questionnaire scale with a subjective question. The study used as research material a new application that is in its final testing phase. The application, called Nicho, is intended to be a virtual space where artisans and artists can promote their work and connect with customers. It also provides information about physical fairs taking place in the city, as well as information for artists and artisans. The app has two main user groups: Artists and artisans and the customers. The main areas of the app are: product, places, saved, follow e chat. Figure 1 show examples of Nicho application screens.

Figure 1. Screen imageshot of the app presentation (left) and the Nicho app home page

3.2 Data Collection and Participants

The purpose of the test was to verify the user experience with the application in the two established user groups. The tests were conducted in remote mode. First, the researchers visited physical fairs held in the city to recruit representative participants for the study. The study targeted different groups of participants: men and women, artists/craftspeople, and customers.

First, participants received an email or Whatsapp message (depending on the participant's choice) to schedule an appointment for the test. Then, participants were briefly informed about the experiment and asked to complete the informed consent form. To participate in this study, participants were required to use an Android phone, as the application only works on an Android platform for now. Participants were required to download the app to their cell phones. Testing was conducted in the Google Meet system, so they had access to the video call through their browser and did not need to download a communication app to connect to the researcher specifically for the test. Participants' activities were recorded during the tests, and they were asked to answer the questions and speak aloud while interacting with the application. There were two ways to access the application: one for clients and one for artists. Customers answered 9 questions and artists answered 10 questions (there was an additional task for artists: they were asked to publish a product). Examples of questions are: (1) Find ceramic plates and see what their price is; (2) Make the purchase of these dishes; and (3) Choose a product you like and save it. After participants answered the questions, the recording was stopped, and participants were asked to answer a Google form containing 4 pieces of personal information (sex, age, occupation, education), 11 scaled questions (1 to 5, strongly disagree to strongly agree), and 2 open-ended questions (one about the application and one about the test).

In agreement with Kaya et al. (2019) that SUS is not a specific scale for mobile applications and therefore may not be as helpful in identifying specific user experience issues for mobile devices, a user experience scale form is proposed that includes questions more related to mobile applications. The user experience tool used in this test included 4 questions adapted from the SUS tool (questions 1, 2, 3, and 5), with the same meaning and almost the same words as the original (only adapted to be more consistent with the other questions, including the term app instead of system), others revised to be more direct and adapted to the context of use, one based on an NPS question, but instead of a scale from 0 to 10, the scale 1 to 5 was kept. The proposed scaled questions of the form (translated from Portuguese) and the open-ended questions were:

App User Experience Scale (AUES):

1. I would use this app often.
2. I found the app easy to use.
3. I think I would need the help of a person with more experience to use it.
4. I think the features of the app would be useful to me.
5. I can imagine learning how to use this app quickly.
6. How likely are you to recommend this app to others?
7. I found the app to be visually appealing.
8. I think this app stands out from other apps like Etsy, Instagram, and Pinterest.

9. I like the content of the app.
10. It took me a long time to find anything.
11. Overall, my expectations for the app were met.

Open questions:

1. Is there anything else you would like to say about the app?
2. What do you think of our survey?

To ensure that the researchers proceeded in the same way for each of the participants, a research route was planned. As Hertzum, Hansen, and Andersen (2009) noted, the variability used to explain the instructions in the think-aloud test may affect the results of the study. Also, considering that the test is conducted in a remote environment, many steps are required, as well as technical equipment (cell phones, operating systems, recording software, contact software, etc.), and prior contact, downloading the application, and more. Considering all these aspects, the research journey for this study was divided into two main phases: the selection of users and the day of the interview.

The test was conducted with 10 participants, but two results were discarded due to problems in recording the test. For this, the data of 8 participants were analyzed: half were artists/craftsmen and the other half were customers. Regarding sex, four were female, 3 were male, and one preferred not to provide any information. The age group of the participants was very diverse: half were between 20 and 20 years old and the others were between 30 and 60 years old or older. The participants had different professions: the clients were civil servants, students, college professors and entrepreneurs, while the artists described themselves as artists, designers and copywriters, plastic artists and illustrators. All of them had at least a college degree.

3.3 Think-Aloud Results and Discussion

Participants took about 10 minutes to answer the questions (minimum 7, maximum 13 minutes). Of all the answers, only one participant could not solve one task (Find the product you previously saved). This indicates that participants had no problems with accuracy when using the app. In general, the time to answer the questions decreased as the test progressed, indicating that familiarity with the app is helpful to the user experience.

It was observed that participants expressed their feelings, preferences, and navigation behaviors when using the app by speaking aloud. For example, one participant found it strange to create a storage folder and suggested the Instagram app as an example of use. In terms of navigation, the results show that thinking aloud helps designers understand where users look first, what grabs their attention, and which path users prefer. This is because users talked out loud about where they look, how they navigate, and what they pay attention to.

Participants' insights or suggestions for improving the Niche app include: increasing the size of the profile photo, linking artists, decreasing the number of levels to reach the purchase screen, and increasing the size of the font in some areas. In addition, it was recognized that the method of thinking aloud captured the emotions of the participants. The joy of finding something they like, or the disappointment of not finding it, or still having difficulty finding an answer to a question, or an estrangement with a function different from what they are used to is captured by this method.

3.4 App User Experience Scale (AUES): Results and Discussion

As explained earlier, the App user experience scale (AUES) proposed in this study includes 11 questions and uses a scale from 1 to 5 (strongly disagree to strongly agree). The proposed questionnaire is based on SUS, but has many differences, including questions about content, visual appeal, content, user expectations, and an NPS question. The AUXS calculation method is the same as for SUS: (1) add the score contributions of each item (from 1 to 5), (2) for positive items related to the application, the score is the position of the scale minus 1, for negative items (items 3 and 10), the score is 5 minus the position of the scale, (3) multiply the sum of the scores by 2.5 to get the total score. The score ranges from 0 to 100.

In terms of frequency, the majority of participants found the app easy to use and that they would use the app frequently. The third question was about the need for help in using the app. But unlike the original question in SUS tools, which asks if the participant thinks he/she "would need the support of a technical person to be able to use this system," it was adapted in this form to ask for help from "a person with more experience." This is meant to sound more common, as users have quicker access to people around them with more experience who can help them with the app than assistance from a "technical person". In this test, most participants felt they did not need help from a person with more experience, confirming the ease of use of the app.

Regarding the NPS (Net Promoter Score) question: How likely are you to recommend this app to others? most participants (87.5%) answered 5, and one participant (12.5%) answered 4. This means that it is valid to spread the application to others. The NPS is considered a simple and effective method for measuring and monitoring customer satisfaction (Sasmito et al., 2019). Moreover, positive NPS (likelihood to recommend) scores indicate that users' willingness to install an app also increases (Wohllebe et al., 2020).

In this study, all participants found the app visually appealing. The beauty of the app was also mentioned by some participants during the Think Aloud test and in the open-ended questions.

This form also differs from that of the SUS tool in that it includes a question about the content of the app. How close or interested users are in the content of the app seems to have an impact on their experience with the app. According to Stoyanov et al. (2015), one of the 5 app quality criteria is the information quality of the app (the other four are: engagement, functionality, aesthetics, and subjective quality categories). The authors divide information quality into seven sub-criteria: accuracy of app description, goals, quality of information, quantity of information, visual information, credibility, evidence base. The Nicho app not only establishes a contact between artists, artisans, and consumers, but also provides information about the artists so that they can be informed about certain laws, rights, deities and opportunities. It also provides a space to inform consumers and interested parties about events such as fairs in a particular city.

The last question was related to the users' general expectation of the app. This question is also important to understand the overall picture of the app for users. Even if users find some points of improvement or difficulties in the user experience, the overall impression may be positive or negative, and the problems found may or may not affect the overall impression and desire to continue using the app. In the case study, participants felt that their overall expectations of the app were I (91.37 out of 100).

3.5 Insights from the Opening Questions

The test contained two opening questions: one related to the app and the other to the survey. These are not required answers to complete the form. Regarding the app, the form included a question asking if the participant had anything else to say about the app. Six of the eight participants answered this question. Some of the participants mentioned good things about the app, such as: easy to learn, very intuitive user interface, great logo. However, others took the opportunity to make other suggestions for the app, such as: Repeat the idea of creating "sub-filters" and gave an example: "Accessories - > silver accessories | gold accessories | with stone...; Ceramics - > painted | nature | vases | dishes | mugs (in this case you could select more than one, such as painted ceramics and mugs" (Participant's text translated from Portuguese)".

The last question of the form was designed to clarify participants' perceptions of the questionnaire, which contained three types of questions: Multiple choice, scaled, and open-ended questions. Five of the eight participants answered this question. All provided positive feedback about the survey, such as: easy to understand and participate in, agile, well-structured and straightforward, calm, and very direct.

4. CONCLUSIONS

The proposed approach to evaluating the user experience of mobile applications in remote environments includes both thinking aloud and a user experience questionnaire with personalized, scaled, and open-ended questions. While it can be considered common to mix thinking aloud and questionnaires in this type of test, the novelty of this study is the description and explanation of the whole approach (including the research journey), as well as the proposal of a new form with questions that not only focus on usability but also include other aspects of user experience, such as user characteristics, product features, and previous user experiences. In addition, the proposed approach focused on the evaluation of mobile applications in remote environments.

This study confirms other studies that claim that the Thinking Aloud method can help understand users' thoughts and identify usability problems when using the app (Nasuddin et al. 2018; Cho et al., 2019). In addition, the results show that the Thinking Aloud method promotes participants' spontaneity and sincerity. The participants' emotions could be captured during the test, with their engagement, difficulties, and surprises.

Finally, the thinking aloud method can also help designers compare their app with the competition, as participants mention features they know from other apps or would like to find in the app they are using.

The proposed scaled questionnaire (called AUXS - App User eXperience Scale) showed to be an effective approach to evaluate the user experience of a mobile application. Like the SUS tool (Brooke, 1995), the proposed tool is easy to answer and quick to apply. The differences in terms of questions, as explained earlier, are in the evaluation of aspects of the user experience that are not mentioned in SUS, but others, such as: User characteristics (information about the user's age, gender, education and profession), internal state (question about the user's general expectations), cultural differences (the form was adapted to the Portuguese language and the context of use by the participants), product characteristics (questions about the usefulness of the functions and the content), brand image (question about visual appearance) and previous experience (question comparing very well-known similar applications). The questionnaire contains different types of questions: multiple choice (for user characteristics), scaled questions (from 1 to 5, strongly disagree to strongly agree), and open-ended questions. It also contains an NPS question aimed at indicating the level of potential recommendation of the app and, related to this, the possibility of installing it (Wohllebe et al., 2020).

Regarding the limitations of this study, it is important to highlight that the study was conducted with few participants. Although studies suggest that as few as 5 participants are sufficient for usability testing (Nielsen, 2000), it seems that the proposed form should be tested in different contexts and with more people to further verify the order of questions and the number of positive and negative statements, among others. Another limitation was that the selected case study so far only works on the Android system (which limited the number of participants). Since it was difficult to find volunteers and organize the tests with them, it was not possible to check if there were differences between the different groups of participants, for example between men and women, young and elderly. Therefore, the tests should be conducted with more participants, different groups of participants and different case studies (with different types of applications).

ACKNOWLEDGEMENT

We would like to thank all the participants who took part in this research. This research was supported by the Department of Design - Art Institute - University of Brasília.

REFERENCES

Brooke, B. 1996. SUS: A 'Quick and Dirty' Usability Scale. In: Usability Evaluation In Industry. Edited by: dited By Patrick W. Jordan, B. Thomas, Ian Lyall McClelland, Bernard Weerdmeester. CRC Press.

Cho H, Powell D, Pichon A, Kuhns LM, Garofalo R, Schnall R. 2019. Eye-tracking retrospective think-aloud as a novel approach for a usability evaluation. Int J Med Inform. 2019 Sep;129:366-373. doi: 10.1016/j.ijmedinf.2019.07.010.

Davison, G. C., Vogel, R. S., & Coffman, S. G. (1997). Think-aloud approaches to cognitive assessment and the articulated thoughts in simulated situations paradigm. Journal of Consulting and Clinical Psychology, 65(6), 950–958. https://doi.org/10.1037/0022-006X.65.6.950

Drew, M.R., Falcone, B., Baccus, W.L. 2018. What Does the System Usability Scale (SUS) Measure?. In: Marcus, A., Wang, W. (eds) Design, User Experience, and Usability: Theory and Practice. DUXU 2018. Lecture Notes in Computer Science(), vol 10918. Springer, Cham. https://doi.org/10.1007/978-3-319-91797-9_25

Ericsson, K. A. and Simon, H. A. 1980. Verbal reports as data. _Psychological Review_ 87 (3):215-251. DOI 10.1037/0033-295x.87.3.215

Fan, M., Zhao, Q. and Tibdewal, V.. 2021. Older Adults' Think-Aloud Verbalizations and Speech Features for Identifying User Experience Problems. In Proceedings of the 2021 CHI Conference on Human Factors in Computing Systems (CHI '21). Association for Computing Machinery, New York, NY, USA, Article 358, 1–13. https://doi.org/10.1145/3411764.3445680

Fan, M., Lin, J., Chung, C. and Truong, K. N. 2019. Concurrent Think-Aloud Verbalizations and Usability Problems. ACM Trans. Comput.-Hum. Interact. 26, 5, Article 28 (October 2019). https://doi.org/10.1145/3325281

Hertzum, M., Hansen, K. D., and Andersen, H. H. K. 2009. Scrutinising usability evaluation: does thinking aloud affect behaviour and mental workload?, Behaviour & Information Technology, 28:2, 165-181, DOI: 10.1080/01449290701773842

Jacobsen, Niels & Hertzum, Morten & John, Bonnie. (1998). The Evaluator Effect in Usability Studies: Problem Detection and Severity Judgments. Proceedings of the Human Factors and Ergonomics Society Annual Meeting. 42. 1336-1340. 10.1177/154193129804201902.

Kaya, A., Ozturk, R., Altin Gumussoy, C. 2019. Usability Measurement of Mobile Applications with System Usability Scale (SUS). In: Calisir, F., Cevikcan, E., Camgoz Akdag, H. (eds) Industrial Engineering in the Big Data Era. Lecture Notes in Management and Industrial Engineering. Springer, Cham. https://doi.org/10.1007/978-3-030-03317-0_32

Maramba, I.D., Chatterjee, A., & Newman, C. 2019. Methods of usability testing in the development of eHealth applications: A scoping review. International journal of medical informatics, 126, 95-104. DOI:10.1016/J.IJMEDINF.2019.03.018

McDonald, S., Zhao, T. and Edwards. H. M. 2016.Look Who's Talking: Evaluating the Utility of Interventions During an Interactive Think-Aloud, in Interacting with Computers, 28 (3), 387-403, May 2016, doi: 10.1093/iwc/iwv014.

Nasruddin, Z.A., Markom, A., Abdul Aziz, M. (2018). Evaluating Construction Defect Mobile App Using Think Aloud. In: Abdullah, N., Wan Adnan, W., Foth, M. (eds) User Science and Engineering. i-USEr 2018. Communications in Computer and Information Science, vol 886. Springer, Singapore. https://doi.org/10.1007/978-981-13-1628-9_1

Nielsen, J. 2000. Why You Only Need to Test with 5 Users. https://www.nngroup.com/articles/why-you-only-need-to-test-with-5-users/

Nielsen, J. 2012. Thinking Aloud: The #1 Usability Tool. https://www.nngroup.com/articles/thinking-aloud-the-1-usability-tool/

Oliveira, E.R., Branco, A.C., Carvalho, D. et al. An Iterative Process for the Evaluation of a Mobile Application Prototype. SN COMPUT. SCI. 3, 262 (2022). https://doi.org/10.1007/s42979-022-01153-6

Ponte, R. P., Sanders, L. L. O., Peixoto Júnior, A. A., Kubrusly, M., Marçal, E. 2019. Development and Usability Assessment of a Mobile Application for Neuroanatomy Teaching: A Case Study in Brazil. Creative Education, Vol. 10 No.3. DOI: 10.4236/ce.2019.103043

Ramey, J., Boren, T., Cuddihy, E., Dumas, J., Guan, Z., van den Haak, M. J. and De Jong, M. D. T.. 2006. Does think aloud work? how do we know? In CHI '06 Extended Abstracts on Human Factors in Computing Systems (CHI EA '06). Association for Computing Machinery, New York, NY, USA, 45–48. https://doi.org/10.1145/1125451.1125464

Reeves, S. 2019. How UX Practitioners Produce Findings in Usability Testing. ACM Trans. Comput.-Hum. Interact. 26, 1, Article 3 (February 2019), 38 pages. https://doi.org/10.1145/3299096

Sasmito, G. W., Zulfiqar, L. O. M. and Nishom, M., 2019. Usability Testing based on System Usability Scale and Net Promoter Score, International Seminar on Research of Information Technology and Intelligent Systems (ISRITI), 2019, pp. 540-545, doi: 10.1109/ISRITI48646.2019.9034666.

Sevilla-Gonzalez M. D. R., Moreno Loaeza L., Lazaro-Carrera L. S., Bourguet Ramirez B., Vázquez Rodríguez A., Peralta-Pedrero M. L., Almeda-Valdes P. 2020. Spanish Version of the System Usability Scale for the Assessment of Electronic Tools: Development and Validation. JMIR Hum Factors. 2020 Dec 16;7(4):e21161. doi: 10.2196/21161.

Sharfina, Z. and Santoso, H. B. 2016. An Indonesian adaptation of the System Usability Scale (SUS), International Conference on Advanced Computer Science and Information Systems (ICACSIS), 2016, pp. 145-148, DOI: 10.1109/ICACSIS.2016.7872776.

Souto, V. T. (2013). Users' perceptions of the arrangement of links in government websites: an investigation using think-aloud and interview methods. InfoDesign - Revista Brasileira De Design Da Informação, 8(2), 01–14. https://doi.org/10.51358/id.v8i2.122

Stoyanov S. R., Hides L., Kavanagh D. J., Zelenko O, Tjondronegoro D, Mani M. 2015. Mobile App Rating Scale: A New Tool for Assessing the Quality of Health Mobile Apps. JMIR Mhealth Uhealth 2015;3(1):e27. DOI:10.2196/mhealth.3422

Weichbroth, P. 2019. A mixed-methods measurement and evaluation methodology for mobile application usability studies. Communication Papers of the Federated Conference on Computer Science and Information Systems pp. 101–106. DOI: 10.15439/2019F299.

Wohllebe, A., Ross, F. & Podruzsik, S. 2020. Influence of the Net Promoter Score of Retailers on the Willingness of Consumers to Install Their Mobile App. International Association of Online Engineering. Retrieved August 23, 2022 from https://www.learntechlib.org/p/218399/.

Zhou L, Bao J, Setiawan IMA, Saptono A, Parmanto B. 2019. The mHealth App Usability Questionnaire (MAUQ): Development and Validation Study. JMIR Mhealth Uhealth 2019;7(4):e11500. DOI: 10.2196/11500

VIRTUAL HAND MODEL AND ANIMATION

Arman A. Hovhannisyan and Artak A. Khemchyan
National Polytechnic University of Armenia
Yerevan, Armenia

ABSTRACT

The human hand is a sophisticated biomechanical system responsible for everyday interactions with the surrounding environment. Like in real life, the hand is considered the primary manipulating mechanism in virtual reality (VR). VR is a computer-generated environment that makes users feel like they act in the real world. This effect, described as immersion, is reached using VR equipment, which usually includes a head-mounted device (HMD) with near-eye displays employing stereoscopy and a mechanism to track the user's position and motions. The degree of immersion and presence are among the main characteristics describing a virtual environment (VE). One way to improve these characteristics is by enabling natural user interactions, made possible by using the user's hands as the main body component for interactions. Prior research indicates that higher immersion and realism in VR systems are still to reach a satisfactory level. This paper aims to increase immersion and presence in VEs, proposing a method for high-fidelity 3D hand models to simulate hand gestures as they appear in real life.

KEYWORDS

Human-Computer Interaction, Virtual reality, Animation, Immersion, Presence

1. INTRODUCTION

Human interaction with the surrounding environment has long been a research topic. The human hand, with its functionality of grasping and manipulating objects, is of particular interest. It is one of the environmental perception organs and the main manipulation organ in the human organism. Like in the real world, hands are considered the main manipulator objects in immersive virtual worlds. The main focus of incorporating a hand model in the Virtual Environment (VE) is to increase the sense of embodiment in users and to give them the illusion that they are literally getting their hands into the VE and directly interacting with virtual objects. This increases the feeling of immersion and presence and lets the users participate in virtual interactive experimentation. As reported by V. Schwind et al. (2017), natural user interactions with the virtual environment are made possible by rendering the user's hand as the primary body component for interaction.

To develop a precise and correct virtual hand model, it is essential to understand human behavior in a virtual world. It is well described in the behavioral loop "Perception-Cognition-Action-Simulation" (Figure 1), defined in (Ahmad et al., 2019) as a variant of a classical "Perception-Cognition-Action" classical model (Cariani, 1989). According to this model, there are three modules: users, behavioral interfaces, and interactive virtual environment. The behavioral interface comprises two components: Motor interfaces, which enable the acquisition of real hand movements, and Sensory interfaces, which communicate the sensory feedback to the user. When a real hand action is performed, this action is tracked by the motor interfaces, translated to virtual hand movements, and interpreted as a request for the modification of the VE. In response to this request, different sensory feedbacks can be transferred to the different sensory interfaces to be rendered, thus giving a proper perception of the virtual world. The correspondence of action and perception has a significant impact on the level of interactivity and immersion. Thus, it can be concluded that a realistic hand model with life-like animated motions is essential to an interactive and immersive VE.

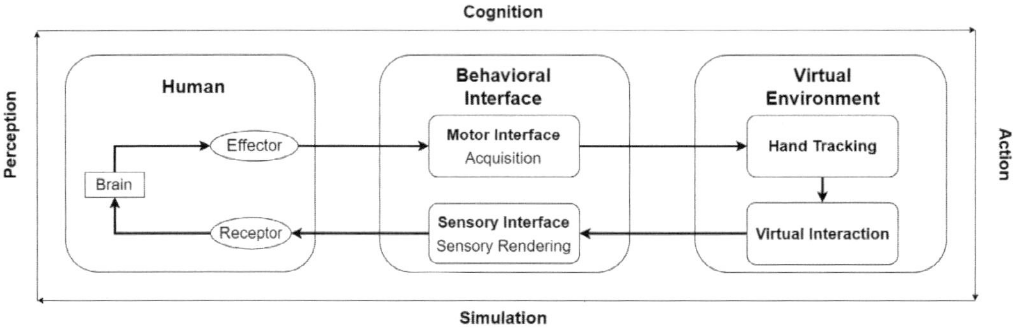

Figure 1. Human behavioral loop in a virtual environment

Much research effort has been afforded to create a virtual hand model. Based on hand anatomy and hand kinematics, E. Peña-Pitarch et al. suggested a 25 DOF hand skeleton model that took into account finger workspace, joint range of motion, and the Denavit-Hartenberg approach to establish joint relationships (Peña-Pitarch et al., 2014). Another hand model was developed by J. Jacobs and B. Froehlich (2011) to make finger-based virtual object operations more reliable. In their research, they make the supposition that each phalanx of the hand model is made up of a number of malleable soft bodies that dynamically conform to the shape of items being grabbed according to the forces being applied. It results in larger contact areas for stronger forces, increasing the friction between hand and object as it would occur in reality. They extend the FastLSM (Lattice Shape Matching) algorithm to consider adaptive stiffness values, which leads to a much-simplified configuration of object and friction parameters. In another work, L. Lin and S. Jörg carried out two studies in which subjects were exposed to six different controllable hand models, including robotic and realistic hands, with each presentation having a different look. The findings showed that realistic models are regarded to have the largest effect of engagement, whereas non-anthropomorphic models had a lower effect. (Lin and Jörg, 2016).

The models mentioned above lack visually realistic results, as opposed to high-fidelity 3D models captured from 2D images. This process is known as a method of 3D reconstruction. The technique of capturing the form and look of actual objects in 3D is known as 3D reconstruction. This procedure can be carried out either actively or passively. One may identify the 3D profile of any object and the 3D coordinate of any point on the profile using 3D reconstruction. There are two main strategies for performing this task: depth sensors (Tang et al., 2014) and RGB sensors (Zimmerman and Brox, 2017). Depth sensors and depth maps are used in active reconstruction methods, where the 3D model is reconstructed by the numerical approximation method. 3D scanning (Daneshmand et al., 2018) may be referred to as an active method of reconstruction. Passive reconstruction techniques merely employ a sensor to detect the illumination reflected or radiated by the object's surface in order to deduce its 3D structure through picture interpretation use RGB sensors in addition to digital photos.

Image understanding systems that exploit deep learning techniques are fast evolving in recent years. In this paper, we consider a system named Hand 3-D Studio, which uses a convolutional neural network (CNN) to detect 2D hand key points, and uses these key points in an iterative pixel growth matching strategy for 3D reconstruction. To get the final hand mesh, the Linear Blend Skinning (LBS) and non-rigid Iterative Closest Points (ICP) algorithms are performed to fit a template hand mesh to the reconstructed point cloud (Zhao et al., 2020).

Another aspect affecting user immersion and presence is the input interface connecting the user to the virtual world. Various methods of input interfaces exist, such as hand-held controllers, data gloves, and vision-based hand-tracking systems. Using data gloves often requires complex calibration and setup procedures to obtain precise measurements (Erol et al., 2007). The vision-based techniques also introduce some obstacles to the natural user interaction. The Leap Motion Controller optical hand-tracking module is reported to have issues with gesture detection in particular. It is a device fixed to the front of the head-mounted device (HMD) and has a single viewpoint of the user's hands. In situations where the user's hand is covered by the palm or the other hand, the software results in tracking inaccurate finger positions (Pietikäinen et al., 2021). Thus, this paper considers the headset hand-held controllers as an input interface. Because the interaction through controllers is held by pressing/releasing various buttons, a method is needed to map these button events to corresponding actions in the virtual world. This paper presents a method for making a high-fidelity realistic hand model performing life-like actions and movements intuitively coupled with the headset controller buttons based on their natural position in hand.

2. METHODOLOGY

First, the 3-D Hand Studio system is used to generate a 3D hand model based on an RGB image. The input image is selected from the public Multi-view 4K dataset. After generating the hand model, hand motion animations for specific hand gestures are created for this model in the Unity Engine. Following that, based on specific criteria described in section 2.3, these animations are paired with the HTC Vive Cosmos Elite headset controller buttons.

2.1 Hand Structure

The human hand is a highly complex biomechanical device, which allows it to perform a great variety of tasks. Therefore, a biomechanical analysis is essential for getting a realistic hand model. The hand consists of a wrist, a palm, and 5 fingers. It includes 19 bones: 5 metacarpal bones (MC), 5 proximal phalanges (PP), 4 middle phalanges (MP), and 5 distal phalanges (DP). There are several constraints called joints limiting the bone positions in the space. These joints are referred to as metacarpophalangeal joint (MCP) for the joint connecting the MC to the PP, proximal interphalangeal joint for the joint connecting the PP and MP, distal interphalangeal joint for the joint connecting the MP and DP, and interphalangeal joint for the joint connecting the PP and DP in the thumb (Figure 2) (Gustus et al., 2012).

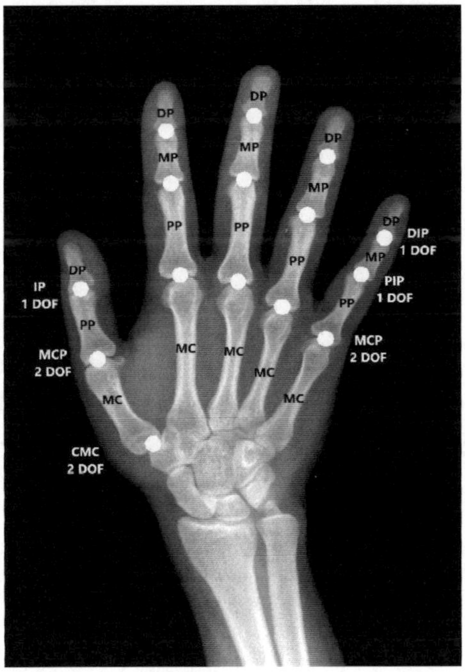

Figure 2. Hand bones and joints

2.2 Model Reconstruction

For generating a 3D hand model from multiple images, we refer to a system named Hand 3-D Studio (Zhao et al., 2020). The system uses customized hardware for hand image capture. It is a holder with adjustable height and angle, with the height ranging between 4.26 feet and 5.90 feet and the angle ranging between 0 and 45 degrees. The setup includes 8 Canon EOS-80D DSLR cameras and 7 Canon EOS-1200D DSLR cameras. The system makes use of 2D hand pose estimation to determine hand key points for further use in reconstruction, multi-viewpoint cloud registration, and non-rigid iterative closest point (ICP) algorithm.

The 2D hand key points are obtained through a cascaded convolutional neural network (CNN) (Wang et al., 2019). Prior research indicated that silhouette is one of the most important cues for hand post estimation. Thus, this network takes advantage of the silhouette information of the hand. The hand pose is represented as k keypoint locations denoted as x_k, with $k \in [1, 21]$, where each keypoint corresponds to a different landmark on the heatmap. A key point detector d maps an input color image $I \in R^{w \times h \times 3}$ to keypoint locations x_k, each with an associated detection confidence c_k:

$$d(I) \rightarrow \{(x_k, c_k), k \in [1, 21]\}$$

The detector is trained on images, hand mask, and keypoint annotations from training examples (I^t, M^t, $\{x_k{}^t\}$), where t denotes a particular color image, M^t denotes the mask for that particular image, and $\{x_k{}^t\}$ includes all the key points. An initial detector d_0 is trained with stochastic gradient descent using a training set T_0 having N_0 samples:

$$T_0 \ = \{(I^t, M^t, \{y_k^t\}), t \in [1, N_0]\}$$

$$d_0 \leftarrow train(T_0)$$

The detector d_0 is used to generate labeled images T_1, which can be used to improve the detector:

$$d_1 \leftarrow train(T_0 \ \cup \ T_1)$$

To detect the 2D hand joints, a convolutional neural network is used, which is composed of 2 stages: mask prediction stage and post prediction stage. To predict the hand mask, the convolutional stages of the pre-initialized VGG-19 network up to conv4_4 are used. It produces a 128-channel feature F, which is then convoluted to produce s 2-channel mask. There are 3 pooling operations in this network, which means for an input image of size m x m, the output is $\frac{m}{8}$.

The second stage of this network is the post-prediction stage, which produces a set of k confidence maps, one for each key point k. This stage is divided into 5 sequential sub-stages, with each stage taking as input the mask prediction stage result and the result from the previous sub-stage.

The softmax loss is used as the loss function of the mask prediction stage:

$$L_m \ = \ -\frac{1}{N_0}\sum \log(\frac{e^{S_y}}{\sum_j e^{S_j}})$$

where $j \in \{0, 1\}$, s_j is the output score for the jth label in the mask prediction stage, and y is the ground-truth label.

The L_2 loss is used as the loss function of the hand pose prediction stage:

$$L_p = \frac{1}{N}\sum \|f - g\|$$

where g is the ground-truth joint heatmaps, and f is the output of the hand pose prediction stage.

The network is designed for images of size m x m x 3, with m = 368. Therefore, before being fed into the CNN, the input images are resized firstly with a ratio τ, where τ is defined as:

$$\tau = \min\left(\frac{m}{w}, \frac{m}{h}\right)$$

To train the network, the public dataset OneHand10K is used, out of which 10000 are used for training, and 1703 are used for validation.

The key point detection process is applied to each input image set for a single hand position. Thus, there are v detections for each key point, where v is the number of input images. After having the 2D key points detected, the next step to accomplish the 3D reconstruction from multiple images is locating these key points in 3D space, referred to as Location Determination Problem (LDP). To solve this problem, the Random Sample

Consensus (RANSAC) algorithm is used (Fischler and Bolles, 1981). A reprojection error of 4 pixels is selected for the inliers. To obtain the final 3D position of the key point, the reprojection error is minimized:

$$x_k^t = arg\min_x \sum_{v \in I_k^t} \|P_v(x) - x_k^v\|_2^2$$

where I_k^t is the inlier set, x_k^t is the located key point in the frame t, and $P_v(x)$ is the projection of 3D point x into the view v.

Finally, Linear Blend Skinning (LBS) and non-rigid Iterative Closest Point (ICP) algorithms are performed to obtain the final hand mesh model. The resulting 3D model is demonstrated in Figure 3. The model mesh data includes 13654 triangles and 40962 vertices.

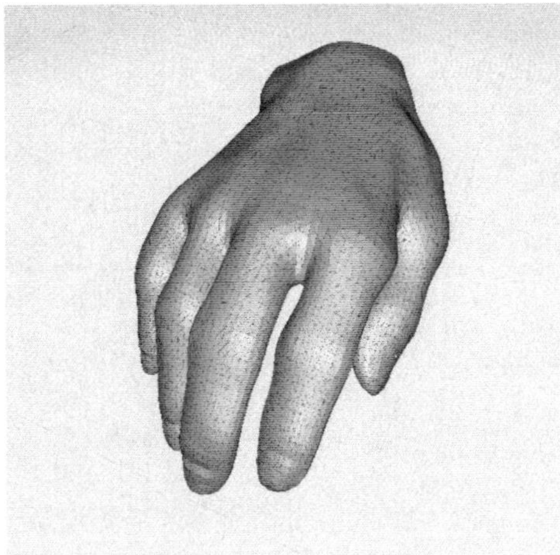

Figure 3. Hand mesh model

2.3 VR Controllers

The HTC Vive Cosmos Elite headset was utilized for simulations throughout this paper. It implements a "room-scale" virtual reality, allowing users to walk around the play area. Two external base stations are put up in the tracked area to monitor the headset and controller placements. The base stations have two infrared lasers coupled to revolving spinners and an array of LED lights that sweep the play area on a regular basis. In order to calculate their relative position in 3D space, the photosensors built into the headset and controllers detect the LED lights and compare their timing to that of the laser sweeps. The headset uses motion controllers (Figure 4) containing circular trackpads, a side button, a trigger button, and an infrared sensor ring with 24 infrared sensors for tracking the base stations and determining the location of the controller. The controllers are tracked with a fraction of a millimeter accuracy due to the update rates 250Hz – 1000Hz.

As already discussed, the vision-based techniques allowing the user to interact with the virtual world using bare hands aren't still at a satisfactory level due to known tracking issues. Thus, the headset controllers serve as an input interface in our system. This, in turn, raises the problem of designing a user-friendly and intuitive input interface. It means that when performing hand interactions in the virtual world using handheld controllers, the hand has to be in its natural position as it would be in real life. For this reason, a method is developed to map the controller buttons to particular hand animations. An essential criterion for this method is that the mappings created should help the user to act in the virtual world, increasing the feeling of immersion and presence and letting the user feel like he is actually performing the action. Below are reviewed the controller buttons and the corresponding action taking place in the virtual world, and the mapping is defined for each button.

The mapping starts from the trigger button, which is used to select or activate an object. To select an item in real life, one would show it. An assumption can be carried out: in this case, the index finger is extended, and the other fingers are flexed. With this assumption in place, the method maps the trigger button press event to animate the hand from the open state to close all the fingers but the index finger, and vice versa for the button release event. This idea is further supported by the fact that the index finger is on the grip button while holding the controller in its normal posture. So, by pressing the button with the index finger user would see his index finger showing at some point in the virtual world. In the same manner, a mapping is defined for the controller grip button, which is used to grasp objects. Naturally, when grasping and holding an object, all the fingers would be in a closed state. Thus, the method maps the grip button push event to bend all the fingers and vice versa for the button release event. In real life, there may be situations where the user wants to bend specific fingers, not necessarily for object interaction. For this reason, a clockwise strategy is selected to apply to the touchpad. The left quarter of the touchpad is selected for the thumb, taking into account that in the controller's natural position, this is the closest button to the thumb. The following is then described for the clockwise strategy: Middle finger, ring finger, and little finger with the touchpad's top quarter, right quarter, and bottom quarter respectively. (Hovhannisyan, 2023).

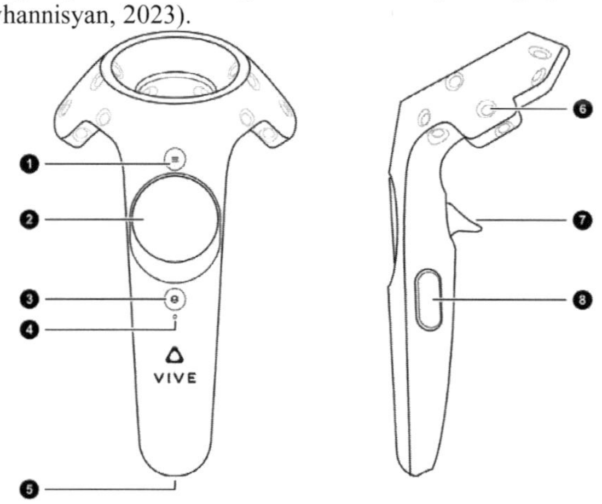

Figure 4. HTC Vive Controllers. (1) Menu button, (2) Trackpad, (3) System button, (4) Status light, (5) Micro-USB port, (6) Tracking Sensor, (7) Trigger, (8) Grip button

2.4 Evaluation

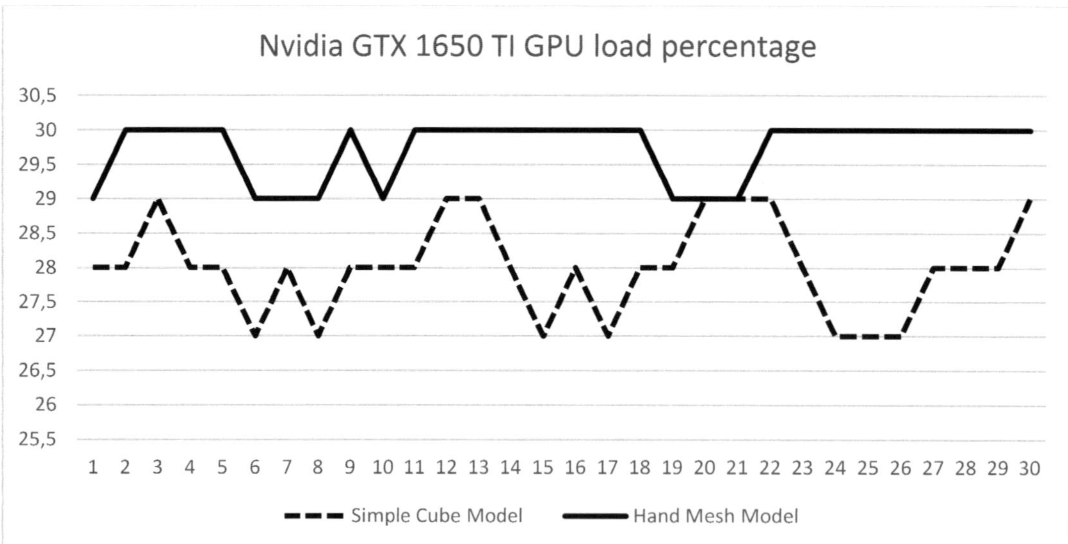

Figure 5. Performance analysis

A performance analysis is provided with 2 models to evaluate the selected model: the selected high-fidelity hand mesh model and the other, a simple cube object not requiring much GPU effort to render. The overall results show that the GPU load is 1% higher on average in the hand mesh model, which is considered acceptable. Thus, it is evaluated that the hand model selected is appropriate for use in our simulation. The results are shown in Figure 5.

3. IMPLEMENTATION

To implement the mapping method described in section 2.3, animations corresponding to natural hand actions are implemented first and then coupled with the controller button press/release events.

3.1 Hand Motion Synthesis

To synthesize hand motions, the keyframing technique is employed. In this method, the finger poses are defined at specific moments, and interpolation curves are applied to control the motion between these keyframes (Jörg et al., 2020). To gain higher-order continuity, the Bézier curve is applied as an interpolation method (Haarbach et al., 2018).

Unity has a rich and sophisticated animation system called Mecanim. It uses a visual layout system similar to a flowchart to represent a state machine to control and sequence the animation clips that are used on objects. The simplest components of animation in Unity are called animation clips. They stand in for a single action, such as Bend or Open, and may be adjusted and combined in many ways to create dynamic outcomes.

To create an animation clip, we first create an animation object. Then, inside this object, all the fingers DP, MP, and PP phalanges are sequentially rotated to a degree where the hand gets a naturally closed look. These rotations are performed after clicking the "Record" button, creating animation clips that include all the rotation phases. Figure 6 illustrates 3 animation phases at 0:00, 0:20, and 0:60 instants.

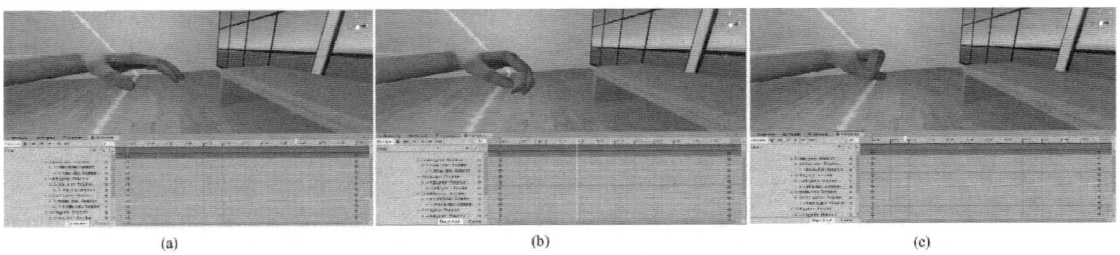

Figure 6. Animation keyframes. (a) – 0:00. (b) – 0:20. (c) – 0:60

The created animation clips are controlled by an Animator Controller. For a character or object, an animator controller enables the arrangement and upkeep of a series of animation clips and related animation transitions. A State Machine, which can be viewed as a flowchart of Animation Clips and Transitions or as a straightforward program written in a visual programming language within Unity, is used by the Animator Controller to manage the various Animation Clips and the Transitions between them. This controller has references to the Animation clips used within it. A state machine consists of states and transitions. The hand positions may be referred to as states. The options for the next state that an object can enter from its current state are referred to as state transitions. A graph diagram can be used to depict the states and transitions of a state machine, with the nodes standing in for the states and the arcs (arrows connecting nodes) for the transitions. Figure 7 illustrates the state machine designed to close/open the hand. The Animator Controller also supports animation masks, which allow one to select specific parts of the object to apply animation to these parts only.

For each interaction event, one state machine is taken into account in the implementation. A conditional variable that is attached to each state machine determines whether the transition should take place at a specific moment. A conditional variable is set to change its value according to interaction events, which in turn causes a state transition to occur and animation to be triggered. The modification of conditional variable is performed within a configurable time period, and the animation clip is set to run at a convenient speed to be performed during within this amount of time.

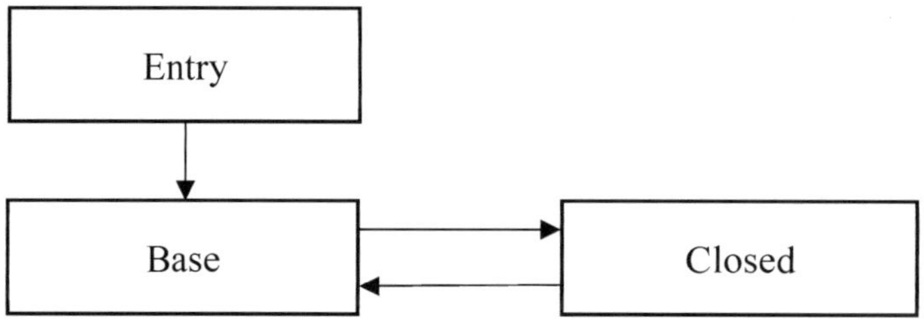

Figure 7. Animation state machine

3.2 Triggering the Animation

In the development environment, the controller buttons are assigned integer values of 1 and 0, representing their pressed and released states, respectively. These values are constantly monitored at each frame, and if a change in value is detected, the associated state machine's conditional variable is adjusted gradually to match the current button state. For example, when the grip button transitions from being released to pressed, the conditional variable of the state machine responsible for animating the grip action is set to incrementally approach a value of 1. This process takes place over a configurable time interval, allowing for control over the speed of the animation. The actual animation is triggered based on a specific value of the conditional variable. This value is determined with respect to the recommended frame rate of 90 frames per second for virtual reality systems, resulting in a time gap of 0.01 seconds between consecutive frames. This time gap serves as the threshold value for the conditional variable, determining when the animations should occur by comparing the current value of the conditional variable with the threshold value.

4. LIMITATIONS AND FUTURE WORK

The animations applied to the hand model are predefined, which is good for bare hand gestures but has drawbacks when interacting with various shape object surfaces. The reliance on predetermined animations restricts the flexibility and adaptability of the hand model because the hand model is not automatically fitted to the object surface. In other words, when grasping various objects, the hand model animates the same way for all the shapes and gets to a fully closed position, intersecting with the object shape, affecting the accuracy and realism of object interactions. In future work, we could aim to overcome these drawbacks by developing methods that allow for the automatic fitting of the model to object surfaces, ensuring more realistic and versatile object interactions.

5. CONCLUSION

This paper proposes a method for high-fidelity VR hand models to simulate real-life hand motions, thus making the virtual world more immersive and giving the user a stronger sense of presence. Firstly, the hand 3D model is reconstructed from multiple RGB images using a convolutional neural network with 2D hand keypoint estimations, 3D keypoint detection with the RANSAC algorithm, and LBS and non-rigid IPC algorithms to register the hand mesh model. For 2D keypoint estimations, a 2-stage CNN is used, with the first stage predicting hand mask (silhouette) and the second stage being the hand pose detection. Afterward, the resulting 3D model is imported into the Unity environment to add animations and map those animations to headset controller buttons. Animations are made according to natural hand gestures for a smooth and life-like experience. For the hand motion synthesis, the keyframing technique is employed, and the Bézier curve is applied as an interpolation method. User input is provided using the HTC Vive Cosmos Elite headset controllers. It is chosen to use the hand-held controllers that come with head-mounted devices despite the fact that there are alternative methods to monitor hand motions to deliver more immersive experiences due to the problems with haptic gloves and vision-based approaches that are already in use. Based on their actual placement in the hand, the controller buttons are assigned to distinct activities in the virtual world. The proposed method can be incorporated in both existing and freshly developed virtual environments, providing the users with a realistic hand model and natural hand gestures.

REFERENCES

Ahmad, A. et al, 2019. Hand pose estimation and tracking in real and virtual interaction: A review. *In Elsevier Image and Vision Computing*, Vol. 89, pp. 35-49.

Cariani, P., 1989. On the design of devices with emergent semantic functions. Ph.D. dissertation.

Daneshmand, M. et al, 2018. 3D Scanning: A Comprehensive Survey. *arXiv preprint arXiv:1801.08863.*

Erol, A. et al, 2007. Vision-based hand pose estimation: A review. *In Elsevier Computer Vision and Image Understanding*, Vol. 108, No. 1-2, pp. 52-73.

Fischler, M. and Bolles, R., 1981. Random sample consensus: a paradigm for model fitting with applications to image analysis and automated cartography. *In Communications of the ACM*, Vol. 24, No. 6, pp. 381-395.

Gustus, A. et al, 2012. Human hand modelling: kinematics, dynamics, applications. *In Springer Biological Cybernetics*, Vol. 106, pp. 741-755.

Haarbach, A. et al., 2018. Survey of Higher Order Rigid Body Motion Interpolation Methods for Keyframe Animation and Continuous-Time Trajectory Estimation. *In Proceedings of IEEE International Conference on 3D Vision*. Verona, Italy, pp. 381-389.

Hovhannisyan, A., 2023. Implementation of Immersive Virtual Hands using Virtual Reality System Controllers. *In SSRG International Journal of Engineering Trends and Technology*, Vol. 71, No. 6, pp. 369-374.

Jacobs, J. and Froehlich, B., 2011. A Soft Hand Model for Physically-based Manipulation of Virtual Objects. *IEEE Virtual Reality Conference*, Singapore, pp. 11-18.

Jörg, S. et al, 2020. Virtual hands in VR: motion capture, synthesis, and perception. *In Proceedings of SIGGRAPH Asia 2020 Courses*. New York, USA, pp. 1-32.

Lin, L. and Jörg, S., 2016. Need a hand?: how appearance affects the virtual hand illusion. *Proceedings of the ACM Symposium on Applied Perception*. Anaheim, USA, pp. 69-76.

Pietikäinen, O. et al, 2021. VRChem: A Virtual Reality Molecular Builder. *In MDPI Applied Sciences*, Vol. 11, No. 22.

Peña-Pitarch, E. et al, 2014. Virtual human hand: model and kinematics. *In Taylor & Francis Computer Methods in Biomechanics and Biomedical Engineering*, Vol. 17, No. 5, pp. 568-579.

Schwind, V. et al, 2017. "These are not my hands!": Effect of Gender on the Perception of Avatar Hands in Virtual Reality. *Proceedings of the 2017 CHI Conference on Human Factors in Computing Systems.* Denver, USA, pp. 1577-1582.

Tang, D. et al, 2016. Latent Regression Forest: Structured Estimation of 3D Articulated Hand Posture. *Proceedings of the IEEE Conference on Computer Vision and Pattern Recognition*. Las Vegas, USA, pp. 3786-3793.

Wang, Y. et al, 2019. Mask-Pose Cascaded CNN for 2D Hand Pose Estimation From Single Color Image. *In IEEE Transactions on Circuits and Systems for Video Technology*, Vol. 29, No. 11, pp. 3258-3268.

Zhao, Z. et al, 2020. Hand-3d-Studio: A New Multi-View System for 3d Hand Reconstruction. *International Conference on Acoustics, Speech, and Signal Processing*. Barcelona, Spain, pp. 2478-2482.

Zimmerman, C. and Brox, T., 2017. Learning to Estimate 3D Hand Pose From Single RGB Images. *Proceedings of the IEEE International Conference on Computer Vision*. Venice, Italy, pp. 4903-4911.

A MOBILE HEALTH DESIGN PROCESS TO IMPROVE COMMUNITY HEALTH WORKERS' ENGAGEMENT WITH MOBILE HEALTH

Tochukwu Ikwunne, Lucy Hederman and P. J. Wall
ADAPT Centre, Trinity College Dublin, Ireland

ABSTRACT

Despite the significance of user engagement for the efficacy of mobile health systems, many such interventions frequently do not include user-engaging attributes. This is because, users' needs and sociocultural contexts of users' groups are frequently not considered in detail during mHealth design, implementation, and operation stages. As users' activities are influenced by their sociocultural contexts, it is important to capture such sociocultural contexts during various stages of mobile health designs. The aim of this paper is to develop a framework that improves user engagement with designed mobile health technology. This framework is intended to be used by mobile health designers and developers and it facilitates specific consideration of any sociocultural context existing. Thirty semi-structured interviews were conducted with end users and mobile health designers to investigate factors that facilitate or hinder user engagement with mobile health technologies. The results of this research show that to understand why and how users engage, continue to engage, disengage, and re-engage with previous mobile health technologies during designs of mobile apps, capturing sociocultural contexts of users during designs of mobile health apps and involving end users in designs of mobile health apps all play significant roles in improving user engagement with mobile health. This research proposes a new sociocultural framework called the **De**sign Pro**c**ess Engagement E**n**hancement Sys**t**em (DECENT) that enables mobile health designers to incorporate users' values as well as the sociocultural contexts of end users into the design process of mobile systems. Global South was the setting in which DECENT is tested.

KEYWORDS

Design Science, User-Centered Designs, User Engagement, Sociocultural Filtration, Sociocultural Contexts, Mobile Health

1. INTRODUCTION

Engagement is a universal goal in the design of content (Doherty & Doherty 2018). However, a lack of engagement may result from an imbalance in the integration of appropriate content and feature that maintain user interest. (Hingle & Patrick 2016; Tang et al. 2015). An important, and often overlooked feature of engagement research is the fit between various conceptions of engagement and the design process (Doherty & Doherty 2018). The design of engaging experiences lies in the appraisal of user engagement. However, little attention has been paid to the integration of measures of engagement within a process of design (Doherty and Doherty 2018). Thus, the need for a better design process of mHealth to improve user engagement. Ikwunne et al. (2022) conducted a systematic review of the user engagement design process and discovered a lack of consideration for sociocultural contexts in the design of mHealth interventions. The systematic review recommended that such sociocultural contexts be considered and addressed systematically by identifying a design process for engaging users in mHealth interventions (Ikwunne et al. 2020). In this research, user engagement is defined as a context-dependent, individual-specific psychological state that emerges from two-way interaction with an object, such as an app (Brodie et al. 2013; Brodie et al. 2011; Hollebeek 2011). The effectiveness of mobile health (mHealth) initiatives thus depends to a large extent on user engagement (Bo¨hm 2020; Grady et al. 2018). However, despite the claimed significance of user engagement for the efficacy of mHealth systems, many such interventions frequently do not include user-engaging attributes (Machado et al. 2016), this led to the research question on the research: how can a design framework be developed to improve user engagement in mHealth technologies? The aim of this research is to develop a framework that supports mHealth designers or developers in creating mHealth technologies that engage their users. This research question results have four specific research objectives: 1) Overview of user engagement and how it is being evaluated for mHealth. 2) review of existing design process frameworks for mHealth. 3) Design of DECENT, and 4) Refine and evaluate the DECENT framework to guide user engagement to improve the user engagement design process for mHealth.

In the globalized economy, for example, new products are frequently developed for international markets. Because user characteristics and needs differ significantly across regions (Omo 2002), product development for global markets requires organizations to design products with these differences in user characteristics and needs in mind. According to Shen et al. (2006, p.7), "Successful interface metaphors should be developed or adapted through cultural requirements by or regarding, representatives of the culture for which they are intended". Culture is defined as the similar patterns of thinking, feeling, and acting of people who belong to the same group but are different in these patterns from other groups (Hofstede 1991). This 'acting' is largely based on unwritten rules and habits passed down from generation to generation (De Angeli 2006).

According to Honold (1999), the approach to learning how to use a new mobile phone, for example, may vary depending on national culture. For example, German users prefer a user manual, whereas Italians prefer "learning by doing." Furthermore, while the salesperson is an important source of information for Chinese users, for Indian users, the entire family is involved in the knowledge acquisition process. Honold's (1999) research shows that culture influences patterns of user-product interaction and engagement, implying that designers should account for these differences in knowledge acquisition approaches. However, determining the nature of this impact may be difficult in the absence of a deeper understanding of how users actually "engage" with technologies (Sonderegger & Sauer, 2013). This emphasizes the importance of providing a framework for assessing users' sociocultural contexts for user engagement designs.

To take such sociocultural contexts into account, this research proposes to develop a new mHealth design framework to improve user engagement in mHealth. This design process will be called Design Process Engagement Enhancement System (DECENT).

This research follows a Design Science (DS) methodology approach which is defined as "a research paradigm in which a designer answers questions relevant to human problems via the creation of innovative artifacts, thereby contributing new knowledge to the body of scientific evidence." (Hevner 2010). Therefore, a DS approach is used to develop DECENT as an artifact, to ensure that it addresses the needs of developers aiming for more user-engaging mHealth.

The remaining part of the paper is structured as follows. Section II discusses related works, while Section III discusses the methodology applied in this paper, which includes data collection, design science approaches for DECENT design, and the data analysis method. Section IV presents results and discussions on factors that facilitate or hinder mHealth engagement. Section V provides a description of DECENT framework and participants involvement refinement of DECENT. Section VI discusses DECENT evaluation by end-users and mHealth designers. Section VII presents the conclusion of the research.

2. LITERATURE REVIEW

The research objectives: 1) analyze an overview of user engagement, and how it is being evaluated for mHealth and 2) extensively review the literature assessing existing design process frameworks for mHealth are achieved in this section as follows:

2.1 Design and Evaluation of User Engagement with mHealth

Even though developing and measuring user engagement with health is a generally recognized goal of interactive system development across many disciplines, there is little guidance available to show designers' efforts to make things engaging (Ikwunne et al. 2022). To assist in creating and evaluating future mHealth interventions, Ikwunne et al. (2022) conducted a review to determine which design process enhances user engagement with mHealth. The review discovered that 1) a rigorous design process for user engagement with mHealth is essential, which incorporates users' sociocultural contexts into the design of mHealth interventions. 2) mHealth designs should clearly incorporate user or human-centered design methodologies, and users should be involved from the start to understand their needs and throughout the mHealth design process. Lalmas

& O'Brien (2014) demonstrated that, while designing for engagement is essential, it cannot be accomplished correctly without understanding how to define and measure user engagement.

Several studies have stressed the importance of understanding user engagement theories with mHealth interventions and analyses of their measurement to build effective interventions that suit users' requirements (Ikwunne et al. 2022; Ikwunne et al. 2022; Yardley et al. 2016; King et al. 2014). Perski et al. (2017) used two notions to measure engagement: subjective and objective measurements. Self-report surveys and qualitative techniques are among the subjective measures. Studies have used self-report questionnaires to assess participation in digital games and digital behaviour change interventions (DBCIs) (Martey et al. 2014; Fang & Zhang 2013). Qualitative methods, such as interviews or think-aloud exercises, have been utilized to acquire a deeper understanding of the nature of users' participation in digital games and DBCIs (Bossen et al. 2013). In the behavioural science literature, objective measures, such as mechanized tracking of use patterns, such as the number of logins, time spent online, and the degree and type of content used during the intervention period, are more commonly used than subjective measures (Morrison & Doherty 2014), whereas in the computer science and HCI literature, psychosocial measures, such as eye tracking, are more commonly used (Jennett et al. 2008).

The understanding of user engagement and the evaluation of user-centered technologies are limited without a means of measuring engagement (O'Brien & Toms 2008). O'Brien & Toms (2008) brought together the threads of many research studies to identify the essential features of engaging experiences and to present a conceptual, process-based model of engagement based on Aesthetic, Flow, and Play theories, the conceptual paradigm, however, the model has not yet been tested and measured in a range of application domains, particularly in mHealth. The assessment of user involvement is crucial in the design of engaging experiences. On the other hand, understanding users and their interactions with technology prompted a shift toward the study of user experience (McCarthy 2004). However, little attention has been made to the integration of engagement measurements inside the process of mHealth design.

2.2 Design Framework for mHealth

The design process is referred to as the solution-based method used in developing mHealth interventions. Six frameworks were utilized in the literature: participatory design, user-centered design, double diamond, human-centered design, Hasso-Plattner Institute, and techno-centric approach (Ikwunne et al. 2022). The existing design framework, its descriptions, and key aspects of the frameworks are described in Table 1.

Table 1. Design frameworks and corresponding descriptions

Framework	Description	Key aspects
Participatory design (PD)	PD is a process that involves all stakeholders in the intervention design process to ensure that the interventions developed are usable and meet the needs of users (Bratteteig & Wagner 2016).	PD is an approach in which designers engage potential users to participate in all stages of the design process. (Bratteteig & Wagner 2016).
User Centered design (UCD)	UCD is the technique that focuses on putting users at the center of product design and development is known as UCD. Its primary goal is to improve the usability of interactive goods by the study of system use and the use of human factors and usability knowledge and methodologies (ISO 2010).	UCD is comprised of four steps: (1) understand and identify the needs of the users; (2) produce design solutions; (3) evaluate the design and (4) implement (ISO 2010).
Double Diamond (DD)	The Design Council developed the double diamond (DD) process is focused on the use of design thinking in business and innovation designs (Tschimmel 2012).	DD consists of four phases which are discovery, definition, development, and delivery (Tschimmel 2012). The DD procedure was utilized sparingly in the literature, with Nyatuka & de la Harpe (2019) examining its usage to improve healthcare delivery, particularly in low-resource settings.
Human-centered design (HCD)	The Innovation, Design Engineering Organization (IDEO) created the human-centered design (HCD) patterns. HCD was employed in the literature to construct a patient-centered e-health solution for	Hearing, producing, and delivering are the three steps of HCD (Das & Svanæs 2013).

	patients receiving weight reduction therapy (Das & Svanæs 2013) and different recommender system (Govoruhina & Nikiforova 2022; Mulrooney et al. 2006).	
Hasso-plattner Institute (HPI)	In the evaluated research, HPI was used to improve the testing of latent tuberculosis infection by health workers (Farao et al. 2020).	The HPI method is divided into six steps: "Understand", "Observe", "Point of View", "Ideate", "Prototype" and "Test" (Farao et al. 2020).
Techno-centric process	A "technocentric approach" unlike UCD is a design technique that emphasizes technological aspects to meet the system design needs.	The technocentric process is centered on "technology-push," in which designers first focus on technology before attempting to apply it (Carayannis et al. 2021).

Though the sociocultural contexts associated with user engagement have been established in the literature as important factors to consider when attempting to achieve user engagement with technology (mccurdie et al. 2012), little work has been done to develop a process (framework) for designing user engaging mHealth apps/technologies to guide mHealth designers and developers, particularly in under-resourced and underserved settings. There is no robust design approach for mHealth user engagement that incorporates users' socio-cultural contexts into mHealth intervention design. There are contributions about theory-based user-engaged mHealth therapies based on behavioural techniques (Ikwunne et al 2022). However, the research emphasizes the importance of developing a framework for incorporating processes that highlight end users' sociocultural backgrounds into the design of mHealth technology.

3. METHODOLOGY

This research adopts design science research methodology (DSRM) which provides a process model for conducting Design Science research (Hevner 2010). The DSRM is divided into six phases below:

1. First we identified the problem and motivation of the study in the introduction.
2. Define Solution Objectives: DECENT's objective is to provide an mHealth design process (framework) that improves user engagement with the designed mHealth; the framework is intended to be used by mHealth designers and developers when developing mHealth apps/technologies, particularly underserved, under-resourced, and under-represented settings.
3. Design and development: Collecting and analysing data from semi-structured interviews to inform the DECENT framework.
4. Demonstration: Refining DECENT mHealth design to suit end-users' needs.
5. Evaluation: DSRM Phase 5 provides an evaluation of the DECENT framework.
6. Communication: Presentation of the research to an appropriate audience in human-computer interaction (HCI) and mHealth fields.

The methodology, including study design and data analysis, is described in the following sections.

3.1 Design Study

To collect data to understand what motivates users to engage in the ways they do and why they engage with mHealth technologies in their individual contexts, an established methodology employed in many HCI research by Jia et al. (2016) is followed as described below.

3.1.1 Research Context

To understand what motivates users to engage in the ways they do and why they engage with mHealth technologies in their individual contexts, we first examine the AIM Health Plus project, a mobile health initiative in Sierra Leone. Since the project's launch in 2017, an mHealth technology component has been a part of it. Sherbro Island and the Imperi neighbourhood are the geographic focus. For use by community health workers (CHWs) during home visits, the AIM Health Plus project equips smartphones with a customized version of Dimagi's CommCare app. Despite the difficulties, the AIM Health Plus project has achieved significant strides in Sierra Leone, where 326 CHWs are using CommCare to deliver timed and targeted counseling (ttC) messages to induce healthy eating and behavior changes in moms of young children under two and pregnant women. The CHWs have also received appropriate training and guidance to ensure the app's long-term use. The app reminds CHWs of the appropriate times to visit households during pregnancy, early childhood, and adolescence.

3.1.2 Experimental Design

A snowballing technique was used to identify potential participants for this research. World Vision Ireland and Sierra Leone through their line managers contacted the participants and asked them to participate in the semi-structured interview process. Those who responded to the request were then sent the Participant Information Leaflet, which detailed the risks and benefits for the participant and provided more information on the study procedures. Within 7 days of receiving the information leaflet, the participant was contacted by the line manager to confirm that they were still interested in participating in the research. If the participant agreed to continue, he or she was asked to complete the consent process before the semi-structured began. Ethical approval was sorted prior to the collection of data.

A total of thirty (30) semi-structured key informant semi-structured interviews including end users, mobile health developers and designs, lasting between 30-90 minutes were conducted. The semi-structured interview questions focused on how participants engaged with their current or previous mHealth technology over time. The semi-structured interview questions were designed to determine which aspects of their mHealth technology they used and which they did not and what made users disengaged or re-engaged with mHealth apps. For semi-structured interviews involving community health workers (CHWs), semi-structured interviews were transcribed in audio in the local language (Mende). On the ground in Sierra Leone, a trained and experienced research assistant carried out the semi-structured interviews and transcribed and translated them. NVivo was used to code and analyze all of the semi-structured interviews

3.2 Data Analysis

The semi-structured interviews were analyzed using Braun and Clarke's (2021) six stages of thematic analysis via a deductive approach. The following is a summary of the thematic analysis phases:

1. Familiarization with data: In this first phase of the analysis, the lead researcher becomes acquainted with the data by reading the transcripts, notes, and audio tapes numerous times. The transcripts of the thirty semi-structured interviews and the reflection notes on each semi-structured interview were all imported into NVivo. NVivo can link different semi-structured interview data sources, allowing for faster retrieval and contextualization of each semi-structured interview. In addition, NVivo mind map tools were used to create a visual representation of concepts and connections linking the different concepts from the semi-structured interview data and research questions and linking them to other factors from the literature that act as facilitators and barriers of user engagement to gain a good understanding of the themes that will be identified from the semi-structured interview data.

2. Systematic data coding: The second phase starts off the coding exploration. NVivo 12 is used to find words, sentences, and paragraphs that discuss a significant topic from the semi-structured interview data using the visual representation of concepts created in phase 1. Based on the meaning subject deduced from the semi-structured interview data, labels were assigned to these isolated words, phrases, and sentences. Until all semi-structured interview transcripts have been coded, each transcript is coded individually.

3. Generating initial themes from coded and collated data: In phase 3, themes were generated from the coded data. Initial themes are created from categories based on the preset themes during this step of the thematic analysis process (Maykut & Morehouse 2002). The authors began grouping the codes that had comparable meanings or were connected to one another once the transcripts had been coded. After clustering the codes, the authors assigned labels to the clusters based on the meaning that the codes shared. For instance, the theme categories "design engagement (process) awareness", "design engagement (process) goals", "design engagement process problem with stakeholder mapping", "negative experience with (not) involvement in design process", and "positive experience with design process" were grouped together under the theme "design process engagement".

4. Developing and reviewing themes: The fourth phase systematically reviewed the evolving thematic framework of nodes. During phase 4, some nodes were merged, while others were clustered together into related code categories. The ideas derived from the data were gradually developed (data reconstruction), and the flat-structured nodes evolved into a more complex hierarchical structure (tree nodes).

5. Refining, defining, and naming themes: In phase 5, the data was revisited, and its breadth and depth were examined (Richards 2020). The themes were connected, and the connections were explained (Ritchie & Spencer 2002). The responses of the participants are summarized in these data-topics-as-themes, but there is no central concept, no shared meaning, only a shared topic. In the initial theme generation described in phase four, for example, the theme "socio-technical facilitator" represents a data topic because it does not provide a shared meaning or a central concept. However, the theme was refined in this phase and renamed to "socio-technical facilitators of user engagement with mobile health technologies".

6. Writing report: The final phase is writing the report. The thematic analysis report was written in the next section (results and discussions) as a qualitative report since the aim of the analysis was to understand what motivates users to engage in the ways they do and why they engage with mHealth technologies in their individual contexts and takes a step further to develop a framework that incorporates the sociocultural contexts of users into the design, based on the user-centered design models and the results of the semi-structured interviews.

4. RESULTS AND DISCUSSIONS

This section provides results and discussions of the application Braun and Clarke's (2021) six stages of thematic analysis of the semi-structured interviews with 30 participants which produced six themes and twenty-three categories as shown in figure 1. However, only one category's findings from each of the six themes that are described below in detail.

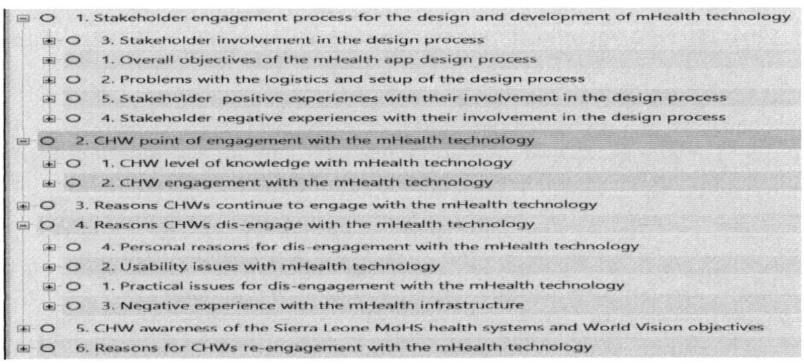

Figure 1. Results of thematic analysis of 30 semi-structured interviews

Theme 1 - Stakeholder engagement process design of the mHealth technology: The first theme is the stakeholder engagement process design of the mHealth technology. This first theme is subdivided into five categories: 1) overall objectives of the mHealth app design process, 2) problems with logistics and setup of the design process; 3) stakeholder involvement in the design process, 4) stakeholder negative experiences with their involvement in the design process and 5) stakeholder positive experiences with their involvement in the design process. The themes' meaning was explained through the categories. There are distinct attributes for each of the five categories. The codes inside each category's content and meaning served as the basis for defining the attributes of each category.

Category 1. Overall objectives of the mHealth app design process: This refers to the health or wellness goals that an individual can achieve while using mHealth technologies. According to CHWs, mHealth technologies were designed to help save the lives of pregnant women and children under the age of five. One interviewee's comment on health or wellness goals demonstrated this:

"The mHealth project was designed to stop maternal and child deaths, which is exactly what we need in this community". (P15)

This category offers resources for incorporating numerous stakeholders in mHealth projects that enhance healthcare delivery.

Theme 2 - CHW's point of engagement with the mHealth technology: The CHW's point of engagement with mHealth technology is the second theme. This is the point at which the CHWs began engaging with the mHealth technology. Participants talked about the start of interesting encounters. Two categories are used to categorize the theme: 1. CHW level of knowledge with mHealth technology; and 2. CHW engagement with the mHealth technology.

Category 1. CHW level of knowledge with mHealth technology**:** This speaks to CHWs' familiarity with the elements of technologies or applications that pique users' interest. An interviewee made the following observation regarding the CHW's use of technology to plan work:

"It also helps me organize my work". (P8)

Theme 3 - Reasons CHWs continue to engage with the mHealth technology: The third theme is the reasons why CHWs continue to use mHealth technology. After describing the point at which they became engaged, CHWs described what was happening and what they felt and thought while engaged, and what made them stay engaged with the mHealth, which formed this theme's six categories, shown in figure 1. CHWs' awareness (level of knowledge) of the mHealth technology to achieve its aims; 2. technological reasons CHWs continue engaging with mHealth technology; 3. social and cultural reasons CHWs continue to engage with mHealth technology; 4. aesthetic reasons for CHW continued engagement with the mHealth technology; 5. CHWs identification of ease of use of the mHealth technology; and 6. CHW positive experiences while using the mHealth technology.

Category 1. CHWs' awareness (level of knowledge) of the mHealth technology to achieve its aims:

This category refers to CHWs' level of understanding of what components of technologies or apps are doing to keep them engaged with mHealth technologies. According to CHWs, there were good impacts on their behaviour and work practice reconfiguration. This is consistent with the following comments from interviewees:

"The use of the CommCare apps impacted my work behaviour because I felt motivated to do more". (P10)

Theme 4 - Reasons CHWs dis-engage with the mHealth technology: The fourth theme focuses on the factors that cause CHWs to avoid using mobile health technologies. It investigates instances in which CHWs chose internally to quit using mHealth technology or in which elements of their external environment led them to stop using it. Four categories make up the fourth theme: 1. usability issues with mHealth technology, 2. practical issues for dis-engagement from the mHealth technology, 3. negative experience with the mHealth infrastructure; and personal reasons for dis-engagement from the mHealth technology.

Category 1. Usability issues with mHealth technology: This is a reference to usability flaws found with mHealth technology or app components that disengage users. One respondent raised the issue of how difficult it is to fix faults and mistakes:

"issue using the app is the area of overdue after registration of the client. If the CHW did not follow up on appointment time, the client would go overdue, and some found it difficult to rectify the issue even after visiting the person. The app administrators will be seen as overdue even though the necessary things have been done but the app failed to synchronise". (P9)

Theme 5 - CHW awareness of the Sierra Leone MoHS health systems and World Vision objectives: The fifth theme is the CHWs' knowledge of World Vision's goals and the Sierra Leone MoHS health systems. If CHWs are aware of their health systems even when they are not using mHealth technologies is explored. Without the aid of technologies or apps, this would assist in evaluating the health or wellness objectives that can be derived from CHWs. The fifth theme is divided into two categories: 1. CHW awareness of the manual health systems (before implementation of the mHealth technology), and 2. CHW issues with the manual health systems (before implementation of the mHealth technology).

Category 1. CHW awareness of the manual health systems (before implementation of the mHealth technology): This is in reference to the health or wellness objectives that CHWs can establish without them using mHealth tools or apps. To register households, one respondent noted that paper was necessary and was used instead of technology:

"Initially, we were using paper-based household registration prior to the mobile health technology known as the CommCare application". (P3)

Theme 6 - Reasons for CHWs re-engagement with the mHealth technology: The sixth theme focuses on the motivations for CHWs' re- engagement with mHealth technology. It investigated whether CHWs would use mHealth technology again. The six theme is divided into four categories: 1. CHWs practical problems with re-engagement with the mHealth technology, 2. what the CHW needs for re-engagement with the mHealth technology, 3. CHW incentives for re-engagement with the mHealth technology, and 4. aesthetics for CHW re-engagement with the mHealth technology.

Category 1. CHWs practical problems with re-engagement with the mHealth technology: This is referring to challenges with re-engaging with the mHealth technology components in a practical sense. One participant in the semi-structured interview stated that the mHealth app does not have stories like those in the paper form:

"The phone they were given did not contain the pictures and stories found in the books. It's just blunt, direct messages". (P18)

5. DECENT PROTOTYPE

Based on the input from the user centered design models, and results from the semi-structured interviews, DECENT prototypes were developed and presented to the participants. The design sessions included participants (end users, mHealth designers) worked together to provide feedback on what they thought and what they understood about the various phases of the DECENT prototypes as well as how the components should be developed to capture their sociocultural contexts and values. This allowed the participants to explore their own ideas for something that might be useful for them. To consider their requirements and values, the participants refine the DECENT prototypes. Participants experimented with, redesigned, or critiqued DECENT prototypes using design tools like paper and sticky notes. Participants did, however, incorporate key concepts and reorganize some tools from the first DECENT prototypes' phase 1 (sociocultural filtration), including personas, capture and postcards, contextual inquiry, and self-built guides. The main difference between the two tools is that while the capture and postcard provide examples of user experiences in the engagement phases of user engagement with mHealth, communication delight provides the same examples with more visual appeal. Even though participants understood and interpreted the communication delight tool without feedback, they thought that once it was added, it would have an impact on it. Figure 2 depicts the DECENT framework, which is a process-oriented user-centered design process that incorporates users' sociocultural contexts into the mHealth design process.

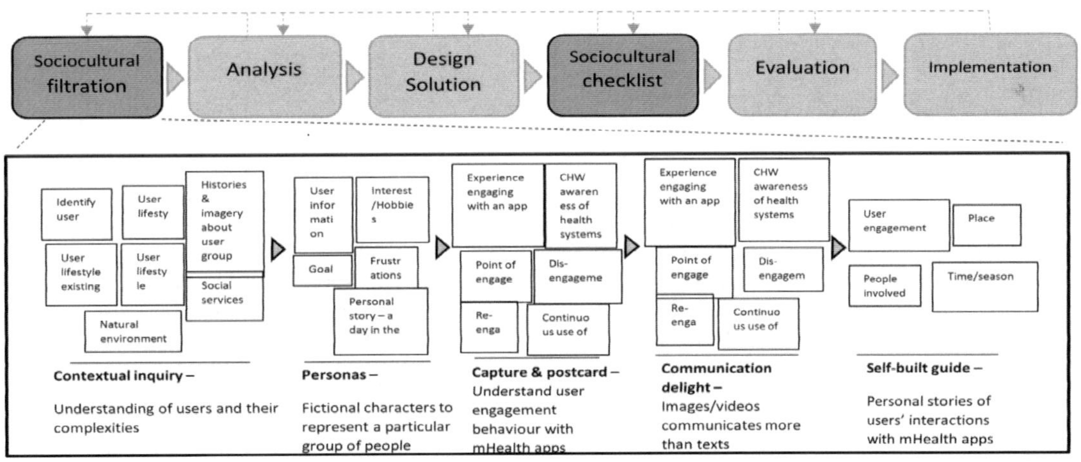

Figure 2. DECENT framework

It places an emphasis on aesthetic, sociocultural, and contextual values, as well as a critical knowledge of the role of design in sociocultural contexts. The DECENT framework is divided into six phases and is based on a user-centered approach. Phase 1: Social and cultural filtration: Many tool sets are employed in this step to understand users' sociocultural contexts. Phase 1 include contextual inquiry, personalities, capture cards and postcards, self-built guides, and communication delight. Other phases of DECENT framework are user needs analysis, design solution development, a socio-cultural checklist, evaluation, and implementation.

6. DECENT EVALUATION

In this paper, it is not possible to say whether the DECENT framework results in more user- engaging mobile health technology. Instead, the assessment procedures looked at DECENT's applicability, comprehension, ease of use, coherence, and engagement, as well as if the steps necessary for the DECENT design process led to mHealth technology that had higher user engagement. It was also established whether the DECENT design process can evaluate end-user requirements, sociocultural contexts and whether the results are engaging and usable. Three mHealth designers evaluated the improved DECENT prototypes at this stage; two of the three participated in the refining of DECENT framework. One of the three mHealth designers Did not participant. Based on what end users liked and disapproved of the DECENT framework was also assessed. Eight end users, comprising six CHWs and one CHW focus as well as a community child monitor (CCM), were also polled to determine whether they had a positive experience taking part in the DECENT design process and whether they thought it would encourage them to interact with the DECENT end-product.

1. Engaging mHealth: This refers to whether mHealth designers and end-users believe that DECENT are likely to result in more engaging mHealth. Participants who are end-users of the DECENT were asked if they thought DECENT would result in mHealth with better user engagement. The participants stated that they were aware that their input from the DECENT design sessions was used in creating the DECENT. As a result, they felt that the DECENT would result in mHealth with better user engagement because the end product would capture their values and reflect their needs.

"In fact, the steps followed in DECENT would produce an outcome that will be very user-friendly". (FG3)

"It will be very perfect, the steps taken were fine and any technology that comes out of it is very usable". (FG1)

2. Usability, effectiveness and other opinions of DECENT: To evaluate whether designer believe that the components of DECENT are likely to be useful and usable, practicable, understandable, easy to follow, coherent, and engaging, mHealth designers were asked to provide their opinions regarding whether DECENT is practical, understandable, easy to follow, coherent, and engaging. One of the mHealth designers (who did involve in the design of DECENT) provided this opinion:

"Yes, it is practical, understandable, etc because it is based on experience and practical's we have already experienced, which is why we recommended the changes. It is coherent and some will be able to use it to gather information". (FG1)

7. CONCLUSION

This paper provides overview of user engagement and how it is being evaluated for mHealth, and reviews existing design process frameworks for mHealth. We conducted 30 semi-structed interview with end-users and mHealth participants to investigate facilitators and barriers to user engagement with mHealth. We offered qualitative insights to explain what motivates users to engage in the ways they do and why they engage with mHealth technologies in their individual contexts and takes a step further to develop a framework that incorporates the sociocultural contexts of users into the design, based on the user-centered design models and the results of the semi-structured interviews. Our work advances user engagement designs with mHealth and HCI research by underpinning the importance of development framework that guides mHealth designers in creating mHealth apps that engages end-users. Future work will apply findings and DECENT framework from this work in developing an mHealth application for delivering health interventions which in turn will be evaluated by end-users. Further studies will also be conducted to determine if our findings would be applicable in other domains besides health.

ACKNOWLEDGEMENT

This research was conducted with the financial support of Science Foundation Ireland under Grant Agreement No. grant 18/CRT/6222 at the ADAPT SFI Research Centre at Trinity College Dublin. The ADAPT SFI Centre for Digital Content Technology is funded by Science Foundation Ireland through the SFI Research Centres Programme and is co-funded under the European Regional Development Fund (ERDF) through Grant 13/RC/2106 P2.

REFERENCES

Böhm, A.K., Jensen, M.L., Sørensen, M.R. and Stargardt, T., 2020. Real-world evidence of user engagement with mobile health for diabetes management: longitudinal observational study. *JMIR mHealth and uHealth*, *8*(11), p.e22212.

Bossen, D., Buskermolen, M., Veenhof, C., de Bakker, D. and Dekker, J., 2013. Adherence to a web-based physical activity intervention for patients with knee and/or hip osteoarthritis: a mixed method study. *Journal of medical Internet research*, *15*(10), p.e223.

Bratteteig, T. and Wagner, I., 2016. Unpacking the notion of participation in participatory design. *Computer Supported Cooperative Work (CSCW)*, *25*, pp.425-475.

Braun, V. and Clarke, V., 2021. One size fits all? What counts as quality practice in (reflexive) thematic analysis?. *Qualitative research in psychology*, *18*(3), pp.328-352.

Brodie, R.J., Hollebeek, L.D., Jurić, B. and Ilić, A., 2011. Customer engagement: Conceptual domain, fundamental propositions, and implications for research. *Journal of service research*, *14*(3), pp.252-271.

Brodie, Roderick J., Ana Ilic, Biljana Juric, and Linda Hollebeek. "Consumer engagement in a virtual brand community: An exploratory analysis." *Journal of business research* 66, no. 1 (2013): 105-114.

Carayannis, E.G., Dezi, L., Gregori, G. and Calo, E., 2021. Smart environments and techno-centric and human-centric innovations for Industry and Society 5.0: A quintuple helix innovation system view towards smart, sustainable, and inclusive solutions. *Journal of the Knowledge Economy*, pp.1-30.

Das, A. and Svanæs, D., 2013. Human-centred methods in the design of an e-health solution for patients undergoing weight loss treatment. *International journal of medical informatics*, *82*(11), pp.1075-1091.

De Angeli, A. and Kyriakoullis, L., 2006, May. Globalisation vs. localisation in e-commerce: cultural-aware interaction design. In *Proceedings of the working conference on Advanced visual interfaces* (pp. 250-253).

Doherty, K. and Doherty, G., 2018. Engagement in HCI: conception, theory and measurement. *ACM Computing Surveys (CSUR)*, *51*(5), pp.1-39.

Fang, X., Zhang, J. and Chan, S.S., 2013. Development of an instrument for studying flow in computer game play. *International journal of human-computer interaction*, *29*(7), pp.456-470.

Farao, J., Malila, B., Conrad, N., Mutsvangwa, T., Rangaka, M.X. and Douglas, T.S., 2020. A user-centred design framework for mHealth. *PloS one*, *15*(8), p.e0237910.

Govoruhina, A. and Nikiforova, A., 2022, September. Digital health shopping assistant with React Native: a simple technological solution to a complex health problem. In *2022 International Conference on Intelligent Data Science Technologies and Applications (IDSTA)* (pp. 34-40). IEEE.

Grady, A., Yoong, S., Sutherland, R., Lee, H., Nathan, N. and Wolfenden, L., 2018. Improving the public health impact of eHealth and mHealth interventions. *Australian and New Zealand journal of public health*, *42*(2).

Hevner, A., Chatterjee, S., Hevner, A. and Chatterjee, S., 2010. Introduction to design science research. *Design research in information systems: Theory and practice*, pp.1-8.

Hingle, M. and Patrick, H., 2016. There are thousands of apps for that: navigating mobile technology for nutrition education and behavior. *Journal of nutrition education and behavior*, *48*(3), pp.213-218.

Hollebeek, Linda. "Exploring customer brand engagement: definition and themes." *Journal of strategic Marketing* 19, no. 7 (2011): 555-573.

Honold, P., 1999. Learning how to use a cellular phone: Comparison between German and Chinese users. *Technical communication*, *46*(2), pp.196-205.

Hostede, G. and Hofstede, G., 1991. Cultures and organizations: Software of the mind. *New York: McGrawHill, 1997*, pp.23-47.

Ikwunne, T., Hederman, L. and Wall, P.J., 2022. Co-creating Digital Health Service: Activity Theory and Communicative Ecology Framework Analysis. https://ceur-ws.org/Vol-3239/paper7.pdf

Ikwunne, T., Hederman, L. and Wall, P.J., 2022. Design processes for user engagement with mobile health: a systematic review. *International Journal of Advanced Computer Science and Applications*, *13*(2).

Ikwunne, T., Hederman, L. and Wall, P.J., 2022. The DECENT Toolkit to Support Design of User Engagement of Mobile Health Technologies from a Practice Theory Perspective. In *Co-creating for Context in the Transfer and Diffusion of IT: IFIP WG 8.6 International Working Conference on Transfer and Diffusion of IT, TDIT 2022, Maynooth, Ireland, June 15–16, 2022, Proceedings* (pp. 94-104). Cham: Springer International Publishing.

Ikwunne, T., Hederman, L. and Wall, P.J., 2022. Theoretical perspectives towards culture-centered user engagement design for mobile health in the global south. In *Proceedings of the Future Technologies Conference (FTC) 2022, Volume 3* (pp. 295-311). Cham: Springer International Publishing.

Ikwunne, T., Hederman, L., & Wall, P. J. (2020). Understanding user engagement in information and communications technology for development: an exploratory study. In *HCI International 2020-Late Breaking Papers: User Experience Design and Case Studies: 22nd HCI International Conference, HCII 2020, Copenhagen, Denmark, July 19–24, 2020, Proceedings 22* (pp. 710-721). Springer International Publishing.

ISO 9241-210, J., 2010. Ergonomics of human-system interaction–Part 210: Human-centred design for interactive systems. *Isotopenpraxis*, *2010*, pp.1-19.

ISO, I., 1999. 13407: Human-centred design processes for interactive systems. *Geneva: ISO*.

Jennett, C., Cox, A.L., Cairns, P., Dhoparee, S., Epps, A., Tijs, T. and Walton, A., 2008. Measuring and defining the experience of immersion in games. *International journal of human-computer studies*, *66*(9), pp.641-661.

Jia, Y., Xu, B., Karanam, Y. and Voida, S., 2016, May. Personality-targeted gamification: a survey study on personality traits and motivational affordances. In *Proceedings of the 2016 CHI Conference on Human Factors in Computing Systems* (pp. 2001-2013).

King, G., Currie, M. and Petersen, P., 2014. Child and parent engagement in the mental health intervention process: A motivational framework. *Child and Adolescent Mental Health*, *19*(1), pp.2-8.

Lalmas, M., O'Brien, H. and Yom-Tov, E., 2014. Measuring user engagement. *Synthesis lectures on information concepts, retrieval, and services*, *6*(4), pp.1-132.

Machado, G.C., Pinheiro, M.B., Lee, H., Ahmed, O.H., Hendrick, P., Williams, C. and Kamper, S.J., 2016. Smartphone apps for the self-management of low back pain: a systematic review. *Best Practice & Research Clinical Rheumatology*, *30*(6), pp.1098-1109.

Martey, R.M., Kenski, K., Folkestad, J., Feldman, L., Gordis, E., Shaw, A., Stromer-Galley, J., Clegg, B., Zhang, H., Kaufman, N. and Rabkin, A.N., 2014. Measuring game engagement: multiple methods and construct complexity. *Simulation & Gaming*, *45*(4-5), pp.528-547.

McCarthy, J. and Wright, P., 2004. Technology as experience. *interactions*, *11*(5), pp.42-43.

McCurdie, T., Taneva, S., Casselman, M., Yeung, M., McDaniel, C., Ho, W. and Cafazzo, J., 2012. mHealth consumer apps: the case for user-centered design. *Biomedical instrumentation & technology*, *46*(s2), pp.49-56.

Morehouse, R., 2002. *Beginning qualitative research: A philosophical and practical guide*. Routledge.

Morrison, C. and Doherty, G., 2014. Analyzing engagement in a web-based intervention platform through visualizing log-data. *Journal of medical Internet research*, *16*(11), p.e252.

Mulrooney, B., McDermott, M. and Earley, N., 2006, April. NutraStick: portable diet assistant. In *CHI'06 extended abstracts on Human factors in computing systems* (pp. 1855-1860).

Nyatuka, D.R. and de la Harpe, R., 2019, May. Evaluating mHealth interventions in an underserved context using service design strategy: A case of Kenya. In *Proceedings of the 3rd International Conference on Medical and Health Informatics* (pp. 153-160).

O'Brien, H.L. and Toms, E.G., 2008. What is user engagement? A conceptual framework for defining user engagement with technology. *Journal of the American society for Information Science and Technology*, *59*(6), pp.938-955.

Ono, M.M., 2002. Emergent strategies for designing new products facing cultural diversity, within the globalisation context. In *2nd conference on innovative research in management, Stockholm*.

Perski, O., Blandford, A., Ubhi, H.K., West, R. and Michie, S., 2017. Smokers' and drinkers' choice of smartphone applications and expectations of engagement: a think aloud and interview study. *BMC medical informatics and decision making*, *17*, pp.1-14.

Richards, L., 2020. Handling qualitative data: A practical guide. *Handling Qualitative Data*, pp.1-336.

Ritchie, J. and Spencer, L., 2002. Qualitative data analysis for applied policy research. In *Analyzing qualitative data* (pp. 187-208). Routledge.

Shen, S.T., Woolley, M. and Prior, S., 2006. Towards culture-centred design. *Interacting with computers*, *18*(4), pp.820-852.

Sonderegger, A. and Sauer, J., 2013. The influence of socio-cultural background and product value in usability testing. *Applied ergonomics*, *44*(3), pp.341-349.

Tang, J., Abraham, C., Stamp, E. and Greaves, C., 2015. How can weight-loss app designers' best engage and support users? A qualitative investigation. *British journal of health psychology*, *20*(1), pp.151-171.

Tschimmel, K., 2012. Design Thinking as an effective Toolkit for Innovation. In *ISPIM Conference Proceedings* (p. 1). The International Society for Professional Innovation Management (ISPIM).

Yardley, L., Spring, B.J., Riper, H., Morrison, L.G., Crane, D.H., Curtis, K., Merchant, G.C., Naughton, F. and Blandford, A., 2016. Understanding and promoting effective engagement with digital behavior change interventions. *American journal of preventive medicine*, *51*(5), pp.833-842.

COMMON AND UNIQUE USER EXPERIENCE PROBLEMS ON E-COMMERCE WEBSITES

Layla Hasan
Faculty of Computing, Universiti Teknologi Malaysia
Johor, Malaysia

ABSTRACT

This research evaluated the user experience (UX) on the top three most visited e-commerce websites in Malaysia, and identified common and unique issues which affected user experience while interacting with such sites. Specific user experience criteria were used in the evaluation, which was adapted from earlier research, and consists of 40 metrics. These metrics were used to evaluate the utilitarian and hedonic features on the websites. The evaluation was conducted using three methods: quantitative questionnaires, qualitative open-ended questions, and qualitative semi-structured interviews. Twenty students participated in this research and they identified ten common user experience problems related to the utilitarian features (e.g., illogical organisation of the websites' content and lack of presenting detailed information about the products); and three unique user experience problems related to the utilitarian features (i.e., not obvious navigation and lack of suggesting complementary products from other shops). Furthermore, the participants identified four common user experience problems related to the hedonic features (e.g., not visually attractive websites, not creative design, and a lack of desirable design elements which evoke users' emotions and gratitude); they also identified seven unique user experience problems on only one of the tested websites (i.e., the website was not motivating).

KEYWORDS

User Experience, UX, e-Commerce, Common, Unique, Malaysia, Utilitarian, Hedonic

1. INTRODUCTION

Nowadays, user experience has become a critical success factor for e-commerce websites. Owners of e-commerce websites should recognize that customers are looking to purchase appropriate products from websites which provide an enjoyable experience (Bernardo et al., 2012). User experience is defined as: "A person's perceptions and responses resulting from the use and/or anticipated use of a product, system or service" (ISO 9241-210:2010, 2010). It includes two aspects of a product (system) relating to the utilitarian (pragmatic/functional) and the hedonic (Mtebe, 2020). The utilitarian aspect relates to the functional characteristics of the product, its utility and usability: i.e., learnability, informativeness, efficiency, customer support, and simplicity (Hassenzahl, 2008; Hassenzahl et al., 2008; Hellianto et al., 2019). The hedonic aspect, however, relates to the emotional experience, customer satisfaction and responses which result from using the product: i.e., attractiveness, entertaining features, and novel functionality (Hellianto et al., 2019; Minge & Thüring, 2018; Hassenzahl, 2005; Dı´az-Oreiro et al., 2021; Febriandika et al., 2020; Hassenzahl, 2001). Customers are concerned about both the utilitarian and hedonic aspects of any e-commerce website. Good and positive user experience on e-commerce websites can increase customer's trust and intention to purchase from a website, and therefore it increases the revenue of the websites (Hellianto et al., 2019; Febriandika et al., 2020; Huang & Wang, 2022; Sudiana et al., 2021).

E-commerce is growing rapidly in Malaysia and it is expected to continue growing in the future (Chan et al., 2018; Kemp & Moey, 2020; Morgan, 2020; GlobalData, 2020). Specifically, e-commerce is expected to reach MYR 51.6 billion (US$ 12.6 billion) in Malaysia by 2024 (GlobalData, 2020). Such growth should be considered and more attention therefore should be paid to improve the user experience of such websites in order to reap the advantages of having positive experience for users. However, the literature review showed that there is a lack of research which has evaluated the user experience on e-commerce websites in Malaysia and which has highlighted common and unique issues which affect the user experience. The aim of this research is to evaluate the user experience on the top three most visited e-commerce websites in Malaysia and to identify common and unique issues which affect users' experience while interacting with them.

2. RELATED WORK

Earlier research investigated user experience in e-commerce websites and identified key factors or attributes which affected the user experience on such websites. For example, Bozzi & Mont'Alvão (2020) investigated the user experience of female apparel e-commerce websites. The results showed that lack of detailed information about products, specifically fit and size, was the most significant problem the users faced which affected their user experience.

Alternatively, the research conducted by Sudiana et al. (2021) identified a total of 43 key success factors which could be considered to make a positive user experience on e-commerce websites. These included obvious navigation, ease of use, quality of information, attractive design, and high speed of downloading. Bonastre and Granollers (2014) also presented a set of heuristics which, if considered, can contribute to positive user experience on e-commerce websites. The heuristics were categorised into six groups based on the stages of the buying decision process. Similarly, Bascur et al. (2021) suggested a set of heuristics which should be considered to create a positive user experience on e-commerce websites. The heuristics included: usability, accessibility, desirability, usefulness, and the extent to which the websites were valuable, findable, and credible. Furthermore, Hinderks et al. (2018) developed a user experience questionnaire to measure user experience for web-based applications. This consisted of six user experience variables, which included: attractiveness, efficiency, perspicuity, dependability, stimulation, and novelty.

Other research was found in the literature which investigated the influence of certain design variables on user experience. For example, Vila et al. (2021) examined the influence of four design variables (content, usability, functionality, and branding) on user experience of tourism websites. The results proved that both usability and branding (detailed information about tourism products and services) had significant effects on the user experience of such websites. Febriandika et al. (2020) also investigated the influence of hedonic features (attractive designs, entertaining features, and gamification) and utilitarian features of an e-commerce website on user experience. The results showed that the hedonic features of an e-commerce website significantly affected the user experience, and the trust in e-commerce. Similarly, Hellianto et al. (2019) examined the effect of functional features and hedonic features on the user experience on an e-commerce website in Indonesia. The results showed that three functional features related to directness, simplicity and informativeness affected the user experience on the site. The results also showed that the hedonic features which affected the user experience on the website related to delicacy and attractiveness. The literature showed that there is a lack of research which evaluates the user experience of e-commerce websites using comprehensive criteria, and which provides a detailed explanation regarding specific issues users face while interacting with these websites.

3. METHODOLOGY

The top three most visited e-commerce websites in Malaysia were identified using the Alexa ranking website (2021), which is one of the major global ranking websites. The three highest ranking according to Alexa for April 2022 were: Shopee.com.my, Lazada.com.my and Pgmall.my. In this paper, we will refer to the three websites as website 1, website 2 and website 3, respectively for simplicity. In order to evaluate the user experience of the three selected websites, the user experience (UX) evaluation criteria, which were developed by earlier research (2022) specifically for e-commerce websites, were used (see Table 1). The criteria included 40 metrics; 27 of them were suggested to evaluate utilitarian quality, and 13 of them were suggested to evaluate the hedonic quality of e-commerce websites.

Table 1. The UX criteria suggested by Hasan (2022)

The UX evaluation criteria	
Metrics to evaluate utilitarian quality	Metrics to evaluate hedonic quality
1. Obvious navigation;	1. Enjoyable experience;
2. Logical and clear structure;	2. Being pleased to interact with the website;
3. Effective internal search engine;	3. Visually attractive interface;
4. A progress indicator is displayed at the top of the checkout pages;	4. Meeting expectations;
5. "Call to action buttons" (i.e., "add to cart" or "buy now") are displayed clearly;	5. Exciting website;
6. Clear advertising of new products;	6. Interesting website;
7. Detailed information about the product is provided;	7. Motivating website;
8. Up-to-date content;	8. Creative website;
9. Clear presentation of order charges;	9. Inventive website;
10. Accurate presentation about the delivery dates;	10. Having innovative features;
11. Related products are recommended clearly;	11. Having desirable design elements which evoke emotion and gratitude;
12. Quick downloading of the website's pages;	12. Having novel functionality;
13. Accessible shopping cart from all the sites' pages;	13. Allowing users to engage in their tasks.
14. Simple registration;	
15. Alternative methods for the delivery of the order are provided;	
16. Alternative methods for the payment are provided;	
17. Consistent interface;	
18. Easy-to-order process;	
19. Easy to learn;	
20. Efficiency;	
21. Availability of privacy policy;	
22. Clear presentation of the shipping, return or exchange policy;	
23. Visible contact information;	
24. Informative frequently asked questions (FAQ) section;	
25. If an error occurs, simple and clear error messages are displayed to get out of the error;	
26. Secure website (i.e., security logos are displayed);	
27. Foreign language and currency support.	

To evaluate the user experience of the three websites using the UX criteria, questionnaires and semi-structured interviews were employed. The questionnaires were designed to collect: background information from the participants, as well as quantitative and qualitative data regarding users' experience while interacting with each of the three websites. The questionnaire included 40 statements corresponding to the 40 metrics of the UX criteria. Twenty voluntary students from the School of Computing at the UTM University participated in this research and evaluated the three websites, using a within-subjects approach. For each website, the participants were asked to rate their agreement to each of the statements using a seven-point Likert scale. The participants were also asked to respond to open-ended questions corresponding to the 40 statements to identify specific problems relating to each statement. After filling-out the questionnaires, the participants were asked to join a semi-structured interview to discuss more about their experience while interacting with the websites. An advertisement for voluntary participants was sent to the students of the Faculty of Computing at the UTM University via WhatsApp, Telegram and Email. The advertisement clarified that the researchers would give each participant an honorarium of RM50.

Regarding the analysis, descriptive analysis was used to describe the background information of the participants. Likert scores were calculated for each statement in each of the questionnaires related to the three e-commerce websites to describe participants' responses to the 40 statements. A Likert score of 1-3 was regarded as a negative response, 5-7 as a positive response and 4 as a neutral one. Negative responses identified several user experience problems on the websites. The qualitative data obtained from participants' responses to the open-ended questions for each of the 40 statements in each of the questionnaires relating to the three e-commerce websites were analysed. These also identified various user experience problems on the websites. The qualitative data obtained from the analysis of the semi-structured interviews were examined and this resulted in identifying more details regarding users' problems on the websites.

It is worth mentioning that in this paper we used method 1 or M1 to refer to the quantitative method used in the questionnaire using Likert scores. Method 2 or M2 refers to the qualitative method used in the questionnaire using open-ended questions while Method 3 or M3 refers to the qualitative method using interviews. User experience problems identified by each of the three methods were compared and this resulted in identifying common and unique problems on the tested websites. The results of the analysis of the three methods and the user experience problems which were identified by each of the three methods are presented in the Results and Discussion Section.

4. RESULTS AND DISCUSSION

This research addressed the gap which was identified in the literature and evaluated the user experience of the top three most visited e-commerce websites in Malaysia using comprehensive criteria. This section presents the results obtained from the analysis of the three methods employed in this research: the quantitative data obtained from the analysis of the Likert scores of the questionnaires; the qualitative data obtained from the analysis of the open-ended questions in the questionnaires; and the qualitative data obtained from the analysis of the interviews. It also presents the common and unique user experience problems on the websites. This section also highlights similar findings obtained from earlier research regarding common user experience problems which were identified previously.

The 20 students who participated in this research were: 18 males and 2 females. Their ages were between 18 to 22 years old. All the participants had experience in purchasing products from e-commerce websites. The results showed that the three tested websites had various user experience problems related to utilitarian and hedonic features. Table 2 summarizes the user experience problems related to the utilitarian features, obtained from the analysis of the three methods, while Table 3 summarizes the user experience problems related to the hedonic features, obtained from the analysis of the three methods. Tables 2 and 3 show that the quantitative analysis of the questionnaire obtained from the analysis of the Likert scores (M1) identified the smallest number of user experience problems, while the qualitative data obtained from the interviews (M3) identified the largest number of user experience problems on the websites.

Table 2. The user experience problems relating to the utilitarian features, which were obtained from the analysis of the three methods

	Problems Related to Utilitarian Features	**Website 1**			**Website 2**			**Website 3**		
		M1	M2	M3	M1	M2	M3	M1	M2	M3
1	The navigation is not obvious throughout the website	×	×	×	×	×	×	×	✓	✓
2	The website has unclear/ illogical structure / hierarchy	×	✓	✓	×	✓	✓	×	✓	✓
3	The website has an ineffective internal search engine	×	×	×	×	×	×	✓	✓	✓
4	Lack of progress indicator at the top of the checkout pages	✓	✓	✓	✓	✓	✓	✓	✓	✓
5	Lack of providing detailed information about the products	×	✓	✓	×	✓	✓	×	✓	✓
6	Inaccurate and unclear information about the delivery dates	×	×	✓	×	×	✓	×	×	✓
7	Lack of recommending related or complementary products from the website	×	×	×	×	×	×	✓	✓	✓
8	Slow downloading of the website's pages	×	×	×	×	✓	✓	✓	✓	✓
9	Lack of providing alternative methods for the delivery of the order	✓	✓	✓	✓	✓	✓	✓	✓	✓
10	The website is inefficient	×	×	×	×	✓	✓	×	✓	✓

11	Lack of suggesting solutions if an error has occurred while interacting with the website	×	✓	✓	×	✓	✓	×	✓	✓
12	Inaccurate foreign language support	×	✓	✓	×	✓	✓	×	✓	✓
13	Lack of foreign currency support	×	✓	✓	×	✓	✓	×	✓	✓

×: A problem was not identified by the method
✓: A problem was identified by the method

Table 3. The user experience problems relating to the hedonic features, which were obtained from the analysis of the three methods

	Problems Related to Hedonic Features	Website 1			Website 2			Website 3		
		M1	M2	M3	M1	M2	M3	M1	M2	M3
1	The user's experience with the website was not enjoyable	×	×	×	×	×	×	×	✓	✓
2	The user was not pleased to interact with the website	×	×	×	×	✓	✓	✓	✓	✓
3	The website was not visually attractive	×	✓	✓	×	✓	✓	×	✓	✓
4	The website did not meet the user's expectations	×	×	×	×	×	×	×	✓	✓
5	The website is motivating	×	×	×	×	×	×	×	×	✓
6	The website was not creative	×	×	×	×	✓	✓	×	✓	✓
7	The website was not inventive	×	×	×	×	×	×	×	✓	✓
8	The website did not have innovative features	×	×	×	×	×	×	×	✓	✓
9	The website did not have desirable design elements which evoked emotion and gratitude	×	✓	✓	×	✓	✓	×	✓	✓
10	The website did not have novel functionality: it was not new or unusual in an interesting way	×	×	×	×	×	×	×	✓	✓
11	The website did not allow users to engage in their tasks	×	×	×	×	×	×	×	✓	✓

×: A problem was not identified by the method
✓: A problem was identified by the method

Specifically, the results obtained from the analysis of the three methods identified 13 user experience problems related to utilitarian features (including 10 common and 3 unique problems), and 11 problems related to hedonic features (including 4 common and 7 unique problems). The following explains in detail the user experience problems which affected the participants while interacting with the tested websites.

- *User Experience Problems Related to the Utilitarian Features*

The participants identified ten common user experience problems on the tested websites related to the utilitarian features, as shown in Table 1. These related to:

1. Illogical and unclear organisation of the websites' content. This problem was identified from the analysis of methods 2 and 3 on all the websites.
2. Lack of displaying a progress indicator at the top of the checkout pages. This problem was identified from the analysis of the three methods on all the websites.
3. Lack of presenting detailed information about the products, such as materials or size. This problem was identified from the analysis of methods 2 and 3 on all the websites. This problem was also one of the most significant problems which affected user experience on e-commerce websites according to earlier research (Hellianto et al., 2019; Sudiana et al., 2021; Bozzi & Mont, 2020; Vila et al., 2021).
4. Inaccurate and unclear information about the delivery dates. This problem was identified from the analysis method 3 only on all the websites.
5. Slow downloading of the website's pages. This problem was identified on website 2 based on the analysis from methods 2 and 3. It was also identified on website 3 based on the analysis of the three methods. It is worth mentioning that earlier research (Sudiana et al., 2021) considered high speed of downloading as one of the key success factors which could be considered to make a positive user experience of e-commerce.

6. Lack of supporting alternative methods for the delivery of the order. This problem was identified from the analysis of the three methods on all the websites.
7. Inefficient website. This was related to the poor organization of website 3, difficulty in finding a product in it and slow downloading of its pages. This problem was also identified on website 2 because it uses many pop-ups which disturbed users and because of the slow downloading of its pages. This problem was identified from the analysis of methods 2 and 3. Efficiency was also considered as one of the user experience variables that should be taken into consideration to result in a positive user experience (Hinderks et al., 2018).
8. Lack of providing simple and clear error messages if an error occurs while interacting with the websites. This problem was identified from the analysis of methods 2 and 3 on all the websites.
9. Inaccurate foreign language support; when the language of the interface of the websites was changed, only a few elements were displayed using the selected language. This problem was identified from the analysis of methods 2 and 3 on all the websites.
10. Lack of foreign currency support; prices of the products were only displayed in Malaysian Ringgit (RM). This problem was identified from the analysis of methods 2 and 3 on all the websites.

The participants also identified three unique user experience problems related to the utilitarian features only on website 3, as shown in Table 1. These related to:

1. The navigation was not obvious throughout the website; this problem was identified from the analysis of methods 2 and 3. Obvious navigation is considered one of key success factors which should be considered to make a positive user experience on e-commerce websites (Sudiana et al., 202).
2. Ineffective internal search engine function; the internal search results included redundant and inaccurate results. This problem was identified from the analysis of all the methods.
3. Lack of suggesting complementary products from other shops. This problem was identified from the analysis of all the methods.

- *User Experience Problems Related to the Hedonic Features*

The participants identified four common user experience problems on the tested websites related to the hedonic features, as shown in Table 2. These related to:

1. The users were not pleased to interact with the websites 2 and 3. The users explained the reasons behind this, which related to it not being easy to return products to website 2 and the excessive number of pop-up advertisements displayed on it. For website 3, the reasons for users being displeased related to its failure to present many products. This problem was identified on website 2 based on the analysis from methods 2 and 3, and it was identified on website 3 based on the analysis of the three methods.
2. The design of the websites was very simple and not visually attractive; this problem was identified from the analysis of methods 2 and 3 on all the websites. Attractive design is one of the key success factors which could be considered to make a positive user experience on e-commerce websites (Sudiana et al., 2021; Hinderks et al., 2018). Also, earlier research showed that unattractive design of e-commerce websites significantly affected the user experience (Hellianto et al., 2019; Febriandika et al., 2020).
3. The design of the websites was not creative. This problem was identified from the analysis of methods 2 and 3 on websites 2 and 3.
4. The design of the websites lacked desirable design elements which evoked users' emotions and gratitude. This problem was identified from the analysis of methods 2 and 3 on all the websites.

The participants also identified seven unique user experience problems only on website 3 relating to the hedonic features, as shown in Table 2. These related to:

1. The users did not have an enjoyable experience while interacting with website 3. This was related to the small font size used in the website, the illogical structure, and the inefficient internal search function. This problem was identified from the analysis of methods 2 and 3.
2. The website did not meet users' expectation because of its slow downloading of the website's pages, the poor organisation, and the ineffective search function. This problem was identified from the analysis of methods 2 and 3.
3. The website was not motivating; it did not display many products and its design was not of high quality. This problem was identified from the analysis of method 3 only.
4. The website was not an inventive website; it lacked continuous improvements of its services to satisfy its customers. This problem was identified from the analysis of methods 2 and 3.

5. The website lacked innovative or unique features, such as a customised internal search function. This problem was identified from the analysis of methods 2 and 3.
6. The website lacked novel functionality. This problem was identified from the analysis of methods 2 and 3. Novelty is one of the user experience variables that should be considered on e-commerce websites to gain a positive user experience (Hinderks et al., 2018).
7. The website did not allow uses to engage in their tasks; this was related to the fact that this website (website 3) had many problems which affected participants' engagement with the website. These included: the lack of an effective internal search engine function; lack of suggesting complementary products; slow downloading of website's pages. This problem was identified from the analysis of methods 2 and 3.

5. CONCLUSION

Owners of e-commerce websites should evaluate and improve the user experience of their websites to reap the benefits of positive user experience such as increased revenue, increased customer's trust and intention to purchase from a website. This research evaluated the user experience on the top three most visited e-commerce websites in Malaysia, and shed the light on specific common and unique utilitarian (functional) and hedonic features which affected the experience of users while interacting with the websites. A total of 20 students participated in this research. Three methods were employed in the evaluation: quantitative (M1), qualitative using open-ended questions (M2), and qualitative using interviews (M3), and the evaluation was conducted based on specific 40 UX evaluation criteria. The results identified 13 user experience problems on the tested websites related to utilitarian features, including ten common and three unique problems. The results also identified 11 user experience problems on the tested websites related to hedonic features, including four common and seven unique problems. The results of this research could help the managers of the tested e-commerce websites to improve the user experience of their websites by addressing the identified problems, helping them, therefore, to reap the advantages of positive user experiences.

REFERENCES

Alexa (2021). Top Sites in Malaysia. On the WWW, July. URL https://www.alexa.com/topsites/countries/MY.

Bascur C., Rusu C., and Quiñones D., 2021. ECUXH: A Set of User eXperience Heuristics for e-Commerce. Meiselwitz G (Ed.): HCII 2021, LNCS 12774, pp. 407–420, Springer Nature Switzerland AG 2021. https://doi.org/10.1007/978-3-030-77626-8_27.

Bernardo M., Marimon F., and Alonso-Almeida M., 2012. Functional quality and hedonic quality: A study of the dimensions of e-service quality in online travel agencies. *Information & Management*, Vol. 49, No. 7-8, pp. 342-347.

Bonastre L., and Granollers T., 2014. A set of heuristics for user experience evaluation in e-commerce websites. *In proceedings of the Seventh International Conference on Advances in Computer-Human Interactions (ACHI 2014).*

Bozzi C., and Mont'Alvão C., 2020. The user experience (UX) on female apparel e-commerce websites in Brazil. *Work*, Vol. 66, No. 4, pp. 945–62. https://doi.org/10.3233/WOR-203239.

Chan S. W., Ahmad M. F., Zaman I., Omar S. S., Ramlan R., and Tam C. X., 2018. Privacy perceptions of online shopping behaviour amongst malaysian lazada online shoppers. *In Proceedings of AIP Conference*, 2018. https://doi.org/10.1063/1.5055438.

Dı´az-Oreiro I., Lo´pez G., Quesada .L, and Guerrero L. A., 2021. UX evaluation with standardized questionnaires in ubiquitous computing and ambient intelligence: a systematic literature review. *Advances in Human-Computer Interaction*, Vol. 5518722, pp. 1–22, https://doi.org/10.1155/2021/5518722.

Febriandika N. R., Millatina A. N., Luthfiyatillah, and Herianingrum S., 2020. Customer e-loyalty of Muslim millennials in indonesia: integrated model of trust, user experience and branding in e-commerce webstore. *In Proceedings of IC4E 2020,* January 10–12, Osaka, Japan.

GlobalData (2020). COVID-19 accelerates e-commerce growth in Malaysia, 2020. On the WWW, July. URL https://www.globaldata.com/covid-19-accelerates-e-commerce-growth-malaysia-says-globaldata.

Hasan L., 2022. Evaluating User Experience (UX) of the Top E-commerce Websites in Malaysia: A Quantitative Study. *In Proceedings of the 40th International Business Information Management Association (IBIMA)*, 23-24 November, Seville, Spain, ISBN: 979-8-9867719-1-5, ISSN: 2767-9640.

Hassenzahl M.. 2001. The effect of perceived hedonic quality on product appealingness. *International Journal of Human–Computer Interaction*, Vol. 13, No. 4, pp. 373-410, https://doi.org/10.1207/ S15327590IJHC1304.

Hassenzahl M., 2005. The thing and I: Understanding the relationship between user and product, in Blythe M, Overbeeke C, Monk A, and Wright, P.S.N. (Eds), Funology: From Usability to Enjoyment, Kluwer Academic Publishers, Norwell, MA, pp. 31-42, doi: 10.1007/1-4020-2967-5.

Hassenzahl M., 2008. User Experience (UX): towards an experiential perspective on product quality. *In Proceedings of the 20th Conference on l'Interaction Homme-Machine,* pp. 1-15, doi: 10.1145/1512714.1512717.

Hassenzahl M., Schöbel M., and Trautmann T., 2008. How motivational orientation influences the evaluation and choice of hedonic and pragmatic interactive products: the role of regulatory focus. *Interacting with Computers*, Vol. 20, No. 4/5, pp. 473-479, doi: 10.1016/j.intcom.2008.05.001.

Hellianto G. R., Suzianti A., and Komarudin, 2019. User experience modeling on consumer-to consumer (c2c) e-commerce website. *In Proceedings of the 1st International Conference on Industrial and Manufacturing Engineering*.

Hinderks A., Schrepp M., and Thomaschewski J., 2018. A benchmark for the short version of the user experience questionnaire. *In Proceedings of the 14th International Conference on Web Information Systems and Technologies (WEBIST)*, pp. 373-377.

Huang J., and Wang X., 2022. User experience evaluation of B2C e-Commerce websites based on fuzzy information. *Wireless Communications and Mobile Computing*, Vol. 6767960, https://doi.org/10.1155/2022/6767960.

ISO 9241-210:2010 (2010). Ergonomics of human-system interaction – part 210: human-centred design for interactive systems.

Kemp S., and Moey S., 2019. Digital 2019 Spotlight: Ecommerce in Malaysia, DATAREPORTAL. On the WWW, July. URL https://datareportal.com/reports/digital-2019-ecommerce-in-malaysia.

Minge M., and Thüring M., 2018. Hedonic and pragmatic halo effects at early stages of User Experience. International *Journal of Human-Computer Studies*, Vol. 109, pp. 13–25.

Morgan, J. P., 2020. E-commerce Payments Trends Report: Malaysia, On the WWW, July. URL https://www.jpmorgan.com/merchant-services/insights/reports/malaysia-2020.

Mtebe S. J., 2020. Examining user experience of eLearning systems implemented in two universities in Tanzania. *Interactive Technology and Smart Education*, Vol. 17, No. 1, pp. 39-55.

Sudiana Y. U., Chandra, and Angela L., 2021. Key success factors for a better user experience in e-commerce website. *In Proceedings of the 2021 International Conference on Information Management and Technology (ICIMTech)*.

Vila T. D., González E. A., Vila N. A., and Brea J. A. F., 2021. Indicators of website features in the user experience of etourism search and metasearch engines. *Journal of Theoretical and Applied Electronic Commerce Research*, Vol. 6, No. 1. pp. 18-36.

PROTOTYPING AN AUTOMATIC AND CONTEXT-ADAPTIVE ACQUISITION METHOD FOR MOBILITY PREFERENCES OF PASSENGERS IN PUBLIC TRANSPORT

Waldemar Titov[1], Christian Rickert[2] and Thomas Schlegel[1]
[1]Institute for Intelligent Interactive Ubiquitous System (IIIUS), Hochschule Furtwangen University
Robert-Gerwig-Platz 1, Furtwangen im Schwarzwald 78120, Germany
[2]Institute of Ubiquitous Mobility Systems (IUMS), Hochschule Karlsruhe University of Applied Sciences
Moltkestrasse 30, Karlsruhe 76133, Germany

ABSTRACT

Planning a trip on public transport is an important step that can be time-consuming and nerve-wracking. Finding the right connection is not always simple, especially since personal preferences influence the selection of the most suitable route. Finding the most suitable route passenger's mobility preferences need to be known by the journey planning system. However, collecting these individually mobility preferences is a time-consuming process. Our contribution applies the contextual inquiring method determining what mobility preferences are most important. Based on these findings, we introduce a prototyping approach automatically determining four of the most important mobility preferences. The detected parameters are used to enrich user's future trip requests, assisting passengers to have pleasant and stress-free journeys from door to door.

KEYWORDS

Detecting Mobility Preferences, Individual Passenger Information, Context-Adaptive Public Transport Information, Contextual-Inquiring, In-App-Questionnaire, Evaluation in Public Transport Domain

1. INTRODUCTION

Travel planning in public transport can be performed on various platforms, including websites, ticket vending machines or smartphones. Due to their great flexibility, smartphones are used in many daily areas, be it shopping, communication or entertainment. The application areas are almost limitless and are becoming more diverse and complex every year. Two of these areas of use are timetable information and travel planning for users. What used to have to be read off information boards or awkwardly folded information maps can now additionally be conveniently accessed from anywhere on the Internet. Added to this is the possibility of personalization, i.e., an experience adapted to the user. A novel term that comes up in this context is "mobility preferences." Mobility preferences are essential for personalizing trip planning. They make it easier for the user to find connections. Likewise, they help the route calculation system in the background to create a customized and individual response. In interaction with journey planner applications installed on the user's own smartphone, optimal route information can thus be offered. According to a 2017 survey, 80% of respondents, aged 18 to 29, reported using their smartphone for connection information (Statista, 2020). A more detailed examination of route requests was carried out in a student thesis at Karlsruhe University of Applied Sciences. The investigation of route requests in the Karlsruhe area led to the conclusion that only a minimal number of requests with additional parameters are performed (Keller et al., 2022). For example, about 25,000 out of 18 million requests were performed that included an additional waypoint. The need for ground level access was indicated in about 5000 requests. A change in walking speed was included in about 55,000 requests. Specifying other parameters was possible, but was done in rare cases. Our contribution aims to provide information about possible reasons. The focus is on the use case in which users have already decided to use public transportation.

The goal of this work is to support users in their travel planning in order to achieve a personalized experience on the one hand and to efficiently use the available resources and potentials on the other hand. Various factors are necessary for this goal, first and foremost mobility preferences. Users specify these only in rare cases. To address the problem, the following two research questions were defined. First, what are the reasons for situational and individually made travel planning decisions? Secondly, what are the reasons for not indicating mobility preferences? To answer these questions, a user study is conducted. The results of this study form the basic building blocks for a concept that will help solve the problem. A system that supports users in specifying their preferences or takes them off their hands will be conceptually designed and tested with our prototype. The results will provide information on possible improvements and pave the way for future work or studies.

Our paper is structured as follows. In the next section, we look at approaches defining individual mobility preferences and finally set definition mobility preferences for this work derived from literature. We will then look at prior published approaches towards context-adaptive acquisition methods for mobility preferences of passengers in public transport in the related work section. Following this section, we will describe our methodology subdivided into the requirement analyses, the conducted user study and the implementation of our prototype. In the last two sections of this paper, we discuss the results of the conducted user study and findings of our development and evaluation process as well as conclude and give an outlook on our future work, pointing out evaluation steps we are planning in the near future.

2. DEFINITION OF INDIVIDUAL MOBILITY PREFERENCES

Mobility Preferences is composed of the word's "mobility" and "preferences". Preferences can be described as a preference or distinct inclination. When a person has a choice between a number of decisions, preferences play a role in making that decision. Additionally, preferences can be assumed to persist over a period of time because they are preceded by a decision-making process based on sufficient information (Piekenbrock, 2020). Preferences appear, among others, in the field of mobility research, for example, in transportation mode choice. In such studies, participants are asked to express their inclination regarding a particular mode of transport (Knapp, 2015). The term "mobility" should be distinguished from transport. Mobility is divided into potential and realized mobility. The former describes a person's mobility in general. The second is the desire for change of place. The realization of the desire for change of place results in turn in traffic (Becker et al., 1999).

In this work, we repeatedly speak of mobility preferences, which is why a comprehensible definition is indispensable. With the help of the previous information, a combination of mobility and preferences is proposed. If mobility is the desire to change location, mobility preferences can be described as those factors that play a role in the decision to carry out the change of location.

(Loepp and Ziegler, 2014) describe the use of a user profile for intermodal navigation. Their goal is to design an exchangeable user profile that can take into account the specific preferences of the users. With respect to mobility preferences, this is an important step because although they are often mentioned in the context of mobility research, a clear classification is not available. Therefore, the user profile proposed by Loepp and Ziegler is used as a basis for mobility preferences. The user profile consists of three parts: Static Profile Data, Static Preferences, and the Situational Context, see Fig. 1. Static profile data describe fixed data such as age, origin, or transportation mode ownership, which usually rarely change. Static preferences include data that express users' inclination regarding different aspects of navigation. The situational context describes factors that cannot be changed in the short term, such as the weather or the time of day. Furthermore, the situational context has an impact on the static preferences.

In a next step, mobility preferences are derived from the static preferences. They form a set of factors that influence the users' travel planning. However, they need to be considered and explained in more detail for the use case of this thesis. The use case refers to the use of public transport only. The proposed user profile of Loepp and Ziegler is too complex for the mentioned use case and therefore has to be adapted.

3. RELATED WORK

Planning a trip by public transport is an important step that can be time-consuming and nerve-wracking. Finding the right connection is not always easy, especially since personal preferences influence the selection of the most suitable route. To find the most suitable route, the journey planner needs to know the mobility preferences of passengers. However, recording these individual mobility preferences is a time-consuming process.

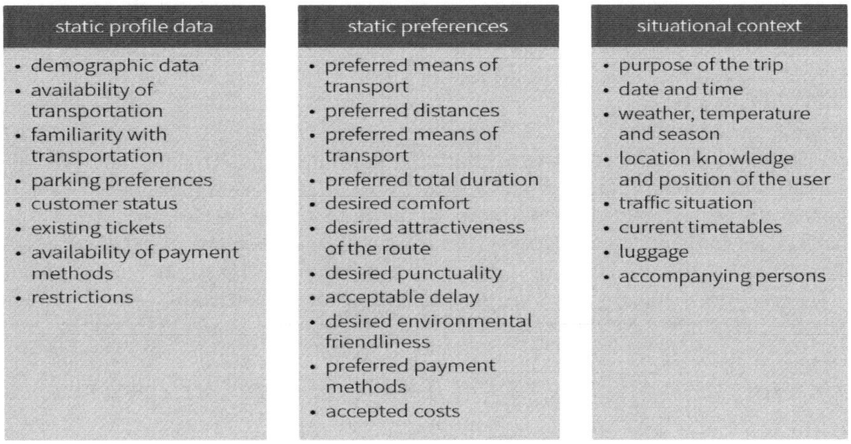

Figure 1. Illustration of the user profile, Loepp and Ziegler (2014).

In their work, (Grotenhuis et al., 2007) investigate what quality of multimodal travel information is required by users and what impact it has on their mode choice. In particular, the different requirements of travel information to the three phases of a trip: Before the trip, at the point of departure, and in the mode of transportation. Before the trip, travel planning takes place. Especially in the area of public transportation, it requires that all necessary information is available so that no further changes have to be made on the way. Information at the point of departure, such as the stop of the train or bus, should only be used for support and not for planning. Information shown on the way in the means of transport also serves as support. For their study of the three phases of travel, they interviewed 191 people, 100 of whom were under 25 and 28 of whom were older than 45. They asked participants about their preferences during the different phases of a trip and what information was important during each phase. Participants could indicate whether they found this information important for different types of information, such as real-time data or duration of the trip. Their results showed that many of the travel information claims are simultaneously necessary for trip planning to occur at all. Information about trip duration, delays, transfers, and departure times are particularly important for trip planning. The ranking of importance was based on how often the respective attribute was selected. The four attributes mentioned were selected by over 80% of respondents.

(Loepp and Ziegler, 2017) conducted an empirical needs analysis focusing on intermodal travel chains. In an initial study, they asked participants about their assessment and use of route planners and journey planner information, among other things. Of the 243 respondents, 103 indicated that trip duration was the most important piece of information. Other important information included real-time data, alternative routes and ease of input. Only 29% of respondents would provide information on their own walking speed. In their second study, they were able to determine with regard to the types of routes that 92% of the 90 respondents, timetable information for unique routes. Furthermore, journey planners are used more for day trips, vacation trips or leisure activities than for commuting or private errands.

In our IP-KOM-ÖV research project, (IP-KOM-ÖV, 2020) is worth mentioning in the context of electronic journey planners. The goal of the project was to increase the quality and efficiency of public transport. One of the work packages includes an interface used for real-time information and was developed within the project. Context, interaction, and classification models were designed to represent the concepts and contexts of public transport.

In our Dynapsis research project (Dynapsis, 2020) is a follow-on project of IP-KOM-ÖV, which aims at connecting passenger information systems and the passenger's daily routine. The user is relieved of the hurdle of mobility planning by having the system consider his schedule and find optimal route suggestions. This can be considered as an approach to automatically calculate a suitable route.

In our currently ongoing SmartMMI research project (SmartMMI, 2022) researcher are focusing on providing information to passengers. The feature of the project is a transparent display to be installed in public transport vehicles. Such a "SmartWindow" supports users with additional and valuable information during the journey. A trip planning or change on the interactive display will be provided. The connection between the SmartWindow and the user's own mobile device is also a relevant feature. While the user is provided with detailed information about the trip on his own end device, the window displays additional, general information.

4. METHODOLOGY

The methodology section summarizes our approach of prototyping an automatic and context-adaptive acquisition method for mobility preferences of passengers in public transport. In the first subsection, the requirement analyses is conducted collecting information about mobility preferences in general. In this phase, we also analyzed the available setting options of selected mobile application used for public transport. Based on the results of the evaluations in first phase, we set up a user study. This user study is described in the second subsection. The results of this user study were incorporated in an interactive prototype. The implementation of this prototype is described in subsection three.

4.1 Requirement Analyses of Mobility Preferences Settings in Mobile Applications

As part of the requirement analyses, we analyzed the setting options for mobility preference available in the six most commonly used German mobile application for public transport travel information. The apps examined contain a variety of setting options, some of which overlap. A comparison of the apps shows that transport mode exclusion can be considered a component of a schedule information app is shown in table 1. The table lists other settings that can be found in the apps, such as transfer time or intermediate stops. "Yes" or "No" means that the apps offer the possibility to make the mentioned setting. For example, in the application, Moovit the walking speed cannot be specified, other than in Öffi where walking speed can be specified as a real value. Relative means that no concrete value can be selected or entered, but only a preference can be expressed. In the case of walking speed, "slow", "normal" or "fast" can be selected. DB's apps allow you to specify a maximum number of transfers, although in the case of DB Navigator this is limited to specifying a direct connection only. Apps that offer a way to optimize the request according to a specific preference, such as "few transfers", can only do this exclusively. Accordingly, it is not possible to optimize for "few transfers" together with "fastest connection" or "shortest walking distance" at the same time. A possible reason for this would be that these specifications are values of the same parameter.

Table 1. Requirement analysis of six commonly used public transport applications in Germany

Parameter	Moovit	Öffi	DB Streckenagent	DB Navigator	Bus&Bahn	KVV.mobil
transportation exclusion	yes	yes	yes	yes	yes	no
walking speed	no	relative	no	no	relative	no
number transfers	relative	relative	absolute	absolute	no	no
transfer time	no	no	absolute	absolute	no	no
accessibility	no	yes	no	no	no	no
bicycle transport	no	no	yes	yes	yes	no
length of footpaths	relative	relative	no	no	relative	no
fastest connection	yes	yes	no	yes	yes	no
stopovers / via's	no	yes	yes	yes	no	no
special means of transport	yes	no	no	no	no	yes

4.2 User Study using the Contextual Inquiry Method

In order to obtain an initial picture of mobility preferences of public transport users, a series of studies were carried out. The study series consisted of three parts and aimed to observe the users' behavior during trip planning. Based on our previous work identifying mobility pattern from commuters using only mobility data we selected them as the main beneficial user group (Gartner et al., 2021). Participants were given a questionnaire while using a journey planner application on their own smartphone. This has the advantage that users do not feel observed during the study and make possible decisions differently (Patton, 2014).

Our user study is based on the method of contextual inquiry. This has the advantage that users are observed in their actions and then questioned for their motivations Moser, 2013. Since the focus is not a usability test of the journey planner application, no usability expert is brought in to perform these tasks. The observation is done by the application on the smartphone and the questionnaire at the end replaces the interview. The conducted user study aimed to investigate users' decision making in route selection. In addition, a first attempt is made to gain an opinion on mobility preferences. The exact questions are explained in the following chapters. The series of studies is intended to help refute or confirm the theses previously established.

Initially the user study was planned to be conducted in the actual usage context of public transport. Therefore, participants would have to fill out the mobile app questionnaire, for example, when starting their journey on the train. According to the circumstances, scenarios were used here, which were processed by the participants at home. The three scenarios were structured as follows: First: A timed appointments such as meeting for dinner require arriving on time and without worries. The criteria for this are the arrival or travel time as well as the number of transfers. Second: A time-flexible appointments only make demands on a suitable arrival time. Third: the criteria for a journey home are also primarily the number of transfers. As shown in Figure 2, we used the evaluation method of contextual inquiring and therefore developed an in-app questionnaire.

Figure 2. In-App questionnaire evaluating user's mobility preferences with contextual inquiring method

Our implemented prototype application called "GoEFA" is intended to test some aspects of the concept. The focus is on the passive determination of mobility preferences for the user. Our evaluation showed the four most important mobility preferences are: favored walking speed, favored transportation mode, favored number of changes and favored travel duration. In addition, we have shown a concept how these preferences can be determined by analyzing user's interaction with the smartphone system. In the next step, we applied the gained information by enriching future connection requests.

4.3 Implementation of the User Study

The implementation of the study proved to be problematic, as rail travel was being avoided due to the situation arising from COVID-19 restrictions. Therefore, participants could not be required to use public transportation as initially planned. An alternative option is to use scenarios. Participants were asked to put themselves in the scenario as best as they can. Participants were given a scenario at weekly intervals. The entire study spans three weeks or three scenarios. These scenarios are to be distinguished from scenarios used in the context of user analysis with personas. In (Keller et al., 2019) we prior introduced our public transport personas based on our research projects IP-KOM-ÖV. The scenarios describe the course of a day on which the journey planner is used. The scenarios are based on a time before the pandemic, in which train travel was part of everyday life. Each scenario has a different task. The first scenario is about the visit of a friend. The starting point, destination and arrival time are given and marked in the description of the scenario. For comprehensibility, the dates have been listed again in the document. The second scenario leaves the choice of departure stop and time open. Scenario 3 suggests three departure times: Before an event, shortly after, or much later. The three scenarios are intended to simulate real-life situations in which users can make as many different decisions as possible. In the background, the system also records which routes the users have looked at. The three scenarios used are presented below.

5. RESULTS OF USER STUDY

At the end of the study period, over 20 submissions could be collected and evaluated. An overview over the results is given in the following chapter. Due to the small number of participants in the study, percentage figures were not provided.

As can be seen in Figure 3, the number of transfers has a great relevance in the choice of connections in Scenario 1 and 3. The reason for this may be the nature of the scenarios. In scenario 1, it is required to arrive on time for a set appointment avoiding the other person having to wait. Transferring passengers could result in not being able to reach a connection. In the follow-up question about why the connection with the few transfers is preferred, participants indicated that transfers are stressful and the connection could be missed. In Scenario 3, on the other hand, it may be more important to arrive home reliably and not too late in terms of time. In scenario 2, it is more important to arrive at the destination at the appropriate time. Although an appointment must also be kept, transfers are less relevant, as it is possible to decide for oneself when to travel to the destination. If none of the answer options was applicable, the participants could give another reason. Particularly in scenario 3, it was indicated in the free text field that connections with long-distance traffic are avoided.

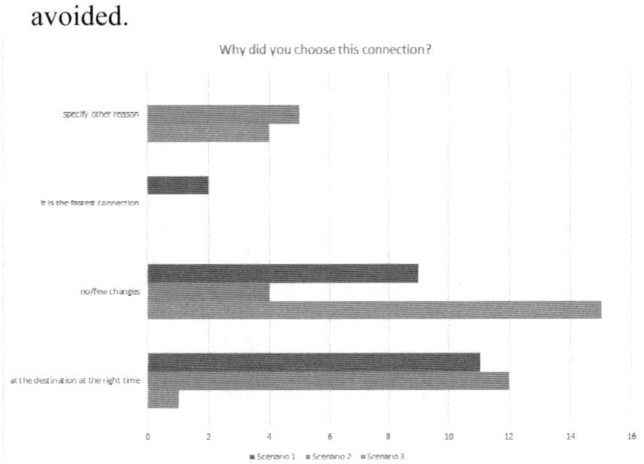

Figure 3. Reasons for choice of a connection

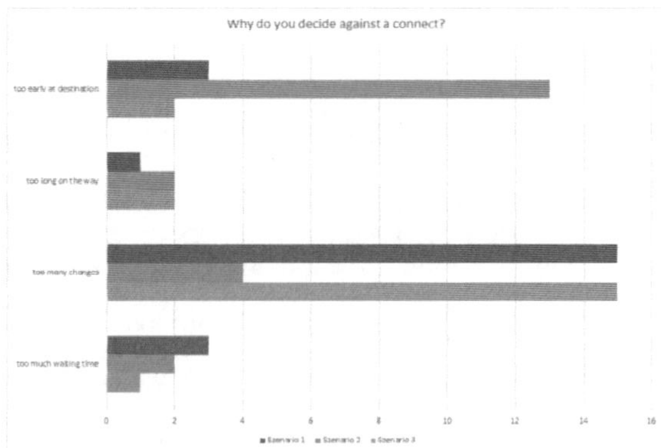

Figure 4. Reasons against choice of a connection

With the second question, a check of the answers from the first question can take place. In Figure 4 can be seen that the answers partially coincide. In scenario 1 and 3, no connections are chosen that have too many transfers. In scenario 2, a large majority indicated that arriving too early at the destination is an exclusion criterion. Travel time and waiting time were only indicated in small numbers.

Figure 5 illustrates that a trade-off is made in the choice of connection. However, how many connections were actually looked at was recorded in the background. The recording shows that ten queries were sent in scenario 1, where only one connection was looked at more closely. In scenarios two and three, there were 14 and 11 respectively. One explanation for the correlation may be that many routes are only looked at more closely if they have transfers. The Figure 6 shows that the common display of connections - descending, with the temporally closest connection first - is preferred. Differences between the scenarios are easy to see, as a certain tendency regarding the prioritization of transfers becomes clear.

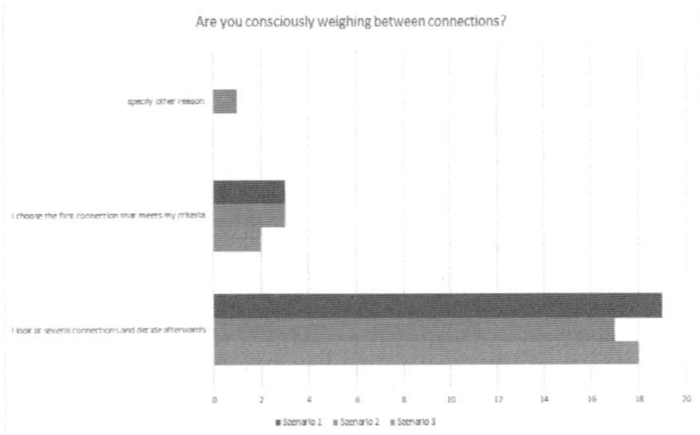

Figure 5. Participants decision weighing

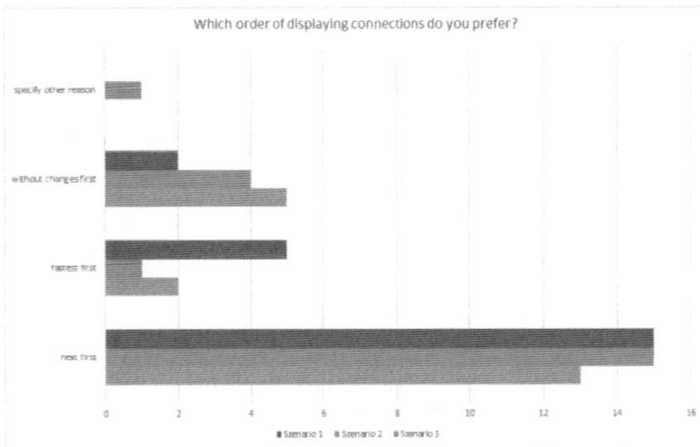

Figure 6. Preference of displayed connections

The answers to the question whether the user would use the option to change the order are available in Figure 7. The purpose of this question is to identify an initial tendency to indicate mobility preferences. The majority of participants indicated that the changeover must be straightforward. The indication that this option is not used decreased from scenario to scenario. A possible explanation could be that participants develop a greater willingness to make this adjustment over the course of the study.

Participants were asked a follow-up question if they indicated that they would not use the option. This again allowed for more specific questions as to why this was the case. The main reason was that the changeover was not needed. Too much effort or fear of doing something wrong was also selected. Due to the small number of responses, however, no reliable statement can be made about a general willingness of users regarding the conversion of settings.

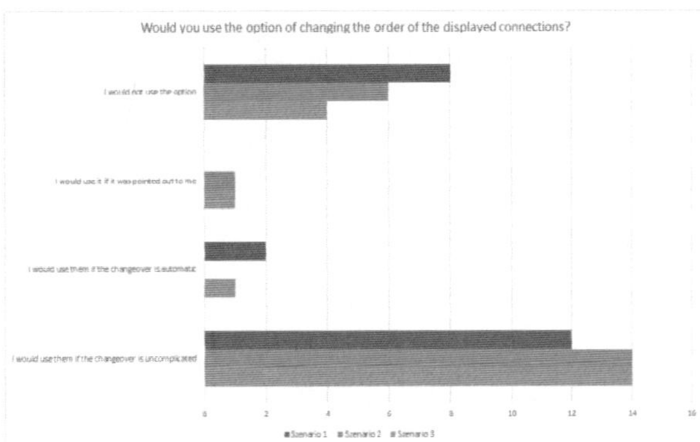

Figure 7. Adaptation preferences of participants

6. CONCLUSION AND FUTURE WORK

In general, our contribution shows the importance and the impact of mobility preferences and describes our analysis and evaluation approaches that we used conducting the user study. We reported on our experiences, the results, the designs of the study we conducted, as well as gave an insight into lessons learned while analyzing user's interaction data. To answer our research question, an in-app user study evaluation using the contextual inquiring method was conducted. Therefore, an in-app questionnaire was formulated to introduce participants to the topic of individual mobility preferences and then ask them directly about their personal mobility preferences. Additionally, the reasons for not stating the individual mobility preferences in mobility application were identified.

The main reason given was not having enough information on the setting, followed by a fear of missing other suitable connections. Some participants indicated that the effort associated with the change would be too great. With the help of these reasons, requirements can be made for possible acquisition methods. The concept includes a preference service that records and validates mobility preferences in the background. This avoids users entering them initially but not updating them later. At the same time, it takes away the effort from users, as well as the fear of setting something incorrectly. A prerequisite for the continuous recording of mobility preferences is an initial measurement. Context is then continuously determined and mobility preferences are created. Future work or future research projects can start here and further investigate mobility preferences.

REFERENCES

Becker, U., Gerike, R., & Völlings, A. (1999). Gesellschaftliche Ziele von und für Verkehr, Heft 1 der Schriftenreihe des Instituts für Verkehr und Umwelt eV (DIVU). Dresden, S, 71.

"Dynapsis" - research project (2020). URL: https://www.tu-ilmenau.de/mtmp/forschung/abgeschlossene-projekte/dynapsys/. Accessed 5 October 2020.

Gartner, T., Titov, W., & Schlegel, T. (2021, July). Identifying Mobility Pattern of Specific User Types Based on Mobility Data. In International Conference on Human-Computer Interaction (pp. 527-534). Springer, Cham.

Grotenhuis, J. W., Wiegmans, B. W., & Rietveld, P. (2007). The desired quality of integrated multimodal travel information in public transport: Customer needs for time and effort savings. Transport Policy, 14(1), 27-38.

"IP-KOM-ÖV" - research project (2020).URL: http://www.ip-kom.net/projekt/. Accessed 5 October 2020.

Keller, C., Struwe, S., Titov, W., & Schlegel, T. (2019, July). Understanding the usefulness and acceptance of adaptivity in smart public transport. In International Conference on Human-Computer Interaction (pp. 307-326). Springer, Cham.

Keller, C., Glück, F., Gerlach, C. F., & Schlegel, T. (2022). Investigating the Potential of Data Science Methods for Sustainable Public Transport. Sustainability, 14(7), 4211.

Knapp, F. D. (2015). Determinanten der Verkehrsmittelwahl (Vol. 10). Duncker &Humblot.

Loepp, B., & Ziegler, J. (2014, September). Komplexe Präferenzprofile für intermodale Navigation. In Mensch & Computer Workshopband (pp. 191-198).

Loepp, B., & Ziegler, J. (2017). Empirische Bedarfsanalyse zur intermodalen Navigation und dem Einsatz von Informationssystemen zur Förderung ihrer Attraktivität. In Innovative Produkte und Dienstleistungen in der Mobilität (pp. 409-426). Springer Gabler, Wiesbaden.

Moser, C. (2013). User experience design. In user experience design (pp. 1-22). Springer, Berlin, Heidelberg.

Patton, M. Q. (2014). Qualitative research & evaluation methods: Integrating theory and practice. Sage publications.

Piekenbrock, 2020. "Definition: Präferenz", URL: https://wirtschaftslexikon.gabler.de/definition/praeferenz-46070, accessed 15 July 2020.

"SmartMMI" research project, Model- and Context-based Mobility Information on Smart Public Displays and Mobile Devices in Public Transport. URL: https://smartmmi.de/project/, accessed 9 May 2022

Statista, 2020. "ÖPNV - Smartphone Nutzung in Deutschland", URL: https://de.statista.com/statistik/daten/studie/713742/umfrage/nutzung-des smartphones-fuerinformationen-ticket-erwerb-im-oepnv-in-deutschland/, accessed 15 July 2020.

BUILDING A FACE DATABASE OF ARAB FACES TOWARD EVALUATING BIAS IN FACIAL ANALYSIS SYSTEMS

Ashraf Khalil[1], Suha Glal[1], Khider Ahmed[2], Sana Zeb Khan[3] and Aysha Abdulgani[4]
[1]*College of Technological Innovation, Zayed University*
Abu Dhabi, UAE
[2]*Mechatronics Engineering Graduate Program, American university of Sharjah*
Sharjah, UAE
[3]*Department of Computer Science and Engineering, American university of Sharjah*
Sharjah, UAE
[4]*United Arab Emirates University*
Al Ain, UAE

ABSTRACT

Machine learning algorithms are fundamentally driven by the data provided by humans; consequently, the decisions made by those algorithms are not free from human bias. This is particularly evident in the case of facial analysis systems that employ machine learning algorithms. Recent studies have shown that the decisions made by many of the commercially available facial analysis systems are prejudiced against certain groups of race, ethnicity, age, gender and culture. Further studies have identified that the underlying reason for such biased decisions is that the open source material available for facial image databases which are used in commerce and academia to train the algorithms has meager diversity in these categories. To compound this issue, facial analysis technology is promoted by influential companies and artificial intelligence service providers without affirming the fairness and accuracy of the decisions given by these systems. To minimize bias and ensure representation of the Middle Eastern population in the imminent growth of this technology, we propose the development of two Arab face databases along with an algorithmic audit involving seven commercially available facial analysis systems. Of the databases, the first, Arab-LEANA, will include 300 Arab subjects' face images with variation in lighting, expression, accessory, nationality and age (LEANA). The second, Arab Public Figures Faces (APFF), will contain images and videos of 300 Arab public figures captured "in the wild". Faces for APFF will be selected manually from the internet since manual selection of faces will result in a high degree of variability in scale, pose, expression, illumination, age, occlusion and make-up. These databases will provide the worldwide community of face recognition researchers with a large-scale, diverse collection of Arab face images for training and evaluating algorithms toward developing a more representative, and therefore more robust, capacity for facial analysis. This, in turn, will facilitate the development of more accurate face recognition technology as it prepares to go mainstream and enter numerous facets of modern life.

KEYWORDS

Arab Face Database, Arab Public Figures Face, Algorithmic Audit, Image Manipulation, Image Processing, Machine Learning

1. INTRODUCTION

Open-source image databases are used for building, training and testing facial analysis software that are used by researchers in academia (Escalera et al, 2016) (Huang et al, 2008) (Klare et al, 2015). However, these open-source databases usually lack diversity, and building a database is an expensive and time-consuming process. Databases such as MORPH (MORPH, n.d.) are built from source materials that lack diversity in terms of race, culture and ethnicity. Escalera et al. have discussed the issues connected with limitations of databases that have a misrepresentative range of facial photos (Escalera et al, 2016). These databases, despite their high degree of skew, are largely utilized for building face recognition software. For example, the dataset IJB-A (Klare et al, 2015) with 500 subjects, containing more than 5712 entries, was developed for unconstrained face detection and recognition. The subjects used in the work had a demographic distribution of Europe (149), North America (135), Asia (89), South America (50), Middle East (29) Oceania (7), and Africa (4). Similarly, the MS- Celeb-1M (Guo et al, 2016) database that was built for the same purpose as IJB-A has 100,000 subjects with 10 million images. The top 5 represented countries of the subjects were the United States, Great Britain, Germany, Canada and France. Similar databases such as LFW (Huang et al, 2008), PubFig (Kumar et al, 2009), Faces (Ebner et al, 2010), CMU-Pittsburgh AU-Coded Face Expression (Kanade et al, 2000) clearly show that the Middle East and North African region (Arabic-speaking people) are underrepresented.

On top of that, despite being the world's second largest religious group, Muslims are generally underrepresented in face databases. Face accessories are very common among Muslims. It is well known that many female Muslim women wear a head cover and many wear a face cover as well. In situations such as face scans at airport departure gates, such women may be required to temporarily uncover their face in the interest of security. However, in scenarios where video surveillance is being used at shopping malls for security or for target marketing, automatic facial analysis will perform poorly in the case of many Muslim women. Figure 1 illustrates some of the very commonly used face accessories.

We predicate that these accessories will be challenging to current state-of-the-art automatic facial analysis or face recognition systems. In this work, we propose the development of two Arab face databases along with an algorithmic audit involving seven commercially available facial analysis systems. The first database, Arab–LEANA, will contain 300 facial images of Arab subjects with variations in lighting, expressions, accessories, nationality, and age. The second database, APFF, will consist of 300 images capturing Arab public figures "in the wild". To the best of our knowledge, it is the first time ever to build a facial database of Arab subjects.

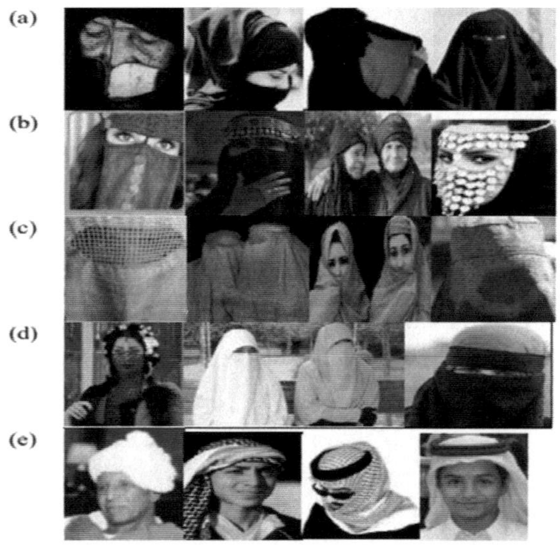

Figure 1. Face cover (called niqab, burqa, or gashowa) worn in various Arab and Muslim countries. (a) represents face cover worn mostly in UAE, KSA, Yemen, and other Gulf countries, (b) Jordon, (c) Afghanistan, (d) Egypt. (e) Traditional head cover for men in some Arab countries

In recent times, researchers working on facial analysis systems have created databases to represent faces of a particular ethnicity or category such as the Indian Face Database (Vidit and Amitabha, 2002), Indian Movie Face Database (Setty et al, 2013), Japanese Female Facial Expression (JAFFE) Database (Lyons, 1998), CAS-PEAL Chinese Face Database (Gao et al, 2007) and CaNAFF Male North African faces (Courset et al, 2018). This is a welcoming move and we applaud the research teams as they play a pivotal role in advancing the accuracy of facial analysis technology. These research groups are considering factors such as race and ethnicity.

The first aim of our project is to create two Arab face benchmark databases. The first database, Arab LEANA, will include Arab subjects' face images (N=300) with different sources of variation, especially lighting, expression, accessories, nationality and age (LEANA). The second database, Arab Public Figures

Faces (APFF), contains images and videos for 300 Arabic public figures taken "in the wild" (without posing). After labeling, all the subjects will be manually localized with bounding boxes for face detection, as well as fiducial nodal points for the center of the two eyes and base of the nose (if visible).

The second goal is to perform an algorithmic audit using the two developed Arab face benchmarks. The audit will evaluate the performance of seven commercial face analysis systems and report the results. Specifically, the audit will include Microsoft, IBM, Face++, Amazon Rekognition, DeepFace, Kairos and Facelytics face recognition software. These softwares were chosen because these companies have heavily invested in artificial intelligence, secured substantial market shares in the machine learning services domain, and provide public demonstrations of their facial analysis technology. Also, six of the seven chosen software have already been involved in a similar algorithmic audit (Raji and Buolamwini, 2019). Therefore, it would be possible for us to compare or at least reference their previous performance in our study. This will be the first algorithmic audit that will examine seven commercial face recognition systems performance in reference to cultural differences.

2. METHODOLOGY

In order to mitigate bias against Arab subjects (both male and female) of Middle-Eastern and North-African regions, we need a large set of unconstrained Arab face images. In this section, the methodology that will be adopted for building an Arab facial image database is presented. The procedure for collection and annotation of Arab Public Figures Faces (APFF) database was motivated by the work of Klare et al. (2015).

2.1 Arab Face Benchmark Databases

2.1.1 Development of Arab-LEANA Database

The first database - Arab LEANA (Lighting, Expression, Accessory, Nationality and Age), will consist of 300 Arab subjects' face images (150 females and 150 males). These images will be collected by taking pictures of Arab subjects with variation in Lighting, Expression, Accessory, Nationality and Age. A brief description of the variations is given below.

- Lighting: Variability in lighting is achieved by positioning 9 lamps in different directions while capturing the image.
- Expression: Each subject gives 6 facial expressions- neutral, happiness, sadness, disgust, fear, and anger.
- Age: Images include a range from young, middle-aged and elderly age groups.
- Nationality: Subjects are from the Middle-Eastern and North-African region - Algeria, Comoros, Djibouti, Bahrain, Egypt, Iraq, Jordan, Kuwait, Lebanon, Libya, Morocco, Mauritania, Oman, Palestine, Qatar, KSA, Somalia, Sudan, Syria, Tunisia, UAE, Yemen.
- Accessories: 6 kinds of accessories commonly in use among Arab men and women are used. This includes (i) head-scarf, (ii) Niqab – face veil, (iii) Agal – head band, (iv) Ghutra – Muslim male attire (v) Burqa – Muslim female attire (vi) Shemagh or Keffiyeh – scarf popularly used by Arabs.

To shoot the Arab subjects' faces, we will set up a special photographic studio room in our computer science laboratory at Zayed University, UAE and the necessary devices will be arranged in the studio: precisely, a camera system, a lighting arrangement, accessories, and various backgrounds. By switching on and off each lamp while the room lights are kept on, altered directional lighting conditions are simulated. A switch matrix will be utilized to control the on/off settings of these lamps.

The sketch map of the cameras' distribution on the semicircle arm and the lamps' location are shown in Figure 2. To generate different lighting conditions, a lighting system will be set using nine fluorescent lamps as shown in Figure 2 (a). As shown in Figure 2 (b), for each subject, seven cameras will be spaced equally in a horizontal semi-circular shelf setup to simultaneously capture images across different poses in one shot. Also, each subject will be asked to look up and down to capture 14 images in another two shots. The camera system will consist of seven digital cameras connected to a computer via USB interface specially configured to support them. We will develop software to control the seven cameras and capture the images in one shot. Images will be stored in a hard drive using a uniform naming convention. Additionally, a professional digital media design student from ZU will be recruited to post-process and edit the images.

In a subsequent validation study, each face will be rated in terms of facial expression and perceived age by young, middle-aged, and elderly females and males (N=300, 50% male). The rating serves two purposes: First, to validate the database and, second, to provide reference for researchers (ground truth). In other words, the aggregated rating will serve as a degree of certainty or confidence interval that the emotion or age presented in the image is perceived in the same way by the raters.

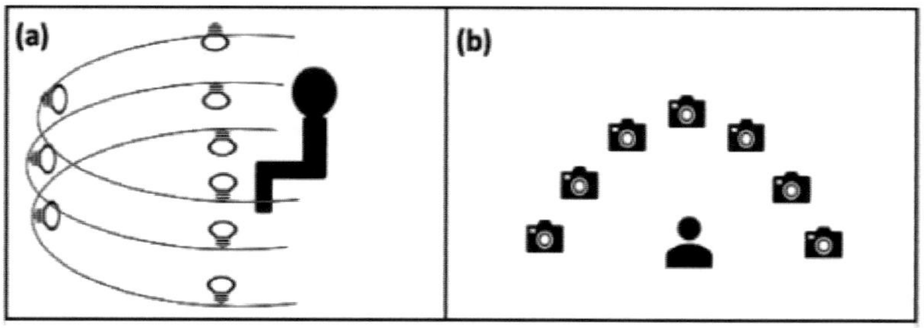

Figure 2. Setup in the photographic room with devices: (a) Lamps positions and configuration (b) Cameras positions

Given the variation we have in the image shooting procedure (ex. pose, expression, age and lighting), we believe 300 subjects for the validation study will be necessary. Also, studies have reported a high turnover among raters due to the difficulty of the task therefore we would like to account for the turnover rate by recruiting a large sample initially. A simple software will be developed for the pictures rating task. Participants of the photo shoot will be compensated with 300 AED each while participants of the validation study will also be compensated with 300 AED each.

2.1.2 Development of Arab Public Figures Face (APFF) database

The second database, Arab Public Figure Faces (APFF) will contain images and videos of 300 Arab public figures captured "in the wild". Faces for APFF will be selected manually from the internet since manual selection of faces will result in a high degree of variability in scale, pose, expression, illumination, age, occlusion and make-up.

The database will be built through the following steps:

1. Subject Specification: Subjects for the database will be manually specified, ensuring a diverse representation across Arab countries.
2. Image and Video Retrieval: Images and videos of the subjects will be located by searching the internet for Creative Commons licensed content. The subject's name, URL, and relevant details will be stored in an Excel file.
3. Scraping and Storage: A scraping software will automatically download the subject's images and save all information in a relational database. For videos, clipped versions and extracted frames will be saved.
4. Annotation: Annotation will be performed using Amazon Mechanical Turk (AMT), a crowdsourcing service. This process will involve creating precise ground truth data, including bounding box positions for faces, subject labels for face recognition, and facial nodal points for research purposes. Additional metadata such as skin tone, sex, facial pose, occlusion, and ambience will also be collected. The annotation task will be executed as given below:

- Errand 1: Annotate bounding boxes around faces in images and video frames, ensuring each head is accurately enclosed. Multiple people in an image will have individual bounding boxes. Five AMT workers will annotate each image, and their annotations will be consolidated into a single set.
- Errand 2: Determine the bounding box corresponding to the person of interest (POI) after annotating all faces. This step helps identify the POI in images with multiple persons. Annotators will compare a reference image with the target image and select the appropriate bounding box. Additional face localization information, such as eye centers and nose base, will be annotated.
- Errand 3: An expert analyst will thoroughly review and manually correct any annotation errors in the consolidated annotations.

Considering variations in image capture (pose, expression, age, lighting), 300 subjects are needed for the validation study. To account for high turnover among raters, a large initial sample will be recruited. A user-friendly software will be developed for picture rating, and the database will be publicly accessible.

2.2 Algorithmic Audit Using Arab Face Benchmark Databases

Researchers who have worked in developing a database of a specific race use their database to evaluate the performance accuracy of state-of-the-art facial analysis software that are commercially available (Courset et al, 2018) (Ebner et al, 2010). In our work, too, we will evaluate the performance accuracy of seven commercial gender classifiers, namely Microsoft Face (Microsoft Azure, n.d.), IBM (IBM Diversity in Faces, n.d.), Face++ (Megvii, n.d.), Amazon Rekognition (Amazon, n.d.), DeepFace (Deepface, n.d.), Kairos (Kairos, n.d.) and Facelytics (Facelytics, n.d.) on our APFF database and Arab LEANA face database. For the auditing purpose, the overall classification accuracy, male classification accuracy, and female classification accuracy will be measured and the positive predictive value (PPV) will be computed. We then evaluate the true positive rate, false positive rate, and error rate (1-PPV) of the following groups: all subjects, male subjects, female subjects, males with traditional accessories, and females with traditional accessories. The performance metrics will reveal whether the databases used in developing these popular facial analysis systems are biased or not.

3. CURRENT STATUS AND FUTURE WORK

The Arab Face Database (AFD) comes with detailed annotations in terms of age, country of origin, and gender. As a first step towards developing AFD, we have already started building the APFF database. The procedure of building APFF database is discussed below. To start with, the famous Arab subjects that are to be included in the database were specified manually. While giving specifications, we took care to ensure that the country of origin of the subjects is well distributed across the Arab region. We have manually chosen Arab public figures from 22 different Arab countries. The subjects are famous in various fields such as business, literature, media, sports, entertainment, politics, religion, & philanthropy. The subjects chosen include a wide range of professionals such as actor, comedian, athlete, music composer, singer, diplomat, director and ceo of companies, judge, jurist, member of royal family, researcher, scholar, scientist, social workers, philanthropist, vocalist, writer, poet, emir, fashion designer, economist, news presenter, model, political party leader, former and present president, prime minister, journalist, minister and military commander. A total of 604 Arab subjects were selected of which 277 are females and 327 are males. A reference image database was manually built by selecting one good quality image of each of the 604 subjects. This database will be given to annotators as a reference image for each subject. Table 1 shows the diversity of the Arab subjects in the built database in terms of country of origin, gender and the various fields in which they are famous.

Table 1. Demographics of Arab subjects in the APFF database in terms of country of origin, gender, professional fields

		Gender		Field					
Country of Origin	No. of subjects	Female	Male	Philanthropy	Business	Litera-ture	Media, Sports & Entertainment	Politics	Religion
Algeria	30	15	15	0	0	4	20	5	1
Bahrain	30	15	15	0	1	4	19	6	0
Comoros	15	4	11	0	0	0	11	4	0
Djibouti	16	0	16	0	0	1	6	9	0
Egypt	30	15	15	0	1	8	14	5	2
Iraq	30	15	15	0	0	1	21	6	2
Jordan	30	15	15	2	2	4	15	7	0
Kuwait	30	15	15	0	2	1	19	6	2
Lebanon	30	15	15	2	0	2	20	6	0
Libya	23	8	15	3	0	1	8	11	0
Mauritania	24	9	15	3	1	2	3	13	2

Morocco	30	15	15	0	0	4	20	5	1
Oman	23	8	15	0	4	1	12	5	1
Palestine	30	15	15	0	1	4	19	6	0
Qatar	30	15	15	0	1	8	14	5	2
KSA	30	15	15	0	0	1	21	6	2
Somalia	30	15	15	2	2	4	15	7	0
Sudan	30	15	15	0	2	1	19	6	2
Syria	30	15	15	2	0	2	20	6	0
Tunisia	23	8	15	3	0	1	8	11	0
UAE	30	15	15	2	2	6	14	5	1
Yemen	30	15	15	5	0	6	8	11	0
All subjects	**604**	**277**	**327**	**24**	**19**	**66**	**326**	**151**	**18**

After manually compiling the list of Arab public figures' names, we located their images. The images and videos of the subjects were located by searching Google images with Creative Commons license. We used a web scraping tool called Octoparse that automates the process of locating the images. The tool takes in the list of subjects' names and, for each subject, it saves the URLs in a database under the subject's name. As the search is for Arab subjects, Google search in Arabic language resulted in more Creative Common (CC) images compared to the search conducted in English. The time taken by the software to scrape the data varied from subject to subject. This is because the search result for each subject is different. On the whole, it took approximately 8 hours to complete the scraping for search results in English and 13 hours for search results in Arabic.

The minimum number of URLs collected for a subject is zero as some of these URLs contain only the mention of the subject and do not have the subject's image. Certain subjects' images appear in a greater number of URLs, for instance, a subject's image appeared in 27 URLs. This implies that we may have as many as 27 images for a subject and on the other hand, we may not have any image for a subject in the database. Hence cleaning the database, that is removing those URLs that do not contain the subjects' images, has to be done and this has to be done manually.

We performed bulk downloading of the images from the set of URLs and saved them under each subject's name. The downloaded image files are saved under the subject's name in a sequential numerical order, such as Abdelmadjid Tebboune_1, Abdelmadjid Tebboune_2. This way, we have built a database of approximately 11,000 images of the 604 subjects, with nearly 6000 images resulting from search in Arabic and 5000 images from search in English.

In case of videos, a clipped version from the original codec and the extracted I-frames, have to be stored. In order to get the images from YouTube videos, we are working on finding a YouTube video scraping tool that can automate the process of collecting various frames/clips of the subject.

After generating the database of images, the next step is to perform annotation of the images. This will be performed through the crowdsourcing service given by Amazon Mechanical Turk (AMT) workers. We will give the annotation task to five AMT workers. We are preparing detailed visual and written guidelines on annotation for the AMT workers. As a part of the guidelines, the annotators will be provided with a good quality reference image of each of the subjects. If an image or video frame contains multiple persons, this reference image will help the annotators to locate the person of interest. Open-source image annotation software available for academic projects and commercial applications can be used to annotate the images. We found an open-source annotator, VGG Image Annotator (VIA), to annotate the images. We will use this VIA to annotate a sample image and the annotated image will be included in the visual guidance. In the guidelines, the AMT workers will be informed to use the same annotator to annotate our image database. The final step after annotation is consolidation of the annotations of the five AMT workers. We are working on finding a code to consolidate the annotations obtained from all the five AMT workers to obtain a label for each subject's image.

The second database, Arab–LEANA will be built using facial images of Arab subjects taken in a purposely-designed photoshoot. For this, the photo studio with arrangements shown in Figure 2 will be set up in the computer science laboratory at Zayed University.

After developing the two databases, we will perform the algorithmic auditing of seven well-known commercially available facial analysis softwares using our facial image database. We conducted a pilot study to evaluate the performance accuracy of Facelytics software in recognizing faces of Arab subjects wearing traditional Arab face accessories. The results showed the vulnerability of the system in identifying the faces. The pilot study result is shown in Figure 3. This study will be extended to the other 6 facial analysis systems mentioned.

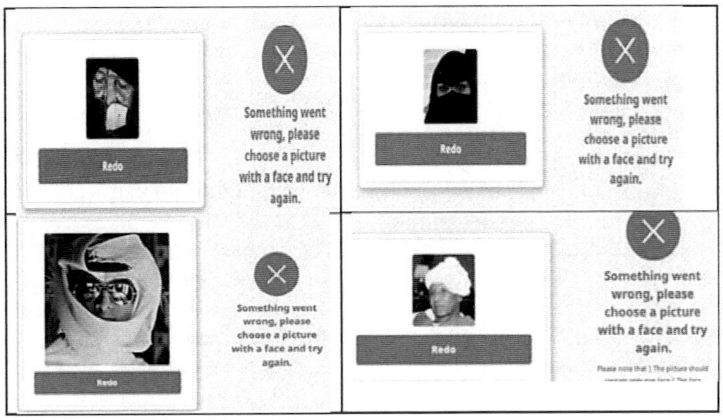

Figure 3. Results of pilot study conducted on Facelytic gender classification for 4 images of Arab Subjects.

4. CONCLUSION

We propose building two Arab facial image databases and conducting an algorithm audit on seven commercial facial recognition algorithms. The first database, Arab–LEANA, will consist of 300 Arab subjects' facial images with variations in lighting, expressions, accessory, nationality, and age. The second database, Arab Public Figure Faces (APFF), will include images of 604 Arab public figures captured from various sources.For the APFF database, we have already selected 604 Arab subjects, including 277 females and 327 males, and located their images using the web scraping tool Octoparse. The database currently contains approximately 11,000 images. We are in the process of selecting a tool to scrape videos from YouTube to gather additional clips or frames. The annotation of the images will be performed by five Amazon Mechanical Turk (AMT) annotators using clear guidelines and a reference image database prepared manually. The annotations will be consolidated to obtain a label for each subject. After completing the APFF database, we will proceed with building the Arab-LEANA database. These databases will enable an algorithmic audit of facial analysis software systems. The aim is to provide the research community with a diverse collection of Arab facial images for training and evaluating algorithms, ultimately enhancing the accuracy and robustness of facial recognition technology.

ACKNOWLEDGEMENT

This work was supported by the Abu Dhabi Award for Research Excellence (AARE) 2019 under Grant 274.

REFERENCES

Amazon, Amazon Web Services. Amazon Rekognition - Video and Image - AWS. Available at: https://aws.amazon.com/rekognition/ Accessed on 7th June 2021.

Courset, R. et al, 2018. The caucasian and north african french faces (CaNAFF): A face database. *International Review of Social Psychology*, *31*(1).

DeepFace: https://pypi.org/project/deepface/ Accessed on 7th June 2021.

Ebner, N.C. et al, 2010. FACES—A database of facial expressions in young, middle-aged, and older women and men: Development and validation. *Behavior research methods*, *42*, pp.351-362.

Escalera, S. et al, 2016. Chalearn looking at people and faces of the world: Face analysis workshop and challenge 2016. In *Proceedings of the IEEE Conference on Computer Vision and Pattern Recognition Workshops*, pp. 1-8.

Facelytics: https://www.facelytics.io/#try-it. Accessed on 7th June 2021.

Gao, W. et al, 2007. The CAS-PEAL large-scale Chinese face database and baseline evaluations. *IEEE Transactions on Systems, Man, and Cybernetics-Part A: Systems and Humans*, *38*(1), pp.149-161.

Guo, Y. et al, 2016. Ms-celeb-1m: A dataset and benchmark for large-scale face recognition. In *Computer Vision–ECCV 2016: 14th European Conference, Amsterdam, The Netherlands, October 11-14, 2016, Proceedings, Part III 14*, pp. 87-102. Springer International Publishing.

Huang, G.B. et al, 2008, October. Labeled faces in the wild: A database for studying face recognition in unconstrained environments. In *Workshop on faces in'Real-Life'Images: detection, alignment, and recognition*.

IBM Diversity in Faces. Available at: https://www.research.ibm.com/artificial-intelli%C2%ADgence/trusted-ai/diversity-in-faces/.

Kairos.: https://www.kairos.com/kairos-2.0/demos. Accessed on 7th June 2021.

Kanade, T. et al, 2000, March. Comprehensive database for facial expression analysis. In *Proceedings fourth IEEE international conference on automatic face and gesture recognition (cat. No. PR00580)*, pp. 46-53. IEEE.

Klare, B.F. et al, 2015. Pushing the frontiers of unconstrained face detection and recognition: Iarpa janus benchmark a. In *Proceedings of the IEEE conference on computer vision and pattern recognition*, pp. 1931-1939.

Kumar, N., Berg, A.C., Belhumeur, P.N. and Nayar, S.K., 2009, September. Attribute and simile classifiers for face verification. In *2009 IEEE 12th international conference on computer vision*. pp. 365-372. IEEE.

Lyons, M.J., 1998. Facial expression database: Japanese female facial expression (jaffe) database. *http://www.kasrl.org/jaffe.html*.

Megvii, Face++ Facial Recognition Database. Available at: https://www.faceplusplus.com/face-detection/ Accessed on 7th June 2021.

Microsoft Azure, *Facial recognition.* Available at: https://azure.microsoft.com/en-in/products/cognitive-services/face/ (Accessed: 22 June 2023).

Ricanek, K. and Tesafaye, T., 2006, April. Morph: A longitudinal image database of normal adult age-progression. In 7th international conference on automatic face and gesture recognition (FGR06) (pp. 341-345). IEEE.

Raji, I.D. and Buolamwini, J., 2019, January. Actionable auditing: Investigating the impact of publicly naming biased performance results of commercial ai products. In *Proceedings of the 2019 AAAI/ACM Conference on AI, Ethics, and Society*, pp. 429-435.

Setty, S. et al, 2013, December. Indian movie face database: a benchmark for face recognition under wide variations. In *2013 fourth national conference on computer vision, pattern recognition, image processing and graphics (NCVPRIPG)* (pp. 1-5). IEEE.

Vidit, J. and Amitabha, M., 2002. The Indian face database.

FACTORS INFLUENCING THE ADOPTION OF FINANCIAL TECHNOLOGY AND NET BENEFIT IN INDONESIAN BANKING

Dekar Urumsah, Estri Ari Respati, Noor Endah Cahyawati and Primanita Setiyono
Accounting Department, Universitas Islam Indonesia

ABSTRACT

The aim of this research is to analyse the factors influencing the adoption of financial technology and net benefit in the banking industry. The method employed was a survey by distributing the questionnaires using convenience sampling among 200 employees working in Indonesian banks. Data was analysed using partial least square (PLS). The results show that performance expectancy, firm readiness, external pressure, and government supports have positive influences on the adoption of financial technology. Nevertheless, perceived risk negatively affects the adoption. In addition, the adoption of financial technology positively influences net benefit. This research results can assist the decision-making process not only for banking industry to take the good opportunity from financial technology but also for government to build regulation of financial technology.

KEYWORDS

Adoption, Financial Technology, Indonesian Bankings, Net Benefit

1. INTRODUCTION

The advanced development of technology enables various industries to grow more effectively and efficiently, including the financial services industry. In recent years, tech-based innovation in financial services industry called Financial Technology (FinTech), which integrates finance and technology in its processes, has been highly sought after in the banking industry (Hochstein, 2015). Currently, almost all financial service providers and e-commerce companies use electronic media to serve their customers. The support of information technology (IT) and favourable regulations has led to the exponential growth of FinTech. In this decade, technology, business models, talent, capital, and consumers are ready to start on the FinTech fever (Knight, 2020). One of the FinTech services which is in demand is e-payment (OJK, 2017). E-payment-based FinTech allows users or customers to quickly and easily access banking services, commonly referred to as e-banking.

The adoption of Fintech presents both opportunities and challenges for businesses. There are several factors influencing the adoption of Fintech in banking, including performance expectancy, which has a positive influence on supporting the use of electronic services (Alraja et al., 2016) and plays a crucial role in technology adoption (Alraja, 2015). Conversely, the adoption of electronic services also faces certain risks. Risk perception is one of the factors that can hinder the implementation of internet banking (Marafon et al., 2018), such as the fear of account hacking by cybercriminals, which can have a negative impact on the adoption of Fintech in banking (Laukkanen & Kiviniemi, 2010). The readiness of an organization to adopt Fintech is a consideration both technically, by providing cutting-edge IT infrastructure, and financially, by having adequate funding for Fintech adoption (Mehrtens et al., 2001). External factors become another factor that influences an organization's decision to adopt new technology (Orlikowski, 1993). In line with this, government support in the form of strong cybersecurity law enforcement to protect customers using online services must be effectively implemented (Chong et al., 2010) to enhance customer trust and encourage Fintech adoption.

There are several theories about technology adoption, one of which is the Technology-Organization-Environment (TOE) theory. TOE classifies three contexts that influence technology adoption, namely technology, organization, and environment (Tornatzky & Fleischer, 1990). This theory has been used to examine the factors that affect technology adoption. AlBar & Hoque (2019) studied the adoption of cloud ERP in relation to technological contexts such as relative advantages, compatibility, and complexity; Abed (2020) investigated the adoption of social commerce in relation to technological contexts including usage and security perceptions, and Park & Kim (2021) also examined the adoption of Big Data in relation to technological contexts that include perceived benefits, system usability, compatibility, security, and privacy.

The adoption of Fintech can be beneficial, especially for banking organizations. This is in line with the theory of Information System Success Model (ISSM), which states that the adoption of information technology can bring benefits to organizations or individuals (DeLone & McLean, 2003). The ISSM theory is also widely used to explain the success of IT implementation, such as the adoption of Fintech in Go-pay (Nurherwening et al., 2021). Based on the description, the researchers used the TOE Theory to investigate the factors influencing the adoption of Fintech in the banking industry. This study aligns the technological context with perceived performance expectations and risks; the organizational context with organizational readiness; and the environmental context with external pressures and government support. The research integrates with the ISSM Theory to demonstrate that the adoption of Fintech can affect the net benefits received by both organizations and individuals. The integration of the TOE and ISSM theories with the research variables has not been extensively explored in previous studies. This research takes the perspective of the banking sector in the adoption of financial technology, which has been relatively unexplored in Indonesia. Previous research has mostly focused on the perspective of users, particularly SMEs (Namira, 2022; Riyanti et al., 2022).

The research outline consists of an introduction followed by a literature review and hypothesis development, where the model is tested quantitatively. The next section presents the hypotheses, followed by sample presentation and data analysis using PLS (Partial Least Squares), as well as the research findings. The last section is the discussion and conclusion.

2. LITERATURE REVIEW AND HYPOTHESIS DEVELOPMENT

2.1 Technology, Organization, Environment (TOE) Model

The TOE framework classifies three dimensions which influence the decision of an organization to use technology innovation, namely technological, organizational, and environmental. Technological involves the sorts of technology used and relevant technical skills owned by an organization. Meanwhile, organizational refers to the internal size of an organization (Oliveira & Martins, 2009). Next, environmental encompasses the external scope where a company runs its business (industry, competitors, and trading partners) (Tornatzky & Fleischer, 1990). This research employs TOE with the development of constructs used, including performance expectancy, risk perception, firm readiness, external pressure, and government support.

2.2 Information Systems Success Model (ISSM)

ISSM is a model used to test the success of an IT adoption which was first introduced by DeLone-McLean in 1992. ISSM explains that system quality estimates the technical success, while information quality measures semantic success. Meanwhile, the technology use, user satisfaction, individual and organizational effects are included in the level of effectiveness. In 2003, DeLone-McLean developed the theory which explained that information quality, system quality, and service quality can affect the interest to use, use, and user satisfaction of information technology. In addition, a high level of use and user satisfaction of IT affects the net benefit received where the user satisfaction can influence the interest to use IT (DeLone & McLean, 2003). This research adopts some of relevant ISSM constructs to elaborate the influence of net benefit on Fintech adoption.

2.3 Performance Expectancy and Fintech Adoption

Performance expectancy is a condition where an individual believes in the use of a system to benefit his performance (Venkatesh et al., 2003). In Ghana, performance expectancy has been found to increase the interest in adopting an electronic voting system (Mensah, 2020). Alraja (2015) reveals that performance expectancy can be assumed as the crucial indicator of IT adoption because it shows that the adoption can increase the productivity and performance of a company or a bank and enable the bank to provide faster services. Accordingly, the first hypothesis is formulated as follows.

H1: Performance expectancy has a positive influence on Fintech adoption.

2.4 Perceived Risk and Fintech Adoption

Perceived risk is the main obstacle in any innovation (Taylor, 1974), and it perches on the top level in financial service innovation (Mitra et al., 1999). The previous research performed by Luarn and Lin (2005) on mobile banking and banking technology indicated several risks, one of which was privacy and security issue of mobile banking of some customers. Perceived risk is revealed to have negative effect on the internet banking adoption by the customers in India (Chauhan et al., 2019). Therefore, the second hypothesis is as follows.

H2: Perceived risk has a negative influence on Fintech adoption.

2.5 Firm Readiness and Fintech Adoption

Firm readiness is an adequate experience of a company in terms of information technology and finance to adopt an innovation in technology. Firm readiness positively influences the adoption of cloud computing (Hiran & Henten, 2019). Similarly, The SMSEs readiness affects the adoption of cloud computing in the industry 4.0 context (Sari et al., 2020). To conclude, the third hypothesis is assumed as follows.

H3: Firm readiness has a positive influence on Fintech adoption.

2.6 External Pressure and Fintech Adoption

External pressure is an indispensable factor from the sources in the surrounding environment (Chwelos et al., 2001). The previous studies mention that external pressure is one of the drives for an organization to adopt new technology (Nelson & Shaw, 2003). External pressure also positively influences the adoption of Performance Measurement System in Yogyakarta Regional Government (Murti et al., 2021). Hence, the fourth hypothesis is proposed as follows.

H4: External pressure has a positive influence on Fintech adoption.

2.7 Government Support and Fintech Adoption

Government support and policy refers to the extent of government activities to influence the company and promote the industry. Government support in relation to open public data and regulatory policy can encourage the adoption of big data (Park & Kim, 2021). Government support positively influences the technology adoption and the interest in continuous use of the technology (Kiwanuka, 2015). Government regulation to support the adoption of technology is one of the measures, and it is found to be influential in the adoption of Internet of Things (IoT) in start-up industry (Purnomo et al., 2021). Therefore, the fifth hypothesis is proposed as follows.

H5: Government support has a positive influence on Fintech adoption.

2.8 Net Benefit and Fintech Adoption

Fintech adoption is the management decision altogether to innovate and develop the online transaction system. The empirical studies have been conducted in several countries and indicated that the banks adopting Fintech show better performance. Thus, Fintech adoption has a positive effect on bank performance (Siddik et al., 2016). Another research conducted by Danuarta and Darma (2019) shows that the adoption of technology positively influences the net benefit of Gopay system. With regard to the explanation, the sixth hypothesis is formulated as follows.

H6: Fintech adoption has a positive and significant influence on net benefit.

3. RESEARCH METHOD

This study employs quantitative method using primary data collected from a survey implementing questionnaire technique. The target population for this study was limited to employees working in the most efficient and the most reliable bank in Indonesia, with the asset category of Rp.100T and more than Rp.100T, including BCA, BRI, Mandiri, and BNI (Tempo.com. 2018). The sampling technique was non-probability convenience sampling. A total 240 questionnaires were distributed and collected online via Google Form, only 200 questionnaires were usable and analyzed using Partial Least Square (PLS) by *Smart*PLS 3.3.9. Each indicator of every variable in this research was measured using 6-point Likert scale. The variables examined include performance expectancy using 3 question items from Martin et al (2014); perceived risk using 4 question items, firm readiness using 4 question items, and external pressure using 3 question items from Xu et al., (2009); government support using 4 question items from Tan & Teo (2000); fintech using 5 question items from Zhou et al., (2010); and net benefit using 3 question items from DeLone & McLean (2003).

4. FINDINGS AND DISCUSSION

4.1 Respondent Characteristics

The number of respondents in this research is 200 consisting of 161 staff (80.5%), 15 manager assistants (7.5%), 13 managers (6.5%), 2 director assistants (1%), and others (4%). The gender distribution is 33.5% of male and 66.5% of female. The majority of the respondents' educational level is undergraduate degree totalling 151 (75.5%), followed by 3-year diploma numbering 25 (12.5%), and senior high school as many as 16 (8%). Referring to the questionnaire responses collected, there was 48% of the companies which already adopt Fintech for 6 years, meanwhile, 141 respondents (70.5%) did more than six online transactions using Fintech in a month.

4.2 Validity Measurement

The results of convergent validity show that the item loading factor scores of more than 0.708 which means that convergent validity minimum value is met. In addition, AVE score of each variable was more than 0.50 as required, therefore, the indicators of this research instrument could be concluded as valid and convergently adequate. The next validity test conducted was discriminant validity which could be analyzed using Heterotrait-Monotrait Ratio (HTMT). HTMT has better sensitivity level compared to traditional validity test like Fornell-Larcker Criterion and Cross Loadings (Henseler et al., 2015). If the HTMT score is high, the issue of discriminant validity is detected. HTMT can be estimated using $HTMT_{90}$ criteria and $HTMT_{inference}$ criteria where if the score of HTMT less than 0.90 and the upper bound of confidence interval less than 1, the research instrument items pass discriminant validity test (Hair et al., 2019). The values of HTMT are presented in Table 1.

Table 1. Heterotrait-Monotrait Ratio (HTMT), Composite Reliability (CR), and R-Square

Construct	EP	FA	FR	GS	NB	PE	PR
EP							
FA	0.465 CI90 (0.191;0.740)						
FR	0.526 CI90 (0.250;0.792)	0.806 CI90 (0.526;0.912)					
GS	0.309 CI90 (0.064;0.635)	0.603 C190 (0.353;0.771)	0.593 CI90 (0.303;0.826)				
NB	0.383	0.894	0.747	0.633			

	CI90 (0.104;0.677)	CI90 (0.694;0.974)	CI90 (0.461;0.888)	CI90 (0.375;0.790)			
PE	0.220 CI90 (0.040;0.569)	0.544 CI90 (0.167;0.882)	0.433 CI90 (0.072;0.786)	0.338 CI90 (0.032;0.669)	0.548 CI90 (0.169;0.860)		
PR	0.111 CI90 (0.069;0.321)	0.332 CI90 (0.166;0.506)	0.235 CI90 (0.074;0.434)	0.345 CI90 (0.112;0.556)	0.321 CI90 (0.139;0.523)	0.168 CI90 (0.092;0.441)	
CR	0.897	0.893	0.872	0.931	0.894	0.944	0.904
R-Squared		0.558			0.559		

Table 1 shows the scores of HTMT less than 0.90, with the highest HTMT score reaching 0.894, and the upper bounds of confidence interval (CI) less than 1, with highest bound reaching 0.974. Hence, the research contructs could be deemed passed the discriminant validity test or valid.

4.3 Reliability Test

Reliability test can be performed by observing the Composite Reliability (CR) value The value of CR between 0.70 and 0.95 can avoid redundant items and be concluded that the construct is reliable (Hair et al., 2019). Table 1 shows that all constructs' CR values were more than 0.70 and less than 0.95, so all constructs of this research were reliable.

4.4 R-Squared (R^2)

R-Squared is used to determine the proportion or percentage of total variance of dependent variable. The R^2 values of 0.75, 0.50, and 0.25 indicate substansial, moderat, and weak criteria (Hair et al., 2019). Table 1 demonstrates the R^2 values of Fintech adoption construct of 0.558 and net benefit of 0.559, therefore, it can be categorized into moderate criteria.

4.5 Goodness of Fit (GoF) Test

Goodness of Fit (GoF) test is conducted by finding the square root of multiplication between AVE (communality) average value and R^2 average value (Henseler & Sarstedt, 2013). GoF values of 0.10. 0.25, and 0.36 are considered small, moderate, and large respectively (Cohen, 1988). The estimation of GoF in the research is as follows.

$$\text{GoF} = \sqrt{\overline{Communality} \times \overline{R^2}} = \sqrt{0{,}6565 \times 0{,}5585} = 0{,}6055$$

The measurement results in the value of GoF as much as 0.6055 which falls under the large category. Hence, it can be concluded that this research produces a robust model.

4.6 Hypothesis Test Results

Structural model was used to test the hypotheses by using path coefficient and T-test (P-value). The hypothesis test results are presented in Table 2.

Table 2. Hypothesis Test Results

Hypothesis	Relation	Path Coefficient	P-Value	Result
Performance Expectancy (H1)	PE → FA	0.234	0.002	Supported
Perceived Risk (H2)	PR → FA	-0.141	0.003	Supported
Firm Readiness (H3)	FR → FA	0.405	0.000	Supported
External Pressure (H4)	EP → FA	0.147	0.004	Supported
Govérnment Support (H5)	GS → FA	0.169	0.010	Supported
Net Benefit (H6)	FA → NB	0.749	0.000	Supported

Significance level < 0.01

4.7 Discussion

4.7.1 Performance Expectancy on Fintech Adoption

Performance expectancy significantly influences Fintech adoption, indicating that if bank staff perceive the expected benefits, adoption is more likely. This perception aligns with TAM's perceived usefulness, a key attribute shaping attitudes toward system usage (Chau et al., 2004). Users believe e-banking enhances performance and are more motivated to use it (Ghalandari, 2012). Similar research by Abrahão et al. (2016) supports performance expectancy as a predictor for new technology adoption. Likewise, Duarte & Pinho (2019) found that performance expectancy crucial for Mobile Health adoption. Consequently, banks should assess if fintech meets performance expectations to benefit the bank and customers in transaction effectiveness and efficiency.

4.7.2 Perceived Risk on Fintech Adoption

Perceived risk negatively influences the adoption of Fintech. This indicates that the more risks a bank perceives, such as financial loss, fraud, and privacy breaches, the more reluctant the bank to adopt Fintech. The anxiety in a person who is doing online transaction can negatively affect the acceptance of the person toward online service (Veeramootoo et al., 2018). This result is seconded by Ryu (2018) who found that perceived risk negatively influences interest in adopting new technology (mobile banking). Additionally, Khayer et al. (2020) reveal the negative effect of perceived risk on Cloud computing.

4.7.3 Firm Readiness toward Fintech Adoption

Firm readiness positively influences the adoption of Fintech. Bank readiness in terms of finance, technology, human resources, and top management support can encourage the adoption of Fintech. Firm readiness is categorized into three aspects, including finance, technology, and human resources (Herath et al., 2020). This finding is supported by the studies performed by Herath et al. (2020) which states that the firm readiness positively influences the adoption of technology. Consequently, banks must ensure the financial, technology, and human resources preparation by giving trainings to their employees to improve their skills. Thus, comprehensive preparation of a company will make the company ready in adopting Fintech.

4.7.4 External Pressure on Fintech Adoption

External pressure positively influences Fintech adoption. This indicates that the existence of external pressure, especially from the competitors which already adopt Fintech, can increase the likelihood of a bank to adopt Fintech. The tough competition in banking industry forces the banks to improve their service innovations to attract more customers. The external arena where a bank runs its business (i.e. industry, competitors, and trading partners) might influence the diffusion of innovations in an organization (Tornatzky & Fleischer, 1990). One of the main stakeholders of a company is customers, and customers' trust is a crucial aspect in business environment nowadays (Herath et al., 2020).

This research result is endorsed by Nurlinda et al. (2020) in the context of e-commerce adoption and by Herath et al. (2020) in relation to the adoption of Information Security Solutions. Evidently, this implies that banks must keep up with envolving business competition and embracing the advancements of the digital era. Companies must be responsive to the recent changes in business sector. The large number of banks in Indonesia forces those banks stay competitive, and gaining the customers' trust is of paramount importance (Herath et al., 2020).

4.7.5 Government Support in Fintech Adoption

Government support positively affects the adoption of Fintech. This result indicates that government endorsement in the forms of facilities and regulations can increase the likelihood of Fintech adoption by the banks. Government support and regulatory policies stimulate industry growth and encourage the adoption of innovative technologies like big data. If the government enacts the regulation on technological innovation compliance where the companies that violate the policy must pay large amount of money, the companies will surely adopt the technology which is in the context is IoT (Purnomo et al., 2021).

This result agrees with the study carried out by Purnomo et al. (2021) which states that government support in the form of regulation has a positive effect on the adoption of internet of things in start-up industry. Similarly, the study conducted by Park and Kim (2021) has revealed that there is a positive influence of the government support and policy on the adoption of big data. Based on the results, the government in Indonesia should enhace fintech adoption by improving internet speed, implementing regulations to encourage the adoption, and data protection for secure transactions. Furthermore, collaborative efforts between the between banking sector and the government are essential to ensure convenience and customer protection.

4.7.6 Influence of Fintech Adoption on Net Benefit

Adoption of Fintech significantly and positively influences net benefit which means that the banks in this research which represented by their employees assume that adopting Fintech can benefit the banks and customers. Fintech presents a new opportunity to empower the community by increasing the transparency to reduce costs or cut off the intermediary agent and by making the information more accessible (Zavolokina et al., 2016). Fintech adoption creates both challenge and opportunity. It has risks, but it is not the only underlying factor for its adoption context because there are also the benefits to be the incentive of the adoption (Ryu, 2018).

This result is corroborated by the findings of Nurherwening et al. (2021) in relation to the net benefit of Gopay and Wibowo (2020) regarding e-Local Return's impact on net benefit which can be interpreted as tax compliance. Despite the challenges, adopting fintech brings significant benefits to both banks and customers, making it an attractive proposition and enabling more effective and efficient transaction.

5. CONCLUSION

Based on the statistical tests, it can be concluded that in the technological context, performance expectancy positively influences the adoption of Fintech, while perceived risk negatively influences the adoption. In the organizational context, firm readiness has a positive effect on Fintech adoption, and in the environmental context, both external pressure and government support have positive influences on the adoption of Fintech. Moreover, the adoption of Fintech positively affects net benefit. These findings contribute to the existing literature in three ways: (1) they provide insights for future research on the adoption of information technology, especially Fintech; (2) they enrich the theories on the adoption of information technology by integrating the TOE and ISSM models, which are currently limited in number; and (3) they enhance the existing model of information technology adoption by presenting a robust research model.

The implications of this study for banking include: (1) the need to keep Fintech performance during adoption to enhance operations and provide better security for the bank and customer data, in order to attract more customers and compete effectively with other banks; (2) the recommendation for banks adopting Fintech to prepare adequate funding, management support, and employee training; and (3) the expectation for banks to adopt Fintech, as it offers benefits that can make banking transactions more effective and efficient. For the government, this study suggests encouraging and supporting the adoption of Fintech by improving internet facilities and regulations.

However, this research also has some limitations: (1) the sample size is limited to 200 respondents from specific areas, which may not represent a comprehensive study; (2) the integration of the TOE and ISSM models is incomplete, as some variables were not included. The future studies are suggested to: (1) expand the scope of research samples to cover more areas; (2) include additional relevant variables, such as customer perception and perceived cost.

REFERENCES

Abed, S. S. (2020). Social commerce adoption using TOE framework: An empirical investigation of Saudi Arabian SMEs. *International Journal of Information Management*, *53*, 1–11. https://doi.org/10.1016/j.ijinfomgt.2020.102118

AlBar, A. M., & Hoque, M. R. (2019). Factors affecting cloud ERP adoption in Saudi Arabia: An empirical study. *Information Development*, *35*(1), 150–164. https://doi.org/10.1177/0266666917735677

Alraja, M. N. (2015). User acceptance of information technology: A field study of an e-mail system adoption from the individual students' prespective. *Mediterranean Journal of Social Sciences*, *6*(6), 19–25.

Chauhan, V., Yadav, R., & Choudhary, V. (2019). Analyzing The Impact of Consumer Innovativeness and Perceived Risk in Internet Banking Adoption: A Study of Indian Consumers. *International Journal of Bank Marketing*, *37*(1), 323–339. https://doi.org/10.1108/IJBM-02-2018-0028

Chong, A. Y. L., Ooi, K. B., Lin, B., & Tan, B. I. (2010). Online banking adoption: An empirical analysis. *International Journal of Bank Marketing*, *28*(4), 267–287. https://doi.org/10.1108/02652321011054963

Chwelos, P., Dexter, A. S., & Benbasat, I. (2001). Research Report: Empirical Test of an EDI Adoption Model. *Information Systems Research*, *12*(3), 304–321. https://doi.org/10.1287/isre.12.3.304.9708

Cunningham, L. F., Gerlach, J. H., Harper, M. D., & Young, C. E. (2005). Perceived risk and the consumer buying process: internet airline reservations. *International Journal of Service Industry Management*, *16*(4), 357–372.

Danuarta, G. L. N., & Darma, G. S. (2019). Determinants of Using Go-Pay and its Impact on Net Benefits. *International Journal of Innovative Science and Research Technology*, *4*(11), 173–182.

DeLone, W. H., & McLean, E. R. (2003). The DeLone and McLean Model of Information Systems Success : A Ten-Year Update. *Jurnal of Management Information Systems*, *19*(4), 9–30. https://doi.org/10.1080/07421222.2003.11045748

Garg, A. K., & Choeu, T. (2015). The Adoption of Electronic Commerce by Small and Medium Enterprises in Pretoria East. *Electronic Journal of Information Systems in Developing Countries*, *68*(7), 1–23.

Grandon, E., & Pearson, J. M. (2003). Strategic Value and Adoption of Electronic Commerce : An Empirical Study of Chilean Small and Medium Businesses. *Journal of Global Information Technology Management*, *6*(3), 22–43.

Hair, J. F., Risher, J. J., Sarstedt, M., & Ringle, C. M. (2019). When to use and how to report the results of PLS-SEM. *European Business Review*, *31*(1), 2–24. https://doi.org/10.1108/EBR-11-2018-0203

Henseler, J., Ringle, C. M., & Sarstedt, M. (2015). A new criterion for assessing discriminant validity in variance-based structural equation modeling. *Journal of the Academy of Marketing Science*, *43*(1), 115–135. https://doi.org/10.1007/s11747-014-0403-8

Herath, T. C., Herath, H. S. B., & D'Arcy, J. (2020). Organizational Solutions: An Information Security Adoption of Adoption and the Based on Innovation Integrative Lens Environment Organization-Technology- Framework. *The Data Base for Advances in Information Systems*, *51*(2), 12–35. https://doi.org/10.1145/3400043.3400046

Hiran, K. K., & Henten, A. (2019). An integrated TOE–DoI framework for cloud computing adoption in the higher education sector: case study of Sub-Saharan Africa, Ethiopia. *International Journal of Systems Assurance Engineering and Management*.

Hochstein, M. (2015). *BankThink Fintech (the Word, That Is) Envolves*. American Banker.

Kaluzny, A. D., Mclaughlin, C. P., & Jaeger, B. J. (1993). TQM as a managerial innovation: Research issues and implications. *Health Services Management Research*, *6*(2), 78–88. https://doi.org/10.1177/095148489300600202

Khayer, A., Talukder, M. S., Bao, Y., & Hossain, M. N. (2020). Cloud computing adoption and its impact on SMEs' performance for cloud supported operations: A dual-stage analytical approach. *Technology in Society*, *60*, 101225. https://doi.org/10.1016/j.techsoc.2019.101225

Kim, S. H., Jang, S. Y., & Yang, K. H. (2017). Analysis of the Determinants of Software-as-a-Service Adoption in Small Businesses: Risks, Benefits, and Organizational and Environmental Factors. *Journal of Small Business Management*, *55*(2), 303–325. https://doi.org/10.1111/jsbm.12304

Kiwanuka, A. (2015). Acceptance Process: The Missing Link between Utaut dan Diffusion of Innovation Theory. *AmericanJournal of Information Systems*, *3*(2), 40–44.

Knight, E. (2020). *FinTech , economy and space : Introduction to the special issue*. *52*(8), 1490–1497. https://doi.org/10.1177/0308518X20946334

Laukkanen, T., & Kiviniemi, V. (2010). The role of information in mobile banking resistance. *International Journal of Bank Marketing*, *28*(5), 372–388. https://doi.org/10.1108/02652321011064890

Luarn, P., & Lin, H. H. (2005). Toward an understanding of the behavioral intention to use mobile banking. *Computers in Human Behavior*, *21*(6), 873–891. https://doi.org/10.1016/j.chb.2004.03.003

Marafon, D. L., Basso, K., Espartel, L. B., de Barcellos, M. D., & Rech, E. (2018). Perceived risk and intention to use internet banking: The effects of self-confidence and risk acceptance. *International Journal of Bank Marketing*, *36*(2), 277–289. https://doi.org/10.1108/IJBM-11-2016-0166

Martins, C., Oliveira, T., & Popovič, A. (2014). Understanding the internet banking adoption: A unified theory of acceptance and use of technology and perceived risk application. *International Journal of Information Management*, *34*(1), 1–13. https://doi.org/10.1016/j.ijinfomgt.2013.06.002

Mehrtens, J., Cragg, P. B., & Mills, A. M. (2001). A model of Internet adoption by SMEs. *Information and Management*, *39*(3), 165–176. https://doi.org/10.1016/S0378-7206(01)00086-6

Mensah, I. K. (2020). Impact of Performance Expectancy, Effort Expectancy, and Citizen Trust on the Adoption of Electronic Voting System in Ghana. *International Journal of Electronic Government Research*, *16*(2), 19–32. https://doi.org/10.4018/IJEGR.2020040102

Mitra, K., Reiss, M. C., & Capella, L. M. (1999). An Examination of Perceived Risk, Information Search and Behavioral Intentions in Search, Experience and Credence Services. *The Journal of Services Marketing*, *13*(3), 208–228.

Murti, R. B., Mahmudi, M., & Nurfauziya, A. (2021). An analysis of performance measurement system used in Indonesia local government. *Journal of Contemporary Accounting*, *3*(2), 64–76. https://doi.org/10.20885/jca.vol3.iss2.art2

Nelson, M. L., & Shaw, M. J. (2003). *Tha Adoption and Diffusion of Interorganizational Systems Standards and Process Innovations*.

Nurherwening, A., Dari, A. W., Urumsah, D., & Wibowo, H. T. (2021). The success of go-pay financial technology service adoption. *Journal of Contemporary Accounting*, *3*(2), 98–111. https://doi.org/10.20885/jca.vol3.iss2.art5

Nurlinda, Napitupulu, I. H., Wardayani, Azlina, Andina, A., Ulfah, A. K., & Supriyanto. (2020). Can E-Commerce Adoption Improve SME's Performance? (Case Studies on Micro, Small and Medium Enterprises with Gojek Services in Indonesia). *ResearchGate*, 1–8. https://doi.org/10.4108/eai.11-12-2019.2290850

Oliveira, T., & Martins, M. F. O. (2009). Determinants of information technology adoption in Portugal. *ICETE 2009 - International Joint Conference on e-Business and Telecommunications*, 264–270.

Orlikowski, W. J. (1993). CASE tools as organizational change: Investigating incremental and radical changes in systems development. *MIS Quarterly: Management Information Systems*, *17*(3), 309–340. https://doi.org/10.4135/9781849209687.n11

Park, J. H., & Kim, Y. B. (2021). Factors Activating Big Data Adoption by Korean Firms. *Journal of Computer Information Systems*, *61*(3), 285–293. https://doi.org/10.1080/08874417.2019.1631133

Pramanita, I. G. A. A. N. G., & Rasmini, K. N. (2020). Sistem E-Filing dan Kepatuhan Wajib Pajak Orang Pribadi: Studi D&M IS Success Model pada KPP Pratama Denpasar Timur. *E-Jurnal Akuntansi*, *30*(11), 2825. https://doi.org/10.24843/EJA.2020.v30.i11.p09

Purnomo, M., Maulina, E., Wicaksono, A. R., & Rizal, M. (2021). Adopsi Teknologi Internet of Things pada Startup Industri F&B. *Techno.Com*, *20*(3), 342–351. https://doi.org/10.33633/tc.v20i3.4824

Ryu, H. S. (2018). Understanding Benefit and Risk Framework of Fintech Adoption: Comparison of Early Adopters and Late Adopters. *Proceedings of the 51st Hawaii International Conference on System Sciences*, 3864–3873.

Sari, R. P., Santoso, D. T., & Puspita, D. (2020). Analisis Kesiapan UMKM Kabupaten Karawang Terhadap Adopsi Cloud Computing dalam Konteks Industri 4.0. *Jurnal Teknik Industri*, *15*(2), 63–72.

Siddik, M. N. A., Sun, G., Kabiraj, S., Shanmugan, J., & Yanjuan, C. (2016). Impacts of e-banking on performance of banks in a developing economy: empirical evidence from Bangladesh. *Journal of Business Economics and Management*, *17*(6), 1066–1080. https://doi.org/doi:10.3846/16111699.2015.1068219

Tan, M., & Teo, T. S. H. (2000). Factors Influencing the Adoption of Internet Banking. *Journal of the Association for Information Systems*, *1*(1), 1–44.

Taylor, J. W. (1974). The Role of Risk in Consumer Behavior. *Journal of Marketing*, *38*, 54–60.

Tempo.co. (2018). *Bank Terbaik Versi Indonesia Banking Award 2018 Diumumkan*. Bisnis.Tempo.Co.

Tornatzky, L. ., & Fleischer, M. (1990). *Technological Innovation as a Process*.

Tseng, S. Y., & Wang, C. N. (2016). Perceived risk influence on dual-route information adoption processes on travel websites. *Journal of Business Research*, *69*(6), 2289–2296. https://doi.org/10.1016/j.jbusres.2015.12.044

Veeramootoo, N., Nunkoo, R., & Dwivedi, Y. K. (2018). What determines success of an e-government service? Validation of an integrative model of e-filing continuance usage. *Government Information Quarterly*, *35*(2), 161–174. https://doi.org/10.1016/j.giq.2018.03.004

Venkatesh, V., Morris, M. G., Davis, G. B., & Davis, F. D. (2003). User Acceptance of Information Technology: Toward a Unfied View. *MIS Quarterly*, *27*(3), 425–478.

Whitman, M., & Mattord, H. (2013). *Management of information security*. MA: Cengage Learning.

Wibowo, H. T. (2020). The effect of e-local tax return usage towards local tax compliance. *Journal of Contemporary Accounting*, *2*(2), 81–96. https://doi.org/10.20885/jca.vol2.iss2.art3

Xu, B., Shao, B., Lin, Z., & Shi, Y. (2009). Enterprise adoption of internet banking in China. *Journal of Global Information Technology Management*, *12*(3), 7–28.

Zavolokina, L., Dolata, M., & Schwabe, G. (2016). FinTech - What ' s in a Name? *In Proceedings of International Conference of Information Systems*.

Zhang, T., Tao, D., Qu, X., Zhang, X., Lin, R., & Zhang, W. (2019). The roles of initial trust and perceived risk in public's acceptance of automated vehicles. *Transportation Research Part C: Emerging Technologies*, *98*, 207–220. https://doi.org/10.1016/j.trc.2018.11.018

Zhou, T., Lu, Y., & Wang, B. (2010). Integrating TTF and UTAUT to explain mobile banking user adoption. *Computers in Human Behavior*, *26*, 760–767.

EMPHASIZING HUMANS IN INDUSTRY 5.0: A CROSS-AGE ANALYSIS OF BEHAVIORAL ENTROPY AND COGNITIVE WORKLOAD IN VR-BASED TELEROBOTICS

Federica Nenna[1], Davide Zanardi[2] and Luciano Gamberini[1]
[1]*Department of General Psychology, University of Padova, Padova, Italy*
[2]*Department of Developmental Psychology and Socialization, University of Padova, Padova, Italy*

ABSTRACT

Human motion patterns have been shown to reflect cognitive processes in psychology and applied Human-Computer Interaction (HCI) research. Specifically, behavioral entropy of users' movement trajectories has been proposed to consistently reflect workload and fatigue in various scenarios, including Virtual Reality (VR). In VR, this measure is typically calculated based on the movements of the VR controllers, known as Entropy of Controller Movements (ECM). While having great potential as a highly sensitive and unobtrusive measure of human workload, the effectiveness of ECM in more applied and realistic instances of VR-based applications (e.g., teleoperation platforms) has not been proven yet. Furthermore, the existing literature is based on young experimental samples, living open the question of whether age-related changes in motor performance might prevent using ECM as a measure of workload. We here covered these aspects by assessing relations between workload and ECM in 15 young and 15 senior participants who physically maneuvered an industrial robot in VR. Specifically, they were asked to guide the robot through a pick-and-place task by using their own physical movements in VR. Our findings evidence some criticalities of ECM as a measure of workload in our VR-based industrial contexts, opening new questions on its applicability and effectiveness.

KEYWORDS

Behavioral Entropy, Virtual Reality, Workload, Industrial Robotics, Entropy of Controller Movements

1. INTRODUCTION

1.1 Virtual Reality in Manufacturing and Industrial Robotics

Industry 5.0 is enabling greater use of robotic and autonomous systems in manufacturing while bringing peculiar attention to humans. Always more considerations are done regarding human workload in the workplace (Coronado et al., 2022; Panagou et al, 2023) and a great deal of effort is spent on better designing human-machine interactions, to lower users' fatigue and provide workers with the best robotic support.

Lately, physical industrial settings are being transferred into digital platforms allowing users to operate or inspect robots and machines also remotely. Such platforms, also known as digital twins (Van der Valk et al., 2020), can exploit the most various interfaces, including Virtual Reality (VR) (Havard et al., 2019). VR is particularly attractive in this sector for the following reasons. First, VR can faithfully reproduce real scenarios, even the most complex ones, with high levels of immersion. This feature is significantly useful in the robotics and manufacturing industry, where it is crucial for usability test settings to be as close as possible to the real ones. Second, implementing novel features in physical robots for usability tests is time-consuming and requires a great deal of work (Dautenhahn, 2018). Also, interacting with autonomous machines can be particularly dangerous in some situations, or even impossible in others (e.g., Guo et al., 2021). By using simulation software in VR, it is possible to overcome issues related to the hardware, generate usability test settings, or even get immersed in physically unreachable environments in a much faster, more efficient, safer, and cheaper way

(Dianatfar et al., 2021; Duguleana et al., 2011). Third, VR allows interactions with any virtual object exploiting human physical and embodied mechanisms. This calls to action human spatiality, which is the innate ability to act in physical space and thus facilitate any interaction with the virtual replica of physical objects (Villani et al., 2018).

1.2 VR-Based User Performance and Workload Metrics

Besides the mere advantage of enabling physical interactions, VR interactivity allows for collecting vast amounts of data related to user behavior and performance. This data can be used to improve the user experience, as well as inform research in fields such as cognitive science, psychology, ergonomics and Human-Computer Interaction (HCI). A broad body of literature in the work sector has demonstrated how workload and performance are strictly related, and how high workload levels are associated with mental fatigue, frustration, errors, and distraction (Galy et al., 2012; Young et al., 2015). Such factors can have important consequences in industrial robotics, and therefore, are particularly worth measuring, also in VR.

In this respect, all VR hardware (i.e., headset, controllers, body trackers) continuously generates time series data about their position and rotation. Such data can be leveraged to compute, for example, the start time and duration of any interaction with a virtual object, the users' movement velocity within a work setting, their position with respect to the digital replica of a robot or a machine, their task efficiency, or their work peace (Nenna et al., 2022; Nenna et al., 2023). All these metrics can report on the users' behaviors within a VR-based industrial or work context, enhancing our understanding of how people interact with virtual environments.

Remarkably, time series data on the VR controller position were further leveraged to gain insights into users' workload (Reinhardt et al., 2019; 2020). More precisely, the authors computed the Entropy of Controller Movement (ECM), which was demonstrated to be significantly modulated by the users' mental workload. While entropy measures have most likely been computed on gaze data and in desktop and mouse- or joystick-based settings within the human research areas (Chatzithanos et al., 2021; Diaz-Piedra et al., 2019; Goodrich et al., 2004; Reinhardt and Hurtienne, 2018; Stillman et al., 2018; Wu et al., 2020), the evidence of the effectiveness of such a measure within virtual environments opens new possibilities for continuous and indirect workload monitoring in VR-based industrial robotics.

1.3 Behavioral Entropy as a Measure of Workload

The concept of entropy refers to the degree of irregularity, randomness, and disorder in a system. It is typically used to quantify the complexity of different structures or processes or to learn about the randomicity of data or component variations (Wehrl, 1978). While it was initially developed to describe physical phenomena, the concept of entropy can actually extend to different kinds of data, including time series data, thus applying to various phenomena and application areas.

In the HCI and ergonomics fields, entropy has been employed to infer human workload, fatigue, or decisional processes by analyzing the unpredictability of specific movement trajectories. Nakayama, Boer, and colleagues (1999; 2000) first employed measures of entropy in the steering wheel of a vehicle to estimate drivers' workload (i.e., steering entropy). Subsequently, this concept was generalized to human activity at large, which is currently known as *behavioral entropy*. Some studies computed behavioral entropy on users' movements via mouse (e.g., McKinstry et al., 2008; Reinhardt and Hurtienne, 2018; Stillman et al., 2018), or VR controllers (Reinhardt et al., 2019; 2020); some others also computed the entropy of eye movements as a measure of workload (e.g., Wu et al., 2020).

In all such cases, when individuals interact with technology, they perform task-related movements whose complexity and accuracy can be influenced by the task demand (e.g., complexity, precision). As the task complexity or precision increases, users may experience greater cognitive and physical demands, resulting in more random and unpredictable movement trajectories. More specifically, Goodrich et al. (2004) proposed that, when operators face high workload or other factors causing degraded performance, they might select less efficient behaviors, anticipate less and react more, therefore resulting in more fragmented or exaggerated actions (i.e., reactive behaviors). Under lower workloads, instead, operators are likely to perform anticipatory behaviors, which are smoother with lower magnitudes and less frequent changes. As a result, examining the entropy of human movements can provide insights into the levels of users' workloads.

Goodrich et al. (2004) tested these hypotheses in seven users teleoperating a robot through direct or shared control, while additionally performing an arithmetic task. They concluded that behavioral entropy allowed to identify the most complex conditions of the teleoperation task. More recently, Chatzithanos et al. (2021) used behavioral entropy in a remote inspection scenario, whereby a sample of three operators teleoperated a robot to navigate an arena through a joypad. Different workload levels were created via dual-tasking and were directly related to the entropy values.

On the measurement of behavioral entropy within immersive virtual environments, Reinhardt et al. (2019) measured the Entropy of Controller Movements (ECM) in twenty-two participants executing a simple rhythm game in VR. They found a clear relation with their workload, indicating ECM as a promising mental workload measurement even in VR. In a subsequent experiment, the same authors tested twenty students performing the e-crossing task in VR, and demonstrated positive relations between the task difficulty, mental workload reported at the NASA-TLX and ECM (Reinhardt et al., 2020).

While the literature on behavioral entropy in immersive VR is not that extensive, ECM seems to have great potential as a highly sensitive and unobtrusive measure of workload in various VR scenarios. Nonetheless, to the best of our knowledge, literature assessing the effectiveness of ECM in more applied and realistic instances of VR-based environments (e.g., teleoperation platforms) is missing. Furthermore, the experimental samples underpinning the current literature are consistently young. On this point, it is known how older individuals demonstrate age-related changes in motor performance and multi-joint trajectories, with decreasing smoothness and accuracy of the movements (Seider et al., 2002). Therefore, it is also crucial to further assess the possible impact of age on the effectiveness of ECM as a measure of workload in VR.

2. THE PRESENT STUDY

With this study, we aim at covering the identified gaps and learn more about the effectiveness of ECM as a measure of workload in VR. We thus addressed a VR-based industrial robotics framework, and compared results obtained by young (<30 years old) and senior users (>50 years old). Specifically, a total of thirty participants - divided into two age groups - guided an industrial robotic arm through a pick-and-place task in VR by physically moving their arms, under low (single-task) and high (dual-task) mental demands. We also administered the NASA-TLX questionnaire to reference the participants' perceived workload after both task conditions. Based on the literature on behavioral entropy (Reinhardt et al., 2019; 2020) and considering the possible age-related motor performance degradation (Seider et al., 2002), we expect: H1) higher ECM and higher scores on the NASA-TLX questionnaire in the dual-task compared to the single-task, independently from the participants' age; H2) a generally higher ECM in the senior compared to the young group.

3. METHODOLOGY

3.1 Participants

15 individuals (9 females) composed the senior group, who reported being more than 50 years old (M_{age}= 57.1, SD_{age}= 6.2), and 15 individuals (6 females) the young group, who reported being less than 30 years old (M_{age}= 27.8, SD_{age}= 6.4). All participants signed informed consent. The inclusion criteria were the following: absence of past or present neurological/psychiatric disorders, being right-handers, possessing normal or corrected-to-normal vision with contact lenses, and normal color vision. The local ethics committee approved the research methodology, and the study was conducted following the principles of the Declaration of Helsinki. One senior participant was excluded due to limited proficiency with technological devices, which caused extremely long training and a severe inability to perform the task. All participants reported to be inexperienced with VR and telerobotics, particularly the senior once.

3.2 Technical Setup and Experimental Procedure

Participants were provided with HTC VIVE Pro Eye and both its controllers. The virtual environment was programmed in Unity (version 2020.2.1f1). All data was automatically saved on the internal storage of the local laboratory computer at the end of each experimental session.

Before starting the experiment, participants conducted a training session based on the same tasks used in the experimental phase to familiarize themselves with the virtual environment and minimize individual differences related to the ability to use the virtual system. Afterward, during the experimental session, all subjects controlled a robotic arm in VR to execute a pick-and-place task under different demands (single- and dual-task) presented in random order. The young group completed 40 trials for each experimental condition. Differently, for the senior group, the number of trials was lowered to 20, as they showed longer training duration and greater difficulties in familiarizing with the tasks. This may be due to their lack of technological literacy (Wildenbos et al., 2018), which may pose a barrier to the repeated execution of VR-based tasks for older adults.

In the single-task, participants were called to physically drive the robot to pick a bolt from the workstation and place it into a blue box. Figure 1 depicts one complete task trial, which was split into two task phases: the Pick phase, which required higher movement precision to accurately align the robot effector with the bolt, and the Place phase, which required less movement precision as the box where to release the bolt is provided with a larger area. Given that the two task phases demanded different levels of precision of the movement trajectories, we computed the ECM within each of them independently. Oppositely to the single-task, in the dual-task participants additionally performed an arithmetic task to create a higher level of task demand. Specifically, they were presented with a series of digits randomly ranging between 1 and 10 every 2sec, with a jitter of 0.3sec. They were thus asked to sum the numbers all the way through the trial, and then report the result of the mental calculations on a virtual numeric keyboard once the trial was completed.

The robot control modality followed the same mechanisms developed by Nenna et al. (2022; 2023). Specifically, participants approached their right hand to the robot effector and then grasped it by pressing the grip button on the controller. Therefore, they dragged the robot to the desired position by physically moving their own arm within the virtual space, producing a movement trajectory. To enable the picking or placing operations, they then pressed the pad button on the left controller and the robot automatically went down on the workstation to either pick or place the bolt. Once the bolt entered the box, a new bolt and box randomly appeared on the workstation, and a new trial started.

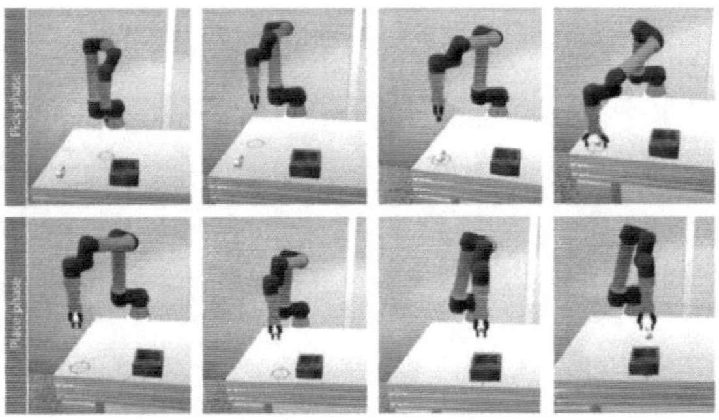

Figure 1. Depiction of one trial of the pick-and-place task, divided into two task phases (i.e., Pick and Place)

3.3 Behavioral and Workload Measures

The levels of perceived mental workload were measured through the NASA-TLX questionnaire (Hart and Staveland, 1988) after the single- and the dual-task. The global workload score was calculated by averaging the scores in its six sub-scales.

For the computation of behavioral entropy, we isolated the movement trajectories performed during the pick and the place action and only included trials exempt from movement disruptions (e.g., the participant lost the robot grip and returned to grasp the robot again, causing fragmented trajectories); therefore, all actions under examination were continuous and uninterrupted. We then choose to determine sample entropy using the method of Richman and Moorman (2000). This method best fits the randomness intrinsic to systems behaving in real-world or complex environments and has been demonstrated to be the preferred method in applied research for mental workload assessments, also in VR scenarios (Reinhardt et al., 2019). Sample entropy can be defined as the negative logarithm of the probability that if two sets of data points of length m are similar, they will remain similar at $m+1$ (Richman and Moorman, 2000). Therefore, if areas in a trajectory that appear similar at one length are no longer similar at a greater length, greater dispersion and complexity are observed in a trajectory, which increases the sample entropy (Hehman et al., 2015). For its computation, we converted the data to normalized time and shifted the absolute controller positions on the three axes (x, y, z) in order to always start from zero (0, 0, 0) in each trial. Based on the overview of statistical tools for calculating sample entropy of Chen and colleagues (2019), we used the function *sample_entropy* in Rstudio (Team, 2020) from the package *pracma* (Borchers, 2022), which allows setting specific parameters like the embedding dimension m (length of sequences to be compared for similarity) and the tolerance r (the threshold for determining similarity between windows). By following the approaches of Hehman et al. (2015) and Reinhardt et al. (2019), we set m=2 and r=0.2; thus, we compared windows with a length of 2, and each sequence was determined to be similar if it was within a tolerance of 0.2 multiplied by the standard deviation of the data. We finally calculated the ECM on the three axes (ECM-X, ECM-Y, ECM-Z) and the ECM-total by averaging the three individual ECMs (Reinhardt et al., 2019).

3.4 Statistical Analysis

All data were analyzed through Generalized Linear Models (GLMs from lme4 package, Bates et al., 2014). We computed a model for each ECM calculation (ECM-X, ECM-Y, ECM-Z, ECM-total) over the factors Task (single-task, dual-task) and Age (young, senior). For the analysis of the NASA-TLX scores, we additionally included the factor Item (mental demand, temporal demand, physical demand, performance, effort, frustration) to further explore possible differences within each of the questionnaire sub-scales. Each model was chosen based on data distribution (Delignette-Muller and Dutang, 2015). Post hoc were performed on each significant interaction with the application of the Bonferroni correction for multiple comparisons (Bonferroni et al., 1936).

4. RESULTS

Table 1. Descriptive statistics of the NASA-TLX questionnaire scores

Dimension	Young Single-task M ± SD	Young Dual-task M ± SD	Senior Single-task M ± SD	Senior Dual-task M ± SD
Global score	5.79 ± 4.85	10.30 ± 5.28	5.54 ± 4.87	11.5 ± 5.89
Mental demand	2.67 ± 1.35	13.80 ± 4.25	4.14 ± 4.44	15.6 ± 2.71
Physical demand	8.40 ± 5.47	11.9 ± 4.48	5.21 ± 4.02	8.14 ± 5.63
Temporal demand	7.27 ± 3.47	7.00 ± 3.40	7.14 ± 4.75	11.2 ± 5.58
Performance	4.33 ± 4.75	7.93 ± 5.64	4.43 ± 3.39	9.36 ± 5.49
Effort	8.27 ± 5.18	13.9 ± 3.83	9.71 ± 6.70	16.8 ± 2.94
Frustration	2.73 ± 2.76	7.47 ± 5.01	2.57 ± 1.40	8.14 ± 5.95

Table 2. Descriptive statistics of the ECMs

Task phase	Axis	Young Single-task M ± SD	Young Dual-task M ± SD	Senior Single-task M ± SD	Senior Dual task M ± SD
Pick	ECM-x	0.026 ± 0.013	0.017 ± 0.015	0.021 ± 0.026	0.010 ± 0.008
	ECM-y	0.199 ± 0.099	0.137 ± 0.086	0.112 ± 0.089	0.104 ± 0.085
	ECM-z	0.093 ± 0.084	0.080 ± 0.041	0.052 ± 0.060	0.033 ± 0.037
	ECM-tot	0.106 ± 0.048	0.078 ± 0.028	0.062 ± 0.040	0.049 ± 0.034
Place	ECM-x	0.044 ± 0.038	0.045 ± 0.042	0.023 ± 0.029	0.019 ± 0.025
	ECM-y	0.216 ± 0.144	0.205 ± 0.145	0.145 ± 0.100	0.111 ± 0.090
	ECM-z	0.064 ± 0.065	0.068 ± 0.072	0.037 ± 0.050	0.028 ± 0.048
	ECM-tot	0.108 ± 0.059	0.106 ± 0.058	0.068 ± 0.042	0.053 ± 0.038

The analysis of the NASA-TLX revealed a main effect for Task ($X^2 = 121.58$, $p < 0.001$) and Item $X^2 = 81.26$, $p < 0.001$). Significant interactions were observed between Task and Item ($X^2 = 41.78$, $p < 0.001$) and Item and Age ($X^2 = 16.57$, $p < 0.01$). No significant main effect was found for Age ($p = 0.19$). Post-hoc tests on the Task-Item interaction showed significantly higher levels of mental demand ($p<.0001$), effort ($p < 0.0001$), and frustration ($p < 0.001$) in the dual- compared to the single-task. Differently, no significant contrasts were found for the Age-Item interaction. Descriptive statistics are resumed in Table 1. For the analysis of behavioral entropy, we resumed the descriptive statistics in Table 2, the results of the GLMs in Table 3, and all the post-hoc contrasts are depicted in Figure 2.

Table 3. Results of the GLMs performed in the pick and place phases on each ECM measure

Axis	Task phase	Task	Age	Task * Age
ECM-x	Pick	$X^2 = 66.66$ ***	$X^2 = 1.62$ ns	$X^2 = 4.03$ *
	Place	$X^2 = 0.04$ ns	$X^2 = 28.53$ ***	$X^2 = 3.07$ ns
ECM-y	Pick	$X^2 = 1.47$ ns	$X^2 = 7.79$ **	$X^2 = 1.33$ ns
	Place	$X^2 = 7.61$ **	$X^2 = 13.22$ ***	$X^2 = 10.53$ **
ECM-z	Pick	$X^2 = 7.27$ **	$X^2 = 15.44$ ***	$X^2 = 0.28$ ns
	Place	$X^2 = .008$ ns	$X^2 = 36.49$ ***	$X^2 = 8.76$ **
ECM-tot	Pick	$X^2 = 15.73$ ***	$X^2 = 17.38$ ***	$X^2 = 0.05$ ns
	Place	$X^2 = 5.52$ *	$X^2 = 22.85$ ***	$X^2 = 18.58$ ***

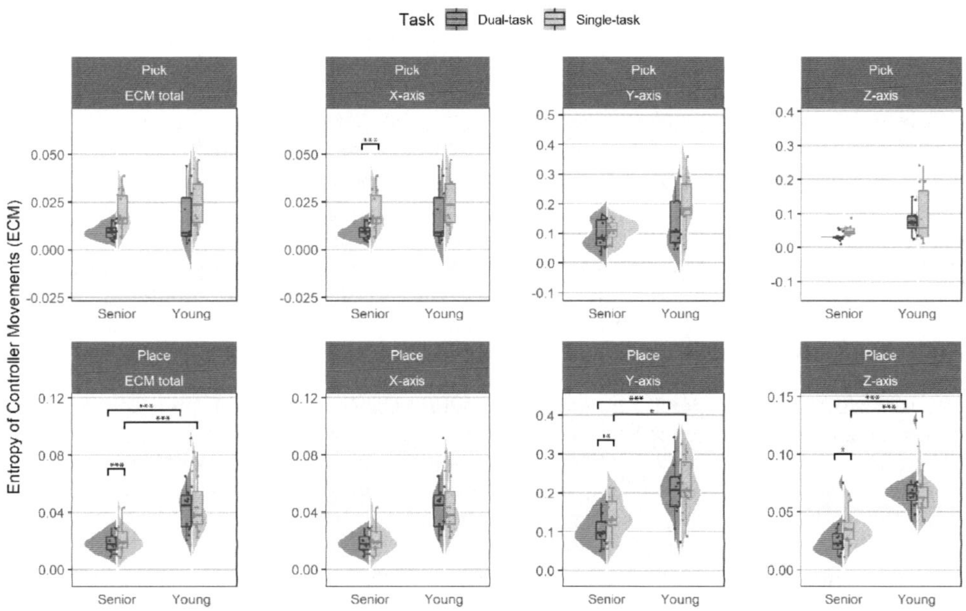

Figure 2. Averaged behavioral entropy in each task phase (pick, place) and task condition (dual-task, single-task), divided by age (senior, young). The dots on the boxplots indicate each participant's averaged entropy. The half violins show the data distribution. The stars indicate the significance levels of the post hoc tests (*$p \leq .05$; **$p \leq .01$; ***$p \leq .001$)

5. DISCUSSION AND CONCLUSIONS

In this study, we applied the concept of behavioral entropy to the trajectory of VR controller movements, exploring its effectiveness in measuring human workload within a VR-based robotic teleoperation scenario. We further explored possible differences between young and senior users, who are prone to decreasing smoothness of movements (Seider et al., 2002), which might affect the effectiveness of ECM as a measure of workload. We thus defined different task demands through the dual-tasking: participants physically drove a robotic arm once as a single task, and once concurrently with an arithmetic task (dual-task). As indicated by the NASA-TLX, regardless of participants' age, the dual-task elicited significantly higher mental demand, effort, and frustration than the single-task. Additionally, young and senior participants self-reported similar workload levels, suggesting no age-dependent differences in perceived workload.

However, unexpectedly, our findings on the ECM deviate from what previously observed (i.e., Chatzithanos et al., 2021; Goodrich et al., 2004; Reinhardt et al., 2019). Specifically, we first hypothesized (H1) higher ECM in the most demanding task condition (i.e., dual-task). Oppositely, we observed systematically higher ECM values in the single-task compared to the dual-task as specifically suggested by ECM-x and ECM-z in the pick phase, ECM-y in the place phase, and ECM-tot both in the pick and place phases, indicating an inverse relationship between the entropy of movement trajectories and the task difficulty. Only senior participants demonstrated slightly higher ECM in the dual- compared to the single-task in the place phase, which aligns with prior research (Chatzithanos et al., 2021; Goodrich et al., 2004; Reinhardt et al., 2019). On this matter, we argue that the secondary task may have intrusively interfered with the primary pick-and-place particularly in the young group, influencing users' motor trajectories. Specifically, in the dual-task, participants summed a series of numbers throughout each pick-and-place action and were always instructed to be as fast and accurately as possible in both tasks. However, the faster they placed the bolt into the box, the fewer mental calculations they had to compute. Differently, in the single-task, they were free to act impulsively while following the instruction of being both fast and accurate. This may have led to more conscious, regular, and smooth motor trajectories in the dual-task to correctly pick and then place the bolt as fast as possible, and more impulsive and dispersive trajectories in the single-task.

An additional note on this regard: previous research, which demonstrated the efficacy of behavioral entropy in detecting varying levels of workload resulting from dual-tasking, was conducted in desktop environments using either a mouse or joypad (Chatzithanos et al., 2021; Goodrich et al., 2004). However, to the best of our knowledge, no study investigated the effectiveness of behavioral entropy in VR contexts leveraging dual-tasking. In their VR-based experiments on behavioral entropy, Reinhardt and colleagues (2019, 2020) always used some inhibition tasks to increase the levels of demand on the user, while no instances of ECM under VR dual-tasking were ever provided. It is thus possible that the presence of a secondary task changes the nature of the primary task, particularly when human physical motion with higher degrees of freedom is involved, like in our VR contexts. This underlines the necessity of a better understanding of behavioral entropy sensitivity in VR, by also considering the impact of secondary tasks on human motion trajectories.

As a second hypothesis (H2), we then expected higher ECM values in the senior group, possibly reflecting their age-related alterations of movement trajectories (Seider et al., 2002). In contrast, we observed consistently higher behavioral entropy in young respect to senior participants. This result is completely reversed compared to our expectations, and therefore, does not allow to define whether it drawn the absence of age-related motor trajectory alterations, or a different behavioral approach to task execution compared to young users.

Nonetheless, as young and senior participants reported similar levels of workload at the NASA-TLX, such findings don't suggest that workload was the cause of differences in motor behavior between young and senior participants. Other factors, such as their particular VR inexperience and low technological literacy, may have influenced their motor behavior. In this view, senior users, being completely new to virtual environments, may have been more cautious when maneuvering the virtual robot, while young users which are typically more familiar with advanced technologies were more impulsive. The study also found that senior users had higher ECM during the dual-task, suggesting they used different strategies than younger users. Furthermore, only senior users demonstrated slightly higher ECM in the dual- compared to the single-task specifically in the place phase. This also indicate that young and senior users have likely adopted different strategies for the task: for easier operations like the place action, senior users actually moved at a more hectic pace under high mental demands, while being smoother under lower demands. The same does not apply to younger individuals, who always kept highly frenetic movement patterns under lower demands.

Overall, behavioral entropy, and ECM in VR, represent valuable unobtrusive and easily computable measures to trace the dispersion of human motion trajectories in digital environments. However, new questions were raised about its effectiveness in reflecting users' workload in VR. Future research should delve into these questions and better understand which are the factors that may affect human motion strategies in VR and to what extent behavioral entropy can inform on users' workloads across different task scenarios.

REFERENCES

Bates, D., Mächler, M., Bolker, B., & Walker, S. (2014). Fitting linear mixed-effects models using lme4. *arXiv preprint arXiv:1406.5823*.

Boer, E. R. (2000, July). Behavioral entropy as an index of workload. In *Proceedings of the Human Factors and Ergonomics Society Annual Meeting* (Vol. 44, No. 17, pp. 125-128). Sage CA: Los Angeles, CA: SAGE Publications.

Bonferroni, C. (1936). Teoria statistica delle classi e calcolo delle probabilita. *Pubblicazioni del R Istituto Superiore di Scienze Economiche e Commericiali di Firenze, 8,* 3-62.

Borchers, H. W., & Borchers, M. H. W. (2022). Package 'pracma'. *accessed on, 4.*

Chatzithanos, P., Nikolaou, G., Stolkin, R., & Chiou, M. (2021, October). Fessonia: a method for real-time estimation of human operator workload using behavioural entropy. In *2021 IEEE International Conference on Systems, Man, and Cybernetics (SMC)* (pp. 1325-1331). IEEE.

Chen, C., Sun, S., Cao, Z., Shi, Y., Sun, B., & Zhang, X. D. (2019). A comprehensive comparison and overview of R packages for calculating sample entropy. *Biology Methods and Protocols, 4(1),* bpz016.

Coronado, E., Kiyokawa, T., Ricardez, G. A. G., Ramirez-Alpizar, I. G., Venture, G., & Yamanobe, N. (2022). Evaluating quality in human-robot interaction: A systematic search and classification of performance and human-centered factors, measures and metrics towards an industry 5.0. *Journal of Manufacturing Systems*, *63*, 392-410.

Dautenhahn, K. (2018). Some brief thoughts on the past and future of human-robot interaction. *ACM Transactions on Human-Robot Interaction (THRI), 7(1),* 1-3.

Delignette-Muller, M. L., & Dutang, C. (2015). fitdistrplus: An R package for fitting distributions. *Journal of statistical software, 64,* 1-34.

Dianatfar, M., Latokartano, J., & Lanz, M. (2021). Review on existing VR/AR solutions in human–robot collaboration. *Procedia CIRP, 97,* 407-411.

Diaz-Piedra, C., Rieiro, H., Cherino, A., Fuentes, L. J., Catena, A., & Di Stasi, L. L. (2019). The effects of flight complexity on gaze entropy: An experimental study with fighter pilots. *Applied ergonomics, 77*, 92-99.

Duguleana, M., Barbuceanu, F. G., & Mogan, G. (2011). Evaluating human-robot interaction during a manipulation experiment conducted in immersive virtual reality. In *Virtual and Mixed Reality-New Trends: International Conference, Virtual and Mixed Reality 2011, Held as Part of HCI International 2011, Orlando, FL, USA, July 9-14, 2011, Proceedings, Part I 4* (pp. 164-173). Springer Berlin Heidelberg.

Galy, E., Cariou, M., & Mélan, C. (2012). What is the relationship between mental workload factors and cognitive load types?. *International journal of psychophysiology, 83(3),* 269-275.

Goodrich, M. A., Boer, E. R., Crandall, J. W., Ricks, R. W., & Quigley, M. L. (2004). *Behavioral entropy in human-robot interaction*. BRIGHAM YOUNG UNIV PROVO UT.

Guo, Y., Freer, D., Deligianni, F., & Yang, G. Z. (2021). Eye-tracking for performance evaluation and workload estimation in space telerobotic training. *IEEE Transactions on Human-Machine Systems*, *52*(1), 1-11.

Hart, S. G., & Staveland, L. E. (1988). Development of NASA-TLX (Task Load Index): Results of empirical and theoretical research. In *Advances in psychology* (Vol. 52, pp. 139-183). North-Holland.

Havard, V., Jeanne, B., Lacomblez, M., & Baudry, D. (2019). Digital twin and virtual reality: a co-simulation environment for design and assessment of industrial workstations. *Production & Manufacturing Research*, *7*(1), 472-489.

Hehman, E., Stolier, R. M., & Freeman, J. B. (2015). Advanced mouse-tracking analytic techniques for enhancing psychological science. *Group Processes & Intergroup Relations*, *18*(3), 384-401.

Leng, J., Sha, W., Wang, B., Zheng, P., Zhuang, C., Liu, Q., ... & Wang, L. (2022). Industry 5.0: Prospect and retrospect. *Journal of Manufacturing Systems, 65*, 279-295.

McKinstry, C., Dale, R., & Spivey, M. J. (2008). Action dynamics reveal parallel competition in decision making. *Psychological Science, 19(1),* 22-24.

Nakayama, O., Futami, T., Nakamura, T., & Boer, E. R. (1999). Development of a steering entropy method for evaluating driver workload. *SAE transactions*, 1686-1695.

Nenna, F., Orso, V., Zanardi, D., & Gamberini, L. (2022). The virtualization of human–robot interactions: a user-centric workload assessment. Virtual Reality, 1-19.

Nenna, F., Zanardi, D., & Gamberini, L. (2023). Enhanced Interactivity in VR-based Telerobotics: An Eye-tracking Investigation of Human Performance and Workload. International Journal of Human-Computer Studies, 103079. https://doi.org/10.1016/j.ijhcs.2023.103079

Panagou, S., Neumann, W. P., & Fruggiero, F. (2023). A scoping review of human robot interaction research towards Industry 5.0 human-centric workplaces. *International Journal of Production Research*, 1-17.

Reinhardt, D., & Hurtienne, J. (2018, March). Cursor entropy reveals decision fatigue. In *Proceedings of the 23rd International Conference on Intelligent User Interfaces Companion* (pp. 1-2).

Reinhardt, D., Haesler, S., Hurtienne, J., & Wienrich, C. (2019, March). Entropy of controller movements reflects mental workload in virtual reality. In *2019 IEEE Conference on Virtual Reality and 3D User Interfaces (VR)* (pp. 802-808). IEEE.

Reinhardt, D., Hurtienne, J., & Wienrich, C. (2020, March). Measuring Mental Effort via Entropy in VR. In *Proceedings of the 25th International Conference on Intelligent User Interfaces Companion* (pp. 43-44).

Richman, J. S., & Moorman, J. R. (2000). Physiological time-series analysis using approximate entropy and sample entropy. *American journal of physiology-heart and circulatory physiology.*

RStudio, T. (2020). RStudio: integrated development environment for R. *(No Title).*

Seidler, R. D., Alberts, J. L., & Stelmach, G. E. (2002). Changes in multi-joint performance with age. *Motor control, 6(1),* 19-31.

Stillman, P. E., Shen, X., & Ferguson, M. J. (2018). How mouse-tracking can advance social cognitive theory. *Trends in cognitive sciences, 22(6),* 531-543.

Van der Valk, H., Haße, H., Möller, F., Arbter, M., Henning, J. L., & Otto, B. (2020, August). A Taxonomy of Digital Twins. In *AMCIS.*

Villani, V., Capelli, B., & Sabattini, L. (2018, August). Use of virtual reality for the evaluation of human-robot interaction systems in complex scenarios. In *2018 27th IEEE International Symposium on Robot and Human Interactive Communication (RO-MAN)* (pp. 422-427). IEEE.

Wehrl, A. (1978). General properties of entropy. *Reviews of Modern Physics, 50(2),* 221.

Wildenbos, G. A., Peute, L., & Jaspers, M. (2018). Aging barriers influencing mobile health usability for older adults: a literature based framework (MOLD-US). *International journal of medical informatics, 114*, 66-75.

WM Van Gerven, Fred GWC Paas, Jeroen JG Van Merriënboer, Henk G. Schmidt, P. (2000). Cognitive load theory and the acquisition of complex cognitive skills in the elderly: Towards an integrative framework. *Educational gerontology, 26*(6), 503-521.

Wu, C., Cha, J., Sulek, J., Zhou, T., Sundaram, C. P., Wachs, J., & Yu, D. (2020). Eye-tracking metrics predict perceived workload in robotic surgical skills training. *Human factors, 62(8),* 1365-1386.

Young, M. S., Brookhuis, K. A., Wickens, C. D., & Hancock, P. A. (2015). State of science: mental workload in ergonomics. *Ergonomics*, *58*(1), 1-17.

ACCESSIBILITY ASSESSMENT OF MOBILE APPLICATIONS: THE CASE OF THE HOMINERE APP

Daniel Alves, Diana Siso, Joana Tavares, Juliana Gouveia, Oksana Tymoshchuk and Rita Oliveira
DigiMedia, Department of Communication and Art, University of Aveiro, Portugal

ABSTRACT

In this article, it is intended to analyze and evaluate the Hominere mobile application regarding its accessibility through manual assessment and automatic tools, guided by the accessibility criteria defined by the Web Content Accessibility Guidelines (WCAG). The automated evaluation with the support of various tools (WAVE - Web Accessibility Evaluation Tool, Access Monitor and SortSite Accessibility Checker and Validator) allowed the authors to identify common accessibility problems, such as missing or mislabeled buttons, non-descriptive links, or inaccessible images. The manual evaluation was complemented with TalkBack allowed the identification of specific accessibility problems that automated tools cannot detect, such as complex user interactions or problems related to visual design and layout. With the evaluation and its analysis, it was possible to identify solutions for the problems presented to make the application more inclusive and accessible, and also to verify that the selected accessibility strategy evaluation is effective and appropriated and can be replicated in the accessibility evaluation of other mobile apps.

KEYWORDS

Accessibility Assessment, Accessibility Principles, Guidelines, Mobile Application, Screen Readers, Web Accessibility

1. INTRODUCTION

With the increasing number of people with disabilities, accessibility has become a critical issue for designers and developers of digital products and services. Mobile applications have become an integral part of people's daily lives, and their usage has increased significantly in recent years. These applications serve as a medium for individuals to access information, communicate, and complete various tasks. However, people with disabilities often face significant barriers when using mobile applications due to accessibility issues. Therefore, evaluating mobile application accessibility is critical to ensure that everyone, including those with disabilities, can use them without any difficulties.

The accessibility evaluation strategies can be classified into two categories: manual evaluation and automated evaluation. Manual evaluation involves expert evaluators who manually inspect the product or service for accessibility issues, and automated evaluation comprises software tools that can automatically check the accessibility of digital products. Manual evaluation can identify accessibility issues that are difficult to detect using automated tools; however, this type of evaluation can be time-consuming and expensive. Automated evaluation, on the other hand, is faster and less expensive, but it may miss certain accessibility issues that can only be detected by human evaluators.

This article focuses on developing a hybrid evaluation strategy that combine both manual and automated evaluation, which can help developers and designers improve the accessibility of mobile applications and provide a better user experience for everyone.

In a context of Challenge Based Learning (CBL), in the school year 2022/2023, integrated in the Master Communication and Web Technologies from the Aveiro's University, it was proposed by the partner of that year – the company BOSCH – the development of digital platforms to reduce energy waste. One of the projects developed was Hominere, a mobile application that aims to solve the lack of motivation regarding energy and water saving and the lack of energy efficiency in people's daily lives, such as food, transportation, and recycling. Furthermore, the application also aims to change users' behavior in the mentioned areas, presenting a motivating and re-educating character through information-sharing publications. There is also the presentation of challenges that aim to help and guide individuals to change bad habits according to their needs.

In this way, in the scope of the Curricular Unit of Digital Accessibility and Compliance, of the mentioned master's degree, the evaluation and analysis of the Hominere app were carried out to detect possible accessibility problems and, through the results obtained, elaborate and present possible solutions to improve the final product, and also to understand if the selected accessibility strategy evaluation is effective and appropriated and can be replicated in other mobile apps assessments.

2. THEORETICAL BACKGROUND

Web accessibility is the degree to which a website/mobile app is usable by the most significant number of people to promote their digital and social inclusion (Kalbag, 2017). Therefore, web accessibility refers to the ability of people with disabilities to access and use digital content, including websites, mobile applications, electronic documents, and other digital resources. This means designing and developing digital content to be easily accessed and used by people with disabilities/incapacities, including those with visual, hearing, physical, cognitive, neurological or some temporary impairment (Cooper et al. 2016; Oliveira et al. 2021).

Digital accessibility is essential because it ensures that people with disabilities have equal access to information, services, and opportunities online. It also helps European organizations comply with legal requirements, such as the Directive (EU) 2019/882 on the accessibility requirements for products and services, also known as the European Accessibility Act.

The World Wide Web Consortium (W3C) defines web accessibility as "essential for developers and organizations that want to create high-quality websites and web tools, and not exclude people from using their products and services" (W3C WAI 2018). Digital accessibility involves ensuring that digital content is perceivable, operable, understandable, and robust for all users, including those who use assistive technologies like screen readers, magnifiers, and alternative input devices (WCAG 2.1). Digital accessibility also includes considerations for usability, such as providing clear and consistent navigation, labelling of form fields, and ensuring that content is easy to read and understand.

The compliance levels of a mobile platform/application depend on the priority check. Thus, the application is assigned conformance level 'A' if all priority one checkpoint is satisfied, conformance level 'AA' if all priority 1 and 2 checkpoints are satisfied, and conformance level 'AAA' if all priority 1, 2 and 3 checkpoints are satisfied (W3C WAI 2018). Accessibility assessment should be a process that combines automatic tools (software) and human assessment (Rutter et al. 2007). Following this line of thought, Slatin & Rush (2002) refer that no automatic tool detects all accessibility problems. However, in combination with a manual check, they are the starting point for problem detection and correction.

3. RELATED WORK

Developing an accessible app is still challenging due to several particularities of mobile phones requiring technical expertise in creating applications that meet the needs of people with disabilities (Ballantyne et al. 2018). Recent studies show that developers need to consider different specialties of mobile phones, e.g. versions of the same mobile operating system, different screen sizes, and the features of assistive tools such as screen readers like VoiceOver and TalkBack (Oliveira et al. 2021; Silva et al. 2021; Tymoshchuk et al. 2021).

In this context, several studies highlight the importance of accessibility testing in the prototyping phase is crucial for ensuring that mobile applications are accessible to everyone (Nilsson 2018; Silva et al. 2021; Vieritz et al. 2016). Dias et al. (2022) conducted a literature review of automated evaluation tools for web and mobile accessibility and despite the existence of various tools either for web or mobile apps, they are not completely effective, covering less than 40% of all the problems encountered. Also, no tool was found capable of adapting the application interfaces according to the type of disabilities that users may present. Ismailova and Inal (2018) carried out a comparison of online accessibility evaluation tools to perceive their effectiveness. The authors observed that each tool generated different evaluation data for the same websites and some of the tools are complementary to each other, meaning the highest coverage and completeness can be possible with the right combination of evaluation tools. Therefore, the authors suggest that different tools should be utilized to provide consistency and obtain reliable data from online evaluation tools, improving tool effectiveness.

Accessibility evaluation requires a deep understanding of accessibility guidelines, specialized knowledge and expertise, and adequate time and resources to conduct the testing properly. In this context, web development courses should offer future developers the opportunity to learn and apply in practice the accessibility guidelines that should be considered in the mobile app development process. Recent studies report that students of web/application development have a low level of familiarity with accessibility guidelines and their practical application (Kearney-Volpe et al. 2021; Cao and Loiacono 2022). These studies underline the importance of educating future developers about accessibility guidelines, promoting their personal connection with disabled people in the educational process, including universal design principles in the development of accessible websites/apps, as well as the business values of an accessible web/app.

4. METHODOLOGY

This study presents a work of accessibility assessment of a mobile app prototype – Hominere developed by five students of the master's degree Communication and Web Technologies, focuses on informing and motivating users for energy efficiency and water saving through challenges and a forum (Figure 1) that help and guide them to save more and change bad habits, depending on their needs.

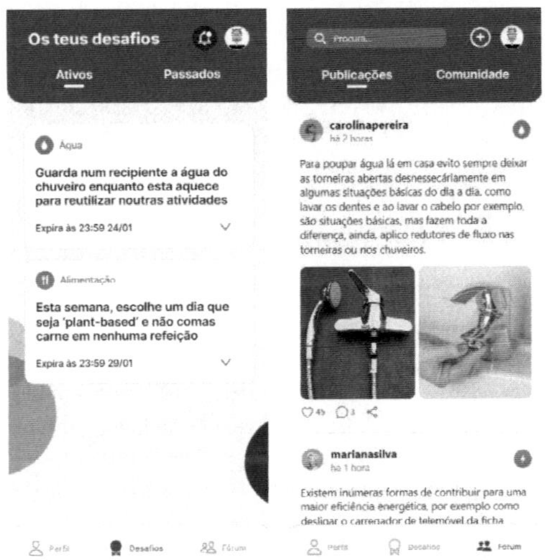

Figure 1. Challenges and Forum areas

To improve the accessibility of the Hominere app, the authors evaluated it by applying the following guidelines and automatic and manual evaluation platforms/tools:

1. Web Content Accessibility (2.1) and Mobile Accessibility (2.0) Guidelines

The analysis was ruled by a set of recommendations defined by the Web Content Accessibility Guidelines 2.0 (W3C WAI 2018), following its principles, guidelines and criteria applied to the content of the mobile application, together with some standards presented by the Mobile Accessibility Guidelines (W3C WAI 2021). In this way, it was weighted for evaluating and analyzing the four main principles: perceivable, operable, understandable, and robust (POUR).

2. Automatic Validation

It was selected a three automatic validation tools for accessibility that proved to be adequate to the context: WAVE – Web Accessibility Evaluation Tool, Access Monitor and SortSite Accessibility Checker and Validator.

3. Manual Analysis through TalkBack

For manual analysis, the authors chose TalkBack, a tool included in Android mobile devices that visually impaired users widely use. The scenario of a visually impaired user was simulated as close as possible to reality using the application with the help of the screen reader.

5. RESULTS

With the use of all the tools mentioned in the previous topic, it was possible to analyse the Hominere application and identify aspects that be unsuccessful in accessibility and define possible solutions to correct these aspects. Next, the results are presented according to POUR principles.

5.1 First principle – Perceivable

The principle of Perceivable states that content should be perceivable to all users (W3C WAI 2018), so the authors highlighted the following aspects:

5.1.1 Small Screen Size - Criterion 1.1 (WCAG 2.0)

The application analysis showed that the application does not guarantee the provision of acceptable sizes on some buttons in terms of their proportions and the spacing around them. Considering that the minimum size a button should have been 44px - 44px, several screens of the application are found buttons with smaller dimensions. In the most severe case, the button to return to the previous page with a proportion of 8px -14px (Figure 2).

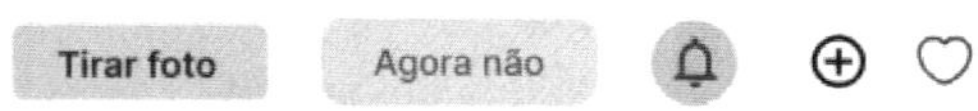

Figure 2. Examples of buttons that do not reach 44px in height

5.1.2 Contrast - Criterion 1.4.3 (WCAG 2.1)

The authors tested the contrast between the elements that make up the app using several tools, such as Stark[4]. Considering that the minimum desired contrast value is 4.5:1 for standard text, it was concluded that the Hominere app presents contrast problems in the chosen color palette (Figure 3).

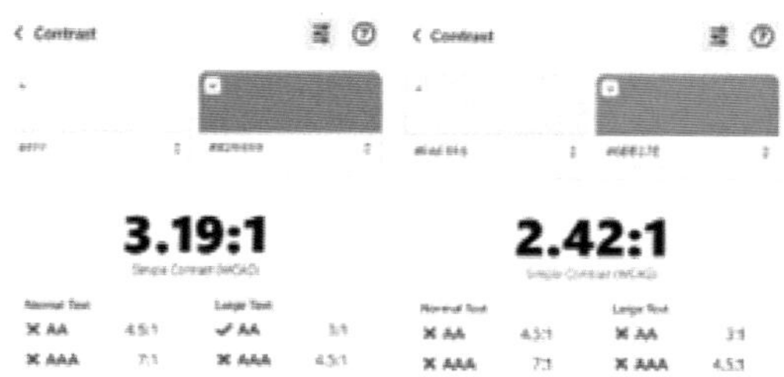

Figure 3. Example of lack of contrast between colors

5.1.3 Visual Presentation - Criterion 1.4.8 (WCAG 2.1)

Regarding the visual presentation of the information, the authors found flaws that do not allow the user to customize the background and foreground colors. In some screens, the minimum line spacing required is not met (this point will also be addressed in criterion 1.4.12).

5.1.4 Text Spacing - Criterion 1.4.12 (WCAG 2.1)

The authors found that the Hominere app does not meet several success criteria regarding text spacing. The line spacing, which ideally would be equivalent to 1.5 of the font size, takes on a value of zero (0). The app also fails to meet the spacing between characters or words, which ideally would be 0.12 and 0.16 of the font size, respectively.

5.2 Second Principle – Operable

According to WCAG 2.1, the operability principle is related to the navigation and interface being operational, so the authors assessed the following aspect: Placing buttons where they are easy to access - Criterion 3.5 in WCAG 2.0. In some situations, the buttons are only positioned for easy access by right-handed users. In addition, some buttons occupy a very high position on the page and without margins, thus compromising their touch since not all devices will present favorable conditions for their display, as is the case of cell phones with the front camera positioned in the upper right corner.

5.3 Third Principle - Understandable

The understandable principle holds that the user must understand the content presented (W3C WAI 2018). Following this definition, the authors found the following aspects:

5.3.1 Consistent Layout/Consistent Navigation - Criterion 4.2 (WCAG 2.0) and Criterion 3.2.3 (WCAG 2.1)

Regarding the consistency of layouts, the authors observed that on the forum page, there is no consistency concerning the other pages, giving the impression that this section does not belong to the platform. This is due to the scarcity of the color palette, which is generally very present and the difference in the background color and aesthetic components characteristic of the Hominere app (Figure 4).

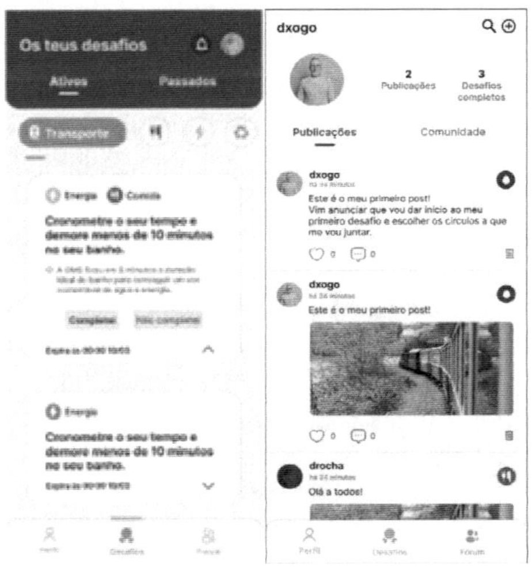

Figure 4. Challenge and forum pages

5.3.2 Error Identification - Criterion 3.3.1 (WCAG 2.1)

This criterion states that if an input error is automatically detected, the error element should be identified and described to the user in text. The authors have detected some problems with this criterion. On the registration page, users may enter invalid values, e.g., fake or incomplete cell phone numbers and e-mails that have not been correctly validated (e.g., aaa@aaa) without being informed of this. In this sense, false accounts can be created very quickly, which may not only impair the use of the application but also complicate accessibility for people with motor disabilities who may be mistaken in their credentials.

5.3.3 Positioning Essential Page Elements before the Page Scroll - Criterion 4.3 (WCAG 2.0)

Regarding the strategic positioning of essential page elements before the page scroll, the authors found that on the registration pages, the progress bar has an element that is at the top, and this is not the most relevant concerning the element that is next (question and options for setting the user profile and its forward button).

5.3.4 Provide a Clear Indication that Elements are Actionable - Criterion 4.4 (WCAG 2.0)

Another aspect at fault in the design is related to touchable elements. The app generally includes a box with rounded edges, a dark green background, and text or icons that are buttons. However, it is possible to see that there are other elements of quite similar structures, but they are not touchable. Furthermore, the aesthetics of the transport, food, energy, and recycle buttons (in a set) differ from the presented aesthetics of the symbols present within each publication, which could create difficulties concerning understanding and association.

5.4 Fourth Principle - Robust

Finally, the robustness principle translates that the content should be robust enough to be interpreted by various agents (W3C WAI 2018). In this respect, the authors found no inconsistencies.

5.5 Other Results

With the use of automated tools, it was possible to find other relevant aspects regarding accessibility and obtain results that meet the problems previously found in the guidelines.

5.5.1 Access Monitor Plus

The authors used the Access Monitor Plus tool for the automatic evaluation of the most relevant pages, and the scores (0-10 points) obtained are shown in Table 1.

Table 1. Scores obtained with the Access Monitor Plus tool

Page	Classification
Challenges	6,9
Profile	6,9
Forum	6,7
Notifications	6,3
Personal information	7,1

The authors still found some common errors among the pages regarding color contrast, as mentioned in the manual analysis through the guidelines. In this evaluation, several errors were found in the CSS file (e.g., with null alts) that do not meet the WCAG 2.1. This point strongly fails in the accessibility of the app since the alternative descriptive text to images decreases possible misinterpretations and improves the user experience.

5.5.2 WAVE – Web Accessibility Evaluation Tools

With the WAVE extension, the authors evaluated the developed project regarding the structure and organization of the code and visual accessibility with a focus on the contrast of the colors used. The page that reported more accessibility problems was the Forum, with one (1) error, three (3) alerts, forty-seven (47) contrast errors and a total of twenty-four (24) features without alternative text (Figure 5).

Using this tool, the authors found that the forum search bar does not have a corresponding label, which configures as an error, and that the color palette used by the Hominere app is not adequate, something that the authors had already concluded before.

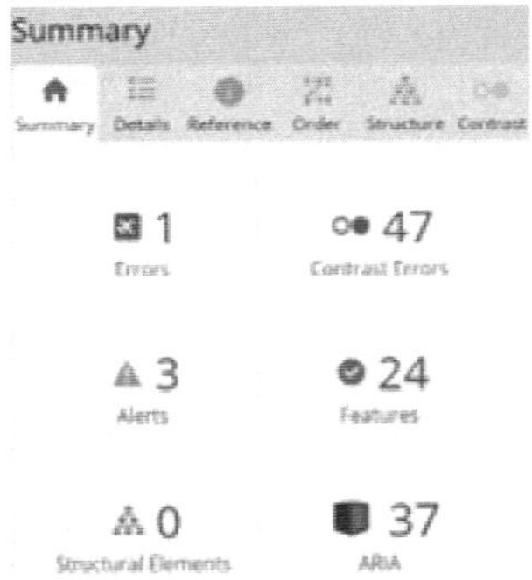

Figure 5. Results obtained on the Forum page using the WAVE extension

5.5.3 Accessibility Checker - PowerMapper

In general, the application did not present many problems when evaluated by the PowerMapper tool (Figure 6), presenting only two grave errors: in search - the application does not respect the Google, Bing and Yahoo guidelines, and in standards - there are validation flaws at the W3C HTML/XHTML level. However, it should be noted that since it is a Single Page Application (SPA), this type of tool cannot evaluate the entire application extension and only evaluates its homepage.

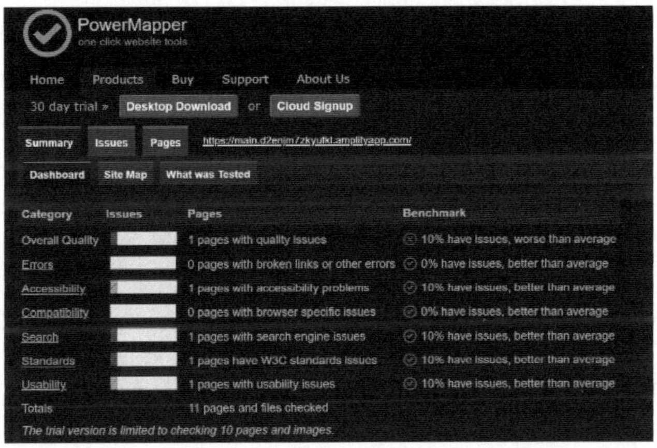

Figure 6. Overview of the PowerMapper evaluation results

5.5.4 TalkBack

To finish the results acquisition stage, the authors used the tool provided by Android mobile devices - TalkBack, to verify accessibility in a scenario where the user presents visual limitations. The evaluation process showed the need to improve several aspects since, in several situations, the user was confused about his progress and could not complete the tasks assigned to him without the help of a second person. Thus, the results revealed that using the Hominere app by people who need screen readers is practically impossible.

6. POSSIBLE SOLUTIONS

As it was possible to observe from the elaborated analysis, the authors identified several points that need to be improved to allow this app to have greater accessibility and a better user experience.

One of the possible strategic solutions to adopt would be to increase the button proportions. They generally present smaller sizes than is advisable, so increase their dimensions to 44px at least is mandatory. In buttons with essential functions, adding a background is also an option so that the element gains more prominence and a larger touch area. Finally, it is necessary to improve the positioning of some buttons and consider implementing them to allow left-handed people to use the application without any inconvenience since buttons are positioned for better access with the right hand.

The palette would need a revamp, as most of the colors failed the contrast test, and a definition to ensure consistency because several shades of green do not differ much from each other. In the Stark tool, it is possible to see some color suggestions within the same color spectrum, which would solve this problem.

Regarding the visual presentation of information, the application could include in the settings page an area dedicated to accessibility, where the user can customize the background and foreground colors. In addition, this accessibility area could include other options, namely text spacing, giving the user freedom to adjust it to their needs, as well as a night mode option.

The application also presented flaws regarding the comprehension principle. The authors used the design guidelines to assess the consistency of layouts/navigation to follow logic and coherence. For example, the main buttons should all have the same color scheme, or the background should have a constant color instead of varying between shades of white and beige. Besides helping the application's consistency, these guides would also solve the problem regarding touchable elements since all these elements would be designed in the same way or with similar logic (depending on the cases).

Regarding positioning the essential elements of the page before the scroll, the suggestion is to invert the order of the elements. The progress bar would be presented at the end of the page, ensuring that the relevant information appears first. As for positioning elements too close to the edges, it is only necessary to set fixed margin values. This way, there is no failure to display information because it is in a position that coincides with the physical elements of the device.

Regarding the null alternative texts, it is necessary to provide descriptive texts to the images that appear throughout the application so that all users can capture them in the best way and have the best experience that the Hominere app can give. This way, add the alt="[description]" field in the code referring to the images so that users have access to this information. In the case of the forum, it would be interesting to allow each user to define their descriptive text for the image post they have published. This is especially important for blind users, as they can hear the description through tools such as TalkBack and understand what images are on the pages and what they represent. However, images are not the only ones that need extra care for reading by the screen reader; buttons and text must be configured to read correctly.

Regarding search engines, the application has several flaws that violate Google Search, Bing Search and Yahoo Search guidelines, which can negatively affect its positioning in search results. One of the leading solutions to improve search engine accessibility would be offering users an HTML site map with links pointing to the critical parts of the site. Links embedded in menus, lists and similar elements are not accessible to search engines unless they are in the site map.

7. CONCLUSION

This study has shown that the selected accessibility strategy evaluation, combining manual evaluation of WCAG and using a mobile screen reader with automated evaluation through specific tools, is effective and appropriated and can be replicated in the accessibility evaluation of other mobile apps.

The mobile application Hominere presents accessibility problems beyond visualization and aesthetics, necessitating correctly structuring the code that composes it. Accessibility elements should be placed in all necessary parts to make it possible for a user with limitations to enjoy the platform without discomfort, which now is not possible, even using tools such as screen readers. However, without restructuring the color palette and the proportions of some elements, achieving a satisfactory result will not be possible either.

Among the study limitations, the authors can mention the time constraints, which did not allow testing the application with people with different types of disabilities. At the moment, the suggested improvements are being made. In the next stage, the application is expected to be tested with end users, including people with some disability/disability.

In conclusion, incorporating accessibility assessment into the development process of this application will allow the development authors to correct the shortcomings identified and create an accessible product for the most significant number of people. This study reinforces the importance of learning and applying accessibility guidelines in platform/mobile application development, which is crucial to create inclusive and accessible digital products that meet legal requirements and provide a better experience for all users. Nonetheless, evaluating and ensuring digital accessibility remains a significant challenge, and more research is needed to develop effective evaluation strategies. The authors believe that to associate a protocol of evaluation by users is the key to a more complete strategy, and that it will be this field of research that they will investigate in the future and take this study to a higher level.

ACKNOWLEDGEMENT

This work is financially supported by national funds through FCT – Foundation for Science and Technology, I.P., under the project UIDB/05460/2020.

REFERENCES

Ballantyne et al., 2018. Study of accessibility guidelines of mobile applications. *Proceedings of the 17th international conference on mobile and ubiquitous multimedia,* pp. 305-315.

Cao, S. and Loiacono, E., 2022. Perceptions of web accessibility guidelines by student website and app developers. *Behaviour & Information Technology*, Vol. 41, No. 12, pp. 2616-2634. https://doi.org/10.1080/0144929X.2021.1940278

Cooper, M., Kirkpatrick. A. and O Connor, J. 2016. *Understanding WCAG 2.0: A guide to understanding and implementing Web Content Accessibility Guidelines 2.0.* https://www.w3.org/TR/2016/NOTE-UNDERSTANDING-WCAG20-20161007/

Dias, J. et al., 2022. Automated Evaluation Tools for Web and Mobile Accessibility: A Systematic Literature Review. In et al. Innovations in Bio-Inspired Computing and Applications. IBICA 2021. *Lecture Notes in Networks and Systems*, vol 419. Springer, Cham. https://doi.org/10.1007/978-3-030-96299-9_43

Ismailova, R. and Inal, Y., 2018. Comparison of Online Accessibility Evaluation Tools: An Analysis of Tool Effectiveness. *IEEE Access*, vol. 10, pp. 58233-58239. https://doi.org/10.1109/ACCESS.2022.3179375

Kalbag, L., 2017. *Accessibility for Everyone*. A Book Apart: New York, New York. ISBN: 978-1-937557-62-1

Kearney-Volpe, C. and Hurst, A., 2021. Accessible web development: Opportunities to improve the education and practice of web development with a screen reader. *ACM Transactions on Accessible Computing (TACCESS),* Vol. 14, No. 2, pp. 1-32.

Nilsson, E., 2018. *Accessibility Evaluation of a Mobile Application UsingWCAG 2.0 - An Evaluation of the CREDENTIAL Project's.* Karlstad University. https://www.divaportal.org/smash/get/diva2:1241573/FULLTEXT02.pdf

Oliveira, R. et al., 2021. Accessibility Solutions for Visually Impaired Persons: A Digital Platform Conceptualization. In *Handbook of Research on Multidisciplinary Approaches to Entrepreneurship, Innovation, and ICTs* (pp. 331-348). IGI Global.

Rutter, R. et al., 2007. *Web accessibility: Web standards and regulatory compliance*. Apress.

Silva Neto, N. G. et al., 2021. Accessibility on mobile devices: an analysis from the perspective of human computer Interaction research in Brazil. *Brazilian Journal of Development*, Vol. 7, No. 4, pp. 34137-34150.

Slatin, J. and Rush, S., 2002. *Maximum Acessibility: Making you Web Site More Usable for Everyone*. Boston: Addison-Wesley.

Tymoshchuk, O. et al., 2021. Accessibility and microcopy remote testing of mobile applications: The case of the CeNTER platform. In *2021 16th Iberian Conference on Information Systems and Technologies (CISTI)* (pp. 1-6). IEEE.

Vieritz, H., Schilberg, D. and Jeschke, S., 2016. Early accessibility evaluation in web application development. *Engineering Education 4.0: Excellent Teaching and Learning in Engineering Sciences*, pp. 685-692.

W3C WAI, 2018. *Web Content Accessibility Guidelines (WCAG) 2.1.* Available at https://www.w3.org/TR/WCAG21/ (Accessed: 05 April 2023)

W3C WAI, 2021. *Mobile Accessibility at W3C.* Available at https://www.w3.org/WAI/standards-guidelines/mobile/ (Accessed: 05 April 2023)

PERSONALIZED AVATARS CREATION BASED ON REALISTIC 3D FACE RECONSTRUCTION

Yueming Ding and Pik Yin Mok*
School of Fashion and Textiles, The Hong Kong Polytechnic University, Hong Kong

ABSTRACT

Personalized 3D human avatars hold great potential in the digital era, and this also enables interesting fashion applications such as virtual try-on, virtual fashion shows, and immersive online shopping experiences. Nevertheless, personalized avatars are seldom used in the fashion industry due to the requirements of specialized equipment and the tedious and computationally demanding nature of traditional personalized face modeling processes. In this paper, a novel method is presented for creating personalized fashion avatars by reconstructing a realistic 3D face from a single image. The proposed method involves transferring customized 3D facial shape and appearance, reconstructed from a single face image, onto full-body avatars with varying topologies suitable for different fashion applications. Through a comprehensive comparison with state-of-the-art face reconstruction methods, the proposed method has demonstrated high realism and richer facial details. This technology has already been applied in an augmented reality (AR) mobile application, enabling users to engage in virtual try-on experience of fashion.

KEYWORDS

3D Reconstruction, Human Avatar, Virtual Try-on, 3DMM

1. INTRODUCTION

With the advancement of Internet and smart mobile devices, virtual reality technology soars in the fashion industry, with personalized fashion avatars playing a pivotal role in engaging applications, such as virtual trying-on (Meng et al., 2010), virtual fashion recommendation (Liu et al., 2014; Zhou et al., 2019), and immersive online shopping (Waltemate et al., 2018). According to Waltemate et al. (2018), personalization of avatar significantly increases self-identification and body ownership to the users (see Figure 1). Nevertheless, most virtual try-on systems do not have personalized avatars. One of the reasons is that personalized avatars require professional equipment, such as camera arrays, and large computing resources, resulting in high costs of customization. In recent years, 3D morphable model (3DMM) provides an economic solution to personalize human face and body shape by reconstruction methods. 3DMM is a type of statistical model of shape and texture learned from 3D scans by principal components analysis (PCA). It utilizes a set of parameters to generate a 3D shape or texture by linearly weighting the principal components. A number of studies use 3DMM to reconstruct personalized human body (Bogo et al., 2016; Loper et al., 2015; Pavlakos et al., 2019).

Another key reason impeding the widespread use of personalized avatars is the diverse model topology. The topology of face models varies in different applications or datasets, making it difficult to implement 3DMM reconstruction across different fashion applications. In this regard, some methods were proposed to combine morphable face model with human body model. For example, Fang et al. (2021) stitched Basel face model (BFM) (Blanz & Vetter, 1999) to their human avatars to realize personalized shape and texture in virtual try-on application. TF-Flame (Li et al., 2017) transferred the parametric texture model of BFM (Blanz & Vetter, 1999) to the texture uv-map of its full head model. However, these models are far from realistic, for example, the BFM model was learned from only 200 identities. The scarce of 3D dataset and the Gaussian nature of statistic model limited the presentation ability of the statistic texture model, which cannot satisfy requirements for personalized appearance and makeup (Liu et al., 2014). In this paper, a new method is proposed to transfer a customized facial shape and appearance reconstructed from single face images to full-body avatars of different topologies for fashion applications.

*Corresponding author: tracy.mok@polyu.edu.hk

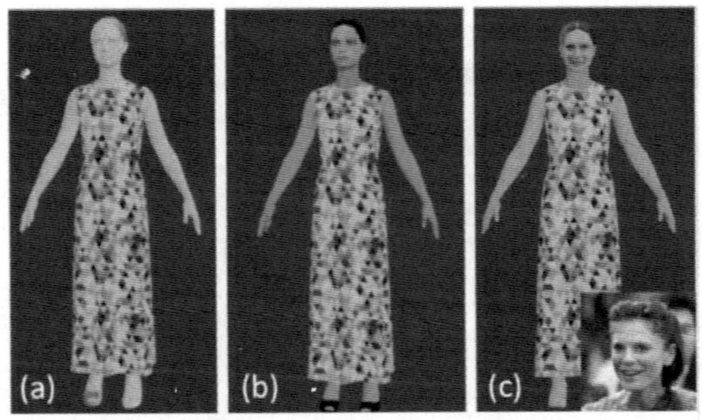

Figure 1. The try-on effect on (a) an avatar without texture, (b) an avatar without personalized texture, and (c) a personalized avatar

2. RELATED WORK

3D human body reconstruction: The research on 3D human reconstruction has mainly concentrated on reconstructing human poses and body shapes, with the face region often being neglected. For instance, in 3D human body reconstruction, a skinned multi-person linear model (SMPL) (Bogo et al., 2016; Loper et al., 2015) was put forward as a statistical full body animatable model to enable fast pose and shape reconstruction for computer games and animation applications. However, SMPL model only has coarse facial and body shape representation. Subsequently, Romero et al. (2022) and Pavlakos et al. (2019) augmented the hand and face model with additional joints and animation for SMPL. Joo et al. (2018) introduced a fusion model that merges the body from SMPL and head from the FaceWarehouse model (Cao et al., 2013) to acquire a comprehensive body model with more facial expression and animation. These models increased their amination ability, yet they still have limited shape and appearance.

3D face reconstruction: For 3D face reconstruction, 3DMM-based methods are widely employed using RGB-D data (Bao et al., 2021), single or multiple images (Bai et al., 2020). Blanz and Vetter (1999) proposed an analysis-by-synthesis reconstruction method using PCA-based face model. Nevertheless, PCA facial texture is often of low resolution and with limited expressions because of its Gaussian nature and small sample size. Feng et al. (2021) presented a self-supervised DECA method to reconstruct detailed head shape based on TF-FLAME model (Li et al., 2017) using in-the-wild images.

For virtual try-on of fashion products, avatars with personalized appearances are definitely beneficial. Considering the difficulty of reconstructing human avatars with highly individualized identities, Yuan et al. (2013) suggested a mixed reality virtual clothes try-on system, which combined the rendered reconstructed body model with the real face image of the user. Nonetheless, the result is not lifelike and presents inconsistent between the face and body. Some scholars proposed a pixel-aligned reconstruction of body with clothes from 2D images through deep neural networks in voxel space, such as PIFu (Saito et al., 2019) and PIFuHD (Saito et al., 2020). However, these voxel-based methods only can output low resolution models due to the high demands on storage and computing resources. In addition, these models do not have uniform topology, models reconstructed by PIFu are not animable and thus not suitable for fashion applications. Recently, for improving the personalization of human avatars in virtual try-on system, Fang et al. (2021) proposed a weak registration method to align a customized face model to a body model, similar to wearing a `mask'. This method can partly provide customized fashion avatar for virtual try-on system which only possess a generic human avatar. However, this method still has a few drawbacks, including distortion of the face model with noisy reference landmarks, only low resolution and less individual identities. In summary, a new method is needed for personalized fashion avatar creation that is ready for customized facial shape and appearance and adaptable to a full-body avatar with various topologies for plug-and-play fashion applications.

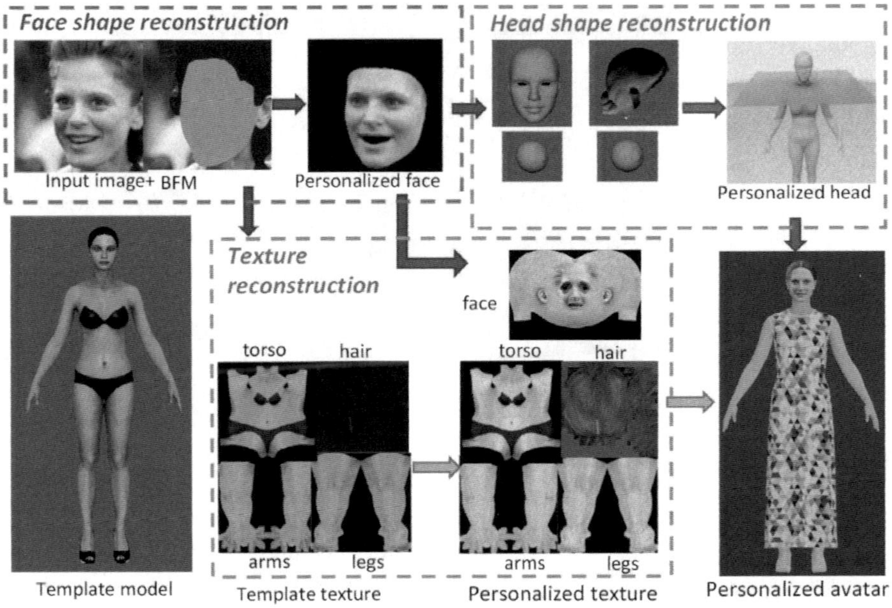

Figure 2. Overview of the personalized avatar reconstruction

3. METHOD

Figure 2 shows the outline of the proposed method for the creation of personalized fashion avatars based on realistic face reconstruction. The creation process of personalized fashion avatars includes four parts: (1) Reconstructing face shape based on input face image; (2) Transferring face shape to a full head model of any fashion avatar which can have varied topology; (3) Reconstructing face texture and aligning skin tone and color from face to full-body texture; (4) aligning and stitching the customized head model to body model.

3.1 Face Shape Reconstruction

3DMM In this work, we employ the Basel Face model (BFM), one of 3DMM face models in face reconstruction stage, to reconstruct the initial face shape and appearance. BFM generates a new 3D face shape $S_f \in R^{3N}$ or face texture $T_f \in R^{3N}$ of N mesh vertices by adding to a mean face shape S_{mean_f} or a mean face texture T_{mean_f} a linear combination of weight parameters α_{S_f}, α_{T_f} and principle parameters P_{S_f}, P_{T_f} respectively, which are formulated as following,

$$S_f = S_{mean_f} + \alpha_{S_f} \cdot P_{S_f}$$
$$T_f = T_{mean_f} + \alpha_{T_f} \cdot P_{T_f}. \quad (1)$$

Preprocessing: Prior to the personalized face reconstruction, face landmark detection and region segmentation are processed. Afterwards, the landmarks of the 3D head model must be estimated. This is because in most fashion avatars, facial landmarks are absent. Thus, the landmarks of the 3D head model must be estimated for following processes.

Landmarks detection. For aligning the face model to face image and initializing face reconstruction, it is necessary to detect facial landmarks from input face images. Because our work requires high accuracy of landmarks localization, we employ Dlib (Kazemi & Sullivan, 2014) to detect 68 points landmarks for this work.

Face segmentation. A face parsing network MaskGAN (Lee et al., 2020) pretrained on CelebAHQ dataset is then used to segment a face image into face skin region and hair region.

Landmarks estimation for 3D head mesh. Most 3D fashion avatars lack annotated facial, however landmarks are necessary for our subsequent processing, such as shape transfer and alignment. Therefore, we have to estimate 3D facial landmarks for any input fashion avatars. Compared to detect landmarks from 3D data directly, detecting landmarks from 2D images has more thoroughly explored. We take advantage of 2D landmark estimation to assist 3D landmark detection. To do so, we render the 3D avatar into an image and use 2D landmarks detector to back-project these landmarks to 3D mesh.

Reconstruction of face model: Reconstructing 3D face from face images through 3DMM can be decomposed into facial shape, texture and pose estimation. As discussed, BFM is employed to reconstruct 3D face from input face image, and orthogonal projection $P(\cdot)$ is assumed as our camera model. In face reconstruction, a 3D face mesh S_f is generated from an input image I first. Next, a face image I' is rendered from the generated face mesh S_f. The reconstruction of face can be considered as optimizing the μ parameters of 3DMM face model including shape α_{S_f} and texture parameters α_{T_f}, as well as the pose parameters $[R, t, s]$ consisting of rotation, translation and scaling factors.

$$\mu = \left[\alpha_{S_f}, \alpha_{T_f}, R, t, s\right] \tag{2}$$

The face reconstruction is optimized by minimizing the loss functions defined below.

Landmark loss measures the difference between the landmarks v^{lmk} of an input image I and the landmarks v'^{lmk} extracted from the rendered image I'

$$L_{lmk}(\mu) = \frac{1}{N_{lmk}} \sum_{k=1}^{N_{lmk}} \left\| v_i^{lmk} - P\left(v'^{lmk}_i\right) \right\|^2, \tag{3}$$

where $P(\cdot)$ represents the orthographic projection operation, v'^{lmk}_i is a landmark point i detected from the input image I, v_i^{lmk} is the corresponding landmark on the 3d face S_f, and N_{lmk} is the total number of detected landmark points.

Contour edge loss is used to fine-tune face shape reconstruction, since landmarks can only provide coarse shape information. Contour loss measures the distance between the points on the detected facial edges of the 2D image and the points on the projected occluding contours from the 3D face S_f, and is defined as follows,

$$L_{edge}(\mu) = \frac{1}{N_C} \sum_{j \in C} \left\| v_i^{cont} - P\left(v'^{edge}_i\right) \right\|^2, \tag{4}$$

where v_i^{cont} is vertex j on the occluding contour of the predicted 3D face model, $j \in C$ and C is the number of vertices on the contour. v'^{edge}_i denotes the pixel location on the detected occluding contours of the input image that is the closest to vertex j. The contour loss is mainly used to fine-tune the reconstructed 3D shape (Bas et al., 2016).

Photometric loss measures the pixel-wise RGB color distance between the input image I and the rendered image I' as follows,

$$L_{photo}(\mu) = \frac{1}{N_R} \sum_{(x,y) \in R} \left\| I_{(x,y)} - I'_{(x,y)} \right\|^2, \tag{5}$$

where the (x, y) represents a pixel in the face region R of an image, and N_R represents the number of pixels in face region, $I_{(x,y)}$ and $I'_{(x,y)}$ present the RGB value of a pixel on input image and the rendered image. This loss is mainly used in shape fine-tune and texture reconstruction.

The total loss function is defined as weighted landmark loss, edge loss and photometric loss as follows

$$L(\mu) = \omega_{lmk} \cdot L_{lmk}(\mu) + \omega_{edge} \cdot L_{edge}(\mu) + \omega_{photo} \cdot L_{photo}(\mu). \tag{6}$$

3.2 Head Shape Reconstruction Based on Face Model

Transfer face shape to head model: We use PCA parameters and linear least squares method to transfer the face shape of S_f to an arbitrary head model S_h. First of all, we random the face shape parameters of S_f and use nonrigid ICP (NICP) method (Amberg et al., 2007) to generate paired synthetic head shape data. Then, the PCA method is used to generate principal components of the head model. The head shape model is defined as:

$$S_h = S_{mean_h} + \alpha_{S_h} \cdot P_{S_h} \tag{7}$$

where S_{mean_h} is the mean head shape and α_{S_h} denotes the parameters of the head principal components P_{S_h}. We mainly consider shape and texture reconstructions by setting the expression parameters of the face model to zero. Transferring face shape S_f of eq. ($\begin{matrix} S_f = S_{mean_f} + \alpha_{S_f} \cdot P_{S_f} \\ T_f = T_{mean_f} + \alpha_{T_f} \cdot P_{T_f} \end{matrix}$ (1) to head model S_h of eq. ($S_h = S_{mean_h} + \alpha_{S_h} \cdot P_{S_h}$ (7) can be considered as a regression problem. After shape registration of face and head models, the head and face shape parameters are represented as matrices $C_h \in R^{n_h \times r}$ and $C_f \in R^{n_f \times r}$, respectively. The face-to-head transformation is solved as a regression matrix (Ploumpis et al., 2020),

$$T_{h,f} = C_h C_f^T C_f C_f^{T-1}, \tag{8}$$

where the $C_f^T C_f C_f^{T-1}$ is the pseudo-inverse of C_f. By solving the regression matrix, the head shape parameters can be calculated by

$$P_{S_h} = T_{h,f} P_{S_f}. \tag{9}$$

Reconstruction of complete 3D full head model: In most 3D full-head models, eyeballs and hairs are usually isolated models in addition to the head shape model (Figure **2**). These models are transformed according to the customized head shape model. To do so, the joint of the head is considered as the point of origin, and the center coordinates $v_{c\{\cdot\}}$ of each eyeball and hair model in the template are transferred to the head local coordinates. When adjusting the size of the isolated models, the scale factors are calculated in three directions by proportion, considering the reference points $v_{i,j} \in \varphi$ estimated head model and $v_{i_0,j_0} \in \varphi_{ori}$ template. Landmarks of eyes $\varphi_{\{eyes\}}$ and vertices on bounding box of cranium $\varphi_{\{hair\}}$ are used as reference points, the isolated scale factors for eyes and hair are formulated as,

$$H_{x,y,z\{eyes,hair\}} = \frac{\left\| \max_{i,j \in \varphi_{\{eyes,hair\}}} v_{i(x,y,z)} - v_{j(x,y,z)} \right\|}{\left\| \max_{i_0,j_0 \in \varphi_{\{eyes,hair\}}} v_{i0(x,y,z)} - v_{j0(x,y,z)} \right\|}. \tag{10}$$

To adjust model location, landmarks as well as the center of the bounding box of hair model are used to compute the translation and rotation matrix,

$$t_{\{eyes,hair\}} = \left[v_{C\{eyes,hair\}} - v_{C0\{eyes,hair\}} \right]^T. \tag{11}$$

The transformation of isolated models is calculated as,

$$M_{eyes,hair} = \begin{bmatrix} H_x & 0 & 0 \\ 0 & H_y & 0 \\ 0 & 0 & H_z \end{bmatrix} R\left(\begin{bmatrix} v_x \\ v_y \\ v_z \end{bmatrix} \right) + t_{eyes,hair}. \tag{12}$$

3.3 Texture reconstruction

The third step of the fashion avatar customization pipeline is texture reconstruction, which covers face texture and body model texture. Parametric face models usually have low resolution texture information. To improve this, we combine the texture sampled from input face images with the reconstructed BFM albedo map as supplement in face texture reconstruction (see Figure 2). The reconstructed head mesh can be unwrapped into UV-space using the cylinder unwarp, then the texture of BFM can be mapped to UV-space through barycentric coordinates. We obtain a face segmentation result from the input face image using MaskGAN, a pretrained face parsing model (Lee et al., 2020). The combination of sampled texture and BFM texture is processed through a segmentation mask with a gaussian kernel with 30-pixel radius.

The paper also presents a method to customize the texture of body and hair by using the color features extracted from face skin and hair as reference. For hair reconstruction, because hair reconstruction is complicated and time-consuming, we mainly focus on hair color reconstruction. In terms of body texture, the skin color is the main attribute for human body texture. Thus, in this process, we first extract color features from the skin and hair segmentation of face image, and color features from template body textures and hair textures. Then, we transfer these features on CIELAB color space. These textures transformation allows a more realistic representation of the hair and full-body skin color of the user in practice (see Figure **2**).

3.4 Align and Stitch Head to Fashion Avatar

Previous research on reconstructing personalized fashion avatars proposed to replace the face part of a full body avatar with a 3DMM face model through cutting and stitching. For example, Fang et al. (2021) used the Bezier curve to stitch the BFM face model with the head of fashion avatar. Unfortunately, this will lead to the compression and distortion of the face model along the depth direction due to the degradation of depth information and inaccurate landmarks. Moreover, the texture of the mesh model in the stitching regions is not smooth and consistent.

In this work, the head is separated from the fashion avatar by cutting along the plane on the neck. After the personalized head is reconstructed, the rigid transformation matrix is calculated using the estimated landmarks, and the head is aligned to the fashion body using rigid transformation. The personalized head is then stitched to the fashion body along the boundary point set.

4. EXPERIMENTS AND RESULT DISCUSSION

Experiments were conducted on a PC with Intel i7 CPU and NVIDIA Titan GPU, and the programming environment is python. We use the differentiable rendered of Pytorch3D to render the reconstructed model.

Dataset: The CelebA dataset (Liu et al., 2015) was used as a face image dataset for simulating application scenarios in our experiment. This dataset contains 10,177 identities and 202,599 face images. The BFM (Blanz & Vetter, 1999) with 35709 vertices was used to reconstruct 3D faces from images. For full-body avatar customization, we used a template body model with 40763 vertices, in which the head region contains 8187 vertices and has different topology than the BFM. In fact, an arbitrary body model can be used in the proposed method.

Face only comparison: For face only customization, the analysis-by-synthesis method from BFM was used as baseline for comparison with the proposed method, and we also compare to other state-of-art methods, including DECA method (Feng et al., 2021) and weak-registration algorithm (Fang et al., 2021).

Quantitative analysis: We use perceptual similarity (Kim et al., 2021) to evaluate the effectiveness of different face reconstruction methods. Perceptual similarity is a metric using the cosine similarity of embedding features extracted from VGGface (Parkhi et al., 2015), a pretrained face recognition model. We conducted experiment on a subset of CelebA dataset (Liu et al., 2015). The results in Table 1 indicate that our method has the lowest mean cosine distance between the reconstructed personal face images with the inputs, compared to other state-of-the-art methods.

Metric. VGGface (Parkhi et al., 2015) is a deep learning facial recognition model developed by the Visual Geometry Group (VGG) at Oxford University. It uses a convolutional neural network (CNN) to extract features from a face image and then compares them to a reference image to measure the perceptual similarity. The cosine distance is used to measure the similarity among the VGGFace-features $F(\cdot)$ extracted from ground true image I and images I' synthesized from different methods, which is formulated as,

$$Cosine\ similarity(I, I') = \frac{F(I)\cdot F(I')}{\|F(I)\|\times\|F(I')\|}. \tag{13}$$

Table 1. Quantitative analysis by perceptual similarity

	BFM (Blanz & Vetter, 1999)	DECA (Feng et al., 2021)	Weak-rigid registration (Fang et al., 2021)	Our method
Subset of CelebA (Liu et al., 2015)	0.57±0.01	0.39±0.12	0.59±0.16	0.37±0.10

Qualitative analysis: The qualitative comparison is shown Figure **3**. As shown, the texture from the method based on BFM has less details, such as in the eyes, and has low resolution due to the nature of PCA-based texture models. This can lead to low self-identity of the facial representations. The DECA model (Feng et al., 2021) realized full head reconstruction based on TF-FLAME morphable face model but without complicated texture. The coarse version of this model can realize head shape reconstruction with sampled texture. The reconstructions resulting from the weak-registration algorithm proposed by Fang et al. (2021) are depicted in column (d). This method enables the fusion of the BFM results with a coarse head model. However, the face model is twisted in the z-axis during the registration process, resulting in an inconsistency between the face and head regions. In addition, the texture is based on BFM model, suffering from the same limitation of BFM. The reconstructions of the proposed method are shown in column (e) of Figure **3**. As shown, our reconstruction results possess high self-identity comparing to BFM, and the connection between face and head is smoother than that of .Fang et al. (2021). In sum, the proposed method has better face reconstruction shape and appearance and is suitable for fashion avatar personalization.

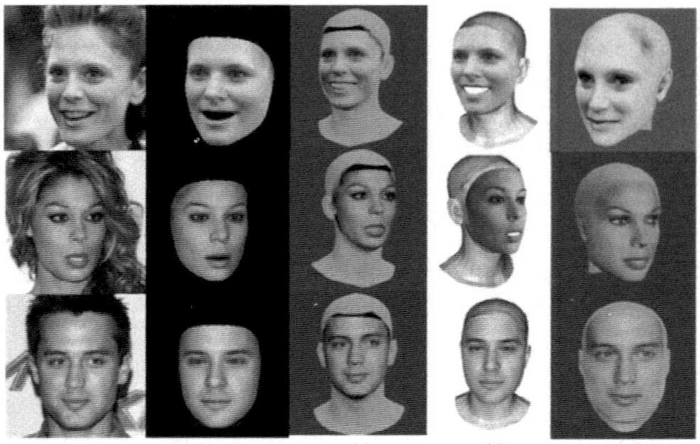

(a) (b) (c) (d) (e)

Figure 3. Comparison with different face reconstruction methods: (a) input images, (b)results by methods of BFM (Blanz & Vetter, 1999), (c) DECA (Feng et al., 2021), (d) Weak-rigid registration (Fang et al., 2021) and (e) ours

Personalized avatar comparison: For personalized full-body avatar, we only conducted qualitative evaluation in comparison to other methods including SMPL-X (Pavlakos et al., 2019) and weak-rigid registration method (Fang et al., 2021). As illustrated in Figure **4**, SMPL-X can reconstruct human models from single images with limited facial details and without full-body texture. The weak-registration method can reconstruct personalized human model; however, the resulting face is twisted and the texture of the face and body are inconsistent. In contrast, our method can reconstruct personalized human avatars with more details and consistent texture and shape. More examples are given in Figure **5**, demonstrating that the proposed method can create avatars with different skin colors and facial shapes. We have applied this personalized avatar reconstruction method to a mobile AR app, and a video is shown in the supplementary information.

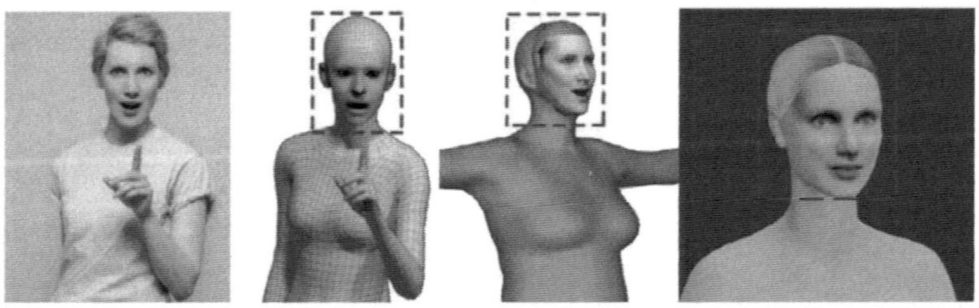

(a) (b) (c) (d)

Figure 4. Comparison with different full-body model customization methods: (a) input image, results of methods by (b) SMPL-X (Pavlakos et al., 2019), (c) weak-registration(Pavlakos et al., 2019), and (d) ours

5. CONCLUSION

This paper develops a new reconstruction method for personalizing fashion avatars that can be used on different platforms, of which avatars have different topology and texture, for virtual try-on application. Compared with pure 3DMM-based human personalization methods, our personalization method for human model personalization can be used on models of arbitrary topology. In addition, this method can also reconstruct facial appearance with higher resolutions and self-identity. When comparing with the method which replace face mesh with rigid registration, our method not only presents high self-identity on face appearance, but also presents consistence on texture and shape. The current method has a few limitations, for instance it only reconstructs static model and the performance will be affected if the avatar has a head mesh with extreme sparse vertices. In the future, we will extend this method to avatars with animation and personalized hair shape. On the other hand, we will try to extend this method to avatars with poor mesh conditions.

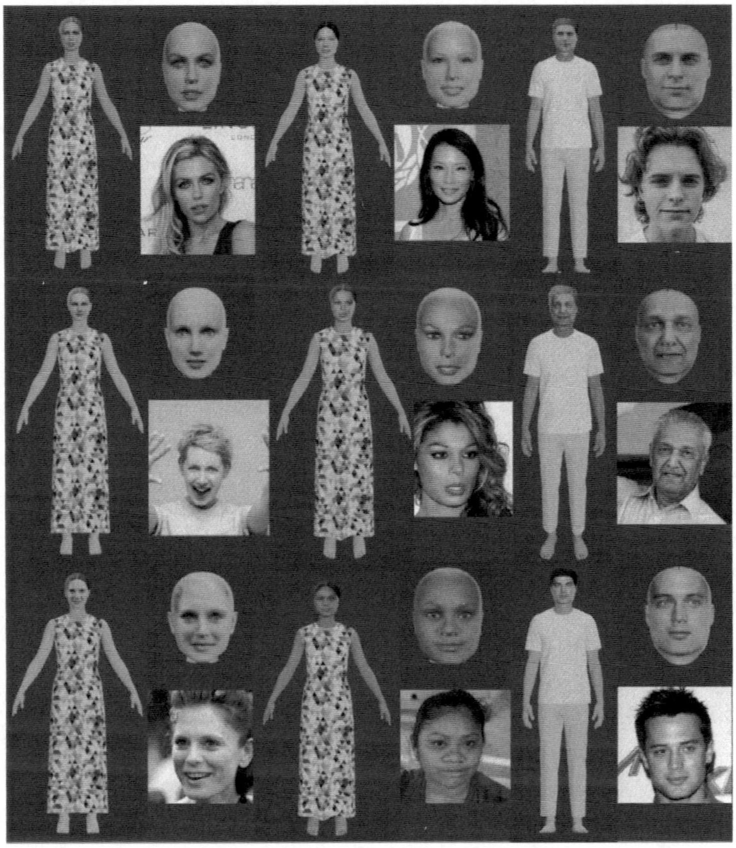

Figure 5. Personalized avatar in try-on application

ACKNOWLEDGEMENT

The work described in this paper was supported by a grant from the Research Grants Council of the Hong Kong Special Administrative Region, China (Grant Number 152112/19E).

REFERENCES

Amberg, B., Romdhani, S., & Vetter, T. (2007). Optimal step nonrigid ICP algorithms for surface registration. 2007 IEEE conference on computer vision and pattern recognition.

Bai, Z., Cui, Z., Rahim, J. A., Liu, X., & Tan, P. (2020). Deep facial non-rigid multi-view stereo. Proceedings of the ieee/cvf conference on computer vision and pattern recognition.

Bao, L., Lin, X., Chen, Y., Zhang, H., Wang, S., Zhe, X., Kang, D., Huang, H., Jiang, X., & Wang, J. (2021). High-Fidelity 3D Digital Human Head Creation from RGB-D Selfies. ACM Transactions on Graphics (TOG), 41(1), 1-21.

Bas, A., Smith, W. A., Bolkart, T., & Wuhrer, S. (2016). Fitting a 3D morphable model to edges: A comparison between hard and soft correspondences. Asian Conference on Computer Vision.

Blanz, V., & Vetter, T. (1999). A morphable model for the synthesis of 3D faces. Proceedings of the 26th annual conference on Computer graphics and interactive techniques.

Bogo, F., Kanazawa, A., Lassner, C., Gehler, P., Romero, J., & Black, M. J. (2016). Keep it SMPL: Automatic estimation of 3D human pose and shape from a single image. Computer Vision–ECCV 2016: 14th European Conference, Amsterdam, The Netherlands, October 11-14, 2016, Proceedings, Part V 14.

Cao, C., Weng, Y., Zhou, S., Tong, Y., & Zhou, K. (2013). Facewarehouse: A 3d facial expression database for visual computing. IEEE transactions on visualization and computer graphics, 20(3), 413-425.

Fang, N., Qiu, L., Zhang, S., Wang, Z., Wang, Y., Gu, Y., & Tan, J. (2021). A Modeling Method for the Human Body Model with Facial Morphology. Computer-Aided Design, 141, 103106.

Feng, Y., Feng, H., Black, M. J., & Bolkart, T. (2021). Learning an animatable detailed 3D face model from in-the-wild images. ACM Transactions on Graphics (TOG), 40(4), 1-13.

Joo, H., Simon, T., & Sheikh, Y. (2018). Total capture: A 3d deformation model for tracking faces, hands, and bodies. Proceedings of the IEEE conference on computer vision and pattern recognition.

Kazemi, V., & Sullivan, J. (2014). One millisecond face alignment with an ensemble of regression trees. Proceedings of the IEEE conference on computer vision and pattern recognition.

Kim, J., Yang, J., & Tong, X. (2021). Learning high-fidelity face texture completion without complete face texture. Proceedings of the IEEE/CVF International Conference on Computer Vision.

Lee, C.-H., Liu, Z., Wu, L., & Luo, P. (2020). Maskgan: Towards diverse and interactive facial image manipulation. Proceedings of the IEEE/CVF Conference on Computer Vision and Pattern Recognition.

Li, T., Bolkart, T., Black, M. J., Li, H., & Romero, J. (2017). Learning a model of facial shape and expression from 4D scans. ACM Trans. Graph., 36(6), 194:191-194:117.

Liu, L., Xing, J., Liu, S., Xu, H., Zhou, X., & Yan, S. (2014). Wow! you are so beautiful today! ACM Transactions on Multimedia Computing, Communications, and Applications (TOMM), 11(1s), 1-22.

Liu, Z., Luo, P., Wang, X., & Tang, X. (2015). Deep learning face attributes in the wild. Proceedings of the IEEE international conference on computer vision.

Loper, M., Mahmood, N., Romero, J., Pons-Moll, G., & Black, M. J. (2015). SMPL: A skinned multi-person linear model. ACM Transactions on Graphics (TOG), 34(6), 1-16.

Meng, Y., Mok, P. Y., & Jin, X. (2010). Interactive virtual try-on clothing design systems. Computer-Aided Design, 42(4), 310-321.

Parkhi, O. M., Vedaldi, A., & Zisserman, A. (2015). Deep face recognition.

Pavlakos, G., Choutas, V., Ghorbani, N., Bolkart, T., Osman, A. A., Tzionas, D., & Black, M. J. (2019). Expressive body capture: 3d hands, face, and body from a single image. Proceedings of the IEEE/CVF Conference on Computer Vision and Pattern Recognition.

Ploumpis, S., Ververas, E., O'Sullivan, E., Moschoglou, S., Wang, H., Pears, N., Smith, W. A., Gecer, B., & Zafeiriou, S. (2020). Towards a complete 3D morphable model of the human head. IEEE transactions on pattern analysis and machine intelligence, 43(11), 4142-4160.

Romero, J., Tzionas, D., & Black, M. J. (2022). Embodied hands: Modeling and capturing hands and bodies together. arXiv preprint arXiv:2201.02610.

Saito, S., Huang, Z., Natsume, R., Morishima, S., Kanazawa, A., & Li, H. (2019). Pifu: Pixel-aligned implicit function for high-resolution clothed human digitization. Proceedings of the IEEE/CVF international conference on computer vision.

Saito, S., Simon, T., Saragih, J., & Joo, H. (2020). Pifuhd: Multi-level pixel-aligned implicit function for high-resolution 3d human digitization. Proceedings of the IEEE/CVF Conference on Computer Vision and Pattern Recognition.

Waltemate, T., Gall, D., Roth, D., Botsch, M., & Latoschik, M. E. (2018). The impact of avatar personalization and immersion on virtual body ownership, presence, and emotional response. IEEE transactions on visualization and computer graphics, 24(4), 1643-1652.

Yuan, M., Khan, I. R., Farbiz, F., Yao, S., Niswar, A., & Foo, M.-H. (2013). A mixed reality virtual clothes try-on system. IEEE Transactions on Multimedia, 15(8), 1958-1968.

Zhou, W., Mok, P., Zhou, Y., Zhou, Y., Shen, J., Qu, Q., & Chau, K. (2019). Fashion recommendations through cross-media information retrieval. Journal of Visual Communication and Image Representation, 61, 112-120.

STREAMLINE TRACING VISUALIZATION OF FLOW ON SURFACES

Fukun Wu[1,2], Yi Cao[2] and Qingli Dong[1,2]
[1]*CAEP Software Center for High Performance Numerical Simulation, Beijing, China*
[2]*Institute of Applied Physics and Computational Mathematics, Beijing, China*

ABSTRACT

To address the visualization problem of surface streamline on complex curved surfaces, we present and implement an efficient surface streamline generation method for visualizing vector field on arbitrary geometry. The intersection calculation on curved surfaces with complex topology is performed to achieve the high-precision underlying vector. Then, this approach adopts an extended Runge-Kutta streamline integration technology for performing streamline tracing on an unstructured mesh, where the adaptive stepsize strategy and intersection acceleration structure are presented for sake of simplicity and efficiency. Finally, this approach is integrated into a visualization software to enhance the visualizing capability. The experimental results demonstrate that our approach can efficiently and accurately generate continuous and consistent geometric surface streamlines on curved surfaces.

KEYWORDS

Surface Streamline, Intersection Calculation, Extended Runge-Kutta, Adaptive Stepsize Strategy

1. INTRODUCTION

The analysis of flow on polyhedral surfaces is of particular importance for design and optimization of complex geometry in computational fluid dynamics, which plays a key role in visual analysis of electromagnetic shielding effects, surface cur-rents on electronic equipment and flow characteristics inside engine combustion chambers from physical sciences and engineering.

A significant body of research is dedicated to vector field visualization such as LIC (Battke et al. 1997, Cabral and Leedom 1993, Mao et al. 1997), ISA (Laramee et al. 2003), or IBFVS (van Wijk, 2003), in order to support exploration of flow on large and unstructured polygonal meshes. Although texture-like representations allow to in-crease the spatial resolution and to depict small details accurately, it is challenging to visualize the flow feature on CAD models for engineering designer. Covering an image with a set of evenly spaced streamlines is a good way to visualize the flow features. However, image quality enhancement need be achieved by using streamline placement algorithms which optimize the placement of a set of streamlines according to an image-based criterion. In other words, these methods can generate sparse or dense representations of vector fields. However, the generation and advection of texture properties in object space is finally projected to image space.

Directly performing streamline tracing on 3D curved surfaces is interesting due to their visual intuitiveness from the view of designer. The work on streamline tracing visualization has been concentrated on Runge-Kutta integration methods which cannot adapt to the constraints of complex geometric surfaces due to the intrinsic properties. It is difficult to generate the continuous and consistent streamline on curved surfaces with the challenge of the robust intersection testing and numerically stable methods. Polthier and Schmies (Polthier and Schmies 2006) introduced straightest geodesics in geometry to solve the initial value problem for geodesics on polyhedral surface. However, their algorithm only uses intrinsic geometric properties of the polyhedral surfaces, not considering underlying discrete triangulation of surfaces in vector field.

This paper proposes an efficient streamline generation algorithm for the analysis of flow on curve surfaces. Different from previous work, we introduce the high precision polygon intersection and interpolation algorithms to achieve vector field extraction on surfaces with complex topology which keep the underlying detail of geometric surfaces in vector field. Then, we present surface streamline integration technology to perform streamline tracing on unstructured mesh where the fourth-order Runge-Kutta integrator is extended to 2D surfaces.

2. RELATED WORK

Visualizing vector fields defined on curved surfaces or manifolds is of particular im-portance for engineering designer in computational fluid dynamics and has received comparatively much attention. Due to the complex topology of CAD geometries with holes and discontinuities, to use a technique based on surface parametrization would be especially difficult. The research on the visualization of vector fields defined on surfaces focuses on texture-based approaches (Laramee 2004, Stalling and Hege 1997, Li et al. 2008). In the early 1990s, Spot Noise (van Wijk 1991) and LIC (Cabral and Leedom 1993, Forssell and Cohen 1995) were presented to generate dense representations based on textures which are limited to curvilinear surface in 2D. An extension of LIC for arbitrary surfaces in 3D were proposed by Mao et al. (Mao et al. 1997) where the convolution of noise image with filter kernels are performed only at visible ray-surface intersections. See Stalling et al. (Stalling and Hege 1997) for more comprehensive overviews of LIC techniques applied to surfaces. In order to overcome computation time hurdle introduced by LIC, two representative approaches, ISA (Laramee et al. 2004) and IBFVS (van Wijk 2003), were proposed to generate dense representation of flow on complex surfaces at fast frame rates. Although texture properties are advected on boundary surfaces in 3D, they essentially realized texture advection in image space in 2D by projecting the surface geometry and its associated vector field to image space and then applying texturing.

Covering an image with a set of streamlines is also a good way to visualize the flow features. A significant body of research is dedicated to using image-based approach to generating streamlines with different streamline seeding strategies for vector fields defined on curved surfaces (Li and Shen 2007, Mattausch et al. 2003, McLoughlin 2010, Spencer et al. 2009, Verma et al. 2000, Ye et al. 2005). These methods can generate sparse or dense representations of vector fields, and image quality enhancement can be achieved by using streamline placement algorithms based on an image criterion. However, the generation and advection of texture properties is still confined to image space.

It is interesting for engineering designer to use geometric streamline approach due to their visual intuitiveness. This can help them analyze the flow feature of arbitrary positions on curved surfaces in order to aid the design of computational fluid dynamics models. However, it is very difficult to perform streamline tracing on an unstructured mesh with the challenge of the robust intersection testing and numerically stable methods of handing special cases (Reshetnyak 1989). Geodesic curves in geometry solve the initial value problem on polyhedral surfaces on smooth surfaces and play a key role to streamline generation (Polthier and Schmies 2006, Spencer et al., Alexander and Bishop 1996). For instance, Polthier and Schmies presented an efficient straightest geodesics method to generate streamlines on polyhedral surface and arbitrary manifolds, which allows to move uniquely on a polyhedral surface in a given direction along a straightest geodesic. Their work only uses geometric properties of the polyhedral surface and not considers the underlying discrete triangulation of the surface. Inspired by their work, we achieve the highly detailed underlying vector by surface extraction and present a novel and conceptually simple method of generating streamlines on curve surfaces.

3. ALGORITHM

The streamline generation algorithm proposed in this paper is applied to vector fields defined on complex curved surfaces. The key to performing streamline tracing is to accurately calculate the integral value of the streamline on curved surfaces.

3.1 Surface Extraction

From the view of engineering designer in computation fluid dynamics, the surface streamline generation algorithm is essentially different from the traditional image-based streamline visualization algorithms

(Laramee et al. 2004, Spencer et al. 2009). It is limited by the geometry model with high-order, discontinuous and multi-scale characteristics, and requires the high-precision acquisition of the vector field on the geometric surface. Here, our algorithm extends the previous polygon clipping approaches presented by Greiner (Greiner and Hormann 1998) and Vatti (Vatti 1992) to 3D curved surfaces to achieve the high-precision surface extraction which keep the underlying detailed structures of geometric surface on vector field.

Considering the fact that vector field may be composed of structured or unstructured grids, this paper applies the grid-related interpolation algorithms to calculate the vector field on extracted surfaces. For unstructured grids, we adopt the trilinear interpolation method to calculate the vector on arbitrary point on curved surfaces. For structured grids, domain-related interpolation methods are applied.

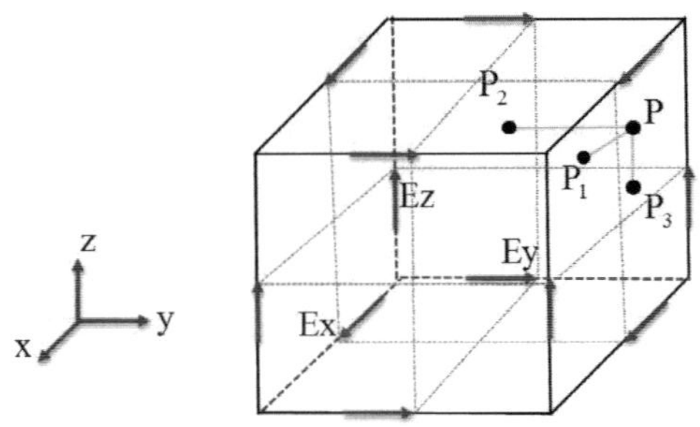

Figure 1. Geometric structure of vector field E defined on the hexahedral cell

Figure 1 shows an example of the structured grid generated by the numerical solver. The physical quantity E in vector field is registered as the center of the grid cell, but the components of the vector E are located at the edge center of the grid cell. In order to calculate the vector value of any node P on the complex geometric surface, three reference planes, as shown in the area enclosed by the three groups of green dashed lines in Figure 2, are introduced for vector field defined on structured grids. The projection points of the point P on the three reference planes are P_1, P_2, and P_3 respectively. P_1 is used to calculate the x-axis component Ex of the vector field E associated with P. P_2 and P_3 are used to calculate y-axis component Ey and z-axis component Ez respectively.

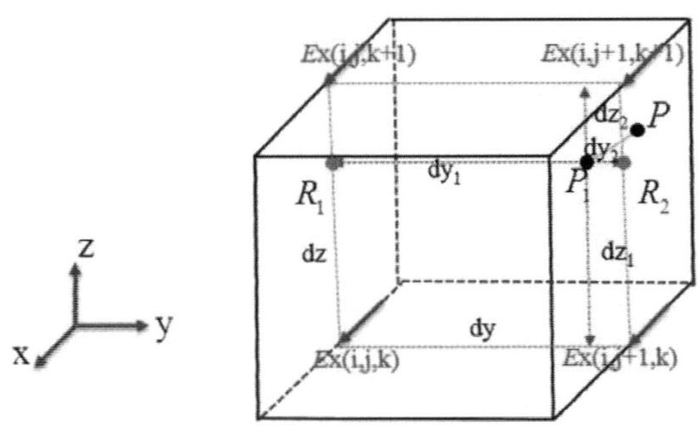

Figure 2. Geometric structure of vector field E defined on the hexahedral cell

Figure 2 shows the example of calculating the projection point P_1, and the complete linear interpolation formula is:

$$Ex(P_1) = \frac{dy_1}{dy} * Ex_{R_1} + \frac{dy_2}{dy} * Ex_{R_2} \tag{1}$$

where,

$$Ex_{R_1} = \frac{dz_1}{dz} * Ex(i,j,k) + \frac{dz_2}{dz} * Ex(i,j,k+1)$$
$$Ex_{R_2} = \frac{dz_1}{dz} * Ex(i,j{+}1,k) + \frac{dz_2}{dz} * Ex(i,j{+}1,k+1) \quad (2)$$

Substituting the Ex_{R_1} and Ex_{R_2} in Equation 2 into Equation 1 can obtain the component of $Ex(P_1)$. $Ey(P_2)$ and $Ez(P_3)$ can be obtained in the same way.

3.2 Surface Streamline Generation

Through extracting vector field using curved surfaces, we can obtain a high precision surface vector field which provides the pre-processing data for streamline generation. Then, according to the initial seed point specified interactively by engineering designer, a streamline moving along the geometric surface needs to be generated. However, due to the limitation from the complex curved surfaces, the classical Runge-Kutta integrators is no longer valid. Focusing on this central challenge, this paper adopts a new and extended Runge-Kutta method based on surface projection for integration calculation, with the aid of an adaptive stepsize strategy and streamline-surface intersection acceleration structure, to accomplish the continuous and consistent surface streamline generation.

3.2.1 Runge-Kutta Integral

The core idea of the surface streamline generation algorithm is to track and calculate the motion trajectory of these seed points on curved surfaces in vector field. The trajectory is a curve, namely, a streamline. For each streamline $x(t)$, its motion equation satisfies:

$$\frac{dx_t}{dt} = V(t,x) \quad (3)$$

Where $V(t, x)$ is the value of vector field at the position $x(t)$, and for the static field, $V(t, x) = V(x)$.

Considering the case that surface streamlines are constrained by geometric shapes, this paper defines an extended Runge-Kutta streamline integral formula as

$$x(t+h) = x(t) + (Proj_{\Omega}(\int_t^{t+h} V(t,x)dt)) \quad (4)$$

Where Ω represents the geometric surface and ProjΩ represents the projection of the integral formula on the geometric surface. The choice of h is more important. If h is too small, the calculation overhead will be too large. If h is too large, it will bring greater errors and reduce the accuracy of streamline generation.

For generating continuous surface streamline in vector field, we need to iteratively calculate the points of the streamline according to the Equation 4, and finally obtain a complete streamline that can show the move status of flow field. We adopt the fourth-order Runge-Kutta method used for concrete calculation. This method is used as the basis of solving the derivative and initial values in differential equations. Specifically, the next step value x_{i+1} of the streamline is determined by the current value x_i plus the projection on the surface of the product of the step interval h and an estimated slope, formulated by

$$x_{i+1} = x_i + Proj_{\Omega}(h(K_1 + 2K_2 + 2K_3 + K_4)/6) \quad (5)$$

Where

$$
\begin{aligned}
&K(1)=V(t_i,x_i)\\
&K(2)=V(t_i+\frac{h}{2},x_i+\frac{hK_1}{2})\\
&K(3)=V(t_i+\frac{h}{2},x_i+\frac{hK_2}{2})\\
&K(4)=V(t_i+h,x_i+hK_3)
\end{aligned}
\tag{6}
$$

3.2.2 Stepsize Adaptive Adjustment

When iteratively performing streamline integration, the stepsize is comprehensively weighed according to the calculation accuracy and efficiency, and it has a decisive influence on the local error. When using a fixed step size, the complexity of the projection calculation becomes a time-consuming problem. As shown in Figure 3, s_1, s_2, and s_3 represent three polygonal cells on the geometric surface, and p_1, p_2, and p_3 represent the projection points of streamline integration on surface. The structural diversity of curved surfaces increase the complexity of generating surface streamlines after projection.

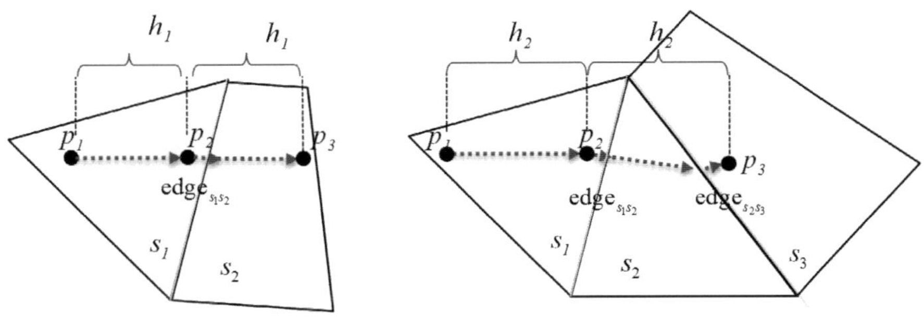

Figure 3. A Surface projection under two types of integration with fixed steps h1 (left) and h2(right)

For solving this problem, we construct an adaptive stepsize method based on the grid size and shape to calculate and generate surface streamline as shown in Figure 4.

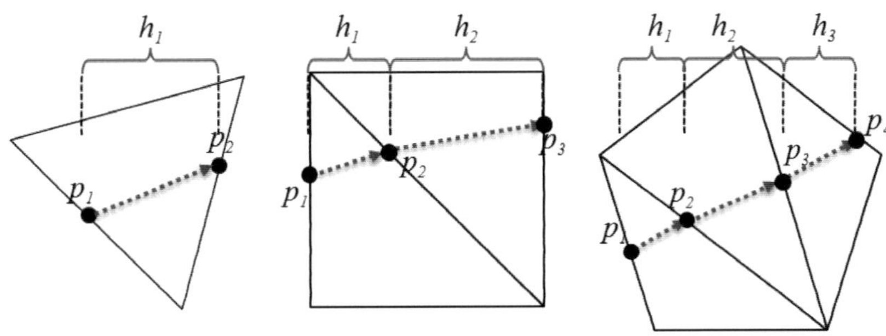

Figure 4. A Surface projection under two types of integration with fixed steps h_1 (left) and h_2(right)

According to the type of polygon cells on curved surface, different stepsizes are processed during surface integration. For a triangle, the integral projection directly crosses the internal field of the triangle, and the step length is only h_1. The quadrilateral or pentagon is triangulated separately to form two step sets h_1h_2 and $h_1h_2h_3$, where there is still only one integration step inside each triangle. This algorithm avoids the complicated calculations when the streamlines are projected on the geometric surface, and at the same time takes into account the grid shape and the changes of cell volume. When visualizing streamlines, we synthesize surface streamlines orderly according to the adaptively generated projection pointsets.

4. EXPERIMENTAL RESULTS AND ANALYSIS

We implemented our surface streamline generation algorithm and integrate it into a general visual analysis platform, namely VisIt (VisIt 2005), in the form of plugin-in component. We also demonstrated its validity by applying our method to representative datasets for visualizing the surface field of objects with regular and irregular geometry. All of the images in this work were produced on a Dell T7600 workstation with a 2.40 GHz Intel Xeon CPU E5-2609.

For geometric models with arbitrary topology, the high-precision extraction algorithm proposed in this paper can obtain the surface vector field with the same mesh density and accuracy as original 3D vector field, meanwhile maintaining the profile of the geometric model. Table 1 provides a concise overview of performance by extracting surface vector field using cylinder and sphere models, where the consumed time can be further reduced with the increase of the cpu cores.

Table 1. Performance comparison of extracting two types of dataset using cylinder and sphere under 6 CPU cores

Type of dataset	Num of cells	Time(cylinder)	Time(sphere)
Structured grid	36000	0.257 s	0.189 s
Unstructured grid	45618700	3.872 s	3.591 s

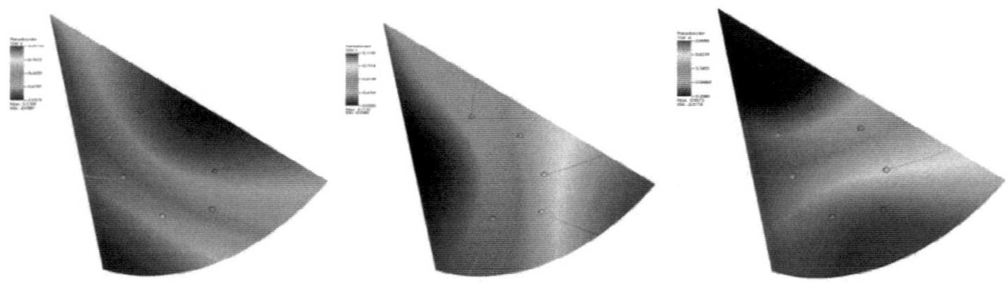

Figure 5. Visualization of coloring surface streamline using different physical variable. The comparison with the underlying scalar field shows the expected better approximation quality

A very important feature in streamline rendering is to support the visualization of streamline colors based on arbitrary physical field values. Figure 5 shows the surface streamline coloring effects based on the four types of scalar fields u, v, and w, with the corresponding scalar field coupled in the background. It can be concluded that our surface streamline generation algorithm can effectively describe the flow characteristics of the vector field and the changing trend of physical quantities.

The complexity of the geometric surface models varies with numerical devices simulated in the field of engineering. As shown in Figure 6, this paper selects another common geometric surface model for surface streamline generation and verification. Figure 6a shows the high-precision vector field obtained after surface extraction. The upper half of the vector diverges upward, and the lower half of the vector diverges downward, that is, there should be two completely different directions of surface flow on the entire surface. Figure 6b shows the continuous and consistent surface streamlines generated using 14 seed points, which is the same as the trend of the surface flow field, where the color is generated based on the physical field u. Figure 6c is a schematic diagram of the coupling of the pseudocolor diagram and surface streamlines. Figure 6c verifies the flexibility and accuracy of the algorithm in this paper when coloring the surface streamline. In particular, the above experiments further prove that the proposed surface streamline method is not limited by the shape of the geometric model and the characteristics of the vector field.

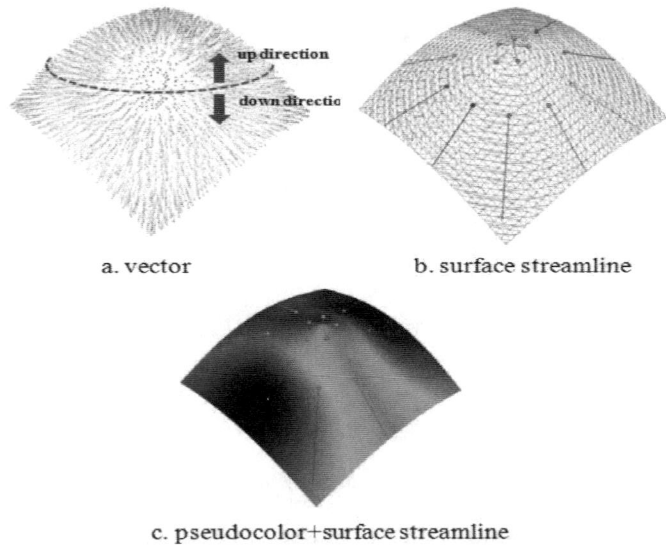

Figure 6. Proximity comparison: (top row) between the underlying direction of motion in vector field and the generated streamlines using our algorithm, (bottom row) between scalar field and our coloring method. The underlying structure of the flow mesh is now more clearly reflected by the streamlines

In addition, a comparison with Tecplot's streamline generation results as illustrated in Figure 7 also demonstrates the expected high approximation quality of our proposed algorithm.

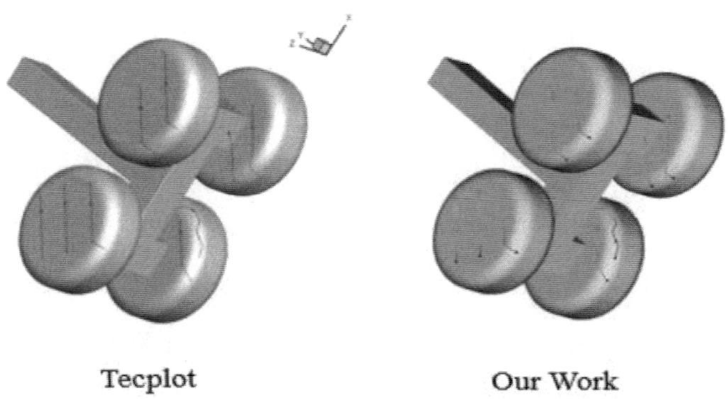

Figure 7. Comparison of generating surface streamlines on curved surface using Tecplot and ours

5. CONCLUSION

In this paper, we have proposed a streamline generation algorithm for vector field defined on curved surfaces. This algorithm achieves the underlying discrete feature of curved surfaces by applying the polygon intersection and the grid-related high-precision interpolation algorithms. Then, we present the surface streamline integral technology, combined with the adaptive stepsize strategy and acceleration structure, in order to support continuous and consistent surface streamline generation, which solves the bottleneck problem of performing streamline tracing directly on curved surfaces. We have shown that this work can aid engineering designer for the design and optimization of major devices by analyzing flow on curved surfaces.

REFERENCES

Alexander, S. and Bishop, R. L., 1996. Comparison theorems for curves of bounded geodesic curvature in metric spaces of curvature bounded above. *Differential Geometry and its Applications*, Vol. 6, No. 1, pp. 67–86.

Battke, H. et al, 1997. Fast line integral convolution for arbitrary surfaces in 3D. *Visualization and Mathematics*, pp. 181–195. Springer, Berlin, Heidelberg.

Cabral, B., Leedom, L. C., 1993. Imaging vector fields using line integral convolution. *Proceedings of the 20th annual conference on Computer graphics and interactive techniques*, California, USA, pp. 263–270.

Forssell, L. K., Cohen, S. D., 1995. Using line integral convolution for flow visualization: curvilinear grids, variable-speed animation, and unsteady flows. *IEEE Transactions on Visualization and Computer Graphics*, Vol. 1, No.2, pp. 133–141.

Greiner, G., Hormann, K., 1998. Efficient clipping of arbitrary polygons. *ACM Transactions on Graphics*, Vol. 17, No. 2, pp. 71–83.

Laramee, R. S., 2004. *Interactive 3D Flow Visualization Using Textures and Geometric Primitives*. Vienna University of Technology, Institute for Computer Graphics and Algorithms, Vienna, Austria.

Laramee, R. S. et al, 2004. The state of the art in flow visualization: Dense and texture-based techniques. *Computer Graphics Forum*, Vol. 23, No. 2, pp. 203–221.

Laramee, R. S. et al, 2003. Image space based visualization of unsteady flow on surfaces. *Proceedings of Visualization*, Los Alamitos, USA, pp. 131–138.

Li, L., Shen, H.-W., 2007. Image-based streamline generation and rendering. *IEEE Transactions on Visualization and Computer Graphics*, Vol. 13, No. 3, pp. 630–640.

Li, G. et al, 2008. Flow charts: visualization of vector fields on arbitrary surfaces. *IEEE Transactions on Visualization and Computer Graphics*, Vol. 14, No.5, pp. 1067–1080.

Mao, X. et al, 1997. Line integral convolution for 3D surfaces. *Proceedings of Eurographics*, Vienna, Austria, pp. 57–69.

Mattausch, O. et al, 2003. Strategies for interactive exploration of 3D flow using evenly spaced illuminated streamlines. *Proceedings of Spring Conference on Computer Graphics*, pp. 213–222.

McLoughlin, T. et al, 2010. Over two decades of integration-based, geometric flow visualization. *Computer Graphics Forum*, Vol. 29, No. 6, pp. 1807–1829.

Polthier, K., Schmies, M., 2006. *Straightest geodesics on polyhedral surfaces*. Association for Computing Machinery, New York, USA, pp. 30-38.

Reshetnyak, Y. G., 1989. Two-dimensional manifolds of bounded curvature. *Encyclopaedia of Mathematical Sciences*, Vol.70, pp. 3–164.

Spencer, B. et al, 2009. Evenly spaced streamlines for surfaces: An image-based approach. *Computer Graphics Forum*, Vol.28, No.6, pp. 1618–1631.

Stalling, D., Hege, H.-C., 1997. LIC on surfaces. *Proceedings of Computer Graphics and Interactive Techniques*. Los Angeles, USA, pp. 51–64.

van Wijk, J. J., 2003. Image based flow visualization for curved surfaces. *Proceedings of Visualization*. Los Alamitos, USA, pp. 123–130.

van Wijk, J. J., 1991. Spot noise-texture synthesis for data visualization. *ACM SIGGRAPH Computer Graphics*, Vol. 25, No.4, pp. 309–318.

van Wijk, J.J., 2003. Image based flow visualization for curved surfaces. *Proceedings of Visualization*. Los Alamitos, USA, pp. 123–130.

Vatti, B.R., 1992. A generic solution to polygon clipping. *Communications of the ACM*, Vol.35, No.7, pp. 56–63.

Verma, V. et al, 2000. A flow-guided streamline seeding strategy. *Proceedings of Visualization*. Los Alamitos, USA, pp. 163–170.

VisIt, 2005. *VisIt User's Manual*. Lawrence Livermore National Laboratory, USA.

Ye, X. et al, 2005. Strategy for seeding 3D streamlines. *Proceedings of Visualization*. Los Alamitos, USA, pp. 471–478.

CONCEPTUAL MEASUREMENT OF INDIVIDUAL PITCHES DURING THE STENT PRODUCTION

Benedikt Haas and Eric Sax
Institute for Information Processing Technologies (ITIV)
Karlsruhe Institute of Technology (KIT)
Karlsruhe, Germany

ABSTRACT

Due to cardiovascular diseases being the main cause of death in Germany in 2020, about 298,557 stents, which can be used to treat these kinds of diseases, were implanted. Stents are medical devices and therefore, need to fulfill corresponding requirements. The requirements, like the geometric form, have to be checked. In practice, in the case of maypole braided stents, this will be performed manually. In order to be more cost-efficient, an automatic visual inspection system is desirable. The proposed concept, representing such a system, consists of six steps: 1) image preprocessing, 2) mandrel detection, 3) dynamic image cropping, 4) pitch measurement, 5) pitch localization, and 6) modeling. Additionally, it allows to measure individual segments of the stent, enabling a precise error localization. Furthermore, the algorithm is designed to be executed during production. Lastly, the industrial environment, as well as requirements, are incorporated, such that an existing product diversity is not restricted.

KEYWORDS

Stents, Machine Vision, Pitch Measurement, Image Processing

1. INTRODUCTION

In the year 2020, in Germany, reportedly 985,572 citizens died. The reason of death for 330,001, which equals 36.4%, of them, are diseases of the cardiovascular system. (Radtke, 2023) One possible treatment for these diseases is an implantation of a stent (Wintermantel et al, 2008). Therefore, in Germany, in 2020, 298,557 stents were implanted (Herzstiftung eV, 2021). According to the German fee-per-case system, the costs for a stent range from 54.80€ to 1,189.69€, depending on the specific stent (InEK GmbH, 2021). One possible reason for these high costs could be the absence of an automatic visual inspection system for (maypole) braided stents (Bermudez, 2017).

This paper proposes a concept for an automatic visual inspection system of single segments of a (maypole) braided stents during production. In specific, it aims to measure the geometric size of the single segments. Therefore, it contributes to the field of automatic quality control and/ or visual inspection systems in the context of an automated stent production.

2. STENTS AND STENT PRODUCTION

The stents relevant to this work are tubular or circular braids produced by a maypole braider (see Figure 1). Its two main components are the carriers and the mandrel. The carriers store the braiding wire, which is connected to the mandrel. When the braiding process starts, the carriers move in a sinewave path around the mandrel, in pairwise opposite directions. During this process, the mandrel moves upwards. Its movement speed is called take-off speed. In addition, a braiding ring can be used optionally. It'll help regulate the braiding process. In the resulting mesh structure, as shown in Figure 2, a single mesh is called a pitch. A pitch can be described using its length and width. The pitch length is the distance between the topmost and bottommost interlacing point of the wire of a pitch. Equivalently, the pitch width is the distance between the leftmost and rightmost interlacing points of the wire. (Koysev, 2014)

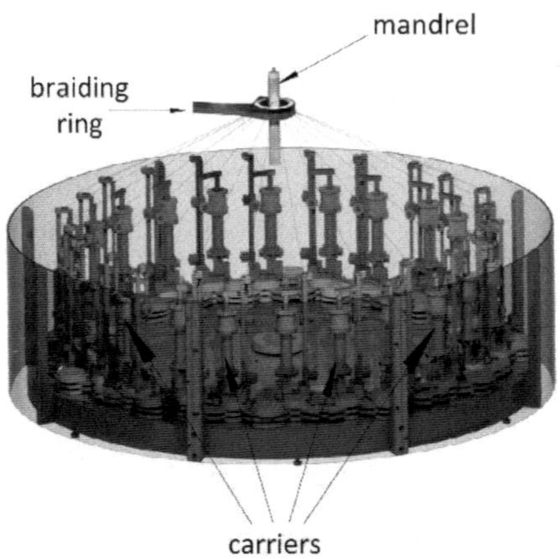

Figure 1. Schematic visualization of a Maypole braider. Marked are the mandrel, the carriers and the braiding ring

Figure 2. Image of a stent during production. Visible are the braided stent as well as the mandrel. (Haas et al, 2021)

3. RELATED WORK

The authors do not know of any approaches and/ or visual inspection systems for maypole braided stents.

Due to the fact, that stents are a specific type of braid, methods analyzing (general) braids could be transferred to the problem at hand. The most common method of analyzing these is to use a Fourier-based approach, like the discrete or fast Fourier transformation (Brigham/ Morrow, 1967) (see (Hunt, 2017), (Hunt/ Carey, 2019), (Vollbrecht et al, 2021), (Ershov, 2022) or (Jiyong et al, 2023)). Less common are:

- the Hough transformation (Duda/ Hart, 1972) being used in (Schmitt/ Mersmann/ Schoenberg, 2009) or (Monnot/ Levesque/ Lebel, 2017),
- a spectral analysis, like proposed from (Zhenkai/ Jialu, 2006), or
- an approach based on convolutional neural networks, like shown in (Şerban/ Barsanescu, 2020).

Additionally, (Hunt/ Carey, 2019) and (Vollbrecht et al, 2021) performed a measurement at the time of production, while (Şerban/ Barsanescu, 2020), (Vollbrecht et al, 2021) and (Jiyong et al, 2023) used the measurement result(s) in some sort of feedback loop to control the braiding system.

All mentioned methods have in common, that the environment was controlled or ideal. In addition, the measurement results weren't used in any kind of modeling. Therefore, a precise error localization wasn't possible. Furthermore, a single measurement was performed using multiple picks. This will smooth the measured values, which will introduce a (measurement) bias. Lastly, the content of the used images is different regarding the number of visible wires. This will influence the number of lines and edges in the image and therefore, the measurement method.

4. REQUIREMENTS

(Haas/ Erlinghagen/ Sax, 2022) already defined requirements regarding the measurement error as well as the execution time. Relevant to this paper are:

- that the maximal execution time of the measurement system has to be small enough, such that every pitch is seen at least once,
- that the image's middle falls onto the mandrel and
- that the mandrel is a cylinder and vertically aligned (with the camera's field of view).

Additionally, the measurement system should not restrict the production process. This does explicitly include production resources like the braiding wire and the mandrel.

5. CONCEPT

In order to solve this, the in Figure 3 shown algorithm is proposed. It consists of roughly six steps. These steps are 1) image preprocessing, 2) mandrel detection, 3) dynamic image cropping, 4) pitch measurement, 5) pitch localization, and 6) modeling.

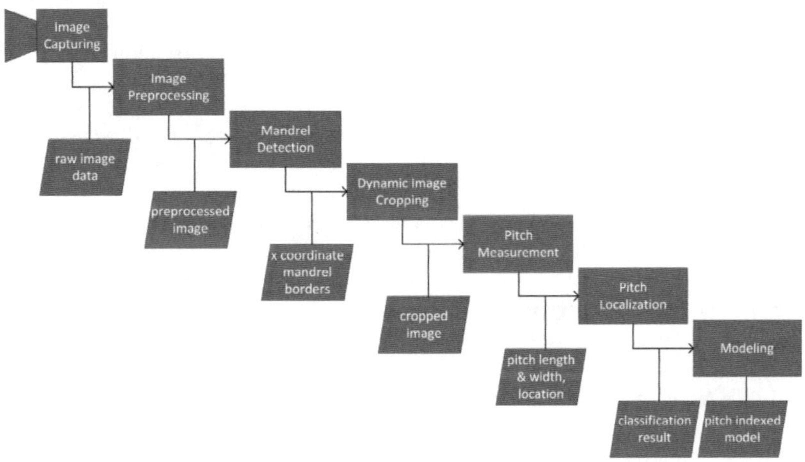

Figure 3. Visualization of the proposed concept including (measured and/ or generated) artifacts

5.1 Image Preprocessing

The image preprocessing receives the raw image data from the camera, which performs the image capturing. Therefore, the raw data has to be converted into a suitable format, like for example RGB. This is done using a demosaicing algorithm. The specific implementation of this algorithm is camera-dependent. While it is camera specific, there are different types of demosaicing algorithms. These range from fast and artifact bias ones like a bilinear interpolation, to slower approaches like the variable number of gradients (VNG), which contains fewer artifacts. (Malvar/ He/ Cutler, 2004) Therefore, the used method is system specific and is dependent on requirements like real-time conditions as well as the allowed measurement error.

5.2 Mandrel Detection

In order to crop the image, it is necessary to know, where the object being measured is. Due to the positioning of the camera relative to the mandrel being noised, this has to be measured. The mandrel being a cylinder, which is assumed to be vertical, it can be described using the left and right border. Each border being a line, can be defined using two two-dimensional points. Because of the verticality of the border, the y coordinate can be disregarded. Additionally, if the mandrel is not skewed, then the lines are parallel to the y-axis. In this case, the x coordinates of both points are identical and only one of them has to be stored. In practice, if the mandrel is skewed or the measurement is noised, then a faulty border is to be expected. Due to the borders being used in the image cropping, faulty borders will lead to faulty image cropping. The result of faulty image cropping can be 1) a too-small cropped image, 2) a too-big cropped image, 3) a false cropping position, or 4) the cropped image contains background. Especially the last point (4) can lead to (huge) measurement errors due to the background influencing the pitch measurement. 1) and 2) can be dealt with by defining minimal and/ or maximal sizes based on prior knowledge about the pitches and the mandrel. Because the borders only influence the horizontal position, a consistency check using the image's middle can be performed and prevent a cropping position (3), which does not include the preprocessed image's middle. If it (the image's middle) is included, it is highly likely, that at least one measurable pitch is shown in the cropped image. Due to these reasons, only one x coordinate will be used the describe a mandrel border.

In a practical implementation, the measurement can be performed using a variety of image processing algorithms. In general, these algorithms consist of three steps, namely (Stiller/ Bachmann/ Duchow, 2009): 1) image preprocessing, 2) feature extraction, and 3) Information extraction. The mapping of specific methods or algorithms to one of the three steps cannot be done in general. However, there are some algorithms or methods which are preferably used in one of those steps. E.g. image filtering like blurring (Beyerer/ León/ Frese, 2016) or using the Sobel operator (Kanopoulos/ Vasanthavada/ Baker, 1988), is usually done in the scope of the image preprocessing. Additionally, methods like the Hough transformation or the Canny operator (Canny, 1986) are used to extract lines or edges. Because lines or edges represent the borders of one or multiple objects, they are categorized as features. Therefore, such algorithms are usually part of the feature extraction. Lastly, methods that extract the desired information are part of the information extraction. This includes e.g. computing the intersection point(s) of lines or counting pixels in order to measure a distance.

Additionally, it is known, that the mandrel is placed in the image's middle (see chapter 4). Using this information, the search space for each border can be restricted to the corresponding half of the image. In addition, the measured borders can be checked for consistency using said information, as well as being in the range of the image dimensions. Moreover, an area, where the borders should be found, can be defined using previous knowledge and/ or the diameter of the mandrel, offering another possibility for a consistency check.

5.3 Dynamic Image Cropping

Using the mandrels borders, the image can be cropped, like presented in (Haas/ Erlinghagen/ Sax, 2022). This approach focuses on a sub-image creation, which contains the same amount of information and got the same dimensions. Due to the reason, that the images show multiple pitches as well as a mandrel, a regulation of the amount of information results in regulating the number of visible pitches. Obviously, the image has to include at least one pitch. Otherwise, there wouldn't be any measurable pitch present. In order to always contain a complete pitch, the size of the cropped image is set to three times the expected size of a pitch. It is necessary because the to-be-measured pitch includes the image's middle but does not have to be centered around it. This results in a sub-image with a size 3×3 expected pitch size, rather than containing 3×3 complete pitches. After the cropping, the sub-image is resized to a fixed size like 512×512. This will result in sub-images, that contain about the same amount of information as well as have the same image dimensions.

Alternatively, the image could be cropped using a fixed-sized rectangle. This would lead to sub-images, which contain a different number of pitches. The specific number is dependent on the pitches' size as well as the rectangles' size. Because the image has to contain at least one measurable pitch, the size will correspond to the size of the biggest measurable pitch. At the same time, in the case of smaller pitch sizes, this will lead to the display of a great number of pitches. If methods based on e.g. Convolution Neural Networks (CNNs) should be used, this can lead to measurement errors due to the variety. Additionally, the generated sub-images of different measurements are not comparable, which could lead to a lack of trust from a potential user as well as an additional problem dimension. Following this, the amount of information (aka pitches), has to be regulated, resulting in sub-images of different sizes. Rescaling these sub-images will lead to noise due to either the compression ("downscaling") or the generation ("upscaling") of the image. Nonetheless, scaling to a fixed size will produce comparable sub-images, which is human-friendly. Additionally, methods, which are based on e.g. CNNs, expect inputs to have the same size and therefore require a rescaling. Lastly, the multiplication factor is used to ensure, that at least one pitch is shown completely and therefore, measurable. It is necessary because

1) the size of the interlacing points is not part of the pitch length and/ or width and 2) the pitch does not have to be centered in the sub-image. 2) can be achieved using a multiplication factor greater than two, as shown in (Haas/ Erlinghagen/ Sax, 2022). At the same time, the factor should be as small as possible. The greater the factor, the greater the sub-images will be and therefore increase the likelihood of a downscaling. Following this, using a factor of three is a reasonable compromise. Additionally, using three covers 1). Moreover, if the expected size of the pitch is unknown, the measurement system cannot be used. This can be approached using the previously measured pitch size instead. Therefore, only an estimation for the first pitch being measured is needed. Lastly, the target dimension of the scale influences the measurement performance. On the one hand, if the target dimension is too small, then the information loss caused by the downscaling will result in a bad measurement performance. On the other hand, if it is too big, artifacts, due to the upscaling, will bias the measurement. Additionally, an increase in image size will lead to higher resource costs and a higher execution time. In the end, the size of 512×512 was chosen due to its popularity in Frameworks like PyTorch (Paszke et al, 2019) or Tensorflow (Abadi et al, 2015).

5.4 Pitch Measurement

Based on these sub-images, a pitch measurement can be implemented. Due to the sub-image being designed to contain one measurable pitch in its middle, the goal of the pitch measurement is to measure the pitch in the sub-images middle. In specific, the target is to compute the pitch length and width, as well as some kind of spatial information. Due to the image being two-dimensional, the location can be described using one two-dimensional coordinate. The process of extracting the pitch length and width as well as its location is equivalent to the one described in chapter 5.2.

5.5 Pitch Localization

The next step, namely the pitch localization, computes the index of the measured pitch dependent on the previously measured ones. In order to be resource efficient as well as have a low execution time, this computation won't be image-based. It'll use the measured location of the current, as well as the previously measured pitch. This will reduce the amount of computation time needed from analyzing at least one image to analyzing two (two-dimensional) locations. Specifically, the location of the previously measured pitch will be propagated to the current point in time using the mandrel's take-off speed as well as the time difference between both measurements. Then, the difference between the current and the propagated location can be interpreted as a difference vector. Incorporating the requirements (see chapter 4), the number of possible indices and therefore, the values (or space) of the difference vectors, are restricted. In detail, the difference vector can be mapped onto nine different indices, as shown in Figure 4. Due to this restriction, the computation of the measured pitches index can be interpreted as a classification task, using the described difference vector. In this classification scheme, class 5 represents the same pitch, while class 9 states, that the measured pitches row index equals the previous one plus two. Examples of methods being able to perform such a classification task are a multi-class SVM (Vapnik, 1963), a decision tree, a random forest (Ho, 1995), or a neural network.

The described approach is iterative; therefore, an alternative would compute the index directly. In order to do so, the complete stent would have to be visible. Otherwise, the computation would be state dependent and iterative. In practice, the complete stent does not have to be visible/ in the camera's field of view. Therefore, this approach is, in practice, not feasible. Even if the complete stent would be visible, it would require analyzing the complete image, which is cost and time inefficient. Also, cost and time inefficient would be, to compute the index iteratively using two cropped images, especially compared to the analysis of two different locations. Additionally, using a classification schema instead of computing the index directly, has the advantage, that a (classification) confidence can be provided. In the case of an error, it (the confidence values) can be used to locate said error. Moreover, if the column (index) is neglected, the confidence values can be summed up representing one row.

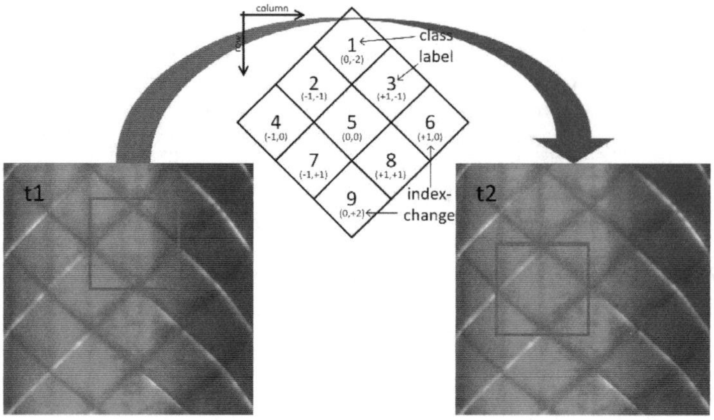

Figure 4. Visualization of the classification scheme used in the pitch localization embedded into an example. In this example, the pitch change from t1 to t2 results, according to the schema, in class 7

5.6 Modeling

The last step is to transform the output of the pitch measurement as well as localization into a consistent representation. Due to the localization being pitch indexed, the resulting model will be the same. Additionally, there will probably be multiple measurements of the same pitch. Therefore, these measurements have to be combined such that one pitch is represented by a single value. This can be done using the median of the measured length and width of the pitch. Compared to the mean, the median is more robust regarding noise and outliers, and therefore the preferred solution. The location information is, in contrast to the pitch length and width, time-sensitive. Additionally, it can be regarded as an interim result. Therefore, it can be saved for traceability reasons or otherwise, be discarded. Lastly, the measurement values can optionally be converted from pixel to an SI unit. The mapping to e.g. millimeters can be retrieved using the mandrel's diameter as well as the distance between the (measured) borders of the mandrel.

6. PROOF OF CONCEPT

The presented concept was implemented in C++ and tested, using data produced by a commercial maypole braider. This was done in cooperation with an industrial partner, in the scope of the project Stents4Tomorrow. As a result, the mandrel detection using a Hough Transformation and the pitch measurement, being realized with a YoloV3 object detector, had a mean measurement error of 2,64 mm (MAPE: 13,2%) and 0,58 mm (pitch length, MAPE: 7,7%) with a mean execution time of 127,55 ms and 66,32 ms. The localization, which was based on the k-nearest neighbors algorithm, achieved an accuracy of 99,99% while needing 0,24 ms on average.

7. CONCLUSION

Analyzing the described measurement process, there are some parts, which could prevent a (successful) practical implementation. The first one is the neglection of a skewed mandrel. This problem can be solved using some kind of camera-mandrel alignment. Such an alignment has to influence the position of the camera because the mandrel's location is fixed. In addition, a falsely set take-off speed will influence the localization leading to, in the worst case, a localization error. This does include the (mandrels) acceleration process, which, if not modeled, will lead to a wrong assumption about the take-off speed value. But, due to the acceleration process being machine-specific, modeling it would not be satisfying. Therefore, the used classification method has to be robust regarding this kind of noise. Alternatively, the take-off speed could be measured. This requires the analysis of two images, which is resource and execution-time inefficient. In addition, using a method, which computes a decision confidence, could offer some transparency in the case of a measurement error. Moreover, the concept does not incorporate measurement errors caused by production diversity, changes in the environment as well as software-based ones. Having said this, the color information can (probably) be disregarded using appropriate color space transformations. While changes in the environment will influence at least the image quality, methods like a histogram equalization can try to compensate for those. Finally, the concept assumes, that the image contains a mandrel and pitches, which is, especially at the beginning of a braiding process, not always true. Therefore, a sub-process, handling the absence of a mandrel and/ or pitches, should be included.

8. SUMMARY & OUTLOOK

In this paper, an algorithm to measure single pitches of a stent, during its production, is proposed. This algorithm contains roughly six steps, namely:

1. Image preprocessing: The method unspecific preparation of the image,
2. Mandrel detection: Image-based measurement of the location of the mandrel's borders,
3. Dynamic image cropping: Cropping of the image to contain the same amount of information as well as having the same size,
4. Pitch measurement: The measurement of the pitch length and width as well as its location,
5. Pitch localization: The computation of the index of the measured pitch and
6. Modeling: The conversion into a consistent representation including the handling of multiple measurements of the same pitch.

Using this procedure, the geometric size of single pitches of a stent can be measured. Following this, the deviation regarding the target geometry (pitche's length and width) can be computed. Additionally, due to the comparison with the target geometry, it will implicitly detect missing pitches.

Future work could thematize the problems mentioned in chapter 7. Additionally, the integration of non-cylindrical mandrels into the described process could be analyzed. Alternatively, the process could be implemented and different methods evaluated in order to satisfy the requirements. In this case, the production diversity, like the pitch length and width, the mandrels diameter as well as the wire's color and diameter, should be included.

ACKNOWLEDGEMENT

Parts of this work have been developed in the project Stents4Tomorrow. Stents4Tomorrow (reference number: 02P18C022) is partly funded by the German ministry of education and research (BMBF) within the research program ProMed. Additionally, the authors want to thank M. Braeuner (Admedes GmbH) and K. Lehmann (Admedes GmbH) for their continuous support and advice.

REFERENCES

Abadi, M., et al., 2016, Tensorflow: Large-scale machine learning on heterogeneous distributed systems. arXiv preprint arXiv:1603.04467.

Bermudez, C. et al., 2017, Automated stent defect detection and classification with a high numerical aperture optical system. In Automated Visual Inspection and Machine Vision II. SPIE. S. 92-102.

Beyerer, J.; León, F.P.; Frese, C., 2016, Automatische Sichtprüfung: Grundlagen, Methoden und Praxis der Bildgewinnung und Bildauswertung. Springer-Verlag.

Brigham, E. O., Morrow, R. E, 1967, The fast Fourier transform. IEEE spectrum, 4. Jg., Nr. 12, S. 63-70.

Canny, J., 1986, A computational approach to edge detection. IEEE Transactions on pattern analysis and machine intelligence, Nr. 6, pp. 679-698.

Duda, R. O., Hart, P.E., 1972, Use of the Hough transformation to detect lines and curves in pictures. In Communications of the ACM, 15. Jg., Nr. 1, S. 11-15.

Ershov, S. V., et al., 2022, Method for Measuring the Braid Angle and its Deviation from the Specified Value in Braided Preforms Using Image Analysis. Fibre Chemistry, 53. Jg., Nr. 5, S. 346-354.

Haas, B., et al., 2021, Evaluation of different methods to measure a stent's pitch length in an industrial environment. In: 2021 International Conference on Electrical, Computer, Communications and Mechatronics Engineering (ICECCME). IEEE, S. 1-6.

Haas, B., Erlinghagen, L., Sax, E., 2022, Pitch length measurement of stents using dynamically cropped images. In: 2022 International Conference on Electrical, Computer, Communications and Mechatronics Engineering (ICECCME). IEEE, pp. 1-6.

Herzstiftung eV, D. 2021. Deutscher Herzbericht 2020. Frankfurt am Main: Deutsche Herzstiftung eV, 2021-06.

Ho, T. K., 1995. Random decision forests. In: Proceedings of 3rd international conference on document analysis and recognition. IEEE, pp. 278-282.

Hunt, A. J. A, 2017, Machine Vision System for the Real-Time Fiber Orientation Measurement of Tubular Braided Preforms.

Hunt, A.J.; Carey, J.P., 2019, A machine vision system for the braid angle measurement of tubular braided structures. In Textile Research Journal, 89. Jg., Nr. 14, S. 2919-2937.

InEK GmbH – Institut für das Entgeltsystem im Krankenhaus, 2021, aG-DRG-Fallpauschalen-Katalog 2022, [online] https://www.g-drg.de/content/download/10834/file/Fallpauschalenkatalog_2022_20211123.pdf [visted 2023-03-13].

Jiyong, F. et al., 2023, Traction control of space tubular shaped mandrel and detection of preform braiding angle. In Textile Research Journal, 93. Jg., Nr. 1-2, S. 392-408.

Kanopoulos, N., Vasanthavada, N., Baker, R.L, 1988, Design of an image edge detection filter using the Sobel operator. IEEE Journal of solid-state circuits, 23. Jg., Nr. 2, pp. 358-367.

Koysev, Y., 2014, Braiding technology for textiles: Principles, design and processes. Elsevier.

Monnot, P.; Levesque, J.; Lebel, L.L., 2017, Automated braiding of a complex aircraft fuselage frame using a non-circular braiding model. Composites Part A: Applied Science and Manufacturing, 102. Jg., S. 48-63.

Paszke, A. et al, 2019, PyTorch: An Imperative Style, High-Performance Deep Learning Library, Advances in Neural Information Processing Systems 32, pp. 8024-8035.

Radtke, R. 2023. Anzahl der Todesfälle nach den häufigsten Todesursachen in Deutschland in den Jahren 2019 bis 2021. Statista.

Şerban, A.; Barsanescu, P.-D., 2020, Automatic detection of fibers orientation on composite laminates using convolutional neural networks. In: IOP Conference Series: Materials Science and Engineering. IOP Publishing, pp. 012107.

Stiller, C.; Bachmann, A.; Duchow, C., 2009, Maschinelles Sehen. Handbuch Fahrerassistenzsysteme: Grundlagen, Komponenten und Systeme für aktive Sicherheit und Komfort, pp. 198-222.

Malvar, H.S.; He, L.-w.; Cutler, R., 2004, High-quality linear interpolation for demosaicing of Bayer-patterned color images. In: 2004 IEEE International Conference on Acoustics, Speech, and Signal Processing. IEEE, pp. iii-485.

Monnot, P.; Levesque, J.; Lebel, L.L., 2017, Automated braiding of a complex aircraft fuselage frame using a non-circular braiding model. Composites Part A: Applied Science and Manufacturing, 102. Jg., S. 48-63.

Vapnik, V., 1963, Pattern recognition using generalized portrait method. Automation and remote control, 24. Jg., pp. 774-780.

Vollbrecht, B. et al., 2021, Developing a camera-based measuring system to feedback control the fibre orientation for the braiding process of CFRP. In Advances in Industrial and Manufacturing Engineering, 3. Jg., S. 100059.

Wintermantel, E. et al, 2008, Stenting und technische Stentumgebung. In Medizintechnik Life Science Engineering: Interdisziplinarität· Biokompatibilität· Technologien·Implantate·Diagnostik Werkstoffe Business, pp. 1009-1041.

Zhenkai, W., Jialu, L., 2006, Braided angle measurement technique for three-dimensional braided composite material preform using mathematical morphology and image texture. AUTEX Research Journal, 6. Jg., Nr. 1, pp. 30-39.

APPLICATION OF GRAPHICAL REPRESENTATIONS FROM VIDEO GAMES TO AMPLIFY CO-PRESENCE IN GROUP VISITS TO VIRTUAL HOUSES

André Freitas, Filipe Santos and Pedro Santana
ISCTE – Instituto Universitário de Lisboa, Portugal
ISTAR - Information Sciences, Technologies and Architecture Research Center, Portugal

ABSTRACT

In real life, the ability that people have of observing the elements of their surrounding space contributes for the sense of presence and social co-presence in that physical space. Digital avatars are often the employed means for providing a similar sense of co-presence in virtual environments. Digital avatars of the users and other co-presence amplification strategies (e.g., co-presence inducing graphical representations) have been extensively studied and employed in multi-player videogames. This paper studies the application of some these strategies to amplify the sense of co-presence of people in virtual group house visits, which is an application scenario with value for real estate industry and participatory design in architecture. For this purpose, a Unity-based collaborative virtual environment was implemented and tested in a user study with 33 participants. The obtained results show that the implemented strategies enrich the sense of co-presence in the virtual environment and trigger interesting collaborative interactions.

KEYWORDS

Co-Presence, Virtual Environment, Videogames, Collaborative Interaction

1. INTRODUCTION

Ideally, users should feel fully present and immersed in the virtual environments with which they interact. However, there are still limitations to these virtual experiences, as they are not yet capable of fully replacing the benefits of real life and technical questions remain about how to effectively use this technology (e.g., how to avoid cyber-sickness), thus demanding for further research.

Virtual environments require strong support for spatial navigation, given that navigation without some assistance can be difficult to perform, inducing disorientation and discomfort to the user (Vinson, 1999). Spatial navigation and reasoning are particularly challenging in Collaborative Virtual Environments (CVE) (Casanueva et al., 2000), as these require users to share the same virtual space and perform collaborative tasks. In these environments, users need to have a sense of co-presence, otherwise they will not be able to collaborate. Digital avatars of the users, i.e., graphical representations of the users, are often employed for this purpose (Churchill and Snowdon, 1998) (Negron et al., 2020).

Digital avatars of the users and other co-presence amplification strategies (e.g., co-presence inducing graphical representations) have been extensively studied and employed in multi-player videogames (Warpefelt, 2016) (Steuer, 1992). Videogames are a special case of CVE, many of them capable of providing the players with a strong sense of co-presence when facing challenging complex collaborative navigation tasks. The value of studying videogames beyond their entertainment role is well established. For instance, previous studies addressed the role of videogames as learning tools in specific age groups and their effects on physical and mental health of the users (Stanney and Cohn, 2009).

This paper studies the hypothesis that some the co-presence strategies employed by videogames are capable of amplifying co-presence in virtual group house visits. Performing virtual group house visits is an important application scenario in the real estate industry. The ability to pre-visit houses virtually is a time and cost saver and being able to do it in group more closely resembles what people do when selecting a house. Group visits to virtual houses can also be a valuable tool for participatory architectural design: clients can be invited to jointly visit early house designs and provide timely feedback to inform subsequent design iterations.

To validate our hypothesis, we have designed and implemented a Unity-based CVE, hereafter VVApp (from Virtual Visit App), in which remote users are able to jointly visit virtual houses, with co-presence amplified by means of graphical representations borrowed from videogames. A user-study with 33 participants was conducted. The behavior of the users was observed during the execution of a set of tasks with the goal of assessing then ability of the implemented co-presence strategies to facility collaborative navigation, communication, and decision making. The obtained results show that the implemented strategies enrich the sense of co-presence in the virtual environment and trigger interesting collaborative interactions.

This paper is organized as follows. Section 2 presents related work. Then, the developed CVE is described in Section 3. The experimental setup and results are presented in Section 4 and 5, respectively. Finally, conclusions are drawn and future is proposed in Section 6.

2. RELATED WORK

Casanueva and Blake (2000) studied the effects that avatars have on co-presence in a CVE, namely the appearance and functionality of the avatar. The conclusion reached by the authors was based on the presence and co-presence scores and survey responses, which turned out to be quite positive. Buck et al. (2019) observed that co-presence can exist in a CVE at a level very similar to that of reality. Podkosova and Kaufmann (2018) concluded that users try not to collide in the virtual world even when aware that they were safe from real collisions. Pimentel and Vinkers (2021) refer the possibility of co-presence in mixed reality. Kim et al. (2018) showed the existence of co-presence between a virtual interlocutor and a human being. Cho et al. (2015) analyzed the influences of co-presence on the performance of virtual staging. They concluded that age and epistemological beliefs significantly influence physical and social presence, as well as the participants' sense of being present together in the CVE. Wienrich et al. (2018) showed that collaborative tasks increase levelsof social presence and cooperation in a positive way in large-scale CVE.

In CVE, the base interaction is typically performed by digital avatars, i.e., graphical representations of the users. However, these interactions are limited. Negrón et al. (2020) concluded that interactions such as interactions verbal/non-verbal, kinesics and proxemics, were used in a positive and discriminating way (Negron et al., 2020). Zhang et al. (2019) developed a CVE and a series of collaborative games dedicated to children suffering from autism spectrum disorder, with the aim of establishing the viability and tolerability of the system. They concluded that their system greatly improved collaborative performance among children. Gamelin et al. (2021) confirmed the importance of avatar's fidelity regarding spatial interaction, since it can affect communication between users, especially when performing collaborative spatial tasks.

The previous studies address the effect that various factors have on collaborative interaction and sense of co-presence; however, most of them explored the digital avatar as the sole cue for inducing co-presence. The videogames industry has devised, implemented, and deployed many other alternatives for entertaining purposes. This paper contributes with a study on the value of these alternatives to amplifying co-presence in virtual house group visits, that is, in a non-entertaining setting.

3. VVAPP DESIGN AND IMPLEMENTATION

3.1 Avatar

A virtual environment is only considered to be a CVE when more than one user is simultaneously present (Casanueva and Blake, 2000) (Buck et al., 2019) (Knapp et al., 2014). Digital avatars are visual demonstrations of the users that contribute for them to feel present in the CVE. The avatar's visual appearance can be selected to be either stylized or realistic if it clearly represents the user in question. According to Buck et al. (2019), adding just one personalization element to a 3D avatar has more impact of distinguishing than adding several personalization elements. Hence, avatars in VVApp, which have a *stickman*-like look, are distinguishedbased solely on their colors. Their faces include a nose to cue partners regarding their gazing direction (Figure 1).

To generate interaction events or navigation events within a CVE, a mapping of controls is required. Cursor keys used to be used more in character-based systems, before new alternative control mappings came along outside the keyboard (Janet et al., 2004). In current 3D games, the cursor keys are less used since the inclusion of the mouse. Instead, the WASD mapping is more often used. User controls in VVApp are divided into two parts. The first part follows the pattern used in current video games to control the avatar, of which W moves it forward, S backwards, A to the left, and D to the right. The second part focuses on the mouse position, a variable that modifies the avatar's orientation and the user's perspective, in which the user sees the world in the first person, through the avatar's eyes.

Hearing reveals significant importance in increasing additional information about a given physical or virtual space. Virtual hearing helps to inform the user the presence and type of sound propagation has occurred. However, it fails to indicate precisely where this sound was propagated in the virtual space. (Török et al., 2015) (Calado et al., 2017). VVApp contains a 3D sound system that fixes this flaw.

3.2 Virtual Houses

The CVE in VVApp presents clues that describe a habitable house so that users feel that they are visiting a real home, such house divisions, textures to identify the type of flooring or wall texture, and furniture for each room. All elements included in the virtual houses fit together correctly, otherwise the CVE would exhibit unfamiliar visual information, breaking the experience. Currently, VVApp includes three virtual houses of different sizes, structurally equivalent to real apartments (Figure 1).

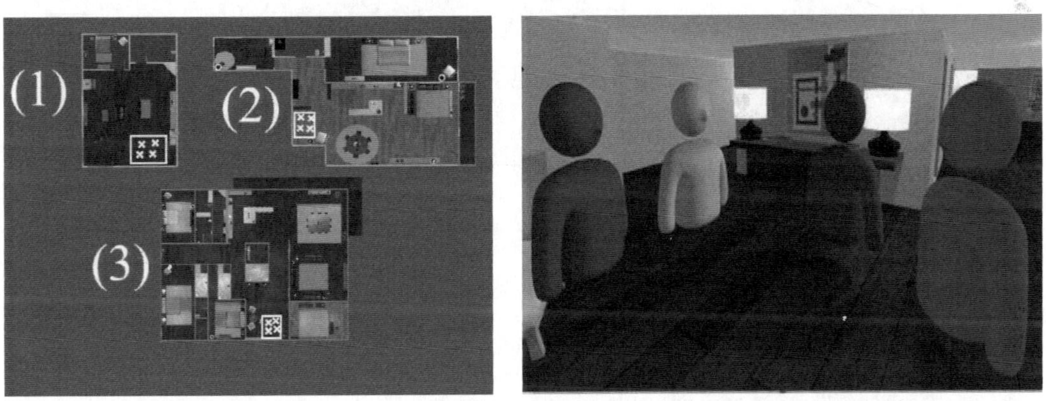

Figure 1. Plan view of the houses CVE_1 (1), CVE_2 (2) and CVE_3 (3). The crosses in the white area indicate the starting position of the four users, i.e., house visitors (Left). Avatar's graphical representations (Right)

House CVE_1 is small but beginner-friendly, comprising a spacious living room with kitchen, a medium-sized bedroom, and a bathroom; it is furnished in a simple and practical way. House CVE_2 is medium-sized, consisting of a large living room, two bedrooms, one bathroom and kitchen; the apartment is fully furnished and decorated. Finally, House CVE_3 is large and comprises a hall, two bedrooms, suite, office, living room, kitchen in open space, laundry, social bathroom, and pantry with wine cellar; a wide corridor guides users to enter the private area; the apartment is fully furnished and decorated.

3.3 Collaborative, Non-verbal and Spatial Interaction

One way to amplify the feeling of co-presence is to share necessary information from all users of the CVE. Each mechanism sends visual feedback about any event in the CVE to the user (Abrams and Gerber, 2013).

Video games, such as *Left For Dead 2* (Valve Software, 2004) or *Apex Legends* (Electronic Arts, 2020), provide the player with information about the partners' avatars state. Similarly, VVApp contains a rectangular *Info-bar* (Figure 2), divided into four parts, each representing the information (name and location in terms of house division) of each user present in the CVE (in the current version only four users are allowed).

Video games often notify players using interfaces about recent events. These events must be clearly notified in advance so that the user experience is not abruptly interrupted. All users in VVApp are also notified of the others' information, giving them the feeling that they are not in an empty space (Churchill and Snowdon, 1998). VVApp includes a transparent interface, called *Text box*, which reports the events registered on the CVE (Figure 2).

Allowing users to mark three-dimensional positions for others to see (a pointing mechanism) helps considerably collaborative task solving (Churchill and Snowdon, 1998). This reduces communication problems in CVE (Gamelin et al., 2021) and potentially amplifies the feeling of co-presence. In this line, the video game Counter Strike Global Offensive (Valve Software, 2012) includes a non-verbal communication tool called *Pointing*, which marks the location defined by a user in three-dimensional space. The similar interface included in VVApp is an animated icon that includes the relative distance, in meters, between the user and the focus point that works like in the mentioned video game (Figure 2).

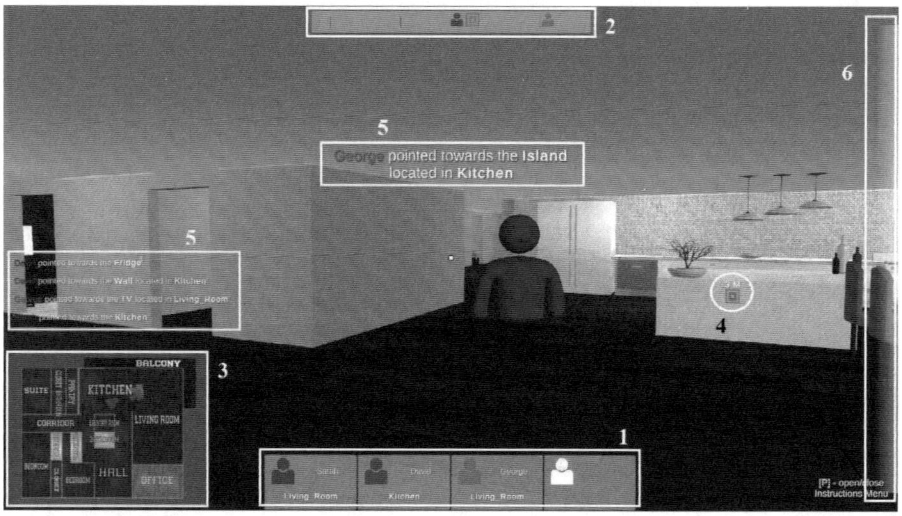

Figure 2. Point of view of Sarah's avatar. In this screenshot, it is shown all the interfaces added to the application: *Info-bar* (1), *Compass* (2), *Mini-map* (3), *Pointing* (4), *Text boxes* (5) and *Collision warning* (6)

Kyriakou et al. (2017) concluded that people feel more present in the virtual environment when there are scenarios with intensive interactions. In videogames, such as *Gran Turismo 7* (Polyphony Digital, 2022), the player is often notified, via small 2D visual elements, when an opponent approaching from behind is too close. VVApp follows a similar approach by presenting to the user two rectangular graphical elements, by the name of *Collision Warning*, each occupying one of the two sides of the screen (Figure 2). The closer a partner is from the user, below a give threshold distance, the opaquer the rectangles become. To convey the information to the user clearly, the active graphic element flashes, regardless of its opacity.

Navigation (i.e., planning a path to a desired destination) in large-scale CVE can be challenging for most users if no access to a navigation guide. To cope with this challenge, videogames often provide the player with a (in)complete (mini-)map of the environment. Maps in CVE must ensure that the user is able to relate two points in the map's graphical representation to the two corresponding points in the environment (Darken and Sibert, 1993). VVApp includes a rectangular *Mini-map* capturing the entire virtual area (Figure 2). To reduce visual clutter, the decorative objects present in the virtual houses are not rendered on the *Mini-map*. However, the *Mini-map* exhibits icons of the avatars present, pinpointing their current position and orientation. To facilitate localization on the *Mini-map*, a label per house's division is overlaid in the map with the division's name.

Although maps contribute positively for navigation, it is not always the most effective tool (Chen and Stanney, 1999). For instance, *The Elder Scrolls V: Skyrim* (Bethesda, 2011) provides the player with a *Compass* that, with its compact format, manages to guide the player in following the current locations of active objectives or enemies. A similar compass is included in VVApp (Figure 2). It indicates the current orientation of the user's partners, as well as the orientation of the points marked with the *Pointing* tool. The interface of the *Compass* presents all the points in a 2D format. The *Compass* does not identify the poles that associate with the traditional *Compass*. It has the potential to amplify the feeling of co-presence, since the user can guide the partners through a pointing marker while the partner follows that marker with the support of the *Compass*.

3.4 Formative Evaluation

To detect points of improvement in an early version of VVApp, a formative evaluation session with a duration of forty minutes was carried out with three remote users. The ages of the participants varied between 22 and 28 years old, two males and one female. This test included the execution of three tasks to be performed in virtual house CVE_3. The participants were verbally questioned about the performance of the mechanics. In general, the test showed positive results regarding the use of interfaces and non-verbal communication mechanisms. Identified issues in the application were later corrected. The results presented in the following sections were obtained with the corrected version of the VVApp.

4. EXPERIMENTAL SETUP

To evaluate the co-presence mechanisms included in VVApp, 11 groups of three participants each (without reposition) were recruited. Participants belonging to the same group are hereafter called *partners* of each other. The ages of the participants varied between 17 and 40 years, with a mean age of 24.03 years ($\sigma = 5.02$), 30 males and 3 females. The experiments were designed to test the following working hypotheses: H1: participants use at least one of the co-presence inducing interfaces to solve tasks; H2: the proposed co-presence inducing interfaces give positive collaborative *feedback*, that is, they are used with some significant frequency by users; H3: the co-presence inducing interfaces, in general, enrich the visits of virtual houses, that is, they are well received by the users.

The experiments were conducted online. Video and sound of all sessions were recorded using *NVIDIA GeForce Video Capture software.* Each group was notified to participate days before the session. Participants had to meet the requirements to remotely enter the application: to use a Laptop or Desktop with a minimum memory capacity of 8 GB, running the operating system *Windows* or *MAC OS*; download the dedicated version and software *Zoom* or *Discord*, so that they could communicate verbally within the group. All participants consented to the recording of the session. At the beginning of the session, the group was introduced to the application through a video tutorial. The video shows an example of a user's POV interacting with VVApp's features. This will help the participants to learn the co-presence inducing interfaces functionality easily. After that, the person responsible for conducting the experiment described the first task and asked the group to achieve the objective of the task. After the group finishes a task, the responsible for running the test asks the participants to leave the server, since the application needs to be closed to download the data files. The server comes back up once everything is ready to move on to the next task. The process is repeated for every task. After completing all tasks, a session sheet containing a short questionnaire to fill in at the time of the session was provided to all groups. The first part of the questionnaire captures the familiarity of the participants with video games and looking for houses to buy or rent as a customer, as well as the experience of using the application. The second part of the questionnaire assesses the usefulness of the co-presence inducing interfaces included in VVApp via a set of statements that are to be responded by the participants with a 5- point *Likert* scale (from 1 for "totally disagree with the statement" up to 5 for "totally agree with the statement").

To being able to isolate the analysis of each co-presence inducing interface, a version of VVApp customized for the experiments was developed. This version disables certain interface elements (*interface* hereafter for the sake of compactness) by default, namely: Interface 1 - *Info-bar*; Interface 2 - *Compass*; Interface 3 - *Mini-map*. To enable them, users must use special keys on the keyboard, each corresponding to one of the three interfaces. Enabling one of the three interfaces results in automatic disabling of the other two. The remaining interfaces remain active regardless of the user's options. Additionally, VVApp contains a data collection system that saves essential data for the analysis of the experiment, in CSV format. Participants had to execute, in sequence, the following three tasks:

- **Task 1 (Evaluation of virtual houses)** - The group visits the three virtual houses. Participants go through what is necessary to be able to evaluate the house based on their own evaluation criteria (e.g., visual, architectural). The group has a time limit of 4 minutes to navigate inside the house and organize their critique. The evaluation is done individually, that is, each participant must transmit one's evaluation about the house in question. When the time limit expires, the person in charge of conducting the test asks the participants individually to evaluate the house, even if their assessment is incomplete. During the evaluation, participants can move and use the available co-presence mechanisms. The task ends when the evaluation of the three virtual houses is concluded.

- **Task 2 (Riddle solving)** - The group is asked to solve six riddles in virtual house CVE_3. The area is large enough to convince participants to explore more cautiously in search for the answers. The answers must be provided collaboratively, that is, all group members must agree with the given decision. The group must answer each riddle within a maximum of 2 minutes and 30 seconds. The group must verbally identify the object they consider to be the solution to the riddle. If they have not reached an answer, the group is given one last opportunity to reach an agreement within a short period of time. Participants are free to use all available tools in the application to find the object. The task is completed once the participants answer all the riddles.
- **Task 3 (Pre-defined route)** - The group must follow a predefined route inside virtual house CVE_3. The route contains several intermediate waypoints points that guide participants to their final waypoint. The task starts after the first waypoint is dictated to the participants and they must navigate to that point. This process is repeated from waypoint to waypoint, until the final waypoint. Participants must stop on the respective waypoint in order to proceed to the next one. The task has no time limit, nor a mandatory trajectory. Participants have the freedom move as desired between waypoints.

5. EXPERIMENTAL RESULTS

5.1 Interfaces Utilization Rate

Figure 3 shows the pie charts of the three co-presence inducing interfaces utilization rate. Of the 33 participants, 6 of them did not activate any of three interfaces in Task 1 (18.18%), which contradicts H1. The recordings reveal that these specific participants discussed in more detail the positions of the furniture, the visual appearance of each room, the proportion of the areas, among others, which may justify their lack of need to use to the co-presence interfaces. For the remaining participants, a variety of results were obtained. Interface 3 (*Mini-map*) exhibits a utilization rate of 52,22% (σ = 33,15%), which is higher than the 16.56% (σ = 20.91%) obtained for Interface 1 (*Info-bar*) and the 13,04% (σ = 16,03%) for Interface 2 (*Compass*). On average, 16.48 transitions between interfaces were recorded (σ = 12.70), which reveals that Interfaces 1 and 2, despite having average utilization rate below 15%, were used occasionally.

In Task 2, we can observe differences in relation to the data obtained in Task 1 due to learning effects. Of the 33 participants, 3 of them did not activate any interface, in which 2 of them are the same participants who did not use any of the interfaces in Task 1. These participants were always close to their partners, in the virtual house, while solving riddles. The data files report that participants who did not use any of the interfaces during Task 1, chose Interface 3 (*Mini-map*) in Task 2. For the remaining participants, different results were obtained compared to Task 1. Interface 3 (*Mini-map*) shows a higher utilization rate compared to Task 1. Interface 1 (*Info-bar*) exhibited a utilization rate of 12,33% (σ = 19,70%), whereas Interface 2 (*Compass*) and Interface 3 (*Mini-map*) exhibited 8,68% (σ = 23,05%) and 69,90% (σ = 36,93%), respectively. On average, 6.70 transitions between interfaces were recorded (σ = 7.27). Compared with the results of Task 1, there was a decrease of 25.54% in the average utilization rate of Interface 1 (*Info-bar*), a decrease of 33.44% in Interface 2 (*Compass*), and an increase of 25.30% in Interface 3 (*Mini-map*). Although participants resorted more to the *Mini-map*, the number of interface transitions indicate that users still used the other two interfaces.

In Task 3, we can observe differences in relation to the data obtained from Task 2. Of the 33 participants involved, the same 3 participants reported in Task 2 did not activate any interface. For the remaining participants, significantly different results were obtained compared to Task 2. Interface 3 (*Mini-map*) once again reveals a higher utilization rate compared to the other two. Interface 1 (*Info-bar*) exhibited an average utilization rate of 2,91% (σ = 6,33\%), Interface 2 (*Compass*) of 1,39% (σ = 4,53%), and Interface 3 (*Mini-map*) of 86,61% (σ = 29,10%). On average, 4.52 transitions between interfaces were recorded (σ = 9.28). Compared with the results of Task 2, there was a decrease of 76.40% in the average utilization rate of Interface 1 (info- bar), a decrease of 83.99% in Interface 2 (*Compass*), and an increase of 19.30% in Interface 3 (*Mini-map*). As Task 3 is purely linked to three-dimensional navigation, most participants opted for Interface 3 (*Mini-map*) due to the provided guidance simplicity.

In general, a mixed use of the three interfaces was observed. Interfaces 1 (*Info-bar*) and 2 (*Compass*) reveal a decrease in utilization rate throughout the entire experiment, whereas Interface 3 (*Mini-map*) reveals an increase. At first glance, the results shows that most participants ignored Interfaces 1 and 2 almost completely in the two last tasks. However, the registered interface transitions indicate otherwise. Participants used Interfaces 1 and 2 enough to learn about the identification of partners within the CVE and their positions. The obtained general results corroborate hypothesis H2, which states that the interfaces provide positive collaborative feedback.

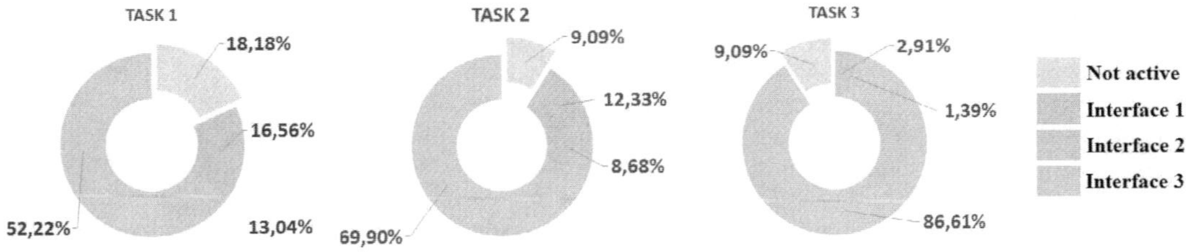

Figure 3. Average interface utilization rate for Interface 1 (*Info-bar*), Interface 2 (*Compass*), and Interface 3 (*Mini-map*)

5.2 Collisions and Pointing

Figure 4 presents the total number of *collisions* between users and the number of *pointing actions* (to insert a marker in the environment). The main objective of this analysis is to study the participant's behavior from the registered number of collisions and pointing actions. The comparison of values between tasks is not included. In Task 1, a total of 430 collisions and 1343 pointing actions were registered, with an average of 39.09 collisions ($\sigma = 27.79$) and of 122.09 pointing actions ($\sigma = 105.46$) per group (roughly 1 collision and 4 pointing actions per minute). Some participants showed care in navigation and curiosity in testing the application in Task 1 (e.g., two of the elements collided on purpose). Most participants used pointing actions to identify objects, furniture, and rooms in their speech, which draw the attention of their partners.

A total of 295 collisions and 1581 pointing actions were registered in Task 2, with an average of 26.82 collisions ($\sigma = 19.74$) and 143.73 pointing actions ($\sigma = 128.98$) per group. The participants resorted considerably to pointing actions, as they help users to jointly identify which object may be the correct answer to the riddle. A total of 506 collisions and 311 pointing markers were registered in Task 3, with an average of 46 collisions ($\sigma = 32.27$) and 28.73 pointing actions ($\sigma = 27.76$) per group. Participants collided more frequently in narrower spaces. The pre-defined route included these narrow spaces with the purpose of observing the trajectories chosen by the participants. The *Pointing* mechanism was used to help participants in indicating a clear space when a misunderstanding occurs.

In Task 1, participants made extensive use of pointing markers to comment on the style of the house or the position of furniture to the partners in the evaluation phase and to identify the objects, rooms, and furniture during their speech. Collisions between partners occurred from time to time. In Task 2, there was clear evidence that the pointing markers significantly helped participants in identifying objects and furniture. The frequency of collisions has decreased, which could mean that the collision avoidance mechanism helped participants navigate cautiously. In Task 3, a high number of collisions and a lower number of pointing markers were observed. This suggests that participants' navigation was compromised although most collisions happened in narrow passages. Participants used the pointing markers to correctly orient their partners.

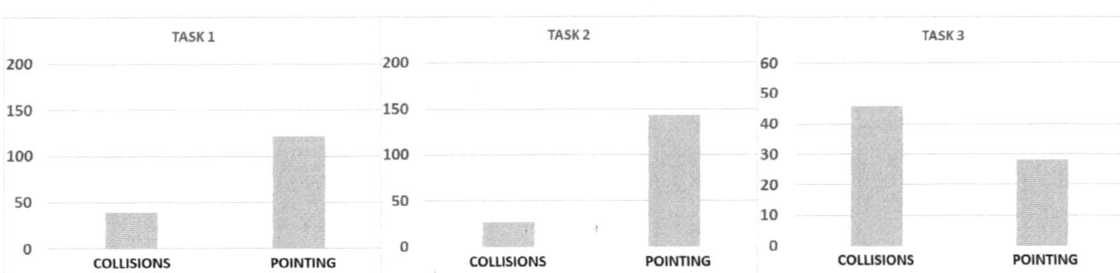

Figure 4. Bar graph of the total number of collisions and pointing

5.3 CO-PRESENCE Mechanisms Subjective Rating

Participants were asked to subjectively rate how often they used each co-presence inducing interface in a 5-point scale (1-not used at all, 5-used very often). Subjective data related to Interfaces 1 (*Info-bar*), 2 (*Compass*), and 3 (*Mini-map*) provided for a given task were discarded for the users that did not actually objectively used anyof these interfaces in that task (data in previous sections).

In Task 1, an average rating of 2.19 (σ = 1.04) was observed for Interface 1 (*Info-bar*), 2.52 (σ = 1.12) for Interface 2 (*Compass*), 4.74 (σ = 0.59) for Interface 3 (*Mini-map*), 4.06 (σ = 1.06) for *Pointing actions*, 3.24 (σ = 1.17) for *text boxes*, and 2.85 (σ = 1.15) for the *collision warnings*. Hence, all interfaces, except for the information bar, revealed a good result in terms of usage by the participants. The *Mini-map* and *pointing actions* were consulted with high frequency. Participants reported a neutral position regarding the *text boxes* and the *collision warning*. Some reported that these two mechanisms helped a lot in performing the task, others indicate the opposite effect. Although with lower frequency, participants reported that have consulted the *Compass* occasionally. *Info-bar* was classified as being even less used because participants studied the avatars' appearance right at the task's onset. In Task 2, an average rating of 2.63 (σ = 1.38) was observed for Interface 1 (*Info-bar*), 2.53 (σ = 1.17) for Interface 2 (*Compass*), and 4.53 (σ = 0.97) for Interface 3 (*Mini-map*), 4.61 (σ = 0.83) for *Pointing actions*, 2.79 (σ = 1.11) for the *text boxes*, and 2.24 (σ = 1.09) for *collision warning*. All implemented mechanisms, except the collision warning, revealed a good result in terms of usage by the participants. The *Mini-map* was heavily consulted, and *Pointing* was considered the top choice for riddle solving. Participants reported a neutral position regarding *text boxes*. The *Compass* and *Info-bar* were consulted a little more than in Task 1. The *collision warning* did not help much in solving the riddle. In Task 3, an average rating of 2.30 (σ = 1.29) was observed for Interface 1 (*Info-bar*), 2.17 (σ = 1.12) for Interface 2 (*Compass*), 4.83 (σ = 0.59) for Interface 3 (*Mini-map*), 3.03 (σ = 1.51) for *Pointing*, 2.30 (σ = 1.24) for the *text boxes*, and 2.76 (σ = 1.32) for the *collision warning*. The *Mini-map*, *text boxes* and *collision warning* reveal positive results in this task. The interface of the *Mini-map* was considered the top choice for navigation. Participants reported a neutral position regarding *text boxes*. The *Compass* and *Info-bar* were consulted less than in Task 2. The *collision warning*, for some participants, did not help in avoiding collisions and, for others, it helped considerably.

The participants consideration of the co-presence inducing interfaces implemented in VVApp varied from taskto task. For task 1, participants reported that the *Mini-map* was the most used to guide themselves inside the virtual houses, while *Info-bar* and *Compass* were used to identify their partner's avatars and position with small frequency. The *Pointing* showed to be a good non-verbal communication mechanism, the *text boxes* were consulted with a certain frequency to identify the registered pointing markers, and the *collision warnings* caught the attention of some. For task 2, participants claim that the interfaces 1 (*Info-bar*) and 2 (*Compass*) are used with some frequency but gave more priority to Interface 3 (*Mini-map*) in solving riddles. The *Pointing* mechanism showed to be very important in identifying objects and furniture, the *text boxes* were consulted with a certain frequency, and the *collision warnings* were not very helpful. For task 3, the participants claim the *Mini-map* to be an essential tool for navigating in the virtual house, using the *Info-bar* and *Compass* as an intermediate support. The *Pointing* mechanism was used only to guide the participants, while the *text boxes* were consulted with a certain frequency. The *collision warnings* got the attention of some participants to be careful when navigating. With this analysis, it can be stated that the implemented co-presence inducing mechanics, in general, enrich group visits to virtual houses, as predicted in hypothesis H3.

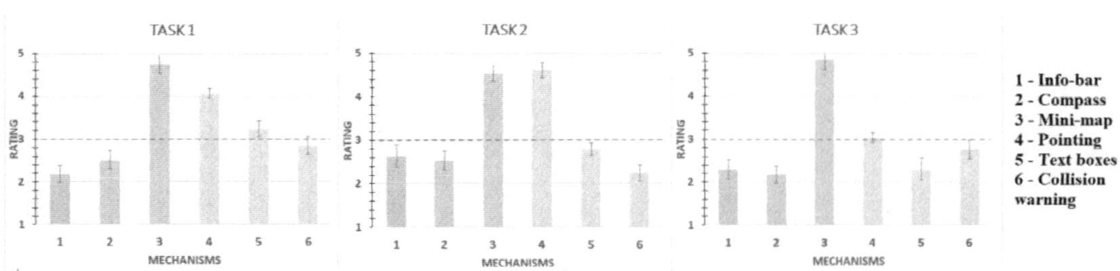

Figure 5. Bar graph of average mechanism rating. It includes a dashed red line that indicates the neutral rating (a value of 3) and the standard error for each mechanism

5.4 Session Form Questionnaire

Table 2 summarizes participants' responses to the session questionnaire: Q1: "Do you have experience with video games?" Q2: "Have you ever played co-op video games with partners you know?" Q3: "Have you been looking for houses to buy/rent before?" Q4: "Would you consider using a system like the one you've been experiencing to help you choose a house in the future?". The responses show that all participants have experience with videogames and recognized the mechanisms implemented in VVApp. All participants, except one, have already played multiplayer videogames with their partners. This reveals that these participants participated in this session with the awareness that they will perform tasks requiring team collaboration. The only participant who had never experienced multiplayer videogames expressed that VVApp's co-presence mechanisms helped a lot in identifying the group partners. A total of 17 participants have already looked for houses to rent or buy. Of these, 12 are over 21 years old. At the end of the session, all participants praised the collaborative experience.

Table 1. Participants' responses to the session questionnaire

Questionnaire							
Q1		Q2		Q3		Q4	
Yes	No	Yes	No	Yes	No	Yes	No
33	0	32	1	17	16	33	0

6. CONCLUSION

A Unity-based collaborative virtual environment, VVApp, designed to include videogame-inspired mechanisms to amplify the co-presence sense of people in virtual group house visits was presented. These mechanisms include an information bar, a visual compass, a small map, pointing actions, text boxes, and user- user collision warnings. Positive results were obtained in a user-study conducted with 33 participants, split in groups of three elements. Concretely, participants frequently used the several co-presence inducing mechanisms to navigate and communicate more efficiently while performing a set of given tasks. All participants had previous experience with multiplayer video games and showed willingness to reuse VVApp. As future work, it would be interesting to study the inclusion in VVApp of two additional co-presence inducing mechanics from videogames: text chat and voice chat. It would also be interesting to study the value of the co-presence inducing mechanisms included in VVApp in different age groups and with users that have no previous experience with videogames.

ACKNOWLEDGMENT

This work was partially supported by FCT under ISTAR projects UIDB/04466/2020 and UIDP/04466/2020.

REFERENCES

Abrams, Sandra Schamroth, and Hannah R. Gerber. (2013). Achieving through the Feedback Loop: Videogames, Authentic Assessment, and Meaningful Learning. *The English Journal*, vol. 103, no. 1, pp. 95–103.

Calado, J., Santana, P., and Lopes., R. (2017). A unity-based framework for sound transmission and perception in video games. In Proc. of the 24º Portuguese Meeting on Computer Graphics and Interaction (EPCGI).

Casanueva, J., Blake, E. (2000). The Effects of Group Collaboration on Presence in a Collaborative Virtual Environment. In: Mulder, J., van Liere, R. (eds) Virtual Environments 2000. Eurographics. Springer, Vienna. https://doi.org/10.1007/978-3-7091-6785-4_10

C. Wienrich, K. Schindler, N. Döllinqer, S. Kock and O. Traupe, (2018). Social Presence and Cooperation in Large-Scale Multi-User Virtual Reality - The Relevance of Social Interdependence for Location-Based Environments, *IEEE Conference on Virtual Reality and 3D User Interfaces (VR)*, pp. 207-214, https://doi.org/10.1109/VR.2018.8446575.

Cho, Y. H., Yim, S. Y., and Paik, S. (2015). Physical and social presence in 3d virtual role-play for pre-service teachers. Internet and Higher Education, vol 25, ISSN 1096-7516, pp. 70-77. https://doi.org/10.1016/j.iheduc.2015.01.002.

Churchill, E. F., & Snowdon, D. (1998). Collaborative virtual environments: an introductory review of issues and systems. *virtual reality*, *3*(1), 3-15.

Darken, R. P., & Sibert, J. L. (1993). A toolset for navigation in virtual environments. In *Proceedings of the 6th annual ACM symposium on User interface software and technology*, pp. 157-165.

Dix, A., Finlay, J., Abowd, G. D., & Beale, R. (2003). *Human-computer interaction*. Pearson Education.

Gamelin, G., Chellali, A., Cheikh, S. *et al.* (2021). Point-cloud avatars to improve spatial communication in immersive collaborative virtual environments. *Pers Ubiquit Comput* 25, pp. 467–484. https://doi.org/10.1007/s00779-020-01431-1

Iana Podkosova and Hannes Kaufmann. (2018). Mutual collision avoidance during walking in real and collaborative virtual environments. In Proceedings of the ACM SIGGRAPH Symposium on Interactive 3D Graphics and Games (I3D '18). Association for Computing Machinery, Article 9, pp. 1–9. https://doi.org/10.1145/3190834.3190845

J. L. Chen and K. M. Stanney. (1999). A Theoretical Model of Wayfinding in Virtual Environments: Proposed Strategies for Navigational Aiding, in *Presence*, vol. 8, no. 6, pp. 671-685, https://doi.org/10.1162/105474699566558.

Kim, Kangsoo, Bruder, Gerd, & Welch, Gregory F. (2018). Blowing in the Wind: Increasing Copresence with a Virtual Human via Airflow Influence in Augmented Reality. International Conference on Artificial Reality and Telexistence and Eurographics Symposium on Virtual Environments. Retrieved from https://par.nsf.gov/biblio/10105838. https://doi.org/10.2312/egve.20181332

Knapp, M. L., Hall, J. A., and Horgan, T. G. (2014). Nonverbal Communication in Human Interaction. Wadsworth, Cencage Learning.

Kyriakou, Marios, Xueni Pan e Yiorgos Chrysanthou (2017). "Interaction with Virtual Crowd in Immersive and semi- Immersive Virtual Reality systems". Computer animations virtual worlds. ISSN 1546-4261, Vol. 28. https://doi.org/10.1002/cav.1729

L. E. Buck, J. J. Rieser, G. Narasimham and B. Bodenheimer, (2019). Interpersonal Affordances and Social Dynamics in Collaborative Immersive Virtual Environments: Passing Together Through Apertures, in *IEEE Transactions on Visualization and Computer Graphics*, vol. 25, no. 5, pp. 2123-2133, https://doi.org/10.1109/TVCG.2019.2899232.

Norman G. Vinson. (1999). Design guidelines for landmarks to support navigation in virtual environments. In Proceedings of the SIGCHI conference on Human Factors in Computing Systems (CHI '99). Association for Computing Machinery, pp. 278–285. https://doi.org/10.1145/302979.303062

Peña Pérez Negrón, A., Muñoz, E. & Lara López, G. (2020). A model for nonverbal interaction cues in collaborative virtual environments. *Virtual Reality* 24, pp. 605–618. https://doi.org/10.1007/s10055-019-00421-w

Pimentel, D. and Vinkers, C. (2021). Copresence with virtual humans in mixed reality: The impact of contextual responsiveness on social perceptions. Frontiers in Robotics and AI. Vol. 8, ISSN 2296-9144, https://doi.org/10.3389/frobt.2021.634520

Stanney, K. M. and Cohn, J. V. (2009). Virtual environments. Human-Computer Interaction, pp. 1031-1048.

Steuer, J., Biocca, F., & Levy, M. R. (1995). Defining virtual reality: Dimensions determining telepresence. Communication in the age of virtual reality, Vol. *33*, 37-39.

Török, Á., Mestre, D., Honbolygó, F. *et al.* (2015). It sounds real when you see it. Realistic sound source simulation in multimodal virtual environments. *J Multimodal User Interfaces* 9, pp. 323–331. https://doi.org/10.1007/s12193-015-0185-4

Warpefelt, H. (2016). The Non-Player Character: Exploring the believability of NPC presentation and behavior (PhD dissertation, Department of Computer and Systems Sciences, Stockholm University).

Zhang, L., Warren, Z., Swanson, A. *et al.* (2018). Understanding Performance and Verbal-Communication of Children with ASD in a Collaborative Virtual Environment. *J Autism Dev Disord* 48, pp. 2779–2789. https://doi.org/10.1007/s10803-018-3544-7

DEFINING INFORMATION VISUALIZATION HEURISTICS BASED ON HEURISTIC GROUPING BY EXPERTS

Juliana Almeida Morroni, Otavio Passarelli Praça, Vitor Augusto Stachetti de Freitas,
Giovana Lodde Girardi and Celmar Guimarães da Silva
School of Technology, University of Campinas
Limeira, São Paulo, Brazil

ABSTRACT

The visualization community has been done some efforts to construct a set of heuristics focused on the qualitative evaluation of a visualization (including usability issues, but not limited to them), which could be used in Heuristic Evaluations (HE). Despite these efforts, we could not find a consolidated (i.e. solid) set of visualization heuristics in use in our community. In this work, we present initial steps for defining a set of heuristics based on heuristics proposed by our community, aiming that such a set can be used in a visualization-focused Heuristic Evaluation and become consolidated after improvements. To develop this work, we started by collecting visualization heuristics and guidelines proposed by our community in papers related to HE; we also collected guidelines extracted from visualization books. A set of experts grouped these heuristics and guidelines using an online card sorting procedure. We summarized these groups in a set of eight heuristics to be used in a regular HE procedure. We assessed these new heuristics in an experiment with professionals and students with visualization background. These participants pointed out that they were able to use the proposed heuristics to identify problems related to visualization concepts in the systems they evaluated. In addition, most participants indicated that the set is well-defined, appropriate, and pertinent to each case found, which is a positive result towards the definition of a consolidated set of heuristics for visualization.

KEYWORDS

Information Visualization, Heuristic Evaluation, Heuristics

1. INTRODUCTION

Heuristic evaluation is a well-known inspection technique for assessing human-computer interfaces. It was proposed initially as a discount method for usability engineering (Nielsen, 1989), given that it can anticipate many relevant interface problems that a usability test would reveal, it is cheaper and faster than that kind of test, and its execution does not involve end users.

Many areas have been defining their own heuristics, such as human-robot interaction, software for children, smartphones, mobile devices and games (Oliveira, 2017). In particular, visualization is also part of this list. This research area has been proposing in the last two decades some sets of heuristics (e.g. the works of Forsell and Johansson (2010), Amar and Stasko (2004), Freitas et al. (2002), Scapin and Bastien (1997), Zuk and Carpendale (2006)), each one with its own concerns about which concepts to focus on and which construction strategy to follow. However, until now we could not perceive a consensual set of "visualization-specific heuristics" (in the terms of Tarrell et al. (2014)), i. e., a set of heuristics that are widely accepted by the visualization community to assess the quality of visualization systems. The opinion of the same authors is that the creation of visualization-specific heuristics would require "a concerted, community-wide effort to be most effective".

Inspired on the need of widely accepted visualization-specific heuristics constructed and validated with the support of the visualization community, this paper presents a small set of heuristics for heuristic evaluation focused on relevant characteristics for information visualization (InfoVis) systems. This set was constructed with the support of InfoVis community members, and it groups 82 heuristics into 8 groups, which originated a new set of eight heuristics. This reduced set was preliminarily evaluated through an experiment with the participation of InfoVis community members, which provided positive feedback about the proposed heuristics.

This paper is organized as follows. We present in Section 2 some works related to the creation of visualization-specific heuristics. In Section 3, we describe our methodology for creating and evaluating our own set of heuristics with support of the InfoVis community. We discuss our results in Section 4, in which we highlight the description of our new heuristic set, the evaluation procedure, and the feedback of the evaluators that used our heuristics. The last section concludes the paper and points out future work.

2. RELATED WORK

As we pointed out in the beginning of this paper, the InfoVis area has been developing a list of heuristic sets for itself for at least twenty years (Freitas et al., 2002; Amar and Stasko, 2004; Zuk and Carpendale, 2006; Scapin and Bastien, 1997; Forsell and Johansson, 2010). Oliveira and Silva (2017) summarize the main contributions of these works. Developing such kind of heuristics is relevant, given that using visualization-specific heuristics would provide more effective assessment of visualizations than using usability heuristics (Tarrell et al., 2014).

Regarding some desired properties for InfoVis heuristics, Santos et al. (2018) argued that these heuristics should not be very specific, because this situation would have the potential to distract the evaluators from finding other, more general problems. Väätäjä et al. (2016) pointed out that the document that describes the heuristic set (in their case, the set of Forsell and Johansson (2010)) should include examples of heuristic violations, should group the heuristics according to a logical order, and should also shorten their descriptions. They also reported the need to include heuristics related to user interactions and aesthetics in that particular set. In a similar way, Santos et al. (2018) pointed out that some of the current proposed heuristics may be hard to use, and suggested that some heuristics could be rephrased and perhaps presented as exemplified guidelines.

Tarrell et al. (2014) and Oliveira and Silva (2017) presented distinct classifications of the approaches for developing heuristics. Tarrell et al. (2014) proposed three classes of approaches for creating visualization-specific heuristics: process-based approaches, in which the heuristics embrace all aspects of a visualization process; performance-based approaches, which propose a small set of heuristics that tries to cover most known problems; and framework-based approaches, which organize heuristics into categories. The authors argued that a framework-based approach would be better that the other two approaches. Oliveira and Silva (2017) defined two main classes of techniques for developing heuristic sets: techniques based on human resources, or based on literature review. In the first case, brainstorming meetings, answering questionnaires, and rating heuristics are some of the mentioned ways in which recruited people (users and/or experts) may help to define the heuristic set. In the second case, literature exploration, transformation of guidelines into heuristics, and derivation of heuristics from a set of problems are some strategies to define heuristic sets.

Apart from these classifications, it is worth noting that Tarrell et al. (2014) pointed out that the development of such set of heuristics is not straightforward, and it would require "a concerted, community-wide effort to be most effective". They proposed that the community should work in a wide, asynchronous iterative task in which the proposed visualization guidelines could be commented on, voted on, and refined.

It is also relevant to consider how visualization-specific heuristics would complement (or be complemented by) other evaluation techniques. The work of Santos et al. (2018) compared problems found in usability tests and those found by heuristic evaluations. These evaluations used Nielsen's usability heuristics (Nielsen, 1994) and the visualization heuristics proposed by Zuk and Carpendale (2006) and Forsell and Johansson (2010). The authors pointed out that usability tests may complement the list of problems found by these visualization heuristics (which is similar to what happens with Nielsen's heuristics), according to their comparison.

Assessing the quality of a given set of heuristics is also a concern. Regarding this topic, Väätäjä et al. (2016) used a qualitative and quantitative methodology for assessing the explanatory quality of the heuristics of Forsell and Johansson (2010). The proposed methodology collects data from evaluators, after a heuristic evaluation session, about how well the heuristics explain the problems found by the evaluators, the usefulness of each heuristic, how easy (or not) was to do the evaluation procedure with these heuristics, and how to improve them. The authors perceived the need to provide better, more comprehensive definitions of these heuristics than those presented by Forsell and Johansson (2010), and these definitions were presented to the evaluators before the evaluation sessions. Väätäjä et al. (2016) concluded that the assessed heuristics have a good explanatory quality, because 65% of the reported heuristic violations gave a complete or fairly complete explanation of these violations to the evaluators. Väätäjä et al. (2016) also indicated that the lack of knowledge of the application domain by the evaluators may hamper the evaluation process.

As far as we know, the three last sets of heuristics presented in the InfoVis literature were the sets of Wall et al. (2019), Zhu and Gumieniak (2021), and Oliveira and Silva (2017) (whose work was partially complemented by Oliveira (2017)). Wall et al. (2019) presented a methodology called ICE-T. It comprises a set of 21 low-level heuristics, which are grouped into ten guidelines and further into components. These components (insight, confidence, essence and time) are supposed to represent the value of the visualization under evaluation. One step that differs ICE-T from other approaches is that the evaluators must provide a score for each heuristic, instead of associating problems with heuristics.

Zhu and Gumieniak (2021) proposed a computer-assisted heuristic evaluation method for data visualization. They exemplify some of the heuristics they considered; however, the complete list of heuristic rules they used is not available in their work. It is noteworthy that they argue that "Many heuristic rules are too abstract to be checked automatically", which enhances the need to have a human inspection of visualization systems.

The set of Oliveira and Silva (2017) and Oliveira (2017) was based on grouping of heuristics proposed by the following authors: Forsell and Johansson (2010), Shneiderman (1996), Amar and Stasko (2004), Freitas et al. (2002), Scapin and Bastien (1997), Nielsen (1994), and Zuk and Carpendale (2006). It is worth noting that Zuk and Carpendale (2006) also define "potential heuristics" based on theories and guidelines from the works of Bertin (1983), Tufte (1991), and Ware (2004). Oliveira and Silva (2017) grouped all these heuristics (a total of 62 ones) based on a matrix with pairwise similarity of heuristics. This matrix was reordered to group similar heuristics, aiming to help the visual identification of groups. They empirically defined the similarity level of each pair of heuristics as "not similar"; "somewhat similar"; "resembling, but not equal", and "equal". Visualizing this similarity matrix as a heatmap helped the authors to propose their groups of interrelated heuristics. After that, they defined each group as a new heuristic, which received a name and a description. They proposed a set of 15 heuristics. Oliveira (2017) conducted a preliminary HE with this new set of heuristics and collected a set of suggestions about how to improve it. Three evaluators conducted the evaluation of a visualization system from the electric power generation sector. They started with an individual session of assessment, followed by a consolidation session. The evaluation returned a set of problems to be solved in the assessed software. Oliveira (2017) pointed out that the empirical values of the similarity matrix could be a source of bias in the work, and that information visualization books could contribute with relevant concepts that possibly were not covered by the proposed heuristics.

3. METHODOLOGY

Our methodology comprises the following steps:

1. *Collecting sets of visualization heuristics published in previous papers*. This step is composed of bibliographic review about heuristic evaluation in visualization.
2. *Collecting a set of guidelines published in visualization books*. We consider this step necessary to fill in some possible gaps regarding visualization concepts that would not have been covered by the set of heuristics proposed in previous works. (Hereafter we will consider that guidelines can be understood as heuristics, and therefore we will use only the term "heuristics" to refer heuristics and guidelines).
3. *Generating groups of interrelated heuristics*. This step involves the participation of visualization experts to group the heuristics. Using the *card sorting* technique (Nielsen and Mack, 1994) supported by an online tool, each expert should individually create clusters of heuristics and provide a representative name to each cluster. It is worth noting the relevance of the participation of experts in this step, aiming to avoid bias.
4. *Creating a new set of visualization heuristics*, based on groups generated in the previous step. This step begins with a review and comparison of the (sometimes conflicting) groups of heuristics defined by each expert. The intermediate result of this process is a single set of groups of heuristics that tries to better represent the opinions of the experts. Based on this result, it is possible to define a new list of heuristics, one for each proposed group. Each heuristic must have a clear name and a description, based on the group of heuristics that the new heuristic represents.

5. *Evaluating the new heuristics*. The proposed preliminary assessing procedure comprises four steps.
   (a) First of all, it is necessary to define which systems will be evaluated by the proposed visualization-based HE. This choice may be guided by the experience of the research team regarding the perceived quality of visualization systems, and by the already known problems these systems present. The pre-selected systems are then inspected to search for problems related to each of the new heuristics, with the aim to find at least one problem per group of heuristics.
   (b) After selecting the systems to be assessed, it is necessary to invite a set of professionals and graduate students, with experience in visualization, to participate of a HE session. The first task of these professionals is to fill a short profile questionnaire; the questions are: highest academic level; formation area; working area; and years of experience with information visualization.
   (c) After filling the questionnaire, the authors must indicate that the participants should execute the individual step of a HE with the proposed visualization heuristics, in the set of systems defined by the authors. Each participant should briefly describe (and illustrate, if possible) the visualization problems they identified on each system. They should also link each problem to some of the new heuristics and to inform the reasoning behind the linking. It is noteworthy that the authors should not provide a set of tasks to guide the participants in exploring the systems in search of heuristic violations.
   (d) According to their own experience when executing the HE with the proposed heuristics, each participant should use a five-point Likert scale score, varying from 1 (completely disagree) to 5 (completely agree), to classify eight statements, one per heuristic. Each statement has the format "The heuristic *N*, "*name*" is suitable for evaluating visualization systems". *N* and *name* are respectively the number and name of the heuristic.
   (e) Besides, the participant should also write a brief analysis of the heuristic set, in which he/she should consider aspects such as suitability, pertinence, objectivity, and usefulness of the set of heuristics, and if the description of each heuristic is adequate.
   (f) The authors are then in charge of the analysis, comparison, and summarization of these results.

4. RESULTS

In this section we present and discuss the results we obtained by following our methodology. We split this section in two parts: definition (Section 4.1) and evaluation (Section 4.2) of the proposed heuristics.

4.1 Defining Heuristics

We summarize the results of the first steps of our methodology, from the selection of heuristics to the definition of a new set of heuristics:

1. *Collecting sets of visualization heuristics published in previous papers*: in this step, we considered as a starting point the papers already selected by Oliveira and Silva (2017), which surveyed works related to heuristic evaluation in visualization. Therefore, we chose the 62 heuristics they collected in their work.
2. *Collecting a set of guidelines published in visualization books*: in this second step, we complemented the selected heuristics with a set of 22 heuristics extracted from the books of Ward et al. (2015) and Mazza (2009). We chose these books due to our own perception about their easy-of-learning style and their
   coverage regarding the main aspects of the visualization area. Therefore, at the end of this step, we collected a set of 84 heuristics (this number includes the heuristics found in the Step 1).
3. *Generating groups of interrelated heuristics*: for this step, we invited a set of five researchers with background in visualization. We used the online tool Proven By Users (https://provenbyusers.com, accessed in August, 2020) to conduct this step. We inserted each of the heuristics from Step 2 into this tool as a card (except two of them, which were omitted due to a manual failure). During the use of the tool, the participants individually grouped the cards with heuristics, according to subjective similarity criteria. Therefore, at the end of this step, we had five distinct ways of grouping the set of heuristics.
4. *Creating a new set of visualization heuristics*: in this step, we compared the groups of heuristics defined by each of the five participants. First of all, we studied the co-occurrence of heuristics in groups.

For each pair (h_1, h_2) of heuristics, we defined a function $c(h_1, h_2)$ that counts how many groups have both heuristics. After that, we constructed a reorderable heatmap that represents this function; rows and columns represent heuristics, and the cells represent the values of the function c. We used a hierarchical clustering method (with average linkage criterion) to reorder and group the heuristics in the heatmap. Based on this reordered heatmap, we identified groups that could be considered as more consensual regarding the experts' grouping. We used these groups as a starting point to define a single set of groups of heuristics. Each of these groups was then considered as a new heuristic. Each new heuristic received a representative name and a description that includes the concepts of the heuristics that it embraces. The process of providing clear descriptions to each new heuristic motivated us to enhance the differences between them. Therefore, we made at this point a new review of the heuristic grouping, where some groups were merged. The final result of this step was the following new list of heuristics:

- **Heuristic 1. Help and error management.**
  - Prevent user errors;
  - Help users undo or redo one or more actions (for error correction or as part of an exploratory process);
  - Help users understand error messages using simple, code-free language;
  - Provide easy-to-find help for users.
- **Heuristic 2. Interaction and view transformation.**
  - Allow users to have an overview of the dataset, adjust the visualization focus (zoom resources), and dynamically select data (dynamic queries);
  - Allow users to get details about a data selection and browse those details, as well as extract selected items and selection parameters.
- **Heuristic 3. Action control and feedback.**
  - Users must receive feedback on the actions they executed on the system, in an appropriate manner and within a reasonable time.
- **Heuristic 4. Decreased visual effort.**
  - Avoid visual overload;
  - Use item grouping, and item distinction by format and localization appropriately;
  - Use proper graphic resources to get immediate users' attention when needed.
- **Heuristic 5. Decreased cognitive effort.**
  - Prevent users from having to remember information from one part of the dialog to another;
  - Use visualizations that are consistent with users' knowledge and experience (idiom, language, symbol understanding, expected order of how a system displays information, expected order to perform actions; and low or high computing or application domain experience).
- **Heuristic 6. Decreased motor effort.**
  - Provide accelerators to increase the interaction speed (such as shortcuts and control keys).
- **Heuristic 7. Ease of obtaining and deriving information.**
  - Provide resources to ease the creation, acquisition and transfer of knowledge or metadata about domain parameters;
  - Expose data uncertainties and their consequences;
  - Support the formulation and confirmation of hypothesis, as well as manual or automatic discovery of correlation models and constraints;
  - Allow users to visualize and understand relationships between data;
  - Add text to the visualization, in an integrated manner, when needed;
  - Use extra codification to help the perception of information elements (such as clusters);
  - Make easy to find information elements in the visualization, as well as understand the general disposition of information elements in the visualization.
- **Heuristic 8. Visual mapping**
  - Follow visual mapping guidelines that are consistent with the types of each variable of the dataset to be visualized (categorical, ordinal or quantitative), aiming to provide an appropriate precision level to the users' analysis task;
  - Consider limitations of the proposed mapping, such as space constraints to show a visualization, constraints on the number of marks and variables to be presented, and constraints of each graphic property regarding the number of elements it is able to represent;
  - Enable changes in scales;
  - Consider the semantic of colors in the source domain of the data, when relevant;

- Consider visual constraints related to accessibility (color blindness especially);
- Promote graphical excellence; do not use inadequate visual mappings that promote data misinterpretations; and present as much ideas as possible, in the lowest possible time, using the smallest amount of ink, using the smallest possible space.

4.2 Evaluating the New Heuristics

To prepare our preliminary evaluation procedure of our new heuristics, we started by selecting two systems to be evaluated: Gapminder's Bubbles (https://www.gapminder.org/tools) and DrasticData's Treemapping (https://www.drasticdata.nl/treemapping.htm) – hereafter mentioned as Gapminder and DrasticData, respectively, for short. These systems were initially selected due to previous experience of our research team using both systems in visualization classes.

We executed a preliminary inspection of these systems, based on our new list of heuristics, aiming to confirm that the systems have visualization problems related to most of these heuristics. We observed that Gapminder violates heuristics 1, 3, 5, and 7 (at least one violation per heuristic), and DrasticData violates heuristics 2, 4, and 8 (one violation per heuristic). We did not note violations to the heuristic 6. Therefore, we concluded that we could use these systems in our experiment.

After selecting Gapminder and DrasticData, we invited 9 people with experience in visualization to use our heuristics in a HE session. Their highest level of formal education is doctorate (4 participants), master's degree (3), MBA (1) and graduation (1). Their study area is "computing"; they used many different names for that, such as computer science, information systems, and systems analysis and development; some reported artificial intelligence and InfoVis. Four participants reported that their current occupation area is InfoVis, while other reported varied areas such as business intelligence, data science, information systems, systems analysis and development, computer science, machine learning, and software development. Four participants reported that they have 3.5 to 5 years of experience with information visualization, two participants reported 6 to 9 years, and three participants informed 10 to 12 years. Therefore, we can conclude that our HE was carried out by professionals who are mostly Ph. D. and masters in computing, work mostly with InfoVis and have an average of 7.3 years of experience in the area. These characteristics contribute to strengthen the analysis of the results that we will present.

Each participant performed a HE of the selected systems using our list of heuristics, as proposed in the methodology. Regarding the Gapminder visualization, the HE revealed a set of 17 violations of heuristics composed by the union of all violations reported by each participant. All heuristics were used at least one time, except the heuristic 5, which was not used. From the 7 problems that were reported by more than one participant, in 5 of them the participants cited the same heuristic to identify the problem (sometimes using a complementary heuristic to enhance the error description). Besides, from the 6 heuristic violations that we previously identified in Gapminder, the participants found 5 of them, and in 3 problems both the authors and the participant(s) classified the violation using the same heuristic.

In the HE performed over the DrasticData system, the union of the heuristic violations observed by the participants comprised 15 violations. In this case, all heuristics were used at least one time, with no exceptions. From the 6 problems reported by more than one participant, in 3 of them the participants identified the problem using the same heuristic (sometimes using a complementary heuristic to enhance the error description, as already happened in the Gapminder's HE). We had previously found only 3 problems in DrasticData, but we classified these problems with different heuristics than the participants, except in one case.

These results raise some considerations about the new heuristics. We can comprehend a heuristic evaluation as a process with two goals: helping to find errors, and helping to classify each of them. In our evaluation experiment, we observed that more errors were found than we expected; we can consider this as a normal situation, given the already known advice of having 3 to 5 evaluators in a HE session (Nielsen, 1994). Regarding the classification of errors, we noted that some errors were associated with more than one heuristic (sometimes by the same evaluator). We highlight that heuristic 7 (Ease of obtaining and deriving information) was reported for a same error than other heuristics were, such as heuristic 8 (Visual mapping) and 4 (Decreased visual effort). Some factors that may justify this situation are the novelty of these heuristics for the evaluators, and the complementarity of the heuristic 7 regarding other heuristics (e.g., a non-appropriate visual mapping can lead to a visualization in which is hard to obtain information). Besides, we did not a consolidation step in which evaluators could aggregated, discuss and refine the errors they found; such step could potentially reduce these multiple classifications.

	Participants										
Heuristics	1	2	3	4	5	6	7	8	9	Mean	Std. Dev.
H1	5	5	5	5	5	4	4	5	5	4.8	0.4
H2	5	5	5	5	3	4	5	5	5	4.7	0.7
H3	5	5	5	5	5	3	5	5	5	4.8	0.7
H4	4	5	3	5	3	4	5	5	4	4.2	0.8
H5	5	5	5	5	5	4	5	5	4	4.8	0.4
H6	3	5	5	5	5	2	2	5	4	4.0	1.3
H7	5	5	5	5	3	4	5	5	5	4.7	0.7
H8	5	5	5	5	3	4	5	5	5	4.7	0.7
Experience with InfoVis (years)	12	10	8	6	5	5	10	3.5	4		

Figure 1. Matrix with five-point Likert scale scores for questions related to each heuristic

Figure 1 presents a heatmap with the Likert scale scores given by each participant to the statements related to each heuristic. The color mapping follows a red-white-blue scale, in which bluish cells represent scores 4 or 5, white cells indicate score 3, and reddish cells represent scores 1 or 2. The overall bluish appearance of this heatmap and the mean scores indicate that in most situations the participants agreed that the heuristics are suitable for evaluating visualization systems.

The opinions provided by the participants about each heuristic revealed some possibilities of improvement for our heuristic set. We highlight the following improvements: enabling evaluators to better distinguish heuristics 2 and 7, and 4 and 8; splitting heuristic 7 into two or three heuristics; removing subjective terms in heuristics 3 and 4; and considering how essential is to add a heuristic related to shortcuts (heuristic 6). It is worth noting that the lowest mean scores of heuristics 4 and 6 are consistent with the problems pointed out in the comments.

Besides the heuristic-focused comments, the participants also provided overview comments about the heuristics. Most of them were positive. The participants made two suggestions: indicating filtering and sampling as visual scalability solutions (maybe as part of heuristic 4); and considering how suitable is the scale of values being used to represent the data space (including distortion aspects and possible interpretation problems).

We must highlight a set of limitations of our work, which need to be considered when trying to follow our methodology. First of all, given the absence of a control group in our experiment, we could not state that our heuristic set is more effective than others proposed by the InfoVis literature. We also cannot state that the results can be generalized to other types of visualizations, given that only two systems were evaluated. The small number of participants involved along the process may also limit this generalization; further research should evaluate more systems with more participants in order to verify this possible generalization. Besides, we believe that the work of Wall et al. (2019) points out a complementary view to our work, and we must consider this work before doing new experiments. We also did not collect data about the participants' previous experience with practical application of HE; their level of expertise could help to better group heuristics, or to better execute HE procedures.

5. CONCLUSIONS

This work presented a proposal of a new set of heuristics for assessing visualization software in a heuristic evaluation method. We created this set based on a process in which experts clustered heuristics which were available in InfoVis literature or were derived from InfoVis books. The proposed groups of heuristics were used as a basis for the proposition of our heuristics.

A set of evaluators with expertise in InfoVis used these heuristics to assess two visualizations available on web, with the goal of experimenting these new heuristics. The evaluators found a set of InfoVis-related problems in these systems, and classified them according to the violated heuristics. They also expressed their opinions related to the experience of using our InfoVis-related heuristics. The scores they provided pointed out that they agree, in average, that these heuristics are suitable for evaluating visualization systems. They provided very constructive comments about how to improve these heuristics, including the need of clarifying terms in some descriptions, adding some missing concepts, and helping to distinguish between some heuristics.

We understand that there is still a long way to reach a wide accepting of the proposed heuristics by the InfoVis community. Future work includes refining the proposed heuristics according to the received comments presented in this paper, as well as conducting more heuristic evaluations using these heuristics. We also plan to measure the coverage of these heuristics and to compare it to the coverage of other heuristics and other evaluation methods, so that we can better understand the pros and cons of using our heuristics to evaluate visualization systems.

ACKNOWLEDGEMENT

This study was financed in part by the Coordenação de Aperfeiçoamento de Pessoal de Nível Superior – Brasil (CAPES) – Finance Code 001. We also thank the grant #2170/23 from FAEPEX/PRP/Unicamp.

REFERENCES

Amar, R. and Stasko, J., 2004. A knowledge task-based framework for design and evaluation of information visualizations. In *IEEE Symposium on Information Visualization*, pp. 143–150.

Bertin, J., 1983. *Semiology of Graphics: Diagrams, Networks, Maps*. University of Wisconsin Press.

Forsell, C. and Johansson, J., 2010. An heuristic set for evaluation in information visualization. In *Proceedings of the International Conference on Advanced Visual Interfaces*, AVI '10. New York, USA, pp. 199–206.

Freitas, C. M. D. S. et al., 2002. Evaluating usability of information visualization techniques. In *Proceedings of 5th Symposium on Human Factors in Computer Systems*, pp. 40–51.

Mazza, R., 2009. *Introduction to Information Visualization*. Springer Publishing Company, 1st edition.

Nielsen, J. and Mack, R. L., 1994. *Usability Inspection Methods*. John Wiley & Sons.

Nielsen, J., 1989. Usability engineering at a discount. In *Proc. of the Third Int. Conference on Human-Computer Interaction on Designing and Using Human-Computer Interfaces and Knowledge Based Systems* (2nd Ed.), USA, pp. 394–401.

Nielsen, J., 1994. Enhancing the explanatory power of usability heuristics. In *Proceedings of the SIGCHI Conference on Human Factors in Computing Systems*, CHI '94. New York, USA, pp. 152–158.

Oliveira, M. R. and Silva, C. G., 2017. Adapting heuristic evaluation to information visualization - a method for defining a heuristic set by heuristic grouping. In *Proceedings of the 12th International Joint Conference on Computer Vision, Imaging and Computer Graphics Theory and Applications* - IVAPP, (VISIGRAPP 2017), pp. 225–232.

Oliveira, M. R., 2017. *Adapting heuristic evaluation for use in information visualization*. Master's thesis, University of Campinas, Limeira, Brazil.

Santos, B. S. et al., 2018. Heuristic evaluation in visualization: An empirical study. In *2018 IEEE Evaluation and Beyond - Methodological Approaches for Visualization (BELIV)*, pp. 78–85.

Scapin, D. L. and Bastien, J. M. C., 1997. Ergonomic criteria for evaluating the ergonomic quality of interactive systems. *Behaviour & Information Technology*, 16(4-5):220–231.

Shneiderman, B. (1996). The eyes have it: a task by data type taxonomy for information visualizations. In *Proceedings 1996 IEEE Symposium on Visual Languages*, pp. 336–343.

Tarrell, A. et al., 2014. Toward visualization specific heuristic evaluation. In *Proceedings of the Fifth Workshop on Beyond Time and Errors: Novel Evaluation Methods for Visualization*, BELIV '14. New York, USA, pp 110–117.

Tufte, E. R., 2001. *The Visual Display of Quantitative Information*. Graphics Press, 2nd edition.

Väätäjä, H. et al., 2016. Information visualization heuristics in practical expert evaluation. In *Proc. of the Sixth Workshop on Beyond Time and Errors on Novel Evaluation Methods for Visualization*, BELIV '16. New York, USA, pp. 36–43.

Wall, E. et al., 2019. A heuristic approach to value-driven evaluation of visualizations. *IEEE Transactions on Visualization and Computer Graphics*, Vol. 25, No. 1, pp. 491–500.

Ward, M. et al., 2015. *Interactive Data Visualization: Foundations, Techniques, and Applications*. A K Peters/CRC Press, Natick, MA, USA, 2nd edition.

Ware, C., 2004. *Information Visualization: Perception for Design*. Morgan Kaufmann Publishers, 2nd edition.

Zhu, Y. and Gumieniak, J. A., 2021. Computer-assisted heuristic evaluation of data visualization. In *Advances in Visual Computing*, pp. 408–420, Cham. Springer International Publishing.

Zuk, T. and Carpendale, S., 2006. Theoretical analysis of uncertainty visualizations. In *Visualization and Data Analysis 2006*, Vol. 6060, pp. 66–79.

ALTERNATIVE HDLOD METHOD FOR LARGE SCENES WITH MULTIPLE DYNAMIC BEHAVIORS

Vasily Shutkin[1], Vitaly Semenov[1,2], Vladislav Zolotov[1] and Nikita Morozkin[1]
[1]*Ivannikov Institute for System Programming of the Russian Academy of Sciences*
25, Alexander Solzhenitsyn st., Moscow, 109004, Russia
[2]*Moscow Institute of Physics and Technology (National Research University)*
9 Institutskiy per., Dolgoprudny, Moscow Region, 141701, Russia

ABSTRACT

Efficient rendering of large dynamic scenes is one of the most important problems of computer graphics, which arises in many applications such as CAD/CAM/CAE, geoinformatics, project management, scientific visualization, virtual and augmented reality, computer games and animation. The previously developed method of Hierarchical Dynamic Levels of Detail (HDLOD) helps alleviate this problem. However, it has some drawbacks when it comes to the applications where 3D scene must be visualized with different dynamic behaviors sequentially or simultaneously in several windows. Also, the method requires to regenerate all representations when dynamic behavior of some objects change. This happens, because HDLOD combines both spatial and temporal information in single data structure. In this paper we present an alternative version of HDLOD method that decouples spatial and temporal information into different interrelated data structures.

KEYWORDS

Levels of Detail, Hierarchical Levels of Detail, Dynamic 3D Scenes

1. INTRODUCTION

The problem of efficient rendering of complex scenes has been studied intensively for over many decades. Proposed approaches include frustum culling, occlusion culling and simplification culling. The concept of simplification culling developed from geometry simplification (Luebke 2001), to generating series of simplified representations, also known as levels of detail (Rossignac and Borrel 1993), to hierarchical levels of detail (HLOD) (Erikson et al. 2001). More detailed information on this topic can be found in the book (Luebke et al. 2003). In this paper we will focus on HLOD methods, which provide levels of detail not only for individual objects, but also for the groups of objects organized into multi-level hierarchy. This allows to achieve high scalability on large scenes by reducing the number of entities that need to be processed, reducing scene graph traverse time and number of draw calls. In addition, simplifying large meshes obtained by merging multiple objects overcomes fragmentation and results in higher visual quality. Their advantages make HLOD one of the best solutions for large static scenes. However, for dynamic scenes HLOD have serious disadvantage in a fact that HLOD representations have to be recalculated each time changes in the scene occur.

In this paper we will consider applications where dynamics has predefined nature. The large scene must be animated using preassigned dynamic profiles for objects: the objects can appear, disappear, change color and move. For example, this is the case of spatial-temporal (4D) modelling and visual planning systems such as Autodesk Navisworks, Bentley Synchro Pro, OpenBIMSystems 7D Modeler, Bexel Manager. Such software is widely used to plan, control and manage project work in the construction of buildings, structures and infrastructure. It allows to simulate construction processes by animating 3D model according to the project schedule. Moreover, such systems often offer multi-view interface, where the same model can be simultaneously animated in multiple windows with different schedules, i.e., to compare planned construction schedule with actual progress on the construction site. As an example, screenshot of the 7D Modeler application is presented in Figure 1. In the right window the 3D scene is visualized according to planned dates, which shows that according to the initial project plan three building floors must have been constructed by the current date. The left window utilizes actual dates and shows that outer walls on the third floor haven't yet been constructed due to some issues or delays on the construction site (i.e., logistic problems, weather factors, shortage of human resources). This is a rather simple example, whereas real industrial projects typically involve complex models with detailed architectural, mechanical, electrical and plumbing data, resulting in 3D scenes consisting of thousands of objects represented by millions of polygons.

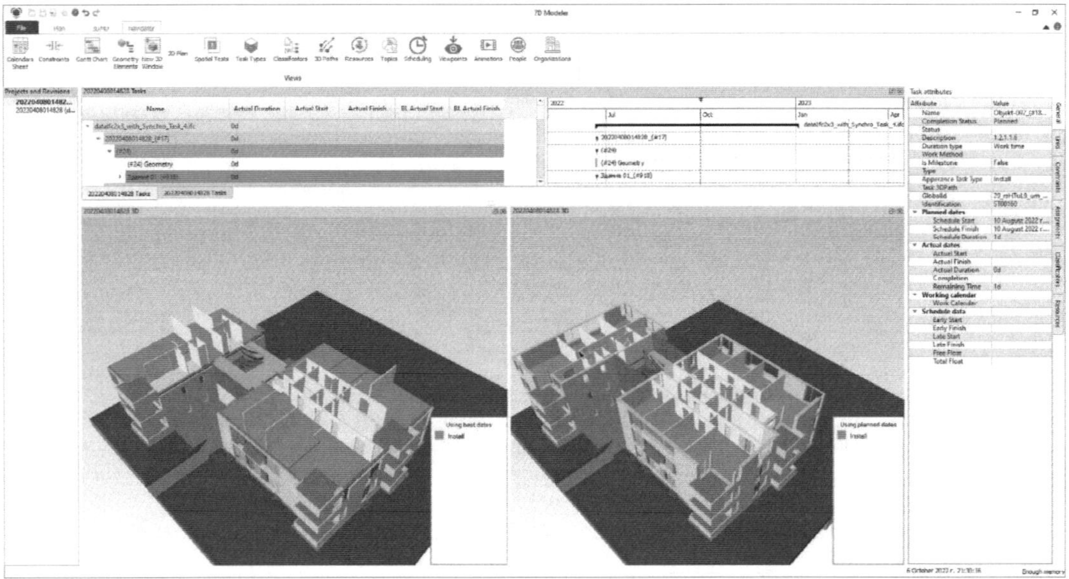

Figure 1. Screenshot of 7D Modeler with a construction scene rendered in multiple views according to different project schedules: actual (left) and planned (right)

Previously, a method of hierarchical dynamic levels of detail (HDLOD) has been developed for efficient visualization of large scenes with predefined dynamics (Semenov 2019). Similar to HLOD, it also assumes preliminary hierarchical clustering of objects. However, it takes into account not only their spatial proximity, but also the similarity of dynamic behaviors. As a result, each HDLOD cluster encapsulates both geometric model and dynamic behavior. This allows to animate the scene throughout the entire time interval without the need to recompute representations. At the same time, such approach can have some drawbacks. For example, when dynamic behavior changes, HDLOD must be regenerated with updated dynamic information. Also, if the scene has to be visualized in multiple windows using different dynamic behaviors (i.e., project schedules, drawing patterns), separate HDLODs have to be generated for each window, which increases CPU/GPU overloads and memory consumption. To address these issues, an alternative HDLOD method has been developed, that decouples spatial and temporal information. This allows to use single HDLOD cluster tree for different purposes while avoiding regeneration of HDLOD clusters due to behavior changes.

The original HDLOD method is shortly described in section 2. The alternative HDLOD method, that is the main result of this paper, is presented in section 3. Section 4 discusses the topics of high performance HDLOD generation and GPU rendering. A comparative study of the original and alternative HDLOD methods using computational experiments and benchmarking is provided in section 5. In conclusions, we briefly outline the key advantages and partial impairs of the proposed method for rendering large scenes with multiple dynamic behaviors.

2. ORIGINAL HDLOD METHOD

The original HDLOD method presented earlier in (Semenov 2019) uses both spatial and temporal information during clustering. If forms the tree of clusters, each of which has its own dynamic behavior. Formally, it can be expressed as follows. Suppose that a scene $S = \{s(g_s, p_s(t), m_s(t))\}$ is represented as a set of objects s that are defined in a 3D Euclidean space E^3 on a simulation time interval $[0, T]$. Each object $s \in S$ has an invariable geometric representation g_s. The presence (or visibility) of the object s may depend on time and is defined by the presence function $p_s(t): [0, T] \to \{0,1\}$ in such a way that the function takes unit values when the object is present and zero values when the object is absent. The position of the object is determined by its movement function $m_s(t): [0, T] \to M$, where M is a set of transformations, defining location and orientation of the object. Transformations can be represented by 4×4 matrices, quaternions or any other data structures.

In terms of dynamic behavior, all objects in the scene can be divided into three non-overlapping classes.

The class of *static* objects includes the objects whose presence and position do not change throughout the entire simulation period, i.e., $\forall t \in [0, T]\ p_s(t) = 1, m_s(t) = I$, where I is the identity transform.

The class of *pseudo-dynamic* objects consists of the objects that appear and disappear without changing their positions: $\forall t \in [0, T]\ m_s(t) = I$, but $\exists t_1, t_2 \in [0, T]$ such that $p_s(t_1) \neq p_s(t_2)$.

Finally, the class of *dynamic* objects implies that both the presence function and movement function of the object vary with time.

Originally, hierarchical dynamic levels of detail (HDLOD) are defined as a tree of clusters $C = \{c(g_c, p_c(t), m_c(t), b_c(t), \delta_c(t))\} \cup \{\prec\}$ represented by a set of clusters c and a set of agglomeration relations $\prec$. Each cluster c is specified by its geometric representation g_c, which doesn't change with time, and the following functions defined over the entire simulation interval $[0, T]$. Similar to the scene objects, clusters have presence function $p_c(t): [0, T] \to \{0,1\}$ and movement function $m_c(t): [0, T] \to M$. Additionally, they have a bounding volume function $b_c(t): [0, T] \to B$, where B is a set of volumes in E^3, which is needed to determine cluster bounds at each moment of time and perform frustum culling during rendering. The main concept, unique to HDLOD, is geometric error function $\delta_c(t): [0, T] \to [0, \Delta_c]$, which describes deviation of the cluster geometry from geometries of its originated objects at different moments of time, with Δ_c being the maximum deviation throughout the whole time period. Each agglomeration relation $c' \prec c$ defines child-parent relationships and means that the parent cluster $c \in C$ was formed from simplified geometric and behavioral representations of the child cluster $c' \in C$. Clusters at the top of the tree contain spatiotemporal representations with lowest levels of detail, while bottom clusters provide representations with higher levels of detail.

During rendering, the cluster tree is traversed starting from the root and descending to the leaves. Visualization is performed at specific moment of time $t_{current} \in [0, T]$. For each visited cluster a decision must be made on whether to render the cluster, skip it, or visit more detailed child clusters. Here, the bounding volume of the cluster $b_c(t_{current})$ is checked against the view frustum. To determine if the quality of the cluster is sufficient, its geometric error $\delta_c(t_{current})$ is converted to the screen-space error and checked against user-defined tolerance. At $t_{current}$, some scene objects are present, some are absent. If we decide to render the cluster, absent scene objects (that have been clustered into that cluster) will be rendered as part of it. If we decide to skip the cluster, present scene objects won't be rendered. This error is included into $\delta_c(t)$ during HDLOD generation and is synchronized with $p_c(t)$, so that $\delta_c(t)$ takes into account geometric error, introduced by rendering absent objects when $p_c(t) = 1$, and geometric error, introduced by not rendering present objects when $p_c(t) = 0$.

HDLOD generation builds the cluster tree from the bottom to the top, by aggregating clusters into larger and more simplified ones. The cluster tree is built for static and pseudo-dynamic objects. Dynamic objects are processed separately. Generation starts by forming leaf clusters from the scene objects without any simplifications. Amongst these clusters, the one with the smallest bounding volume b_{min} is found. Typically, to compare bounding volumes, linear dimensions can be used, i.e., diagonal of the bounding box or radius of the bounding sphere. The clustering is performed in steps. At each step n, the algorithm tries to form clusters with the size of $b_n = n \cdot r \cdot b_{min}$, where r is a parameter of the algorithm that defines how quickly the sizes of the clusters will grow with each step. For each cluster, neighbors are sought in both spatial and temporal dimensions. Spatially, the clusters must be close enough in order to not exceed the size limit b_n. Temporal distance is calculated using the formula:

$$D_p(p_A(t), p_B(t)) = \frac{1}{T} \int_0^T |p_A(t) - p_B(t)| dt.$$

Temporal distance at each step must not exceed b_n / b_s, where b_s is a bounding box of the whole scene. At the step when $b_n \geq b_s$ clustering process finishes. The neighboring clusters are grouped together into new cluster that becomes their parent. Its geometric representation is obtained by merging and simplifying child representations. The target geometric error of simplification depends on the size of the cluster $\varepsilon_c = e \cdot b_c$, where e is a parameter of the algorithm. The presence function of the cluster can be calculated from the children:

$$p_c(t) = \frac{\sum_{c'<c} f_{c'}(t) b_{c'}}{\sum_{c'<c} b_{c'}}.$$

It takes values in interval $[0,1]$. Then, geometric error function can be calculated:

$$\delta_c(t) = \begin{cases} \varepsilon_c(2p_c(t) - 1) + (1 - p_c(t)) \cdot 2b_c \ when \ \frac{1}{2} \leq p_c(t) \leq 1 \\ p_c(t) \cdot 2b_c \ when \ 0 \leq p_c(t) < \frac{1}{2} \end{cases}$$

In the end of the clustering process all presence functions must be rounded up to take values $\{0,1\}$.

Dynamic objects can move along different trajectories, so generally it is not reasonable to try to cluster them with each other. Thus, they are stored as a flat list next to the cluster tree. However, it is possible to generate series of simplified clusters for each dynamic object, where each cluster will have only one child.

3. ALTERNATIVE HDLOD METHOD

The original HDLOD method has proven to be efficient for dynamic scenes. However, for some applications it can have some drawbacks. For example, if an application has to visualize the same model in multiple 3D views with different dynamics in each view. Since dynamics is a part of HDLOD and dynamic behavior is stored as a part of the cluster, such application would require to generate separate HDLOD for each 3D view. This is not only computationally expensive to perform clustering multiple times, but also memory expensive to store multiple HDLOD representations. Another issue is changes in dynamic behavior that require the entire HDLOD to be regenerated from scratch. Trying to address these problems, the authors of the paper have come up with the solution that stores dynamic information separately from clusters, allowing to apply multiple different dynamic behaviors to the clusters and update only the corresponding dynamic information in case of changes.

In the alternative method, HDLOD is the tree of clusters $C = \{c(g_c, b_c, \delta_c)\} \cup \{<\}$. Here, cluster parameters don't depend on time anymore, which makes them similar to the traditional HLOD (Erikson et al. 2001). The geometric representation of a cluster $g_c = \{g_{prim}(id_s)\}$ now is a set of primitives. Each primitive corresponds to some scene object s and stores its globally unique identifier id_s. This is somewhat similar to 3D Tiles concept of batched 3D model (Cesium 3D Tiles). The batched 3D model is a polygonal mesh, where each vertex can have associated information provided by the batch table. For the HDLOD method, we don't concretize the kinds of primitives for cluster representation, they can be some solid shapes (sphere, box, cylinder, cone), extrusion, polyhedron or surface, defined analytically or as a polygonal mesh. Also, cluster can have single representation with identifiers stored for each vertex or face. The latter case is especially important for efficient rendering, because it allows to operate cluster as a single object to minimize overhead on processing and draw call count. What is important, is that for each part of cluster representation an identifier of the original scene object must be known. This allows to style parts of the cluster according to the appearance of the original objects at specific time.

All time-dependent parameters are moved to the set of dynamics $D = \{d_s(p_s(t), m_s(t), \sigma_s(t), \tau_s(t))\}$. Dynamics d_s stores information about dynamic behavior of scene object s. Alongside familiar presence function $p_s(t)$ and movement function $m_s(t)$ here we introduce color function $\sigma_s(t)$ and transparency function $\tau_s(t)$. Generally, for dynamic scenes not only simulation of presence and movement of objects may be required, but also simulation of color and transparency change with time.

Rendering algorithm is similar to that of the original method, but there are some differences. First of all, to perform frustum culling, bounding volume of the cluster must be obtained. For static and pseudo-dynamic clusters, their bounds are obtained as parameter b_c. Dynamic clusters don't cluster with each other, which means that the whole geometric representation of the dynamic cluster corresponds to single object. Identifier of the object id_s can be obtained from geometric representation of the cluster, then sought in D to find corresponding dynamics d_s, get movement function $m_s(t)$ and find transformation $m_s(t_{current})$. This transformation can be applied to b_c to get bounding volume at the desired moment of time $b_c(t_{current})$.

The presence, color and transparency are determined for each primitive of the cluster using id_s, searching for corresponding d_s and computing $p_s(t_{current}), \sigma_s(t_{current}), \tau_s(t_{current})$.

Geometric error δ_c of the cluster is converted to screen-space error using well-known formula:

$$SSE = (\delta_c \cdot h) / \left(2 \cdot d \cdot \tan \frac{fov_y}{2} \right),$$

where h is the height of the screen in pixels, d is the distance from the camera to the cluster and fov_y is the camera vertical field of view. If the screen-space error of the cluster doesn't exceed the user-defined tolerance, the cluster is selected for rendering, otherwise child clusters are visited.

HDLOD generation algorithm changes in a sense that now it doesn't need to take temporal proximity into account during clustering. Neighbors are sought only in spatial dimension, which can generally result in better cluster tree in terms of cluster density compared to the original HDLOD method.

4. IMPLEMENTATION NOTES

Although in the formal definition of the alternative HDLOD method we have defined cluster geometry representation as a set of primitives $g_c = \{g_{prim}(id_s)\}$, it is worth mentioning that in practice, the main advantage of HDLOD and other HLOD-like methods comes down to the facts that they reduce scene complexity by reducing the number of entities that have to be processed and allow for better quality drastic geometry simplification because they merge geometric representations. That is why, in practice, cluster representations typically are triangulated meshes, with identifiers associated with each vertex or face. Merging meshes and then simplifying is typically better than simplifying parts. For example, when scene consists of large number of rather simple objects, which cannot be significantly simplified by themselves. However, when simplifying merged representation, it can be useful to still differentiate parts of the representation that relate to different objects. In our implementation of the HDLOD method we used mesh simplification algorithm that merges vertices. It picks a vertex and searches for potential candidate vertices in ε_c radius to be merged into that vertex. We have found out, that for some models it is necessary to prevent vertices with different color from merging. As an example, let's consider a building model, where wall consists of two planes — the outer plane has grey color, and the inner plane has yellow color. Merging yellow vertex to grey vertex will result in yellow color appearing on the facade of the building, which will significantly distort visual representation despite geometric error being within the desired tolerance.

For the generation algorithm to perform clustering, only bounding volumes are required. This allows for the algorithm to be implemented memory-efficiently in an out-of-core fashion. Geometric representations can be stored on disk and loaded only when they are needed to form parent cluster representation. In our implementation, the algorithm starts with all representations in main memory and unloads them as soon as parent cluster is formed, since they won't be required afterwards. The representations are written to the disk in separate thread, in parallel with clustering. The clustering is performed in steps. On each step n we iteratively pick an arbitrary clusters and search for neighbors. AABBs are used as bounding volumes. To quickly find neighbors we sort AABBs of all clusters that participate in the current step by their min and max points. Cluster and its neighbors that don't exceed size limit b_n form new cluster. Some clusters may not have neighbors on this step, they are moved to the next step.

During rendering it is required to determine presence, color and transparency of different parts of the cluster by fetching id_s corresponding to that part of cluster's geometric representation g_c, getting d_s and computing $p_s(t_{current}), \sigma_s(t_{current}), \tau_s(t_{current})$. To efficiently render cluster as a single mesh we pass RGBA color information to the vertex shader. RGB values are computed for each part of the cluster using id_s of that part and finding $\sigma_s(t_{current})$. Presence and transparency are combined in alpha value of the color. If $p_s(t_{current}) = 0$, alpha is set to 0 in order to hide corresponding part of the mesh in shader by discarding fragments. If $p_s(t_{current}) = 1$, alpha is set to the value of transparency function $\tau_s(t_{current})$. Our implementation uses OpenGL for rendering. RGBA colors are passed to the vertex shader via shader storage buffer object (SSBO). Each vertex of the mesh has integer vertex attribute that is an index to the SSBO. Before rendering each mesh, we compute colors for each part of the mesh and send them to the GPU using SSBO. They are fetched in the vertex shader and passed to the fragment shader to compute Phong shading. Fragment shader discards fragments with zero alpha and computes shading for other fragments. We use weighted blended order-independent transparency algorithm (McGuire and Bavoil 2013) for rendering transparent surfaces. Most approaches for rendering scenes with transparent objects require to divide all objects into opaque and transparent, render opaque objects first with depth-testing, then render transparent objects with depth-testing against opaque, but not writing into depth buffer. This means that as RGBA colors for clusters are calculated, the cluster should be marked as transparent and postponed for later rendering, if it $0 < \alpha < 1$ for at least one of its parts. Otherwise, if the cluster is fully opaque, or has some invisible parts (with $\alpha = 0$), it is considered opaque and can be rendered immediately. It is also worth mentioning that by using id_s other material properties like specular color, emissive color, shininess or even textures can be matched with the primitive and applied to the parts of the cluster. Also, id_s allows to implement selection of objects in 3D window on mouse click, since identifier of the object can be obtained from each vertex of face of the cluster. Compared to the original, alternative HDLOD method has slightly higher rendering costs, due to necessity to process cluster parts and search for their dynamic data by object identifier. However, we argue that this is a reasonable price for the flexibility that the alternative method provides.

5. COMPUTATIONAL EXPERIMENTS

In order to compare rendering performance of the alternative HDLOD method to the original, a series of computational experiments have been carried out. The experiments are organized in such a way that that the camera is moving through the scene along the predefined path over 500 frames and the frame times are measured. The camera starts far away from the scene, then goes towards the center of the scene, rotates and flies away from the opposite side (see Figure 2).

Figure 2. Camera movements around the scene in ongoing computational experiments

As test scenes, the real industrial 4D models simulating construction of skyscraper and stadium has been chosen. The skyscraper scene consists of 79378 meshes with the total number of 3668091 triangles. The stadium scene has 53805 meshes and 7252950 triangles. The benchmark has been performed for two scenarios: static and animation (Figure 3). The static scenario means that model time is fixed on the finish date of the project plan, thus visualizing the constructed facility, while the camera is moving along the path. The animation scenario means that model time changes from project start to project finish as the camera is moving along the path, thus visualizing the construction process. HDLODs are pre-generated and stored in main memory before running the benchmarks, dynamics doesn't change during benchmark.

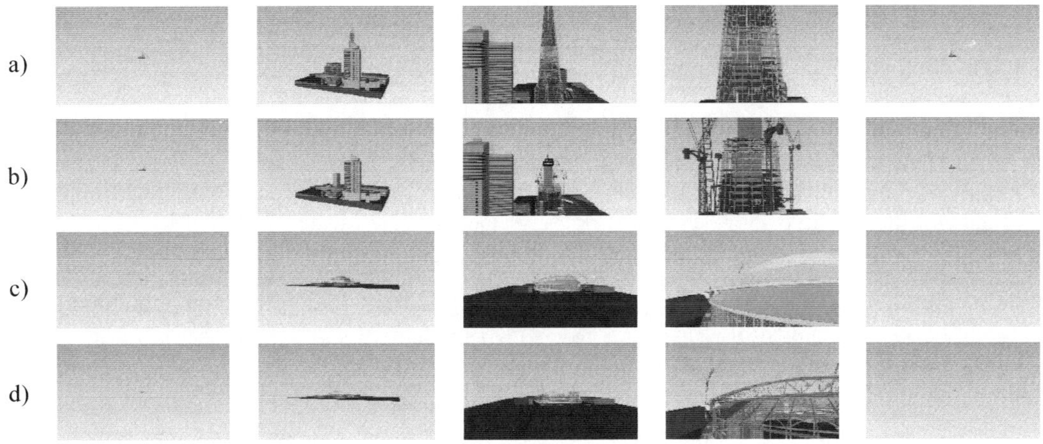

Figure 3. Screenshots taken during benchmarks: a) skyscraper static, b) skyscraper animation, c) stadium static, d) stadium animation

The Table 1 shows the summary of results. It showcases performance measurements obtained using the original and the alternative HDLOD methods with the same error thresholds, as well as without using any levels of detail. Performance values are shown as minimum, maximum and average frames per second values. Also, a total time it took to render all 500 frames is presented in the last column of the table.

Table 1. Results of performance benchmarks

Benchmark	Min. frames/s	Max. frames/s	Avg. frames/s	Total time
Skyscraper Static Original HDLOD	1.08	1076.89	36.40	13 s
Skyscraper Static Alternative HDLOD	6.57	257.86	20.41	24 s
Skyscraper Static No LODs	6.31	67.86	13.21	37 s
Skyscraper Animation Original HDLOD	15.26	1065.42	77.76	6 s
Skyscraper Animation Alternative HDLOD	7.17	251.66	20.19	24 s
Skyscraper Animation No LODs	1.25	7.23	2.65	3 m 8 s
Stadium Static Original HDLOD	7.86	677.87	33.34	14 s
Stadium Static Alternative HDLOD	6.69	549.36	22.03	22 s
Stadium Static No LODs	7.36	86.00	21.12	23 s
Stadium Animation Original HDLOD	11.36	2666.67	65.10	7 s
Stadium Animation Alternative HDLOD	6.12	544.31	21.54	23 s
Stadium Animation No LODs	1.65	7.23	3.39	2 m 27 s

It can be observed that the original HDLOD method is the fastest among all the benchmarks. As expected, the alternative HDLOD method is slightly slower due to higher costs of processing clusters during rendering (i.e., computing presence for all cluster parts and sending color data to the GPU). The original HDLOD method exhibits the highest performance in animation scenario. This is because in the original method each cluster has its own presence function. At the start of the animation most of the clusters are absent and are thus not rendered. During animation the facility is being constructed, building elements appear, but overall, total number of rendered meshes (and triangles) during the animation is lower for the original method because of the absence of clusters for some period of time. In the alternative method, clusters are selected for rendering by taking into account only their geometric error. Absence of objects is implemented by hiding corresponding parts of the cluster in fragment shader. So, for the alternative method, the static and the animation scenarios yield the same number of rendered meshes and tringles, resulting in the same performance. The method of rendering without LODs that has been used for these benchmarks is not a naïve scene graph traverse. Rather, it is an algorithm that pre-builds data structures for efficient frustum culling and minimizing scene graph traverse time. It performs quite well for the static scenario, although still slower than HDLODs. However, on the animation scenario it performs really bad due to the necessity to update data structures to take into account presence and absence of objects. At the same time, HDLOD is already a spatiotemporal structure optimized for the animation scenario.

Table 2. Comparison of HDLOD generation times

Method	Skyscraper	Stadium
Alternative HDLOD	3 m 53 s	2 m 57 s
Original HDLOD	6 m 3 s	3 m 17 s

The HDLOD generation performance has also been measured for the alternative and the original methods. Results are presented in Table 2. The alternative method exhibits faster generation time because it doesn't take temporal factor into account, whereas the original method has to estimate temporal distance D_p and compute functions $p_c(t)$ and $\delta_c(t)$ during generation. But most importantly, the alternative method doesn't require regeneration in case of changes in dynamic behavior, whereas the original method would require to wait several minutes when dynamic behavior changes (i.e., user editing project schedule in a 4D modelling application). Another main advantage of the alternative method is less memory usage in the scenario when the scene is visualized in multiple views with different dynamic behaviors (Table 3).

Table 3. Memory cost of windows with different dynamic behaviors for the same scene

Method	One window	Two windows	Three windows	Four windows
Alternative HDLOD	186 MB	238 MB	439 MB	587 MB
Original HDLOD	203 MB	579 MB	884 MB	1219 MB

6. CONCLUSION

In this paper the alternative HDLOD method has been presented. In comparison to the original method, that stores dynamic behavior as part of each cluster, the alternative method decouples spatial and temporal information. This allows to reuse the same simplified LOD representations with different dynamic behaviors and to make changes to the temporal information without the need to regenerate clusters. The rendering performance of the alternative method is slightly worse than that of the original method, since it requires more processing during cluster rendering and unable to skip absent clusters. Nevertheless, we argue that alternative method is a better choice for many applications due to the flexibility it provides. For instance, the alternative HDLOD method should be recommended for applications with multiple 3D windows that allow to edit data (i.e., 4D modelling and planning desktop editor application where user can visualize the scene according to different schedules and modify these schedules), whereas the original HDLOD method is best for single-view applications (i.e., web viewer that allows to efficiently visualize prepared model without the ability to modify it).

REFERENCES

Cesium 3D Tiles, Specification for streaming massive heterogeneous 3D geospatial datasets. URL: https://github.com/CesiumGS/3d-tiles.

Erikson, C. et al., 2001. HLODs for Faster Display of Large Static and Dynamic Environments. *I3D '01 Proceedings of the 2001 symposium on Interactive 3D graphics*. New York, USA, pp. 111-120.

Luebke D.P., 2001. A developer's survey of polygonal simplification algorithms. *In IEEE Computer Graphics and Applications*, Vol. 21, No. 3, pp. 24-35.

Luebke D.P. et al, 2003. *Level of Detail for 3D Graphics*. Morgan Kaufmann, San Francisco, USA.

McGuire M. and Bavoil L., 2013. Weighted Blended Order-Independent Transparency. *In Journal of Computer Graphics Techniques (JCGT)*, Vol. 2, No. 2, pp. 122-141.

Rossignac J. and Borrel P., 1993. Multi-resolution 3D approximations for rendering complex scenes. *In: Falcidieno B., Kunii T.L. (eds) Modeling in Computer Graphics*. IFIP Series on Computer Graphics. Springer, Berlin, Heidelberg, Germany, pp. 455-465.

Semenov V. et al, 2019. Faster rendering of large pseudo-dynamic scenes using hierarchical dynamic LODs. *Proceedings of International Conference on Computer Graphics, Visualization, Computer Vision and Image Processing*. Porto, Portugal, pp. 275-282.

FACE RECOGNITION USING DEEP CONVOLUTIONAL NEURAL NETWORKS: A SURVEY

Khalid Alharbi and Sudhanshu Semwal
Department of Computer Science
University of Colorado at Colorado Springs
1420 Austin Bluffs Pkwy, Colorado Springs, CO 80918, USA

ABSTRACT

Face recognition technology uses Deep Convolutional Neural Network (DCNN) to extract biometric features for identity authentication. It has been used in various application domains, including military, law enforcement, finance, public security, and other daily life applications. This paper reviews the updated progress of DCNN architectures used for face recognition. It also explores pretrained models along with training datasets that exist. Furthermore, some face recognition applications are summarized. The limitations and further research directions are pointed. Although face recognition is an emerging technique, it raises security concerns.

KEYWORDS

Face Recognition, Deep Face, Deep CNN

1. INTRODUCTION

Face recognition (FR) technology identifies or verifies faces in a static image, video data, and data stream. FR consists of four processes: face detection, alignment, feature extraction, and feature matching Almabdy and Elrefaei (2019); Jain and Li (2011); Masi et al. (2018). Figure 1 illustrates the flow of these processes. Face detection locates a face in an image and marks it with a bounding box, determining the face location, size, and pose. Face alignment normalizes the face to be consistent with coordinates (i.e., photometric). Feature extraction extracts essential information (i.e., feature vector) from the face. The feature vector is required for the feature matching process. Feature matching performs matching feature vectors against one or more known faces in a prepared database. Overall, the FR produces a face identification (so-called FaceID) that exists in the faces' database or does not exist, which refers to an unknown person.

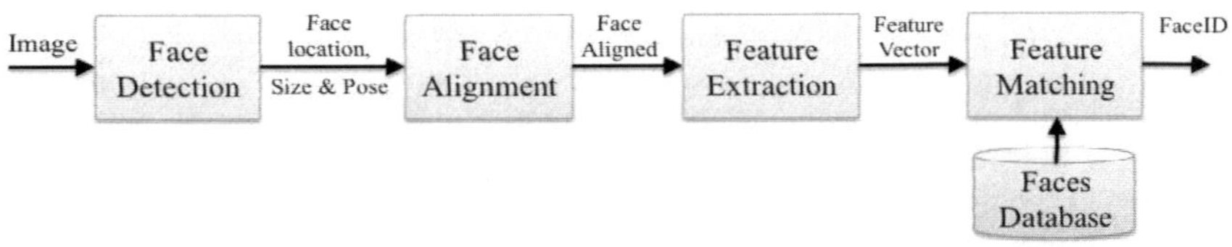

Figure 1. Face Recognition Processes Pipeline

FR technology has been used in various application domains Adjabi et al. (2020); Ali et al. (2021). It is used in law enforcement as police officers instantly identify individuals in the field. Forensic investigations automatically recognize individuals in security footage or other videos. It can also be utilized to find missing children and victims of human trafficking. FR is used in social media applications. For instance, Facebook automatically recognizes members appearing in photos. It is practical for users to locate photos they are in and suggest when particular people should be tagged in photos. It helps the blind person by alerting with a vibration when people are smiling, for example. FR is used in finance. It is currently being used at ATMs to protect people's identities. FR is used in other daily life applications. Smartphones are now using FR to unlock phones. Airlines have already started using FR to help people check bags, check into flights, and board planes faster.

Restaurants use FR as customers place orders through a digital menu and then use face scan as a payment option. FR is used to control restricted access areas. It ensures that only authorized individuals get into facilities like labs, boardrooms, bank vaults, and other sensitive locations.

This survey presents a classification scheme that categorizes the literature on face recognition. It then classifies a set of related articles that were recently published into sub-categories according to specific criteria. The survey explains each sub-category. It also discusses the limitations of face recognition along with points to future research directions.

The rest of this paper is organized as follows. Section 2 introduces the classification scheme used to categorize the FR literature into subsets. In section 3, different Deep CNN network architectures are presented. Section 4 presents various pretrained models and section and section 5 presents the training datasets. Section 6 classifies face recognition applications. In section 7, the limitations of face recognition technology and further research directions are discussed. Section 8 concludes this paper and clarifies the findings.

2. LITERATURE CLASSIFICATION SCHEME

We built a new classification scheme to filter the literature on face recognition and categorize it into subcategories. The classification scheme is designed based on various characteristics that are extracted from the surveys recently published.

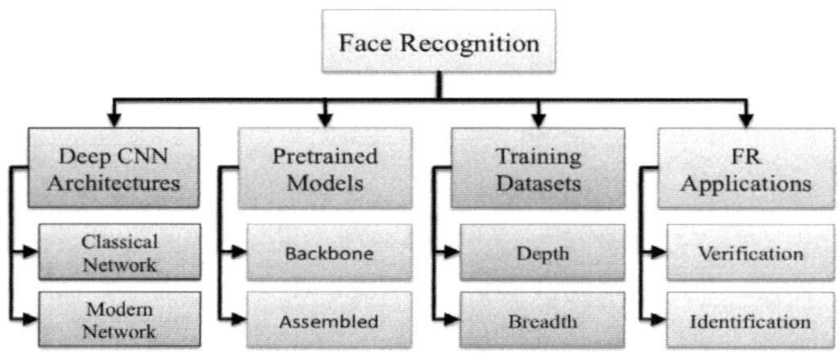

Figure 2. Face Recognition Literature Classification Scheme

As illustrated in Figure 2, the FR literature classification scheme consists of four main categories: DCNN Architectures, Pretrained Models, Training Datasets, and FR Applications. Each includes two sub-categories. The Deep CNN architectures are classified as classical networks, and modern networks Ali et al. (2021); Khan et al. (2020). Classical networks utilize stacked convolutional layers, while the modern networks explore novel approaches for constructing convolutional layers to increase learning efficiency. A Pretrained model is a DCNN model previously trained for face recognition on large benchmark datasets. Based on the DCNN architecture used to train a model, the Pretrained models are grouped into the backbone-based and assembled models. The backbone model uses a single network to extract features from an input image, while the assembled-based model uses multiple networks that are assembled for features extraction Ali et al (2021); Gwyn et al. (2021). The training datasets are classified into two types, depth, and breadth datasets Hupont and Fern´andez (2019). The depth datasets contain many images per subject, usually more than 30 images on average per subject. In contrast, the breadth datasets include many subjects but fewer images per subject. The FR applications are grouped into verification and identification applications. The verification application matches face information to registered facial data to determine whether the two faces are of the same identity. It is the process of asking, "are you who you say you are?" The identification application compares face information to a database of identities to match it and discover its identity. It is the process of asking, "who are you?"

The classification scheme is applied to a set of 24 publications published from 2019 to early 2023. These publications include conference papers and journal articles. Books were ignored unless they were used for terms definition. The FR literature targeted in this survey covers novel contributions, extended work, and other surveys. The following sections explore each group of the publications and organize them based on the contributions and findings provided.

3. DEEP CNN ARCHITECTURES

A neural network includes three layers: input, hidden, and output. The input layer initializes data for the neural network Gulli and Pal (2017). The hidden layers, intermediate layers between the input and output layer, simultaneously perform multiple mathematical functions (i.e., activation functions) to map the values from one layer to the next. The output layer produces the result for given inputs. The neural network also consists of a function (so-called loss function) that minimizes the error, which is the difference between actual and predicted values Gulli and Pal (2017). A simple neural network consists of only one hidden layer (so-called a shallow neural network), while a deep neural network uses a cascade of multiple hidden layers of processing units for feature extraction and transformation Elhassouny and Smarandache (2019); Gulli and Pal (2017).

A Convolutional neural network (i.e., ConvNet or CNN) is a deep neural network. Besides input and output layers, CNN includes three main layers: convolutional, pooling, and fully connected layers. The convolutional layer is the essential building block of a CNN. The first layer represents a set of neurons (i.e., kernels) that receive data from the input layer and map the data to convolutional layers. The convolutional layers are supported by either additional convolutional or pooling layers. The convolutional layers shrink as they become deeper, primarily by divisible input factors. The last layers are fully connected layers that pass on the data to the output layer Albawi et al. (2017); Elhassouny and Smarandache (2019); Gulli and Pal (2017). The CCN depth refers to the number of layers, convolutional, pooling, and other layers, while the CNN width refers to the number of parameters the CNN carries out.

Table 1. Deep CNN Architectures

CNN Architecture	Reference	Width	Depth	Activation Function	Loss Function
Classic	Radman et al. (2022)	1728	25	ReLU	CE
	Ben Fredj et al. (2021)	2.7k	21	ReLU	Softmax
	Boyd et al. (2023)	14400	11	ReLU	CE
Modern	Ketab et al. (2023)	23328	14	ReLU	CE
	Niu et al. (2021)	2304	14	Maxout	Log
	Brown (2022)	50176	26	ReLU	Softmax

Table 1 classifies the DCNN architectures used for face recognition into classical networks and modern networks. Classical networks are stacked convolutional layers, while modern networks whose convolutional layers are constructed in many ways to improve learning efficiency. Table 1 also describes the DCNN's width and depth along with the activation and loss functions used. The activation function is set either at the end of or between neural networks. It supports determining if the neuron would fire or not. Several types of activation functions exist, including Sigmoid, hyperbolic tangent (tanh), Rectified Linear Units (ReLU), Leaky ReLU, and Exponential Linear Unit (ELU) Nwankpa et al. (2018). For layer minimization, several types of loss functions exist, including Mean Squared Error (MSE), Softmax, Cross-Entropy (CE), and Binary Cross-Entropy (BCE) Srivastava et al. (2019). Table 1 shows that most of the architectures use the ReLU activation function and CE loss function, while the Softmax loss function is barely used. It also shows that a loss function can be developed for specific purposes. For instance, in Niu et al. (2021), the authors try to maximize the values to eliminate the influence of noise signals in the image. Thus, they used the Maxout activation function and developed a specific loss function using a logarithmic equation for prediction loss.

3.1 Classical Networks

Radman et al. (2022) design a deep residual neural network (i.e., DResNet), a type of DCNN, to handle a forensic face sketch synthesis. ResNet learns a deep mapping between photos and sketches. The DResNet contains nine stacked residual blocks, and each consists of convolutional, batch normalization, and rectified-linear unit (ReLU) layers. The input and output layer does not have batch normalization; as a result, the network's depth is 25 layers. The DResNet uses 64 filters of size 3x3x64 that allow 64 feature maps, limiting its width to 1728 parameters. It also uses the Cross-Entropy loss function. An experiment was conducted on the network to train a model. For training, the authors used 699480 photo-sketch patch pairs from three datasets (CUHK, AR, and the XM2VTS database). The results show that DResNet outperforms other existing models for face sketch recognition. The proposed DResNet achieves an average of 0.40% Visual Information Fidelity (VIF) scores over others. Overall, the proposed DResNet presents robustness to handle forensic photos, which validates the potential value of the DResNet for real applications.

Ben Fredj et al. (2021) present a DCNN to learn robust face verification in an unconstrained environment using large-scale data with a massive noisy and occluded face. The DCNN was built based on GoogLeNet style Inception models. It consists of 21 layers, including 3 convolutional and 18 Inception layers. It uses the ReLU activation function and Softmax loss function. The DCNN provides 2.7k parameters. For verification, experiments were conducted on the Labeled Faces in the Wild (LFW), which contains 13,233 images of 5749 people, and YouTube face (YTF), containing 3425 videos of 1595 different people. The results show that the trained model reaches the classification rate of 94.5% on LFW and the face recognition accuracy of 97.7%. Overall, the proposed DCNN achieves comparable performances on LFW and YTF for face verification.

Boyd et al. (2023) propose a DCNN to handle real-time face recognition. They use the Open-Source Neural Network library (Keras running on top of Tensorflow) to build the network. The proposed DCNN consists of 11 layers, including 3 convolutional, 2 max pooling, 3 dropouts, 1 flatten, and 2 dense layers. It uses the ReLU activation function and the Cross-Entropy (CE) loss function and handles 14400 parameters. The process first starts with a real-time input image captured from a camera, and then it is fed to the Viola-Jones algorithm for face detection. The face image is then converted into grayscale, resized to 120×120 pixels, and fed to the first convolution layer comprising 32 filters of size 3×3 pixels. A performance evaluation was conducted using a standard AT&T dataset containing 10 images from 40 individuals, leading to 400 images. Out of 400 images, 320 images (8 images from 40 individuals) were used for training and the remaining 80 images for testing. The result shows that the proposed DCNN reaches maximum recognition accuracy of 98.75%. The authors offer that the DCNN can be adapted to various applications such as face detection-based home automation, device control, attendance system, and intruder detection.

3.2 Modern Networks

Ketab et al. (2023) propose a DCNN to deal with low resolution face recognition. DCNN architecture has two branches. One projects high-resolution images to space, and the other one maps low-resolution images into space. The proposed DCNN architecture consists of 14 layers, including 10 convolutional and 4 max-pooling layers. It uses the ReLU activation, Cross-Entropy (CE) loss functions, and handles 23328 parameters. The DCNN was used to train a model of over 90,800 face images with variations in pose, expression, illumination, and age. An experiment was conducted on FERET, LFW, and MBGC datasets for evaluation. The proposed DCNN shows significant improvement and robustness against expression, illumination, and age variations. It outperforms competing methods across various resolutions of probe images. It shows significant performance improvement (5%) when applied to low-resolution images. The proposed method shows the reliable performance when faces are in the wild and taken by surveillance cameras.

Niu et al. (2021) introduce multiscale fusion lightweight convolution neural network for hyperspectral face recognition. Hyperspectral imaging combines traditional imaging and spectroscopy technologies to acquire spatial and spectral information for robust face recognition; however, the structure of hyperspectral images is more complicated than ordinary grayscale or RGB images. The proposed DCNN has a depth of 15 layers, integrating 5 convolution layers, 3 Network in Network (NIN) layers, 5 Second-Order Efficient Channel Attention (SECA) models, Max-Feature-Map layer, and max-pooling layer. It uses the Maxout activation, logarithmic loss functions and handles 2304 parameters. An experimental evaluation was conducted on three benchmark hyperspectral face databases, PolyU, CMU, and UWA. The results show that the proposed DCNN has achieved competitive accuracy and efficiency, significantly reducing storage space and computation overheads. These characteristics also show its broad applicability on the edge and mobile devices.

Brown (2022) proposes a DCNN of a bimodal system for enhancing security. The DCNN processes face and iris biometrics from a single image. The author uses the OpenCV library to build the network. The DCNN architecture consists of 26 layers, including 4 convolutional, 6 batch normalizations, 4 activations, 2 max-pooling, 3 dropouts, 2 dense, 1 input, 1 random translation, 1 resizing, and 1 flatten layer. It uses the ReLU activation, Cross-Entropy (CE) loss functions, and handles 50176 parameters. An experiment was conducted on IITD-Iris and CASIA-Iris-Distance datasets for evaluation. The result indicates that a smaller designed CNN achieves impressive results on challenging iris data. It shows that the proposed DCNN effectively outperforms other approaches.

4. PRETRAINED MODELS

A Pre-trained model is a DCNN that had been trained on a large dataset. The Pretrained models are classified based on the DCNN architectures used for training into the backbone-based and assembled models. The backbone architecture consists of a single network to extract features from an input image, while the assembled-based architecture has multiple networks that are assembled for features extraction Ali et al. (2021); Gwyn et al. (2021). Lots of pretrained models are available. However, the survey covers the modern models that trained using popular CNN architectures, including VGG19, ResNet50, Inception-v3 (GoogLeNet), EfficientNet-B3, and MobileFaceNet. The pretrained model is evaluated according to the challenge it deals with and the classification accuracy. The classification accuracy is the rate of correct predictions to the total number of input samples Mahdianpari et al. (2018).

Table 2 shows that pretrained models that deal with simple face challenges such as prediction accuracy and Thermal images achieve high classification accuracy (above 90%). The models exploited for complex challenges such as facial emotion, masked face, and preference prediction reach low classification accuracy (below 70%). Preference prediction relates to the process mobile device gallery of photos and videos and predicts preferences based on scene recognition, object detection, and facial analysis. In general, pretrained models provide acceptable results when used as they have been trained. Otherwise, they must be retrained or transferred to learn to handle challenges that they did not train for, which require specific datasets.

Table 2. Deep CNN Pretrained Models

Architecture Based	Reference	Model Name	Challenge	Accuracy
Backbone	Singh et al. (2022)	VGG19	Facial Emotion	69.10%
	Cheng et al. (2023)	FaceNet	Masked Face	93.00%
Assembled	Anand et al. (2020)	Inception-v3	Prediction Accuracy	91.43%
	Chen and Ross (2019)	Mobile-FaceNet	Thermal Image	99.30%
	Savchenko et al. (2022)	EfficientNet-B3	Preference Prediction	63.82%

4.1 Backbone

Singh et al. (2022) use VGG19 pretrained model to recognize facial emotions such as anger, disgust, fear, happiness, sadness, surprise, and neutral. VGG19 was built by the University of Oxford and trained on more than 1 million images from the ImageNet database and can classify up to 1000 objects. The authors run the VGG19 model against the Face Expression Recognition dataset (FER2013) that contains 35,887 various images with emotions for evaluation. The authors observed that the size of the dataset plays a vital role in facial expression recognition. The VGG19 model achieved better accuracy on facial emotions with more samples, such as happy, neutral, and angry, than other emotions.

Cheng et al. (2023) utilize ResNet-50 to identify people with face-masks due COVID-19 mandatory of use face masks. The ResNet-50 was built by the Microsoft Corporation and trained on the ImageNet database. The authors run the ResNet-50 model against the Real-world masked face recognition dataset (RMFRD) that contains 5000 masked faces of 525 people and 90000 unmasked faces for evaluation. The model has been more trained on unmasked faces than the masked faces dataset. Thus, the results show that the ResNet-50 model did better on the masked than on the masked dataset. The ResNet-50 model achieved an accuracy of 89.7016% for unmasked faces while 47.91% for masked faces.

4.2 Assembled

Anand et al. (2020) create a new dataset to train the Inception-v3 (GoogleNet) model to achieve higher accuracy. The Inception-v3 was built by the Google Corporation and trained on the ImageNet database. The authors created the dataset based on two principles, provide as many unique faces as possible and provide the maximum number of faces for everyone. They use the transfer learning method to increase the model training level. The transfer learning is done by adjusting the weight of the fully connected layers in the inception model with the new dataset. The results show improvement for the recognition accuracy reaching 91.43%. The authors indicate that transfer learning a model over many datasets enhances its performance and accuracy.

Chen and Ross (2019) challenge matching face images obtained in the thermal spectrum with those obtained in the visible spectrum. They experiment with the MobileFaceNet model against multispectral face datasets, Pinellas County Sheriff's Office (PCSO), and Army Research Laboratory (ARL) datasets. The PCSO and ARL datasets consist of face images acquired in the middle-wave infrared (MWIR) and long-wave infrared (LWIR) spectra. The MobileFaceNet model was developed by the School of Computer and Information Technology, Beijing University, trained on the CASIA-Webface dataset. The experimental results show that the MobileFaceNet model effectively synthesizes the visible spectrum images from thermal spectrum images and enhances cross-spectral face matching accuracy. The face matching accuracy reaches 99.30%. Nevertheless, the PCSO and ARL datasets are small; thus, further investigation is required to experiment with the MobileFaceNet model on a large-scale dataset.

Savchenko et al. (2022) use the EfficientNet-B3 model preferences prediction that processes mobile device gallery of photos and videos predict preferences of hobbies and lifestyle. Preferences prediction is based on scene recognition, object detection, and facial analysis. The Inception-v3 was built and released by the Google Corporation in 2019 Tan and Le (2019). The authors experimented with the Inception-v3 model on Photo Event Collection and Web Image Datasets for Event Recognition and Amazon Fashion data. The experimental results of the model reach a prediction accuracy of 63.82%. The authors provided the implementation publicly as Android application various personalized mobile services such as target advertisements, marketing, and recommender systems.

5. TRAINING DATASETS

The datasets play a critical role in training and testing DCNN models and improving performance. The ImageNet Large- Scale Visual Recognition Challenge (ILSVRC) announces that premier deep FR models were commonly trained on data larger than 0.5M images and 20K people Oloyede et al. (2020); RoyChowdhury et al. (2020). The training datasets are classified into two types, depth, and breadth RoyChowdhury et al. (2020). A depth dataset has a limited number of subjects but many images for each subject. It enforces the trained model to address a wide range of intraclass variations, such as lighting, age and pose. A breadth dataset contains many subjects but fewer images per subject. It ensures the trained models cover enough variable appearance of various people.

Table 3 covers the popular datasets used for face recognition, including the MS-Celeb-1M, CASIA-WebFace, VGGFace2, MegaFace, UTKFace, Facial Expression Comparison (FEC), and Labelled Faces in the Wild (LFW). These datasets are classified based on the dataset type (depth and breadth), the number of identities, and the total number of images. The numbers are inexact. The following sections explain the characteristics and objectives of these datasets and show the exact numbers of identities and images.

Table 3. Deep CNN Pretrained Models

Dataset Type	Reference	Dataset Name	#Identities	#Images
Depth	Song et al. (2020)	CASIA-WebFace	10.5k	500k
	Fariza et al. (2019)	CASIA-WebFace	10.1k	200k
	Singh et al. (2023)	VGGFace	9.1k	3.3M
	Abdelmaksoud et al. (2020)	LFW	5.7k	13.2k
Breadth	Peng et al. (2021)	MS-Celeb-1M	100k	10M
	Xu et al. (2021)	MageFace	672k	4.7M
	Vemulapalli and Agarwala (2019)	GFEC	500K	156K

5.1 Depth Datasets

Song et al. (2020) use CASIA-WebFace to train a DCCN model for similar face recognition. CASIA WebFace is the first public dataset consisting of 10,575 people, 494,414 face images collected from the web. Each person has 45 face images on average. The images are 250 x 250 pixels and taken with various light intensity levels, posture, and expression. The CASIA-WebFace dataset is typically used for scientific research of unconstrained face recognition; for face verification and face identification tasks. The authors note that the dataset includes some error labels and images; thus, dataset cleaning is required.

Fariza et al. (2019) utilize the UTKFace dataset to evaluate the performance of DCNN for age estimation of the range 1-100 years old. The UTKFace is a large-scale face dataset with an extended age range of 0 to 116. It includes 23,708 images with age, gender, and ethnicity annotations worldwide. The images are 240 x 240 pixels covering significant variations in pose, facial expression, illumination, occlusion, resolution. It is typically used for age estimation, age progression, and age regression tasks.

Singh et al. (2023) use the VGGFace dataset train DCNN for low resolution face recognition. The VGGFace dataset was developed by researchers at the Visual Geometry Group at the University of Oxford. It provides a large-scale training dataset of 3.31 million images of 9131 identities, with 362.6 images an average for each identity. The images are 240 x 240 pixels collected from Google Image Search. The VGGFace varies pose, age, illumination, ethnicity, and profession (e.g., actors, athletes, politicians). It is typically used for training and evaluating effective face recognition models and verification performance.

Abdelmaksoud et al. (2020) employ Labelled Faces in the Wild (LFW) dataset to train Super-Resolution Generative Adversarial Network (SRGAN) to overcome the low-resolution problem of face recognition with a single sample per person. The LFW dataset consists of 13,233 images of faces of 5749 identities collected from the web. The LFW is public and commonly used for face verification; however, it is not suitable to evaluate CNNs designed to recognize images with complicated conditions such as poor lighting, extreme pose, strong occlusions, low resolution. It is typically designed for research purposes of face recognition verification.

5.2 Breadth Datasets

Peng et al. (2021) compare the MS-Celeb-1M to other two datasets in the ethically problematic face and person recognition. Microsoft Corporation created the MS-Celeb-1M, consisting of 10 million face images collected from the Internet, including 100K identities; each identity has an average of 100 facial images. Each image is linked to an entity key identified by a unique key and associated with property information helps to conduct disambiguation and improve the recognition accuracy. The MS-Celeb-1M is a public dataset designed to develop face recognition for a large-scale classification problem.

Xu et al. (2021) use MageFace dataset to evaluate the performance of a training technique that speeds up capturing discriminative information for face recognition. The MageFace provides extensive training data to the research community. The MageFace is a public dataset containing 4.7 million images with 672K identities and a significant age variation, collected from Yahoo's Flickr. It evaluates the performance of face recognition algorithms in identification and verification.

Vemulapalli and Agarwala (2019) introduce Facial Expression Comparison (FEC) dataset used for analyzing and recognizing facial expression. The FEC is a large-scale face dataset with expression comparison annotations. Google Corporation designs it, consisting of 500k expression triplets (identities) with 156k face images and annotations that specify which two expressions in each triplet are most similar. The FEC is typically used for expression-based image retrieval, photo album summarization, emotion classification.

6. FACE RECOGNITION APPLICATIONS

Face recognition has received attention from research and commercial communities due to the wide range of real-world applications Adjabi et al. (2020); Ali et al. (2021). FR has been used in law enforcement, forensic investigation, controlling restricted access, social media, finance and banking, and other daily life applications such as unlocking smartphones, airline 7 checking-In and boarding, ordering in restaurants. The FR applications serve as face verification or identification. Face verification applications verify face information to registered facial data to confirm whether it is the person who says he/she is or not, while the FR identification applications compare face information to a database of identities to determine the person's identity. Table 4 illustrates challenging FR applications and classifies them based on the application type (verification and identification) and the application domain.

Table 4. Face Recognition Applications

Application Type	Reference	Application Domain
Verification	Porselvi et al. (2021)	Banking & Security: Face-based access to Automatic Teller Machine (ATM)
	Kuchta et al. (2022)	Service: Face-based airlines check-in and boarding services
	Al-Amoudi et al. (2022)	Security: Face-based schools attendance system
Identification	Rikwith et al. (2021)	Security: Face recognition & fingerprint for Electronic Voting Machine
	Kute et al. (2019)	Forensic: Partial face images recognition for forensic applications
	Ortega-Delcampo et al. (2020)	Security: Detect morphing presentation attacks in border control system

6.1 Face Verification

Porselvi et al. (2021) use face recognition as facial identification for processing banking transactions of ATM system. The system compares the face scans with similar face information uploaded by the bank's personnel to verify the customer's identity. They use Haar Feature-based Cascade Classifiers for face detection, then pass on the face information to a deep belief network (DBN), one type of DCNN, for recognition. The process starts with the new user should register his/her face to get an account number; along with that, the user needs to fill in personal details like Username, Password, and Mail ID. The authors state the security advantages of using face recognition as facial identification for the banking system, reducing the danger of hackers, banking fraud, and misused once a user registers mobile is lost.

Kuchta et al. (2022) study the use of face recognition to increase the efficiency of the processes of check-in and boarding services. They analyzed ten face recognition systems, including Accenture, Aware, BioID, Certibio, Fulcrum Biometrics, Thales, HYPR, Idemia, Leidos, and NEC. The check-in and boarding services include passenger identity validation, baggage registration and handling, and seating assignment. The study shows that the check-in and boarding services provoke queues, requiring additional identity control processing. Therefore, using face recognition systems as identity control significantly reduces check-in queues, and the workforce is only required circumstances or when additional control is required.

Al-Amoudi et al. (2022) propose an automatic school attendance system using face recognition. The system consists of attendance, student profile, and training. A lecturer needs to take a photograph of the student and upload it to the system. The authors use Multi-Task Cascaded Convolutional Neural Network (MTCNN) for face detection and FaceNet for face recognition. They trained the system on 908 images of 21 students. The testing result showed 100% for face detection and 87.03% for face recognition.

6.2 Face Identification

Rikwith et al. (2021) present enhancement for Electronic Voting Machine (EVM) performance using biometric fingerprint and face recognition. The face recognition process includes collecting voters' image IDs, unique feature extraction, classification and storage in XML files, and voter prediction by matching input image features with the saved XML files. A voter's face is captured only if the face is well illuminated and classified using Eigen's face. The process runs until 50 viable images are collected from the person for data collection efficiency. The experiment shows that the system effectively allows only authenticated voting persons to be identified based on their fingerprint and face recognition and prevents unregistered voters from voting.

Kute et al. (2019) use partial face images available for forensic recognition purposes (so-called component-based face recognition). They utilize the transfer learning method using the knowledge gained from complete face images to classify components of the face. The essential face components used for recognition are ears, lips, and nose. They use Fisher's LDA, a transfer DCNN, to extract features and regularization block for probability minimization. They also utilize the K-nearest neighbor classifier for classification. The authors experimented with the system on the Faces94 dataset that contains face images of 153 individuals with 20 images per person. They also cropped various parts of a face from the Faces94 dataset, including half faces (left, right, upper, and lower half, and left, right, upper, and lower diagonal), nose, ears (left and right), and lips. The results show that nose features are better than lip and ear features for recognition accuracy.

Ortega-Delcampo et al. (2020) use face recognition for automated border control to prevent biometric attacks, which are presentation attacks. One of the biometric attacks is morphing, which is hard to detect. The authors use DCNN to de-morph a passport with a fake face image (morphed image). The process checks between the actual image of a person located in the automated border control system and the morphed image. An experiment was conducted on the FRAV-ABC database that consists of 1170 individuals, 640 females and 530 males. Each has two images, morphing and the actual one. Although the accuracy rate reached 98%, the equal error rate (EER) was low, which requires. The authors state that paying more attention to feature selection for CNN would improve the outcomes.

7. LIMITATIONS & RESEARCH DIRECTIONS

Face recognition technology has been adopted in real-world applications and shows remarkable success in well-controlled environments. However, face recognition is limited to accuracy and efficiency in real-life scenarios due to the face acquisition process with unconstrained environments, including illumination, pose variation, occlusion, face expression, plastic surgery, aging, and low resolution. The trained DCNN models perform well on the same dataset, but Recognition accuracy decreases when they perform on various datasets. Moreover, DCNN face recognition is limited to robustness for presentation attacks, such as masked face and digital manipulation attacks, threatening the security of face recognition systems.

7.1 Limitations

The set of 26 publications studied in this survey indicates that face recognition using DCNN is limited to:

- **Uncontrolled Environments:** Face images captured with low resolution, illumination, occlusion, and other detection issues, are difficult to detect; as a result, they fail to be recognized.
- **Masked Faces:** Many DCNN were developed for masked face recognition, especially with the COVID-19 pandemic; however, the classification accuracy is still low, and the equal error rate (EER) is unsuitable.
- **Face Expression:** Face emotions recognition is profitable; however, it lacks accuracy and efficiency, especially for face expression similarity.
- **Training Mechanism:** Training a DCNN model for face recognition lacks the diversity of the training datasets.
- **Partial Face Images:** forensic face recognition limits face classification and recognition due to the low effectiveness of the existing DCNN used for Partial face images classification.
- **Face Recognition Security Attacks:** Detection and recognize morphable faces is an open issue because the existing DCNN models provide unsuitable accuracy and high equal error rate.

These limitations are connected. Overcoming a limitation would help solve another issue of face recognition. For instance, increasing the face classification accuracy in uncontrolled environments improves the security attacks prevention for face recognition.

7.2 Research Directions

According to the face recognition limitations and the future works included in the studies covered in this survey, the further research directions are:

- **Detection Accuracy:** Detection of face images in uncontrolled environments requires advanced DCNN to be developed, trained, and evaluated in real-life scenarios.
- **Diversity of Datasets:** Diversifying datasets to train and test DCNN is necessary for face recognition.
- **Use other's Knowledge:** Transfer learning is practical to increase the effectiveness and efficiency of the DCNN for face recognition.
- **Standard Evaluation Metric:** Developing a standard evaluation metric for training and testing DCNN models of face recognition ensures the DCNN models' quality and reduces incidental ambiguity.
- **Security Attacks:** Increasing the precision over other evaluation factors of DCNN models might lower the equal error rates and tolerate the security attacks for face recognition.

8. CONCLUSION

This survey paper reviewed academic literature of 26 papers published from 2019 to early 2023 on using Deep Convolutional Neural Network (DCNN) for face recognition. A classification scheme that categorizes this literature was introduced. The classification scheme groups the 24 papers into four categories, DCNN architectures, pretrained models, training datasets, and applications.

The classical and modern DCNN architectures used for face recognition were explored, including hidden layers and types of activation and loss functions that distinguish these architectures. Popular pretrained models including VGG19, ResNet50, Inception-v3 (GoogLeNet), EfficientNet-B3, and MobileFaceNet were explored, and their classification accuracy was discussed.

The survey also covers the popular datasets used for training and testing face recognition models, including the MS-Celeb-1M, CASIA-WebFace, VGGFace2, MegaFace, UTKFace, Facial Expression Comparison (FEC), and Labelled Faces in the Wild (LFW).

Critical applications that used DCNN face verification and identification, such as ATM banking, forensic investigation, airline checking-In and boarding, and electronic voting machine, were discussed and evaluated. Finally, DCNN face recognition limitations were explained, and further research directions were highlighted.

Using DCNN for face recognition is promising; however, accuracy and efficiency are limited, especially in real-life scenarios. It is due to the lack of training on practical and diverse training datasets. The DCNN face recognition is also limited to robustness for presentation attacks, introducing security concerns.

REFERENCES

Abdelmaksoud, M., Nabil, E., Farag, I., and Hameed, H. A. (2020). A novel neural network method for face recognition with a single sample per person. IEEE Access, 8:102212–102221.

Adjabi, I., Ouahabi, A., Benzaoui, A., and Taleb-Ahmed, A. (2020). Past, present, and future of face recognition: A review. Electronics, 9(8).

Al-Amoudi, I., Samad, R., Abdullah, N. R. H., Mustafa, M., and Pebrianti, D. (2022). Automatic attendance system using face recognition with deep learning algorithm. In Proceedings of the 12th National Technical Seminar on Unmanned System Technology 2020, pages 573–588. Springer.

Albawi, S., Mohammed, T. A., and Al-Zawi, S. (2017). Understanding of a convolutional neural network. In 2017 International Conference on Engineering and Technology (ICET), pages 1–6.

Ali, W., Tian, W., Din, S. U., Iradukunda, D., and Khan, A. A. (2021). Classical and modern face recognition approaches: a complete review. Multimedia Tools and Applications, 80(3):4825–4880.

Almabdy, S. and Elrefaei, L. (2019). Deep convolutional neural network-based approaches for face recognition. Applied Sciences, 9(20):4397.

Anand, R., Shanthi, T., Nithish, M. S., and Lakshman, S. (2020). Face recognition and classification using GoogleNET architecture. pages 261–269, Singapore. Springer Singapore.

Ben Fredj, H., Bouguezzi, S., and Souani, C. (2021). Face recognition in unconstrained environment with CNN. The Visual Computer, 37(2):217–226.

Boyd, A., Tinsley, P., Bowyer, K. W., and Czajka, A. (2023). Cyborg: Blending human saliency into the loss improves deep learning-based synthetic face detection. In Proceedings of the IEEE/CVF Winter Conference on Applications of Computer Vision, pages 6108–6117.

Brown, D. (2022). Deep face-iris recognition using robust image segmentation and hyperparameter tuning. In Computer Networks and Inventive Communication Technologies, pages 259–275. Springer.

Chen, C. and Ross, A. (2019). Matching thermal to visible face images using a semantic-guided generative adversaria network. In 2019 14th IEEE International Conference on Automatic Face & Gesture Recognition (FG 2019), pages 1–8. IEEE.

Cheng, W.-C., Hsiao, H.-C., and Li, L.-H. (2023). Deep learning mask face recognition with annealing mechanism. Applied Sciences, 13(2):732.

Elhassouny, A. and Smarandache, F. (2019). Trends in deep convolutional neural networks architectures: a review. In 2019 International Conference of Computer Science and Renewable Energies (ICCSRE), pages 1–8. IEEE.

Fariza, A., Arifin, A. Z., et al. (2019). Age estimation system using deep residual network classification method. In 2019 International Electronics Symposium (IES), pages 607–611. IEEE.

Gulli, A. and Pal, S. (2017). Deep learning with Keras. Packt Publishing Ltd. Gwyn, T., Roy, K., and Atay, M. (2021). Face recognition using popular deep net architectures: A brief comparative study. Future Internet, 13(7):164.

Hupont, I. and Fern´andez, C. (2019). Demogpairs: Quantifying the impact of demographic imbalance in deep face recognition. In 2019 14th IEEE International Conference on Automatic Face Gesture Recognition (FG 2019), pages 1-7.

Jain, A. K. and Li, S. Z. (2011). Handbook of face recognition. Springer. Ketab, F., Russel, N. S., Selvaraj, A., and Buhari, S. M. (2023). Parallel deep learning architecture with customized and learnable filters for low-resolution face recognition. The Visual Computer, pages 1–12.

Khan, A., Sohail, A., Zahoora, U., and Qureshi, A. S. (2020). A survey of the recent architectures of deep convolutional neural networks. Artificial Intelligence Review, 53(8):5455–5516.

Kuchta, D., Sergi, D., and Ucal Sari, I. (2022). Selection of the best face recognition system for check in and boarding services. In Intelligent and Fuzzy Techniques in Aviation 4.0, pages 361–384. Springer.

Kute, R. S., Vyas, V., and Anuse, A. (2019). Component-based face recognition under transfer learning for forensic applications. Information Sciences, 476:176–191.

Mahdianpari, M., Salehi, B., Rezaee, M., Mohammadimanesh, F., and Zhang, Y. (2018). Very deep convolutional neural networks for complex land cover mapping using multispectral remote sensing imagery. Remote Sensing, 10(7):1119.

Masi, I., Wu, Y., Hassner, T., and Natarajan, P. (2018). Deep face recognition: A survey. In 2018 31st SIBGRAPI conference on graphics, patterns and images (SIBGRAPI), pages 471–478. IEEE.

Niu, J.-Y., Xie, Z.-H., Li, Y., Cheng, S.-J., and Fan, J.-W. (2021). Scale fusion light cnn for hyperspectral face recognition with knowledge distillation and attention mechanism. Applied Intelligence, pages 1–15.

Nwankpa, C., Ijomah, W., Gachagan, A., and Marshall, S. (2018). Activation functions: Comparison of trends in practice and research for deep learning. arXiv preprint arXiv:1811.03378.10.

Oloyede, M. O., Hancke, G. P., and Myburgh, H. C. (2020). A review on face recognition systems: recent approaches and challenges. Multimedia Tools and Applications, 79(37):27891–27922.

Ortega-Delcampo, D., Conde, C., Palacios-Alonso, D., and Cabello, E. (2020). Border control morphing attack detection with a convolutional neural network de-morphing approach. IEEE Access, 8:92301–92313.

Peng, K., Mathur, A., and Narayanan, A. (2021). Mitigating dataset harms requires stewardship: Lessons from 1000 papers. arXiv preprint arXiv:2108.02922.

Porselvi, A., ME, A. S., Meena, P., and Nishitha, K. (2021). A secure banking by face recognition method. Radman, A., Sallam, A., and Suandi, S. A. (2022). Deep residual network for face sketch synthesis. Expert Systems with Applications, 190:115980.

Rikwith, S. L., Saiteja, D., and Jayaraman, R. (2021). Enhancement of electronic voting machine performance using fingerprint and face recognition. In 2021 2nd International Conference on Smart Electronics and Communication (ICOSEC), pages 757–763. IEEE.

RoyChowdhury, A., Yu, X., Sohn, K., Learned-Miller, E., and Chandraker, M. (2020). Improving face recognition by clustering unlabeled faces in the wild. In European Conference on Computer Vision, pages 119–136. Springer.

Savchenko, A., Demochkin, K., and Grechikhin, I. (2022). Preference prediction based on a photo gallery analysis with scene recognition and object detection. Pattern Recognition, 121:108248.

Singh, A., Bhatt, S., Nayak, V., and Shah, M. (2023). Automation of surveillance systems using deep learning and facial recognition. International Journal of System Assurance Engineering and Management, pages 1–10.

Singh, V., Gandhi, S., Kumar, R., Yadav, R., and Joshi, S. (2022). Deep neural network for facial emotion recognition system. pages 397–402. Springer.

Song, A.-P., Hu, Q., Ding, X.-H., Di, X.-Y., and Song, Z.-H. (2020). Similar face recognition using the ie-cnn model. IEEE Access, 8:45244–45253.

Srivastava, Y., Murali, V., and Dubey, S. R. (2019). A performance evaluation of loss functions for deep face recognition. In National Conference on Computer Vision, Pattern Recognition, Image Processing, and Graphics, pages 322–332. Springer.

Tan, M. and Le, Q. (2019). Efficientnet: Rethinking model scaling for convolutional neural networks. In International Conference on Machine Learning, pages 6105–6114. PMLR.

Vemulapalli, R. and Agarwala, A. (2019). A compact embedding for facial expression similarity. In Proceedings of the IEEE/CVF Conference on Computer Vision and Pattern Recognition, pages 5683–5692.

Xu, J., Guo, T., Xu, Y., Xu, Z., and Bai, K. (2021). MultiFace: A generic training mechanism for boosting face recognition performance. Neurocomputing, 448:40–47.

SP3F-GAN: SEAMLESS TEXTURE MAPS GENERATION BY ADVERSARIAL EXTENSION FOR FASHION

Honghong He[1,2], Zhengwentai Sun[1], Jintu Fan[1,2] and Pik Yin Mok[1,2]
[1]*School of Fashion and Textiles, The Hong Kong Polytechnic University, Hunghom, Hong Kong*
[2]*Laboratory for Artificial Intelligence in Design, Hong Kong Special Administrative Region, Hong Kong*

ABSTRACT

Creating seamless textures is essential for achieving realistic virtual objects and environments. This paper proposes a method for automatic seamless texture synthesis by designing a tiled latent space in the generator of an adversarial expansion network, resulting in a continuous texture output at the seam intersection area. In addition, considering the different properties of virtual environment rendering materials, the spatially varying BRDFs (albedo, normal, roughness and displacement map) are all designed in the proposed model to handle multi-layer texture representation. Qualitative and quantitative experiments on the describable textures dataset (DTD) show that the generated texture maps are not only seamlessly tiled but also exhibit superior visual quality in preserving details compared to previous deep texture synthesis methods.

KEYWORDS

Generative Adversarial Network (GAN), Seamless Texture Synthesis, BRDFs

1. INTRODUCTION

Seamless textures are an essential component of many digital art and 3D applications, as they allow artists and designers to create realistic or stylized surfaces with ease. These textures are designed to be applied multiple times without any noticeable repetition or breaks in the pattern, resulting in a continuous and visually appealing surface. However, creating seamless textures is a challenging task, as it requires careful planning and attention to detail to ensure that the edges of the texture match up perfectly when tiled. Due to this complexity, the creation of such textures is usually done by skilled artists using specialized software to capture (Guo et al., 2020; Li et al., 2018) and reconstruct the details of real-world materials (e.g., leather, human skin), or they create their own patterns from scratch. Recent advances in convolutional neural networks (CNNs) and generative adversarial networks (GANs) have been applied to texture synthesis problems showing unprecedented levels of realism and quality (Hertz et al., 2020; Liu et al., 2020; Mardani et al., 2020). However, the output of these methods is not always seamless when it is tiled. This means that while these methods can generate visually appealing textures, they may not be suitable for use in certain applications where seamless tiling is necessary. While some recent techniques have attempted to address the problem of tileable texture synthesis (Bergmann et al., 2017; Frühstück et al., 2019), they either require a certain degree of regularity or produce textures that lack visual fidelity. Furthermore, many existing methods for synthesizing textures focus on generating a single RGB image. Accurately simulating the appearance of real-world materials in virtual environments requires a spatially varying BRDF (Montes & Ureña, 2012; Zhou et al., 2022) to represent complex materials that exhibit different properties at different locations on the surface. The BRDFs typically consists of multiple images, such as albedo, normal, roughness etc., which are used collectively to accurately represent the properties of the material. Therefore, a single RGB image is usually insufficient to capture the complexity of the material's appearance.

In this paper, we take these 4 types of texture maps into account (albedo, normal, roughness, and displacement map) and propose a **GAN-based method** for synthesizing **Seamless Patterns for 3D Fashion** (**SP3F-GAN**) from any arbitrary content input. We train a generative network using an adversarial extension model SP3F-GAN, which differs from the model (Zhou et al., 2018) in that SP3F-GAN involves tiling feature maps obtained from decoded input textures. The tiled feature map is then cropped in the central region and decoded to produce a seamless output image. The discriminator is trained to distinguish between actual blocks from examples and blocks generated by the generator. The discriminator is trained to classify whether a $2k \times 2k$ texture block is real (a crop from the input exemplar) or fake (synthesized by generator). In addition, to allow texture maps synthesis, we design 4 decoders to cope with the generation of different texture maps and demonstrate the texture maps synthesis of 4 maps. Our method is shown to outperform state-of-the-art solutions for seamless texture synthesis. Unlike prior work on deep texture synthesis, our model is designed and optimized not only to generate visually pleasing texture effects but also to enable the generation of infinite texture patterns suitable for printing on various surfaces such as floors, clothing, walls, and more. This capability is demonstrated in Figure 1.

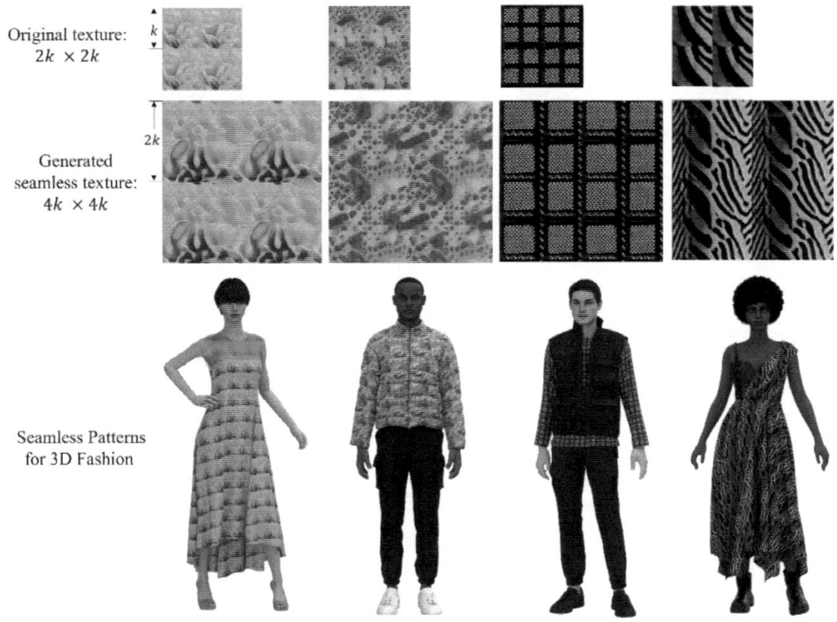

Figure 1. Tiling the original texture creates a discontinuity at the intersection of the seams, as shown in the top row. Our method can generate seamless textures, which are able to apply to fabric pattern swatches, 3D garments, etc.

2. RELATED WORK

Texture synthesis: Traditional texture synthesis algorithms are methods used to generate textures by analyzing a given input texture and synthesizing new textures with similar properties, mainly including texture mapping (Madaras & Ďurikovič, 2012; Piponi & Borshukov, 2000) and patch-based texture synthesis technology (Barnes et al., 2009; Cohen et al., 2003; Kaspar et al., 2015; Levin et al., 2004; Liang et al., 2001). These algorithms, while successful at generating a wide range of textures, often struggle to generate high-quality and realistic textures, especially for complex materials such as hair, fur, and natural landscapes. As a result, deep generative models have gained popularity due to its superior generation capability. Specifically, in terms of texture synthesis, they have been shown to successfully generate high-quality and diverse texture samples from images or image datasets that are visually similar to the input texture or dataset (Bergmann et al., 2017; Frühstück et al., 2019; Hertz et al., 2020; Zhou et al., 2018).

Seamless texture synthesis: Several recent works have explicitly explored the tileability of texture synthesis. The Periodic Spatial GAN proposed by Bergmann et al. (2017) can create textures from a set of random numbers that represent the expected general image, local variation, and periodic repetition of learning in generated images. GANosaic (Jetchev et al., 2017) extends such method to generate textures by optimizing the latent noise space to produce textures that match the overall content of a given guidance image. While these methods produce smoother transitions between texture patches, they still suffer from issues relating to texture scalability and variability. Rodriguez-Pardo and Garces (2022) solves the scalability problem by completing textures into tiles through tile search and feature repetition. However, their method requires training each texture synthesis network from scratch, resulting in high computational costs. Inspired by (Zhou et al., 2018) in non-stationary texture synthesis task, in which we modified its network structure and extended it to BRDFs for generating tileable texture maps.

3. METHOD

Our ultimate goal is to generate seamless texture maps, which can then be used for downstream tasks, such as 3D garments. These seamless texture maps are perceptually similar to smaller input texture samples being tiled. However, by default, the input texture samples are tiled with significant seams. Our main idea is to eliminate the seams by automatically learning from the network to generate tileable texture maps from arbitrary texture input examples. The GAN (Goodfellow et al., 2014) is used in our method to learn the implicit representation of textures in two neural modules, generator G and discriminator D. Given a $k \times k$ source block S_A cropped from the input sample, the generator is trained to generate a new $2k \times 2k$ output $\hat{T}_A$. Among them, the other maps of the input sample are normal map, roughness map and displacement map, respectively denoted as S_N, S_R and S_D, which corresponding to the generated new texture maps represented as $\hat{T}_N$, $\hat{T}_R$ and $\hat{T}_D$. Discriminator D is trained to distinguish between these 4 $2k \times 2k$ texture maps are real (cropped from input samples) or fake (synthesized by G). Synthetic seamless texture maps can be applied to 3D garments for visualization and presentation. The diagram in Figure 2 depicts our proposed method of SP3F-GAN.

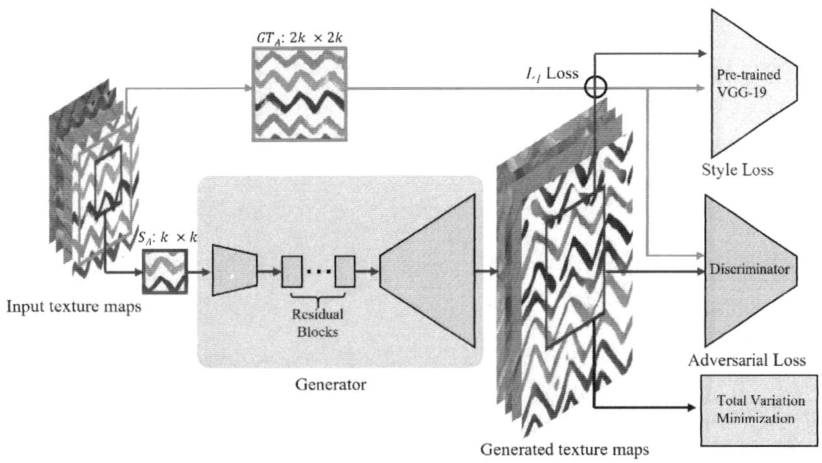

Figure 2. Illustration of the proposed method for seamless texture maps generation

Network architecture: The network architecture of SP3F-GAN is adopted from (Rodriguez-Pardo & Garces, 2022; Zhou et al., 2018), including a residual connected encoder-decoder, convolution generator G, and convolution discriminator D. However, their methods mainly focus on 2D textures. To achieve 3D seamless textures, we extend their methods with two major aspects. First, instead of synthesizing a single RGB image, we extend Generator's outputs to 4 texture maps (albedo, normal, roughness and displacement map). Second, to keep the continuity in the seam region, we applied Total Variation Loss as a regularization term.

Generator: The proposed generator consists of three main components: (i) the encoder, (ii) residual blocks and (iii) the decoder. First, the encoder encodes the input texture maps, taking the albedo map S_A as an example, to obtain feature map x_0 (the spatial resolution is 1/4 of the input albedo map S_A). The feature map x_0 is first tilled (2*2) to obtain the tiled feature map x'(the spatial resolution is 1/2 of the input albedo map S_A). The tiled feature map x' is then cropped in the central region to obtain x_c'. Then, a set of residual blocks learn a compact representation of the input texture. Finally, a bunch of decoders decode the output of the last residual block to the output texture $\hat{T}_A$. Synthesizing multiple texture maps with a single generative model presents additional challenges for the case of a single texture map because different texture maps produce different visual expressions. Inspired by (Rodriguez-Pardo & Garces, 2022), we extend the decoder to four decoding texture maps for each of the four different data types.

Discriminator: Since we are not performing a pixel-by-pixel estimation of the whole image, the discriminator is designed as a PatchGAN architecture, allowing local evaluation of the synthetic texture quality for better local texture detail and global structural consistency. The discriminator has not been altered in this task, (Isola et al., 2017; Zhou et al., 2018; Zhu et al., 2017) can find more analysis on the patchGAN-based discriminator.

Loss Function: We train the network according to the standard GAN framework (Goodfellow et al., 2014), and iterate between the training D and the real texture maps GT_A, GT_N, GT_R and GT_D and the generated texture maps $\hat{T}_A$, $\hat{T}_N$, $\hat{T}_R$ and $\hat{T}_D$. In addition to the standard adversarial loss function L_{adv}, we used three additional loss terms: L_1 loss , style loss L_{style} (Gatys et al., 2015) and total variation loss L_{tv} (Larsen Greiner et al., 2022).

$$L_{tv}(x) = \sum_{i,j} \left(\left(x_{i,j+1} - x_{ij}\right)^2 + \left(x_{i+1,j} - x_{ij}\right)^2 \right)^{\frac{1}{2}} \quad (1)$$

where x stands for the synthesized image, x_{ij} is a pixel from image x at location (i, j). The L_1 loss is extended to 4 texture maps: L_1^a, L_1^n , L_1^r and L_1^d. The L_{style} and L_{tv} are calculated as the sum of the perceptual losses and total variation losses between the target and the generated albedo, normal, roughness and displacement texture maps. We weight the total style loss by weighting different layers in the same way described in (Gatys et al., 2016; Zhou et al., 2018). Our total loss function is defined as follow:

$$L = \lambda_{adv} L_{adv} + \lambda L_1^a + \lambda L_1^n + \lambda L_1^r + \lambda L_1^d + \lambda_{style} L_{style} + \lambda_{tv} L_{tv} \quad (2)$$

4. EXPERIMENT

In this section, we evaluate our two main contributions. First, we examine the impact of the design choices of Generator G on multilayer texture maps (Section 4.1), and second, we compare our SP3F-GAN with the SOTA method (Section 4.2).

4.1 Consistency of Texture Maps

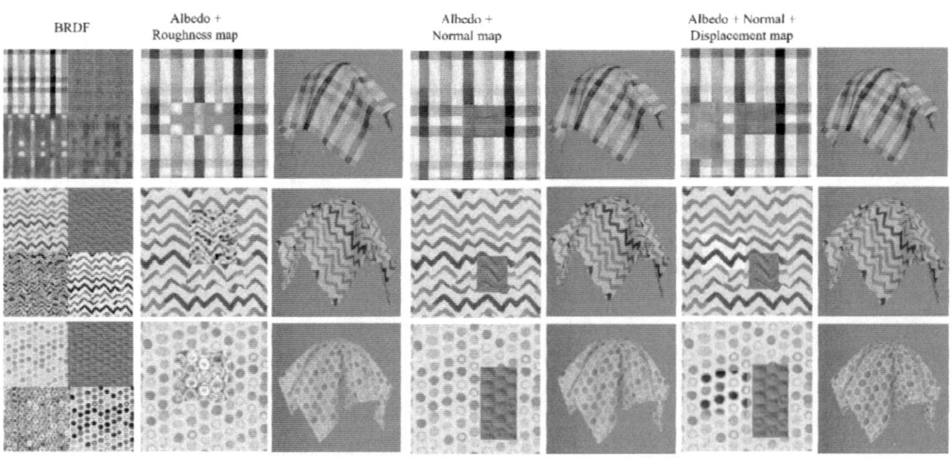

Figure 3. Illustration of consistency of synthesized texture maps

Our generator G can generate high-quality seamless texture maps but cannot guarantee that the pattern of these texture maps is consistently at a specific location. Gradients may not be shared in texture maps because L_{style} and L_{tv} are calculated independently for each map. In this section, we demonstrate the usefulness of our generator through a practical application. For the four generated seamless texture maps, we randomly select two or three maps (e.g., albedo + roughness map, albedo + normal map, and albedo + normal + displacement map) to overlay on the fabric swatches for 3D garments and observe whether the pixel-level consistency between the maps is preserved. Figure 3 shows the consistency of synthesized texture maps.

4.2 Comparison Experiment

4.2.1 Qualitative Comparison

We compare with the SOTA texture synthesis method proposed by Bergmann et al. (2017)'s PSGAN, using samples from the describable textures dataset (DTD) (Cimpoi et al., 2014). 300 samples were randomly selected from DTD to compare with the PSGAN method. The Figure 4 shows some representative texture seamless generation results.[1] In the line, dot and marbled pattern examples, due to the relatively simple texture structure, both methods work convincingly, capturing different repeating patterns. In the second row of chequered pattern and the first row of grid pattern, PSGAN generates images with obvious artifacts, and the details of the texture are not well preserved (e.g., generated distorted chequered pattern). PSGAN performs reasonably when texture structure changes can be achieved locally at the seams but fails when the required changes are global (meaning that the effect is not good for 2*2 tiling). Textures can be applied to fabric pattern samples or 3D garments where seamless tiling is a minimum expectation. Our proposed SP3F-GAN can not only generate tractable textures but also preserve the high-level semantic structure, thereby yielding clear and realistic synthetic textures. Particularly, SP3F-GAN provides high-quality output for textures with non-uniform illumination (e.g., the second row of chequered pattern), irregular textures (e.g., striped and bubbly pattern) and gradient color textures (e.g., grid and smeared pattern).

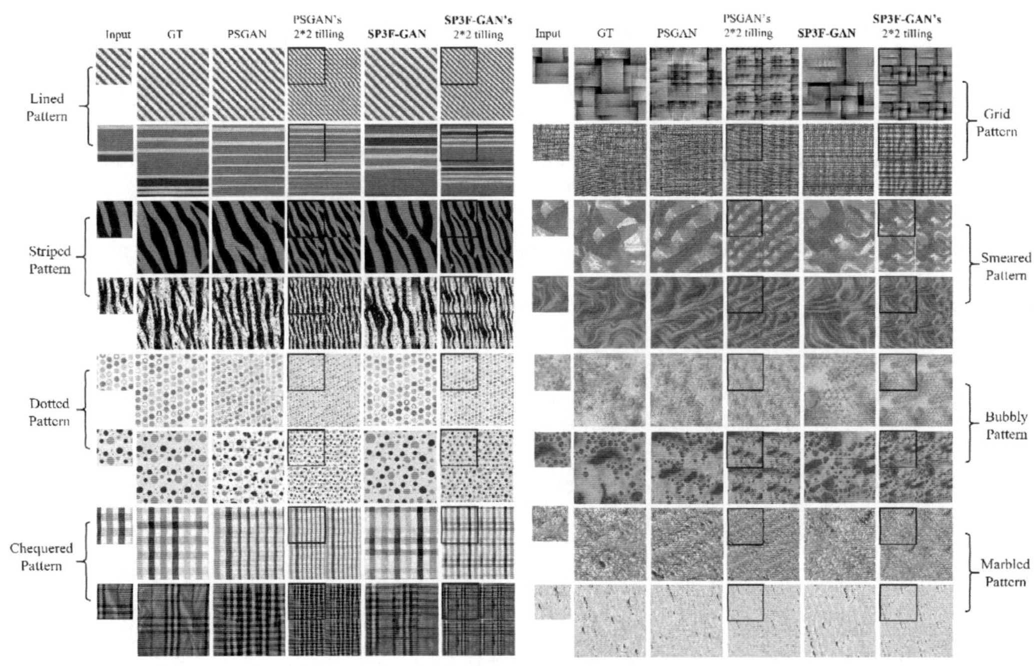

Figure 4. Qualitative comparison with SOTA method. On the left column, we show the input textures cropped from the ground truth. From left to right, the synthesized results of PSGAN (Bergmann et al., 2017) and the proposed SP3F-GAN Outputs are tiled a similar number of times (at least twice in each dimension) for better visualization. Our method generally captures better the overall structure of the texture, while providing seamless and semantically coherent borders, for enhancing tileability

[1]More qualitative results can be obtained through e-mail: tracy.mok@polyu.edu.hk

4.2.1 Quantitative Comparison

In the quantitative evaluation, we compare the performance of the generated texture with the ground truth texture (GT) using standard metrics: SSIM and LPIPS. The Structural Similarity Index Metric (SSIM) (Wang et al., 2004) is a perceptual-aware metric that acts on pixel space to measure the similarity of structural information and may be suitable for evaluating synthesized textures. In addition, we use learning perceptual image block similarity (LPIPS) (Zhang et al., 2018) as perceptual distance metric in deep image space. This metric is widely used to evaluate generative models (Huang et al., 2018; Karras et al., 2020; Zhan et al., 2022). Experiments were conducted in a fair comparison between describable textures dataset (DTD) and the deep learning-based method PSGAN (Bergmann et al., 2017). We first compared the composite image and GT. Our method obtained better SSIM and LPIPS scores, as shown in Table 1. Then, we also compared the 2*2 tiled generated textures and GT. However, the metrics used for this experiment require both to have the same resolution. To achieve this, a 2*2 tiled generated image is cropped in the center so that it has the same resolution as the corresponding GT. Similarly, scores better than PSGAN are both in SSIM and LPIPS. This shows that our method can better preserve the stylistic and semantic content of the generated texture by combining various loss functions. In addition, our potential spatial manipulation algorithm allows seamless boundaries between tiling, superior to PSGAN in terms of structural similarity.

Table 1. Quantitative comparison of PSGAN and the proposed SP3F-GAN. Higher is better for SSIM, while lower is better for LPIPS

	PSGAN (Bergmann et al., 2017)	Center cropped PSGAN's 2*2 tiling	SP3F-GAN	Center cropped SP3F-GAN's 2*2 tiling
↑SSIM	0.1763	0.1896	0.2354	**0.24566**
↓LPIPS	0.5957	0.5236	**0.4327**	0.5063

5. CONCLUSION

In this paper, an automatic seamless texture synthesis network architecture is proposed to process multi-layer texture maps. Extensive experiments on a describable texture dataset (DTD) show that the proposed wearable GAN can generate seamless texture maps with superior visual quality in terms of detail preservation compared to previous deep texture synthesis methods.

ACKNOWLEDGEMENT

The work described in this paper was funded in part by a grant from the Laboratory for Artificial Intelligence in Design (Project Code: RP1-1) under the InnoHK Research Clusters, Hong Kong Special Administrative Region Government and by the Innovation and Technology Commission of Hong Kong, under grant ITP/028/21TP.

REFERENCES

Barnes, C., Shechtman, E., Finkelstein, A., & Goldman, D. B. (2009). PatchMatch: A randomized correspondence algorithm for structural image editing. *ACM Trans. Graph.*, *28*(3), 24.

Bergmann, U., Jetchev, N., & Vollgraf, R. (2017). Learning texture manifolds with the periodic spatial GAN. *arXiv preprint arXiv:1705.06566*.

Cimpoi, M., Maji, S., Kokkinos, I., Mohamed, S., & Vedaldi, A. (2014). Describing textures in the wild. Proceedings of the IEEE conference on computer vision and pattern recognition,

Cohen, M. F., Shade, J., Hiller, S., & Deussen, O. (2003). Wang tiles for image and texture generation. *ACM transactions on graphics (TOG)*, *22*(3), 287-294.

Frühstück, A., Alhashim, I., & Wonka, P. (2019). Tilegan: synthesis of large-scale non-homogeneous textures. *ACM transactions on graphics (TOG)*, *38*(4), 1-11.

Gatys, L., Ecker, A. S., & Bethge, M. (2015). Texture synthesis using convolutional neural networks. *Advances in neural information processing systems*, *28*.

Gatys, L. A., Ecker, A. S., & Bethge, M. (2016). Image style transfer using convolutional neural networks. Proceedings of the IEEE conference on computer vision and pattern recognition,

Goodfellow, I. J., Pouget-Abadie, J., Mirza, M., Xu, B., Warde-Farley, D., Ozair, S., Courville, A., & Bengio, Y. (2014). Generative adversarial networks (2014). *arXiv preprint arXiv:1406.2661*, *1406*.

Guo, Y., Smith, C., Hašan, M., Sunkavalli, K., & Zhao, S. (2020). Materialgan: reflectance capture using a generative svbrdf model. *arXiv preprint arXiv:2010.00114*.

Hertz, A., Hanocka, R., Giryes, R., & Cohen-Or, D. (2020). Deep geometric texture synthesis. *arXiv preprint arXiv:2007.00074*.

Huang, X., Liu, M.-Y., Belongie, S., & Kautz, J. (2018). Multimodal unsupervised image-to-image translation. Proceedings of the European conference on computer vision (ECCV),

Isola, P., Zhu, J.-Y., Zhou, T., & Efros, A. A. (2017). Image-to-image translation with conditional adversarial networks. Proceedings of the IEEE conference on computer vision and pattern recognition,

Jetchev, N., Bergmann, U., & Seward, C. (2017). GANosaic: Mosaic creation with generative texture manifolds. *arXiv preprint arXiv:1712.00269*.

Karras, T., Laine, S., Aittala, M., Hellsten, J., Lehtinen, J., & Aila, T. (2020). Analyzing and improving the image quality of stylegan. Proceedings of the IEEE/CVF conference on computer vision and pattern recognition,

Kaspar, A., Neubert, B., Lischinski, D., Pauly, M., & Kopf, J. (2015). Self tuning texture optimization. Computer Graphics Forum,

Larsen Greiner, T. A., Lie, J. E., Kolbjørnsen, O., Kjelsrud Evensen, A., Harris Nilsen, E., Zhao, H., Demyanov, V., & Gelius, L.-J. (2022). Unsupervised deep learning with higher-order total-variation regularization for multidimensional seismic data reconstruction. *Geophysics*, *87*(2), V59-V73.

Levin, A., Zomet, A., Peleg, S., & Weiss, Y. (2004). Seamless image stitching in the gradient domain. Computer Vision-ECCV 2004: 8th European Conference on Computer Vision, Prague, Czech Republic, May 11-14, 2004. Proceedings, Part IV 8,

Li, Z., Sunkavalli, K., & Chandraker, M. (2018). Materials for masses: SVBRDF acquisition with a single mobile phone image. Proceedings of the European conference on computer vision (ECCV),

Liang, L., Liu, C., Xu, Y.-Q., Guo, B., & Shum, H.-Y. (2001). Real-time texture synthesis by patch-based sampling. *ACM transactions on graphics (TOG)*, *20*(3), 127-150.

Liu, G., Taori, R., Wang, T.-C., Yu, Z., Liu, S., Reda, F. A., Sapra, K., Tao, A., & Catanzaro, B. (2020). Transposer: Universal texture synthesis using feature maps as transposed convolution filter. *arXiv preprint arXiv:2007.07243*.

Madaras, M., & Ďurikovič, R. (2012). Skeleton texture mapping. Proceedings of the 28th Spring Conference on computer Graphics,

Mardani, M., Liu, G., Dundar, A., Liu, S., Tao, A., & Catanzaro, B. (2020). Neural ffts for universal texture image synthesis. *Advances in neural information processing systems*, *33*, 14081-14092.

Montes, R., & Ureña, C. (2012). An overview of BRDF models. *University of Grenada, Technical Report LSI-2012-001*.

Piponi, D., & Borshukov, G. (2000). Seamless texture mapping of subdivision surfaces by model pelting and texture blending. Proceedings of the 27th annual conference on Computer graphics and interactive techniques,

Rodriguez-Pardo, C., & Garces, E. (2022). SeamlessGAN: Self-Supervised Synthesis of Tileable Texture Maps. *arXiv preprint arXiv:2201.05120*.

Wang, Z., Bovik, A. C., Sheikh, H. R., & Simoncelli, E. P. (2004). Image quality assessment: from error visibility to structural similarity. *IEEE transactions on image processing*, *13*(4), 600-612.

Zhan, F., Yu, Y., Wu, R., Zhang, J., Lu, S., & Zhang, C. (2022). Marginal contrastive correspondence for guided image generation. Proceedings of the IEEE/CVF Conference on Computer Vision and Pattern Recognition,

Zhang, R., Isola, P., Efros, A. A., Shechtman, E., & Wang, O. (2018). The unreasonable effectiveness of deep features as a perceptual metric. Proceedings of the IEEE conference on computer vision and pattern recognition,

Zhou, X., Hasan, M., Deschaintre, V., Guerrero, P., Sunkavalli, K., & Kalantari, N. K. (2022). TileGen: Tileable, Controllable Material Generation and Capture. SIGGRAPH Asia 2022 Conference Papers,

Zhou, Y., Zhu, Z., Bai, X., Lischinski, D., Cohen-Or, D., & Huang, H. (2018). Non-stationary texture synthesis by adversarial expansion. *arXiv preprint arXiv:1805.04487*.

Zhu, J.-Y., Park, T., Isola, P., & Efros, A. A. (2017). Unpaired image-to-image translation using cycle-consistent adversarial networks. Proceedings of the IEEE international conference on computer vision

HE IS NOT YOUR HERO: GENDERED EXPERIENCE UNVEILED THROUGH GAMEPLAY VIDEOS (A CASE STUDY OF GENJI FROM OVERWATCH)

Chuxuan Zhang
University of Edinburgh
Holland Annexe, 18 Holyrood Park Road, Edinburg, Scotland, UK

ABSTRACT

The gaming industry has predominately exhibited a significant gender disparity, resulting in the portrayal of game characters, including avatars, in a manner that reinforces gender stereotypes. This study aims to investigate the impact of avatar portrayal on the overall gaming encounter among individuals with diverse gender identities. To achieve this objective, gameplay videos are analysed as valuable sources of players' experiences. The case study focuses on Genji, an avatar from the video game *Overwatch* (2016) and its subsequent sequel and replacement. By employing multimodal discourse analysis, the study examines the impact of avatar characteristics on player engagement in the context of *Overwatch (2016)* and *Overwatch 2 (2022)*. The findings reveal that avatar characteristics significantly influence player engagement, particularly in terms of gameplay mechanics, surpassing that of the narrative. The endorsement of heteronormative representations, as the character Genji exemplifies, could conspires with the toxic environment. The research advocates that promoting gender inclusivity in the gaming industry requires the integration of a wide range of avatars that not only reflect queerness in the narrative but also in the game mechanics, thereby fostering a more inclusive gaming atmosphere.

KEYWORDS

Avatar, Gameplay Video, Gendered Experience, Overwatch

1. INTRODUCTION

Video gaming has long been recognised as a masculine space. The phenomenon is evident in various forms, including problematic depictions found in gaming artefacts, gender disparities in the gaming industry labour force, and associated social media buzz (Bailey et al., 2021; Cote, 2020; Maloney et al., 2019; Tompkins and Martins, 2022). The origins of the game are often ascribed to these phenomena. Throughout history, a predominant focus has been on on marketing games towards a male demographic (Friedberg, 2015). This may limit the variety of content types that dominate consumer landscapes and gaming offerings. Men are the main contributors to the discourse shaping of the gaming domain. Numerous scholars assert the enduring validity of this statement within the present context (Bailey et al., 2021; Maloney et al., 2019; Tompkins, 2021).

The subsequent discussion will shed light on the gendered representations in games, in alignment with the research concerns delineated in the text. In her scholarly work, Shaw (2014, p.6) criticises the gender representation of characters in game artefacts as non-progressive. This may manifest as character portrayals that follow gender stereotypes or uneven representation of diverse gender identities (Malkowski, 2017). However, it has been observed by scholars like Süngü (2020) that efforts have been made to enhance the representation of diverse characters within the game.

Avatars are distinct representative characters facilitating player interaction with the game environment and other characters via the screen. Schröter and Thon (2014) propose a comprehensive framework for analysing the portrayal of video game characters, encompassing three essential perspectives: their role within the narrative structure, their contribution to gameplay mechanics, and their involvement in social dynamics. In addition to the functions above, playable avatars allow players to assume various identities within the virtual environment. This enables interactions in the game world to exceed those encountered in real life. (Bowman & Banks, 2021). Avatars possess the capacity to assume diverse attributes, encompassing gender, race, and species, empowering players to detach themselves from their identity temporarily. Hence, it is imperative to thoroughly investigate the potential impact of the avatar on the player, thereby establishing its significance.

Several scholarly investigations have explored the potential correlation between the selection of gendered avatars and the gender identity of players (Ratan et al., 2019; Tompkins, 2021). This study aims to investigate the correlation between different factors in the context of the play experience, with a focus on maintaining objectivity rather than being influenced by personal biases. This study examines the impact of narrative and gameplay characteristics of avatars on the gaming experience of players with different gender identities. Specifically, it explores the relationship between avatar attributes and gaming experience. The issues will be investigated by utilising gameplay video as a research tool. The character Genji, who appears in both the games *Overwatch* (2016) and *Overwatch 2* (2022), has been chosen as a subject of analysis to explore the aforementioned inquiries. The subsequent section will elaborate on the gameplay video and the various cases involved.

2. RESEARCH CONTEXT AND METHODS

Overwatch (2016) and its sequel and replacement production, *Overwatch 2* (2022), are first-person shooters published by Blizzard Entertainment. Given the substantial similarities in narrative context and gameplay mechanics between *Overwatch 2* (2022) and its predecessor, the subsequent discussion will utilise the designations *Overwatch 1&2* (2016, 2022) when explaining both iterations. *Overwatch 1&2* (2016, 2022) showcases a wide array of heroes representing various backgrounds and characteristics. The game emphasises teamwork and offers a selection of 32 playable hero avatars, which can be divided functionally into three categories, attack, support, and tank. While portraying these avatars, the games manage to grant a vibrant setting in the avatar narrative. Meanwhile, it has a higher proportion of female players than its counterpart (Choi et al., 2020). Taken together, *Overwatch 1&2* (2016, 2022) is a suitable playground for addressing research inquiries.

This research examines the utilisation of gameplay and narrative aspects concerning avatars. The gameplay dimension investigates the avatar's mechanics, dynamics, and associated emotional experiences, drawing inspiration from the work of Hunicke et al. (2004). On the other hand, the narrative dimension places greater emphasis on the backstory of the avatar. This distinction arises from the separation of focus between the avatar's gameplay attributes governed by game mechanics and its narrative depiction portrayed through peripheral productions within the context of *Overwatch 1&2* (2016, 2022).

Genji is an attack hero. In contrast to specific characters whose creators openly express their emphasis on either gameplay (e.g., Brigitte) or narrative (e.g., Ana) during the design phase, the origin of Genji is not explicitly mentioned. Nonetheless, his mechanics and appearance were likely intertwined by the developers. The design and concept of Genji are characterised by his distinct portrayal as a cyber ninja, wielding a great sword and exhibiting agile movements. This depiction is widely acknowledged and easily identifiable, as are the thematic colours associated with him.

This concept fundamentally delineates his performance concerning the mechanics of the game. The integration of Genji's offensive mechanics presented considerable difficulty due to the inherent complexity of incorporating melee weapons into a first-person shooter video game (Technica, 2017). However, per his conceptual framework, the ultimate design choice was to outfit Genji with shurikens to engage in long-range combat while still retaining his proficiency in close-quarters combat for his ultimate ability. The individual's mechanical abilities grant him vital offensive capability and improved mobility in diverse environments. Consequently, he significantly demonstrates the ability to disrupt the adversary's forces during combat encounters.

Meanwhile, the in-game voice packages, the game archives, and its franchises effectively portray the narrative surrounding Genji and his relationship with certain avatars. He is portrayed with a relatively comprehensive narrative: As the younger son of the Shimada Clan, he faced a perilous threat to his life due to intrafamilial disputes instigated by his sibling. Eventually saved by the Overwatch organisation (mainly Mercy, who plays a prominent role in his modification and healing), Genji undergoes significant mechanical enhancements, ultimately serving as a Cyborg Ninja for Blackwatch (carrying out black ops missions of Overwatch. Genji grapples with existential confusion as a cyborg and eventually departs from the organisation in search of the meaning of life.

According to Jenkins (2013), fandom offers an avenue for fans to express their perspectives on matters related to sexuality and gender. Gameplay videos have emerged as prevalent manifestations of fan engagement within the video game sector. Critics argue that gameplay videos hinder the essence of games, which is the dynamic and interactive relationship between mechanics and user input (Oberg, 2021, as cited in McKitrick et al., 2023). In addition, from the perspective of the game industry, the videos may also threaten the interests of gaming companies (Carey, 2019) and prevent the gaming experience from being fully appreciated (Tekinbaş, 2004). Regarding video content, gameplay videos have been questioned for fraudulent content due to their desire for popularity and reach (Oberg, 2021).

In contrast, scholars who hold favourable views towards gameplay videos perceive the performative aspect as the primary focus rather than interpreting them as deliberate misrepresentations. They argue that creators boost the entertainment value of these videos by assuming multiple roles simultaneously, acting as operators, performers, and spectators (Nguyen, 2016). Similarly, Fernández-Vara (2019, p.123) argues that these videos have the potential to serve as a reliable source of data for assessing game experience. This research endeavour will employ gameplay videos as a primary data source to examine the gendered experiences within the realm of gaming.

In order to examine the relationship between gendered avatars and players, the study made an effort to prioritise Genji gameplay videos that were relevant to gender-related analysis. Four videos were carefully chosen, each containing specific information as presented in Table 1. The aforementioned data constitutes the primary dataset examined within the scope of this scholarly research article. A critical analysis was conducted on the game contribution and player interaction for the four samples.

This study aims to evaluate the gendered aspects of gaming in the context of *Overwatch 1&2* (2016, 2022), utilising a comprehensive analysis of a collection of gameplay videos. In order to accomplish this objective, the researchers tried to employ the term 'Genji' as a primary keyword in conjunction with other keywords related to gender, including 'female', 'male', 'gender', 'transgender', and 'girl'. A total of eighteen videos were identified and documented. Subsequent filtration was conducted to acquire additional interpretive data regarding the interaction among the players. As a result, four videos were chosen for the conclusive examination. These videos were specifically chosen due to their inclusion of pivotal gameplay moments and their substantial representation of interactions between the player and other participants.

Table 1. The selected Genji gameplay videos

Video No	Uploader Username	Video Title
V1	ChristalRaine	Mercy? Nah, I'll lock Genji instead ;)
V2	Cannaestia	When A Girl Plays Genji –Overwatch
V3	Necros	Impressing an EGIRL in Overwatch | NECRIZZ
V4	Diggums	GENJI PLAYS WITH HIS GIRL? Overwatch

These gameplay videos serve as performance texts that aim to construct, maintain, or problematise gender norms around Genji. They are sites of gendered experience, exposing us to the construction of gendered discourses in gaming and the power structures embedded in the conventions of these discourses.

Based on the manner of presentation of the gameplay video, multimodal critical discourse analysis is employed here to analyse the data. As noted by Kress (2012), this method involves examining and interpreting any text as a comprehensive and meaningful semiotic entity. Its purpose is to describe and analyse the elements and dynamics present within the text, including the manifestation of power in social interactions. It is characterised by the ability to consider multiple modes as a relevant cultural resource for producing meaning (representation) by individuals belonging to a specific social group within a specific temporal context.

The utilisation of multimodal critical discourse analysis confirms to be highly valuable in examining gameplay. As per Kress's (2010, p.5) definition, the term 'mode' encompasses the various means of generating meaning and experience, including spoken and written language, gesture, gaze, layout, and image. The video medium is a typical example of a multimodal text, encompassing various semiotic elements such as written text, static and moving visual images, sound, and other forms of communication. The study utilised multimodal critical discourse analysis to investigate the gameplay experience offered by the character Genji and the role of gender representation in the avatars used in the game. This analysis integrated both the material capabilities and the social influence of various semiotic elements.

3. RESULTS

3.1 Titles and Thumbnails

The initial procedure involved thoroughly analysing the thumbnails and titles of the chosen gameplay videos. Prior studies, including Christel (2006) and Yoon and Kim (2019), have demonstrated the significance of video thumbnails and titles as crucial elements in conveying discourse. These visual and textual components convey information about the video's content and entice prospective viewers. One could argue that these findings also shed light on the specific style of Genji gameplay that garners greater viewer attention within the gaming context of *Overwatch 1&2* (2016, 2022). Based on the title, it seems that the different uploaders adhere to an antagonistic dynamic, wherein they position Genji within a binary framework alongside either Mercy or the female persona of the player. This dynamic could potentially be interpreted as a subordinate association, wherein Mercy is relegated to the role of "his girl." These relationships are also perpetuated in thumbnail images.

Regarding thumbnails, an examination of the analytical framework proposed by Kress and van Leeuwen (2020) reveals a notable visual metaphor wherein the portrayal of gender identity aligns prominently with the heteronormative norm, thereby openly endorsing heterosexuality. The heteronormative intimacy between Genji and Mercy is particularly evident in their portrayal, characterised by non-verbal cues like gazing. The emergence of the two avatars within the frame initiates a dynamic interaction characterised by reactivity. According to Kress and Van Leeuwen (2020, p.67), a vector can be defined as the directional line of sight from Mercy to the relevant content of Genji, conceptualised as a 'phenomenon'. The male individual assumes the actor's role, while the female individual fulfils the role of a devoted admirer of his performance, reinforcing Genji's central position. Depending on the nature of the video, the individual's focus is either the performance metrics of Genji's players, such as their kill statistics, or the physical attributes of Genji, specifically his buttocks.

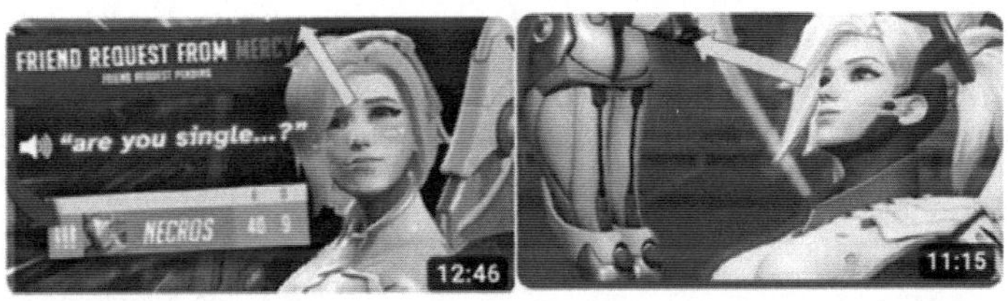

Figure 1. Interaction between Genji and Mercy (left to right: cover of V3 and V4)

Meanwhile, the visual depiction in the cover image sustains an explicitly binary structure through the composition. Mercy adopts an upward gaze towards Genji, implying an unequal power relationship and a sense of admiration for him. At the same time, concerning the left-right structure, according to Kress and Van Leeuwen (2020, pp. 196-198), the left stands for 'the given, the taken for granted' and the right for 'the now/present'. Caution must be taken that this symbolic construction is rooted in a Western reading tradition, or at least a left-to-right reading tradition. While establishing character dynamics, Genji is presented as being submitted to, while the adoring Mercy shows affection towards him. Similarly, when female players are introduced, whether competitively or entertainingly, feminine semiotic entities oppose Genji.

Figure 2. Binary structure of the composition (left to right: cover of V1 and V2,)

The incorporation of colour is intricately intertwined with the underlying structure of dyadic gender paradigms. The utilisation of the colour pink by creators, irrespective of gender, serves as a symbolic representation of femininity, aligning with prevailing societal categorisations of colour (Cunningham & Macrae, 2011). The selection of colour holds significance when the creator is free to engage in design decisions. Unlike the green and pale-yellow colours that frequently appear on covers and subtitles, perpetuating the official visual design of the characters, the image identified as female is often deliberately highlighted in pink. The colour pink appears in the modification of the theme colours of Genji, the movements of the figures, and the textual representation of female player spoken content. In brief, the titles and thumbnails designed by either male or female players are littered with evidence of the logic of dichotomous gender constructions centred on Genji.

Figure 3. The usage of colour pink (left to right: cover of V1, V2, and V3)

3.2 Play of the Game: The Cult of Gameplay Capabilities

The video exposes the diverse collection of game contributions that *Overwatch 1&2* (2016, 2022) provide to players. These include but are not limited to digital text presentation of kills, assisted kills, deaths, and voice incentive of multiple kills. The 'Play of the Game' feature, determined by an algorithm, highlights an impactful action performed by a player during a match. Displayed at the end of each match, it showcases the player's significant contribution from their perspective.

In parallel, the determination of a player's position can be achieved through a rigorous analysis based on data, wherein the magnitude of their contribution is assessed and taken into account. The discourse among players illustrates that the act of eliminating an adversary who has already engaged in combat with a fellow teammate is commonly referred to as 'stealing'. The fundamental performance metrics within the game are consolidated in the combat panel and career profile of the player. These statistics serve as a reference point for players to assess their performance. The pursuit of victory and the feedback system in *Overwatch 1&2* (2016, 2022) result in an evolving power dynamic between players, using their relative skills as a reference point.

> [Scene: Genji (Cannaestia, female Genji player) eliminates an enemy that is attacked by Reaper (Male Player O)]
>
> Male Player F: Rob (Male Player O), Jen(Cannaestia, , female Genji player) is trying to steal your goal. (Content of V2)

These gameplay videos reveal the positive (killing for recognition) and negative (being killed as a joke) aspects of gaming skills as their primary content. The videos have been meticulously edited to emphasise instances where players demonstrate superior performance in the aforementioned aspect. This editing process involves the removal of less captivating sections and deliberate highlighting of moments wherein players successfully eliminate multiple adversaries. Comedic elements manifest in situations where players emphasise their mistakes or subpar performance, such as their inability to deal damage or encountering unexpected eliminations.

> [Screen: Play of the Game: RAINE (female Genji player) as Genji]
>
> Raine: [looks at the camera] Easy (Content of V1)
>
> [Scene: Genji (Cannaestia, female Genji player)) being trapped and eliminated, with hit sound effects, all players laughes together]
>
> Male Player F: Yeah. Way to go. You just distracted them with your stupidity...Fucking good play. You're a good distraction. They feel like... What the fuck is she doing? (Content of V2)

Simultaneously, the team's interests are crucial in the avatar selection process. The gameplay footage showcases players actively participating in dialogues pertaining to their avatar selection. Effective communication and coordination among team members can optimise overall productivity. Nevertheless, it is essential to acknowledge that team members may also face evaluation or mistreatment from their peers, contingent upon their competencies. Sarcasm, humour, and teasing are commonly observed in such contexts.

In certain instances, players may dispute acquiring and utilising a specific avatar, particularly when it is not readily accessible.

Cannaestia(female Genji player): Rob (Male Player O), grab heal.
Male Player F: Healer, Rob (Male Player O).
Male Player O: Don't tell me. I don't wanna heal. (Content of V2)

3.3 A Critical Reading of Genji's Player Experience with Mercy as Comparison

Avatars in the game create their demands on the players. Genji, one of the attack heroes, requires a subtle mastery of gameplay abilities. The player must possess accurate aim, sound command of the map, and dynamic abilities to go along with Genji's agility and mobility. Proper use of Genji's abilities can result in consistent damage to the enemy, especially with his ultimate skill. Some players clip footage of themselves multi-killing with Genji to prove their proficiency as Genji players. This echoes the context mentioned in the previous section, where a player's ability to damage enemies as Genji can be seen as proof of their worthiness to be called a 'Genji Main/Player'.

The analysis of video content, particularly V1, demonstrates the pervasive existence of gender identity-based discrimination and inequitable treatment. Female players frequently encounter instances of harassment, which can create perceived barriers that hinder their ability to participate in playing the character Genji. The disclosure of gender identity frequently becomes inevitable due to the necessity of verbal communication for effective team coordination in gaming contexts such as *Overwatch 1&2* (2016, 2022). In certain instances, the interactions involve harassment targeting the players' sex and gender identity, exemplified by derogatory remarks such as 'rub one out' or 'make sandwiches.

Furthermore, female Genji players in video content also encounter unpleasant interactions influenced by Genji's role as a referee. They often face unwarranted harassment, irrespective of their skill level or ability to effectively play the Genji role. In other terms, a female participant can face disqualification as a Genji player due to her gender. This incident occurs when she selects Genji as her chosen avatar. Instances of harassment persist even in cases where her demonstrated proficiency in playing the character Genji and her valuable contributions to the team have been established.

Male Player 1: Why aren't you playing Mercy? Why are you not playing Mercy?
Male Player 2: [laughter]
[Raine ((female Genji player)) looks into the camera several times, purses her lips with a speechless expression] (Content of V1)
[Scene: Raine(female Genji player) activates the Genji Ultimate Ability and eliminates five enemies]
Raine (female Genji player): Anymore? [raises eyebrows] I should play Mercy, by the way, I wish I knew how to play Genji [looks into the camera].
Male Player 1: That's right, that's exactly right. Oh my gosh. She just noticed it. The hysteria has worn off (inaudible – 01:56). (Content of V1)

The employment of Genji as an avatar by male players in the game can be seen as a manifestation of a parallel logic that aligns with the construction of heteronormative gender roles. In V3 and V4, individuals are exempt from scrutiny or evaluation of their gaming proficiency. Male players who demonstrate exceptional proficiency in playing the character Genji are often portrayed as highly skilled and assertive individuals, showcasing their dominance over other players, particularly those who play as Mercy. The Genji player receives a trophy in the form of a friend request from the Mercy player in V3, which is prominently featured in the title, thumbnail, and video content. In instances where gender is not a prominent theme (V3 and V4), gender conflicts remain concealed as the Genji performance aligns with societal expectations associated with this avatar.

Necros (male Genji player): Rizz her up? Shut the fuck up, chat. She wants you. Bro, yeah. She interacted with me, that's true, a massive time. (Content of V3)

This can be further supported by empirical evidence of acts of Mercy. The videos (V2, V3, and V4) highlight the reliance on the character Mercy within the game. Mercy is widely recognised as a hero who demands less proficiency to play due to her role as a support hero, primarily providing offensive or healing support to allies through an auto-targeted beam. Although she possesses a secondary weapon in the form of a pistol, its significance is secondary to her primary role as a support hero. Mercy's unique abilities include reviving deceased teammates and flying to the aid of her teammates in need. While Mercy players effectively communicate crucial information on the battlefield, the mechanics of her character inherently create a sense of dependence on other heroes, irrespective of their gender. Moreover, prioritising support (commonly known as "pocketing") towards a specific ally can sometimes be perceived as favouritism.

> Cannaestia(female Genji player): [screams] I need healing!
>
> Male Player F: (plays as Mercy) OH, FUCK YEAH!!! [these words are also presented on screen in text format serving as an emphasis] That's what I needed. that's what I needed. OH. I need someone to be stupid. OH, keeping stupid anything. (Content of V2)

3.4 You Jump, I Jump: The Impact of Narrative Interpretation on Game Involvement

> [Scene: Genji falls out the map and dies, Mercy also jumps off the map and eliminates herself]
>
> Genji Player: [sings] Near, far, wherever you are-
>
> [Screen: text at the bottom in green: [Titanic song commences.]]
>
> Male Mercy Player: [laughter] (Content of V4)

The emphasis on narrative (V4) allows the win-lose dichotomy to be diluted transiently. Nourishing an interesting role-playing interaction with happenings encountered in the game as raw ingredients is the aim of the players in V4 or the outcome the footage pursues. The actions above are counterproductive to the game's victory and the other teammates' efforts. The actions exhibited by the individuals in question reflect their deliberate assessment of the plausibility of the narrative connection, which is contingent upon the roles they portray and the comedic impact they generate. The romantic affiliation between the two individuals contributes to a compelling progression in Mercy's martyrdom. Similarly, the video segments are collectively evaluated based on their comedic impact on the overall presentation.

Furthermore, when players interact with the character of Genji through his narration and even in a voiceover format, they tend to prioritise behaviours that align with the Genji syllogism rather than behaviours that directly contribute to achieving victory in the game. The narrative and emotional elements embedded within his backstory possess the potential to exert an influence on the player's behavioural patterns. Conforming to the narrative, offering assistance to non-Genji avatars is teased as 'cheating'. Meanwhile, Genji expresses his disapproval out of envy when other players seek Mercy's healing services. This practice contradicts the principles of rational resource allocation in pursuit of achieving victory.

> Genji Player: Why are you healing other people?
>
> Male Mercy Player: I'm sorry. Don't cheat on me... （Content of V4）

The video narrative alludes to the relationship between Genji and Mercy, which mirrors the allusion to the romantic relationship between the two avatars within the broader context of the game franchise. Furthermore, the conversation resonates with the official narrative of Mercy's role as the individual responsible for Genji's cyborg enhancements. Nevertheless, it is frequently overlooked in discourse throughout the game, with only sporadic references made in V4.

> Genji Player: [singing]: You whore......
>
> Male Mercy Player: Oh, Shi- That better not be for me! For all the shit I've done for you! Bitch, I'll rebuild you into a fucking meatloaf sandwich!

4. DISCUSSION

In the context of *Overwatch 1&2* (2016, 2022), the level of player involvement is predominantly influenced by the gameplay attributes of the avatar, owing to the game's strong emphasis on skill-based mechanics. *Overwatch 1&2* (2016, 2022), a team-based combat game, requires players to pursue success by employing accurate aiming, strategic deliberation, efficient communication, and comprehensive map awareness. The game promotes constructive involvement by implementing a comprehensive feedback mechanism that enhances the game's visual appeal and offers great positive reinforcement, commonly referred to as 'juiciness' (Juul, 2010). This complex feedback method further enhances players' admiration of their gaming abilities.

The overarching game environment in *Overwatch 1&2* (2016, 2022) establishes a hierarchical structure among avatars, which is determined by the skill requirements imposed on players by each diverse avatar. The character of Genji embodies remarkable gaming abilities, presenting a formidable challenge to players while providing opportunities for substantial advancement within the game. The distinct narrative and gameplay mechanics inherent in each *Overwatch 1&2* (2016, 2022) avatar contribute to a hierarchical structure among avatars, as the admiration of gaming skills becomes a prominent factor. The portrayal of Genji in media has the potential to acquiesce the perpetuation of stigmatisation towards other avatars, thereby creating an environment conducive to discrimination. To put it precisely, individuals compete to showcase their superior skills by favouring the character 'Genji', and they may experience a sense of dissatisfaction if they are labelled as a 'support main'.

It is crucial not to disregard the significance of narrative, as there is a substantial and inherent connection between narrative and the game's mechanics. A cohesive connection between the two dimensions is established by contextualising Genji's in-game identity as a skilled combatant and agile mover within his narrative framework. Although the precedence between Genji's narrative and gameplay traits remains agnostic, they exhibit high consistency.

Nonetheless, remnants of the narrative persist beyond the aspects closely aligned with gameplay mechanics. Occasionally, when players adhere strictly to the logic of the narrative, it may lead to queer gameplay experiences that contradict the player dynamics invited by the game mechanics. These instances can be regarded as narrative performances that expand the canonical territory within the game. However, the gameplay footage shows that Genji's complex persona is rarely invoked when the narrative does not explicitly drive player engagement. In cases where game mechanics clash with narrative properties, the narrative usually yields to the dominance of game mechanics (V1, V2, and V3).

The validity of the game mechanism over narration is outstanding in the relationship between Genji and Mercy. Narratively, Mercy is portrayed as the technical owner of Genji, but the game mechanics force her to be frail, incapable, and dependent. This institutionalised symbolic violence is encoded within the avatars and inevitably impacts players. When Genji interacts with Mercy, heteronormative norms come to the forefront. The avatar actively narrates and idealises masculine performance, shaping players' perceptions of what it means to embody Genji or Mercy. Genji is constructed as a hero, while Mercy assumes the role of a mother, providing care and compassion (Jung, 2014). This dynamic is reflected in the concept of 'pocketing', a metaphor for the womb where a supporting hero provides additional support and attention to a teammate.

The video evidence presented provides insight into the presence of a toxic atmosphere within the *Overwatch 1&2* (2016, 2022) context, consistent with the assertions made by Blamey (2022). The toxicity here is marked by a hostile and harmful environment, which promotes and sustains patriarchal privilege to uphold its dominant position (Consalvo, 2012). The presence of a toxic environment can pose difficulties for female players in developing a positive rapport with Genji, often limiting their interactions to utilising him solely as a tool to demonstrate their proficiency. Female players may experience pressure to select heroes with lower skill requirements, such as Mercy. Alternatively, they encounter challenges in being recognised as credible competitors, despite possessing equivalent skill levels compared to their male counterparts.

Certain individuals who engage in toxic behaviours may attribute lower gaming proficiency to biological determinism, leading to mistreating female players through derogatory actions. This mistreatment is based on the belief that female players inherently lack competence in gaming. However, empirical evidence from Terlecki et al. (2011) indicates that sexual differences have minimal influence on gaming proficiency. Despite their high skill level, proficient female professional gamers continue to face prejudice and intimidation, highlighting the significant role of gender identity in inciting harassment. This finding is consistent with the studies conducted by Taylor et al. (2009) and Ericsson and Bergström (2020), which demonstrate that gender rather than actual skill levels primarily provoke mistreatment.

However, *Overwatch 1&2* (2016, 2022) deserves recognition for its commendable efforts in promoting narrative diversity. Upon contemplation of the gameplay encounter in V4, it becomes evident that there exists a notable defiance against a toxic cultural environment within the storyline presented by *Overwatch 1&2* (2016, 2022), thereby corroborating prior scholarly investigations. The diverse selection of playable characters and their intricate narrative backgrounds possess the capacity to confront the negative aspects of a competitive system based on merit and encourage the representation of various gender identities through virtual personas. The game's inclusion of a diverse range of characters, encompassing various genders, ethnicities, and occupational backgrounds, has been lauded by scholars as a commendable development (Choi et al., 2020).

In addition, the game endeavours to disrupt the traditionally male-dominated realm of shooter games to cultivate a more inclusive virtual environment that appeals to individuals who typically have limited involvement with first-person shooter games (Lin, 2019). According to Hayday and Collison (2020), the positive outcome observed in *Overwatch 1&2* (2016, 2022) can be attributed to the inclusive practices implemented by game developers. This serves as an illustration of how game developers can effectively promote social justice within the domains of gaming and esports. However, the results of this study demonstrate that unintentional reinforcement of discriminatory practices can occur even when well-intentioned actions are taken to encourage and celebrate the achievements of female players.

While acknowledging the positive aspects of *Overwatch 1&2*'s (2016, 2022) diverse range of contextual avatars, it is essential to exercise caution when discussing the representation of queerness, particularly concerning the portrayal of Genji's character. Whether it pertains to the cover or the title, the narrative framework employed in the characters of Genji and Mercy appears to reflect a deep-seated misogyny that is ingrained within the gaming culture (Bègue et al., 2017; McCullough et al., 2020). The perception exists that Mercy and female players, by default, are considered less capable compared to Genji and male players. Their stance on their own positions on the spectrum of gameplay competence, aligned with what they critique, is predicated on surrendering to the universality of 'girl'.

The issue of toxicity within the game is undeniably problematic. In instances where female players exhibit exceptional competence or choose not to engage in interactions, they continue to be labelled as 'game girlfriends' or 'mothers' pocketing others. However, the narrative of the avatar potentially enables Mercy players to justify and modify their identity, influencing their actions accordingly. In a similar context, the interplay between Genji, masculinity, and toxic male players gives rise to a complex amalgamation that manifests as an aggressive hybrid, which in turn serves as a destructive force that undermines the game's attempts at diversity.

5. CONCLUSION

The purpose of this study is to examine the influence of avatar representation on the overall gaming experience among a diverse population of individuals with different gender identities. The attributes of avatars have a substantial impact on player engagement, specifically regarding gameplay mechanics. *Overwatch 1&2* (2016, 2022) employs a hierarchical framework to organise and present avatars. This system positions Genji as a prominent game avatar, specifically as an attack hero characterised by a significant level of operational complexity and his contribution to game progression. When structured hierarchically, the alignment of game mechanics with gendered avatars can mirror the toxic environments prevalent in certain games and reinforce the narrative frameworks that prioritise heterosexual experiences. This alignment can inadvertently contribute to perpetuating toxic gaming culture and reinforce heteronormative ideologies.

The findings of this study suggest that incorporating a more comprehensive range of gender identities and representations for avatars, both in terms of narrative and game mechanics, might offer more significant opportunities to deviate from heteronormative norms and enhance the player's experience. This development has the potential to yield positive outcomes for the gaming industry by addressing the longstanding criticism surrounding its inadequate gender representation and promoting gender inclusivity.

Nevertheless, it is crucial to recognise the inherent limitations in extrapolating these findings. The lack of comprehensive data from players hinders the understanding of the precise actions and contextual factors of social groups. Simultaneously, the analysis is predicated upon the contextual framework of the first-person shooter *Overwatch 1&2* (2016, 2022). The significance of the avatar's gameplay mechanics and narrative characteristics in shaping players' gendered gaming experiences may vary in its explanatory capacity across different game genres. Future research endeavours could investigate a broader spectrum of avatars originating from various cultural backgrounds to examine their potential for universality. The incorporation of quantitative analyses would enhance the robustness of this interpretation by offering more substantial evidence.

REFERENCES

Ars Technica. 2017. Blizzard answers unsolved mysteries of the Overwatch universe | ars technica. [Accessed 30 June 2023]. Available from: https://www.youtube.com/watch?v=CVxWCV-Mfqo.

Bailey, E. N. et al., 2021. Gender composition of teams and studios in video game development. *Games and Culture*, Vol. 16, No.1), pp. 42–64.

Bègue, L. et al., 2017. Video Games Exposure and Sexism in a Representative Sample of Adolescents. *Frontiers in Psychology*, [Online] Vol. 8 No. 11, pp.466–466. https://www.frontiersin.org/articles/10.3389/fpsyg.2017.00466

Beres, N. A. et al., 2021. Don't you know that you're toxic: Normalization of toxicity in online gaming. *Proceedings of the 2021 CHI Conference on Human Factors in Computing Systems*, New Orleans, LA, pp. 1–15.

Blom, J. 2022. The Player's Interpretative Agency and the Developer's Disruptive Powers: How Blizzard Enforces Authorial Intention in Overwatch. In *Modes of Esports Engagement in Overwatch* , pp. 49–66.

Bowman, N. D., and Banks, J. 2021. Player-avatar identification, relationships, and interaction: Entertainment through asocial, parasocial, and fully social processes. in P., Vorderer, and C., Klimmt (eds), *The Oxford Handbook of Entertainment Theory (online edn, Oxford Academic)* [Accessed 30 June 2023]. Available from: https://doi.org/10.1093/oxfordhb/9780190072216.013.36.

Carey, J. 2019. Economic and social patterns in the adoption of new media. In Z., Vukanovic et al. (eds), *Digital Value Migration in Media, ICT and Cultural Industries* , pp. 1–11

Choi, Y. et al., 2020. Deep strike: Playing gender in the world of Overwatch and the case of Geguri. *Feminist Media Studies*, Vol. 20, *No.* 8, pp.1128–1143.

Christel, M. G. 2006. Evaluation and user studies with respect to video summarization and browsing. *Proceedings of SPIE.* pp. 196–210. California, USA.

Cole, K. K. 2015. "It's like she's eager to be verbally abused": Twitter, trolls, and (en) gendering disciplinary rhetoric. *Feminist Media Studies*, Vol.15, No.2), pp. 356–358.

Consalvo, M. 2012. Confronting toxic gamer culture: A challenge for feminist game studies scholars., *A Journal of Gender, New Media, and Technology,* pp.1-7.

Cote, A. C. 2020. *Gaming Sexism : Gender and Identity in the Era of Casual Video Games / Amanda C. Cote*. [Online]. New York University Press, New York, USA.

Cunningham, S. J., and Macrae, C. N. 2011. The colour of gender stereotyping. *British Journal of Psychology*, Vol. 102, No.3, pp. 598–614.

Dewinter, J., and Kocurek, C. A. 2017. "AW FUCK, I GOT A BITCH ON MY TEAM!": Women and the Exclusionary Cultures of the Computer Game Complex. In J. , Malkowski and T. M., Russworm, (Eds.), *Gaming Representation* ,pp. 57–73. Indiana University Press, Indiana, USA.

Drakett, J. et al., 2018. Old jokes, new media–Online sexism and constructions of gender in Internet memes. *Feminism and Psychology*, Vol. 28, No.1, pp. 109–127.

Ericsson, N., and Bergström, H. 2020. *How toxicity differ between male and female players in competitive Overwatch.* Bachelor thesis. Uppsala University

Fernández-Vara, C. 2019. *Introduction to game analysis*. Routledge, New York, USA.

Friedberg, J. (2015). *Gender games: A content analysis of gender portrayals in modern, narrative video games*.MA. thesis, Georgia State University.

Genovesi, M. 2017. Choices and consequences: The role of players in the walking dead: a telltale game series. *Open Cultural Studies*, Vol 1, No. 1, pp.350–358.

Jenkins, H. 2013. *Textual Poachers: Television Fans and Participatory Culture*. Routledge, New York, USA.

Hunicke, R. et al., 2004. MDA: A formal approach to game design and game research. *Proceedings of the AAAI Workshop on Challenges in Game AI*, *4*(1), Vol. 4, No. 1, p. 1722.

Janik, J. 2018. Game/r-Play/er-Bio-Object. Exploring posthuman values in video game research. *Proceedings of The Philosophy of Computer Games Conference*, Msida, Malta, pp.1–8.

Janik, J. 2021. Intra-acting bio-object: A posthuman approach to the player–game relation. *Journal of Gaming and Virtual Worlds*, *13*(1), Vol. 13, No.1, pp.21–39.

Jung, C. G. 2014. *Four archetypes*. Routledge, New York, USA.

Juul, J. 2010. *A casual revolution: Reinventing video games and their players/ Jesper Juul*. MIT press, Massachusetts, USA

Kasumovic, M. M., and Kuznekoff, J. H. 2015. Insights into Sexism: Male Status and Performance Moderates Female-Directed Hostile and Amicable Behaviour. *PLOS ONE*, Vol. 10, No. 7, e0131613.

Kaye, L. K. et al., 2018. Do casual gaming environments evoke stereotype threat? Examining the effects of explicit priming and avatar gender. *Computers in Human Behavior*, Vol. 78, pp.142–150.

Klevjer, R. 2012. Enter the avatar: The phenomenology of prosthetic telepresence in computer games. *The Philosophy of Computer Games*, 17–38.

Kordyaka, B. et al., 2020. Towards a unified theory of toxic behavior in video games. *Internet Research*, Vol. 30, No. 4, pp.1081–1102.

Kress, G. 2012. Multimodal discourse analysis. In J. P. Gee and M. Handford (eds.) *The Routledge Handbook of Discourse Analysis*, pp.35–50.Routledge, New York, USA.

Kress, G., and van Leeuwen, T. 2020. *Reading Images: The Grammar of Visual Design*. Taylor and Francis Group, Oxfordshire, UK.

Kress, G., 2010. *Multimodality: A social semiotic approach to contemporary communication*. Routledge, London, UK.

Lawless, T. et al., 2020. Is it really just a joke? Gender differences in perceptions of sexist humor. *Humor*, Vol. 33, No. 2, pp. 291–315.

Malkowski, J. 2017. "I TURNED OUT TO BE SUCH A DAMSEL IN DISTRESS": Noir Games and the Unrealized Femme Fatale. In J. Malkowski and T. M. Russworm (Eds.), *Gaming Representation* ,pp. 19–37. Indiana University Press. Indiana, USA.

Maloney, M. et al., 2019. Introduction. In M. Maloney, S. Roberts, and T. Graham (Eds.), *Gender, Masculinity and Video Gaming: Analysing Reddit's r/gaming Community* , pp. 1–21, Springer International Publishing. New York, USA.

Martey, R. M. et al., 2014. The strategic female: Gender-switching and player behavior in online games. *Information, Communication and Society*, Vol. 17, No. 3, pp.286–300.

McCullough, K. M. et al., 2020. Female Video Game Players and the Protective Effect of Feminist Identity Against Internalized Misogyny. *Sex Roles*, Vol. 82, No. 5, pp. 266–276.

McKitrick, B. et al., 2023. "What are you Bringing to the Table?": The Something Awful Let's Play Community as a Serious Leisure Subculture. *Games and Culture*, Vol. 18, No., 3, pp.402–421.

Newman, H. 2019. How Baptiste, Brigitte, genji, and other overwatch heroes got made. Forbes. [Online]. [Accessed 30 June 2023]. Available from: https://www.forbes.com/sites/hnewman/2019/06/30/how-baptiste-brigitte-genji-and-other-overwatch-heroes-got-made/.

Nguyen, J. 2016. Performing as video game players in Let's Plays. *Transformative Works and Cultures* [Online] Vol. *22*.

Papale, L. 2014. Beyond identification: Defining the relationships between player and avatar. *Journal of Games Criticism*, Vol. 1, No.2, pp. 1–12.

Paul, C. A. 2018. *The toxic meritocracy of video games: Why gaming culture is the worst*. University of Minnesota Press, Minnesota, USA.

Ratan, R. A. et al., 2019. Women Keep it Real: Avatar Gender Choice in League of Legends. *Cyberpsychology, Behavior, and Social Networking*, Vol. 22, No. 4, pp. 254–257.

Ratan, R. A. et al., 2015. Stand by your man: An examination of gender disparity in League of Legends. *Games and Culture*, Vol. 10, No. 5, pp.438–462.

Schröter, F., and Thon, J.-N. 2014. Video game characters. Theory and analysis. *Diegesis*, Vol. 3, No. 1, p.40.

Shaw, A. 2014. *Gaming at the edge sexuality and gender at the margins of gamer culture / Adrienne Shaw*. University of Minnesota Press, Minnesota, USA.

Shifman, L., and Lemish, D. 2010. Between feminism and fun (ny) mism: Analysing gender in popular internet humour. *Information, Communication and Society*, Vol. 13, No. 6, pp.870–891.

Süngü, E. 2020. Gender Representation and Diversity in Contemporary Video Games. In B. Bostan (Ed.), *Game User Experience And Player-Centered Design* ,pp. 379–393. Springer International Publishing, New York, USA.

Taylor, N. et al., 2009. Cheerleaders/booth babes/Halo hoes: Pro-gaming, gender and jobs for the boys. *Digital Creativity*, Vol. 20, No. 4, pp.239–252.

Tekinbaş, K. S. 2004. *Rules of play: Game design fundamentals / Katie Salen and Eric Zimmerman*. MIT Press, Massachusetts, USA.

Terlecki, M. et al., 2011. Sex differences and similarities in video game experience, preferences, and self-efficacy: Implications for the gaming industry. *Current Psychology*, Vol. 30, pp. 22–33.

Tompkins, J. E. 2021. *Does the Character Matter? Avatar Gender, Identification, and Player Agency Among Women Who Play Digital Games*. Ph.D. thesis, Indiana University.

Tompkins, J. E., and Martins, N. 2022. Masculine pleasures as normalized practices: Character design in the video game industry. *Games and Culture*, Vol. 17, No.3, pp.399–420.

Lin, X., 2019. *Gender In Overwatch: Virtual Space And Social Realities*, Bachelor Thesis. National University of Singapore.

Yoon, S. H., and Kim, H.W. 2019. What content and context factors lead to selection of a video clip? The heuristic route perspective. *Electronic Commerce Research*, Vol. 19, pp.603–627.

USING ELECTROENCEPHALOGRAPHY TO SURVEY THE PHYSIOLOGY OF IMMERSION AND FLOW

Ehm Kannegieser[1], Sarah Münch[2] and Johannes Ratz[2*]
[1]*ORCID: 0000-0001-8869-7946, Fraunhofer Institute of Optronics, System Technologies and Image Exploitation*
Fraunhoferstr.1, 76131 Karlsruhe, Germany
[2]*Karlsruhe Institute of Technology*
Kaiserstraße 12, 76131 Karlsruhe, Germany
**ORCID: 0009-0008-9719-0512*

ABSTRACT

Deep focus states, like Immersion and Flow are important parameters when it comes to an enjoyable experience during learning activities. Exploring the Physiology of deep focus, in the course of prior studies, physiological data of participants was recorded during activities and inspected for correlations with Flow and Immersion. As no significant correlations were found, the experimental setup was extended by Electroencephalography (EEG) sensors to broaden the sprectrum of physiological data available for analysis, before further studies were conducted. In this paper, after shortly revisiting prior research, the results of the EEG-measurements are presented.

KEYWORDS

Electroencephalography, Flow, Immersion, Serious Games

1. INTRODUCTION

One of the central questions in games research and psychology and of particular interest for the development of serious games is how video games are percieved as enjoyable, more so how this fun can be transferred into learning or working contexts, as enjoyment is proven to be linked to an effective learning process (Deci and Ryan, 1985; Krapp, 2009).

Mihály Csíkszentmihályi defined "the optimal experience of an action" as Flow, which is achieved when the individual is so engrossed in the activity that nothing else seems relevant anymore. It is a deep sense of enjoyment, that occurs when a "person's body or mind is stretched to its limits in a voluntary effort to accomplish something difficult and worthwhile" (Csikzentmihaly, 1990). A similar experience in the video game domain is commonly called Immersion, describing the transfer of consciousness into a virtual world. Cairns et al. define game Immersion by dividing it into three levels: Engagement, Engrossment, and Total Immersion. These levels are used to describe the degree of involvement with the game (Brown and Cairns, 2004; Cairns et al. 2006).

Both Flow and Immersion are linked to an intrinsic motivation in the task or game, which means deriving enjoyment from the action itself rather than from external gains like money or a fear of punishment for not completing a task. Due to the similarities of definitions and conditions for Immersion and Flow, authors suggest on unifying and not separating both terms for further research, especially in the video game domain (Michailidis et al., 2018). A combined model of Immersion and Flow based on the definitions by Csíkszentmihályi and Cairns was proposed (Kannegieser et al., 2018) and later extended by additional emotional dimensions (Kannegieser et al., 2021) which builds the theoretical basis for the following work.

Until now, the method of choice to measure Flow and Immersion has been the usage of questionnaires, which are answered by the subject after the task at hand. However, this method is potentially inaccurate due to the delay in elicitation and the subjectivity of the answers. An alternative way of measuring deep focus states could be, to record subjects' physiological data during an activity and look for correlations between the physiological data and elicited states of Flow and Immersion, thus establishing a more robust and objective measurement method, theroretically rendering the usage of questionnaires obsolete.

Beside various physiological channels like galvanic skin response (GSR) and electrocardiography (ECG), the subjects' brain activity, measured using electroencephalography (EEG) is of particular interest, and will be the focus of this paper: By non-invasively recording the electrical brain activity from the scalp, EEG is easy to use in medicine and research and still provides a lot of information on the mental states of subjects.

Based on previous studies and experiences gathered in the previous iterations (Kannegieser et al. 2018; Kannegieser et al. 2021) a study was conducted with 23 participants, in which EEG data were analyzed and evaluated for potential correlations with states of deep focus. Thus, this work will concern itself with the following hypotheses:

H1: States of deep focus will result in different activations of specific frequency bands between the activity and a neutral state of mind (baseline) during the activity at hand,

H2: States of deep focus will result in different activations of specific frequency bands during the activity at hand.

2. RELATED WORK

EEG is a common method for measuring the electrical activity of the brain by recording voltage fluctuations between electrodes positioned on the scalp. The fluctuations are mostly generated by the firing of cortical neurons, which are located on the outer layer of the brain and range between 5 and 100μV (Hu and Zhang, 2019). They result in typical sinusoidal wave shapes which are analyzed for amplitude and frequency. In general, the waves are classified into different frequency bands: Delta (1-4 Hz), Theta (4-8 Hz), Alpha (8-13 Hz), Beta (13-30 Hz), and Gamma (30-40 Hz). The frequency bands are associated with different levels of brain activities. When the subject is awake mostly alpha and beta waves are noticed. The alpha waves are the most extensively studied rhythm of the human brain and can be usually observed while being in a relaxed awake state or having eyes closed (Teplan et al., 2002). They are associated with cortical inactivity and mental idleness as well as attentional demand (Ray and Cole, 1985). Beta waves indicate a normal state of wakefulness and are usually most evident in the frontal cortex. They are connected to cognitive processes, decision making, problem solving and information processing (Ray and Cole, 1985). Delta and theta waves are most prominent during sleep (for adults). Delta waves are more present at deep sleep, more specifically during non-rapid eye movement (NREM) phases (Teplan et al., 2002). Theta waves play a greater role in REM sleep and general drowsiness (Teplan et al., 2002). They are also connected to daydreaming, creativity, intuition, memory recall, emotions, and sensations (Aftanas and Golocheikine, 2001). In some cases, gamma waves can be observed at very high concentration and Flow of information. It is also seen during cross-modal sensory processing (combining two or more senses, such as sound and sight) (Kisley and Cornwell, 2006) as well as deep meditation (Vialatte et al., 2009).

There are several different types of EEG devices or systems to choose from, e.g. headsets, single electrodes or closed electrode caps. While closed electrode caps usually provide better conduction quality (Hu and Zhang, 2019), smaller devices like headsets offer better mobility and comfort. Electrodes are positioned after the International 10-20 system, which uniquely labels each electrode with letters for the brain area (F: Frontal, C: Central, P: Parietal, T: Temporal, O: Occipital) and numbers for the horizontal position (odd numbers left hemisphere, even numbers right hemisphere; higher numbers are more outward than lower ones) encoding the exact position on the head. The voltage is measured between an active electrode and one of two additional reference electrodes placed on the bone behind each ear.

The neural basis of Flow has been analyzed in several studies in the past as shown in the review article by Alameda (Alameda et al., 2022), who reviewed 25 studies, which were related to measuring brain activity in the context of Flow. While EEG measurement seems to be the most popular way of recording brain activity, there are also studies involving functional magnetic resonance (fMRI), functional near-infrared spectroscopy (fNIRS) or even the manipulation of brain activity with transcranial direct stimulation (tDCS).

Apart from different physiological measurements studies also differ in the elicitation methods of the Flow state. Many studies use a difficulty-based approach, where the same task is carried out with different levels of difficulty (e.g., Ulrich et al., 2014; Katahira et al., 2018; Knierim et al. 2018). As Flow is connected to a balance of challenge and skill, this approach is evident, and allows a direct comparison of Flow levels for the same subject. However, often the tasks are very small and do not last longer than 10 minutes, which could make it hard for participants to deeply immerse into a different world. Another approach more similar to the work in this paper are video game studies (e.g., Klasen et al., 2012), where subjects are assigned to play a certain video game for a longer period of time without interruption. Afterwards researchers analyzed the game's content and classified situations based on Flow dimensions (e.g., skill-difficulty balance, focus, clear goals, and control) to identify high probability Flow moments. A problem with this method is the subjectiveness of the researchers and the players not assessing their mental states themselves.

Studies involving the measurement of EEG report different results when it comes to linking the Flow state to specific brain rhythms (i.e., theta, alpha, beta and gamma). Katahira et al. as well as other authors observed higher power in theta activity in the frontal electrodes during Flow, which might be related to the high cognitive control demands required by the task. Also, they report a rising power in alpha activity with increasing difficulty. Lim et al. found a higher beta activity in the frontal, temporal and occipital lobe to be involved in the Flow state (Lim et al. 2019). Wolf et al. observed a higher asymmetry between the temporal lobe of the left hemisphere and the temporal lobe of the right hemisphere during Flow states, which they link to a suppression of analytical-verbal activity and irrelevant cognitive processes (Wolf et al., 2015).

In a previous study (Kannegieser and Ratz, 2021), a method of measuring EEG in the context of game Immersion and Flow was presented. The experiment was tested with an initial test study involving three participants. The data recorded during this experiment was analyzed for correlations with elicited states of deep focus. This analysis resulted in the average spectral power density in the respective frequency band per channel for each of the five mental states (Baseline, Engagement, Engrossment, Total Immersion, and Flow).

In the study, theta power appeared to increase compared to baseline in the frontal areas during Engagement and especially Engrossment. Total Immersion and Flow on the other hand did not show a big difference to the baseline. Beta activity was overall higher compared to baseline during both Immersion and Flow. The other frequency bands did not show any correlations. Throughout all frequency bands, Total Immersion and Flow are very similar in their power distribution, which could indicate a close relation between total Immersion and Flow as suggested by our proposed model. Although the results indicated a correlation between Immersion, Flow and EEG, the statistical significance of its results remained to be proven because of the small number of participants.

3. EXPERIMENT

The experiment's main goal is to gather physiological data during game play that can be used to find a correlation between physiological measurements and Flow/Immersion states. It mainly consists of a custom-made measurement application, which sets the structure of the experiment and manages different data inputs and outputs. Apart from EEG, various other physiological input sources such as sensors for GSR, ECG/heartrate and EMG can be connected, thereby extending the data pool for statistical correlation analysis between physiological data and elicited states of deep focus.

3.1 Study Conduct

A study was conducted with 23 self-selected participants (21 male, 2 female), most of them university students in their twenties who all had at least some experience with video games in the past. Participants were gathered using posters and word-of-mouth advertising, thus representing a group of people interested in gaming and the study itself. One underage person with a lot of gaming experience participated with full parental consent.

The study took place in a prearranged lab room, containing the experimental setup including a PC system for gaming and data recording as well as the physiological sensors. EEG was measured using the Emotiv EPOC+, a 14-channel EEG headset, that only requires its electrode covering felt pads to be covered in a saline solution before attachment. It offers a sampling rate of 256 Hz and uses a wireless connection via Bluetooth, making it easy to install and comfortable to wear during the experiment. This increases the likeliness for participants to reach the desired mental states compared to closed electrode caps, which use a contact gel for conduction and are possibly less comfortable to wear.

3.2 Procedure

The experiment was split into four phases: Setup, Baseline, Gaming and Assessment. During the setup phase, the game was selected, and the sensors are placed on the participant. Game selection was free, as participants were allowed to bring their own games or use a distribution platform like Steam to install a game of their choice, with Minecraft, Valorant, and League of Legends beeing the most popular game titles. Free game selection was chosen to improve the odds of players reaching higher Flow and Immersion states, at the cost of game-specific analysis options. While there can be benefits in evaluating the same game among all participants, the goal for this study is rather to find general correlations between any reported deep focus states and physiological measurements.

During the second phase of the experiment, the baseline phase, physiological data is recorded for one minute, while the subject is in a calm state of mind. The physiological measurements were monitored by the examiner of the study on a separate monitor screen, showing the incoming data streams in real time. After finishing setup, the gaming phase began, in which the subject played the chosen game for 30 minutes without interruption. The duration was chosen based on test runs, as 30 minutes were found to be sufficient to reach the Flow / Total Immersion states. While the participant was playing, the physiological data as well as the gameplay and webcam footage was recorded and stored for analysis.

During the assessment phase, participants watched a recording of their game session as well as web cam footage of themselves. While watching this footage, Flow and Immersion questionnaires about how immersed the participant was at the time of the recording were answered repeatedly, thus gathering more accurate data without interrupting the Flow/Immersion during the game session itself, as shown in a similar study by Rajava and Kivikangas (Ravaja and Kivikangas, 2008).

Three questionnaires were used in the experiment, with one of them being split into two parts. The first questionnaire used was the Immersion questionnaire presented by Cheng et al. based on their improvement upon the hierarchical model presented by Cairns (Cheng et al., 2015; Cairns et al. 2006). The questionnaire was chosen, as it can be used to measure the likeliness to be in each of the individual Immersion levels. As the questionnaire was too long to be measured multiple times without worsening the results, it was split into an Immersive Tendency questionnaire asked at the beginning of playback and an iterative questionnaire asked every minute during playback. For Flow, the Flow Short Scale questionnaire by Rheinberg was used (Rheinberg et al., 2003). It was originally designed for being used multiple times in a row, making it perfect for this iterative approach. During playback, it was asked every two minutes. The final questionnaire used was the Game Experience questionnaire (IJsselsteijn, et al., 2013). It measures a more general set of questions and was asked once after playback was finished.

An overview of the experimental structure is presented in figure 1.

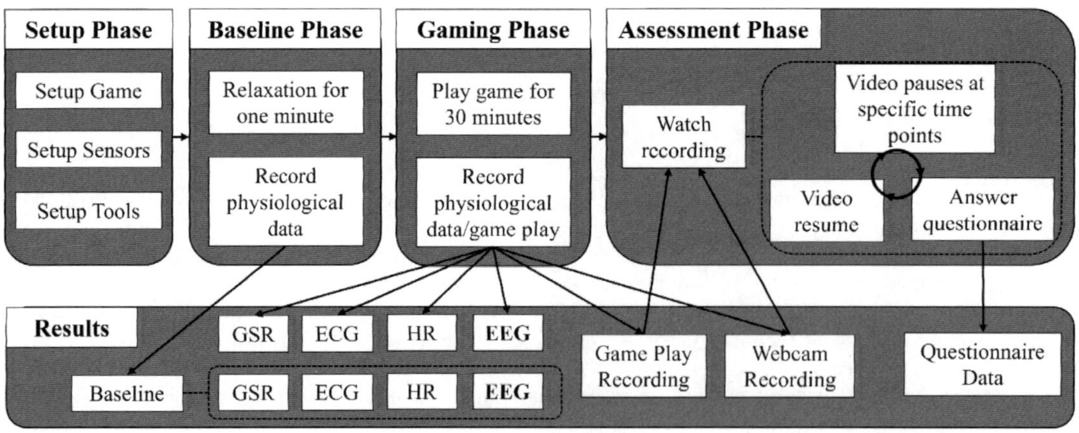

Figure 1. Experiment procedure

3.3 Analysis

The questionnaire data was combined and Engagement, Engrossment, Total Immersion and Flow levels were calculated for each 60 second stage. The raw EEG data was processed using the EEGLAB extension for MATLAB. The data was preprocessed using EEGLAB's inbuilt bad channel removal and independent component analysis functions. The remaining data was subdivided into stages with a duration of 60 seconds, corresponding to the shortest interval covered by a questionnaire. After preprocessing, artefact recognition and removal were performed manually. For the remaining data, the power spectra were averaged per stage and frequency band (Delta: 1-4 Hz, Theta: 4-8 Hz, Alpha: 8-13 Hz, Beta: 13-30 Hz and Gamma: 30-40 Hz) for each channel. Both sets of experimental data and the baseline data were then combined for statistical anlysis. As the results from both the Flow and Immersion questionnaires did not follow a normal distribution, Spearman correlation was used (Landau et al., 2004) to test for H0, H1 and H2.

4. RESULTS

While questionnaires revealed higher Flow possibility, theta activity was significantly higher than in the baseline condition (paired t-test $p < 0.001$). However, Flow level and theta activity during task performance were slightly negatively correlated in the frontal region. Overall, no significant positive correlation between Flow level and theta activity was evident. Additionally, during task performance, there was no statistically significant difference between theta power in Flow and theta power while the subject was not in Flow. This suggests that the increase in theta power is not directly linked to the Flow state but may be due to the nature of the gaming task in general. As Engagement was generally high during task performance and was also high when Flow was rated as low, Engagement may be the main contributor to the increase in theta power (see figure 2).

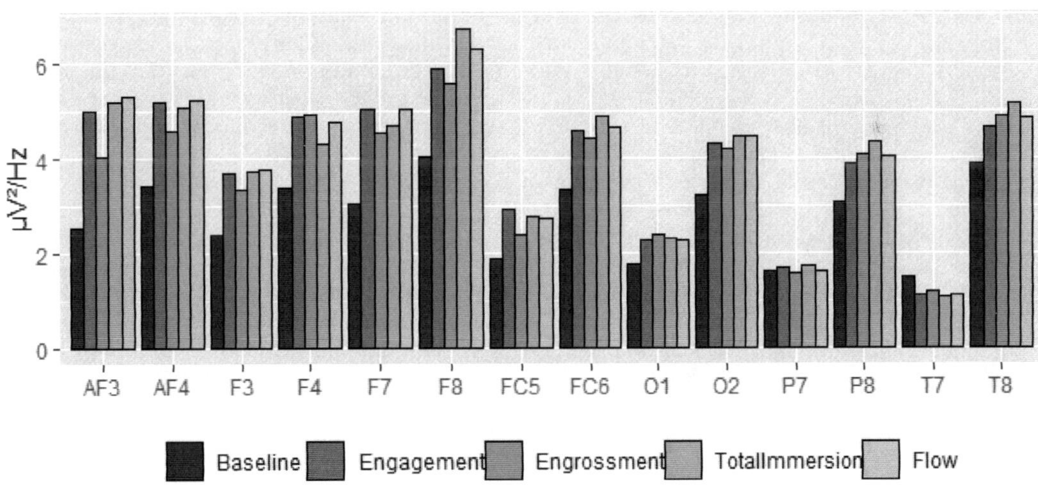

Figure 2. Theta power in each channel regarding different mental states

Frontal EEG asymmetry and particularly asymmetrical frontal alpha activation have also been found as potential neurocognitive indicators of Flow. Activation was measured by calculating the per-subject difference between baseline alpha power and alpha power during task performance. While there was a statistically significant difference between left alpha activation and right alpha activation ($p < 0.005$) while in Flow, there was no significant difference in alpha power while in Flow (see figure 3).

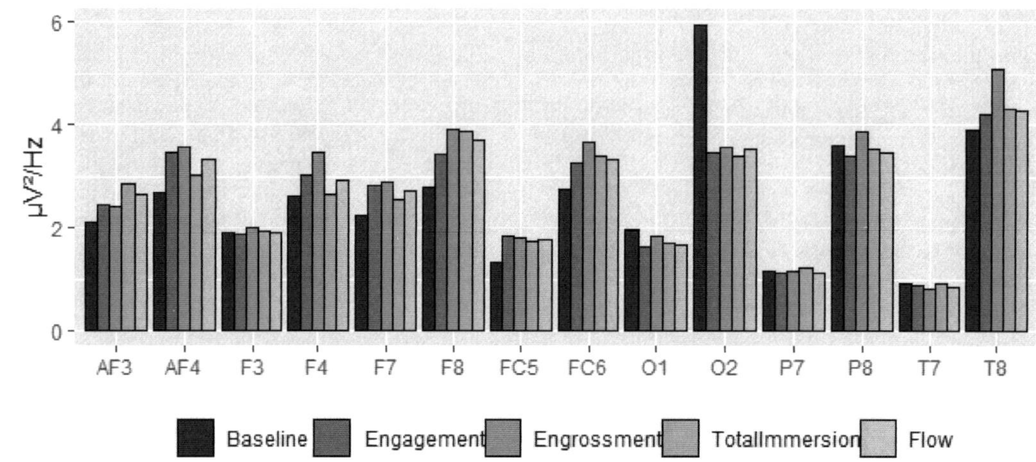

Figure 3. Alpha power in each channel regarding different mental states

Additionally, as with theta power, there was no significant difference in activation between Flow and no Flow during task performance. This further suggests that being in Flow does not explain the observed differences in spectral power density between baseline and experimental condition. Hindering further analysis of potential asymmetries was that across all data obtained during the experiment, electrodes positioned on the right hemisphere consistently measured higher spectral power densities. This might be due to a malfunctioning reference electrode or the equipment used in the experimental setup. Hence, the observed asymmetry is not in line with or comparable to previous findings.

Across all frequency bands, Flow and spectral power were negatively correlated at the dorsolateral prefrontal cortex (F3, F4). The DLPFC is associated with higher order processing, particularly working memory and decision making, but has also shown to be relevant to self-awareness (Yuan, Raz, 2014) and one's sense of time (Fuster, 1995). Therefore, a decreased *activation* in this area may directly tie into the Flow experience. Alpha activation of the DLFPC was not significantly correlated with Flow, though left alpha activation in the Flow condition was negative, whereas right alpha activation was slightly positive. This may be partly explained due to the fact that in young adults, the right and left DLFPC are more specialised with the left DLFPC being activated more strongly during verbal and spatial processing and right DLFPC during visual processing (Reutzer-Lorenz et al, 2000). As the games played involve more visual processing, a higher activation of the right DLFPC can be expected.

The disparities in selected games may account for parts of the activation patterns that were seen. Increased left frontal and temporal alpha activity/activation are associated with enjoyment and positive affect or motivation. If the game includes different design elements, activation patterns may differ based on that, inducing a range of different emotions.

5. CONCLUSION

This paper gave an overview about the current state of work in the field of physiology of Flow and Immersion by means of taking psychophysiological measurements during the activity under test (Kannegieser et al. 2018). Obtained results yielded by a study with an extended sensor set for Electroencepalography (EEG) were explored and the implementation of measuring deep focus states with EEG in addition to the sensor set used in prior studies were discussed in comparison with the initial test study (Kannegieser and Ratz, 2021). While other studies have shown an increase in frontal activity while in Flow (Katahira et al. 2018) and significantly higher theta activity was observed in this study compared to the theta baseline in line with hypothesis H1, no positive correlation for theta activity and alpha/theta power where found during episodes of deep focus contrary to the formulated hypothesis H2.

Further research will focus on improving data bandwith by using more psychophysiological inputs, enhancing data quality, especially dealing with the occurance of EEG-artifcats which invalidated a significant portion of the EEG data available for analysis.

Based on the theory that different game titles might lead to different frequency activations, the sample size for the most favorized game titles/genres will be increased to allow for more statistical relevance and improving task comparability.

REFERENCES

Aftanas, L., & Golocheikine, S., 2001. Human anterior and frontal midline theta and lower alpha reflect emotionally positive state and internalized attention: High-resolution eeg investigation of meditation. *Neuroscience letters*, 310(1), pp 57–60.

Alameda C, Sanabria D, Ciria LF., 2022. The brain in Flow: A systematic review on the neural basis of the Flow state. *Cortex*.;154:348-364. doi: 10.1016/j.cortex.2022.06.005. Epub 2022 Jul 5. PMID: 35926367.

Brown, E., & Cairns, P., 2004. A grounded investigation of game Immersion. *CHI '04 Extended Abstracts on Human Factors in Computing Systems*, pp 1297–1300.

Cairns, P., Cox, A. L., Berthouze, N., Jennett, C., & Dhoparee, S., 2006. Quantifying the experience of Immersion in games. *CogSci 2006 Workshop: Cognitive Science of Games and Gameplay*.

Cheng, M.-T., She, H.-C., & Annetta, L. A., 2015. Game Immersion experience: Its hierarchical structure and impact on game-based science learning. *Journal of computer assisted learning*, 31(3), pp 232–253.

Csikzentmihaly, M., 1990. *Flow: The psychology of optimal experience*. Harper & Row, New York.

Deci, E. L., & Ryan, R. M. (1985). Intrinsic Motivation and Self-Determination in Human Behavior. Berlin: Springer Science & Business Media. https://doi.org/10.1007/978-1-4899-2271-7

Hu, L., & Zhang Z., 2019. EEG Signal Processing and Feature Extraction. Springer, Singapore.

IJsselsteijn, W. A., de Kort, Y. A., & Poels, K., 2013. The game experience questionnaire. *Eindhoven: Technische Universiteit Eindhoven*, 46(1).

Kannegieser, E., Atorf, D., & Meier, J., 2018, Surveying games with a combined model of Immersion and Flow. *IADIS International Conference Information Systems 2018,* Lisbon, Portugal.

Kannegieser, E., Atorf, D., & Meier, J., 2019, Conducting an Experiment for validating the Combined Model of Flow and Immersion, *CSEDU 2019 11th international conference on computer supported education,* Heraklion, Crete – Greece.

Kannegieser, E., Atorf, D., Herold, J. (2021). Measuring Flow, Immersion and Arousal/Valence for Application in Adaptive Learning Systems. In: Sottilare, R.A., Schwarz, J. (eds) Adaptive Instructional Systems. Adaptation Strategies and Methods. HCII 2021. *Lecture Notes in Computer Science()*, vol 12793. Springer, Cham.

Kannegieser, E., & Ratz, J. (2021). MEASURING GAME IMMERSION AND FLOW WITH ELECTROENCEPHALOGRAPHY. *Proceedings of the 15th International Conference on Interfaces and Human Computer Interaction 2021 and 14th International Conference on Game and Entertainment Technologies 2021*.

Katahira, K., Yamazaki, Y., Yamaoka, C., Ozaki, H., Nakagawa, S., & Nagata, N., 2018. EEG correlates of the Flow state: A combination of increased frontal theta and moderate frontocentral alpha rhythm in the mental arithmetic task. *frontiers in Psychology,* 9, pp 300-311.

Kisley, M. A., & Cornwell, Z. M., 2006. Gamma and beta neural activity evoked during a sensory gating paradigm: Effects of auditory, somatosensory and cross-modal stimulation. *Clinical neurophysiology*, 117(11), pp 2549–2563.

Klasen, M., Weber, R., Kircher, T. T., Mathiak, K. A., & Mathiak, K. (2012). Neural contributions to Flow experience during video game playing. *Social Cognitive and Affective Neuroscience*, 7(4), 485–495. https://doi.org/10.1093/scan/nsr021

Knierim, M. T., Nadj, M., Hariharan, A., & Weinhardt, C. (2018). Flow Neurophysiology in Knowledge Work: Electroencephalographic Observations from Two Cognitive Tasks: *Proceedings of the 5th International Conference on Physiological Computing Systems*, 42–53. https://doi.org/10.5220/0006926700420053

Krapp, Andreas. "Kapitel 14 Pädagogische Psychologie: Lernmotivation und Interesse." *Psychologie–Experten als Zeitzeugen* (2009): 166.

Landau, S., Everitt, B.S.: *A Handbook of Statistical Analyses Using SPSS. Statistics* (Chapman & Hall/CRC). Taylor & Francis. (2004)

Lim, S., Yeo, M., & Yoon, G., 2019. Comparison between concentration and Immersion based on eeg analysis. *Sensors 2019*, 19(7), pp 1669-1672.

Michailidis, L., Balaguer-Ballester, E., & He, X., 2018. Flow and Immersion in video games: The aftermath of a conceptual challenge. *frontiers in Psychology,* 9, pp 1682-1690.

Rheinberg, F., Vollmeyer, R., & Engeser, S., 2003. Die erfassung des Flow-erlebens. *Diagnostik von Motivation und Selbstkonzept*, pp 261–279.

Shu-Fen Wu, Yu-Ling Lu, Chi-Jui Lien, Detecting Students' Flow States and Their Construct Through Electroencephalogram: Reflective Flow Experiences, Balance of Challenge and Skill, and Sense of Control. 2021

Ray, W. J., & Cole, H. W., 1985. Eeg alpha activity reflects attentional demands, and beta activity reflects emotional and cognitive processes. *Science*, 228(4700), pp 750–752.

Reuter-Lorenz, P. A., Jonides, J., Smith, E. E., Hartley, A., Miller, A., Marshuetz, C., & Koeppe, R. A. (2000). Age differences in the frontal lateralization of verbal and spatial working memory revealed by PET. *Journal of cognitive neuroscience*, *12*(1), 174–187. https://doi.org/10.1162/089892900561814

Rheinberg, F., Vollmeyer, R., & Engeser, S., 2003. Die Erfassung des Flowerlebens. Diagnostik von Motivation und Selbstkonzept, pp 261–279.

Teplan, M. et al., 2002. Fundamentals of eeg measurement. *Measurement science review*, 2(2), pp 1–11.

Ulrich, M., Keller, J., Hoenig, K., Waller, C., & Grön, G. (2014). Neural correlates of experimentally induced Flow experiences. *Neuroimage*, 86, 194–202. https://doi.org/10.1016/j.neuroimage.2013.08.019

Vialatte, F. B., Bakardjian, H., Prasad, R., & Cichocki, A., 2009. Eeg paroxysmal gamma waves during bhramari pranayama: A yoga breathing technique. *Consciousness and cognition*, 18(4), pp 977–988.

Wolf, S., Brölz, E., Keune, P. M., Wesa, B., Hautzinger, M., Birbaumer, N., & Strehl, U. (2015). Motor skill failure or Flow-experience? Functional brain asymmetry and brain connectivity in elite and amateur table tennis players. *Biological Psychology*, 105, 9.

RANDOM REWARD MECHANISMS (LOOT BOXES): BEHAVIORAL ECONOMICS AS A REGULATORY SOLUTION IN BRAZILIAN LAW

Laiane Maris Caetano Fantini
PUC Minas. Centro DTIBR
Belo Horizonte, MG., Brazil

ABSTRACT

The paper seeks to reflect on ways to create an effective regulation by understanding the aspects of random reward mechanisms in video games, also known as loot boxes. Players acquire digital assets of a game through microtransactions, and pays with in-game currency or real money. Among these digital assets, several games also offer loot boxes, which are systems of "surprise boxes" with a certain price but whose reward is unknown to the player (and is only revealed when the box is purchased and opened). A simple way of selling a digital asset has serious implications for players, mainly due to the similarity with gambling in making the reward relegated to chance. Also, adults and children players are encouraged to exhibit addictive behaviors, spending time and money without any control. Brazilian law does not have enough apparatus to protect consumers from these practices and banning loot boxes from the market does not seem to be the solution, as similar mechanisms could arise even worse. This way of marketing digital assets hides the real transaction costs and makes consumers make decisions based on heuristics, and that's why the Behavioral Economic Theory can offer better solutions to protect players.

KEYWORDS

Loot Boxes, Regulation, Gambling, Behavioral Economics, Brazilian Law

1. INTRODUCTION

The concept of loot boxes, also known as random reward mechanism (RRM), has become increasingly prevalent in the videogame industry, with many games offering them as a means of obtaining virtual goods with in-game currency or real money. While loot boxes can provide a sense of excitement, realization and unpredictability, according to studies cited in this research, there are growing concerns about their impact on consumers, particularly children, and their potential to encourage vicious and gambling-like behaviors.

Brazil has legal tools that can help subsume loot boxes within the legal system. First, it is necessary to discuss whether loot boxes are or not gambling, because the practice of gambling is prohibited in the country, although it has recently found flexibility with betting websites and apps.

If loot boxes not being considered gambling, which is prohibited by law, it is possible to use the Consumer Protection Code (Código de Defesa do Consumidor), the Internet Legal Framework (Marco Civil da Internet) and the General Data Protection Law (Lei Geral de Proteção de Dados). All of this may not be enough to protect consumers from the vulnerabilities brought about by the virtual environment, and especially children. Therefore, this work proposes a complementary way to study regulation in Brazil.

Behavioral economics, as a field of study, is concerned with the ways in which human behavior deviates from the idealized assumptions of traditional economic models. It assumes that people are influenced by psychological biases and emotional factors, and that these influences can impact decision-making. In the context of loot boxes, understanding the psychological factors that contribute to their appeal can help inform the development of effective regulations to protect consumers.

In previous research, the legal instruments available to the Brazilian legal system to protect consumers were studied. However, during a previous research, it was identified that the current legal apparatus was not enough to protect consumers from harmful behavior and the solution was found in the Behavioral Economic Theory.

2. LOOT BOXES: DEFINITION AND IMPLICATIONS

Loot boxes have been widely studied by professionals from the most diverse areas in recent years, being identified as a problem that goes beyond the technical field of developing a game. There are studies in psychology, psychiatry, sociology and law that seek to understand the effects of this system on players and the social and legal implications.

In recent years, the video game industry has adopted a new way of monetizing game assets: microtransactions, also known as IAP (*in-App purchases*). In video games, microtransactions consist in purchase of virtual goods, using virtual currency or real world money, and then traded for a virtual good, which can be any asset, including loot boxes. (King, Delfabbro, 2018; Neely, 2018). By themselves, microtransactions already have the controversy of operating in a non-transparent system of supply and demand based on personalized ads based on data and an artificial scarcity.

Loot boxes consist of a reward delivery system within the game, usually represented by a chest or crate that will be opened, which gives the player a selection of random items (King; Delfabbro. 2018) with uncertain value. It can be owned by gameplay or waiting time or by microtransactions, by real-world money or in-game currency. This is the initial cost, according to economic theory.

Despite the name referring to a "box", they can have other formats. Hence the proposal for a more appropriate name, such as random reward mechanism (Xiao, 2022) or random reward machines (Nielsen, 2019). Both nomenclatures are technically correct and should be used for legislative technical purposes, although loot boxes are the more popular term in the game industry.

Despite loot boxes having emerged as a revenue tool in free or freemium games, big game companies and publishers increasingly began to implement them in major titles, changing the classical sales models to insert in-game purchases (Perks, 2019).

Random reward mechanisms may have three components in common (Nielsen; Grabarczyk. 2019). The first one is the eligibility condition which concerns how the player is able to trigger the random mechanism. The cost can be linked to spending on microtransactions or achieving an objective within the game. The second element is the random procedure, created by any algorithm that determines when the player can get the reward and what kind of reward. The third element is the reward itself, which consists of any element that can only be used within the game in which the crate was purchased.

According to the policy paper commissioned by the European Parliament (Cerulli-Harms et al. 2020), loot boxes have four main characteristics[1]:

Table 1. Four main characteristics of loot boxes

Access and cost	It can be obtained through game development (gameplay), waiting time, time spent viewing ads or can be acquired via microtransactions.
Transparency and probabilities of obtaining different items	Some loot boxes return different results given similar probabilities, but there is a calculation where rare items have a low probability of dropping in rewards, while common items have a higher probability. This probability is not always informed to the player.
Content	The content ranges from purely cosmetic items to functional items, which affect gameplay, and in all cases may prove useful or valuable to players.
Value conversion	Rewards obtained may, in some cases, be converted into in-game currency or real currency. This is usually the predominant feature to define whether or not loot boxes are games of chance. It is also called transferability (Griffiths, 2018).

As we can see, loot boxes and gambling are also a game of chance, according to Caillois (2017).

A new understanding by the Dutch Gambling Authority may rekindle the debate on the elements that link loot boxes to gambling (Otto, 2022). According to the decision, issued in March 2022, loot boxes are no longer considered games of chance under Dutch law if, cumulatively:

1) The loot boxes are part of a game whose winner is decided by skill criteria;
2) Loot boxes are obtained and opened within the game environment;
3) Loot boxes can be obtained both during the game and through microtransactions;

[1]And those are way too similar to gambling.

4) The vast majority of loot boxes are obtained during the game, without there being a situation where players buy boxes on a large scale with the sole intention of selling the content received as a reward.

The decision brought new evaluation criteria to understand loot boxes that can be adopted in other countries around the world. One of them is the analysis based on the percentage of boxes that can be received during the game in relation to those that are actually purchased by the players. The other is the relationship of autonomy in relation to the game, since being merely accessory, the relationship with gambling is removed.

In Brazil, it was only in 2021 that the Associação Nacional dos Centros de Defesa da Criança e do Adolescente (ANCED) filed several public civil actions against developers and publishers, provoking the judiciary to take a position on the banning of loot boxes in the country. The process, despite being in the knowledge phase, has already received a favorable opinion from the Public Prosecutor's Office.

3. FRAMEWORK OF BRAZILIAN LAW

3.1 Brazilian´s Legal Players Protection

In normative terms, there is no legislative approach to digital goods in Brazil, either in the Código de Defesa do Consumidor (general law to protect consumers, despite the lack about virtual consumption), in the Marco Civil da Internet (which regulates the use of the internet in the country and determines the transparency duty of suppliers) and in the Lei Geral de Proteção de Dados (which determines rights and duties in relation to personal data processed in Brazil). Contracts for software consumption are, as a rule, terms of adhesion, provided for in the Código de Defesa do Consumidor. However, the legal basis for certain behaviors that occur within the virtual environment requires the application of other norms, such as Decreto n. 7.962/13 which reinforces the consumer's right to information and expressly ensures the right to regret purchases via e-commerce.

Despite concerns about the effects of microtransactions, the biggest challenge in regulating online gaming and protecting virtual consumers is still the lack of consent or clarity about the classification of the legal status of certain types of in-game purchases. These are issues that deal directly with basic consumer rights provided for in the Brazilian consumer law.

In a general aspect, the Consumer Law protects the consumer against an objective misleading advertising which can be materially demonstrated, that is intentionally created to mislead the consumer. On the other hand, it says nothing about subtle or aggressive advertising that aims to suggest the consumer in order to convince him that that choice for a particular consumer good is necessary, immediate or better than the others available.

In the analysis of the legal provisions applicable to loot boxes in the country today, there is a problem in relation to the offer that affects freedom of choice (article 6, III and article 30 of the Código de Defesa do Consumidor), since the consumer does not know exactly what you are acquiring, as it is not the acquisition of the box itself that motivates the player, but its content and the expectation of perhaps – believing that the randomness criterion is observed – receiving an digital item of value. The structure of loot boxes creates an asymmetry in detriment of the consumer and the Brazilian law is not prepared to deal with this asymmetry because it assumes that the consumer will normally make "rational choices", even when he is being "deceived".

The market failure identified in the consumption of loot boxes lies mainly in the lack of information to the virtual consumer, but it impacts the consumer even before the consumption relationship, reflecting on his choice process, an area of study of behavioral economics discussed later. Other effects of this failure were widely addressed in the study when dealing with aspects of microtransactions, behavioral problems related to addiction and problematic gambling and the way in which the consumption of these assets affects different consumers.

3.2 Gambling in Brazil

In Brazil, gambling is currently prohibited by Decreto-lei n. 2980/43, also known as the Lei das Contravenções Penais. The law defined games of chance as those in which the gain and loss depend exclusively on luck. So, if random reward mechanisms were considered, in Brazil, as games of chance, they would be automatically prohibited by law.

However, there may be exceptions, taking two situations as a reference. Lotteries are prohibited in Brazil by the same law that prohibited gambling, except in the case of the exploitation of lotteries by the Government, which was authorized by Decreto-lei n. 204/67. So, any law can make exceptions for certain gambling practices, making them legal.

This is what happened with the second example: the virtual bets that became extremely popular with the Fifa World Cup. The activity has been carried out in Brazil since the enactment of the Lei das Apostas Esportivas (Lei 13.756/2018). The law regulated lotteries in the form of fixed-quota bets, creating a specific fund for the allocation of activity resources. With a series of gambling laws in progress in the National Congress, it seems to be just a bureaucratic issue to Brazil legalizing random reward mechanisms in video games that are sold in Brazil.

4. BEHAVIORAL ECONOMICS

Classical economic theories assume that all human actions are part of rational, stable and constant choices in order to allow safe and reliable forecasts and, consequently, solid regulations. (Ribeiro, Domingues. 2018). This means that, according to this theory, the consumer will make rational decisions in any circumstances, even if he is faced with an appealing advertisement, products selected from preferences shaped by algorithms or other digital marketing methods intended to stimulate purchase behavior in the virtual environment.

Realizing a flaw in this perspective, since people also make irrational consumption choices, Behavioral Economics emerged from research by Amos Tversky and Daniel Kahneman (1974). This theory, also known as behaviorism, countered the dogmatic assumption of rationality and proposed a new analytical basis for individuals' decisions, based on the idea that people may have subjective motivations for their choices and therefore not even these will be endowed with rationality and therefore, great.

Richard H. Thaler (2019) was one of the main voices for disseminating behavioral theory and defended the insufficiency of the normative model of traditional economic theory to describe the consumer choice process in the real world. In another research with Christine Jolls and Cass Sunstein (1998), they found that economic agents are rationally limited and, since they are inserted within an environment of uncertainty, the choices will depend, if and how, the information is or will be presented and willingness to take risks.

The Economic Theory of Behavior seeks to study the motivation of conscious impulses and behavior in the face of incentives to reflect on ways that the Public Power can use to help the economic agent, that is, the consumer, to make more efficient and less expensive decisions. susceptible to subjective elements (Ribeiro, Domingues. 2018. P. 462). That is why the Brazilian legal norm it's not enough to protect consumers: because it assumes human rationality.

4.1 Hidden risks, heuristics and motivations in loot boxes

The relationship between the consumer and video games goes beyond the mere entertainment perspective and breaks the boundaries created by the Huizinga's magic circle. Faleiros Júnior and Densa (2022) emphasize the exploratory nature of the application of loot boxes, since "complex algorithms that can turn electronic entertainment games into games of chance" are usually used, without the consumer knowing that he is facing a game of chance. As the authors point out, with the development of games with clear elements characteristic of gambling, companies operate in a zone of regulatory obscurity and take full advantage of it.

According to Whitson and Simon (2014), unlike a game of chess, an electronic game like Call of Duty has rules determined by the algorithm which are not shared with the player, but create a feeling of freedom to act and make choices when, in fact, there is a complex data inference to understand the consumer's profile and create mechanisms for their actions to occur within what is expected. This is a reflection of the language of immersion and engagement provided by games.

According to the authors, "the more immersed you are in a video game, the less you will be concerned about the conditions that produced that experience". This represents one of many factors that make it difficult for players to understand the risks of microtransactions.

There are resources that use heuristics and reinforce consumption, and, despite being lawful, they transit through the abusiveness provided for in the consumer law by compromising the dissemination and accuracy of information, labeling and veracity of the offer. They are known as nudges and they are framing, anchoring and bundling (Faleiros Junior; Densa. 2021). This is why current Brazilian law fails to fully protect consumers from random reward mechanisms in video games.

Framing, or "price framing", creates the idea that individuals' choices are influenced according to the way the problem is presented. Just as the rarity of game items is artificially created, here there is an inauthentic definition of price as a way to influence the consumer regarding an advantage that, in fact, does not exist. This becomes even more serious when, by purchasing in-game currency, players lose track of the real value of the goods being purchased through microtransactions.

The anchoring effect, created by Tversky and Kahneman (1974), concerns the way in which people tend to base their choices on irrelevant information. According to the authors, with this, decisions are made from typically insufficient adjustments, called anchors, so that different starting points produce different estimates, although all are biased. In addition to anchoring in artificially stipulated prices, the studies used showed that, at least in principle, players spend money on loot boxes not for the act of purchase itself, but based on the expectation of being able to receive a surprise item that is rare or considered desired. The motivation is based on a created expectation, that the purchase of the loot box will confirm the receipt of a desired digital asset.

Bundling consists of a grouped sales technique, in an offer, of a set of services or products as a package, with the apparent advantage over the separate acquisition of goods. It is similar to the combined sale, but it differs since the products can be purchased individually. In the context of microtransactions and loot boxes, in-game stores often offer a value for the purchase of a box, and another substantially advantageous value for consumers who want to purchase a set of boxes. All of the practices listed enhance the environment of uncertainty and undermine the clarity of the consumer.

Also, there's a transparency problem. In a study of reward probabilities carried out by Chen et al (2019), it was found a lack of transparency in disclosing the allocation of reward probabilities. With that, if on the one hand the developer informs the consumer that the chance of receiving a certain rare item is 1%, the real chance is 0.0005% and, without knowing this, the wrong information brings a false sense of loss – or reduced sense of loss – and turns out to be another driving factor in the repetitive purchase of loot boxes.

As we have seen, it is intrinsic to the very concept of loot boxes: uncertainty and unpredictability. People are naturally drawn to unpredictable outcomes, as they can provide a sense of excitement and anticipation. This is known as the "endowment effect" (Tversky; Kahneman. 1974), which is the idea that people value items more highly simply because they own them. In the case of loot boxes, this can lead to players spending more money in the expectation of obtaining valuable virtual items. Another psychological factor is the concept of "near misses" (Tversky; Kahneman. 1974). This refers to the phenomenon where people feel that they have come close to winning a prize, but just missed out. This can increase the motivation to keep playing, as players feel that they are close to obtaining the desired outcome.

All of these are common practices in the digital asset market and even in electronic games. Brazilian law does not have enough resources to protect players when the problems go beyond the lack of supply and the false sense of transparency.

4.2 The appeal and impact of loot boxes on players

The uncertainty and unpredictability of loot boxes can have negative consequences for players, particularly for children who may not have the maturity or judgment to understand the risks involved. No wonder, academic and political concern has grown around the effects of these random reward systems on players.

Research has shown that exposure to loot boxes can increase the likelihood of problem gambling behaviors, and that children who play games with loot boxes are more likely to develop gambling-related issues later in life. Although there are not many studies about it, it can also affect an elderly population that is highly vulnerable in the virtual environment.

There are several studies that link the consumption of loot boxes with typical symptoms of gambling addiction disorders. Griffiths (1995) presented one of the pioneering studies that linked loot boxes with gambling, in addition to identifying that electronic games attract younger people due to their familiarity with technology. Hing et al (2022) reviewed about sixteen studies on the relationship between loot boxes and gambling, and found that purchases with random reward mechanisms is significantly associated with spending on gambling, indicating an important convergence in both behaviors.

Some studies found that teenage gamblers are more likely to engage in gambling activities and those who spend money on loot boxes are more likely to have problem gambling behavior. This can lead to problems such as indebtedness, alcohol dependence and exposure to gambling content on social networks, facilitating access and fostering addiction (Delfabbro, 2009; Zendle, Meyer, Over, 2019; Zendle, Cairns, 2019).

Barton et al (2017), in a systematic literature review of more than 50 researches published between 1991 and 2015, found that slot machine players and other forms of electronic gambling, even in the face of near misses and disguised losses the wins, presented high value to the victory. Put another way, the researchers concluded that "winning" is not the only way players get excited about consuming electronic gambling items.

There are several studies that link the consumption of loot boxes with typical symptoms of gambling addiction disorders. Griffiths (1995) presented one of the pioneering studies that linked loot boxes with gambling, in addition to identifying that electronic games attract younger people due to their familiarity with technology. Hing et al (2022) reviewed about sixteen studies on the relationship between loot boxes and gambling, and found that purchases with RRM is significantly associated with spending on gambling, indicating an important convergence in both behaviors.This can lead to problems such as indebtedness, alcohol dependence and exposure to gambling content on social networks, facilitating access and fostering addiction (Delfabbro, 2009; Zendle, Meyer, Over, 2019; Zendle, Cairns, 2019).

Barton et al (2017), in a systematic literature review of more than 50 works published between 1991 and 2015, found that slot machine players and other forms of electronic gambling, even in the face of near misses and disguised losses the wins, presented high value to the victory. Put another way, researchers concluded that "winning" isn´t the only way players get excited about consuming items in electronic gambling.

Not surprisingly, many countries have banned loot boxes in games. Belgium (Kansspelautoriteit, 2018), Germany and the Netherlands (Zendle; Cairns, 2019) understood that this system violated national rules on gambling. In the United Kingdom, the Gambling Commission of the House of Commons stated, in 2019, that loot boxes were a form of gambling, depending on how they were offered. Seeking to mitigate the randomness factor, the Chinese government required, in 2016, that electronic game developers start disclosing the perception probabilities of possible items in loot boxes, a practice that is also required in the country for casinos (Perks, 2017). It indirectly recognized the strong similarity denied by countries such as North America (ESRB, 2020).

5. HOW BEHAVIORAL ECONOMICS CAN HELP UNDERSTAND LOOT BOXES AND BUILD AN APPROPRIATE REGULATION TO PROTECT PLAYERS

The regulation of loot boxes aims to cause a smaller impact on the market, as agents will know the limits of action in creating random reward mechanisms, and there will be greater security for consumers. The problems pointed out go beyond informational asymmetry: they demand behavioral and contextual analysis of consumers of electronic games.

In this way, the Brazilian consumer law can be revised to cover its own rules on virtual consumption inspired by COPPA (Children's Online Privacy Protection Rule), in the USA, or The Digital Markets Act in Europe. In other words, it is suggested that specific provisions on virtual consumption, algorithmic transparency, rights to review or cancel transactions made during a certain period of time and protection of the virtual consumer be added to the law.

In addition, the Ministry of Justice, the administrative body responsible for creating policies in favor of consumers, can trigger game companies that market their products in the country to provide information on the consumption of assets of random reward mechanisms and ask what measures are adopted to effectively protect Brazilian consumers.

Also, it can create manuals and establish parameters suggesting that companies adopt measures such as periodic spending limits, minimum age, history of spending on amounts in in-game currency and real money and spending control tools, have tax benefits, for example.

They can also limit that the rewards obtained in the loot boxes cannot be sold (in or out of the game), restricting transferability, and that the player can exercise the right of repentance, within a time limit, if he wants to recover the money spent on these mechanisms. In addition, in a joint effort with other authorities, tax benefits can be offered to companies that present a certain degree of compliance with consumer protection parameters.

These are measures based on the assumption that the player, within the game environment, is normally not in a position to make rational consumption choices and therefore needs greater protection to circumvent possible psychological and financial damages.

6. CONCLUSION

Classical Economic Theory assumes that players will make rational decisions under any circumstances, so they will not be influenced by random reward systems, visual and sound stimuli, and advertisements shaped by algorithms that are intended to stimulate buying behavior. On the contrary, the Behavioral Economic Theory assumes that the player, in an environment of uncertainty, may make irrational decisions influenced by heuristics, without having sufficient elements to identify the existing hidden risks. Therefore, the adoption of this theory to guide the regulation of these mechanisms may provide greater protection to consumers.

In addition to the aforementioned legislation being applicable to microtransactions and other aspects related to the trade of digital goods within electronic games in Brazil, there are regulatory gaps that weaken consumer relations and make consumers even more vulnerable, subject to predatory and abusive practices and the harmful consequences of consumption.

Thus, considering the evidence presented and analyzing the normative context of both loot boxes in the world and gambling in Brazil, measures were proposed for regulation based on informational asymmetry and Behavioral Economic Theory as a way to intensify consumer protection.

REFERENCES

ANCED (2021). *ANCED entra na justiça pedindo a proibição de sorteios ilegais em jogos eletrônicos*. Available in: https://www.ancedbrasil.org.br/anced-entra-na-justica-pedindo-proibicao-de-sorteios-ilegais-em-jogos-eletronicos/. Access: 8 feb. 2023.

Barton, K. R.; Yazdani, Y.; Ayer, N.; Kalvapalle, S.; Brown, S.; Stapleton, J.; Brown, D. G.; Harrigan, K. A. (2017). The Effect of Losses Disguised as Wins and Near Misses in Electronic Gaming Machines: A Systematic Review. Journal Of Gambling Studies, 33, 1241–1260.

Caillois, Roger (2017). Os jogos e os homens: a máscara e a vertigem. Editora Vozes, 1º ed. Petrópolis, RJ, Brazil.

Cerulli-Harms, Anette; Munsch, Marlene; Thorun, Christian; Michaelsen, Frithjof; Hausemer, Pierre (2020). Loot boxes in online games and their effect on consumers, in particular young consumers. Publication for the committee on the Internal Market and Consumer Protection (IMCO), Policy Department for Economic, Scientific and Quality of Life Policies, European Parliament, Luxembourg. Available in: https://www.europarl.europa.eu/thinktank/en/document/IPOL_STU(2020)652727. Access: 4 feb. 2023.

Chen, Ningyuan; Elmachtoub, Adam N.; Hamilton, Michael L.; Lei, Xiao (2019). Loot box pricing and design. Agosto. Available in: https://papers.ssrn.com/sol3/papers.cfm?abstract_id=3430125. Access: 12 feb. 2023.

Coase, Ronald H. (2008). The Problem of Social Cost.The Berkeley Electronic Press. USA.

Delfabbro, P.; King, Daniel; Lambos, C.; Puglies. S. (2009). Is Video-Game Playing a Risk Factor for Pathological Gambling in Australian Adolescents? Journal Of Gambling Studies, 25, 391–405.

ESRB (2020). Introducing a new interactive element: In-game purchases (includes random items). Available in: https://www.esrb.org/blog/in-game-purchases-includes-random-items/. Access: 12 dec. 2022.

Faleiros Junior, J. L. de M.; Densa, R. (2021). Para além das loot boxes: responsabilidade civil e novas práticas abusivas no mercado de games. In: Proteção de dados pessoais na sociedade da informação. Coord.: João Victor Rozatti Longhi, José Luiz de Moura Faleiros Junior, Rodrigo Gugliara. Foco. Indaiatuba, SP, Brazil.

Griffiths, M. D. (1995). Adolescent gambling. Routledge

Hing, Nerilee; Rockloff, Matthew; Russel, Alex M.; Browne, Matthew; Newall, Philip; Greer, Nancy; King; Daniel L.; Thorne, Hannah (2022). Loot Box Purchasing is Linked to Problem Gambling in Adolescents when Controlling for Monetary Gambling Participation. Journal Of Behavioral Addictions.

Jolls, Christine; Sustein, Cass R.; Thaler, Richard (1998). A behavioral approach to law and economics. Standford Law Review 1471. Available in: https://chicagounbound.uchicago.edu/cgi/viewcontent.cgi?article=12172&context=journal_articles. Access: 26 dec. 2022.

Kahneman, D. & Tversky, A. (1974), Judgment under uncertainty: heuristics and biases. Science, Vol. 185, Issue 4157.

Kansspelautoriteit (2018). Sommige loot boxes in strijd met kansspelwet. Retrieved May 17, 2018. Available in: https://www.kansspelautoriteit.nl/nieuws/alle-nieuwsberichten/2018/april/artikel-0/. Access: 12 feb. 2023.

King, Daniel L.; Delfabbro, Paul H. (2018). Video Game Monetization (e.g., 'loot boxes'): a Blueprint for Practical Social Responsibility Measures. International Journal of Mental Health and Addiction.

Neely, Erica (2018). Come for the game, stay for the cash grab: the ethics of loot boxes, microtransactions, and freemium games. ETHICOMP Conference, Poland.

Nielsen, Rune Kristian Lundedal; Grabarczyk, Paweł (2019). Are loot boxes Gambling? Random Reward Mechanisms in Video Games. DIGRA - Digital Games Research Association. Vol 4, No 3 (2019). 171-205. Available in: http://todigra.org/index.php/todigra/article/view/104. Access: 21 dec. 2022.

Otto, Renè (2022). Dutch Gambling Authority vs Electronic Arts, and the future of loot boxes. GameIndustry.biz. Available in: https://www.gamesindustry.biz/articles/2022-04-25-dutch-gambling-authority-vs-electronic-arts-the-end-of-loot-boxes-as-legislative-black-boxes. Access: 25 apr. 2022.

Perks, Matthew (2017). Why A Conversation Around Loot Box Regulation, Responsability, and Harm Needs to be Happening. Medium Corporation. Available in: Https://Medium.Com/@Perks_matthew/Why-A-Conversation-Around-Loot-Box-Regulation-Responsibility-And-Harm-Needs-To-Be-Happening-636acf0e99ba. Access: 14 feb. 2023.

Perks, Matthew (2019). How does games critique impact game design decisions? A case study of monetization and loot boxes. Games and Culture, 15(8).

Ribeiro, Marcia Carla; Domingues, Victor Hugo (2018). Economia comportamental e direito: a racionalidade em mudança. Revista Brasileira de Políticas Públicas. Economia comportamental e direito: a racionalidade em mudança. Org. Marcia Clara Pereira Ribeiro e Victor Hugo Domingues. V. 8, n.2. P. 457-471.

Thaler, Richard H; Sustein, Cass R. (2019). Nudge: como tomar decisões sobre saúde, dinheiro e felicidade. Trad.: Ângelo Lessa. 1ed. Rio de Janeiro, RJ. Brazil.

United Kingdom. Gambling Commission (2019). Young people and gambling survey 2019. A research study among 11-16-year-olds in Great Britain. Birmingham: Gambling Commission.

Whitson, Jennifer; Simon, Bart. (2014). Game Studies meets Surveillance Studies at the Edge of Digital Culture: An Introduction to a special issue on Surveillance, Games and Play. Surveillance & Society, 12(3).

Xiao, L.Y. (2022). Which Implementations of Loot Boxes Constitute Gambling? A UK Legal Perspective on the Potential Harms of Random Reward Mechanisms. In: International Journal of Mental Health and Addiction. 20, 437–454.

Zendle, David; Meyer, Rachel; Over, Harriet (2019). Adolescents and Loot Boxes: Links with Problem Gambling and Motivation for Purchase. Royal Society Open Science. Disponível em: https://royalsocietypublishing.org/doi/pdf/10.1098/rsos.190049. Acesso em 14 feb. 2023.

ANALYSIS OF THE PROCEDURAL GENERATION ALGORITHM OF EDGAR PRO TOOL WITH A FASTER VARIETY CREATION IN DUNGEON LAYOUT

Cristina Souza de Araujo[1], Ana Carolina Brandão Salgado[1], Gabriel Barroso da Silva Lima[2],
Jucimar Maia da Silva Junior[2], Clairon Lima Pinheiro[2] and Luis Cuevas Rodriguez[2]
[1]CESAR SCHOOL
Recife, Brazil
[2]Escola Superior de Tecnologia - EST
Universidade do Estado do Amazonas - UEA, Manaus, Brazil

ABSTRACT

This article describes the process of analysis the procedural generation package Edgar for Unity game engine. This package focuses on generating dungeon layouts for top-down 2D games. The generation works with the developer creating room models and a non-directional graph for the dungeon, with the package generating a random layout from these inputs. The purpose of this article is to expand the variety of layouts that the package generates, creating a greater variety of results for the player without losing the randomness factor that comes from procedural generation.

KEYWORDS

Procedural Generation, Games, Unity, Game Development

1. INTRODUCTION

During the game design process, many elements are taken into account regarding game development: mechanics, UX, UI, platforms, progression, accessibility [Motta, Junior 2013]. One of these elements refers to the replayability factor of the game, that is, how much new content the game can offer for each new playthrough. Many games offer unlockable difficulties, new game modes, or achievements to be obtained. However, other games go beyond that.

Roguelike games have two characteristics that differentiate them from other genres: one is permanent death, which refers to the loss of progress (or part of it) when the player loses; and the other is procedural generation of new maps for each playthrough, allowing new experiences to be enjoyed by the player in every new game [Cerny, Dechterenko 2015]. The type of procedural generation can vary greatly depending on what the game design of the project requires and the game engine used can do.

The Edgar procedural generation package is a tool for creating dungeon layouts focused on top-down 2D games [Nepožitek 2018]. With it, it is possible to create and edit rooms and assemble the layout of the dungeon to be generated, allowing the developer to procedurally generate maps without losing control of the game's level design. This tool was based on the work of Chongyang Ma, where many of the concepts and techniques used were presented [Ma, Vining, Lefebvre, Sheffer 2014, May]. This article describes the process of replicating the artificial intelligence used by the Edgar package in its procedural generation of 2D dungeons, but applying techniques that avoid creating similar layouts in near generations, making the player to feel a greater variety of results that the algorithm can provide.

1.1 Justification

The Edgar procedural generation package is a great tool for 2D dungeon procedural generation, but in Ondřej Nepožitek's article, there is no mention of something that tries to avoid creating layouts similar to those created in past generations, which can be a problem, especially in games that have procedural generation as a fundamental part of their design (such as roguelike games).

To solve this problem, this article presents an approach to the procedural generation technique of the Edgar package, but applying validation functions that verify and ensure that new layouts are visually different from dungeons generated in past generations. This allows the variety of maps to be better explored and, therefore, increases the replayability of the game, giving more value to the final product. The algorithm works based on tilesets. This working method was chosen because it makes replication of the Edgar package less complex, in addition to aligning with the results of the Edgar package.

2. DUNGEON ELEMENTS

This algorithm works in three parts: the first part involves obtaining configuration spaces between rooms, which are the positions where a room connects correctly to another; the second part involves breaking the planar graph of the dungeon layout into subgraphs, determining the generation priority order between the obtained subgraphs; and the third part involves generating the rooms from the subgraphs, using the configuration spaces to determine the position of a new room and whether a generated layout is valid or not.

To compare with previously generated dungeons, points such as the angle of the new room with the room it connects to, similarity between the arranged rooms, the number of connections the room has, and how old the old layout being compared is are checked. All these factors contribute to assigning a value that determines whether a new room is different enough to be arranged or whether a new generation needs to be made. These steps contribute to generating a dungeon efficiently, with the minimum processing and time required and effectively.

The dungeon layout graph is the logical representation of the desired dungeon progression, containing information about which rooms (or set of rooms) connect with each other. This information is loaded into the generation algorithm, which translates these values into a procedural dungeon.

Since rooms cannot overlap, it is required that the dungeon layout can be represented in a planar graph. In a planar graph, its edges can be rearranged so that there are no edge crossings [Bondy, Murty 1976]. In addition to being planar, the layout must be simple enough for the generation algorithm to create a dungeon with great variety and without major issues. A complex graph or one with more restrictions will eventually cause greater processing time, and graphs that are impossible (with constraints that prevent any possibility of dungeon creation) should be avoided at all costs.

The dungeon is a connected set of rooms, and each room, like the dungeon itself, also has its properties. Rooms can have distinct characteristics such as enemies, bosses, shops, customizable events, but they all have two fundamental parameters: the list of corners and the list of openings. Since rooms are composed of tiles, both corners and openings must be aligned to the game grid.

The list of corners informs the position of the corners and delimits the area of the room. The wall of a room is determined by the line that starts from a corner to the next corner on the list (in the case of the last corner, it connects to the first corner, closing the area of the room). The list of openings informs the allowed areas for connection, which are attached to the walls and inform which walls are successive to be replaced by a connection through a corridor. These two properties are crucial for the elaboration of configuration spaces.

Corridors are special types of rooms whose purpose is to connect rooms in a dungeon. They are characterized by being rectangular and having their openings at their respective ends: horizontal corridors have openings only on the left and right walls, and vertical hallways have openings on the top and bottom walls.

Before starting the generation process, a calculation is made based on the corridors inputted by the developer, determining the size of the openings, the width, and orientation of the hallways. This is important information that allows for the creation of a greater variety of possibilities for room connection.

3. CONFIGURATION SPACES

Configuration spaces are positions where two rooms can connect correctly without one overlapping the other [Nepožitek 2018] [Ma, Vining, Lefebvre, Sheffer 2014, May]. This greatly speeds up procedural generation as it is not necessary to randomly place the room and check if the connection is valid, just place the room in one of the available configuration spaces.

To obtain the configuration spaces, one room must remain static while the other moves around it. During the movement, the positions where the moving room is correctly connected to the static room (intersection greater than or equal to minimum size and no overlap between the rooms) are recorded. At the end of the process, all the found positions are saved to be accessed later during the dungeon generation.

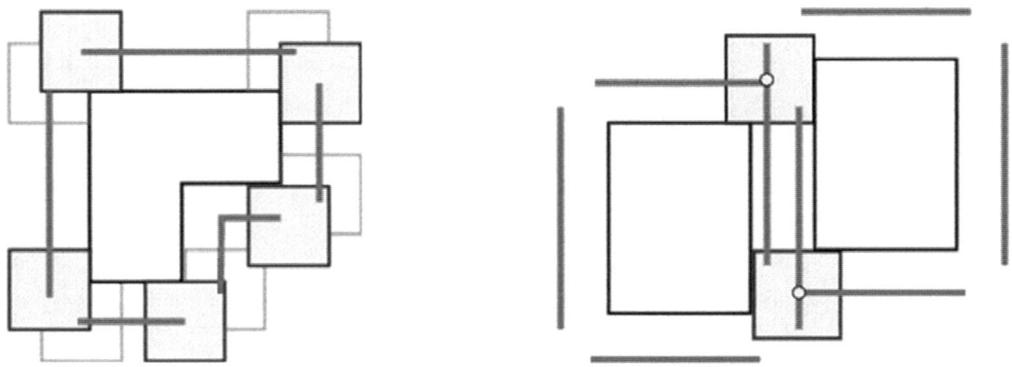

Figure 1. Configuration spaces: room move around fixed room, getting all valid connection positions. A configuration space intersection means a room can connect to more than one placed room

3.1 Configuration Space Creation

The process begins with the selection of two rooms, one static and one mobile. Initially, both are placed on top of each other, then the mobile room is moved one unit upwards until there is no more overlap, and starts to move around the static room. The rotation of the mobile room around the fixed room is straight until it encounters an overlap or the mobile room is no longer in contact with the fixed room. This loop continues until the room returns to its initial position, at which point the process is finished with all configuration spaces saved.

At each position of the mobile room, two checks are made: the first is to analyze whether the mobile room overlaps with the fixed room or there is no contact between the two rooms. If neither of these cases occurs, then the openings between the two rooms are checked. Each saved configuration space has information about the opening, which is important during the placement of corridors after the dungeon layout is finalized. configuration spaces are saved in the fixed room.

For each valid connection, a search is made for available corridors, taking into account the orientation of the contact. This is done so that during the arrangement of the rooms, it is not necessary to correct the position to accommodate the corridors, as the positions already allow this naturally. For example, if a valid position is found and this valid position is on an upper wall in the fixed room, it is understood that the mobile room should move upwards, as it is the direction in which it moves away from the fixed room. It is also understood that this connection occurs in the vertical orientation, as it is the orientation in which the room moves.

All saved configuration space has information about the opening, which is important during the placement of corridors after the dungeon layout is finalized. This information includes: connection orientation, room orientation, distance from the room, opening size, socket values of the openings in contact, and the position where the corridor should be placed for a perfect connection.

3.2 Wall Intersection Check

The wall intersection check between the rooms is extremely important for obtaining the configuration spaces, since in order for a position to be valid for connection, it is necessary to meet some prerequisites, which are: not overlapping the other room and the number of connecting openings is at least the minimum required. Each of these prerequisites has its own functions that perform this check.

For each point, three checks are performed: if the point is far enough to discard any comparison; if the point position is on the wall of the static room (position passed if it falls between the two corner values) and if the point is inside the static room (even-odd rule [Foley, Van, Van Dam, Feiner, Hughes 1996]). These checks are performed in this order and, if one of them is true, it is not necessary to perform subsequent checks.

These functions use techniques to speed up the checking process as much as possible, avoiding unnecessary repetitions and comparisons. Basically, they involve traversing the points of the walls of the mobile room and comparing them to the points of the walls of the static room. Because the rooms are located within a grid, it is not necessary to analyze decimal values since each room can only be located within the grid, with its position being an integer value. The points of a wall are the integer values that the wall occupies: if a room has a wall that goes from (0, 0) to (0, 6), the points of the wall are all the integer values that are on that line, in this case: (0, 0), (0, 1), (0, 2), (0, 3), (0, 4), (0, 5), and (0, 6).

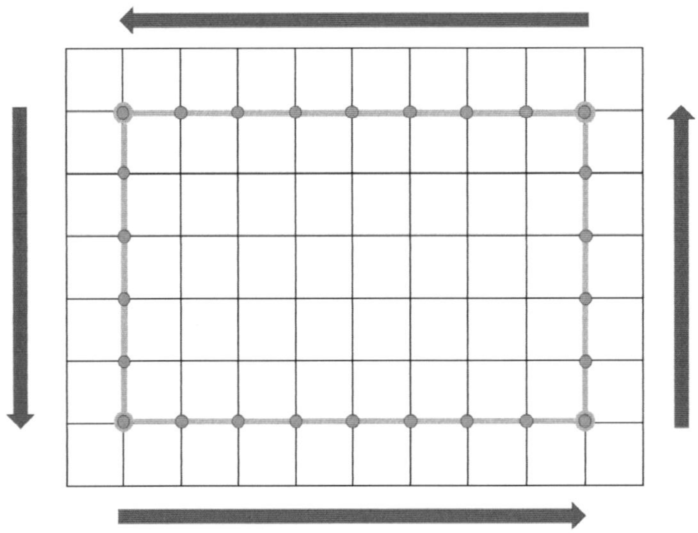

Figure 2. Starting from the first corner, all wall points are traversed until all points of the grid that the walls of the room occupy have been checked

The second and third checks help to decide the direction that the mobile room will take in the next iteration: if no contact is identified between the rooms or there is overlap, the room returns to the previous position and follows the next path. If there is contact without overlap, then the algorithm is able to check the intersection of the openings of the rooms.

3.3 Opening Intersection Check

If the wall intersection check verifies the current position of the room is a valid position, the opening intersection check verifies if the current position of the room is valid for capturing configuration spaces from the fixed room to the mobile room. This is validated from the intersections between the openings of the rooms where the largest consecutive intersection determines if the current position is a configuration space or not.

The verification is done similarly to the wall intersection check of the rooms with the difference that, instead of the function traversing point by point the walls, it traverses the openings of the mobile room and checks if they are within reach of the openings of the fixed room. Another difference is that, in this case, the function seeks to track the longest sequence of points that intersect the openings of the fixed room. A valid position for capturing configuration spaces is characterized when the longest sequence of intersections found is equal to or greater than the width of the opening defined by the room plus one.

4. GRAPH DECOMPOSITION

The ordering of the chains is done as follows: all cycles within the graph are identified using a technique similar to graph coloring [Jensen, Toft 2011], where all nodes are traversed, saving the addresses of the visited nodes, and when a repetition is detected, an array is saved in a list of found cycles with all addresses from the repetition to the last visited node. This list is then sorted from the array with the smallest size to the largest.

The ordering of the subgraphs has as priority the smallest cycle found, followed by the smallest cycles adjacent to the previously arranged cycles. When there are no more cycles connected to the subgraphs, a breadth-first search [Beamer, Asanovic, Patterson 2012] is performed where each node connected to the obtained subgraphs is arranged one by one into the set of subgraphs. If a new cycle is found, the process of inserting cycles into the list of chains is repeated. The process of breaking the graph into subgraphs is terminated when all elements of the received graph are within one of the chains in the created list.

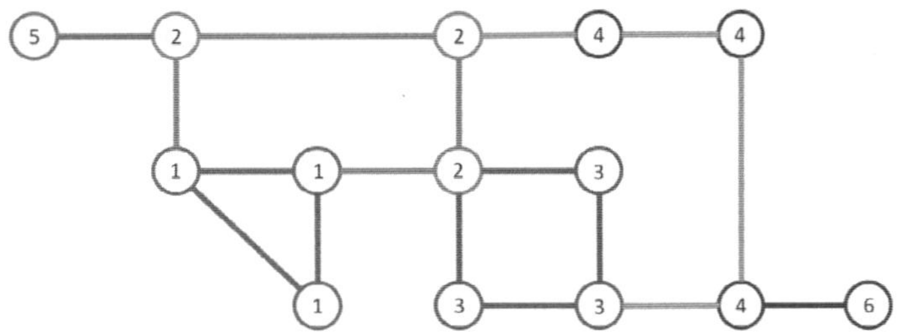

Figure 3. Order of breaking the graph into subgraphs, starting from the smallest cycle, then adding the smallest cycle connected to the previous ones, and finally the acyclic nodes

5. DUNGEON LAYOUT CREATION

The ordering of the chains is done as follows: all cycles within the graph are identified using a technique similar to graph coloring [Jensen, Toft 2011], where all nodes are traversed, saving the addresses of the visited nodes, and when a repetition is detected, an array is saved in a list of found cycles with all addresses from the repetition to the last visited node. This list is then sorted from the array with the smallest size to the largest.

5.1 Finding a Room Position

When receiving a chain, the algorithm first allocates the rooms in their proper positions. All rooms are based on the configuration spaces of the rooms they connect to, in order to define their position (the first room of the first current will have (0, 0) as position).

New rooms choose a random valid position among those listed in the configuration spaces (without overlapping with other rooms). However, for rooms that connect to only one already-disposed room, an evaluation is also made that checks how different each position is from layouts created in both this generation and past generations. This evaluation assigns a weight to the position. The higher the value, the more different the new room in that position is from other layouts. For a position to be considered different enough, it must have a minimum weight of 1.

The position selection function stores the list of configuration spaces to connect in a backup list. In case there are no intersections between configuration spaces (in cases where rooms connect to more than one room already placed) or if no valid positions are found during the position verification, the function returns a random position from the created backup, already indicating that the returned position did not meet the acceptance criteria.

5.2 Old Layouts Comparison

For each valid position available for the new room, a weight is assigned to determine if the position is different enough from other layouts created, both in the current generation and in past generations. This function takes into account three factors: the angle of the room in comparison to the room it connects to, if the comparison is between two instances of the same room, and the generation of the layout to which the room is being compared.

Initially, the weight and multiplier of rooms from past generations are calculated. The initial value of the weight is the angle of the new room's central point with the central point of the room it connects to. This angle is defined from the horizontal axis: with the center of the room exactly to the left of the center of the room it connects to, without being slightly up or down, its angle is 0, and as the room moves counterclockwise, the angle value increases: being below the room it connects to, the angle is 90, to the right, 180, up, 270, until returning to 0.

The multiplier of this weight defines how lenient or strict the comparison will be. Larger values make the weight assignment more lenient, while smaller values make it more restrictive. Older layouts or rooms not identical to the room being checked tend to the multiplier to a larger value, while newer layouts and identical rooms tend to a smaller value.

Having saved the angles of the rooms and their multipliers, the function stores, in a new list, the distances of all the rooms, in angles, from the saved layouts, and then removes all indices whose distances are greater than double the average distance, avoiding values that may negatively contribute to the desired distance calculation. After that, the calculation of the angle of the new room is made, using the same principle applied to the other rooms. The more distant the new room angle is from the other layouts angles, the higher the result of the division.

5.3 Biased Random Choice

To choose the position of a room based on its weight, a biased random choice is made where the higher the weight of the room, the greater its chances of being chosen. First, the sum of all weights is stored and a variable is created that receives a random value between 0 and the sum of the weights.

The function then creates a zeroed variable that will help to iterate through the positions' weights: if this variable plus the current weight is equal to or greater than the obtained random value, the function returns the current index. Otherwise, the variable receives itself plus the weight value and the same verification is done for the weight of the next index. This method ensures that larger weights have a greater chance of being chosen, and to further reinforce this aspect, all weights are squared before calling this function, so that larger weights become even more valuable compared to smaller weights.

5.4 Chain Energy

After the rooms in the chain are placed in their defined positions, the energy of the current chain is calculated. This energy is defined based on two factors: the total area of overlap between the rooms and the squared distance between connected rooms in the dungeon graph that are not connected in the generated layout. The energy of a chain refers to how close the set of placed rooms is to becoming a valid set, i.e., correctly connected. The calculation of the chain is given by the following function [Ma, Vining, Lefebvre, Sheffer 2014, May]:

$$E = e^{A/m} \cdot e^{D/m} - 1$$

In this equation, 'E' represents the total energy; 'A' represents the total overlap area; 'D' represents the sum of squared distances of non-connected rooms, and 'm' represents how much the function tends to accept higher energy chains. Is recommended a value of 'm' that allows for greater chances of creating a valid chain without compromising the optimization of the code too much. In the article "Game Level Layout from Design Specification" by Chongyang Ma, it is mentioned that empirically, a value of one hundred times the average area of the rooms was found to satisfy both proposed requirements.

For 'D' the process is simple: it is possible to create a triangulation with the center of the two unconnected rooms in order to form a right triangle, and from the Pythagorean theorem formula $a^{\wedge 2} + b^{\wedge 2} = c^{\wedge 2}$ [Maor 2019].

For ‘m’, the algorithm counts all blocks occupied by the room, starting from the uppermost line to the lowers. The area of a room is the sum of all blocks occupied by each row. Then, after getting the area of all rooms, the result is divided by the room amount and then multiplied by one hundred to get the desired value.

For ‘A’, The process starts at the first corner of a room, traversing, point-by-point, the walls of the room. When it identifies an overlap with the other room, that is, the current point is inside the other room, the function starts storing all the corners that it traverses in a list. When it is identified that the current point is no longer inside the other room, the previous position is stored as a corner, and the function starts traversing the wall of the other room in the direction where the point is inside the first room. After getting all intersection corners, the area is calculated using the same method to get the ‘m’ value. ‘A’ is the sum of all overlap areas.

5.5 Simulated Annealing

Simulated annealing is an optimization metaheuristic that seeks to find a low-cost solution without excessive time cost. Its characteristic is the possibility of accepting higher cost results to avoid minimal locals, and this probability decreases with each iteration [Kirkpatrick, Gelatt Jr, Vecchi 1983].

After arranging the rooms in a chain, its energy is calculated, and the chain becomes the reference layout for future changes. If the chain has an energy higher than 0 (not a valid layout), a change is made in a random room of the chain. After that, the energy of the layouts is compared: if the energy of the altered layout is lower, it becomes the reference for creating new layouts; otherwise, it can still be chosen as the reference if the following condition is met [Ma, Vining, Lefebvre, Sheffer 2014, May]:

$$e^{-\Delta E/(a*t)} < Random(0{\sim}1)$$

In this condition, 'ΔE' represents the energy difference between the reference layout and the new layout, 'a' represents the average of energy differences during the creation of layouts based on other references. 't' represents the current temperature of the algorithm and *'Random (0~1)'* is a random number between 0 and 1 generated during the comparison. The 't' variable decreases with each cycle of comparisons, reducing the chance of layouts with higher energy costs being accepted as a reference.

5.6 Corridors Placement

With all rooms arranged in their respective positions, the position of the corridors that connect the rooms can be defined. In the configuration spaces of the rooms, each position returns a list of information on how the corridor should behave for the chosen position specifically.

During the creation of the configuration spaces, two directions are saved that are important to define the position of the room. The first is the direction in which the mobile room was going, and the second is the direction in which the room moves away from the fixed room. These two directions define which opening point the corridor will use as a reference when defining its position. All corridors have four opening points: the two that form the left opening and the two that form the right opening in the case of horizontal corridors, and the two at the bottom opening and the two at the top opening in vertical corridors.

6. RESULTS AND FUTURE WORKS

For the generated dungeon, the following characteristics were determined: the first room will always be the starting room, the following rooms will consist of a normal package of three rooms, and the last room will always be the final room. In the graph, the second and third rooms connect to the first, the fourth room connects to the second and third, the fifth and sixth rooms connect to the fourth, the seventh connects to the fifth and sixth, and the eighth room connects to the seventh.

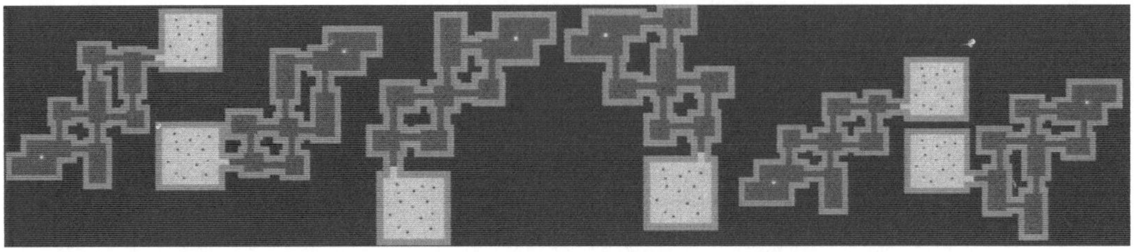

Figure 4. Dungeons generated by passing the room packages, their connections, and corridors.

Having the algorithm already capable of creating dungeons from inputs defined by the developer, the next step is to apply it to a game in development. By being inserted into the logic of a game, it will be analyzed whether the algorithm can consistently, quickly and efficiently meet the requirements of the game designer.

Another step is to directly compare the results of the algorithm with the results produced by the procedural generation package Edgar, replacing the package in a game that uses it, comparing the dungeons and verifying if the algorithm presented in this article succeeded in generating greater varieties of dungeons in fewer interactions.

ACKNOWLEDGEMENT

The authors thanks to the Universidade do Estado Amazonas (UEA), Transire Eletrônicos, Tec Toy S.A. and Ludus Lab for their support. The results were published through the research and development activities of project ARKADE AD ASTRA, sponsored by Transire Eletrônicos and Tec Toy S.A, with the support of SUFRAMA under the terms of Federal Law No.8.387/1991.

REFERENCES

Baghdadi, W., Eddin, F. S., Al-Omari, R., Alhalawani, Z., Shaker, M., & Shaker, N. (2015). A procedural method for automatic generation of spelunky levels. In *Applications of Evolutionary Computation: 18th European Conference, EvoApplications 2015, Copenhagen, Denmark, April 8-10, 2015, Proceedings 18* (pp. 305-317). Springer International Publishing.

Beamer, S., Asanovic, K., & Patterson, D. (2012, November). Direction-optimizing breadth-first search. In SC'12: *Proceedings of the International Conference on High Performance Computing, Networking, Storage and Analysis* (pp. 1-10). IEEE.

Bondy, J. A., & Murty, U. S. R. (1976). *Graph theory with applications* (Vol. 290). London: Macmillan. (pp. 135-139).

Cerny, V., & Dechterenko, F. (2015). Rogue-like games as a playground for artificial intelligence–evolutionary approach. In *Entertainment Computing-ICEC 2015: 14th International Conference, ICEC 2015, Trondheim, Norway, September 29-October 2, 2015, Proceedings 14* (pp. 261-271). Springer International Publishing.

Foley, J. D., Van, F. D., Van Dam, A., Feiner, S. K., & Hughes, J. F. (1996). *Computer graphics: principles and practice* (Vol. 12110). Addison-Wesley Professional. (pp. 127)

Itch Corp (2023). *Most used Engines*. itch.io/game-development/engines/most-projects

Jensen, T. R., & Toft, B. (2011). *Graph coloring problems*. John Wiley & Sons.

Kirkpatrick, S., Gelatt Jr, C. D., & Vecchi, M. P. (1983). Optimization by simulated annealing. *science, 220*(4598), 671-680.

Ma, C., Vining, N., Lefebvre, S., & Sheffer, A. (2014, May). Game level layout from design specification. In *Computer Graphics Forum* (Vol. 33, No. 2, pp. 95-104).

Maor, E. (2019). *The Pythagorean theorem: a 4,000-year history* (Vol. 65). Princeton University Press.

Motta, R. L., & Junior, J. T. (2013). Short game design document (SGDD). *Proceedings of SBGames*, 2013, 115-121.

Nepožitek, O. (2018). Procedural 2D Map Generation for Computer Games.

GENERATIVE AI FOR THE SUPER GAME DESIGNER

JaeJun Lee and JunHee Lee*
Department of Film, TV and Multimedia, College of Art, Sungkyunkwan University
Seoul, Korea

ABSTRACT

This paper explores the transformative impact of generative AI on the game development process, with a focus on changes to the game project proposal process. While the rise of AI in video games has already resulted in smarter monsters, NPCs, and richer game content, generative AI can revolutionize the way games are created. This paper compares two commercially developed cases to illustrate the possible significant impact of generative AI on game design and predicts the emergence of a "super game designer" who can do market sensing, artwork creation and playable prototype development and more. The study showcases the same game designer using generative AI to change how they propose game projects in just three years. The paper highlights the potential of generative AI to empower game designers, revolutionize the industry and unlock new levels of creativity and innovation.

KEYWORDS

Game Design, Game Proposal Documentation, Generative AI, Game Artwork, Midjourney, Novel AI

1. INTRODUCTION

Content designers need to persuade their team members, management and investors by presenting and formalizing their ideas in a visualized, tangible form. Initially, designers may explain their ideas using words, writings or drawings. However, accurately conveying ideas to the counterparts can be one of the most challenging aspects of the design process particularly in multidisciplinary fields like game design, where planning requires diverse and complex elements. Although designers can communicate their ideas more effectively by possessing various communication skills, such as drawing and perhaps making working prototypes, such skills should not be the essential requirements for game designers.

In this study, we argue that generative AI based services can enhance content designers' capabilities immensely. By comparing two in-production commercial game design document examples, one that was created in traditional way and one that was created with the help of generative AI services, we seek to explore how the new technology can empower the game designers to an extent that was not quite imaginable just a decade ago.

After the pen-and-paper prototype stage with the core mechanics of the game may be firmly established in the game designer's mind, depending on the project type or the needs of the stakeholders, detailed artwork or a working protocol may be required for approval. The process often represents laborious work involving a team of skilled people and a demanding schedule in addition to significant expenses. If a single designer or a micro team can match the same output, it can be viewed as a significant innovation in a game design process. AI-based tools offer the potential to create such a "super game designer." We will discuss how generative AI is revolutionizing the project proposal stage by comparing the case of Project Walking Dead and Project Nox, both developed by the same designer, focusing on the in-production game idea and pitching the proposal.

2. AI AND GAMES

Traditionally, AI in games has been understood to be used to control NPCs or enemy characters, or in sports games to control teammates. More specifically, it mimics intelligence by acting as a finite state machine with

*corresponding author

seemingly autonomous behavior within a very limited domain, or by sensing the current state of the game and making limited knowledge acquisition (Funge, 1999). In addition, generative technologies have been continuously studied in games, and various contents such as maps and levels can be automatically generated through procedural content generation for games (PCG-G) (Hendrikx et al, 2013), with varying degrees of success in different fields (Lara-Cabrera, & Fernández-Leiva, 2012), (Cardamone et al., 2011), and (Hartsook et al,. 2011), from the graphical elements of games to game scenarios including space, environmental systems such as paths and tracks, and puzzles. Entering the era of Deep Learning, we can find various attempts to incorporate AI into almost every facet of gaming. We have already seen AlphaGo beat the world's best players in highly complex strategy games as a player, and efforts are underway to create video game players (Oh et al, 2022). Within the screen, NPCs are interacting with players at a much higher level (Karpouzis & Tsatiris, 2022), helping game production with level design (Mehta A. et al, 2022), or using them as a platform for creative ideas (Guzdial, M. et al., 2019). Riedl & Zook have shown the potential for AI to support the game design process (2013). In addition, generative AI services such as Midjourney are already being actively experimented in the field of architecture as a tool to support conceptual design (Jaruga-Rozdolska, A., 2022), (Ploennigs, J. & Berger, M., 2022). Game designers, who need to communicate their ideas to people of different disciplines, can also use the prompts of these generative AI services as a way to expand their talents.

The process of game design may vary slightly depending on the region, industry and game genre, but a typical commercial game production process in the case used in this study is market sensing, project proposal (documentation – prototyping - segmentation), production and service (including marketing, Quality Assurance 'QA', and Game Management 'GM'). The project proposal stage is led by the game producer and game designer. The project proposal phase can be divided into game design mechanics development, proposal documentation, and prototype software development to demonstrate the game's core fun or pitching presentation. A typical project proposal includes game design, artwork, scenario, production method, production technology and engine, BM, marketing plan, operations plan and production plan, all of which are developed centered around the core mechanics of the game. Therefore, the final documentation is done by the game producer or game designer, but at this stage, a team with various artists, programmers, and marketers is formed and has been involved.

During the documentation process, the game's main mechanics, worldview, and scenarios are proposed by the game producer and game designer, so many of the game's arts are naturally proposed by them. When drawing concept art that describes the vision of the game and creating art resources for prototypes to be used in-game, game designers will suggest various keywords. They may use word clouds or perception maps to convey the image they have in mind. They also use search engines or curation services such as Pinterest to present the images they have in mind. This is where the collaboration between game designer and artist comes in. The following examples illustrate how and how much the process of creating these proposals differs between traditional way and with generative AI.

3. CASE 1: WALKING DEAD

Project Walking Dead approached the game proposal in a generic way. The production company ('the company', henceforth) had a license agreement with American publisher Skybound to gamify the Walking Dead IP, and wanted to develop an art concept that would be suitable for a video game, but still capture the ambience of the original Walking Dead IP. The art style of a video game is a different endeavor than that of a comic book, and because of the different levels and dimensions of details required for the medium means that the style of the original comic cannot be used directly. The company outsourced the artwork in July 2019, communicating the game genre and key game design elements, as well as information about the target market and various reference texts and images to illustrate the desired style. The work lasted about two months, with weekly discussions. The initial artwork was for one character, three zombies, and one background. Unfortunately, the style did not quite align with the game designer's original intentions and deemed unsatisfactory.

The designer spent three months planning and explaining the specific references, keywords, and uses of the artwork and requested the artwork to be redone based on the artwork that was in line with the original intention. The art concept development started again at the end of December 19 and lasted for another month.

In the second round of work, the design team was able to secure a number of concept designs that met the intent of the game design as requested. While the outsourced art company created the concept art, the internal development team implemented the core game mechanics created by the client programmers and game designers in collaboration. This was done by first prototyping with dummy images, and then replacing the dummy with real image once the artwork was complete. This process took a total of 7 months to create the game design mechanics, create the story and artwork to match the game design, and make the business pitch to Skybound in the U.S. and the company's investor after first coming up with the idea of developing a game based on The Walking Dead. Employed were 8 man-months per month, and specifically, 1 game producer, 1 game designer, 1 character artist, 1 background artist, 3 UI artists, 0,5 animators, and 0,5 client programmers. The total cost of labor and outsourcing was approximately KRW 157,500,000 (roughly equivalent to US$ 135,000 at the time of development).

The project Walking Dead demonstrated the importance of clear communication between game designers and art teams, as well as the need to plan and explain specific references and keywords to ensure that the artwork matches the original intention. It also highlights the significant investment of time, effort, and cost required to develop and pitch a successful video game.

The difficulty of sharing vision between game designers and artists and the delay in the iteration cycle is not an issue that only arises in the process of outsourcing. After the completion of the project pitching, the Walking Dead development team recruited in-house artists who had a similar style to the art used in the pitching in order to internalize the development power. The Walking Dead game required illustrations for over 100 different characters, and as many illustrations as the number of characters were demanded. In addition, the levels of artwork for the 100 or so characters should be appropriately distributed according to the designer's intention, from low to high levels, and the characteristics of the skills or attributes of each character should be reflected in the artwork. Therefore, each character illustration is a planned product drawn by an artist within the guided vision provided by the game designer. In this process, the artist intentionally creates low-quality artwork and clearly understands the intention of the game designer in order to reveal the functional characteristics of the character.

To create new characters, the game designer provides a 'Character Design Guide'. This document contains the external characteristics of the character, setting and story, function in the game, and art planning focused on costume and pose that the game wants to express. The game designer attaches reference images found through text and search engines to explain the characteristics of the character to be produced (Figure 1). Such guide is usually about 7 pages of PowerPoint document per each character and there were 100 characters so creating document just to communicate is a daunting task for the designer.

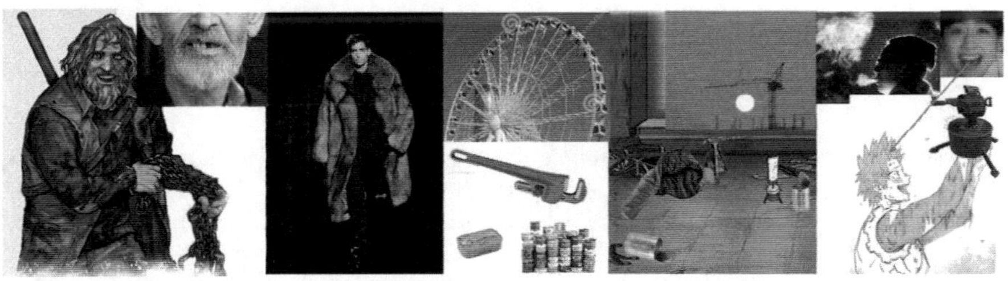

Figure 1. Example of images given for costume design and pose guide

The Costume design guide is provided with the following information:

- Consider the image provided, outfits look warm perhaps picked up from the luxury shop inside the building.
- Compared to the illustration, the image is relatively clean because it's from the past.
- Clothes have no blood on them but do not seem to have been washed in more than a few weeks.
- Shorter hair and beard
- Various tools for making traps

The pose guide is provided with the following information:

- Interior suggesting inside the High Rise Hell (skyscraper)
- The top of the Ferris wheel that can be seen out the big window tells that the building is a skyscraper in Atlanta. The sun is setting so the reddish light seeps into the room.

- Crudely made turrets and uninstalled traps are scattered around the room.
- Here and there, refrigerator food packages and opened cans of food are rolling around. There's an old sleeping bag in the corner with the shape of a human impression.
- Beaming looking up the camera and seems satisfied with the birth of a masterpiece (the turret)
- The facial expression would convey the state of confusion best when looking directly like the image provided. White breath to show that it is cold

Upon receiving the game designer's instructions, the artist listens to the plan and proceeds with the sketch. After the sketch stage, a colored version that can convey the original's feel is created, and at this stage, the direction is checked with the game designer. When the consultation is completed at this stage, the final coloring is done, and the character illustration is completed.

On average, it takes three days for the game designer to come up with the character's ideas and write a 'character design guide'. After that, it takes one day to explain and sketch to the artist, and one day to color the base and reflect feedback from the game designer. After that, it takes two days to finish coloring. As a result, it takes at least 7 days to produce a new character illustration. In the "character design guide" stage, modification of the plan is required, or additional time is required depending on the feedback of the work after the sketch (Figure 2).

Figure 2. Approved sketch to coloring and completed image

4. CASE 2: PROJECT NOX

Once the game mechanics were agreed upon between investors and designers, Project NOX began by creating the world and artwork that would appeal to the target audience. During this process, generative AI was actively used to generate character and background artwork and write new scenarios. The designer would organize keywords related to the concepts he had in mind and then prompt Midjourney to generate images, a process that was virtually identical to outsourcing concept art on previous projects, but with immediate results and the opportunity to spark additional ideas and make numerous revisions and experiments with the deliverables. In addition to the time and cost savings, there was a realization that there basically was no need to have to make any effort to communicate with the outsourced artists and avoided the inefficient process of receiving artwork, discussing revisions, receiving the revised artwork and communicating the revisions back, or having to find an artist again if the desired output level was not met. Achieved results were impressive in creating illustrations of specific characters, story scenes, loading screens, title screens, etc. In the process of creating the UI, it was also very helpful in generating various icons and original artwork required for the UI. Generative AI proved to be a great co-worker by stimulating the imagination of human designers and generating and showing them what they envisioned, with remarkable speed and efficiency. Only by this time the designer assembled a team of 3 ('the team', henceforth) with an assistant designer and an artist to make detailed adjustments to the generated outputs.

The design goal was a game that blended Simcity-like city-building with RPG elements and needed to come up with compelling concept artwork. The market sensing phase yielded the following keywords 'Voxel', 'Warcraft3 style deform', and 'supercell color'. Using these three keywords as the focus of the Midjourney prompt commands, generated a representative building image, a windmill.

The team generated an image of a windmill by repeatedly requesting regeneration using the same prompt command until the image matched the windmill's imagined form. Since the first prompt produced a result quite close to the desired image, regeneration was performed without changing the prompt. A total of 77 windmill images were generated, and the process took approximately 6 hours. 76 unselected windmills were rejected due to awkward or unintended voxel cube size or poor shape. During this process, the same prompt that created the final selected artwork was continually used, and Midjourney created various images with the same prompt command (Figure 3).

Figure 3. Selected windmill image (large image) and various rejected windmill images (small images)

The designer also created characters in the same way as the building was created. According to the first visual concept, the team tried to create a character of the voxel image and created characters from classes commonly found in RPG games. Archer was created as a representative character, and this process took 40 minutes. After setting keywords that can determine styles while creating buildings, it became relatively easy to create similar styles of artwork. In order to create a character, various prompts were entered and repeated until the desired artwork was obtained.

The team wants to develop an Archer character design that incorporated multiple stylistic elements, including voxel graphics, Warcraft 3-style deformations, Supercell-inspired colors, and a dynamic pose that effectively conveyed the action of firing arrows. To accomplish this goal, the team input several prompts to generate Archer characters that aligned with team's design objectives. Additionally, the team included specific keywords such as bow usage, attacking and shooting an arrow, to generate a posture that accurately reflected the character's role as an archer. To further refine the design, the character images were generated repeatedly with the same prompt until the desired appearance was achieved. This iterative approach allowed us to enhance the character's visual impact and optimize the design for maximum aesthetic appeal (Table 1).

Table 1. Generated archer images with various prompt

Result	Images	Prompt
Selecte		voxel 3d, voxel pixel art of supercell color, Medieval archer character, game character, using a bow, attacking, shooting an arrow,' witty shape, large top and small bottom, warcraft character shape, isometric voxel::3, bright atmosphere, vivid colors, made with three-dimensional pixels, super deformed, pixel art intricate, pixel art, hd, 3d, unreal engine, realistic photograph, hyper real hyper detailed. diorama, mounted on a square pedestal with multicolored tiles. bright background, full frame shot --q 5 --ar 2:3 --s 800 --no beard --no cross --no skull
Rejecte		voxel 3d, voxel pixel art of supercell color, Medieval archer character, game character, witty shape, large top and small bottom, warcraft character shape, isometric voxel::3, bright atmosphere, vivid colors, made with three-dimensional pixels, super deformed, pixel art intricate, pixel art, hd, 3d, unreal engine, realistic photograph, hyper real hyper detailed. diorama, mounted on a square pedestal with multicolored tiles. bright background, full frame shot --q 5 --ar 2:3 --s 800 --no beard --no cross --no skull
Rejecte	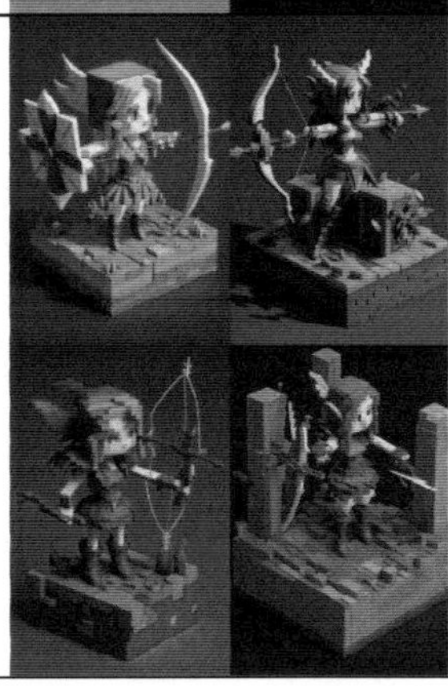	voxel 3d, voxel pixel art of supercell color, Medieval archer character, game character, using a bow with both hands, attacking, witty shape, large top and small bottom, warcraft character shape, isometric voxel::3, bright atmosphere, vivid colors, made with three-dimensional pixels, super deformed, pixel art intricate, pixel art, hd, 3d, unreal engine, realistic photograph, hyper real hyper detailed. diorama, mounted on a square pedestal with multicolored tiles. bright background, full frame shot --q 5 --ar 2:3 --s 800 --no beard --no cross --no skull

Following the creation of a character using Midjourney, a paired illustration based on this image was generated using Novel AI, which proved to be efficient. In the game, voxel characters are used as in-game resources, while illustrations can be used as images to be displayed on character acquisition and picture screens. Novel AI was suitable for such purposes because it creates illustrations while maintaining a sense of shape and pose. However, the shape of the fingers was unnatural, and the perspective was awkward. Moreover, it was challenging to produce other styles as it was created mainly with images that were close to anime-styles. The process of creating the illustration took place within an hour, and the quality was evaluated as a result that could be applicable for the game if a human designer polished a generated artwork.

Table 2. Combination of artwork from Midjourney and artwork from Novel AI

Character Type	Generated by Midjourney	Generated by Novel AI	Prompt for Novel AI
Archer			american game art style, archer character, rpg game character, masterpiece, highres, high_quality, high_quality_anime, high_resolution, sidelighting, super detail, hyper detail, intricate_details, detailed *sth*, {{archer}}, sleeveless green onepiece wear, green hair band, white long bow, blond short hair, bowstring pose Strength: 0.75 Noise: 0.03

The Designer's next attempt was to create concept art for the game's main character, utilizing Midjourney to generate as many different images of the same person as possible, given the same prompt. The result was an illustration that, while slightly different, could be categorized as a character from the same game. Images could not be used as game resources in an animated form, but still useful to share the designer's vision by showing different aspects of the characters to describe the game world. For the main character concept art, the team decided on the following character. "A small, student character around 15 years old, wearing a hooded sweatshirt and leather boots, carrying a backpack going on an adventure." The description as in 'Concept image' from Table 3 was applied to Midjourney.

Midjourney allows for the inclusion of images as well as text in the prompt. The generated criterion was used to assemble the image of the character with a different appearance. The "https://s.mj.run/pZdrd5MQY_c" component in the prompt refers to the link of the reference image used, and the command was entered to reference the image which is 'Concept image' in Table3. As a result of execution of prompt that shown in Table 3, three different images (image1, image2, image3 in Table 3) were created that were thought to be the same character as the original concept image. However, not all of the desired settings were applied as anticipated. Specifically, the study attempted to create a fantasy in which a part of the character was transformed into a voxel but was unsuccessful in doing so. Generating unlearned results that were not generally accepted was a challenge still.

Table 3. Main character concept artwork and variation art works generated with Midjourney

Image Type	Generated Image	prompt
Concept image		a school girl with a back pack, Floating slightly in space where voxel 3d pixels are happening on the floor, Part of it is changing to voxel 3d, 3d illustration, front view, A schoolgirl looking at her hands in amazement, both hands turning into voxels, Two hands are in voxel 3d, Hooded sweatshirt, leather boots, Amazing anime style + tanned skin + impressive detailed doe eyes + intricate detailed brown hair + detailed face + smug expression + wear headphone, intricate hyperdetailed outfit, doe eyes, dynamic pose, very very cool and gorgeous illustration, hyperrealistic, octane render, hyper realistic, detailed petrified angel, location tomb, ultra detailed, dynamic lighting, atmospheric lighting, natural light effect, 32k, super-resolution, intricate, cgi
image 1		<https://s.mj.run/pZdrd5MQY_c> a school girl with a back pack, Floating slightly in space where voxel 3d pixels are happening on the floor, Part of it is changing to voxel 3d, 3d illustration, front view, A schoolgirl looking at her hands in amazement, both hands turning into voxels, Two hands are in voxel 3d, voxel 3d, Hooded sweatshirt, leather boots, Amazing anime style + tanned skin + impressive detailed doe eyes + intricate detailed brown hair + detailed face + smug expression + wear headphone, intricate hyperdetailed outfit, doe eyes, dynamic pose, very very cool and gorgeous illustration, hyperrealistic, octane render, hyper realistic, detailed petrified angel, location tomb, ultra detailed, dynamic lighting, atmospheric lighting, natural light effect, 32k, super-resolution, intricate, cgi --ar 9:16 --v 4 --no backside
image 2		<https://s.mj.run/pZdrd5MQY_c> a schoolgirl with a back pack, Part of it is changing to voxel 3d, 3d illustration, front view, A schoolgirl looking at her hands in amazement, both hands turning into voxels, Two hands are in voxel 3d, voxel 3d, Hooded sweatshirt, leather boots, Amazing anime style + tanned skin + impressive detailed doe eyes + intricate detailed brown hair + detailed face + smug expression + wear headphone, intricate hyperdetailed outfit, doe eyes, dynamic pose, very very cool and gorgeous illustration, hyperrealistic, octane render, hyper realistic, detailed petrified angel, location tomb, ultra detailed, dynamic lighting, atmospheric lighting, natural light effect, 32k, super-resolution, intricate, cgi --ar 9:16 --v 4 --no backside
image 3		<https://s.mj.run/pZdrd5MQY_c> 3d illustration. a schoolgirl with a backpack. She is making a surprised expression while looking at her hand. Light Blue Hooded sweatshirt. Dark Blue Short Skirt. Brown leather boots. Blue Backpack. Amazing anime style + tanned skin + impressive detailed doe eyes + intricate detailed brown hair + detailed face + smug expression + wear headphone, intricate hyperdetailed outfit, doe eyes, dynamic pose, very very cool and gorgeous illustration, hyperrealistic, octane render, hyper realistic, detailed petrified angel, location tomb, ultra detailed, dynamic lighting, atmospheric lighting, natural light effect, 32k, super-resolution, intricate, cgi --ar 9:16 --v 4 --no backside --s 300

The game designer was required to create both concept artwork and simplified voxel characters to reside in a virtual village. Using Midjourney, the designer produced Minecraft-like voxel characters that were suitable for the concept image. The prompt was created by adding two reference images. In the case of simplified voxel characters, the density of descriptions is reduced, allowing for recognition of the same character based on matching hair color, hair style, shirts color, and skirt color. A prompt was then written based on such observation.

Surprisingly, during the execution of the prompt, Midjourney automatically generated an image that was assumed to be the back of the same character. Although the image was not intentionally created to depict the same person, as the description of the bag was not the same, it was possible to generate multiple images with different compositions in one frame simultaneously, as shown in Table 4. Once a suitable method for generating multiple angles of the same person is found, this could be very useful. A repeated attempt to generate different compositions of the same character was ultimately unsuccessful.

Table 4. Generation of simplified voxel art matching concept illustration

Input images	Generated Image	prompt
		<https://s.mj.run/353L2oymjPY>, <https://s.mj.run/-5r6L5slacM> Draw a student character made with the exact voxel standard. Draw the x-axis, y-axis, and z-axis in a standardized form so that they do not clump or diverge, girl with backpack, Gender: Female, Archetype: Adventurer, Body Type: Small, Hairstyle: ponytail, Scheme: Brown and Blue, Clothing: light blue hooded T-Shirt and dark blue Shorts, Features: Small and Cute, Wide Eyes, Button Nose --s 300

However, during the development process, it became apparent that the technology has certain limitations that can affect the quality of the final output. One of the major limitations of Generative AI was observed with Midjourney, which often generated images with incorrect perspective and incorrect number of fingers, particularly with character images. Additionally, the tool was not effective in generating multiple poses of the same character and could not generate the necessary resources to create sprite animations.

The study also evaluated the use of Novel AI and Stable Diffusion, which generate images based on sketches. However, the images generated by these tools did not align with the intended design objectives, and often produced images with a different feel than what was desired. Table 5 highlights an example in which a sketch of a building was inputted into Novel AI to generate a voxel-style building. However, when increasing the style, the shape was not maintained, and when a value was set to maintain the shape, the style was not applied, resulting in an undesired image.

Table 5. How variation in prompt changes the image in Novel AI, following prompt "building, voxel style, masterpiece, high-res, high-quality, high-quality-anime Strength: (variable) Noise: 0.03"

Input sketch	Strength 0.3	Strength 0.4	Strength 0.5	Strength 0.6	Strength 0.66

There were other limitations in the use of generative AI. Firstly, despite numerous repetitions, the design of the user interface (UI) was not successful, and efforts to create a storyboard for opening video did not yield meaningful results. Secondly, looking to generate something entirely original would not work as keywords such as 'never seen before' were not effective. In light of these challenges, it is recommended that designers aim to generate images with a meaningful difference rather than images that are beyond pre-trained models.

5. CONCLUSION

This study highlights the emergence of a new era in which designers and artists who possess the skills to create effective and creative prompts, and who have access to super assistants such as Midjourney, Stable Diffusion, and Novel AI creative, can become a 'super game designer'. Aside from cost and time savings, the most significant difference for game designers is the ability to visualize their creative thoughts without losing them in communication. However, the designer could now broaden the domain of game design even further. For example, the game designers can narrow down what kind of game they want to make without the help of marketing or strategy departments by using market sensing, that is, testing what kind of format, genre, and visuals the market responds to by sending out feelers made with generative AI. Furthermore, with very well-structured trained designers can even create a playable prototype by generating the necessary C# code for Unity3D using a service such as chatGPT. This would be a huge change from the traditional game design process and would actually change the production phase and the overall structure of how game companies do the business. While generative AI has the potential to revolutionize the game design process, there are still limitations and challenges that must be addressed to fully realize its potential.

ACKNOWLEDGEMENT

This research was conducted based on a case study developed with the support of research funding from FLASK.

REFERENCES

Cardamone, L. et al. (2011, July). Interactive evolution for the procedural generation of tracks in a high-end racing game. In *Proceedings of the 13th annual conference on Genetic and evolutionary computation* (pp. 395-402).

Funge, J. D. (1999). *AI for games and animation: a cognitive modeling approach*. AK Peters/CRC Press.

Guzdial, M. et al. (2019, May). Friend, collaborator, student, manager: How design of an ai-driven game level editor affects creators. In *Proceedings of the 2019 CHI conference on human factors in computing systems* (pp. 1-13).

Hartsook, K. et al. (2011, August). Toward supporting stories with procedurally generated game worlds. In *2011 IEEE Conference on Computational Intelligence and Games (CIG'11)* (pp. 297-304). IEEE.

Hendrikx, M. et al. (2013). Procedural content generation for games: A survey. *ACM Transactions on Multimedia Computing, Communications, and Applications (TOMM)*, *9*(1), 1-22.

Jaruga-Rozdolska, A. (2022). Artificial intelligence as part of future practices in the architect's work: MidJourney generative tool as part of a process of creating an architectural form. *Architectus*.

Karpouzis, K., & Tsatiris, G. A. (2022). AI in (and for) Games. *Advances in Machine Learning/Deep Learning-based Technologies: Selected Papers in Honour of Professor Nikolaos G. Bourbakis–Vol. 2*, 27-43.

Lara-Cabrera, R. et al, (2012, November). Procedural map generation for a RTS game. In *13th International GAME-ON Conference on Intelligent Games and Simulation* (pp. 53-58). Malaga (Spain): Eurosis.

Mehta, A. et al., (2022, February). Exploring the viability of Conversational AI for Non-Playable Characters: A comprehensive survey. In *2021 4th International Conference on Recent Trends in Computer Science and Technology (ICRTCST)* (pp. 96-102). IEEE.

Oh, I. et al., (2021). Creating pro-level AI for a real-time fighting game using deep reinforcement learning. *IEEE Transactions on Games*, *14*(2), 212-220.

Perez-Liebana, D. et al., (2019). General video game ai: A multitrack framework for evaluating agents, games, and content generation algorithms. *IEEE Transactions on Games*, *11*(3), 195-214.. General video game ai: A multitrack framework for evaluating agents, games, and content generation algorithms. *IEEE Transactions on Games*, *11*(3), 195-214.

Ploennigs, J., & Berger, M. (2022). AI Art in Architecture. *arXiv preprint arXiv:2212.09399.*

Riedl, M. O., & Zook, A. (2013, August). AI for game production. In *2013 IEEE Conference on Computational Intelligence in Games (CIG)* (pp. 1-8). IEEE.

Zhao, M. (2020, December). Analysis on the connection between nonplayer character and artificial intelligence. In *2020 International Conference on Intelligent Computing and Human-Computer Interaction (ICHCI)* (pp. 105-108). IEEE.

TEACHING METHODS FOR SHARING THE CREATION OF ELECTROACOUSTIC MUSIC WITH INEXPERIENCED PEOPLE

Miki Matsumoto[1], Takumi Mashita, Soma Arai[1],
Hidefumi Ohmura[2], Hiroyuki Yaguchi[1] and Takuro Shibayama[1,3]
[1]*Tokyo Denki University*
Ishizaka, Hatoyama, Hiki, Saitama 350-0394, Japan
[2]*Tokyo University of Science*
2641 Yamazaki, Noda, Chiba 278-0022, Japan
[3]*Tokyo Collage of Music*
1-9-1 Kamimeguro, Meguro, Tokyo 153-0051, Japan

ABSTRACT

Our lab holds a workshop using computers to create electroacoustic music (EAM) for a variety of inexperienced people. Since EAM is positioned as an extension of contemporary music, which has a large philosophical component, it has not gained as many creators and listeners as popular music. The reason for this may be that, compared to music meant for entertainment, both the structure in music theory and the concepts in expressive practice create the impression among many people that EAM is difficult to understand. However, we observed that numerous people enjoy creating EAM in workshops. This may be because EAM is created not by following the rules of ordinary music theory, but by producing a montage of sound materials formed from fragments of recorded sounds along a computer timeline, allowing the listener to hear a near-perfect acoustic representation in real time through intuitive manipulation. Through our creative method, we taught participants to capture their impressions of fragmented acoustic materials using metaphorical adjective pairs such as 'high–low' and 'hard–soft' and to maintain the intensity of the contrast between them. This study is based on an analysis of the works created in university courses that share the same teaching techniques as our workshops. The analytical procedure of the present study was as follows: (1) We selected an 'excellent' completed piece of music. (2) We individually extracted the acoustic materials that made up the piece. (3) We used pairwise comparison to examine the participants' impressions of all acoustic materials used in the given piece. (4) We carried out an analysis to determine whether the original piece maintained a high degree of contrast in the impression of the acoustic materials, thereby validating our instructional technique, which we empirically derived from past workshops.

KEYWORDS

Computer Music, Electroacoustic Music, Educational Method, Pedagogy

1. INTRODUCTION

'Contemporary music' originates in the breakdown of tonality that emerged from the end of the 19th century to the beginning of the 20th century, the subsequent practice of creating atonal music in the early 1900s, and the creation of noise music by the Italian Futurists of the 1910s. Electroacoustic music (EAM) was first produced in France in the late 1940s; it is also known as *musique concrète*, established by Pierre Schaeffer (1910–1995) in France and as *Electronische Musik*, established by Herbert Eimert (1897–1972) and Karlheinz Stockhausen (1928–2007) in Germany. While 'electronic music' involves the use of generators to synthesise sounds and compose music, 'concrete music' is characterised by the fact that it is produced not by 'musical sounds' played on musical instruments but by 'unpitched sounds' recorded on media (such as records and magnetic tapes) and their montage (Brindle, 1987). Nowadays, with the development of digital sound processing technology and the low cost of computers, the boundary between 'concrete music' and 'electronic music' has become blurred, and music created with both technologies is collectively called 'electroacoustic music' or EAM. Currently, EAM continues to be spread through education and culture in specialised institutions and in universities with information and arts departments.

2. THE POSSIBILITY OF EAM BEING ENJOYED BY EVERYONE

2.1 The Possibilities Offered by the Experience of Creating EAM

EAM, like other contemporary music, seems 'esoteric' to most people; for this reason, it has not gained many listeners or creators. Ordinary music may consist of a totality of acts, such as singing or dancing to a beat, either in a 'chorus' or an 'ensemble'. Such musical acts can be viewed auspiciously as a kind of 'musicking' that encompasses the totality of the act (Small, 1998). The creative workshops that we conduct involve producing 'concrete music' as part of EAM. In other words, the music generated in the workshops does not have the rhythm, melody, or harmony of normal music. This creative approach is based on (1) the use of objects in daily life that are not musical instruments brought in by the participants; (2) recording sounds by hitting or rubbing the objects together or against other objects; (3) creating acoustic materials by further fragmenting and processing the recorded sounds; and (4) composing a montage of the acoustic materials (Shibayama et al, 2021). Another reason why EAM has not attracted many listeners and creators is that it is positioned as an extension of contemporary music, which many people often perceive as difficult. Contemporary music belongs to the latter category in the division between entertainment and philosophical music, which began in the early 1900s and was closely linked to Adorno's later emphasis on contemporary music as avant-garde to cultivate a critical spirit toward the consumerist society that emerged with the rise of popular music (Adorno, 1962).

Shibayama reported his experience from practice that EAM tends to seem 'difficult' to many people, while its creation can be enjoyable for many inexperienced individuals (Shibayama et al 2018, 2020). Thus, we considered it necessary to understand the structure of EAM from the perspective of cognitive science, and we explicitly addressed the validity of our creative teaching method. We believe this clarification will help to expand the realm of the mind such that more people can enjoy EAM.

2.2 Understanding the Structure of EAM

To achieve the abovementioned aims, we must first understand the structure of EAM from the standpoint of cognitive science. Concrete music is characterised by the fact that it is composed of a montage of non-musical recorded acoustic material, so it is considered difficult to position its creation as an extension of traditional compositional techniques. Non-musical recorded sound is 'unpitched'; this is distinguished in music theory from 'musical sound', which has musical elements (such as pitch) played by usical instruments. In ordinary music, the structure of transitive articulations is based on music theory, consisting of 'musical tones', whereas in 'concrete music', the acoustic material does not have a clear pitch in the first place, so the structure cannot be analysed according to conventional music theory. Schaeffer (1966) compiled this theoretical system of concrete music into a systematic theory in 1966. However, his creative theory is limited to the morphological classification of acoustic materials and conceptualization based on Saussure's linguistics, and is not based on the acquisition of quantitative data during listening by the listeners.

Roy (2004) detailed methods and examples of analysis of EAM by Nattiez, TenHoopen, and Delalande, among others. Nevertheless, their analyses are rooted in the work of each established composer and his/her respective discourse; hence, their analyses cannot be considered studies for purposes such as how the broader public perceives a given work. On the other hand, the tool designed by Couprie to visualize the structure of electroacoustic music is considered one of the most practical approaches at present (Couprie, 2016).

However, the application of these research on the composition of EAM through cognitive experimental testing remains unexplored.

2.3 Goals of this Study

We aimed to establish a practical theory for sharing the creation of EAM—which many people perceive as difficult—with multiple individuals. The basis for this is the three possibilities offered by the creation of EAM for educational purposes:

(a) EAM is fundamentally different from conventional musical composition rooted in music theory, allowing for repeated trial and error while listening to a creation directly on the spot.

(b) Since the goal of completion is not grounded in the concepts of right or wrong in relation to music theory norms, everyone has a chance to experience the creation involved, regardless of lever of expertise.

(c) The creator can experience the process of discovering and solving his/her own problems.

We aimed to (1) share the process of feeling joy in creating music, which is difficult for many people to achieve; (2) explicitly address the reasons for the 'fun' felt by the participants using quantitative data; (3) to establish these data as an educational model; and (4) to propose and share the model's usefulness with society. In other words, we identified factors that transform 'previously unenjoyable experiences' into 'enjoyable experiences' for numerous inexperienced people and we propose expanding the notion of enjoyment. Shibayama (2018) proposed the process as the Figure 1, which refers a state that only A can be accepted as enjoyable music, on the other hands, the centre refers a state that A and B are able to be accepted as enjoyable music with the expansion of the mind. Creative attitude directs the right end that exploring the out of A, B and C as an universal realm of human mind. Such a mental orientations can explore D, E and F that are not shown in the figure. As a small step toward fulfilling this purpose, we analysed music composed by inexperienced individuals and verified whether our creative instruction was appropriate.

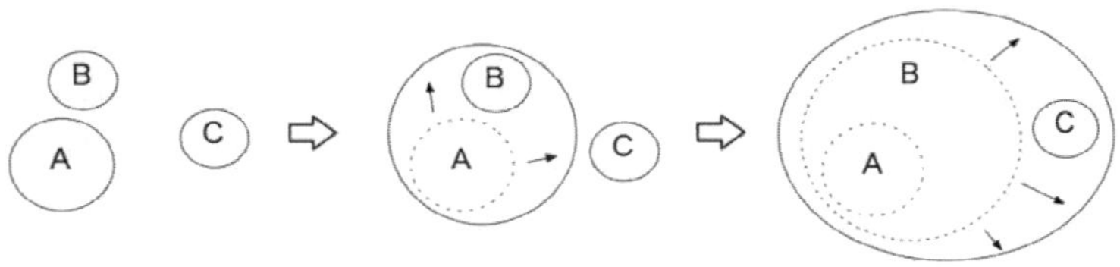

Figure 1. Expansion of the mental realm and enjoyable music (Shibayama, 2018)

3. VERIFICATION OF THE HYPOTHESIS

We attempted to determine the validity of ours and others' workshops, as well as university methods for teaching creative music composition. The instructions consisted of the following steps: (a) attaching figurative language labels to fragments of acoustic material; (b) maintaining a high contrast in the figurative language labels; and (c) completing the resulting work in such a way that movement could be felt. We hypothesised that 'from the works completed as a result of creative instruction, a high degree of contrast in metaphorical language labels may be maintained in the arrangement over time of fragments of acoustic material used in pieces that were rated as "moving" by the instructors' and verified the hypothesis.

3.1 Methods of Teaching Composition Practice as a Prerequisite for the Hypothesis

To verify the hypothesis, we decided to test its validity in teaching sound design in 'Introduction to Formative Design', a course for first-year students enrolled in the Department of Information Systems Design at the Faculty of Science and Engineering at Tokyo Denki University in Japan. We targeted the completed works of this class for analysis because (1) it was difficult to hold the workshop due to COVID-19; and (2) this class was designed in accordance with the teaching methods used in previous workshops, so it was appropriate as a target for analysis.

The flow of the practice was as follows:

(a) the distribution of sound materials for use in creation;

(b) instruction on montage techniques using Digital Audio Workstation (DAW) software;
(c) instruction in sound editing in DAW software;
(d) montage instruction based on linguistic figurative impressions of, and contrasts with, the acoustic material used.

In class, the teacher demonstrated the operation to the learners, and they were given one week to complete a 10-second piece of music as homework. In the off-campus workshop, we started by recording the sound materials to be used, but in 'Introduction to Formative Design', because the time for creation was limited, we distributed seven pre-prepared sound materials, which all students used to create their own music. As a creative point to keep in mind regarding the above (b), the sound material could not be used as it was. Instead, very short fragments of .1 to .5 seconds had to be cut from the given sound materials, and these fragments had to be woven into a montage. The reason for this was that the given acoustic materials lasted from one second to a few seconds; therefore, if the original acoustic materials had been montaged as they were, there was a chance that musical 'movement' might not be fully created. In addition, d) in this flow is the pillar of this study, the teaching method that encourages participants to be aware of the metaphorical impressions of the fragmented acoustic materials. As a result, they imagined their impressions of each acoustic material by relying on the five figurative attributes of *height*, *length*, *hardness*, *coldness*, and *smoothness*, and they were told to create a montage by considering the contrasts of their impressions.

3.2 Selection of the Target Piece and Analysis of the Acoustic Sound Fragments

Among the pieces produced by the students during the training, we selected one piece that we deeply evaluated and dismantled for each of the acoustic fragments that made up the piece. We based our selection on the effectiveness of the teaching method, i.e. the aurally evident characteristics of the piece exhibiting movement. Because the piece consisted of seven sounds and one reverse-playback processed sound (a total of eight sound fragments), we labelled these eight fragments of acoustic material as A–H according to their temporal order of appearance. F is the acoustic material played backwards from E. We obtained the results (see Table 1) by counting the acoustic materials used in the music.

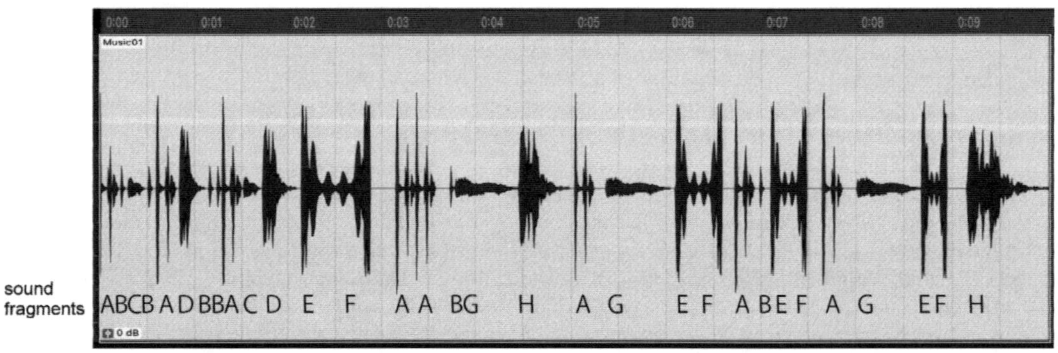

Figure 2. Results of the analysis of sound fragments composing a piece of music

Table 1. Acoustic materials, labelled A–H, that appear in the music and the number of times they appear

Sound fragments	A	B	C	D	E	F	G	H
Number of appearances	8	6	2	2	4	4	3	2

3.3 Preparing the Experiment to Capture Participants' Impressions

To examine the participants' impressions of the sound fragments, we conducted our preliminary experiment in June 2021; we administered a questionnaire using the semantic differential (SD) method on a 5-point scale and obtained online responses from the participants.

To perform the experiment, we needed to quantify the participants' relative impressions of the sound fragments; hence, we decided to use pairwise comparison to scrutinise all sound fragments that made up the analysed piece. The next issue was that the number of items on the questionnaire would increase, and the response time would increase if all eight acoustic materials were compared. A longer response time heightened the possibility of causing participants to lose their focus. Consequently, there was concern that it would be difficult to ensure the accuracy of the results. To solve this problem, we decided to investigate the participants' impressions in the following way:

(a) We constructed mixed groups of α, β, and γ with all participants, carefully ensuring that the number of students in each group was equal.

(b) We created a reduced set of fragments of the target acoustic materials for each group.

(c) In order to align the relative impressions between all sets of fragments, each set contained identical fragments for reference.

(d) We equalised the number of questionnaire items for each group.

As we used pairwise comparison to capture the participants' relative impressions, we determined that the overall findings could be obtained by adding the results procured for each group. By dividing the set of participants and the set of fragments to be auditioned into several groups, we considerably reduced the time required for each participant to answer the items. Because our preliminary experiment confirmed the methodology, we decided to conduct the main experiment with a larger number of participants.

Table 2. Groups of participants and sound material fragments

Groups for the questionnaire	Sets of sound material fragments
α	A, B, C, F
β	C, D, E, F
γ	E, F, G, H

3.4 Participants

In December 2021, we conducted an experiment to capture 30 participants' impressions using a one-pair comparison method. We recruited the participants in two ways. First, we selected participants from among students who had taken the music composition class. We selected eight participants based on the condition that their reports on music composition practice contain many words and excellent content. Second, we chose 22 participants by recruiting students who had no experience in music composition practice; these students were studying at the Tokyo University of Science and had not had the opportunity to create EAM or to listen to it on a regular basis. We recruited all participants and explained the study's content via e-mail.

3.5 Items of the Questionnaire

We created the questionnaire using Google Forms and used the audition materials for pairwise comparison with the Google Drive sharing function. The questionnaire consisted of Section 1, which contained items about gender, age, occupation, musical genres, and musical experiences, and Section 2, which entailed participants' impressions of the audition materials (obtained via pairwise comparison) to identify the attributes. We set up the impressions of sound fragments along five axes consisting of items about *length*, *height*, *hardness*, *coldness*, and *smoothness* based on the adjectives used in the practice. The questionnaire asked, For instance, when the questionnaire asked about the impression of length 'Which of the two acoustic materials seems longer?' By the same way, we replaced *length* with *height, hardness*, *coolness*, and *smoothness*, respectively.

3.6 Grouping of Participants and the Question Sets

In order to evaluate the participants' impressions through pairwise comparison, we divided the eight acoustic materials, labelled A–H, into three groups of four tones each, and we classified each group as α, β, and γ (see Table 2). We included common acoustic materials in each group. The common sounds were used as a basis for merging the results of the questionnaire for α, β, and γ. To eliminate variations in response conditions among the groups, we prepared several versions of the questionnaire with the same number of sounds in the set of acoustic materials, and we shuffled the order of the items on each questionnaire. We also did this to remove the influence of the order in which the participants listened to the acoustic materials on their impressions of the sounds. To shuffle the items on the questionnaire for this purpose, a uniform random number was generated by computer and we manually rearranged the order of the items based on the output of the numbers. We did this because Google Forms does not have such a function, although it would be ideal for the items to be shuffled at the time of submission.

4. RESULTS

4.1 Results: Capturing Participants' Impressions Through Pairwise Comparison

We asked a total of 30 participants divided into three groups (α, β, and γ) to compare their impressions of *length*, *low*, *hardness*, *coldness*, and *smoothness* of the four sound fragments assigned to each group in a round-robin fashion. After evaluating the impressions for each group, we integrated the results for the three groups to obtain the outcomes (see Figure 5).

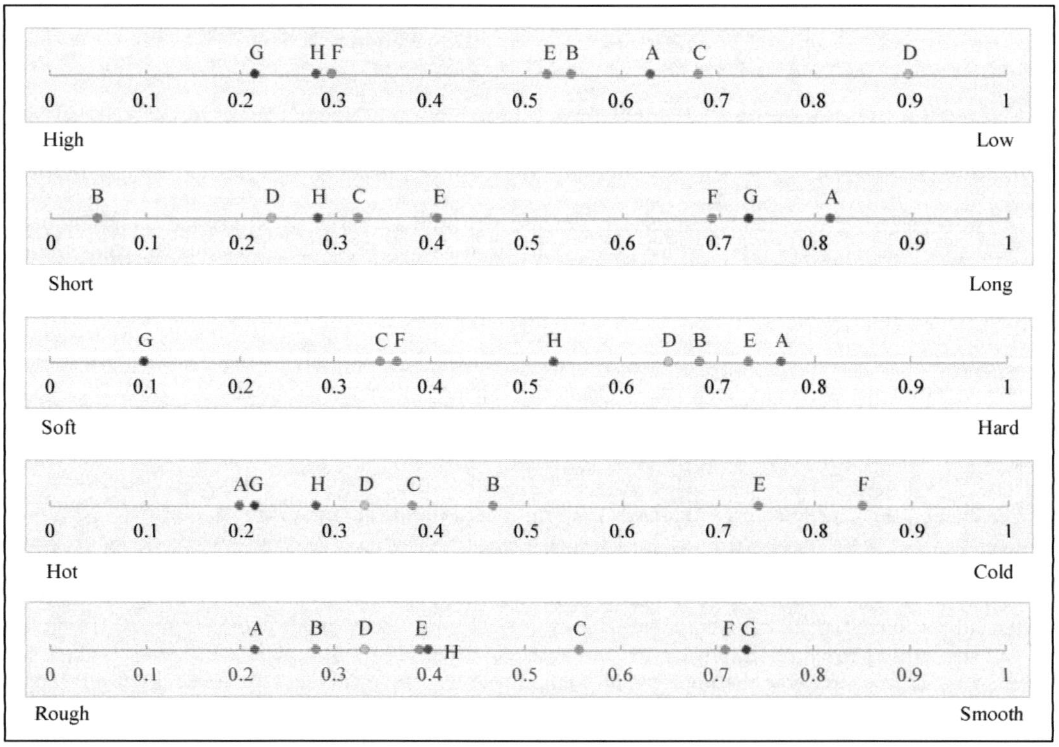

Figure 3. Results of the participants' overall impressions

4.2 Re-analysis of the Piece Based on Data Obtained from Pairwise Comparison

We plotted the acoustic materials in the range of 0 and 1 in each index of *length*, *height*, *hardness*, *coldness*, and *smoothness*; it is possible to clearly show the relative relationships among all acoustic materials in each index. Based on these relationships, we analysed the original musical pieces by examining the amount of contrast in each index in chronological order of the acoustic materials of the original musical piece (see Figure 3). We obtained the data presented in Figure 4 by administering the questionnaire with the original music. The differences in impressions from the immediately preceding sounds are outlined in figures 5 and 6. In previous classes, we taught students that it is possible to compose musical movements by maintaining a high contrast in figurative images. When we applied the data to the temporal arrangement of the acoustic materials of the original piece, we found that the original piece had a high contrast in adjective pairs. Our results demonstrate the validity of this approach.

	A	B	C	B	A	D	B	B	A	C	D	E	F	A	A	B	G	H	A	G	E	F	A	B	E	F	A	G	E	F	H
High - Low	0.63	0.55	0.68	0.55	0.63	0.9	0.55	0.55	0.63	0.68	0.9	0.53	0.3	0.63	0.63	0.55	0.22	0.28	0.63	0.22	0.53	0.3	0.63	0.55	0.53	0.3	0.63	0.22	0.53	0.3	0.28
Short - Long	0.82	0.05	0.33	0.05	0.82	0.23	0.05	0.05	0.82	0.33	0.23	0.41	0.69	0.82	0.82	0.05	0.73	0.28	0.82	0.73	0.41	0.69	0.82	0.05	0.41	0.69	0.82	0.73	0.41	0.69	0.28
Soft - Hard	0.77	0.68	0.35	0.68	0.77	0.65	0.68	0.68	0.77	0.35	0.65	0.73	0.37	0.77	0.77	0.68	0.1	0.53	0.77	0.1	0.73	0.37	0.77	0.68	0.73	0.37	0.77	0.1	0.73	0.37	0.53
Hot - Cold	0.2	0.47	0.38	0.47	0.2	0.33	0.47	0.47	0.2	0.38	0.33	0.74	0.85	0.2	0.2	0.47	0.22	0.28	0.2	0.22	0.74	0.85	0.2	0.47	0.74	0.85	0.2	0.22	0.74	0.85	0.28
Roug - Smooth	0.22	0.28	0.56	0.28	0.22	0.33	0.28	0.28	0.22	0.56	0.33	0.39	0.71	0.22	0.22	0.28	0.73	0.4	0.22	0.73	0.39	0.71	0.22	0.28	0.39	0.71	0.22	0.73	0.39	0.71	0.4

Figure 4. Data obtained by applying the survey results to the original piece

	A	B	C	B	A	D	B	B	A	C	D	E	F	A	A	B	G	H	A	G	E	F	A	B	E	F	A	G	E	F	H
High - Low	—	0.08	0.13	0.13	0.08	0.27	0.35	0	0.08	0.05	0.22	0.38	0.23	0.33	0	0.08	0.33	0.07	0.35	0.42	0.31	0.23	0.33	0.08	0.03	0.23	0.33	0.42	0.31	0.23	0.02
Short - Long	—	0.77	0.28	0.28	0.77	0.58	0.18	0	0.77	0.49	0.09	0.18	0.29	0.12	0	0.77	0.68	0.45	0.53	0.08	0.33	0.29	0.12	0.77	0.36	0.29	0.12	0.08	0.33	0.29	0.41
Soft - Hard	—	0.08	0.33	0.33	0.08	0.12	0.03	0	0.08	0.42	0.3	0.08	0.37	0.4	0	0.08	0.58	0.43	0.24	0.67	0.63	0.37	0.4	0.08	0.05	0.37	0.4	0.67	0.63	0.37	0.16
Hot - Cold	—	0.27	0.08	0.08	0.27	0.13	0.13	0	0.27	0.18	0.05	0.41	0.11	0.65	0	0.27	0.25	0.07	0.08	0.02	0.53	0.11	0.65	0.27	0.28	0.11	0.65	0.02	0.53	0.11	0.57
Roug - Smooth	—	0.07	0.28	0.28	0.07	0.12	0.05	0	0.07	0.34	0.23	0.06	0.32	0.49	0	0.07	0.45	0.33	0.18	0.52	0.34	0.32	0.49	0.07	0.11	0.32	0.49	0.52	0.34	0.32	0.31

Figure 5. Differences in impressions from the immediately preceding sounds

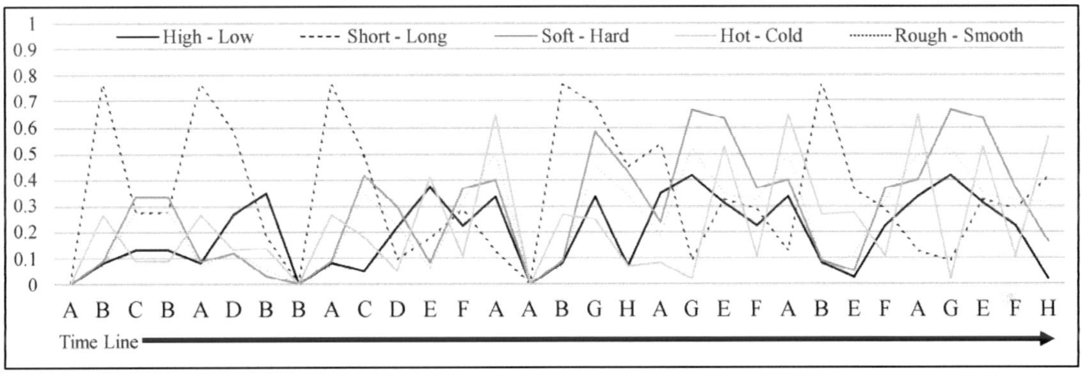

Figure 6. Differences in impressions from the immediately preceding sounds, visualized in a line graph

5. DISCUSSION

We selected the pieces chosen for this study if we graded them as 'excellent'. We decomposed the pieces into fragments of the acoustic materials that comprised them. Through a pairwise comparison of the participants' impressions of each fragment, we clarified the relative relationships among the five adjective pairs. We then plotted these relative distances for the original music, and we found contrasts by adjective pair. Consequently, we confirmed the validity of our creative teaching method.

In the future, if the axes of adjective pairs are made biaxial through principal component analysis, the relative relationships of individual acoustic materials could be plotted in 2D space, which could be applied to a model for the automatic generation of EAM. Moreover, we believe that the validity of our study could be further verified by conducting an experiment to evaluate impressions of music by automatically generating listening materials with adjusted contrasts based on our data. In addition, we did not deal with the temporal timing of the appearance of acoustic materials, and it would be possible to obtain more accurate data by adding the temporal distance of each material and its relationship with the silent part to the items to be verified.

We are currently attempting to elucidate the structure of EAM from the angle of cognitive science. One of our goals is to recapture Schaeffer's perspective on the reception of sound from the standpoint of sound affordance theory. Schaeffer's theory classifies sound reception into four categories: (1) *écouter* (to listen); (2)

ouïr (to perceive aurally); (3) *entendre* (to hear); and (4) *comprendre* (to understand). This theory emphasises 'reductive listening', which is a form of listening that focuses on 'what kind of sound it is' rather than grasping the acoustic material as a symbol and asking 'What is the sound emitted from'? This kind of listening corresponds to the classification of 'musical' and 'ordinary' listening in acoustic affordance theory (Gavor, 1993). These perspectives are also considered highly compatible with those proposed by Meyer (1954), Huron (2007), and Narmour (1991), who positioned music as a continuum of anticipation. This is because they regarded music as an anticipation of subsequent musical scenes. In EAM, where there is no clear theoretical structure, we consider treating fragments of acoustic materials that appear over time as a series of events to be an appropriate next step. We also believe that the pedagogical method of using figurative language labels for fragments of the acoustic materials addressed in this study could be further explored with the aid of Lakoff's theory of metaphor (1980).

6. CONCLUSION

We posited that there would be a high degree of contrast between figurative language labels in the arrangement of fragments of acoustic materials over time, used in pieces completed as a result of creative instruction, which we evaluated as having 'movement'. Our findings confirmed our hypothesis. The novelty of this study is that captures the primordial factors of why concrete music is perceived as "musical", whereas previous studies have mainly focused on the works of composers who have already established their social status and prestige. This approach is expected to provide an opportunity to share the 'creation' and 'listening' of concrete music—which are recommended by a very limited number of people—with a larger number of individuals.

ACKNOWLEDGEMENTS

This work was supported by JSPS KAKENHI (grant #19K00227, #20K12126, and #23K00243), and by Research Institute for Science and Technology of Tokyo Denki University Grant #Q23-02.

REFERENCES

Adorno, T. W., 1962. *Einleitung in die Musiksoziologie,* Bloomster, Suhrkamp Verlag, Frankfurt, Deutschland.

Brindle, R. S., 1987. *The New Music: The Avant-garde Since 1945*, Oxford University Press, Oxford, United Kingdom.

Couprie, P., 2016. EAnalysis: developing a sound-based music analytical tool, in Emmerson. S., ed., 2016. *Expanding the horizon of Electroacoustic Music Analysis*, pp. 170–194, Cambridge University Press, Cambridge, United Kingdom.

Gaver, W., 1993. What in the World Do We Hear? An Ecological Approach to Auditory Event Perception. *Ecological Psychology*, Vol. 5, No. 1, pp. 1–29.

Huron, D., 2007. *Sweet Anticipation: Music and the Psychology of Expectation*, MIT Press, Boston, USA.

Lakoff, G., et al., 1980. *Metaphors We Live by*, University of Chicago Press, Chicago, USA.

Meyer, L. B., 1954. *Emotion and Meaning in Music*, University of Chicago Press, Chicago, USA.

Narmour, E., 1991. *The Analysis and Cognition of Basic Melodic Structures*, University of Chicago Press. Chicago, USA.

Schaeffer, P, 1966. *Traité des Objets Musicaux: Essai Interdisci-plines*. Seul, Paris, France.

Roy, S., 2004. *L'Analysedes musiques électroacoustiques: Modèles et propositions*, Edition L'Harmattan, Paris, France.

Shibayama, T. et al., 2018. A Tentative Assumption of The Electro-acoustic Music As an Enjoyable Music for Diverse People, *Proceedings of 14th International Conference on Advances in Computer Entertainment Technology (ACE) 2017*, London, United Kingdom, pp. 139–152.

Shibayama, T. et al, 2020. Proposal for the Field Design for Co-Creation of Experimental Fine Art Music with Diverse People, *Environmental Arts*, Vol. 24, pp. 132–139.

Shibayama, T. et al., 2021. Proposal for the Design of the Workshop Method for the Denshi Onkyo People Project, *Environmental Arts*, Vol. 26, pp. 50–55.

Small, C., 1998. *Musicking: The Meanings of Performing and Listening*, Wesleyan University Press, Middletown, USA.

SHORT

PAPERS

IS GESTURE-BASED INTERACTION EQUALLY VIABLE IN MANUAL AND AUTONOMOUS DRIVING?

Lisa Graichen[1] and Matthias Graichen[2]
[1]*TU Berlin*
Marchstrasse 23, 10587 Berlin, Germany
[2]*Independent Researcher, Germany*

ABSTRACT

Reducing driver distraction is important for road safety, as manual driving requires the driver to keep their eyes on the road. In the era of autonomous driving, drivers will still need to be able to rapidly take control of the vehicle, but constant observance will no longer be required. Therefore, it is desirable to both focus the driver's attention on the traffic situation and to provide stimulation to avoid driver fatigue. Previous studies have shown that, compared to touch-based interaction, the use of gestures to perform secondary tasks on an infotainment system results in higher ratings of user experience, acceptance, and trust as well as reduced workload. In an autonomous vehicle, the driver's hands do not need to stay on the wheel for the entire driving time, and decreasing visual distraction is less important than in manual driving. In the forthcoming study described in this paper, we plan to investigate whether the subjective advantages for gestures in secondary task interaction are present in both manual and autonomous driving.

KEYWORDS

Gestures, Driver Distraction, Secondary Tasks, User Experience

1. INTRODUCTION

In manual driving, distraction plays a crucial role in driving safety. In 2020, driver distraction was implicated in approximately 13% of all crashes in the US, 14% of injury crashes, and 8% of fatal crashes, leading to a total of over 3,000 deaths (National Center for Statistics and Analysis 2022). Driver distraction is defined by the shifting of the driver's attention from the primary driving task to a secondary task (see Lee *et al.* 2009, Regan *et al.* 2009b), for example using the in-vehicle infotainment system (IVIS), talking to a passenger, or using a mobile phone. Studies have shown that distracted drivers exhibit poorer driving performance (for an overview, see Regan *et al.* 2009a, Regan *et al.* 2013). In autonomous driving, the criticality of driver distraction may be reduced, as the driver is not required to observe the traffic situation constantly. Nonetheless, the driver may still be required to take control of the vehicle and should therefore still be aware of the current situation. However, driving an autonomous vehicle can also be uneventful for the driver: it does not require a high level of attention and may lead to driver fatigue. Therefore, it would be beneficial to provide positive stimulation using modern in-vehicle interaction technologies, such as gesture-based interaction (GBI), in order for the driver to maintain an appropriate level of situational awareness and to avoid fatigue. Studies on GBI in manual driving have found that gesture-based systems are associated with higher user experience ratings (e.g. Chiesa and Branciforti 2012, Loehmann *et al.* 2013, Häuslschmid *et al.* 2015, Fariman *et al.* 2016) and can increase the driver's awareness of the driving situation, leading in particular to increased reaction times in hazardous situations (e.g. Graichen *et al.* 2020).

In previous studies, we observed that GBI garnered higher ratings of acceptability, trust, and user experience compared to a conventional touchscreen when drivers performed secondary driving tasks using an IVIS (Graichen *et al.* 2019a). Because autonomous driving will likely enter the market in future, it would be interesting to investigate whether these advantages hold for autonomous driving as well. In the forthcoming study, we will address the following research questions:

RQ1: Is GBI rated similarly positively in terms of acceptance, trust, and user experience when used in autonomous driving compared to manual driving?

RQ2: How distracting, in terms of looks to the display, are gestures when used for autonomous driving?

RQ3: Does subjective workload receive similarly low ratings when using gestures for manual and autonomous driving?

2. METHODS

2.1 Design and Independent Variables

A one-way repeated measures design has been chosen, where two types of driving mode (manual vs. autonomous) make up the factor. To increase task variety for the secondary tasks, we will implement interaction stories with the IVIS to represent basic, frequently used functions and tasks that would require more complex operations when performed using a touchscreen. Table 1 presents the task details and gestures used. All participants will experience both driving modes. One driving scenario has been selected from the set of pre-delivered scenarios provided by the simulation software. This scenario allows drivers to perform three IVIS tasks during manual and automated driving, respectively. The driving mode will remain constant during each trip, and the sequence of tasks during the trip as well as the task type alternations will be balanced according to the standard Latin square. Within each scenario, the timing of the interaction tasks will be fixed to provide participants with sufficient time to perform them without time pressure.

2.2 Participants

An opportunity sample will be obtained and will consist primarily of students from the Technical University of Berlin in Germany. No restrictions will be established regarding driving experience or visual aids. This study will comply with the tenets of the Declaration of Helsinki such that informed consent will be obtained from each participant.

2.3 Facilities and Apparatus

A fixed-based driving simulator will be used for the study. Participants will sit in a driving simulation mock-up with automatic transmission. We will use Carla as a driving simulation environment (Dosovitskiy *et al.* 2017). To record driver interactions with the IVIS, a camera will be placed on a table close to the mock-up and angled towards the driver. To investigate participants' visual behavior towards the displays, a Pupil Labs eye tracker will be used (see https://pupil-labs.com/).

Figure 1. Experimental situation

The driving scenario is a city scenario that was selected from the tracks provided in Carla. A 15-inch screen will be mounted on the center console to display the IVIS (see Figure 1). The screen will be connected to a gesture recognition device (Leap Motion). Although the gesture detection rate of the Leap Motion is relatively high, we will use the Wizard of Oz method (WoO; Dahlbäck *et al.* 1993) for the interaction, meaning that all user inputs will be enacted by the examiner. This method will be employed to avoid sensor-related errors;

long screen response times; or participants performing the incorrect gesture, which may confound individual evaluations of the interaction system. Carla itself can perform automated driving in most driving situations (such as stabilization and some maneuvering tasks). However, in one situation, the vehicle is required to overtake a stopped vehicle. Here, the examiner is required to use the WoO technique and manually steer the vehicle using a joystick in order to provide a continuous experience of autonomous driving.

The IVIS screens are based on the original displays of a Seat Leon ST brand vehicle to ensure that they are realistic. They will be used to display the information needed to perform the secondary tasks. The display figures are embedded in a slide show format that the examiner will control. For both driving modes, three interaction tasks have been derived from typical IVIS tasks. Two of the tasks can be performed by operating a single control element in a conventional touch-based IVIS. The completion of the remaining task usually requires more complex operations and several interaction steps in a conventional touch-based interface.

To ensure that gestures are suitable for performing the respective tasks, a pre-study with 31 participants was conducted. Participants were presented with images of various gestures and were asked to choose the most appropriate gesture for each task. They could also report that no gesture would be suitable. In the present study, we selected three gestures that had been rated as highly appropriate for the chosen interaction tasks. Table 1 presents the IVIS task descriptions and their corresponding gestures. Each task interaction includes an audio snippet of acoustic feedback (e.g., a song snippet that is stopped for the "mute radio" task) to signal to participants that the task has been completed without requiring them to look at the interface.

2.4 Procedure

Upon arrival, participants will complete questionnaires pertaining to their demographics and technical affinity. They will then be introduced to the IVIS tasks and the general use of the gesture-based functionalities. Each participant will be given as much time as they need to learn and practice the interaction tasks and their respective gestures. Participants will be tested repeatedly on their interaction performance in order to reduce training effects during the experiment and lower the odds of participants performing the incorrect gesture during an interaction task. Gesture recognition functionality will be demonstrated using an online visualization of the Leap Motion on the screen which illustrates the device tracking of the participant's fingers and palm. Before the experiment starts, participants will be introduced to the eye-tracking device, which will then be calibrated individually. The first trip will familiarize the participant with the vehicle and the simulator setting. The two remaining trips will include one driving scenario and three IVIS tasks for each driving mode, respectively. Participants will be instructed to drive according to the German Road Traffic Act and perform the tasks only when they feel comfortable doing so. After each trip, participants will complete a questionnaire pertaining to acceptance, trust, user experience, and workload in relation to their recent interaction. At the end of the experiment, participants will complete further questionnaires pertaining to their engagement in the secondary tasks, their impressions of immersion and presence, and their evaluation of the system. Overall, the experiment will take approximately 1 h to complete.

Table 1. Tasks with corresponding gestures and procedures for completion.

Driving Mode	Task	Gesture	Initial Situation	GBI Subtasks	Result
Manual/ Autonomous	Mute Radio	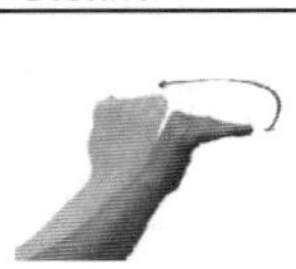	Radio menu displayed Song snippet played	Perform gesture	Song snippet is stopped
Manual/ Autonomous	Start Call		Start menu is displayed	Perform gesture	Instruction of navigation device is repeated at higher volume
Manual/ Autonomous	Increase Navigation Volume		Navigation map is displayed	Perform gesture	Dial tone is presented

2.5 Dependent Variables

Gaze behavior will be assessed using metrics such as the number and duration of looks to the display during each trip. The subjective rating of the interaction types will be measured using questionnaires on acceptance (Van der Laan *et al.* 1997), attractiveness (Hassenzahl *et al.* 2003), and workload (Hart and Staveland 1988), as well as the distraction engagement subscales of the Susceptibility to Driver Distraction Questionnaire (Feng *et al.* 2014). At the end of the experiment, participants will be asked to rate their affinity to new technical devices using the TA-EG (Karrer *et al.* 2009) as well as their feelings of immersion and presence when using the simulator (Lessiter *et al.* 2001).

3. IMPLICATIONS

Autonomous vehicles have the potential to increase driving safety and driver comfort, making it possible for drivers to shift their attention to other activities. However, it is important that drivers and other traffic participants are able to build suitable levels of trust in these systems, as trust is a key determinant of the willingness to use and accept such systems. On the one hand, previous studies suggest that users tend to overtrust technical systems in general, as they misunderstand application functionalities, are unaware of system constraints, or use systems for purposes for which they were not intended (Itoh 2012). On the other hand, drivers also demand an unrealistically high level of safety from autonomous vehicles before they are willing to use them (Shariff *et al.* 2021). Most drivers deem themselves to be more skilled than the average driver, which likely explains this demand (Alicke and Govorun 2005). For the driver to be able to assume control of the vehicle when necessary, it is important to sustain their attention by creating suitable levels of stimulation during autonomous driving, for example by using interaction types that offer a positive user experience. At the same time, visual driver distraction should be minimized to allow drivers to keep their eyes on the road and the traffic situation. In previous studies, we have observed that gestures not only offer this desired level of stimulation and user experience but are also rated as highly acceptable and trusted by users (Graichen *et al.* 2019b). However, in these studies, we investigated the use of GBI to perform secondary tasks on an IVIS system during manual driving. Therefore, the question arises as to whether GBI used in autonomous vehicles will yield similar results.

REFERENCES

Alicke, M.D. and Govorun, O., (2005). The Better-Than-Average Effect. In: M.D. Alicke, D.A. Dunning, and J. Krueger, eds. The Self in Social Judgment: Psychology Press, 85–106.

Chiesa, M. and Branciforti, A., (2012). Experimenting Kinect interactions in the car. In: A.L. Kun, et al., eds. AutomotiveUI 2012: 4th International Conference on Automotive User Interfaces and Vehicular Applications (Adjunct Proceedings). October 17-19, 2012, Portsmouth, New Hampshire, US.

Dahlbäck, N., Jönsson, A., and Ahrenberg, L., (1993). Wizard of Oz studies. In: W.D. Gray, ed. Proceedings of the 1st international conference on Intelligent user interfaces. New York, NY: ACM, 193–200.

Dosovitskiy, A., et al., (2017). CARLA: An Open Urban Driving Simulator. In: Proceedings of the 1st Annual Conference on Robot Learning, 1–16.

Fariman, H.J., et al., (2016). Designing a user-defined gesture vocabulary for an in-vehicle climate control system. In: H. Duh, et al., eds. Proceedings of the 28th Australian Computer-Human Interaction Conference (OzCHI 2016): 29 November - 2 December 2016, University of Tasmania. New York, NY, USA: ACM, 391–395.

Feng, J., Marulanda, S., and Donmez, B., (2014). Susceptibility to Driver Distraction Questionnaire. Transportation Research Record: Journal of the Transportation Research Board, 2434, 26–34.

Graichen, L., Graichen, M., and Krems, J.F., (2019) a. Evaluation of gesture-based in-vehicle interaction: User experience and the potential to reduce driver distraction, 1–19.

Graichen, L., Graichen, M., and Krems, J.F., (2019) b. Evaluation of Gesture-Based In-Vehicle Interaction: User Experience and the Potential to Reduce Driver Distraction. Human Factors: The Journal of the Human Factors and Ergonomics Society, 61 (5), 774–792.

Graichen, L., Graichen, M., and Krems, J.F., (2020). Effects of Gesture-Based Interaction on Driving Behavior: A Driving Simulator Study Using the Projection-Based Vehicle-in-the-Loop. Human Factors: The Journal of the Human Factors and Ergonomics Society, 18720820943284.

Hart, S.G. and Staveland, L.E., (1988). Development of NASA-TLX (Task Load Index): Results of empirical and theoretical research. In: Human Mental Workload: Elsevier, 139–183.

Hassenzahl, M., Burmester, M., and Koller, F., (2003). AttrakDiff: Ein Fragebogen zur Messung wahrgenommener hedonischer und pragmatischer Qualität. In: G. Szwillus and J. Ziegler, eds. Mensch & Computer 2003: Interaktion in Bewegung. Stuttgart, Leipzig: B.G. Teubner, 187–196.

Häuslschmid, R., Menrad, B., and Butz, A., (2015). Freehand vs. micro gestures in the car: Driving performance and user experience. In: 2015 IEEE Symposium on 3D User Interfaces (3DUI): IEEE, 159–160.

Itoh, M., (2012). Toward overtrust-free advanced driver assistance systems. Cognition, Technology & Work, 14 (1), 51–60.

Karrer, K., et al., (2009). TA-EG Fragebogen zur Technikaffinität – Einstellung zu und Umgang mit elektronischen Geräten (29).

Lee, J.D., Young, K.L., and Regan, M.A., (2009). Defining driver distraction. In: M.A. Regan, J.D. Lee, and K.L. Young, eds. Driver distraction. Theory, effects, and mitigation. Boca Raton: CRC Press.

Lessiter, J., et al., (2001). A Cross-Media Presence Questionnaire: The ITC-Sense of Presence Inventory. Presence: Teleoperators and Virtual Environments, 10 (3), 282–297.

Loehmann, S., et al., (2013). Culturally independent gestures for in-car interactions. In: D. Hutchison, et al., eds. Human-Computer Interaction – INTERACT 2013. Berlin, Heidelberg: Springer Berlin Heidelberg, 538–545.

National Center for Statistics and Analysis, (2022). Distracted driving 2021 (Research Note. Report No. DOT HS 813 309.

Regan, M.A., Lee, J.D., and Victor, T.W., eds., (2013). Driver distraction and inattention. Advances in research and countermeasures. Farnham, Burlington: Ashgate.

Regan, M.A., Lee, J.D., and Young, K.L., (2009) b. Driver distraction: Toward a common definition. In: First International Conference on Driver Diststraction and Inattention. 28-29 September 2009, Gothenburg, Sweden.

Regan, M.A., Lee, J.D., and Young, K.L., eds., (2009) a. Driver distraction. Theory, effects, and mitigation. Boca Raton: CRC Press.

Shariff, A., Bonnefon, J.-F., and Rahwan, I., (2021). How safe is safe enough? Psychological mechanisms underlying extreme safety demands for self-driving cars. Transportation Research Part C: Emerging Technologies, 126, 103069.

Van der Laan, J.D., Heino, A., and Waard, D. de, (1997). A simple procedure for the assessment of acceptance of advanced transport telematics. Transportation Research Part C: Emerging Technologies, 5 (1), 1–10.

VISUAL ANALYTICS FOR THE MARRIAGE NETWORK IN THE GORYEO DYNASTY, KOREA

Seongmin Mun[1], Hyunju Lee[1*] and Sangkuk Lee[2†]
[1]Department of Humanities Research Institute, Ajou University
Ajou University, 206, World cup-ro, South Korea
[2]Department of History, Ajou University
Ajou University, 206, World cup-ro, South Korea

ABSTRACT

Political marriage has been a historically productive and important matter to maintain or extend social power. This kind of relationship is also found in Korean history. For instance, in the history of the Goryeo dynasty (i.e., AD 918~ 1392 in Korea), the royal families of the Goryeo dynasty used marriage as a political strategy to maintain or extend their power. Qualitative studies have found that royal families used marriage as a means of maintaining political power, but there is still a lack of quantitative research supporting the outcomes of these studies. For this reason, we adopt computational approaches to advance our understanding of the role of political marriage in the Goryeo dynasty, in Korea. In addition, to simulate the change of power by their origin (i.e., region), we made a visualization system to explore the marriage network of royal families. We note two major findings of this current study. First, the marriage strategies of royal families are divided into three types: (1) exogamous marriages, (2) endogamous marriages, and (3) the combination of exogamous marriages and endogamous marriages. The royal family of Goryeo expanded their external relationship through exogamous marriages and reproduced their power through intra-family marriages. Second, we found that the power of a region was greater when the king was born through wedlock in that region, as opposed to when many marriages were made with the royal family. As a whole, the success of our computational approaches adds to the quantitative evidence for the historical strategies of political marriage in the Goryeo dynasty, in Korea.

KEYWORDS

Visual Analytics, Network Analysis, Political Marriage, Goryeo Dynasty, History of Korea

1. INTRODUCTION

Political marriages have historically played a very important role in the ruling elite group to maintain or extend their power (e.g., Rollins & Bahr, 1976). Likewise, in Korean history, political marriage has been a means for the ruling elite group including the royal families of the Goryeo dynasty to form, maintain, and expand their power (e.g., Lee, 1984). In particular, the first king, Taejo, the founder of the Goryeo dynasty (i.e., AD 918~ 1392 in Korea), used political marriage as a means of strengthening royal authority. In addition, political marriage was also an important way for local groups to become the ruling elite group (e.g., Ha, 1968; Jeong, 1984; Kim, 2009). Most of the previous historical studies have been conducted by using qualitative research methods and have found that royal families used marriage as a means of maintaining political power, but there is still a lack of quantitative research supporting the outcomes of these studies. In order to fill the gap between qualitative and quantitative research methods, we aim to analyze the marriage network to see how royal families of the Goryeo dynasty use marriage as a political strategy to maintain or extend their power and how local groups use marriage to grow the ruling elite group. For this aim, we employ three network analysis algorithms (i.e., degree centrality, closeness centrality, and betweenness centrality) and develop a visualization system to get a better interpretation of the marriage network.

Network analysis method expresses the relationship between information by using nodes and links, and has been widely used in research to express the relationship between people. For instance, Ha et al., (2019)

[*]These authors contributed equally to this work.
[†]Corresponding author(s). E-mail(s): okllsskh@ajou.ac.kr

used network visualization to see the change pattern of voting relationship between people in the Joseon dynasty, Korea. In this study, they noted that network visualization could contribute to research easier to compare the relationship between people than other visualization technics. Considering the results of previous studies that network analysis is useful for exploring and understanding the relationship between people, our study investigate the marriage network of royal families in the Goryeo Dynasty through network analysis by developing a visualization system named *DiachronicPowerChanges* (Available at: http://202.30.16.152/DiachronicPowerChanges/).

2. METHODS

2.1 Creating the Marriage Network Data

Historical data on the marriage relationship for the royal family of the Goryeo dynasty is recorded in the Goryeosa (i.e., History of the Goryeo Dynasty), a government-published book of Goryeo dynasty's history, but there was no computerized data that can be used for our research. For this reason, we manually coded the marriage relationship data by examining and exploring the historical records of the Goryeo dynasty, in Korea. Data annotation was progressed by professionals who majored in the history of the Goryeo dynasty, in Korea. The entire process of the annotations is described as follows.

Based on the historical records including Goryeosa (Figure 1), we extracted information about people who have a relationship with the king and the queen within in the marriage network. We further added more people such as great-grandfathers, great-grandmothers, maternal grandfathers, and maternal grandmothers, including the parents of the king and the queen. At the final, we added personal information of each person such as where they were born (i.e., origin), their final grade, etc. The final data include information about royal marriages from 918 to 1031, the family relationship between the king and queen, and the area of their origin (including 137 people and 752 relationships).

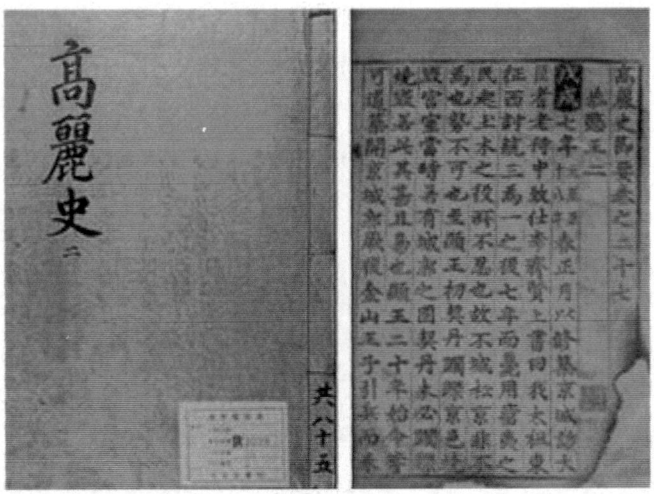

Figure 1. Goryeosa (the historical records of the Goryeo Dynasty; adapted from Kyujanggak. (2023))

2.2 Developing the Visualization System

For better exploring and understanding of the marriage network, we designed a visualization system with JavaScript, HTML, and CSS environments, using the final data including the marriage relationships between people in the Goryeo dynasty, Korea. For the interface of the system, we created three areas for the exploration of the marriage network: data selection interface, network map between origins, and social network between people and details table of the people.

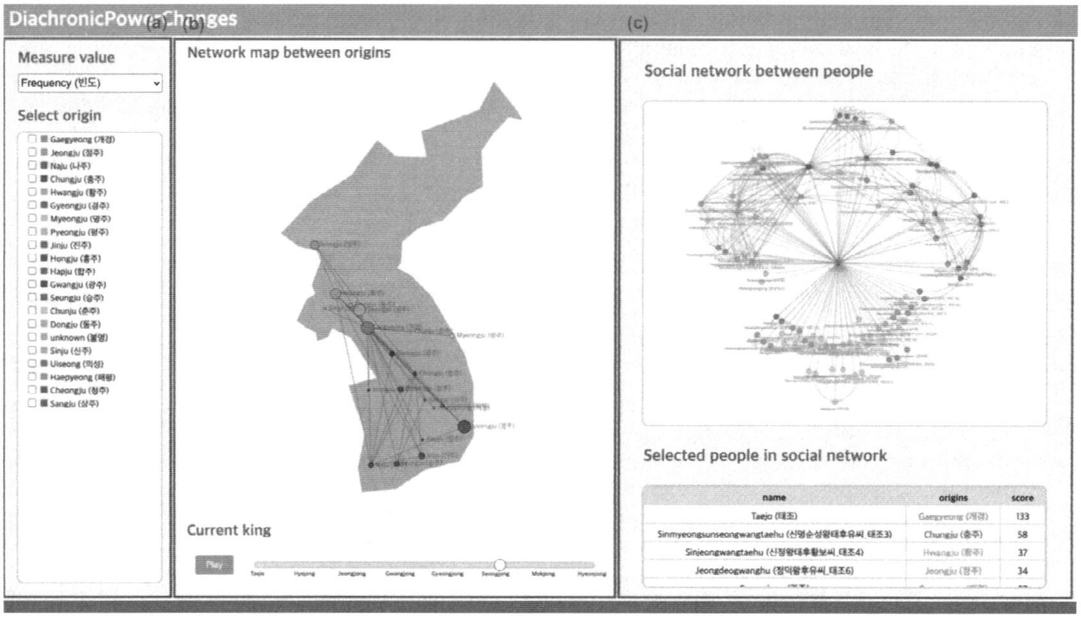

Figure 2. The overall interface of the visualization system (Available at: http://202.30.16.152/DiachronicPowerChanges/)

As shown in Figure 2(b), the network map presents the relationship between origins based on the selected measure values involving different origins (represented as dots and colors). A slider at the bottom of the map allows for changing the kings; the patterns of the network change as the slider moves. Each dot shows the details of the origin (e.g., an index/name of the selected origin, the score according to the selected measure value) once the mouse pointer is located on the dot. For the manipulation of visualization outcomes, Figure 2(a) provides options to select the measure values and checkboxes to highlight interesting origins.

The right side of the system as in Figure 2(c) provides users social network between people, and a details table of the people. This section is also interlocked with the data selection part so that highlights interesting people by the selected origins. The table at the bottom right side of the system presents the details of the people in the social network. This table provides several people's information such as name, origin, and score according to the selected origin and measure value.

3. RESULTS: TWO CASE STUDIES

To assess how our visualization system works, we conducted two case studies.

3.1 How Royal Families of The Goryeo Dynasty use Marriage as a Political Strategy to Maintain or Extend their Power?

Our visualization system showed that the royal families of the Goryeo dynasty used marriage as a political strategy to extend or maintain their power as shown in Figure 3. For instance, in Figure 3(a), marriage in the early Goryeo dynasty was a strategy to unify and dominate local power. King Taejo of the early Goryeo dynasty had more marriages with the different origins (i.e., regions) than other kings. On the other hand, the marriage pattern of other kings showed that they used marriage to maintain their power. For example, in Figure 3(b), the period of King Hyeonjong had more marriages with Gaegyeong than other origins. Considering that the Gaegyeong was the central city of royal families, this fact showed us that they had endogamous marriages to maintain their power.

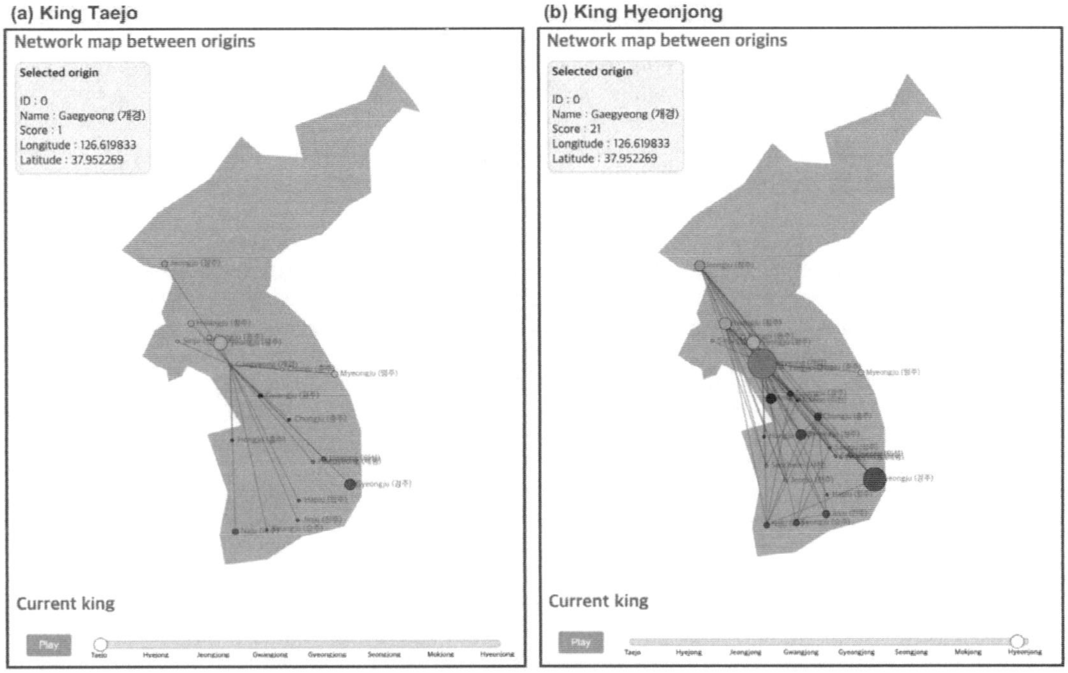

Figure 3. The marriage network between origins (Left: King Taejo; Right: King Hyeonjong)

As a whole, the marriage strategies of royal families can be divided into three types: (1) exogamous marriages, (2) endogamous marriages, and (3) the combination of exogamous marriages and endogamous marriages. The royal family of Goryeo expanded their external relationship through exogamous marriages and reproduced their power through endogamous marriages.

3.2 Which Origin Generates the Most Power Through the Marriage Network?

For the network analysis algorithms, we used three different algorithms (i.e., degree centrality, closeness centrality, and betweenness centrality) in *Python*, by adapting functions provided by *networkx* (Barnowski, 2022). A high degree centrality value of a person means that the target person has direct relationships with many people, a high degree of closeness centrality means that the target person has a close relationship with all other people on average, and a high degree of betweenness centrality indicates that the target person plays a large intermediary role in all people relationships. We used the three algorithms described above to find important people within the marriage network and applied those scores to the visualization system.

Table 1. Ranking of important origins according to frequencies and network analysis algorithms (used all marriage network data from King Taejo to King Hyeonjong)

	Frequencies	**Degree centralities**	**Closeness centralities**	**Betweenness centralities**
1st origin	Gaegyeong (21)	Gaegyeong (3.438)	Gaegyeong (11.341)	Gaegyeong (0.854)
2nd origin	Gyeongju (16)	Hwangju (0.956)	Gyeongju (7.952)	Jeongju (0.035)
3rd origin	Pyeongju (9)	Jeongju (0.752)	Pyeongju (4.455)	Hwangju (0.033)
4th origin	Hwangju (8)	Chungju (0.664)	Hwangju (4.211)	Chungju (0.026)

Table 1 shows the total sum of the people appearing in the marriage network by each origin (i.e., frequencies) and the total score according to each algorithm calculation method by origin (i.e., degree centralities, closeness centralities, and betweenness centralities). As a result of the analysis, Gyeongju was the origin (i.e., region) with a large number of marriages with the royal family, but Jeongju, Hwangju, and Chungju were the origins that played an important role in the marriage network relationship. For instance, Queen

Seonuiwanghu of Jeongju had the highest degree/betweenness centrality score, indicating that Queen Seonuiwanghu played an important role in the marriage network by giving birth to the King Seongjong. This means that the origins where the king was produced through marriage have greater power than the origins which made more marriages with the royal family.

4. CONCLUSION

In this study, we made two major findings. First, marriage in the Goryeo dynasty was an important strategy to maintain or extend power. Furthermore, the marriage strategies of the Goryeo dynasty can be divided into three types: (1) exogamous marriages, (2) endogamous marriages, and (3) the combination of exogamous marriages and inter-family marriages. The royal family of Goryeo expanded their external relationship through exogamous marriages and reproduced their power through endogamous marriages. Second, the power of the origin (i.e., region) is higher in the origin where the king was produced through marriage (i.e., Jeongju) than in the origin where many marriages were made with the royal family (i.e., Gyeongju). For instance, Jeongju became an important origin in the marriage network by producing King Seongjong, although the number of marriages with the royal family was less than other origins.

The findings of this study should be further verified by comparing more historical records with respect to the marriage network of the Goryeo dynasty, which we plan to pursue next. Any future study will also benefit from considering other network algorithms or visualization techniques to better ascertain the advantage of network analysis in this kind of task.

We believe our visualization system will contribute to extending the current understanding of how the marriage network works as a political strategy to maintain or extend royal families' power.

REFERENCES

Barnowski, Ross. (2022). networkx. Available online: https://github.com/networkx/nx-guides/ (accessed on 17 January 2023).

Ha, H., Mun, S., Choi, G., Hong, E., Lee, S., & Lee, K. (2019). Visual Analysis on the Political Orientation of Historical Characters in the Joseon Dynasty: Focusing on Seo, Geojeong. Archives of Design Research, 32(1), 147-161.

Ha, Hyun-kang. (1968). Royal Marriage System during the Early Koryo Period. The history review of Ewha Womans University, 7, korea. 9-10.

Jeong, Yongsook. (1984). The Transition of Policy about Marriage and Completion of the Endogamy of the Royal Family in the Early Koryo Dynasty. Journal of Korean studies, 10(4): 65-66.

Kim, Kap-Dong. (2009), The Study on empress's acceptance of surname of mother in former Koryo dynasty, The Society for Studies of Korean History, 37, korea, 125-126.

Kyujanggak Institute for Korean Studies. (2023). Goryeosa. Seoul National University, Available online: https://kyudb.snu.ac.kr/book/view.do (accessed on 04 April 2023).

Lee, Ki-baik. (1984). A New History of Korea. Harvard University Press, USA.

Rollins, Boyd C. & Bahr, Stephen J. (1976). A Theory of Power Relationships in Marriage. Journal of Marriage and Family, 38(4): 619-627.

GRADIENT PATTERN ANALYSIS APPLIED FOR COMPUTER VISION IN MEDICAL ULTRASOUND DIAGNOSIS

Rubens Andreas Sautter[1], Reinaldo Roberto Rosa[1], Debora Cristina Alavarce[2] and Daniel Guimarães Silva[2]
[1]Applied Computing Program (CAP), National Institute for Space Research (INPE)
Av. dos Astronautas, 1.758, CEP 12245-027, São José dos Campos/SP - Brazil
[2]Hipocampus EdTech - Digital Learning
R. do Serimbura, 320, CEP 12243-360, São José dos Campos/SP - Brazil

ABSTRACT

This paper describes a new application of the technique known as Gradient Pattern Analysis (GPA), focused here on computer vision. In the GPA domain, the image is translated into a tessellation triangulation field based on the vectors positions that make up the gradient lattice of the matrix image. The GPA version considered here generates three attributes (G1, G2 and G3) that can be used as labels for a supervised machine-learning model. The case study presented here shows that GPA is a useful tool for real-time fetal biometry from 2D ultrasound images. The application in obstetrics indicates that the technique can also be useful for learning diagnostic imaging in gynecology, hepatology and oncology. The generalization of the technique to other applications in practical learning in health is discussed.

KEYWORDS

Gradient Pattern Analysis, Computer Vision, Supervised Machine Learning, 2D Endoscopic Ultrasound Biometry

1. INTRODUCTION

Gradient Pattern Analysis (GPA) is a technique for analyzing the dynamics of nonlinear 2D-spatiotemporal systems, which is based on the gradient symmetry-breaking properties of a matrix snapshot sequence. Originally, GPA has found numerous applications in 2D dynamic systems [Rosa et al., 1999, da Silva et al., 2000, Faria et al., 2007; Baroni et al., 2006, Freitas et al., 2010]. GPA was originally inspired by 2D turbulence analysis in space (Andrade et al., 2006) and environmental physics (Velho et al. 2001). In the last five years, the technique has been improved for automatic morphological classification associated with supervised training of machine learning models, especially with hybrid Deep Learning (CNN combined with RNN). In the scope of computer vision, GPA "sees" different morphologies in both the gradient field and the correspondent triangulation domains from where a set of metrics are extracted as in the application in galaxy morphology (Barchi et al., 2019, Rosa et al, 2018). The gradient field metrics (the so-called "gradient moments") are extracted based on the geometry of the gradient field (via Delaunay triangulation) and also on the norm and phase matrices of the correspondent gradient field. GPA is therefore a set of computational operations on a given numerical lattice (as a matrix) and on the gradient pattern of a digital image.

In the field of medical images, diagnostic ultrasounds offer information about internal areas and parts of the body, such as the liver, kidneys health, and reproductive organs. The main application explored here examines an unborn baby and checks its health and growth status. Therefore, identifying the baby (especially the head and face) by 2D ultrasound is a detection task that will be used here as a case study to test the feasibility and usefulness of GPA in diagnostic medical imaging.

2. DATA, METHODOLOGY AND RESULTS

Our approach uses ultrasound recordings provided by the Projeto FAPESP database (process No 2021/15114-8) in partnership with the Brazilian company Hipocampus EdTech. The basic example consists of a set of 2 movies composed by 542 snapshots each, recorded in gray scale, for an 18 and 15-week-old baby.

The GPA as an analytical method explores a new paradigm proposing to analyze, instead of the absolute values of the matrix amplitudes, the symmetry breaking in the gradient field of a given matrix. The symmetry to be broken, considered in the original version of the technique (Rosa, Sharma, Valdivia, 1999; Rosa et al., 2018), are the bilateral symmetries in relation to the vertical and horizontal axes. In the first operation of GPA, the Matrix Gradient Lattice is computed in the x-direction and the y-direction, whenever possible, with Central Finite Difference. The boundaries are measured with forward and backward finite differences. The gradient lattice (GL) of a matrix is composed of V vectors of which a portion V_A is asymmetric (bilaterally symmetric pairs in the gradient lattice are those that, for a given tolerance, have the same module and opposite phases). After obtaining the GL from a matrix, the first three gradient moments are calculated as follows:

$$G_1 = \frac{T_A - V_A}{V_A} \tag{1}$$

where T_A is the number of edges that represent the connection between the V_A asymmetric vectors obtained from the Delaunay triangulation performed on the GL. The measure, G_2, based on the norms of *each asymmetric vector* v_i, is de defined as:

$$G_2 = \frac{V_A}{V}\left(1 - \frac{\left|\sum_{i=0}^{V_A} v_i\right|}{2\sum_{i=0}^{V_A}|v_i|}\right) \tag{2}$$

Note that if all vectors are symmetrical, G_2 = 0.0. The measure, G_3, based on the phase of *each asymmetric vector* v_i, depends on the vector phases (φ) and the angle of each vector with respect to the symmetry center (θ) of the matrix, and is defined as:

$$G_3 = \frac{1}{2}\left(\frac{V_A}{V} + \frac{1}{2V_A}\sum_{i=0}^{V_A}(u_i.v_i + 1)\right) \tag{3}$$

Note that, the dot product is maximum ($u.v = 1$) when the position of the vector is aligned with its phase, zero when they are perpendicular, and minimum ($u.v = -1$) when they are opposite.

Figure 1 shows the application of preprocessing GPA on a snapshot of the one of the ultrasound videos analyzed in this work. In order to enable visualization of the corresponding gradient lattice, the original image is reduced (to 32x32) in order to intensify the typical bilateral asymmetry of the baby's head contour (image (b) immersed in the original image (a)). The corresponding gradient lattice is shown in Figure 1c. The yellow grid with vertical and horizontal axes identifies the references for bilateral symmetry breaking. The tip of the baby's nose, for example, imposes a strong break in symmetry between the fourth and second quadrants. For the calculation of G_1 the triangulation between the vectors is performed. As shown in Figure 2, the triangulation is also useful to highlight fluctuations in norms and phases throughout the dynamics whose main objective is to identify the baby in the video.

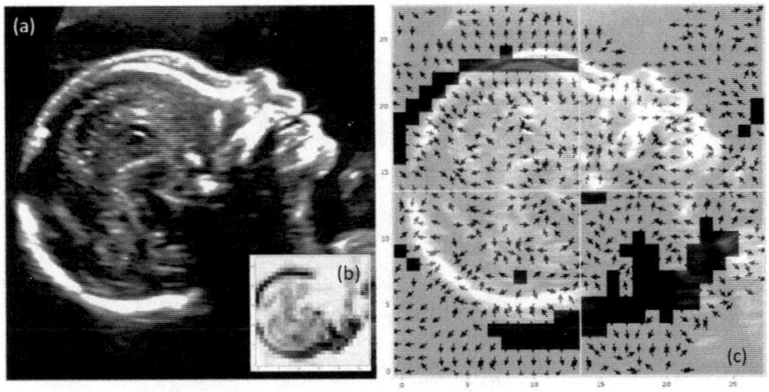

Figure 1. (a) The original image (a snapshot from the ultrasound video); (b) the reduced image and (c) the superposed correspondent gradient lattice with the bilateral symmetry axis

In our approach GPA is applied to each snapshot within a dashboard context. As shown in Figure 2, the measures G_1, G_2 and G_3 work as monitoring scores and are shown on a dashboard developed in Python (dash library). Figure 2 shows the application of the dashboard on the complete ultrasound, in a monitored way, and indicates the moment (peak) in the G_3 metric (of the phases) when the head (with details of the face and arm) are detected with great emphasis. The dashboard shows the original snapshot (left), the same with triangulation (middle) and the histogram of all phases of the vectors that make up the gradient field.

Figure 2 shows the application of the dashboard on the complete ultrasound, in a monitored way, and indicates the moment (peak) in the G_3 metric (of the phases) when the head (with details of the face and arm) are detected with great emphasis. The dashboard shows the original snapshot (left), the same with triangulation (middle) and the histogram of all phases of the vectors that make up the gradient field.

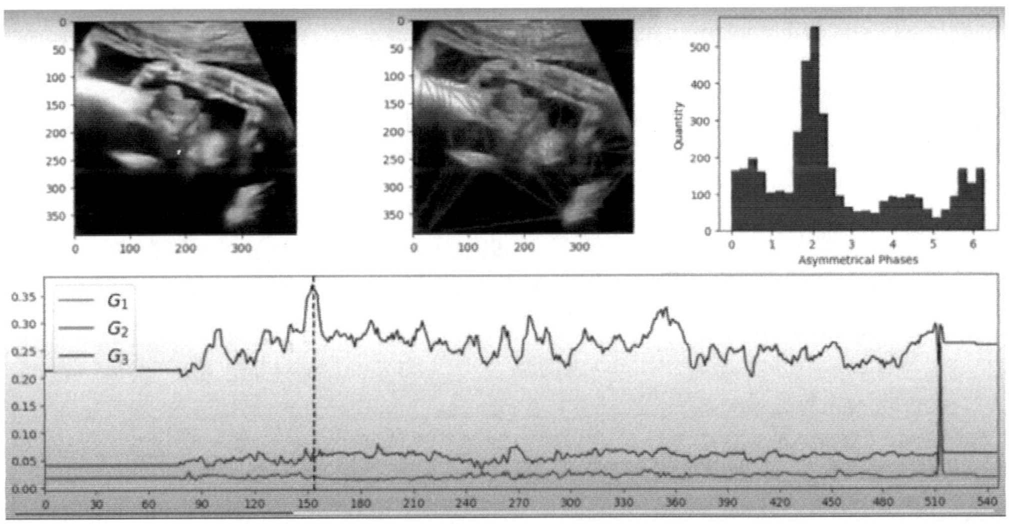

Figure 2. The GPA dashboard for the Ultrasound Diagnosis. The high performance of G_3 is remarkable even when the arm of the baby is in scene. The histogram of the phases of the asymmetric vectors works as a less accurate indicator of target detection

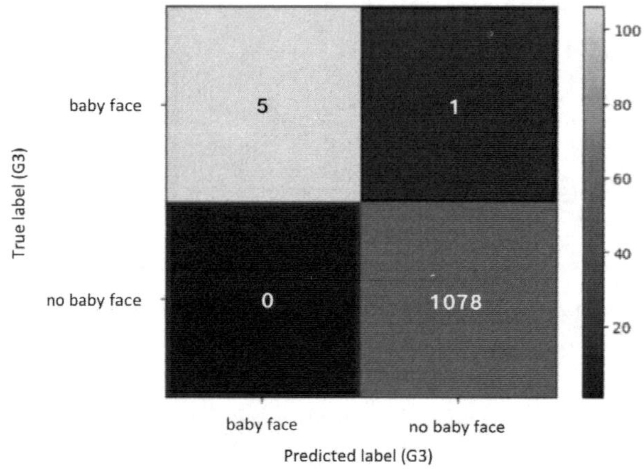

Figure 3. Confusion Matrix based on G_3 as a label

The total sample has 1084 snapshots. Of this total, the sought pattern (baby face) was identified 3 times in each one, totaling 6 positive identifications. The G_3 label was within the range from 0.27 to 0.38 for 5 identifications and only one identification was outside of this range (G_3=0.21) for a snapshot that was also visually validated. Based on this sample, a confusion matrix prototype was created (Figure 3) with these values to guide the exploration of supervised training based on GPA (G_3).

3. CONCLUSION

The preliminary analysis applied to the chosen case study makes it clear that the GPA-G_3 metric is adequate to capture the morphological information sought in ultrasound imaging diagnosis (especially when applied in real time). In two applications having 6 positive patterns in a sample of 1084 snapshots, the expected positive result was 83% (5/6). This result indicates the G_3 metric as the most suitable to be used as a label for supervised training of a hybrid deep learning model that is under development (using CNN with LSTM).

It is noteworthy that the methodology presented here can be useful in diagnosis by medical imaging in other paradigms of health sciences, emphasizing that it can also be effective in the training and learning process in identifying patterns in ultrasound exams and other techniques that require training to detect patterns in endoscopic medical footage or equivalent applications in other fields of computer vision. More recently, testing of new computer vision techniques for diagnostics based on AI is encouraged within the space medicine program under the ISI and Artemis mission (Krittanawong et al. 2023).

ACKNOWLEDGEMENT

The authors would like to thank FAPESP for financial support via Project N° 2021/15114-8.

REFERENCES

Andrade, A.P., Ribeiro, A.L.B., Rosa, R.R., 2006. Gradient pattern analysis of cosmic structure formation: Norm and phase statistics, Physica D, Vol. 223(2), pp. 139-145. DOI: 10.1016/j.physd.2006.08.025.

Barchi, P.H. et al, 2020. Machine and Deep Learning applied to galaxy morphology - A comparative study, *Astronomy and Computing*, Vol. 30, No. 1, pp. 100334. DOI: 10.1016/j.ascom.2019.100334.

Baroni, M.P.M.A. et al, 2006. Modeling and gradient pattern analysis of irregular SFM structures of porous silicon, *Microelectronics Journal*, Vol. 37, No. 4, pp. 290-294. DOI: 10.1016/j.mejo.2005.05.029.

Costa-Junior, R.A. et al, 2005. Gradient pattern analysis of extended convection-diffusion, *Physica A: Statistical Mechanics and its Applications*, Vol. 344, No. 3-4, pp. 447-455. DOI: 10.1016/j.physa.2004.06.013.

da Silva, F.A., Rosa, R.R., Roman, L.S., Veje, E., Pepe, I., 2000. Characterization of asymmetric fragmentation patterns in SFM images of porous silicon, *Solid State Communications*, Vol. 113(12), pp. 703-708. DOI: 10.1016/S0038-1098(99)00557-8.

de Freitas, R.M. et al, 2010. Using Gradient Pattern Analysis for land use and land cover change detection, *IEEE International Geoscience and Remote Sensing Symposium*, Honolulu, Hawaii, pp. 3648-3651. DOI: 10.1109/igarss.2010.5650698.

Faria, L.N. et al, 2007. A parallel application for 3D reconstruction of coronal loops using image morphing, *Image and Vision Computing*, Vol. 25, No. 1, pp. 95-102. DOI: 10.1016/j.imavis.2005.12.007.

Krittanawong, C. et al. 2023. Human Health during Space Travel: State-of-the-Art Review, Cells, Vol. 12, pp. 12-32, DOI: 10.3390/cells12010040.

Rosa, R.R. et al, 1999. Characterization of asymmetric fragmentation patterns in spatially extended systems, *International Journal of Modern Physics C*, Vol. 10, No. 1, pp. 147-163. DOI: 10.1142/S0129183199000103.

Rosa, R.R. et al, 2000. Gradient pattern analysis of Swift-Hohenberg dynamics: phase disorder characterization, *Physica A: Statistical Mechanics and its Applications*, Vol. 283, No. 1-2, pp. 156-159. DOI: 10.1016/S0378-4371(00)00144-8.

Rosa; R.R., et al, 2018. Gradient pattern analysis applied to galaxy morphology, *Monthly Notices of the Royal Astronomical Society: Letters*, Vol. 477, No. 1, pp. L101—L105. DOI: 10.1093/mnrasl/sy054

Velho, H.F.C. et al., 2001. Multifractal model for eddy diffusivity and counter-gradient term in atmospheric turbulence, Physica A, 295 (1-2), pp. 219-223. DOI: 10.1016/S0378-4371(01)00077-2.

Veronese, T.B. and Martins, M.P.A., 2010. Biologically Motivated Fuzzy-like Measure for Complex Structures Perception, *Journal of Computational Interdisciplinary Sciences*, Vol. 1, No. 3, pp. 233-239. DOI: 10.6062/jcis.2010.01.03.0025.

PROTOTYPING VISUALIZATIONS AS A SUPPORT FOR SELECTING REPRESENTATIVE MODELS OF PETROLEUM RESERVOIRS

Miguel Angelo Mena Póvoa, Samuel Oliveira da Silva and Celmar Guimarães da Silva
School of Technology, University of Campinas, Brazil

ABSTRACT

Petroleum engineers usually create a set of hundreds of models of a given oil reservoir under analysis to represent its uncertainties. Assisted optimization approaches may help engineers to select a subset of these models (a.k.a. representative models, or RMs for short), which is used in computational flow simulations in replacement of the original set, aiming to reduce the total simulation runtime without changing the quality of these results. Despite the power of visualization techniques to help people to understand multidimensional datasets like the ones provided in this scenario, we noted a few efforts that use these techniques to help petroleum engineers to assist the selection of RMs. In this context, our research aims to test the hypothesis that it is possible to improve how interactive visualization resources are currently used to aid decision-making regarding the selection of RMs, mainly in the presence of multiple sets of RMs or multiple variables (obtained from running model simulations). This work presents our first steps towards this goal: (a) literature review and (b) definition of visualization prototypes that aim to help the analysis of RMs regarding the values of the variables provided by simulation outputs, and the risk curves associated with these variables. As preliminary results, we present our proposed interactive visualizations and briefly point out the design rationale behind these prototypes.

KEYWORDS

Information Visualization, Oil Reservoir Model, Risk Curves, Cross Plots, Multivariate Data, Representative Models

1. INTRODUCTION

Oil reservoir development and management activities involve risks due to various physical, operational, and economic uncertainties (Schiozer et al., 2019), which are associated with the recoverable reserves of the oil wells and the flow characteristics, the availability of the production system, the oil price, investments, and operational expenses, among others. Besides, these activities also involve defining a production strategy, which consists of the sequencing of drilling, opening, injection and positioning of wells, among other activities. Due to these intrinsic uncertainties, defining this kind of strategy becomes a complex problem, whose solution embraces the analysis of numerous models that sample the possible combinations of the uncertain reservoir characteristics under analysis. Model reduction techniques are highly desirable, in order to reduce the time-expensive execution of flow simulations (up to days) for each possible production strategy and each model under analysis. This reduction should produce a viable set of models that is representative of the entire problem (Meira et al., 2016).

In this context, the RMFinder methodology and software (Meira et al., 2020) use an optimization-based approach proposed to automatically identify, according to the analysts' preferences, subsets of oilfield models, called Representative Models (RM), that represent a set of originally provided models. Although it is possible to select a set of RMs (a.k.a. "solution") in an automated way, the selection of RMs is an assisted optimization procedure, whose results must be inspected by petroleum analysts, which verify if the selected RMs appropriately represent the complete set of models. The RMFinder output sets of cross plots (which resemble scatterplot matrices) and charts with risk curves (a.k.a. complimentary cumulative distribution functions, or CCDFs) related to variables of the models, so that analysts could visually analyze the representativeness of a solution and make decisions such as accepting a given solution from a set of solutions, or rerunning RMFinder with distinct initialization parameters (e.g., with preselected models as RMs).

Despite these initial charts provide some support to analysts, we consider that there is a gap related to the almost absence of interactive visualization resources being used to support decision-making regarding the selection of RMs provided by the RMFinder technique. We focused our efforts to fill this gap in our current research, which aims to propose and improve the use of interactive visualizations to enhance this decision-making. Our focus is on the analysis of output variables of the models and their risk curves. We aim to help analysts to define if a given solution is really representative, and to compare solutions regarding this representativeness.

In this paper, we present our first steps regarding this goal. In Section 2, we briefly discuss the state-of-the-art on the use of visualizations for the selection of RMs. In Section 3, we describe our methodology, present our prototypes and point out their support to improve decision-making. The last section concludes the paper and points to future work.

2. RELATED WORK

We found some optimization-based approaches for the selection of RMs. On the other hand, we noted that few Information Visualization (InfoVis) techniques have been used in recent years as support for the analysis of one or more sets of RMs. Meira et al. (2017, 2020) used three visualization techniques to allow the user to check the quality of a solution: a set of scatter plots (cross plots) to allow visual analysis of the representativeness of RMs regarding each pair of output variables; superposed or juxtaposed risk curves of multiple variables and solutions; and bar charts to discuss the differences of the discretization of continuous attributes. Amaral (2021) added interactions to these views, such as zooming, brushing, selecting a specific model, or expanding a selected chart with model details.

Some works use multidimensional projection and clustering techniques to support the selection of RMs. Anupam and Tewar (2021) use PCA, t-SNE and k-means to select RMs. Zheng et al. (2018) and Sahaf et al. (2018, 2019) apply MDS and k-means to represent the influence of production uncertainties and select RMs. Regarding risk curves, Silva et al. (2020) used reorderable heatmaps to show the dissimilarities of risk curve pairs (e.g., area between risk curves).

Besides, Silva et al. (2019) used a *small multiples* layout of spatial heatmaps of model maps clustered by similarity of spatial petrophysical variables. Highlighting RMs enable analysts to contrast these RMs and the defined clusters of model maps, given that RMFinder does not deal with spatial data to select RMs.

3. METHODOLOGY AND PRELIMINARY RESULTS

To develop this user-centered information visualization project, our methodology is inspired by the iterative development cycle presented by Kulyk et al. (2017). It comprises the following steps: users, data, and tasks characterization; designing a visualization method; implementation of visualization methods; and reviewing and testing the visualization methods (return to the first step if needed). We added a preliminary step, in which we hypothesized, with support of the experience of our research group, the characteristics of the RMFinder users, and the main tasks they want to accomplish to better select RMs or compare sets of RMs. We also prototyped visualizations that aim to provide insights to these analysts. Through interviews with users, we will validate our point of view regarding their tasks and the usefulness of our prototypes.

The analysts are engineers and students, within a broad spectrum of ages (approximately between 22 to 65 years old) and years of experience in reservoir engineering (2 to 20 years). We expect that they had previous contact with RMFinder and with the problem of selecting RMs. Their main tasks, as far as we aware, can be described as: (a) analyzing the representativeness of a solution; and (b) comparing a set of solutions to find the most representative one. Understanding the so-called representativeness is a challenge because it has explicit and tacit components. The explicit components are those already defined in the RMFinder optimization functions. The tacit components, as such, must be obtained by provoking reflections from the analysts – a task that we plan to accomplish when discussing our prototypes with them.

Our dataset may be defined as follows. The RMFinder's input dataset comprises a set M of models. Each model has values for a set V of variables, such as net present value (NPV), oil production (Np), water production (Wp), and oil recovery factor (ORF). The RMFinder defines one or more solutions to its optimization problem, where each solution S_i is a subset of M. For each S_i, the RMFinder tries to minimize a function that considers cross plot-based and risk curve-based representativeness. The *two variable-based representativeness* (2VR) of a solution is the sum of the quadratic distances between each RM and its nearest models in every possible cross plot (w_i, w_j), where $\{w_i , w_j\} \subset W$, and $W \subset V$. This concept reproduces the analysts' praxis when evaluating cross plots (i.e., the shorter the distances, the better the representativeness). The *risk curve-based representativeness* (RCR) of a solution S_i for each variable $v_k \in V$ is defined as a measure of the similarity between the risk curve for M and its risk curve for S_i (i.e., the closer the curves, the better the representativeness). RCR may be considered as the area between a pair of risk curves (as in the work of Meira et al. (2020)) or as the two-sample Kolmogorov-Smirnov statistic (a.k.a. K-S) of a pair of risk curves (Mahjour et al. (2020)). Also, it is worth providing a way to visually analyze the *variability* of a given set of solutions regarding the set of RMs they use.

Hereafter we briefly list a subset of our visualization prototypes (Figure 1 and 2):

- A binary, interactively reorderable heatmap of models used by each solution, so that the analyst may find relevant patterns in sets of solutions regarding their variability, such as common subsets of RMs (Figure 1a).
- A multidimensional projection of risk curves of the solutions in the set $\{M, S_1, ..., S_n\}$, regarding a distance measure based on the RCR related to a set of interactively filtered variables. Supported by clustering after projection, this visualization shows the similarity of the solutions and their representativeness regarding M (Figure 1b).
- A solutions-by-variables heatmap, such as the one from Silva et al. (2020), whose cells present RCR regarding the risk curve of a variable V_k for a solution S_i (e.g., the area between risk curves, or the K-S measure between risk curves) (Figure 2a).
- A plot of the risk curves (one per variable) of M enhanced with confidence bands that summarize sets of risk curves from multiple solutions, so that analysts can better analyze RCR and features of the set of risk curves (Figure 2b).
- An overview heatmap whose cells' colors represent the 2VR per solutions (Figure 2c). A second version of this heatmap uses dimensional stacking to detail the 2VR measure also per RMs (Figure 2d). These visualizations should enable analysts to quickly understand the quality of the presented solutions, as well as perceive possibly incorrect choices of RMs.
- Cross plots comparing models and RMs of a single solution regarding pairs of variables, enhance with convex hulls that outline each RM and the models next to it, aiming to provide visual cues about poorly represented models regarding 2VR (Figure 2e). The RMs are highlighted in bold.

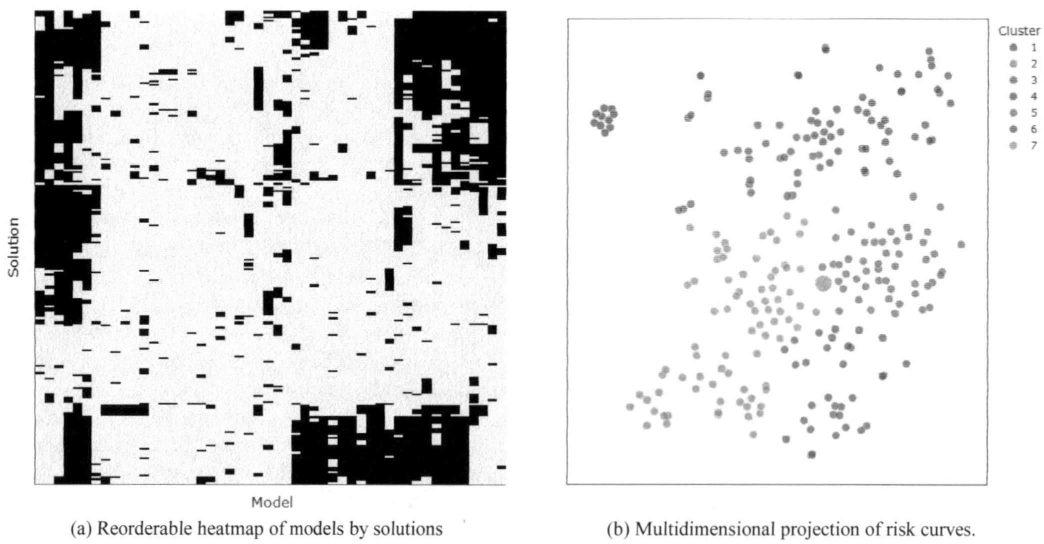

(a) Reorderable heatmap of models by solutions (b) Multidimensional projection of risk curves.

Figure 1. Visualization prototypes using data from the Olympus (Fonseca et al., 2020) and UNISIM-I-D (Gaspar et al., 2015) case studies

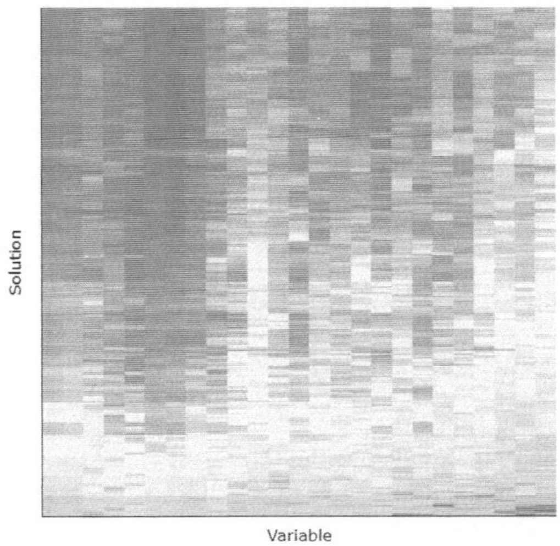

(a) Reorderable heatmap solutions by variables

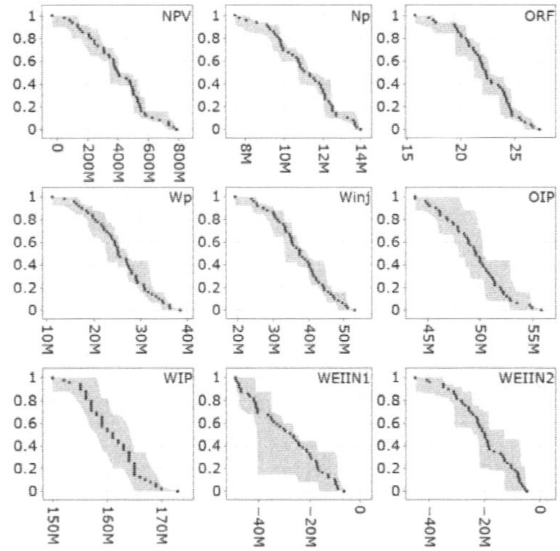

(b) Risk curves with confidence bands.

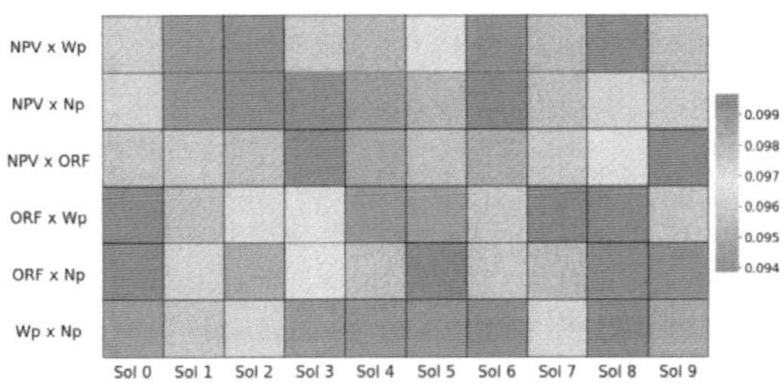

(c) Representativeness heatmap by solutions and pairs of variables.

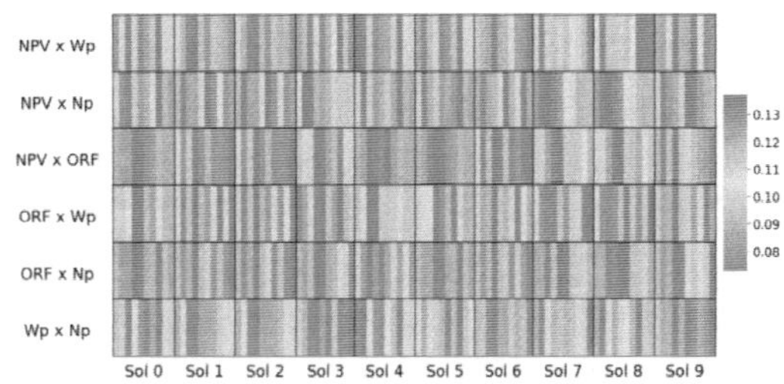

(d) Representativeness heatmap by solutions, pairs of heatmaps and RMs.

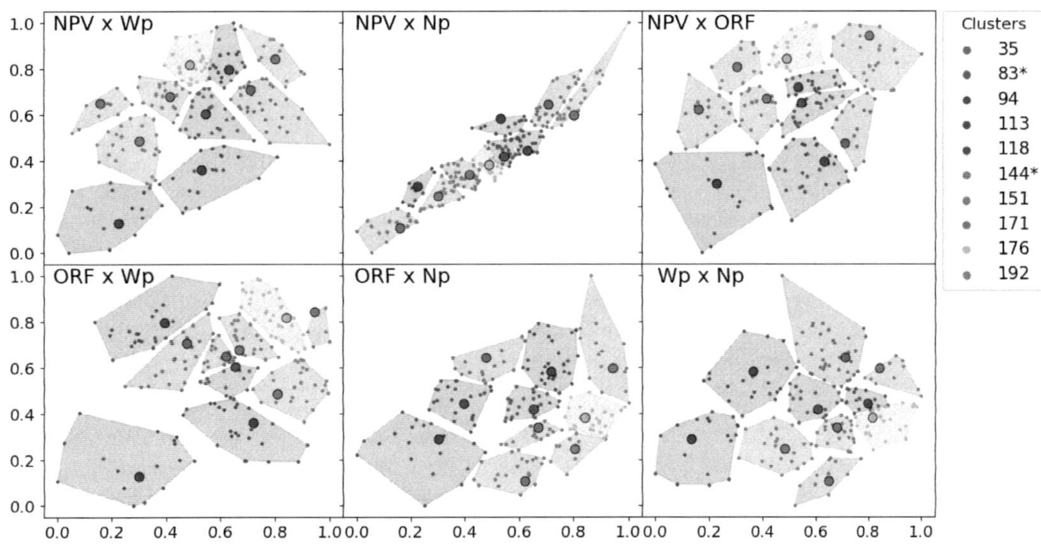

(e) Cross plots of pairs of variables with convex hulls of clusters for each RM.

Figure 2. Visualization prototypes (continuation of Figure 1)

4. CONCLUSIONS

This paper presented our first efforts to aid reservoir engineers using visualizations. We aim to aid the engineers in better selecting representative models based on representativeness and variability criteria applied to single or multiple sets of RMs. We briefly explained and exemplified our proposed multidimensional visualizations for analyzing problem variables and their respective risk curves. Future works include discussing with users how these prototypes fit their needs regarding these tasks and evolving them in that direction.

ACKNOWLEDGEMENT

We gratefully acknowledge the support of Energy Production Innovation Center (EPIC), hosted by the University of Campinas (UNICAMP) and sponsored by Equinor Brazil and FAPESP – São Paulo Research Foundation (2017/15736-3). We acknowledge the support of ANP (Brazil's National Oil, Natural Gas and Biofuels Agency) through the R&D levy regulation. Acknowledgements are extended to the Center for Petroleum and Energy Studies (CEPETRO), School of Mechanical Engineering (FEM), and School of Technology (FT). This study was partially financed by the Coordenação de Aperfeiçoamento de Pessoal de Nível Superior – Brasil (CAPES) – Finance Code 001.

REFERENCES

Amaral, L. D. B. *Visualização de informação aplicada à análise de resultados de processo de seleção de modelos representativos de reservatórios de petróleo*. Undergraduate final project dissertation. University of Campinas. 2021.

Anupam, A.; Tewari, R. Easy Steps in Probabilistic Dynamic Modelling in FDP. In: *Int. Petroleum Technology Conf.* 2021.

Fonseca, R. M. et al. Introduction to the special issue: Overview of OLYMPUS Optimization Benchmark Challenge. *Computational Geosciences*, 24(6), 1933-1941. 2020.

Gaspar, A. T. F. S. et al. UNISIM-I-D: Benchmark Studies for Oil Field Development and Production Strategy Selection. *Int. Journal of Modeling and Simulation for the Petroleum Industry*, v. 9, n. 1, p. 21-30, 2015.

Kulik, O. et al. Human-Centered Aspects. In: Kerren, A. et al. (Ed.). *Human-Centered Visualization Environments*. Berlin: Springer, 2017. p. 13–75.

Sahaf, Z. et al. A visual analytics framework for exploring uncertainties in reservoir models. In: *VISIGRAPP 2018-Proceedings of the 13th Int. Joint Conf. on Computer Vision, Imaging and Computer Graphics Theory and Applications*. Funchal, Madeira, Portugal: SciTePress, 2018. v. 3, p. 74–84.

Sahaf, Z. et al. An ROI visual-analytical approach for exploring uncertainty in reservoir models. In: *Communications in Computer and Information Science*. Funchal, Madeira, Portugal: Springer Verlag, 2019. v. 997, p. 121–142.

Silva, C. G. et al. Visualization of Ensembles of Oil Reservoir Models Based on Pixelization, Small Multiples and Reservoir Similarities. In: *Offshore Technology Conference Brasil*. Rio de Janeiro, BR: Offshore Technology Conference, 2019.

Silva, C. G. et al. Using Reorderable Matrices to Compare Risk Curves of Representative Models in Oil Reservoir Development and Management Activities. In: *Proc. 14th Int. Conf. on Computer Graphics, Visualization, Computer Vision and Image Processing. IADIS*, 2020. p. 19–26.

Schiozer, D. J. et al. Model-based decision analysis applied to petroleum eld development and management. *Oil and Gas Science and Technology*, Editions Technip, v. 74, 2019.

Mahjour, S. K. et al. Developing a workflow to select representative reservoir models combining distance-based clustering and data assimilation for decision making process. *Journal of Petroleum Sci. and Eng.*, Elsevier B.V., v. 190, 2020.

Meira, L. A. A. et al. Selection of Representative Models for Decision Analysis Under Uncertainty. *Computers and Geosciences*. Elsevier B.V., v. 88, p. 67-82, 2016.

Meira, L. A. A. et al. RMFinder 2.0: An Improved Interactive Multi-Criteria Scenario Reduction Methodology. In: *SPE Latin America and Caribbean Petroleum Eng. Conference. Society of Petroleum Engineers*. 2017.

Meira, L. A. A. et al. Improving representativeness in a scenario reduction process to aid decision making in petroleum elds. *Journal of Petroleum Science and Engineering*, Elsevier B.V., v. 184, p. 1–19, 2020.

Zheng, J. et al. A Cluster-Based Approach for Visualizing and Quantifying the Uncertainty in the Impacts of Uncertain Shale Barrier Configurations on SAGD Production. In: *SPE Canada Heavy Oil Conference*. 2018.

HOW TO TEACH PROGRAMMING WITH ELECTRONIC GAMES

Ronald Carvalho Boadana, Cristina Souza de Araujo, Jucimar Maia da Silva Junior,
Clairon Lima Pinheiro and Luis Cuevas Rodriguez
Escola Superior de Tecnologia - EST
Universidade do Estado do Amazonas - UEA, Manaus, Brazil

ABSTRACT

This article describes the process of development of electronic games using the programming language Python which aims to focus on upgrading the student's programming skills. This way to learn turns out to be interesting by the fact that using arcade games that are daily plenty popular among the young who dedicate a lot of their time to playing. The process of game creation is more exciting to apply development tools than programming lists by college subjects.

KEYWORDS

Programming, Games, Skills, Learning

1. INTRODUCTION

Programming is a task which it requires much time and dedication to be learned correctly [Nilo, 2019]. At the university, there's specific programming's subjects which are very important at development of course, besides being present in all engineering courses. It is complete natural that the students ask themselves about the benefits with studies of programming languages concepts [Sebesta, 2011].

Electronic games can be categorized as the first touch with a computer of a young person that can be with PCs, consoles and smartphones, besides also being entertainment software, which focus on holding attention for a long period of time. Many players have the wish of learning how to create a game and especially, how to create their own games in many times they thought that their game ideas are better than those of most commercial gamer's designers [Schell, 2015]. When it comes to learning programming, creating games can be a highly effective and engaging way to learn. Games are interactive, fun, and can help learners to understand the logic behind programming in a practical and engaging way [Sweigart, 2015].

2. OBJECTIVES

The programming language Python is very interesting as the first language programming which a person has touch by its simplicity and clarity [Nilo, 2019]. Writing a clean and organized code makes the code better to understand and keep [McConnell, 2004]. Here there is some of main programming good practices:

- Use descriptive names for variables, functions, and classes. This helps make the code easier to understand [Martin, 2008];
- Avoid code duplication. This helps reduce complexity and makes the code easier to maintain [Fowler, 2018];
- Use a version control system to track changes made to the source code [Chacon et.al, 2014];
- Write automated tests to ensure that your code is working correctly [Beck, 2002].

Software engineering is a branch which works with software development of several kinds and having good practices is very essential for a future professional. On game development, there is good practices that must be followed as well as any development environment. According to Sommerville, rigorous software testing and iterative and incremental software development are important practices which must be adopted by developers because it can make the software development easier and adaptable to handle difficulties what can happen.

According to Martin, there is some techniques and practices which can used to improve the teammate is collaboration as an agile software development such as Scrum or Kanban. Also adopting a coding standard can be good for the project. Knowing how to handle with conflicts that can be emerge or problems among teammates is important, because at harmonic environment there's a higher level of enjoying, satisfaction and productivity increases.

3. JUSTIFICATION

Programming teaching at universities is widely used on graduation courses which involves technology like all engineering areas, computer science and information systems for application development is projects. Also, students cannot see how it relates to their interests or personal goals, because must be a way to make coding relevant and interesting by connecting it with their interests [Payne, 2015]. It is easier to notice the student's difficulties at high dropout rates at graduation courses previously mentioned.

In Brazil, the biggest evasion rate is realized on courses related to technology areas [G1, 2012], being that for each 4 students enrolled only one gets the graduation. This is a big problem, because there are always missing professionals to meet the market demand, a lot of jobs are created and some of them are filled.

The education must be unbounded of standard thought that is still the traditional axis of schools [Shaffer, 2006-a]. So, the electronic game development as a learning process looks ideal. Besides this strategy, also can highlight the active teaching methodologies which are very used in projects as the way to fix the learning.

4. METHODOLOGY

During the game development is necessary to use the active teaching methodologies as a form to get the enough learning to solve complex problems and the possibility to work with a team [Bacich el. al, 2018].

This section describes the materials and methods used during the project development:

• Python: During this process, Python was adopted because the students had familiarity with them and there's graphics libraries to develop.

• Turtle Graphics: This graphics library Python is used to draw on screen using simple commands. It was used for the first game, Pong, by its simplicity.

• PyGame: Python library specific to game development, when compared to Turtle with its functionality and commands, PyGame becomes very interesting by its quantities of commands which makes the code more simple and more functional. It was used in all games mentioned earlier.

• Linux: It's an operational system very used by programmers and made for them. It was used by students to get more immersion on programming and, it's a standard operating system used at universities to teach programming.

• Git: Also known as the version control system which helps the programmer to manage the code of a project. Is very used by programmers to team software development and keeping the code available to everyone from any computer.

• PyCharm: It's an IDE (Integrated Development Environment), so, a development integrated environment that assembles several development tools in one single program. It was developed by JetBrains, and it is very used by students for game development.

The actives methodologies are other pedagogy way which put the focus of teaching process and learning learner involving by discovery learning, investigation or problem is solving [Bacich el.al, 2018]. Learning by Doing is an active methodology, applied to the project, which focuses on hands-on projects, coding challenges, and interactives simulations as this way a programming educator can help the students to develop skills and knowledge they need [Kolb, 2014].

5. DEVELOPMENT

This section will explain how the development process for the game chosen and how learning techniques have applied.

5.1 Pong

The Pong [Atari, 1972] version using the Turtle graphics was the first game developed. This version had errors (bugs). These errors were: the ball was stuck behind the players rackets making it impossible to play and it was the main characteristic of the original game, the ball has velocity and angulation constants. The problem of fixing code also is known as debug which is technique that the programmer verifies each code lines on trying to find errors. Besides this, there was a program good practice to be applied: refactoring (technique used to rewrite/organize a code according by the programmer opinion).

On Pong 2.0, new possibilities have been presented to students with the Pygame library that improves the performance of the game and code, besides making available new more practical functionalities. A good example is the relationship to game sounds, using Turtle it is necessary to use another library that changes according to the operational system. Beyond it was applied software engineering techniques to show the students the importance and how this can make the development easier. Worth highlighting one specific function on this version that was implemented: the second racker was controlled by an AI simulation (Artificial Intelligence).

5.2 Snake

Different from the two previous Pong versions which were given a code with errors to fix, this Snake [Blockade, 1976] version the game was created by zero by students. Also, it started the process to make the code organized using Python functions. On game development, knowing how to handle deadlines is essential to the ethical posture of a developer, starting at this point it should create a weekly plan to show everything will be developed during the week.

The technique applied to this Snake 2.0 was modular programming (instead of writing the code on one file, this technique allows to separate the code in many files which it can communicate itself using an import statement). This kind of program focuses on:

- Joining functions and variables related in single file.
- Game division in modules (which module is responsible of a part of game, per example, the snake module is responsible for the snake on game).
- Making the code maintenance easier.

The introduction of this technique had the goal to prepare for Oriented Object Programming (OOP). The OOP is a programming paradigm that uses objects – data structures that contain data and code to design applications. The OOP promotes modular code, code reuse (it's a technique which the programmer can reuse a code already used previously), encapsulation (it's a technique which protects data and prevents it from being accessed or modified by other part) and a natural way to model real-world concepts and systems [Lafore, 2010].

Beyond the module programming, the Snake 3.0 should use OOP to create the new Snake version, but this time the development process was made with a team. Besides, it should have a snake which has autonomy to fight with the player, it should avoid all the obstacles and eat all fruits.

5.3 Asteroids

From all games developed until now, the Asteroids [Atari, 1979] was the best because it brought all the techniques learned with OOP, modular programming and refactoring. At this game, it should be applied a *Design Pattern* which is a recurring solution to problems that arise when designing software within a particular context and it is a way to reusing knowledge about how to solve a particular type of problem [Gamma et.al, 1994]. The design pattern adopted for this game was *Abstract Factory* which is way to incorporate easily new types of objects (this case these objects actually is the asteroids) or families of objects without requiring major changes to the system itself [Gamma et.al, 1994]. The most common way to create was using arrays and counters, but the optimization was necessary therefore the *Abstract Factory* is better to simplify the code and make the system more flexible [Gamma et.al, 1994].

6. CONCLUSION

The programming teaching at universities is looked at as a complex and tiring task by many students, but it is essential to graduation. So, finding a way to become something bad seen in something funny and interesting is essential. Thus, using game development to teach looks promising at university, but it is not limited to teaching the basics, but also improving the skills already existing. The arcade games look very good to start with their simplicity when compared to present games and by its simple mechanics as Pong, Snake, Asteroids were very important in it is golden age at last century and until now as teaching tools. How there is different ways to create games, the library specific use from a programming language is very used. As an example, the Turtle graphics used to make draws with geometric forms for the first game, but there are specific libraries to game development as Pygame which it offers more functionalities.

ACKNOWLEDGEMENT

The authors thanks to the Universidade do Estado Amazonas (UEA), Transire Eletrônicos, Tec Toy S.A. and Ludus Lab for their support. The results were published through the research and development activities of project ARKADE AD ASTRA, sponsored by Transire Eletrônicos and Tec Toy S.A, with the support of SUFRAMA under the terms of Federal Law No.8.387/1991.

REFERENCES

Bacich L., Moran J., (2018). *Metodologias ativas para uma educação inovadora: uma abordagem teórico-prática.* Penso Publisher, Porto Alegre, Brazil.

Beck K., (2002). *Test Driven Development: By Example.* Addison-Wesley Publisher, USA.

Chacon S., Straub B., (2014). *Pro Git.* Apress, USA.

Fowler M., Beck K., (2018). *Refactoring: Improving the Design of Existing Code.* Addison-Wesley Publisher, Boston, USA.

G1, (2022). Indice de evasão de alunos é maior na área de tecnologia da informação. Available on https://g1.globo.com/sp/sao-carlos-regiao/noticia/2012/09/indice-de-evasao-de-alunos-e-maior-na-area-de-tecnologia-da-informacao.html

Gamma E., Helm R., Johnson R., Vlissides J., (1994). *Design Patterns: Elements of Reusable Object-Oriented Softwares.* Addison-Wesley Professional Publisher, Indianapolis, USA.

Kolb D. A., (2014). *Experiential Learning: Experience as the Source of Learning and Development.* Pearson Education, New Jersey, USA.

Lafore R., (2010). *Object-Oriented Programming in C++.* Sams Publishing, USA.

Martin C. M., (2008). *Clean Code: A Handbook of Agile Software Craftmanship.* Prentice Hall Publisher, Boston, USA.

Martin R. C., (2003). *Agile Software Development, Principles, Patterns and Practices.* Pearson, USA.

McConnell S., (2004). *Code Complete.* Microsoft Press, Washington, USA.

Menezes C. N. Nilo, (2019). *Introdução a Programação com Python: Algoritmos e lógica de programação para iniciantes.* Novatec Publisher, São Paulo, Brazil.

Payne, B. (2015). *Teaching Kids to Code: An Introduction to Python Programming.* No Starch Press, San Francisco, USA.

Sebesta W. R, (2018). *Concepts of Programming Languages.* Pearson, USA.

Shaffer D. W., (2006). *How Computer Games Help Children Learn.* Palgrave MacMillian, New York, USA.

Sommerville I., (2015). *Software Engineering.* Pearson, Indianapolis, USA.

A MOBILE CONDUCTING APP WITH A SWITCHING BEAT-FOLLOWING ALGORITHM

Zengguang Wu, William Raffe and Andrew Johnston
University of Technology Sydney, Australia

ABSTRACT

Conducting an orchestra had been a privilege reserved for professional conductors, until there are music conducting systems that can follow the user's lead. The music playing and beat tracking components of conducting systems have been well developed, but the beat-following algorithm has room for improvement. In this paper we present a mobile conducting app with a novel beat-following algorithm, which can switch between different behaviours to accommodate different musical situations and user preferences, and allow the user to make their own interpretations of classic orchestral works.

KEYWORDS

Mobile, Conducting App, Switching, Beat-Following Algorithm

1. INTRODUCTION

Orchestral music has a significant impact on human culture as a kind of music that can bring emotions and tell stories with a group of instruments. Conducting an orchestra had traditionally been a privilege reserved for highly trained professional conductors. However, with modern interactive conducting systems, a wider audience of enthusiasts can now experience the creative freedom of conducting a large digital orchestra.

As a form of play, a conducting system is an example of *paidia* as opposed to *ludus* (Caillois, 1958/2001). As a game, a conducting system is a *non-game*, "a form of entertainment that really doesn't have a winner, or even a real conclusion" (Iwata, 2005), similar to simulation games like SimCity and The Sims. As a music game, a conducting system is an *instrument game* (Pichlmair & Kayali, 2007), which has a reverse mechanism to rhythm games. In a rhythm game, the user follows the music, and performs actions when they need to; in a conducting system, the user gives beats when they want to, and the music follows their lead.

2. BACKGROUND: MUSIC CONDUCTING SYSTEMS

Music conducting systems have appeared in various forms: multimedia installations, such as Personal Orchestra (Borchers et al., 2004), Mendelssohn Effektorium (WHITEvoid Studio, 2014); computer programs, such as Semi-conductor (Google Creative Lab, 2018), Live Tempo of Avid Sibelius (Avid Technology, 2023); and mobile apps, such as Bravo Gustavo (Hello Design, 2010), vMaestro (Lim & Yeo, 2014), Airconductor (Micro App Brewery, 2019). All these systems have three major components: a music player, a beat tracker, and a beat-following algorithm to let the music follow the beats. The music playing and beat tracking components have been well developed, but the beat-following algorithm has room for improvement.

2.1 The Music Player

A conducting system can work with either a MIDI sequencer (vMaestro, Airconductor) or some recorded sound (Personal Orchestra, Bravo Gustavo). MIDI sequencers are more flexible with tempi, and can chase or wait for the user without the sound quality being compromised. Recorded sound in conducting systems is often performed by prestigious artists, with the artistic value being an objective of the system.

2.2 The Beat Tracker

Beat tracking has previously been achieved with various types of input. Common input devices such as keyboards (Avid Sibelius) and touch screens (Bravo Gustavo) are simple but efficient ways to get beats from the user. Physical devices with sensors such as accelerometer (Bravo Gustavo) and gyroscope (vMaestro) can gather beats from the user's motions, and therefore enable the use of real-world conducting gestures. Cameras (Semi-conductor) provide the most freedom for the user, allowing them to conduct with bare hands, but they also pose the biggest challenge for the algorithm.

2.3 The Beat-Following Algorithm

Looking at past and present conducting systems, we see two core beat-following algorithms, one responsive and flexible, the other smooth and stable; and two complex algorithms that combine the core ones, one by mixing them, and one by weighting between them.

To show how these algorithms work, we use position-time graphs as below. The horizontal t-axis is time in the real world; the vertical x-axis is time in the music file, which is also referred to as position. On the graph, each orange is a beat from the user. The solid line is the system's position in the music file, with a steep slope indicating a fast tempo. A vertical section of the solid line shows the system fast-forwarding to chase the user; a horizontal section of the solid line means the system pausing to wait for the user.

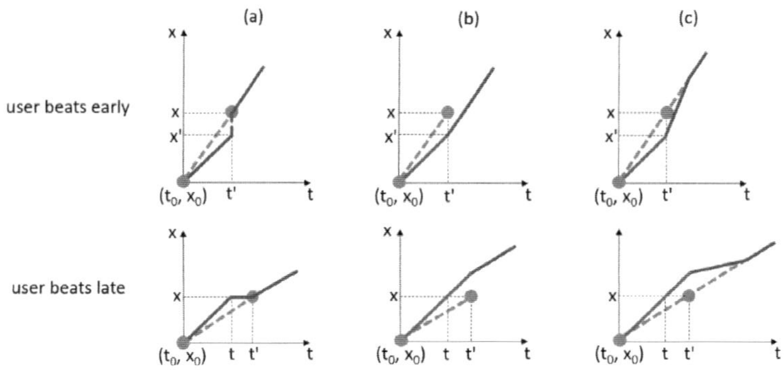

Figure 1. Position-time graphs of existing algorithms

Figure 1(a) shows the algorithm of Bravo Gustavo. In this responsive algorithm, every beat from the user corresponds to a beat in the music. If the user beats early, the music fast forwards to the corresponding beat; if the user beats late, the music waits before the corresponding beat. At each beat from the user, a new tempo is calculated from the time difference between the last two beats, referred to as "the simplest option" (Dannenberg & Bookstein, 1991), and no averaging is involved. This algorithm gives the user more control over the music, but can cause disruptions in playback.

Figure 1(b) illustrates the algorithm of several MIDI-based systems (vMaestro, Airconductor, Mendelssohn Effektorium). In this smooth algorithm, there is no chasing or waiting. At each beat from the user, the tempo is set to the average rate of the last several beats, referred to as "a history buffer" (Dannenberg & Bookstein, 1991). This algorithm can prevent the tempo from shaking up and down, and provide smooth playback. But there is no correspondence between beats in the music and beats from the user, and the music cannot follow the user's individual beats.

Figure 1(c) shows a solution by Personal Orchestra, a mix of the two simple algorithms. In this algorithm, chasing is not fast forwarding, but playing at a tempo faster than the user's desired tempo, to catch up with the user after a certain time; waiting is done in a similar but opposite way. This algorithm allows chasing and waiting without causing disruptions in the playback, although going further than the user's intended tempo change may not sound natural.

In comparison, the algorithm of the Live Tempo feature of Avid Sibelius is a weighting between the two simple algorithms. In the options, there is a "sensitivity" slider with "smoother" at one end and "more responsive" at the other, which can be adjusted according to the character of the piece and the preference of the user. But during a performance, the slider is not accessible, and the weighting remains the same.

However, passages and beats in music are not all the same. For example, Dannenberg and Bookstein (1991) "found a conflict between the necessity for fine control of tempo in the slow, expressive passages, and the necessity in very rhythmically stable passages for the computer to be less sensitive". Such differences in musical situation need to be accommodated by the algorithm of a conducting system. Baba et al. (2010) used performance templates to help with differences in musical situation, but when the user's intention is significantly different from the template, it may not work well. Such differences in user preference also need to be accommodated by the algorithm of a conducting system.

3. IMPLEMENTATION: A MOBILE CONDUCTING APP

Having identified the beat-following algorithm as a niche area of music conducting systems, now we present our implementation, a mobile conducting app with a switching beat-following algorithm. This algorithm is our main focus, so for the music playing and beat tracking components, we took simple but effective approaches previously used in other systems.

3.1 The Music Player

The app uses Swift's AVMIDIPlayer, and works with specially made MIDI files, where the tempo is set to 60 beats per minute (bpm) despite the actual tempo. 60 bpm is one beat per second, so the beat positions are exactly the integer positions of the MIDI file, which makes it easy for the app to find the beat positions.

3.2 The Beat Tracker

The app uses iPhone's gyroscope to catch the user's beats. The user is expected to hold the mobile phone in their right hand, with the top of the phone pointing to the front, and the screen facing to the left. In real-world conducting, each beat of the conductor is a downward motion followed by an upward bounce (McElheran, 2004, Ch. VI), and the orchestra responds when the conductor's hand hits the lowest point and starts the bounce. In our mobile conducting app, such gestures bring a positive rotation around the z-axis followed by a negative rotation, and the app detects a beat when the rotation rate goes first above 3 and then below 0.

3.3 The Beat-Following Algorithm

The app has a novel beat-following algorithm, which can switch between different behaviours to accommodate different musical situations and user preferences. In the app, each MIDI file for the MIDI player comes with a text file for the algorithm. In the text file, each row corresponds to a beat in the music, and contains settings of the app's behaviour at this beat. The settings can be adjusted via a user interface.

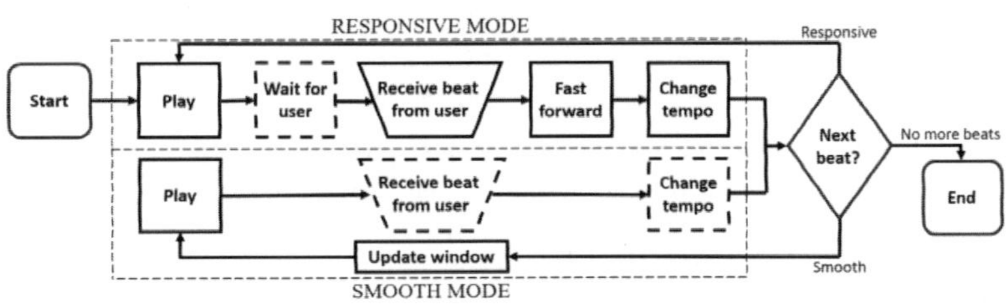

Figure 2. The switching beat-following algorithm

Figure 2 is an illustration of the algorithm. The switching is our main innovation; the responsive mode is the same as the responsive algorithm mentioned above; the smooth mode is similar to the smooth algorithm, but here each beat from the user corresponds to a beat in the music. In the responsive mode, the app follows the user closely, and can wait for/chase the user; the user's beat is compulsory, and the music will only play on when it receives a beat from the user. In the smooth mode, there is no waiting or chasing; the user's beat is optional, and the music plays on whether the user beats or not; for each beat in the music, there is a time window for the user to give the beat; beats received between windows can be ambiguous, and will be ignored.

$$c = \frac{t' - t_0}{t - t_0}$$

$$c' = \frac{c + m}{1 + m}$$

$$v' = \frac{v}{c'}$$

Figure 3. The calculation of the new tempo

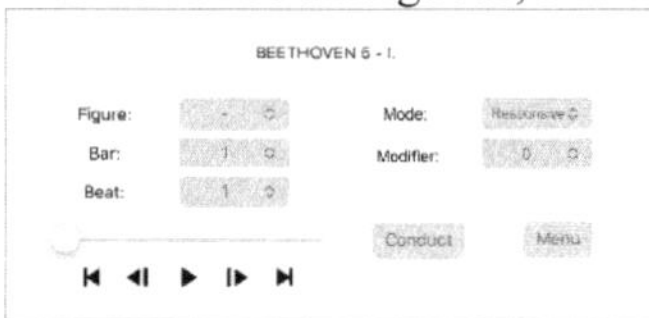

Figure 4. The User interface

In both modes, the new tempo is calculated as shown in Figure 3. Suppose the previous beat of the music was at time t_0, the current beat is expected at time t, and the user's beat is received at time t'. First, the indicated duration change c is calculated as the ratio between the new beat duration t'-t_0 suggested by the user's beat and the old beat duration t-t_0 at the current tempo. Then, the modified duration change c' is calculated from $(c+m)/(1+m)$, where m is a modifier that determines the app's resistance to tempo change. A positive m would shrink the change and stabilise the tempo; the larger m, the stronger the impact; an m between 0 and -1 would magnify the change. Finally, we multiply the current tempo v by the reciprocal of the duration change, $1/c'$, which is the tempo change, and get the new tempo v'.

Figure 4 shows the app's user interface. The user can navigate inside the piece with the slider or the buttons underneath (previous figure, previous beat, play, next beat and next figure). When the user presses the play button, the app plays a pre-recorded performance of the piece. The pickers on the left are another way to navigate, and the pickers on the right allow the user to specify the app's behaviour at this beat, namely the mode and the modifier m. When the user is ready to conduct, they hit the "Conduct" button, and the gyroscope will start catching the user's beats.

4. THE ALGORITHM IN ACTION

Similar to the corresponding separate algorithms, the responsive mode is more flexible, and gives the user more control; the smooth mode is more stable, and keeps the music flowing. For the modifier m, setting it to zero would let the app follow the user's tempo change as it is, while setting it to a very large number would prevent the tempo from changing. With these settings, the app can accommodate beats of different natures, passages of different characters and users of different preferences. To see this, here are some examples.

Figure 5. Beethoven: Symphony No. 5 (1808, excerpt)

Figure 5 is the opening of Beethoven's Fifth Symphony. At the start of a piece, the orchestra needs two instructions from the conductor: when to start, and at what tempo. [6, Ch. XIV] Before the first beat of the music (beat 1), the conductor often gives an extra beat (beat 0); the orchestra start playing at the conductor's beat 1, at the tempo indicated by beats 0 and 1. These beats are supposed to be followed closely, so here we use the responsive mode.

For a fermata, the app clearly needs to allow waiting for the beat after the fermata, but this is not enough. After a fermata it is a new start, and we need an extra beat for the user to set the tempo. In this example, for the first fermata, beat 3 has been added to the score to help with beat 4; for the second, the fermata has been moved from beat 6 to beat 5, this has no impact on the long note, but allows beat 6 to help with beat 7. Beats 3, 4, 6 & 7 all need to be followed closely, and call for the responsive mode.

At the above beats, the app gives the user full control by allowing waiting and chasing, but at beats 2 and 5, such control is unwanted. Sitting on these beats are the fourth notes of the fate motif, and playing them early or late would upset the rhythm, so an early or late beat from the user is more likely an error than an intention. Therefore, here we use the smooth mode to keep the fate motif in good shape. As shown here, the app can accommodate beats of different natures, and handle them in the appropriate ways.

Beat	1	2	3	4	5	6	7	8	9	10	11	12	13	14	15
Mode	S	S	S	S	S	S	S	S	S	R	R	R	R	R	R
m	1	1	1	1	1	1	1	1	1	0	0	0	0	0	0

Figure 6. Brahms: Symphony No. 1 (1876, excerpt)

This excerpt from the finale of Brahms's First Symphony (Fig. 6) features good examples of "rhythmically stable passages" and "slow, expressive passages" in the words of Dannenberg and Bookstein. The first four bars are densely populated with a three-note phrase derived from the main theme of the movement, which is very rhythmic, and tends to keep flowing without being disrupted. For such a passage, we cannot allow waiting or chasing, so we use the smooth mode; tempo changes are possible, but a sudden tempo change would break the momentum, so we set the modifier to 1, and hence reduce the user's tempo changes by a half. The last four bars recall a chorale theme from the movement's introduction, which is a series of long chords, and invites the conductor to do anything they want with the tempo. For such a passage, we need to allow waiting and chasing, and use the responsive mode; the modifier is set to 0, and the user's tempo changes are followed faithfully. In this example, passages of different characters are treated in the way they are supposed to be treated.

		Beat	1	2	3	4	5	6	7
Option 1	Mode		S	S	S	S	S	S	S
	m		24	24	24	24	24	24	24
Option 2	Mode		S	S	S	S	S	R	S
	m		1	1	1	1	24	0	24

Figure 7. Rachmaninov: Symphony No. 2 (1908, excerpt)

Some passages, such as the final bars of Rachmaninov's Second Symphony (Fig. 7), can be played in very different ways. As a typical loud and fast ending, it can be kept to a fast tempo, bringing the symphony to a straightforward close. To do this, we simply set all beats to the smooth mode, and m to a large number to prevent the tempo from changing. But if we want, we can also add some drama here. The first five beats have to be in the smooth mode, but m can be small to allow tempo changes. At beat 5, there is only one chord on the beat, forming a break between beats 5 & 6, making it possible for us to change to a slower tempo at beat 6 to add some weight to the final chords. To do this, we set beat 6 to the responsive mode with an m of zero. Then, the final chords will be played at the tempo suggested by beats 5 and 6 from the user. With the proper setting, the app can play any passage in the user's preferred manner.

5. CONCLUSION

In the current implementation, the new tempo at each beat is a modification of the current tempo according to the beat from the user. Some musical situations, such as "rit. … a tempo" (gradually slow down, then suddenly return to the original tempo), cannot be handled by this mechanism, and call for more options. We are going to polish the beat-following algorithm, combine it with more sophisticated music playing and beat tracking, and aim for a better conducting experience.

Orchestral music is a true pearl of human culture. We hope that, with our mobile conducting app, more orchestral music enthusiasts will be able to make their own interpretations of classic orchestral works, and more human hearts will be blessed with the profound sound of orchestral music.

REFERENCES

Avid Technology (2023). Avid Sibelius [Computer software].

Baba, T., Hashida, M., & Katayose, H. (2010). "VirtualPhilharmony": A Conducting System with Heuristics of Conducting an Orchestra. Conference on New Interfaces for Music Expression, 2010.

Beethoven, L. v. (1808). Symphony No. 5 in C minor, op. 67.

Borchers, J., Lee, E., Samminger, W., & Mühlhäuser, M. (2004). Personal orchestra: A real-time audio/video system for interactive conducting. Multimedia Systems, 9(5), 458-465.

Brahms, J. (1876). Symphony No. 1 in C minor, op. 68.

Caillois, R. (1958/2001). Man, play, and games. University of Illinois press.

Dannenberg, R. B., & Bookstein, K. (1991). Practical aspects of a midi conducting program. Proceedings of the 1991 International Computer Music Conference.

Google Creative Lab (2018). Semi-Conductor [Computer software].

Hello Design (2010). Bravo Gustavo [Mobile app].

Iwata, S., (2005). Keynote speech at the Game Developers Conference. https://www.ign.com/articles/2005/03/11/gdc-2005-iwata-keynote-transcript

Lim, Y. K., & Yeo, W. S. (2014). Smartphone-based Music Conducting. Conference on New Interfaces for Music Expression, 2014.

McElheran, B. (2004). Conducting technique: For beginners and professionals. Oxford University Press.

Micro App Brewery. (2019). Airconductor [Mobile app].

Pichlmair, M., & Kayali, F. (2007). Levels of Sound: On the Principles of Interactivity in Music Video Games. DiGRA Conference.

Rachmaninov, S. (1908). Symphony No. 2 in E minor, op. 27.

WHITEvoid Studio (2014). Mendelssohn Effektorium [Multimedia Installation].

AN AUGMENTED REALITY GAME FOR IOS SMARTPHONES

Felipe Luna Tersi[1] and Ilana de Almeida Souza-Concilio[2]
[1]*Eldorado Institute of Research*
Campinas - São Paulo, Brazil
[2]*AmbevTech*
Campinas - São Paulo, Brazil

ABSTRACT

Augmented reality is a technology that is constantly expanding and has great potential for application in the most diverse areas. This technology is able to integrate virtual objects in physical spaces in a natural way. In addition, games stimulate cognitive and perceptual learning skills, especially when there is a challenge and strategy that has to make the user think to achieve a certain action. This article presents the development of an augmented reality game for mobile devices with iOS operating system. In the game the player is a drone and needs to destroy other drones that protect a city, for that he needs to project the game in a physical space to shoot and deflect the firing of these drones, collect power ups that are virtual objects, bringing interactivity between the real world and the virtual world generated by technology.

KEYWORDS

Augmented Reality, Mobile Applications, Digital Games

1. INTRODUCTION

Human being has always tried to generate representations of reality, through paintings, theater, cinema and other ways. With the emergence of the computer, these attempts to represent reality became virtual, through games, animations and videos according to Romero Tori.

According to Kirner and Siscoutto, before 1945, people used natural interfaces to interact with the world and their surroundings. They hardly needed to interact with any machine to push a button or pull levers.

However, with the appearance of the first ENIAC computer, everything changed and people needed to adapt to new technologies, through training and every decade the people had to adjust their lives to the use of computers.

What people needed before to adapt to the machines, now the machine needs to adjust to the user's needs. The feasibility of use of computers by people and the advancement of these technologies, are allowing the real environment to be intensified with objects and information, promoting a possible new phase of human-computer interaction.

With the evolution of these computers, the first expressions of "beyond the monitor screen" began to emerge, the human being invited to use virtual tools in the physical and real world. The rise of the real world with virtual elements is a variation of mixed reality, known as Augmented Reality (AR).

According to Thompson and Potter, a fundamental principle of augmented reality is the incorporation of digital elements in the real world, that, for mobile AR, tends to depend on contextual markers (usually visually).

This article aims to present the conception of an application with use of augmented reality for smartphones on the iOS platform, using ARKit, RealityKit and SceneKit frameworks provided by Apple.

2. AUGMENTED REALITY

Kirner and Kirner claim that: "Augmented Reality is the insertion of virtual objects in the physical environment, shown to the user, in real time, with the support of some technological device, using the real environment interface, adapted to visualize and manipulate real and virtual objects".

It can be said, then, that AR complements the real world. Through the projection of virtual objects and components, like images, videos and three-dimensional elements, an enriching experience is provided to the user due to the new interaction of the real environment and the new virtual objects.

According to Azuma et al., an AR system must have three properties: integrate the real ambience with virtual objects; have real-time interactivity and make these objects appear to be on the same plane.

AR is a technological tool that can be used in infinite sectors. Some cases and areas of AR applications are: Medicine for surgical training and teleoperations, Dentistry also for surgical training, Engineering to assistance in projects, works and constructions, military training, Entertainment, among others.

2.1 Digital Games and Augmented Reality in Mobile Phones

Until a few years ago, the processors of mobile devices didn't have enough capacity to allow the development of more robust applications. Due to the evolution of the hardware in these devices, this reality has been transformed. Nowadays, cell phones have a hardware architecture suitable for interacting with augmented reality games and applications.

One of the great advances in these devices is that, in addition to the location detection capability, now most of these devices have features and support for orientation through accelerometers, gyroscope and magnetometer.

The union of localization capacity, along with orientation detection allow increasingly real experiences in AR games.

Games have always been used by people as a form of entertainment or cognitive development, however, these games had planar representations, that is, for boards or with immersion limitations such as video games that needed joysticks to play.

Due to all this evolution, technology provides the use of AR in games, bringing virtual games to the user's physical space, bringing a new and unique experience for players according to P. Milgram.

Projected and developed as a platform game for mobile devices, Whack It! aims to stimulate children's physical play through augmented reality interactive games. The authors claim that AR games allow children to experience an enlarged 3D space that will significantly influence them, especially related to motor manipulation and spatial cognition.

Plecher et al. present a serious AR game for tablets - Dragon Tail, whose purpose is teaching the Japanese Kanji language. The authors justify the choice of mobile devices due to the large and intuitive touch screens for drawing kanji and the possibility of using gestures.

2.2 Development

Apple Inc. provides some important frameworks for developing applications with AR. The first one is the Augmented Reality Kit (ARKit) now in its version 3.5. It is a framework SDK that essentially processes data sensors to provide AR experiences.

One of the features in this framework is the Collaborative Sessions, that enables the development of augmented reality applications with real-time sessions between multiple users in a more simple and quicker way. It recovers and shares the projected virtual environment among users, enriching their experiences while interacting synchronously, integrating their scenarios.

The other framework is the Reality Kit that implements, simulates and renders high performance 3D elements and objects for AR applications. It uses the information provided by the ARKit structure, enabling a perfect integration of virtual objects in the real world environment.

Reality Kit provides Reality Composer, a feature that allows the user to import 3D objects with sophisticated compositions, containing meshes, materials and textures. With it users may also animate these objects, incorporate physics simulations and pre-programmed movements, in addition to audio environments, allowing unique immersions for the user.

Another important framework is SceneKit, that enables the creation of 3D games, not necessarily of AR, but the user can also easily add animations, physical simulations, particle effects and very realistic physics-based renderings. This tool has a high performance rendering engine with an API capable of rendering, manipulating and importing 3D objects and it only requires a description of the content in the scene and the actions or animations it must perform.

In this project, the methodology used was Challenge Based Learning (CBL), which consists of three phases, Engage, Investigate and Act. Each of these steps has unique and fundamental activities in order to find the best solution for the project in question.

All steps are fully collaborative and, the more people involved in the project, the greater the chances of proposing better solution ideas, taking into account that people who aren't from the area can also be part of the process. Each stage performed must be registered and documented. Evaluation was carried out at each step in order to promote reflection of the process and lessons learned. It is important to highlight that this is a cyclical methodology and users can come and go during the phases.

The first phase called Engage is when a great area of knowledge known also as Big Idea is stablished. In a second moment, an Essential Question is formulated, representing a problem from this Big Idea that needs special attention. Then a challenge is proposed in order to engage users to guide the research and to work in a solution to solve the proposed problem.

The Investigate phase is when the users become immersed in the problem and challenge, creating guiding questions and stablishing resources that would help them find the answers. Those questions should guide the direction of the research, helping to understand the problem, finding out which solutions already exist, among others. Questionnaires, interviews and gathered data may also help to answer those questions that must be analyzed to assist the users to come up with great solutions.

The third phase is Act and, as the name says, it is an action and development stage. With an analysis of all the proposed solutions based on the set of data and information gathered in the previous phase, it's when the user chooses the one that best meets the solution of the problem and implements it. After the idea has been developed, batteries of tests must be made to collect feedback about what worked and what needs to be improved.

Regarding the game presented in this article, the Big Idea was "Dystopian Game" and the Essential Question was "How to develop a dystopian game for iOS?".

With the first phase defined, the second stage began - Investigate, a series of questions were documented in order to be able to answer the Essential Question. Some of them were: "What is dystopic?", "What are the most common dystopian themes?", "What are our references of dystopian games?", "What are our references of dystopian iOS games?", "How is the game mechanic?, “How is the game aesthetic?", "What is the technology used?", "What is the loop of the game?".

During the investigation phase with research on websites, articles, questionnaires and books, it was possible to answer all of these questions and then move on to the Act stage.

In the third and final phase Act, the Minimal Viable Product (MVP) solution proposal was synthesized at first, and it consisted of an iOS game using AR technology with cyberpunk theme in a dystopian sense. The player would interact with virtual objects overlapping the real environment around him/her and would have to destroy drones and collect items shoot them*.

2.3 Application

Developed using the Apple technologies described above, the game was implemented in two versions, first a single player version and then a second multiplayer version.

2.3.1 Single Player

In the single player version of the game, a storytelling was created, which is, in short, a dystopian world, devastated by pollution, where the ozone layer no longer exists. A nano material was developed by a group of scientists financed by a corporation, which developed a dome with this technology in order to recreate a habitable atmosphere.

The player is a drone and his mission is to invade this city by destroying the drones that protect it and the dome, thus winning the game.

The choice to use the AR tool in this application was made while answering the guiding questions, specifically the one: "Which mechanics to use?". After some research, some answers were proposed such as avoider, beat'em up, tower defense and infinity run. In the end, avoiding creating just another game using these mechanics, AR was chosen along with a cyberpunk aesthetic and the player would be engaged in the proposal and story of the game. It was concluded that AR is the technology most capable of immersing the player as if it were a drone and that would most fulfill the game's need and that Scene Kit, ARKit and Reality Kit frameworks would give the right tools for the game development.

On the game's home screen, there's a message saying "The city is hidden, scan the area and when the element turns green, tap to start". The reason of this tutorial is that in AR the user must always make a recognition of the real ambience with the camera in order to find a sufficient number of feature points. When placing the virtual object in the real scene, everything should work perfectly and providing a tutorial integrated into the game's story, the player should automatically perform the requirements of AR but without feeling to be out of the game, as if it were apart.

After starting the game (Figure 1) the virtual object of a city, covered by a dome surrounded by drones is shown. These drones are spinning around the city orbit and fire missiles every time they pass in front of the player's camera. The player's goal is to destroy all the drones, without running out of energy. However, each shot consumes 1 energy and every time the player is hit by a drone shot, he also loses 1 energy.

Figure 1. Game scenario projected in physical ambience

In order to bring a greater immersion of the user in this game, power ups of energy were spread, as shown in Figure 2. The only way to collect them is by going through them, that is, the player needs to walk to the element to pick it up, bringing greater interactivity to the game. In addition, the user can also fly around the virtual city making it easier to destroy the other drones as well as being able to deviate the shots fired by them.

Figure 2. Power ups spread across the virtual scene

The SceneKit tool made it possible to insert audio elements and tactile feedback as vibrations that provide a more enriching experience to the player during the game. Every time a shot is fired, a sound is emitted and every time a drone is targeted it has a confirming sound. About the vibration, every time the drone is hit, the cell phone vibrates and every time the user passes to collect the powerup, it has a vibration as confirmation but with another intensity so as not to be confused that it was hit by a drone.

In addition to these elements, SceneKit also made it possible to insert particle elements. As an example, when a drone is hit by the missile an explosion particle appears (Figure 3).

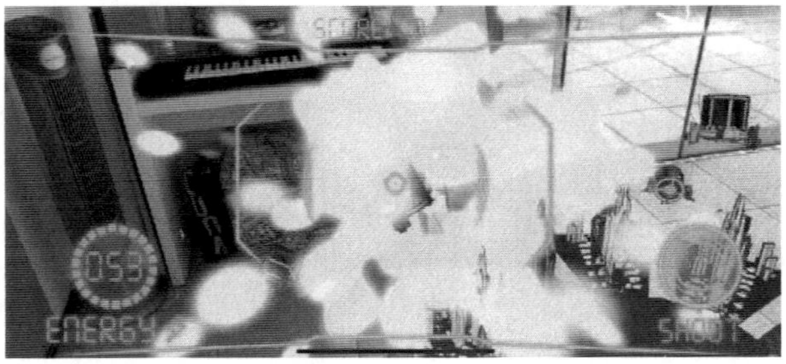

Figure 3. Drone destroyed by the player.

All these elements, such as making the user move to capture the powerups, having feedback for vibrations, visuals and particles, were designed to make the user feel that he's really inside a drone, increasing his interactivity and immersion in the game.

The game's HUD itself was designed with the aim of giving a greater impression that the player was in charge of a drone. Research was also done about colors and how to have an effect that could be visible in any environment, thinking about interaction design and user experience.

2.3.2 Multiplayer

With the launch of RealityKit, that provides the Collaborative Sessions tool, it became easier to develop AR games with sharing virtual scenarios in real time with other players in a physical environment. For this purpose, the multiplayer version of the game which is actually a player versus player, is still under development.

At first, users need to scan the same physical environment to have the recognition of the features points of the physical space and then share the same game scenario.

After this step, the users can see each other and, in place of the cell phone, a drone is projected and the mission is to shoot at each other until one of them defeats the opponent.

3. CONCLUSION

Augmented Reality is a technology that is constantly growing and its application is well diversified and is becoming increasingly easier.

This article presents the process of developing an iOS application that is an AR game where a player needs to destroy drones by deflecting their shots, collecting power ups across the stage to have more energy and destroying the dome to win. For this purpose, frameworks provided by Apple were used, such as ARKit, Reality Kit, Reality Composer and SceneKit.

Despite all the tools, technologies, frameworks and resources used, the process of developing an AR game is not an easy task. In addition to requiring a lot of physical movement and thus considerable space to test it, it is necessary to determine minimum feature points to scan the environment and anchor the virtual scenario.

It is important to highlight the potential of AR, regardless of the application area, since the development of products with this technology can accelerate in exponential size and solve real problems

REFERENCES

Azuma, R. et al. (2001). Recent Advances in Augmented Reality, *In IEEE Computer Graphics and Applications,* v .21, n.6: 34 – 47. DOI: 10.1109/38.963459

Behzadan, A. H. et al. (2011). A collaborative augmented reality based modeling environment for construction engineering and management education. In *WSC '11: Proceedings of the Winter Simulation Conference,* 3573–3581.

Bowman, D. A., Kruijff, E., LaViola Jr, J. J. e Poupyrev, I. (2004). 3D User Interfaces: Theory and Practice, Addison-Wesley, 2004.

Broll, W., et al. (2005). An Infrastructure for Realizing Custom- Tailored Augmented Reality User Interfaces. In *IEEE Transactions on Visualization and Computer Graphics*.

Hedayati, H., Walker, M., and Szafir, D. (2018). Improving Collocated Robot Teleoperation with Augmented Reality. In *HRI '18: Proceedings of the 2018 ACM/IEEE International Conference on Human-Robot Interaction.* Pages 78–86. DOI: https://doi.org/10.1145/3171221.3171251

Huang, Y.-H. et al. (2018). CatAR: A Novel Stereoscopic Augmented Reality Cataract Surgery Training System with Dexterous Instrument Tracking Technology. In *CHI '18: Proceedings of the 2018 CHI Conference on Human Factors in Computing Systems.* Paper No.: 465 Pages 1–12. DOI: https://doi.org/10.1145/3173574.3174039

Kirner, C. (2011). Realidade Virtual e Aumentada: definições. Available at <http://www.ckirner.com/realidadevirtual/?DEFINI%C7%D5ES>. Accessed in: April, 08th 2020.

Kirner, C. and Kirner, T. (2008). Virtual Reality and Augmented Reality Applied to Simulation Visualization. *In El Sheikh, A.A.R.; Al Ajeeli, A.; Abu-Taieh, E.M.O. (Ed.). Simulation and Modeling: Current Technologies and Applications.* 1 ed. Hershey-NY: IGI Publishing.

Kirner, C. and Siscoutto, R. (2007). Realidade Virtual e Aumentada: conceitos, projetos e aplicações. In *IX Symposium on Virtual and Augmented Reality*, 290p.

Luis E. Bautista R., et al. (2018). Augmented Reality User interaction to Computer Assisted Orthopedic Surgery system. In *MexIHC '18: Proceedings of the 7th Mexican Conference on Human-Computer Interaction.* Article No.: 5 Pages 1–9. DOI: https://doi.org/10.1145/3293578.3293590

Mark Nichols, et al. (2016). *Challenge Based Learner User Guide.* Redwood City, CA: Digital Promise.

Milgram, P., et al. (1994.) Augmented Reality: A Class of Displays on the Reality-Virtuality Continuum. In *Telemanipulator and Telepresence Technologies*, SPIE, V.2351.

Nielsen, J., and Loranger, H. (2007). Usabilidade na Web projetando sites com qualidade. Rio de Janeiro: Elsevier.

Nor F. N. M. Daud and Muhammad H. L. Abdullah. Stimulating Children's Physical Play through Augmented Reality Game. In *Journal of Advanced Computing Technology and Application* (JACTA), Vol. 2, No. 1, (May 2020), PP 9-13.

Phattanapon Rhienmora, et al. (2010). Augmented Reality Haptics System for Dental Surgical Skills Training. In *VRST '10: Proceedings of the 17th ACM Symposium on Virtual Reality Software and Technology.* Pages 97–98. DOI: https://doi.org/10.1145/1889863.1889883

Plecher, D. A., et al. (2018). Dragon Tale – A Serious Game for Learning Japanese Kanji. In *CHI PLAY'18 Extended Abstracts*, (October 2018). Melbourne, Australia.

Romero Tori et al. (2006). *Fundamentos e Tecnologia de Realidade Virtual e Aumentada.* Porto Alegre: SBC. Available at:http://www.ckirner.com/download/capitulos/Fundamentos_e_Tecnologia_de_Realidade_Virtual_e_Aumentada-v22-11-06.pdf> Accessed in April, 09th 2020.

Santos, M. E. C. et al. (2016). The COMPASS Framework for Digital Entertainment: Discussing Augmented Reality Activities for Scouts. In ACE '16: Proceedings of the 13th International Conference on Advances in Computer Entertainment Technology. Article No.: 28, 1–6. DOI: https://doi.org/10.1145/3001773.3001799

Stevens, J. and Eifert, L. (2014). Augmented Reality Technology in U.S. Army Training (WIP). In *SummerSim '14: Proceedings of the 2014 Summer Simulation Multiconference*. Article No.: 62, 1–6.

Thompson, A. and Potter, L. E. (2018). Taking the 'A' Out of 'AR': Play Based Low Fidelity Contextual Prototyping of Mobile Augmented Reality. In *CHI PLAY'18 Extended Abstracts*, (October 2018). Melbourne, Australia.

A GAMIFIED APPLICATION FOR MITIGATING PLASTIC POLLUTION IN COASTAL AREAS

Dimitra Tzanetou, Stavros T. Ponis, George Plakas, Eleni Aretoulaki and Antonios Kitsantas
School of Mechanical Engineering, National Technical University Athens
Heroon Polytechniou 9, Zografos 15780, Athens, Greece

ABSTRACT

Marine pollution constitutes an environmental and socioeconomic threat of paramount importance, as millions of tons of debris accumulate in marine ecosystems every year, resulting in the decrease of various touristic activities. The research presented in this paper directs its attention to the mitigation of aesthetic and other consequences of this severe global issue, which has multiple deleterious implications on the economy of many seaside countries. To that end, the proposed paper demonstrates a platform that will integrate data into a gamified application in order to motivate citizens' behavioral change towards proper waste disposal and marine ecosystems protection. After the concise description of the integrated methodology, which will be supported by an innovative technology solution utilizing drones, sensors and station pad technologies, more emphasis will be put on the definition of the gamification methods and elements that will be combined and selected to increase users' engagement and incentivize them to adopt eco-friendly attitudes.

KEYWORDS

Marine Littering, Gamification, Serious Games, Wireless Sensors, Behavioral Change, User Engagement

1. INTRODUCTION

Marine littering is undoubtedly a ubiquitous problem that is becoming extremely intense in the course of time, as approximately 4.8 to 12.7 million tons of plastic and other types of waste end up in marine environments every year (Jambeck et al., 2015), causing detrimental impacts on various ecosystems, the economy and subsequently, human life (Jang et al., 2014). To make matters worse, according to a WWF research (2018) the anthropogenic activity of tourists who travel to a great number of Mediterranean shores, increases the produced waste by 40%. In addition, the aesthetic consequences stemming from marine littering are immensely crucial, given that the factor of cleanliness plays a cardinal role affecting the beach choice for tourists and local residents (Balance et al., 2000). As a result, the high concentration of plastic waste can lead to the decrease of touristic activities, which are the financial backbone of many coastal countries. According to Leggett et al. (2014) cleaning beaches on a regular basis and removing 75% of the existing plastic waste would increase beach visitors by 43%, while the total benefit would be roughly $53 million.

In light of the above and considering that climate change remains a critical issue to be tackled; it comes as no surprise that marine littering should be solved without any further delay. Nevertheless, lack of education has driven citizens away from adopting sustainable methods and recycling habits. As a consequence, innovative and interactive techniques have been investigated in order to raise awareness about practices that mitigate global warming (Ouariachi et al., 2020). More specifically, it is believed that game-based learning, which is the utilization of games that have educational purposes can enhance the adaptation of people so that they can handle the upcoming demands that stem from complicated learning fields and teach them how to adopt multiple habits in a creative way (Ifenthaler et al., 2012; Digital Learning Institute, 2022). Even so, the use of gamification has emerged as a promising tool, which leverages game-design methods for impelling users to become engaged in non-entertainment environments (Bunchball, 2010; Schoech et al., 2013). Since "gamification" and "serious games" share a lot of characteristics, their terms are often being mixed up. The former is the embedding of a number of game-design elements, into non-game contexts in order to increase users' engagement and motivation, whereas serious games put more emphasis on the game's objective, which is beyond entertainment and apply all the elements (Hammady & Arnab, 2022; Preeti GT, 2023). Furthermore, gamified learning is the application of game elements, such as leaderboards, points, badges, rankings, levels, narrative, competition, achievement, avatars, suitable environment, game fiction, interaction among the users, engagement, and specific goals in order to enrich the users' experience and lead them towards the desirable learning behaviors (Landers, 2014; Limantara et al., 2019). Hence, it is observed that the correlation between gamification and learning is a combination based on four essential substances: instructions, game elements, behaviors, and related outcomes aiming at the increase of motivation to cultivate new attitudes (Landers, 2014). Additionally, Toda et al. (2019) has classified gamification elements according to five dimensions:

— the performance dimension elements, e.g., points and levels that demonstrate the user's progress.

— the ecological dimension elements, e.g., time pressure which sets the temporal boundaries for the implementation of a task.

— the social dimension elements which define whether the gamified environment should be competitive or cooperative.

— the personal dimension elements which are based on the user's experience that is created by the application.

— the fictional dimension elements, e.g., storytelling; an activity that uses words to create new worlds and experiences in users' imagination or narrative which is achieved through personalized characters.

In general, gamification has a great potential as an immersive, persuasive technology that initiates environmentally friendly behavioral patterns and stimulates sustainable habits, which adoption is maintained even after the users' engagement with the application (De Guinea et al., 2009). Truelove and Gillis (2018) identify four main dimensions that can influence pro-environmental behavior: the environmental impact, the money saved by the person performing the behavior, the monetary cost of performing the behavior, and the behavioral cost. In addition, according to Li et al. (2019), the factors affecting pro-environmental behavior can be distinguished into two major categories: a) external variables, such as social norms and rules, cost and convenience, and b) individual variables, which include demographic and psychological variables such as attitudes, social capital, previous recycling experience and socio-economic characteristics. Given that the gamified application contains a specific amalgamation of persuasive techniques, it can encourage the required behavior and encourage users to change their attitudes based on the game's purpose.

Some of the most important gamification methods are: set clear goals, so that users are committed to a specific purpose, provide feasible challenges, which will impel users to overcome obstacles, provide feedback, in order to constantly monitor their progress regarding the desired outcome, offering awards, e.g., points, badges, when they reach milestones in their progress or providing leaderboards, levels, in order to demonstrate and compare their progress with other users, and emphasize on the element of fun, by creating narratives, stories and customized characters (Cugelman, 2013). Furthermore, based on Ourdas and Ponis (2023) free choices, badges, points, avatars, narrative, as well as feedback increases the usage of the application and leads to feelings of satisfaction, whereas gamification elements that intensify competitive emotions among users (leader boards, progress bars, ranking etc.) seem to make the experience less pleasant. Especially for environmental behavioral change, it has been evident that achievements, rewards, points, and leaderboards, as well as feedback based on personalized avatars stimulates users' interest and incentivize them to adopt eco-friendly habits (Berengueres et al., 2013; Gnauk et al., 2012; Liu et al., 2011).

2. THE PROPOSED SOLUTION

The project presented in this paper demonstrates a holistic management methodology for tackling marine littering reinforced by underwater and ground sensors, two types of Unmanned Vehicles (Aerial and Underwater), equipped with imaging and environmental sensors and supported by autonomous station pads, as well as a specialized web platform, leading to the data documentation and distribution to project stakeholders and users. More specifically, the imaging sensors that are embedded into the Unmanned Vehicles implement daily monitoring across the beach, especially early in the morning, in order to avoid causing noise pollution for the beach users and at least once per day for the regular collection of imaging information (e.g., photos and videos) about the inspected coastline. On the other hand, environmental sensors are applied for real-time monitoring and measuring specific environmental conditions (e.g., sound levels, air pressure, ambient temperature, CO_2 and CO emissions, humidity, wind speed etc.). As a result, the input value of the unmoving ones is advanced by sharing more information about the status of the beach and resulting in the integrated enhancement of tourists' experience. It is also, worth mentioning that the Unmanned Vehicles are recharged by the station pads which analyze and quantify the accumulated waste on the beach and the underwater sections of marine ecosystems, as well as distribute the collected data to a cloud server, so that all involved stakeholders can process it, at any time. Last but not least, the most essential part of the proposed methodology that is presented in this paper is the game planning mechanism, consisting of two parts; the gamification platform and the project's application. A schematic of the aforementioned management system is demonstrated in Figure 1:

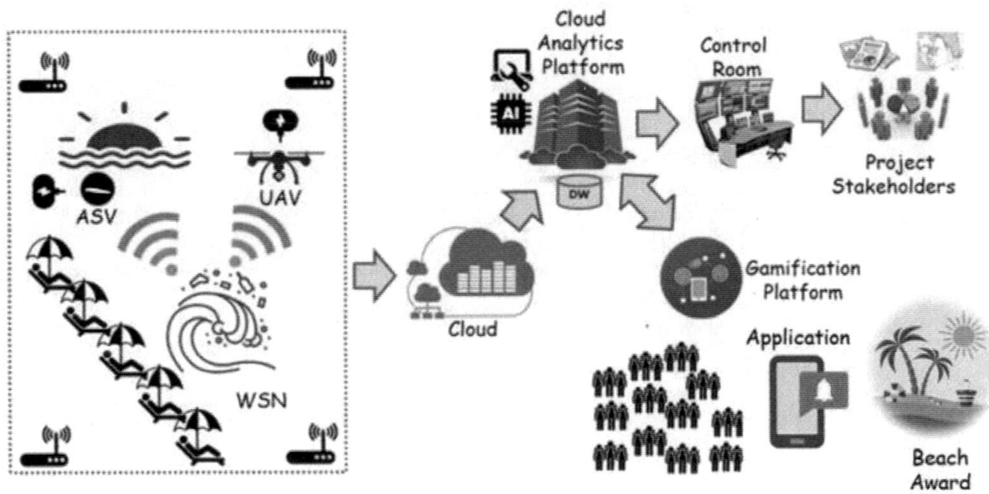

Figure 1. Management system of the proposed solution

This paper directs its attention to the gamification methods and elements that are leveraged for its application, as well as its effective combination which creates a friendly environment for the users and impel them to protect marine ecosystems, thus reinforcing the touristic industry. The applied game methodology has a twofold purpose. The first one is to inform beach visitors about the cleaning status of the selected beach via an algorithm that calculates the real-time debris concentration on the beach, whereas the second one is to raise awareness and encourage citizens to properly deposit their waste, as well as be engaged in cleaning activities. It should be also, noted that the algorithm is reinforced by the accumulated environmental data of the sensors in order to provide an integrated evaluation of the recreational experience of the beach user.

After downloading the project's application, the user has the ability either to get informed about the project and its technical aspects or select information about the participating beaches. According to the authors, a step of paramount importance, is to set a **specific goal**, otherwise the feeling of confusion dominates. Hence, the involved beaches compete with each other regarding its cleaning progress which is calculated by the extracted data from the imaging and environmental sensors and it is visible to the users, at any time. At the end of the week, one of the participating beaches is declared as the winning one and is awarded for contributing to the preservation of marine ecosystems and supporting tourism. It is also, worth highlighting that the start of measurements documentation has been implemented one week before the data documentation and distribution started, so that the progress of each beach is noticeable. Another essential method is to provide **feedback**, utilizing distinct gamification elements. As already mentioned, for environmental behavioral change it is observed that features that exacerbate competitive feelings (e.g., leaderboards and rankings) seem to discourage users from participating in applications that promote sustainability. Thus, progress bars with weekly targets for each participating beach, are being used which have a positive effect on engagement and appear to positively influence competence. Therefore, this gamification element demonstrates the real-time progress of the beach, in comparison to previous week's cleaning conditions. Furthermore, the **element of joy** should not be overlooked, as it has the ability to hold the users' attention and interest. As a consequence, a customized level-up dart for each beach is utilized and demonstrates its overall cleaning status based on the extracted data from the imaging and environmental sensors. To be more precise, the darts' levels fluctuate between 1 and 6, with level 6 being the cleanest one and motivating users to ameliorate its cleaning conditions, as the beach with the highest score gets recognition on a global scale. In addition, each beach collects badges based on weekly targets, rendering the application more enjoyable for the users because they demonstrate users' accomplishments and status, as well as encouraging them to strive for more tasks and to compete with other users. Lastly, the user is guided to a link that leads to documents about marine littering and methods of contributing to the beach's cleaning improvement. A demonstration of the application's mock-ups is presented in Figure 2:

Figure 2. Indicative screens of the project's application

3. CONCLUSION

The research project presented in this paper demonstrates an innovative management methodology designed to mitigate marine littering reinforced by state-of-the-art technologies, as well as the optimal amalgamation of gamification elements that should be embedded into the proposed application. The integrated solution combines two types of Unmanned Vehicles with Internet of Things, while the collected data is distributed and the cleaning status of the inspected coastal area is visualized to all involved citizens. Furthermore, a plethora of gamification elements is leveraged in order to drive citizens towards green behaviors that are in alignment with circular economy and recycling basic principles and raise their awareness about marine pollution. It is also, worth noting that the proposed project could be implemented at any shoreline or beach, as its characteristics are generic and can contribute to the gradual tackling of marine pollution and the upscaling of the area's tourist industry.

ACKNOWLEDGEMENT

This research is co-funded by the European Union and Greek national funds through the Operational Program "Competitiveness, Entrepreneurship and Innovation" (EPAnEK), under the call "RESEARCH-CREATE-INNOVATE" (project code: T2EDK- 03478 and Acronym: GOLDEN SEAL).

REFERENCES

Balance, A.*, Ryan, PG** and Turpie, J. (2000). How much is a clean beach worth? The impact of litter on beach users in the Cape Peninsula, South Africa. South African Journal of Science, 96(5), 210-213.

Berengueres, J., Alsuwairi, F., Zaki, N., & Ng, T. (2013, March). Gamification of a recycle bin with emoticons. In 2013 8th ACM/IEEE International Conference on Human-Robot Interaction (HRI) (pp. 83-84). IEEE.

Bunchball, I. (2010). Gamification 101: An introduction to the use of game dynamics to influence behavior. White paper, 9, 1-18.

Cugelman, B. (2013). Gamification: what it is and why it matters to digital health behavior change developers. JMIR serious games, 1(1), e3139.

De Guinea, A. O., & Markus, M. L. (2009). Why break the habit of a lifetime? Rethinking the roles of intention, habit, and emotion in continuing information technology use. MIS quarterly, 433-444.

Digital Learning Institute, 2022. Webinar Highlights: Gamification and Game-Based Learning. Retrieved from: bit.ly/44a5TPQ

Du, H. S., Ke, X., & Wagner, C. (2020). Inducing individuals to engage in a gamified platform for environmental conservation. Industrial Management & Data Systems.

Gnauk, B., Dannecker, L., & Hahmann, M. (2012, March). Leveraging gamification in demand dispatch systems. In Proceedings of the 2012 Joint EDBT/ICDT workshops (pp. 103-110).

Hammady, R., & Arnab, S. (2022). Serious gaming for behaviour change: A systematic review. Information, 13(3), 142.

Ifenthaler, D., Eseryel, D., & Ge, X. (2012). Assessment for game-based learning (pp. 1-8). Springer New York.

Jambeck, J. R., Geyer, R., Wilcox, C., Siegler, T. R., Perryman, M., Andrady, A., ... & Law, K. L. (2015). Plastic waste inputs from land into the ocean. Science, 347(6223), 768-771.

Jang, Y. C., Hong, S., Lee, J., Lee, M. J., & Shim, W. J. (2014). Estimation of lost tourism revenue in Geoje Island from the 2011 marine debris pollution event in South Korea. Marine pollution bulletin, 81(1), 49-54.

Landers, R. N. (2014). Developing a theory of gamified learning: Linking serious games and gamification of learning. Simulation & gaming, 45(6), 752-768.

Leggett, C. G., Scherer, N., Curry, M. S., Bailey, R., & Haab, T. C. (2014). Assessing the economic benefits of reductions in marine debris: a pilot study of beach recreation in Orange County, California. Cambridge, MA, USA: Industrial Economics, Incorporated.

Li, D., Zhao, L., Ma, S., Shao, S., & Zhang, L. (2019). What influences an individual's pro-environmental behavior? A literature review. Resources, Conservation and Recycling, 146, 28-34.

Limantara, N., Hidayanto, A. N., & Prabowo, H. (2019). The elements of gamification learning in higher education: A systematic literature review. Int. J. Mech. Eng. Technol, 10(02), 982-991.

Liu, Y., Alexandrova, T., & Nakajima, T. (2011, December). Gamifying intelligent environments. In Proceedings of the 2011 international ACM workshop on Ubiquitous meta user interfaces (pp. 7-12).

Ouariachi, T., Li, C. Y., & Elving, W. J. (2020). Gamification approaches for education and engagement on pro-environmental behaviors: Searching for best practices. Sustainability, 12(11), 4565.

Ourdas, C., & Ponis, S. (2023). Evaluating the Effects of Gamification in Behavioural Change: A Proposed SEM-Based Approach. Sustainability, 15(6), 5442.

Preeti GT, 2023. The Key Difference Between Serious Games and Gamification in eLearning. Retrieved from: https://blog.elblearning.com/the-key-difference-between-serious-games-and-gamification-in-elearning#:~:text=Serious%20games%20are%20games%20that,to%20increase%20engagement%20and%20effectiveness.

Schoech, D., Boyas, J. F., Black, B. M., & Elias-Lambert, N. (2013). Gamification for behavior change: Lessons from developing a social, multiuser, web-tablet based prevention game for youths. Journal of Technology in Human Services, 31(3), 197-217.

Toda, A. M., Klock, A. C., Oliveira, W., Palomino, P. T., Rodrigues, L., Shi, L., ... & Cristea, A. I. (2019). Analysing gamification elements in educational environments using an existing Gamification taxonomy. Smart Learning Environments, 6(1), 1-14.

Truelove, H. B., & Gillis, A. J. (2018). Perception of pro-environmental behavior. Global Environmental Change, 49, 175-185.

WWF, 2018. The Mediterranean at risk of becoming 'a sea of plastic', WWF warns. Retrieved from: https://wwf.panda.org/wwf_news/?329099/The-Mediterranean-at-risk-of-becoming-a-sea-of-plastic-WWF-warns

Zhou, F., Mou, J., & Kim, J. (2022). Toward a meaningful experience: an explanation of the drivers of the continued usage of gamified mobile app services. Online Information Review, 46(2), 285-303.

THE IMPACT OF PERCEIVED CHALLENGE ON NARRATIVE IMMERSION IN RPG VIDEO GAMES: A PRELIMINARY STUDY

José Miguel Domingues[1], Vítor Filipe[1], Filipe Luz[2] and André Carita[3]
[1]*University of Trás-os-Montes and Alto Douro (UTAD), Vila Real, Portugal*
[2]*Lusófona University, Lisboa, Portugal*
[3]*Lusófona University, Porto, Portugal*

ABSTRACT

The challenge is a fundamental aspect of almost every gameplay, and immersion is one of the most widely recognized concepts in the video game industry. Since this is currently a work in progress, this study aims to preliminary research how player's perceived level of challenge affects narrative immersion during gameplay in the role-playing game (RPG) genre. This study will outline the procedures that will be undertaken, including the utilization of the Challenge Originating from Recent Gameplay Interaction Scale (CORGIS) instrument and a questionnaire to measure player immersion. These instruments will enable the assessment of the impact of the perceived challenge on narrative immersion in each use case.

KEYWORDS

Narrative Immersion, Perceived Challenge, Video Games, Role-Playing Games (RPG)

1. INTRODUCTION

Researchers employ a variety of methods to study video games and their related aspects. The analysis of video games, and especially their content, serves as an important methodological approach to understanding, for example, the structure and representations within games, (Egenfeldt-Nielsen et al., 2013; Daneels et al. 2022) the experiences available to players (Daneels et al. 2022), or the effects video games can have on players (Slater, 2013; Daneels et al. 2022). Although in the recent past, it has not been common to use video game analysis in all fields of research, as is the case with human-computer interaction (Barr, 2008), it is already starting to be a topic of interest to researchers more and more, to understand agents' motivations in video games, behavioral implications, adaptations of video games to player preferences, as well as needs for possible more immersive experiences. However, video game analysis has for some time now been widely used in the field of video game studies to examine a wide range of topics, such as narrative aspects in FPSs (Breuer et al., 2012), mission ramifications in the genre RPG (Karlsen, 2008), characters in video games focused on classical antiquity (Vandewalle et al., 2020) and even to investigate specific titles such as Super Mario Galaxy (Linares, 2009).

For game designers, two of the main tasks are to design a game that has a challenging enough difficulty curve to keep the player's interest (Wong et al., 2006), as well as the progression of the narrative throughout the game experience (Aarseth, 2012).

However, as far as we know, there is currently very little literature on how different games with different difficulty perception levels influence how immersed people are during the experience.

This could be attributed to the fact that the dimensions of challenge and immersion in video games are not readily identifiable or well comprehended, owing to the intricacy of experiences associated with them (Bowman, 2019).

Therefore, this research aims to empirically investigate how a player's perceived challenge affects narrative immersion during gameplay RPG genre. To experimentally evaluate this effect, we suggest using three different RPG video games and introducing them to a group of players who already had a certain degree of experience in video games. In this work, we provide a rigorous evaluation of the effects of this approach on player experiences, such as narrative immersion and perceived challenge, in the RPG genre.

2. RELATED WORK

2.1 Immersion

Immersion is one of the most well-known concepts in the field of video games, but also recently in other multimedia communities (Schmidt, 2022). Nilsson et al. (2016) analyzed a variety of perspectives on immersion and created a three-dimensional taxonomy with core concepts of system immersion, narrative immersion, and challenge-based immersion. System immersion is also addressed as an objectively measurable property of the system, not the product of a user's reaction to that system. They go on to explain that narrative immersion is characterized by a degree of mental absorption or intense preoccupation with the story, as well as with space and characters. Finally, challenge-based immersion is a user's mental absorption, provoked by the experience of challenges requiring mental and/or sensorimotor skills (Witmer & Singer, 1998; Nilsson et al., 2016).

Agrawal et al. (2020) later defined immersion as a phenomenon experienced by an individual, when in a state of deep mental engagement in which their cognitive processes (with or without sensory stimulation), cause a shift in their state of attention in a way that is possible to experience the dissociation of consciousness from the physical world. Later, Morgado and Beck (2020) combined the three-dimensional taxonomy (Nilsson et al., 2016) and the definition of immersion (Agrawal et al., 2020)

According to a study on cyberpsychology by Wood et al. (2007) experiencing dissociation of consciousness from the physical world is a common occurrence in video games, with 99% of the respondents (N = 280) reporting losing track of time while playing. This research further found that narrative-focused video games were most frequently associated with the loss of time during gameplay.

Riva et al. (2004) emphasized that for narratives to have a positive impact on the sense of presence, players need to assume the role of a character and become immersed in the story, while emotionally or intellectually significant events can induce a prolonged state of presence. Narrative immersion is defined as the feeling of being inside a story, completely involved and accepting the world and events of the story as real. Having a stimulating plot, an interesting character, and dramatic situations are prerequisites for a narrative immersion experience and on unfolding narrative events, the attention should be intense and focused. Such attention should reduce the risk that players engage in real-world reflections and judgmental decisions that are fundamental to them (Adams, 2014).

Qin et al. (2009) explored and analyzed computer game narrative factors that influence players immersed in the game story world. They applied two surveys on the internet to a group of people (N=734), and data were collected. From this work, they concluded that when analyzing narrative immersion in video games, should be considered a seven dimensions factor: Curiosity: Looking forward to exploring and learning about the game narrative. Concentration: Being able to get focused on the game narrative for a long time. Challenge and skills: Having a balanced challenge/skill during the game narrative. Control: Having the power to exercise a sense of control over the game narrative. Comprehension: Interpreting the content and structure of the storyline in the best way possible. Empathy: Getting involved in the imaginary game world while playing the game and allowing themselves to belong there. Familiarity: Having previous knowledge about the game's story and world.

The questionnaire to measure player immersion in video games was derived from this process, resulting in a comprehensive set of 27 questions distributed among the seven dimensions. These questions were formulated to be assessed using a 7-point Likert scale.

Based on its extensive validation across multiple studies (Agrawal et al., 2020; Pianzola, 2021; Moinnereau et al., 2022), this instrument has garnered substantial support as the most appropriate approach for effectively measuring narrative immersion.

While some identify the narrative as the most presence sense influencer (Wood et al., 2007), others say that is a well-balanced flow experience that can enhance the player's immersion (Csikszentmihalyi, 2013).

2.2 Flow and Perceived Challenge

According to flow theory (Csikszentmihalyi, 2013), it is necessary to increase the level of skill to accommodate increasing challenges, in the form of experiencing or staying in a state of flow.

Momentary feedback that is perceived as positive may be what allows someone to maintain flow, while feedback that is perceived as negative indicates challenges that are too high to overcome, causing the flow experience to be interrupted or even incapacitated. So, if the game is too challenging the player gets frustrated, but if the player succeeds too easily, he might get bored. Therefore, being able to maintain the balance of challenges/skills needed to start and stay in a flow experience may depend to some extent on one's feedback perceptions at any point during a flow-producing activity (Csikszentmihalyi, 2013).

Consequently, it is secure to affirm that a well-balanced perceived challenge in a video game is essential to maintain the player in a state of flow.

As pointed out by Adams (2014) the challenge is at the core of almost every gameplay.

Difficulties and challenges are determined by the objective of the video game and the obstacles that prevent the player from achieving it. These denote a task or problem rather than a specific experience. Lomas et al. (2017) define difficulty as "the probability of failing the task", which can be objectively measured in the video game. Contrarily, "challenging" and "difficult", are considered relational attributes concerning how challenges and difficulties are experienced by the player.

According to Denisova et al. (2020) difficult and challenging are terms normally used with different meanings. We use the word "difficult" for tasks that we struggle to keep going, but "challenging" is used more positively to describe a demanding but invigorating problem or task. We can say that a difficult video game can be uncomfortable and even frustrating. On the other hand, the challenging video game is stimulating, and challenged players are motivated to respond to tasks, to which their actions are differentiated, and they feel in control of the results (Lazzaro, 2009). Above all, the challenge depends on the player's skills, which are shaped by experiences in previous video games.

Video games expose players to several types of challenges simultaneously, complicating the perception of the boundary between each challenge. A study by Denisova et al. (2020) concluded that it was important to separate the types of challenges to be qualified to elaborate an instrument capable of measuring the perceived challenge, CORGIS.

The questionnaire CORGIS was validated by a group of players (N=1000), and it was built to measure the perceived challenge in 30 questions, based on four distinct factors: Cognitive Challenge (COG), refers to the player's memory, observation, and problem-solving ability. Performative Challenge (PERF) addresses the player's abilities concerning speed and reaction times, as well as the precision and accuracy of the actions performed. Certain video games also exercise the player's physical resistance, dexterity, and coordination. Emotional Challenge (EMO), the things they thought about outside of the video game, are involved in the emotions they had during the gameplay. Decision-Making Challenge (DM) refers to the player's making difficult or regrettable choices during the gameplay.

In the context of this study, it's suggested that while not imperative, for optimal outcomes, the application of the CORGIS should be immediately after the gaming session, utilizing a 7-point Likert scale.

Based on the established empirical evidence and the demonstrated validity of the CORGIS instrument and the questionnaire designed to measure player immersion in video games, a high degree of confidence can be placed in the utility and significance of these measurement tools for assessing the dimensions of narrative immersion and perceived challenge within the context of this investigation. The deliberate inclusion of these instruments will form an essential cornerstone for conducting a comprehensive analysis and gaining insights into the intricate interplay between players' perceived level of challenge and narrative immersion during gameplay, within the RPG genre.

3. METHOD

We start by choosing three RPG video games with varying difficulties and strong narrative elements. Secondly, an online survey study will be conducted to ascertain participants' experience with the three previously selected RPGs, their proficiency in playing RPG video games, and their self-assessed level of skill in this genre. Only participants who meet the criteria of having no prior experience with the selected video games and possessing a significant level of proficiency in the RPG genre will be included to proceed with the study. This follows the dispatch of an email to notify the participants who have been selected, accompanied by a consent agreement document, to proceed with the study. In the third stage, we expect to conduct three different gameplay in-person sessions for each participant, corresponding to the three video games chosen, one per session. Immediately after each participant gameplay session, two surveys will be applied, the CORGIS and the questionnaire to measure player immersion in video games, with a total of 57 items (7-point Likert scale), to evaluate the four perceived challenge factors and the seven narrative immersion dimensions. Upon completion of data collection, all analyses will be performed using SPSS for Mac OS.

4. RESEARCH STRATEGY

To answer our question: "how player's perceived challenge affects the narrative immersion during gameplay in the RPG genre?", we have outlined a research strategy involving four specific points:

1. Carry out case studies to identify possibilities for games of the RPG genre.
2. Select a group of players with previous experience in the RPG genre.
3. Measuring player's narrative immersion and perceived challenge after playing, in these cases.
4. Looking for patterns that might emerge from the correlation between the degree of narrative immersion and the perceived challenge.

To commence the study, a careful selection process will be undertaken to identify three video games within the RPG genre that boast a compelling narrative. With its inclusion of a highly regarded recognition for excellence in narrative, the Games Awards assumes a pivotal role in assisting us with the identification and selection of games about this matter. Our preference is to choose three narrative award-winning RPG video games from the most recent three to four years. If there are not three winning RPGs within that timeframe, we will also consider the nominees. Initially, we will select the three RPGs that have received awards in the past four years. If the desired number is not met, we will include additional games from the pool of nominees, starting from the previous year.

The study will be conducted amongst video game students, who have demonstrated an inclination towards video games and will therefore serve as a suitable cohort for the analysis. To ensure optimal results, this group of students will be selected based on their experience within the RPG genre and subsequently introduced to the selected video games. Promptly after finishing every gameplay, both the narrative immersion and perceived challenge questionnaires will be administered individually to each participant. These questionnaires hold significant importance as they serve as essential tools to gather comprehensive information from each participant regarding their experience with all three video games in terms of narrative immersion and perceived challenge.

Upon collecting and analyzing all questionnaires and data, comparative analyses will be conducted to identify relationship patterns between narrative immersion and perceived challenge in RPG video games. This will serve as a crucial component of the study, enabling us to draw in-formed conclusions that will aid in understanding the correlation between narrative immersion and perceived challenge within the RPG genre.

5. CONCLUSION AND FUTURE WORK

Within the scope of this paper, our primary objective is to introduce and differentiate the concepts of narrative immersion and perceived challenge as discrete theoretical constructs within the realm of video games. Additionally, we aim to elucidate our proposed research methodology to enhance the understanding of our approach. By building upon the groundwork laid by the aforementioned study, our aim is to establish a significant correlation between narrative immersion and perceived challenge in three RPG video games, identifying patterns that can provide insights into the impact of perceived challenge, as well as the individual factors of cognition (COG), performance (PERF), emotion (EMO), and decision-making (DM), on the phenomenon of narrative immersion. Considering the preliminary nature of this investigation, our future work aims to present a comprehensive exposition of the research, encompassing an intricate analysis of the chosen video games, elucidating the precise criteria employed for their selection, meticulously documenting the duration of each gaming session, and disclosing the exact number of participants involved.

REFERENCES

Aarseth, E. (2012). A narrative theory of games. In Proceedings of the international conference on the foundations of digital Games.

Adams, E. (2014). Fundamentals of game design. Pearson Education.

Agrewal, S., Simon, A. M. D., Bech, S., Bærentsen, K. B., & Forchammer, S. (2020). Defining immersion: Literature review and implications for research on audiovisual experiences. Journal of the Audio Engineering Society, 68(6).

Barr, P. (2008). Video game values: Play as human-computer interaction. (Doctoral dissertation, Open Access The Herenga Waka-Victoria University of Wellington).

Bowman, N. D. (2019). Video games as demanding technologies. *Media and Communication* 7.4,144-148.

Breuer, J., Ruth, F., & Thorsten, Q. (2012). Digital war: An empirical analysis of narrative elements in military first-person shooters. Journal of Gaming & Virtual Worlds, 4(3), 215-237.

Csikszentmihalyi, M. (2013). Flow: The psychology of happiness. Random House.

Daneels, R., Denoo, M., Vandewalle, A., Dupont, B., & Malliet, S. (2022). The Digital Game Analysis Protocol (DiGAP): Introducing a Guide for Reflexive and Transparent Game Analyses. Game Studies, 22(2).

Denisova, A., Cairns, P., Guckelsberger, C., & Zendle, D. (2020). Measuring perceived challenge in digital games: Development & validation of the challenge originating from recent gameplay interaction scale (CORGIS). International Journal of Human-Computer Studies, 137.

Egenfeldt-Nielsen, S., Smith, J. H., & Tosca, S. P. (2013). Understanding video games: The essential introduction. Routledge.

Karlsen, F. (2008). Quests in context: A comparative analysis of Discworld and World of Warcraft. Game Studies.

Lazzaro, N. (2009). Why we play: Affect and the fun of games. In Human-computer interaction: Designing for diverse users and domains (pp. 679-700). Springer.

Linares, K. (2009). Discovering Super Mario Galaxy: A Textual Analysis. DiGRA Conference.

Lomas, J. D., Koedinger, K., Patel, N., Shodhan, S., Poonwala, N., & Forlizzi, J. L. (2017). Is difficulty overrated? The effects of choice, novelty and suspense on intrinsic motivation in educational games. In *Proceedings of the 2017 CHI conference on human factors in computing systems*.

Moinnereau, M. A., de Oliveira, A. A. Jr., & Falk, T. H. (2022). Immersive media experience: a survey of existing methods and tools for human influential factors assessment. *Quality and User Experience* 7(1).

Morgado, L., & Beck, D. (2020). Unifying protocols for conducting systematic scoping reviews with application to immersive learning research. In 2020 6th International Conference of the Immersive Learning Research Network (iLRN) (pp. 231-242). IEEE.

Nilsson, N., Nordahl, R., & Serafin, S. (2016). Immersion revisited: A review of existing definitions of immersion and their relation to different theories of presence. Human technology, 12(2).

Pianzola F. (2021). Presence, flow, and narrative absorption questionnaires: a scoping review. *Open Research Europe, 1.*

Qin, H., Patrick Rau, P. L., & Salvendy, G. (2009). Measuring player immersion in the computer game narrative. International Journal of Human–Computer Interaction, 25(2), 107-133.

Riva, G., Waterworth, J. A., & Waterworth, E. L. (2004). The layers of presence: A bio-cultural approach to understanding presence in natural and mediated environments. CyberPsychology & Behavior, 7(4), 402-416.

Schmidt, S. (2022). Assessing the quality of experience of cloud gaming services. Springer Nature.

Slater, M. D. (2013). Content analysis as a foundation for programmatic research in communication. Communication Methods and Measures, 7(2), 85-93.

Vandewalle, A., & Malliet, S. (2020). Ergodic characterization: A methodological framework for analyzing games set in classical antiquity. DiGRA'20–Proceedings of the 2020 DiGRA International Conference: Play Everywhere.

Witmer, B. G., & Singer, M. J. (1998). Measuring presence in virtual environments: A presence questionnaire. Presence, 7(3), 225-240.

Wong, K. W., Fung, C. C., Depickere, A., & Rai, S. (2006). Static and dynamic difficulty level design for edutainment game using artificial neural networks. In Edutainment 2006: Technologies for E-Learning and Digital Entertainment, 16-19, 2006. Proceedings 1 (pp. 463-472). Springer Berlin Heidelberg.

Wood, R. T. A., Griffiths, M. D., & Parke, A. (2007). Experiences of time loss among videogame players: An empirical study. Cyberpsychology & behavior, 10(1), 45-56.

REFLECTION

SIMPLE MEASUREMENT OF USER RESPONSE

Melanie Steiner and Dieter Meiller
Ostbayerische Technische Hochschule (OTH) Amberg-Weiden
Kaiser-Wilhelm-Ring 23, 92224, Amberg, Germany

ABSTRACT

This article deals with the measurement of human reactions for the evaluation of the user experience, the user experience when using software. The basic question behind this is how our increasingly activating systems can be evaluated even better in terms of the user. We can think of applications with augmented reality, mixed reality or virtual reality approaches, as well as those that use AI algorithms and thus change noticeably for the user with each use, or even for special approaches such as persuasive design. From the perspective of the user experience concept, the human being is the focus of consideration. Accordingly, knowledge of his behavior, his reactions, his emotions, is essential for the development and improvement of digital products. Here, not only proven methods such as usability testing, observation, questioning, etc. are used, but also reactions of the human body are considered in the context of evaluating a human-machine interaction. The article presents 10 methods from the multitude of possible procedures with a short description. It discusses their applicability in terms of user experience evaluation and clusters the methods by type for a good overview.

KEYWORDS

User Experience, Measurement of Human Reactions, Software Engineering, Evaluation, Electrical Activity

1. INTRODUCTION

Contemporary software development follows the principles of the user experience concept and uses the human-centered design process (HCD) for this purpose. The methods used in the evaluation phase range from usability tests, observation and surveys to psychophysical methods such as eye tracking. In recent years, however, many other evaluation methods have been gaining ground that have been used for decades in medicine and psychology to make body reactions measurable and interpretable in a proven manner. However, the measurement of body reactions for the evaluation of people or the customer journey have already become firmly established in neuromarketing.

The background of this development is the improvement and simplification of the measurement systems for body reactions. For this purpose, the handling of hardware and software has also been adapted for layman use. There are also many offers of measurement systems that can be used 24 hours a day and in a mobile context (e.g. pulse watch).

Another important aspect is the simple access to the relevant measurement methods. If we think of pulse measurement, for example, simple wearables for home use are now available to everyone from pharmacies, retailers and the Internet without any great effort or queries to the doctor. The costs are very low compared to professional devices used for clinical diagnostics.

Also, for laboratory tests (e.g. urine tests) more and more simple offers for everyone are offered in the meantime. These can be performed at home with instructions and then sent to a laboratory for evaluation. The results are then often made available in digital and visually appealing form. Such tests are generally not suitable for medical diagnostics. However, they can be used in an evaluation context, as they can clearly show trends in user responses.

Despite this strong simplification such systems and tests supply useful results which can be used in the context of the software evaluation. Depending on the research question and study design, however, careful consideration should be given to which systems and tests are used. Also, with regard to a study design that is to work with several different body reactions and the results to be obtained from them, is now associated with feasible effort. For the latter, multi-measurement systems are the obvious choice.

2. STRAIGHTFORWARD MEASUREMENT OF HUMAN REACTIONS

Numerous methods can be used to measure human reactions. The first step is therefore to formulate the specific question and the survey scope in detail. Particularly for use in software evaluation, methods and procedures are usually required that require little effort on the part of the users and also for the study design.

Another aspect for the use of simple systems is their mobile suitability. Systems designed for everyone often offer quite good quality here, because the results from such measurements are offered as a basis for subsequent medical diagnostics.

To minimize barriers to participation in a User Experience (UX) study, the type of procedure also plays a significant role. In the following, 10 procedures are briefly described that are helpful for measuring body reactions. In this context, information is also given on whether the respective procedures are available as invasive (with needle) or as noninvasive methods.

2.1 Procedures of Measuring Body Response

The following 10 procedures for measuring body responses may be useful in analyzing human-computer interaction:

Table 1.

Procedure	Invasive / noninvasive procedure	Effort
Blood pressure (BP)	noninvasive	low
Blood glucose (BG)	invasive, less invasive	high
Blood oxigen saturation (BOS)	invasive, noninvasive	low
Electrocardiography (ECG)	noninvasive	middle
Electrodermal Activity (EDA)	noninvasive	low
Electroenzyphalography (EEG)	invasive, noninvasive	high
Electrocardiography (ECG)	nonivasive	middle
Elektromyography (EMG)	invasive, noninvasive	low
Electrooculography (EOG)	noninvasive	low
Pulse	noninvasive	low

2.2 Measuring the Blood Without or With Less Invasive Procedures

The measurement of pulse or blood pressure (BP) is widespread, uncomplicated, and therefore very common. The use of a finger clip electrode, wearables as a pulse volume wristband, in the form of a watch, or even as an arm cuff for measurement on the upper arm is also possible around user experience context. Wristbands and watches mostly use the photometric method by sending green light into the tissue. The light intensity of the reflected light portion serves as the basis for measuring fluctuations. When measuring blood pressure, the systolic blood pressure (SBP) as well as the diastolic blood pressure (DBP) are given as standard. Some devices also offer the value of the arterial medium pressure (AMP). Pulse pressure (pulse amplitude), the difference between SBP and DBP, is also a parameter that even mid-priced systems provide. The main determinants of these measurements are both cardiac function and vascular function (Weber 2010, p. 9-10).

The blood glucose level (BG) is also of interest for application in the UX context (nervousness, anxiety, etc. in the case of hypoglycemia). Here, a first distinction can be made between the classic invasive method of blood glucose measurement and methods without pricking for blood collection. There are measuring devices which, in combination with an enzyme-soaked test strip, make the applied blood measurable. Here, the blood glucose content is determined either photometrically, by light measurement, or by measuring the electrical conductivity (amperonic) in mmol/l (minimol per liter, used internationally). In Continuous Glucose Monitoring (CGM), a small sensor is implemented in the subfatty tissue. This then measures the sugar content of the tissue fluid at regular intervals. The data is usually transmitted to a cell phone app, which provides documentation, evaluation, visualization and age. Another technological procedure is flash glucose monitoring

(FGM). Here, too, a sensor is placed that provides data. However, an alert function is not implemented here (Schmeisl 2015, p. 21-32).

Blood oxygen saturation (BOS) is another option that is of particular interest for applications involving a lot of movement. In a diagnostic context, oxygen saturation is often determined by analyzing the blood. The focus is on the arterial oxygen saturation (SaO2) and the venous oxygen saturation (SvO2). However, simple pulse oximeters make the measurement easily tradable as a noninvasive method. Pulse oximetric oxygen saturation can be determined using photometric methods (SpO2) (Machetanz 2017). Electrodes and measuring devices are available for the finger, the forearm or, for example, integrated into wearables such as wristbands and watches.

2.3 Methods of Derivation of Electrical Activity

An Electrocardiograhpy (ECG) is a very proven method that derives electrical impulses of the heartbeat. The first considerations in this regard go back to Carlo Matteucci who was able to prove the connection of cardiac activity with electrical processes in pigeon experiments as early as 1843 (Diepgen et al. 1960, p. 64). Usually, special ECG electrodes are used for this purpose, which are placed at predefined locations close to the heart. Measurement by means of a chest strap is widely used. Here the heart rate, or more precisely the R-pulses, are measured by means of skin electrodes implemented in the belt. Manufacturers of special wearables already offer these electrodes implemented in clothing and wireless, so that they can also serve for mobile use (ECG T-shirt, Ambiotex GmbH, co-developed by the Technical University of Brandenburg, Germany). However, there are also variants of optical ECG measurement that are available as wristbands or watches and can be well integrated for use in the context of a software evaluation.

One method that is already well established and used in evaluation is electrooculography (EOG). This noninvasive method measures the change in resting retinal potential or eye movements. Electrodes are placed above and below or to the side of the eye. They measure the change in voltage between the front and back of the retina. The method can also be used with the eyes closed and provides results. For example, they are available for the UX context as wearable EOG glasses (Bulling 2008). Even though it seems to be the case, this method is rarely used in today's mobile eye trackers and can be applied as an alternative or combined method. Mobile head-mounted eye trackers usually rely on the corneal reflex method and thus the reflection of light sources on the cornea, as well as their distance to the pupil. Simple systems suitable for evaluation measure electrical resistance by means of 3 electrodes, with one electrode serving as a reference electrode.

A noninvasive method that can be used for evaluation is also the measurement of electrodermal activity (EDA) of the skin. In general, this includes all electrical phenomena that can be measured on the skin (Brown 1967). Such changes have been demonstrated since the 1940s, for example, during sleep. Changes of potentials between 2 measuring points reflect the phasic (active) electrical changes of a skin resistance curve. They can occur as a reaction to a specific stimulus, but can also have unspecific causes. The EDA gives an indication of the excitation of the sympathetic nervous system. The tonic (passive) activity of the skin can also be measured. It shows the activity of the sweat glands. Simple measurement systems provide dual electrodes that are placed on the user's fingers during use, for example. It is usually measured in microsiemens (µS), with a range of 0-25 µS providing sufficiently qualitative results for the UX context (Biosignalsplux 2023).Electromyography (EMG) is the appropriate imaging technique to measure the electrical activity of muscles and to draw conclusions about the reactions of users. Here, the changes in electrical membrane potentials of a muscle or muscle group are measured. It can be performed invasively or intramuscularly (iEMG, use of needle electrodes) as well as non-invasively. The latter variant is particularly suitable for evaluation.

The last method presented here is electroencephalography, or EEG for short. It measures the electrical activity of the brain and is a highly interesting method that is not only used in clinical diagnostics, but also in brain-computer interfaces. However, it is considered to be rather laborious, as it usually involves working with a system of 10-20 or 30-40 fixed in an EEG cap. Nevertheless, there are now EEG systems that use much fewer electrodes and simple adjustment using a rubber band on the head. Also, EEGs can be used in a UX context with low to moderate movement. However, too much movement of the head leads to artifact formation. EEG can be used as a non-invasive procedure, or with needle electrodes as an invasive procedure. It offers the possibility to provide qualitative measurement results over longer periods of time.

3. CONCLUSION

There is a wealth of methods from the medical and psychological fields that are also of great interest for the context of user experience evaluation. If a study design is created, the effort for a first overview of possible methods that can be considered for the study context is often very large and therefore there are still barriers to the use of body signal measurement. During the literature review, methods are described in detail and often in technical terms. The emphasis is on ease of use with acceptable quality of results. However, the presented review shows that there are now many technical solutions for home use. Depending on the use case, these are also suitable for UX evaluation and can be used there as a single or multi-system. They are suitable as in combination of proven methods such as the interview survey, the survey with questionnaires or an observation during the usability test.

REFERENCES

Beck, K. and Ralph, J., 1994, Patterns Generates Architectures. *Proceedings of European Conference of Object-Oriented Programming.* Bologna, Italy, pp. 139-149.

Berger, H., 1929, Uber das Elektrenkephalogramm des Menschen. *Psychiatrie. und. Nervenkrankheiten.* Vol. 87, pp. 527–570.

Brown C. C., 1967, A proposed standard nomenclature for psychophysiologic measures. Psychophysiology 4, pp. 260–264.

Biosignalsplux, 2023, Electrodermal Activity (EDA) Sensor Datasheet, https://support.pluxbiosignals.com/wp-content/uploads/2021/11/Electrodermal_Activity_EDA_Datasheet.pdf, retrived 23.05.2023.

Bulling A., Roggen D., Tröster G. 2008, It's in Your Eyes – Towards Context-Awareness and Mobile HCI Using Wearable EOG Goggles. In: UbiComp 2008. Proceedings of the 10th International Conference on Ubiquitous Computing. September 21–24, 2008, Seoul, Korea. Association for Computing Machinery, New York NY 2008, ISBN 978-1-60558-136-1, S. 84–93, doi:10.1145/1409635.1409647.

Diepgen P., Goerke H., 1960 Aschoff/Diepgen/Goerke: Kurze Übersichtstabelle zur Geschichte der Medizin. 7., neubearbeitete Auflage. Springer, Berlin/Göttingen/Heidelberg, pp. 64.

Machetanz L., 2017, Sauerstoffsättigung, 8. Dezember 2017, https://www.netdoktor.de/laborwerte/sauerstoffsaettigung/ reviewed 23.05.2023.

Weber, T., 2010, Journal of Hypertension 2010, *Grundlagen: Zentraler Blutdruck,Pulswellenreflexion, Pulswellengeschwindigkeit*, Vol. 14 (2), pp. 9-13.

POSTER

MESH DECIMATION FOR SHADOW TERMINATOR

Kristian Spoerer and Weibin Wang
School of Computer Science
University of Nottingham, UK

ABSTRACT

In rendering, low complexity 3D meshes can result in aliasing at the shadow terminator. This study aims to develop a novel mesh decimation algorithm that maintains a smooth shadow terminator. By concentrating on regions away from the shadow terminator, the proposed algorithm can reduce computational demands without compromising the render. We demonstrate the algorithm's effectiveness and compare it with existing methods.

KEYWORDS

Shading and Rendering, Geometric Modeling

1. INTRODUCTION

In 3D real time graphics, which can be used in videogames, medicine (Nogimori, et al., 2020), and in AR/VR (Kwak, et al., 2020), triangle meshes can be used to represent smooth surfaces for fast rendering. Higher complexity meshes appear more like the target shape but also take more time to render. Shadows help to improve realism and perception of the scene, but problems can include aliasing at the shadow terminator (Akenine-Möller, et al., 2018). When rendering the shadow using shadow mapping and simulating light rays in the fragment shader, some of the geometry near the shadow terminator will be unlit, and some lit, leading to artifacts (Jen-Yuan Chiang, et al., 2019). The problem is apparent when the 3D mesh complexity is low.

Figure 1 (a) shows a low complexity mesh where many surface points are facing away from the light source and will not be lit resulting in the incorrect shadow terminator shown in (b). Figure 1 (d) shows more complex geometry and in (e) there is no apparent problem on the shadow terminator.

(Snyder & Barr, 1987) performed early investigations to solve this problem, specifying an epsilon variable that moves the calculation point away from the low-complexity geometry, which can be implemented in the fragment shader. (Hanika, 2011) proposed a method to calculate this epsilon value based on Bezier patches. This generated sample point, p, is shown in Figure 1 (c). The problem with this method is that the generated point is not guaranteed to be on the intended geometry.

2. METHOD

Rather than generate sample points we propose to use actual complex geometry. Our method starts with a complex mesh and decimates it away from the shadow terminator using a decimation algorithm. (Garland & Heckbert, 1997) iteratively contracts two vertices into one vertex according to the error introduced which is the distance from the original vertex position, such that the vertices with smallest error will be contracted first. Our algorithm contracts two vertices based solely on their distance apart and is fast to compute. To calculate if a triangle is on the shadow terminator region, we use the method shown in Figure 2, which works by calculating the angle of the triangle normal compared with the light source direction to see if it is within a threshold.

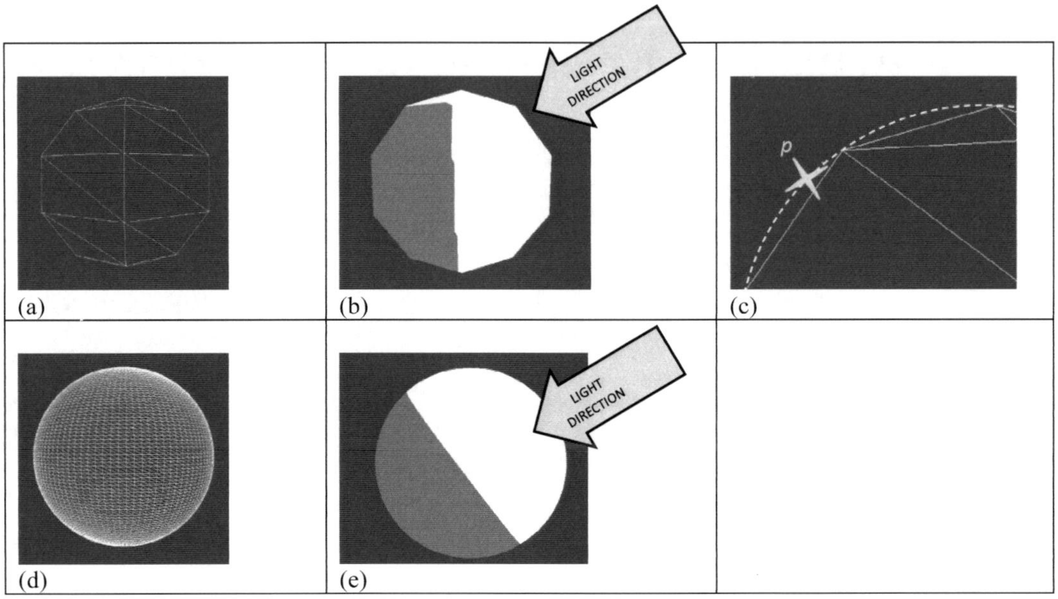

Figure 1. Showing the shadow terminator problem

```
n: normal of mesh triangle (unit vector)
l: vector pointing towards light source (unit vector)
d: dot product of n and l

angle = acos(d)
if (abs(abs(angle)-90)) <= theta
   return true
return false
```

Figure 2. Pseudocode to calculate if triangle is on shadow terminator

3. RESULTS

We tested our method using a procedurally generated sphere and a GLSL implementation of shadow mapping, with geometry decimated to 14% of original model complexity. Figure 3 illustrates the dynamic nature of the method. Each row from top to bottom shows the light source in a different position as can be seen from the position of the shadow on the flat plane above the sphere and the angle of the shadow terminator. Figure 3 can be compared with the result shown in (Figure 4-4 top row second column) in (Hanika , 2021) and as can be seen our method produces a shadow terminator which is comparable to existing state of the art results. It should be noted that the decimation cannot currently be achieved in real-time.

4. CONCLUSION

We have proposed a method for tackling aliasing problems on the shadow terminator. Our proposed method uses complex geometry rather than generated points, which we hope will produce more accurate rendering. Our method will work for local lighting and global lighting. Also, we have considered the shadow terminator region during mesh simplification. We have demonstrated its effectiveness in a dynamic scene and have also showed that it is comparable to existing results. Future work will aim to provide evidence that our method is more accurate than existing methods, will test alternative faster methods which run in real time, and will also aim to demonstrate use in practical applications.

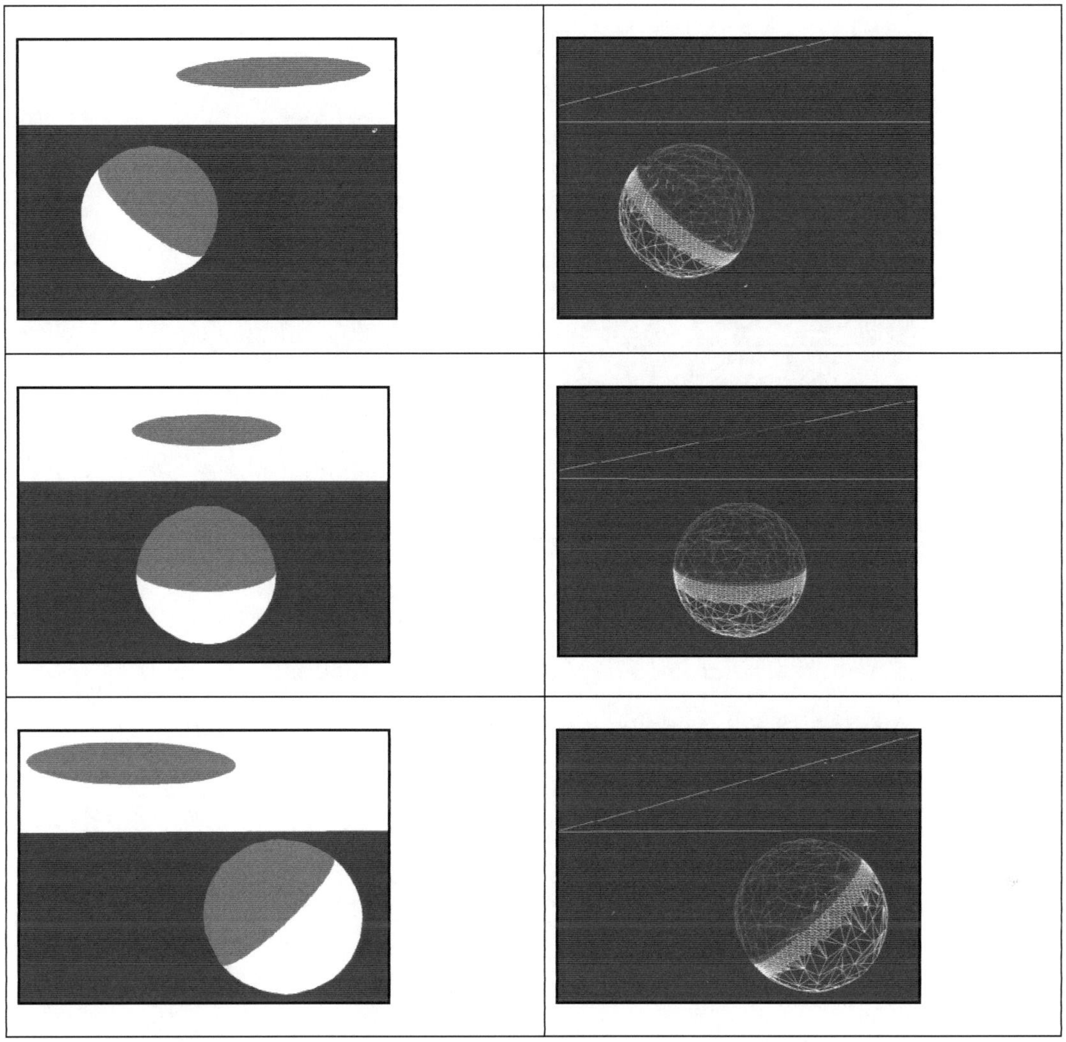

Figure 3. Results showing the dynamic nature of our method

REFERENCES

Akenine-Möller, T., Haines, E. & Hoffman , N., 2018. *Real-Time Rendering.* 4 ed. : CRC Press.

Garland, M. & Heckbert, P., 1997. Surface Simplification Using Quadric Error Metrics. *SIGGRAPH,* pp. 209–216.

Hanika , J., 2021. Hacking the Shadow Terminator. In: *Ray Tracing Gems II: Next Generation Real-Time Rendering with DXR, Vulkan, and OptiX.* Berkeley, CA: Apress , pp. 65–76.

Hanika, J., 2011. *Spectral light transport simulation using a precision-based ray tracing architecture,*: MSc Thesis.

Jen-Yuan Chiang, M., Karl Li, Y. & Burley, B., 2019. Taming the Shadow Terminator. *SIGGRAPH ,* pp. 1–2.

Kwak, S., Choe, J. & Seo, S., 2020. Harmonic rendering for visual coherence on mobile outdoor AR environment. *Multimedia Tools and Applications,* Volume 79, pp. 16141–16154.

Nogimori, Y., Seo, H. & Ueda, H., 2020. A three-dimensional computer graphics tool for congenital heart diseases. *Pediatrics International,* 62(6), pp. 738–740.

Snyder, J. & Barr, A., 1987. Ray tracing complex models containing surface tessellations. *Computer Graphics,* 21(4), pp. 119–128.

AUTHOR INDEX